lonely planet

Tasmania

D0054531

Devonport &
the Northwest
p200

Launceston
& Around
p171

The
East
Coast
p137

Midlands
& Central
Highlands
p127

Cradle Country
& the West
p233

Hobart & Around
p46

Tasman Peninsula
& Port Arthur
p97

The
Southeast
p108

THIS EDITION WRITTEN AND RESEARCHED BY

Anthony Ham, Charles Rawlings-Way and Meg Worby

LAUNCESTON P173

REDZAAL /GETTY IMAGES ©

MT WELLINGTON P56

ANDREW BAIN /GETTY IMAGES ©

SALAMANCA MARKET P53

JODIE GRIGGS /GETTY IMAGES ©

BATHURST HARBOUR P257

ANDREW BAIN /GETTY IMAGES ©

Contents

UNDERSTAND

SURVIVAL
GUIDE

SPECIAL FEATURES

Welcome to Tasmania

Some say islands are metaphors for the heart. Isolation mightn't be too good for romance, but Tasmania has turned remoteness into an asset, with unique wilderness and hip arts and food scenes.

Wilderness & Wildlife

From the squeaky white sand and lichen-splashed granite of the east coast to the bleak alpine plateaus of Cradle Mountain–Lake St Clair National Park, Tasmania punches well above its weight when it comes to natural beauty. Hiking opportunities range from short forest trails leading to waterfalls, to multiday wilderness epics with no one else in sight. You can explore the island's craggy coastlines and wild rivers by kayak, raft, yacht or cruise boat. Tassie's native wildlife is ever-present: spy Tasmanian devils after dark, share the Southern Ocean swell with seals and dolphins, or watch penguins waddling home at dusk.

Tasmania Tastes Good

First it was all about apples...but now the Apple Isle's contribution to world food extends to premium seafood, cheese, bread, honey, nuts, stone fruit, craft beer, whisky and intensely flavoured cool-climate wines. Many smaller producers are owned and operated by passionate foodies: Tasmania is seemingly made for a driving holiday visiting farm-gate suppliers and providores. After you've sampled the produce, book a table at a top restaurant and see how the local chefs transform it.

History Lesson

To understand Australian colonial history, you first need to understand Tasmanian history. The often tragic story of the island plays out through its haunting convict sites: the sublime scenery around Port Arthur only serves to reinforce the area's grim history. It's just as easy to conjure up visions of the raffish past in Hobart's Battery Point and atmospheric harbourside pubs. Elsewhere, architectural treasures include the stoic convict-built bridges at Ross, Richmond and Campbell Town, and Launceston's quality cache of heritage houses. Meanwhile, the state's ongoing obsession with the (probably) extinct Tasmanian tiger continues – are you out there, thylacine?

Festival Frenzy

From wine, beer and food festivals to hot-ticket arts and music events, Tasmania packs a lot of parties into the year. Hobart's beautiful docks play host to many, from the Taste of Tasmania to the heritage glories of the Australian Wooden Boat Festival. Art and culture get their game on during MONA FOMA and Ten Days on the Island, and winter's brooding, edgy Dark MOFO. Festivale brings the party to Launceston. Escape for a long weekend – how many more reasons do you need?

Why We Love Tasmania

By Charles Rawlings-Way & Meg Worby

As Tasmania's biggest fans, we've come to appreciate the island in different ways. Charles spent his childhood in Hobart, careening between the beach and the bush. It was the '70s, man – Tasmania was a magical, laid-back place to be a kid. Lured by the island's natural beauty, Meg arrived in the new century to walk the Overland Track, then moved on to the cafes, the bookshops, the pubs... These days we visit Tasmania every year, and are thrilled to see MONA firing the cultural scene and turning Australia's understanding of Tasmania on its head.

For more about our authors, see page 320

Above: View from Mt Wellington (p56), Hobart

Tasmania

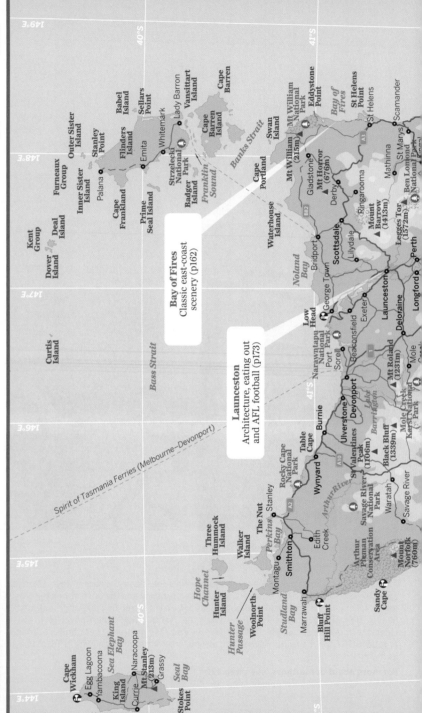

Bay of Fires
Classic east-coast scenery (p162)

Launceston
Architecture, eating out and AFL football (p173)

Spirit of Tasmania Ferries (Melbourne–Devonport)

50 km
25 miles

The Overland Track
The definitive Tasmanian bushwalk (p250)

Rafting the Franklin River
Experience Tasmania's legendary wild river (p249)

Huon Valley
Fresh produce and foodie delights (p119)

Bathurst Harbour
Kayak and camp in remote splendour (p257)

Bruny Island
Wilderness, waves and wine: mini-Tasmania (p111)

Hobart
Where history and hipness collide (p48)

Port Arthur Historic Site
Convict history in a gorgeous setting (p105)

Maria Island National Park
Wilderness and wildlife just offshore (p140)

Freycinet National Park
Wineglass Bay and brilliant bushwalks (p146)

ELEVATION

1600m
1200m
800m
400m
0

TASMAN SEA

SOUTHERN OCEAN

42°S
43°S
44°S

145°E
147°E
149°E

Tasmania's
Top 15

MONA

1 The brainchild of Hobart philanthropist David Walsh, MONA (p57) has turned the Australian art world on its head. Subversive, confronting, funny and downright weird, this is art for grown-ups. Give yourself half a day to explore the darkened underground galleries. Laugh, be appalled, be turned on, then have a glass of wine...there's nothing quite like it anywhere else in the country. To get here, catch a ferry upriver from the Hobart waterfront and eyeball the museum, carved out of a sandstone headland like a vast rusty bunker, from the water.

Port Arthur Historic Site

2 One of the 11 Unesco World Heritage Australian Convict Sites, Port Arthur Historic Site (p105) on the super-scenic Tasman Peninsula was a brutal convict prison between 1830 and 1877. Thousands suffered here, and there's an undeniable tinge of sadness to the place – completely at odds with its gorgeous natural setting. Make sense of it all on an excellent interpretive tour, then explore the Tasman Peninsula further: sea caves, 300m-high sea cliffs, surf beaches and rampant native wildlife. Below right: Penitentiary guard tower

COPYRIGHT JAMES TURRELL. PHOTO CREDIT: MONA/RÉMI CHAUVIN. IMAGE COURTESY MONA MUSEUM OF OLD AND NEW ART, HOBART TASMANIA, AUSTRALIA

ANDREW WATSON / GETTY IMAGES ©

Cradle Mountain

3 A precipitous comb of rock carved out by millennia of ice and wind, Cradle Mountain (p249) is Tasmania's most recognisable – and spectacular – mountain peak. For unbelievable panoramas over Tasmania's alpine heart, take the all-day hike (and boulder scramble) to the summit and back. Or stand in awe below and fill your camera viewfinder with the perfect mountain views across Dove Lake. If the peak has disappeared in cloud or snow, warm yourself by the fire in one of the nearby lodges... and come back tomorrow. Top: Dove Lake

Hobart

4 Australia's southernmost state capital has really come into its own in the last decade. Affordable airfares, internet exposure and the arrival of the astonishing MONA art museum have conspired to put Hobart (p48) on the map, and put a spring into the city's collective step. Don't miss history-rich Battery Point, the Saturday morning Salamanca Market, a tour of Cascade Brewery, a trip up the leafy flanks of Mt Wellington and a beer at Knopwood's Retreat, the quintessential Hobart pub, by the harbour. Bottom: Knopwood's Retreat (p76)

IGNACIO PALACIOS / GETTY IMAGES ©

SUZANNE LONG / ALAMY ©

IAN CONNELLAN / GETTY IMAGES ©

RACHEL LEWIS / GETTY IMAGES

ANDREW HARRIS / GETTY IMAGES ©

Freycinet National Park

5 Ice-clear water, blindingly white beaches and pink granite headlands splashed with flaming-orange lichen – Freycinet National Park (p146) is a gorgeous natural domain. It's also home to Tasmania's most photographed beach: Wineglass Bay. Climb to the lookout over the bay then descend to the sand and dunk yourself under the waves. Escape the camera-clutching crowds on the three-day Freycinet Peninsula Circuit, or explore the peninsula on a cruise, in a kayak or from the air. Luxe accommodation awaits at the end of the day. Above left: Wineglass Bay (p148)

The Overland Track

6 The famed six- to eight-day Overland Track (p250) in Cradle Mountain–Lake St Clair National Park is bushwalking nirvana. Strike out solo and pitch a tent, or take a luxury guided walk fuelled by Tasmanian food and wine, with comfy huts to sleep in at night. Either way you're in for a close encounter with Tasmania's remote highland wilderness and abundant native critters. Detours up Tasmania's highest peak – 1617m Mt Ossa – and the much-photographed Cradle Mountain are hard to resist. Top right: Overland track boardwalk

Gourmet Produce

7 Tasmania – aka the Apple Isle – has much more than just Huon Valley apples in its lunch box these days (p273). The island's fresh air, fertile soil and clean waters sustain truffles, walnuts, blueberries, pears, plums, gooseberries, raspberries, stone fruit, artisan cheeses, honey, seafood, trout, beef, lamb and premium wine, beer and whisky...the whole island is one big food bowl! Festivals and farmers markets present the best local produce, all on tap for local restaurateurs. Bottom right: Cheese tasting in Burnie (p217)

JOHN SONES SINGING BOWL MEDIA / GETTY IMAGES ©

SAM ILLTCHEEVAS / GETTY IMAGES ©

GRANT DIXON / GETTY IMAGES ©

Bruny Island

8 A 15-minute ferry chug from Kettering in the southeast, windswept Bruny Island (p111) is a sparsely populated microcosm of Tasmania. A thriving foodie scene has emerged here, producing artisan cheeses, oysters, smoked seafood, berry products and wines from Australia's most southerly vineyard. Rampant island wildlife includes penguins, seals and marine birds: check them out on a boat cruise around Bruny's jagged south coast. Bushwalking and surfing opportunities abound in South Bruny National Park, while Bruny accommodation is often a relax-at-all-costs experience! Above left: Climbing the steps to the Truganini Memorial (p111)

Launceston

9 Tasmania's northern hub, Launceston (p173) is an affable, arty town that has shed its redneck rep and become the perfect pocket-sized city. Against a backdrop of amazingly well-preserved domestic architecture, lush parks, misty riverscapes and the wilds of Cataract Gorge, 'Lonnie' is a foodie's delight. Expect top-notch restaurants, cafes, patisseries and providores. It's the ideal winter weekender: catch some AFL football, get beery with the uni students at a city bar then explore the Tamar Valley wineries the next day. Top right: Boag's Centre for Beer Lovers

Rafting the Franklin River

10 Rafting the Franklin River (p249) in Tasmania's remote southwest may be the ultimate wilderness journey. Deeply (and often literally) immersed in nature, you'll feel as far from the rest of humanity as it's possible to be. River trips involve up to 10 days on the water, navigating as the river dictates: floating in a world of reflections, battling surging white water and chasing rapids through deep, echoing gorges. Nights are spent in rainforest-fringed camp sites where the river hushes you to sleep.

Guided Bushwalks

11 Tasmania's wilderness is just begging to be explored on foot (p27). But if you're new to bushwalking, cringe at the prospect of sleeping in a tent and can afford a little luxury, a catered guided hike could be for you. There are half-a-dozen of these upmarket experiences across the state, including walks along the Overland Track and around Maria Island, the Bay of Fires and Freycinet Peninsula. Accommodation is often in flashy bush lodges, and meals are very gourmet (not a two-minute noodle in sight). Top: Cradle Mountain Huts (p252)

Bay of Fires

12 Licked by azure ocean and embraced by eucalypt forests and granite headlands, the Bay of Fires (p162) is arguably Tasmania's most scenic slice of coast. To the south, Binalong Bay is perfect for surf or a rough-and-tumble swim, and has dive sites full of crayfish and abalone. Mt William National Park in the north is full of wildflowers, bounding kangaroos and beachfront camp sites. Visit the bay under your own steam or be guided by the experts on the Bay of Fires Lodge Walk.

ANDREW BAIN / GETTY IMAGES ©

Salamanca Market

13 Every Saturday morning since 1972, Hobart's historic waterside Salamanca Pl has filled with trestle tables, food stalls and locals selling everything from home-grown cucumbers to Huon pine fruit bowls. Salamanca Market (p53) is arty, crafty and endearingly homespun. Spend a few hours negotiating the labyrinth, then grab some takeaway lunch and head for the lawns. The upstart rival, the Farm Gate Market in the city centre on Sundays, is challenging for the crown, but Salamanca will always be king.

Maria Island National Park

14 Exquisite Maria Island (p140) is like an island zoo – minus the fences. You don't even need to leave the historic settlement of Darlington to see kangaroos, pademelons, wombats and Cape Barren geese. On a bushwalk you might spot a prickly echidna, Tasmanian devil or a forty-spotted pardalote, one of Tasmania's rarest birds. Oh, and did we say historic? There's World Heritage convict history here too, complete with an ex-penitentiary you can bunk down in for the night. Bottom left: Miner's cottage

Bathurst Harbour & Port Davey

15 Within Southwest National Park in Tasmania's deep south, the hushed, mirror-still waterways of Bathurst Harbour and Port Davey are true natural wonders. Tannin-tinged waters, craggy peaks, white quartzite beaches and underwater kelp forests – there can be few places left on the planet quite so untouristed and untouched. Fly in by light plane from Hobart to the gravel airstrip at Melaleuca (p260) – an adventure in itself – then kayak and camp your way around this incredible watery wilderness. Above: Bramble Cove, Bathurst Harbour (p257)

Need to Know

For more information, see Survival Guide (p293)

Currency
Australian dollars ($)

Language
English

Visas
All visitors to Australia need a visa, except New Zealanders. Apply online at www.immi.gov.au for an ETA or eVisitor visa, each allowing a three-month stay.

Money
ATMs widely available in cities and larger towns. Credit cards accepted for hotels, restaurants, transport and activity bookings.

Mobile Phones
European phones work on Australia's network, but American and Japanese phones don't. Use global roaming or a local SIM card. Telstra has the best coverage.

Time
Tasmania is on Australian Eastern Standard Time (AEST), which is GMT/UCT plus 10 hours.

When to Go

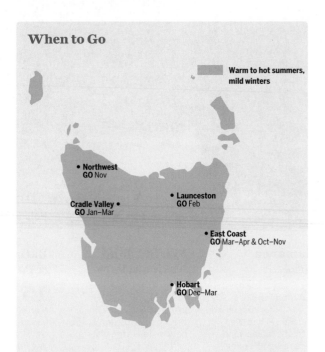

Warm to hot summers, mild winters

Northwest
GO Nov

Cradle Valley
GO Jan–Mar

Launceston
GO Feb

East Coast
GO Mar–Apr & Oct–Nov

Hobart
GO Dec–Mar

High Season
(Dec & Jan)

➡ Accommodation prices scale lofty heights: book ahead.

➡ Festival season hits its straps, and beaches are at their best.

➡ Expect crowds at big-ticket destinations (and the cricket).

Shoulder
(Feb–Apr, Oct & Nov)

➡ Easter is busy with Aussie families on the loose.

➡ Book ahead for Easter camping grounds, motels and ferries.

➡ April is harvest time, with brilliant produce statewide.

Low Season
(May–Sep)

➡ Accommodation prices plunge to manageable levels.

➡ Outside Hobart and Launceston, some eating and sleeping options close their doors.

➡ Snow closes some bushwalking tracks... but you can ski (just!).

Useful Websites

Lonely Planet (www.lonely-planet.com/australia/tasmania) Destination information, hotel bookings, traveller forum and more.

Tourism Tasmania (www.discovertasmania.com) Tasmania's official tourism site.

Tasmanian Travel & Information Centre (www.hobarttravelcentre.com.au) Statewide info and bookings.

Parks & Wildlife Service (www.parks.tas.gov.au) National parks information, maps and passes.

Tasmania Food Guide (www.tasmanianfoodguide.com.au) Restaurant reviews and foodie events.

Important Numbers

Regular Tasmanian phone numbers have a ☎03 STD area code, followed by an eight-digit number. Drop the 0 if calling from overseas.

Ambulance, fire & police	☎000
Australia country code	☎61
Directory assistance	☎1223
International access code	☎0011
Tasmania STD area code	☎03

Exchange Rates

Canada	C$1	$1.02
China	¥1	$0.21
Euro zone	€1	$1.42
Japan	¥100	$1.07
New Zealand	NZ$1	$0.94
UK	UK£1	$1.90
US	US$1	$1.26

For current exchange rates see www.xe.com.

Daily Costs

Budget: Less than $100

➡ Hostel dorm beds: $25–35

➡ Double room in a hostel: $80

➡ Budget pizza or pasta meal: $10–15

➡ Local bus ride: from $3

Midrange: $100–$280

➡ Double room in a motel or B&B: $100–200

➡ Breakfast or lunch in a cafe: $20–40

➡ Car hire per day: from $35

➡ Short taxi ride: $25

Top End: More than $280

➡ Double room in a top-end hotel: from $200

➡ Three-course meal in a classy restaurant: $80

➡ Guided wilderness day tour: from $120

➡ Quality bottle of Tasmanian wine: from $30

Opening Hours

Opening hours for attractions tend to wind back in winter and outside of Hobart and Launceston. The following is a general guide.

Banks 9.30am to 4pm Monday to Thursday, to 5pm Friday

Cafes 7am to 5pm

Pubs & bars 11am to midnight

Restaurants breakfast 8am to 10.30am, lunch noon to 3pm, dinner 6pm to 9pm

Shops 9am to 5pm Mon to Fri, 9am to noon or 5pm Saturday, late-night city shopping to 9pm Thursday or Friday

Supermarkets 7am–8pm

Arriving in Tasmania

Hobart Airport (p304) Door-to-door Hobart Airporter shuttle buses to central Hobart meet every flight. Book ahead. A taxi into the city (20 minutes) costs $42 to $50.

Launceston Airport (p304) Door-to-door Launceston Airporter shuttle buses to central Launceston meet every flight. Book ahead. A taxi into the city (15 minutes) costs about $35.

Devonport Spirit of Tasmania (p206) Redline and Tassielink buses meet every ferry and offer express services into Launceston ($25), continuing to Hobart ($60). Book ahead. Tassielink buses don't run on Sundays.

Getting Around

For many visitors, a major planning consideration is whether to fly to Hobart or Launceston and collect a rental car, or bring a car on the *Spirit of Tasmania* ferry from Melbourne. Check airfares, ferry costs/timings and car-rental prices. For families in particular, the ferry often works out cheaper.

Air Short distances make intrastate flights quick but expensive.

Bus Reliable, affordable but often infrequent services around the state.

Car The best way to get around. Travel at your own tempo and explore remote areas with no public transport. Hire cars available in major towns. Drive on the left.

Train Sadly, Tasmania has no passenger train services.

For much more on **getting around**, see p306.

If You Like...

Gourmet Food

Farm Gate Market Grab a bag full of top local produce at Hobart's Sunday-morning farmers market. (p48)

Agrarian Kitchen Get creative with local produce at Tasmania's first hands-on, farm-based cookery school. (p88)

Bruny Island Laid-back Bruny is home to a cheesemaker, an oyster farm, smokehouse, berry farm and a fudge maker. (p111)

Freycinet Marine Farm Briny oysters, mussels, octopus, rock lobster and crayfish, fresh from the sea. (p152)

King Island Dairy Showstopping dairy on remote King Island with a walk-in tasting room... enjoy! (p231)

Stillwater Settle into a long lunch or linger over dinner at Launceston's best restaurant. (p182)

Summer Kitchen Bakery This little bakery hidden in the southeast bakes the best sourdough you'll ever taste. (p121)

Bushwalking

Cradle Mountain Give yourself a full day to reach the summit of this iconic mountain. (p251)

Wineglass Bay You've seen the photos...now do the walk. It's a three-hour return hike over the saddle to the sand. (p148)

Bay of Fires Lodge Walk Four-day guided walk with all the perks of luxury accommodation and gourmet food. (p163)

Mt Wellington Check out some challenging tracks a short drive from Hobart. And how about them views! (p56)

Mt Field National Park In spring and summer Mt Field's high-country tracks are awash with wildflowers, chuckling streams, tarns and waterfalls. (p89)

Overland Track Tassie's big-ticket trail is an epic through 65km of majestic highlands and forests. (p250)

Maria Island Walk Luxury guided (and catered) four-day hike along Maria Island off the east coast. (p142)

Beer, Wine & Whisky

Jansz Wine Room The 'Méthode Tasmanoise' sparkling white from Jansz is liquid happiness. (p192)

Nant Distillery Nose your way into some fine single malt at this Central Highlands whisky distillery. (p133)

Seven Sheds Railton's microbrewery is home to organically brewed boutique beers. (p214)

Puddleduck Vineyard A charming family-run vineyard in the Coal River Valley. Sip some wine and picnic by the lake. (p83)

Bruny Island Premium Wines The wines from Australia's southernmost vineyard buddy-up nicely with island oysters and cheeses. (p115)

Cascade Brewery Take a guided tour of Australia's oldest brewery and sample the superb product. (p56)

Weldborough Hotel This is a one-stop shop for Tasmanian craft beers – plan on staying the night. (p164)

Hellyers Road Distillery Hellyers makes vodka too, but golden single malt is why you're here. (p217)

History

Port Arthur Historic Site Beautiful coastal scenery masks (almost) the tragic melancholy infused in every building. (p105)

Callington Mill Organic flour from this meticulously restored 1837 mill in Oatlands is transformed into baked treats around the state. (p129)

Hobart Historic Tours Take a guided walking tour and uncover the history of Australia's second-oldest capital city. (p61)

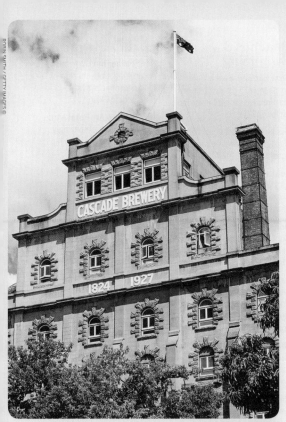

Midland Towns Piece together Tasmania's rural history in photogenic Oatlands, Ross and Campbell Town. (p129)

The Ship That Never Was Hear a true tale of convict escape in this entertaining production in Strahan. (p238)

Evandale The whole town is listed by the National Trust – ignore the cars and this could be 1870-something. (p197)

Woolmers Estate Longford farming estate dating from 1819, and one of the 11 Unesco World Heritage Australian Convict Sites. (p195)

Stanley Historic northwest fishing village sheltering beneath the Nut. (p222)

Wildlife

Maria Island For all things furry and feathered. The wombats are supersized! (p140)

Mt William National Park Rare Forester kangaroos gambol on the grassland behind the beaches. (p164)

Trowunna Wildlife Park Check out some Tasmanian devils, koalas and wombats in the northwest. (p212)

Tasman Island Cruises Astonishing coastal scenery and the chance to see seals, dolphins and the occasional passing whale. (p62)

Bonorong Wildlife Centre Conservation-savvy wildlife centre, starring Tasmanian devils, koalas, wombats, echidnas and quolls. (p83)

Bruny Island Winning bird-watching, including penguins and mutton birds at Bruny Island Neck. (p111)

Top: Cascade Brewery (p56), Hobart
Bottom: Wineglass Bay (p148)

Festivals

Falls Festival Get your rocks off at this touring music fest, visiting Marion Bay around New Year's Eve. (p64)

Dark MOFO Cometh the winter solstice, cometh Dark MOFO – an eerie, unnerving and very hip winter festival. (p63)

MONA FOMA Annual Festival of Music & Art at MONA in Hobart (too many acronyms?). (p63)

Taste of Tasmania Tassie's top food festival is a true gourmet feast. (p63)

Cygnet Folk Festival Folky good times and groovy summer vibes south of Hobart. (p118)

Rosebery Festival The west coast can be bleak, but this folk festival warms up the mood a bit. (p237)

Ten Days on the Island Tasmania's loftiest arts and culture festival. (p63)

Tasmanian Breath of Fresh Air Film Festival Left-of-centre Launceston film fest with red-carpet glam, forums and screenings. (p177)

Beaches & Swimming

Boat Harbour Beach Water so clear you'll think you're in Martinique...except for the 'brrr' factor. (p221)

Ocean Beach Long, wild beach walks, giant waves and west-coast sunsets. (p239)

South Cape Bay It's a two-hour walk from Cockle Creek to one of the world's wildest ocean beaches.

Douglas-Apsley National Park Cool off with a swim in the deep, dark waterholes of Douglas River. (p157)

Seven Mile Beach Hobart's best beach: safe swimming, undulating dunes and nearby camping. Righto, that's summer sorted. (p82)

Fortescue Bay Gloriously isolated and definitely worth the national-park entrance fee. Camping a must! (p103)

Binalong Bay The southernmost beach in the Bay of Fires is just begging for swimmers. (p163)

Luxury Stays

Red Feather Inn Gorgeous accommodation and slow-food cookery classes at Hadspen. (p194)

Henry Jones Art Hotel A true Hobart highlight: amazingly unpretentious for such a hip hotel. (p66)

Saffire Freycinet Hands-down Tasmania's most spectacular accommodation, amid the improbable landscapes of the Freycinet Peninsula. (p151)

Tarkine Wilderness Lodge Outstanding new luxury lodge in the forests behind Rocky Cape National Park. (p230)

Avalon Coastal Retreat A glass-and-steel east-coast haven with endless views ('beach house' just doesn't cut it). (p146)

Horizon Deluxe Apartments Luxe hilltop apartments near Stanley with all the requisite indulgences. (p224)

Peninsula Amazing 19th-century homestead near Dover, with Asian-chic design and a private beach. (p124)

Month by Month

January

The summer festival season kicks off with two very different events in Tasmania's south. It's school-holiday time across Australia, so expect high demand for family-friendly motels and camp grounds.

✯✯ MONA FOMA

MONA FOMA (MOFO; www.mofo.net.au) is MONA's Festival of Music & Art. Under the auspices of Brian Ritchie, the bass player from the Violent Femmes, it's as edgy, progressive and unexpected as the museum itself.

✯✯ Cygnet Folk Festival

More woolly sock than arena rock, the Cygnet Folk Festival (www.cygnetfolkfestival.org), south of Hobart, is a three-day hippie fiesta with good vibes, performances and workshops.

February

Hobart's salty maritime heritage comes to the fore on and off the sea (which is at its warmest – go for a swim!). Meanwhile, Launceston's biggest party of the year is a chance to sip some Tamar Valley wines. Book ahead for accommodation, especially on weekends.

✯✯ Festivale

Launceston's City Park hosts three days of eating, drinking, arts and entertainment at Festivale (www.festivale.com.au). It's a chill-out-on-the-grass affair, with Tasmanian food, wine and beer and plenty of live tunes.

✯✯ Evandale Village Fair

The National Penny Farthing Championships happen south of Launceston at the annual Evandale Village Fair (www.evandalevillagefair.com). In between wobbly bike races there are markets and musical interludes from pipe bands.

✯✯ Australian Wooden Boat Festival

In odd-numbered years, the Australian Wooden Boat Festival (www.australianwoodenboatfestival.com.au) brings a fleet of beautifully crafted yachts, dinghies and tall ships to Hobart's waterfront, filling the harbour with heritage nautical vibes.

✯✯ Royal Hobart Regatta

The three-day Royal Hobart Regatta (www.royalhobartregatta.com) sees the Derwent River bobbing with aquatic craft of all shapes and sizes. Don't miss Hobart's resident tall ships, the *Lady Nelson* and *Windeward Bound*.

March

Summer's warmth lingers into dusky evening – the perfect backdrop for an island-wide celebration of music and arts. March is also harvest time: grape vines glow with autumn colours and roadside stalls are crammed with fresh produce. Book ahead for Easter accommodation.

✯✯ Ten Days on the Island

Towing a trad-arts line, 10 Days on the Island (www.tendays.org.au) is the state's premier arts event, running for (you guessed it) 10 days biennially. Theatre, music, visual arts, literature and film across the state.

Taste of the Huon

Ranelagh showgrounds near Huonville hosts the two-day Taste of the Huon (www.tasteofthehuon. com), a showcase of the best Huon Valley produce. Apples, cherries, wine, salmon, mushrooms, honey, bread...no one goes home hungry. Bucolic splendour!

April

As autumn kicks in, cool days and cooler nights become the norm. Easter often falls in April, so book ferry crossings, motels and camping grounds as far in advance as humanly possible. Oh, and football season gets started!

Football Season

Competing in the Australian Football League (AFL; www.afl.com.au), the North Melbourne Kangaroos play some home games at Hobart's Blundstone Arena, while the Hawthorn Hawks play a few at Launceston's Aurora Stadium. Grab a beer, a meat pie and get into it.

May

Cool blue-sky days make May the perfect time for a Tassie sojourn. The low late-autumn light is stellar for photography, and accommodation owners sometimes offer off-peak discounts. Hobart's cosy eateries host the Savour Tasmania Food Festival.

Savour Tasmania Food Festival

The annual Savour Tasmania Food Festival (www.

savourtasmania.com) showcases Tasmanian produce and fine foodie creations. Sign up for red-wine weekends, chef-run workshops and long-table lunches. Held in Hobart for four days, before moving to Burnie and Launceston in early June.

June

Winter is here. Yes, it's colder than elsewhere in Australia, but crisp mornings and Hobart and Launceston's wood-smoky ridge lines are deeply atmospheric. With the coming of the winter solstice, Hobart gets its gothic going.

Dark MOFO

In the still depths of the Hobart winter, MONA's Dark MOFO (www.darkmo-fo.net.au) arrives. Skirting the frayed edges of Tasmania's guilty conscience, this noir package delivers a taut, seductive and joyful series of happenings, installations and performances that will rattle your rusty cage.

July

As winter rolls on, hunker down for the indoor pleasures of choirs and chocolate. Outside of Hobart and Launceston, expect some accommodation to be closed, especially in coastal areas.

Latrobe Chocolate Winterfest

Chocolate! Don't deny it – you love it. And it's a tasty way to warm the heart in the depths of the Tasma-

nian winter. The Latrobe Chocolate Winterfest (www. chocolatewinterfest.com. au) hosts chocolate-inspired festivities, including the essential 'Chocolate High Tea'.

Festival of Voices

The quirky Festival of Voices (www.festivalofvoices.com) turns Hobart into a singing city for three days. Gospel gangs, choirs and a cappella groups showcase the versatility of the human voice.

August

Winter snow dapples Tasmania's Central Highlands. Unless you're masochistic, it's probably best to leave the bushwalking to experienced hikers. Some tracks become impassable and, besides, hotel accommodation is at its cheapest around the state.

Ski Season

When winter blows in (roughly from June to September), snow bunnies and powder hounds dust off their skis and head for Ben Lomond National Park (www.skibenlomond. com.au). Coverage can be unpredictable: check snow reports before you head for the mountain.

September

As winter packs itself away, spring heaths bloom in the Central Highlands and muddy tracks start to dry out. Time for a bushwalk? Accommodation is still affordable: treat yourself to a boutique hotel when you wander in from the wilderness.

✿ Junction Arts Festival

Launceston's offbeat Junction Arts Festival (www. junctionartsfestival.com.au) is five days of live music, theatre, installations, street art, walking tours and dance. A real shot in the arm for the arts up north.

October

Spring is sprung with (usually) more settled weather. In Hobart and Launceston, the city-meets-country Royal Shows put pressure on accommodation: book ahead.

✿ Bloomin' Tulips Festival

Celebrate spring with food, music, burgeoning blooms and maybe a bit of a dance at Table Cape's annual Bloomin' Tulips Festival (www.bloomintulips. com.au).

✿ Royal Hobart & Launceston Shows

Tasmania's rich agricultural heritage collides with dodgy carnies, terrifying rides, fairy floss and junky plastic show bags at the Royal Hobart Show (www. hobartshowground.com.au) and the Royal Launceston Show (www.launceston-showground.com.au).

✿ Bruny Island Bird Festival

Twitchers rejoice! The gloriously isolated landscapes and coastlines of Bruny Island host the annual three-day Bruny Island Bird Festival (www.bien.org.au). Bring your binoculars.

November

Accommodation around the state is still reasonably priced before the peak tourist season arrives (mid-December to January).

☆ Tasmanian Breath of Fresh Air Film Festival

Held at Launceston's Inveresk Park, the Tasmanian Breath of Fresh Air Film Festival (BOFA; www.bofa. com.au) is an inspiring, left-field and innovative flicker fest. Art house and independent to the core.

✿ Tasmanian Craft Fair

Run over four days before the first Monday in November, Deloraine's Tasmanian Craft Fair (www.tascraft-fair.com.au) lures around 30,000 artsy bods from around Australia. Pottery, textiles, glassware and sculpture all get an airing.

🍷 Tasmanian Beerfest

Craft beer is really taking off in Tasmania. Apart from Tassie brews, you can try hundreds of beers from around the world at Hobart's Tasmanian Beerfest (www. tasmanianbeerfest.com.au). Beer-and-food-matching masterclasses also transpire. Educate me now.

December

School's out! Accommodation is at a premium, especially after Christmas and around New Year's Eve when Hobart cranks up the festival schedule. Book well in advance.

☆ Cricket Season

Cricket fans can catch Tasmania's state team, the Tasmanian Tigers (www. crickettas.com.au/teams/tasmanian-tigers), cracking the willow over summer. From zeroes to heroes, the Tigers have been rampantly successful of late. In the quick-fire Big Bash League, the Hobart Hurricanes (www.hobarthurricanes. com.au) are also value for money.

🍴 Taste of Tasmania

Tassie's big-ticket culinary event, Hobart's Taste of Tasmania (www.thetaste-oftasmania.com.au) is a frenzied waterfront food fest over a week around New Year's Eve. It generates a huge buzz: grab a glass of something cold, a plate of something hot and tune in to some live bands.

🏃 Sydney to Hobart Yacht Race

The world's most arduous open-ocean yacht race is the Sydney to Hobart (www.rolexsydneyhobart. com), departing Sydney Harbour on Boxing Day. The winners sail into Hobart around 29 December...four days at sea is a good excuse for a party!

☆ Falls Festival

Tasmania's biggest outdoor rock fest, the Falls Festival (www.fallsfestival.com. au) happens at Marion Bay south of Hobart around New Year's Eve. Expect left-of-centre internationals (Arctic Monkeys, Fleet Foxes) and a slew of Australian talent (Dan Sultan, Angus and Julia Stone). BYO tent.

Itineraries

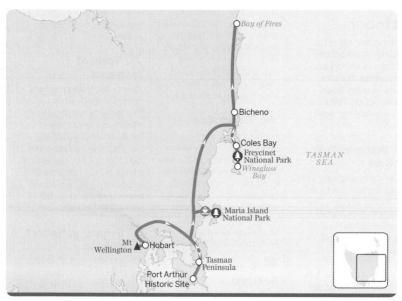

 East Coast Classic

Hobart, Port Arthur, Freycinet and the gorgeous Bay of Fires: check out four of Tasmania's greatest hits on this sunny east-coast cruise.

Hear the heartbeat of **Hobart**: great pubs and cafes, brilliant restaurants and heritage vibes. Don't miss Salamanca Place (and Salamanca Market if it's Saturday morning), an afternoon at the amazing MONA and the view from atop **Mt Wellington**.

From Hobart, head southeast to the dramatic coastal crags of the **Tasman Peninsula** and the grim convict stories of **Port Arthur Historic Site**. Near Copping, shortcut to the east coast via the Wielangta Forest Drive. Hop on a ferry out to **Maria Island National Park** for mountain biking, camping, bushwalking, wildlife spotting and west-facing beaches (rare for the east coast).

Get your camera primed for a trip to **Freycinet National Park** and **Wineglass Bay**, and follow with sea kayaking and oyster appreciation at **Coles Bay**. Continue north to the chilled-out fishing town of **Bicheno** for some penguin spotting then unwind with some serious downtime among the rocky lagoons and headlands of the **Bay of Fires**.

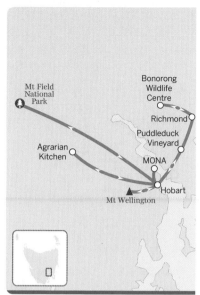

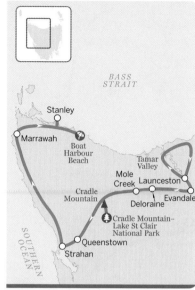

4 DAYS Hobart & Around

Fancy a long weekend in Hobart? Take advantage of Tasmania's short driving distances, by day-tripping around the hip southern capital.

Spend a day mooching around the **Hobart** waterfront and Battery Point, taking a boat trip up the Derwent River to the dazzling **MONA**, and ending with dinner at Garagistes and drinks at Knopwood's Retreat. Next day, drive out to history-rich **Richmond**. Don't miss the stoic Richmond Bridge, **Bonorong Wildlife Centre** and a lazy picnic lunch at **Puddleduck Vineyard**.

On day three, continue the foodie theme with a cooking class at the **Agrarian Kitchen** near New Norfolk. The day-long 'Agrarian Experience' is a paddock-to-plate celebration of the seasons, with fresh fruit and veggies from the kitchen garden.

If you have another day up your sleeve, truck out to **Mt Field National Park** for an accessible alpine bushwalk, or book a place on the Mt Wellington Descent – a 22km downhill mountain-bike run from the summit of **Mt Wellington** behind Hobart to the waterfront.

2 WEEKS Cradle Country & the Northwest

Launceston, the west coast, Cradle Mountain and the northwest: this is certainly the least-visited corner of Tasmania.

Kick off with a couple of days in much-improved **Launceston**: check out Cataract Gorge and the excellent Queen Victoria Museum & Art Gallery (QVMAG), and have dinner at Stillwater and drinks at Saint John.

From Launceston, explore the eclectic enticements of the **Tamar Valley**: seahorses, gold mines, lighthouses and wineries. Loop south through historic **Evandale** before drifting west to **Deloraine** and the **Mole Creek** caves. Don't miss a few days walking in impressive **Cradle Mountain–Lake St Clair National Park**.

From Cradle Mountain, skate southwest to the lunar landscapes of **Queenstown** and ride the West Coast Wilderness Railway to **Strahan**. From Strahan, head north through the vast **Arthur Pieman Conservation Area**; check out the surf at **Marrawah**; and clamber up the Nut in **Stanley**. An ocean dip at photogenic **Boat Harbour Beach** is the perfect journey's end.

PLAN YOUR TRIP ITINERARIES

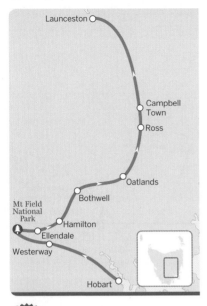

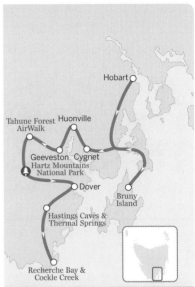

10 DAYS Highlands & Midlands

The historic Midlands is Tasmania's agricultural heartland; the Central Highlands are the state's alpine core.

Get started in **Hobart** with coffee at Jackman & McRoss and a waterfront walk. Check out Saturday's sensational Salamanca Market and the engaging new Mawson's Huts Replica Museum.

From Hobart head northwest to **Mt Field National Park** for waterfalls and bushwalking – just a hint of the vast southwest wilderness beyond.

Track along the Derwent Valley through pretty **Westerway**, **Ellendale** and **Hamilton**, continuing to soporific **Bothwell**. Tee off at Ratho, Australia's oldest golf course, then hit Nant Distillery for some peppy Tasmanian whisky.

Back east in the Midlands, **Oatlands** offers the restored Callington Mill and more Georgian sandstone buildings than any other Australian town. **Ross** is a gorgeous colonial village with a great bakery and an historic bridge. **Campbell Town** makes a handy stop en route to laid-back **Launceston**: reward yourself with a tour of the hallowed Boag's Brewery.

1 WEEK Southern Rambler

Tasmania's southeast is an agricultural and scenic smorgasbord, with an actual smorgasbord of local produce on offer.

From **Hobart**, trundle south to Kettering to catch the car ferry across to easygoing **Bruny Island**. Give yourself at least two nights to appreciate Bruny's charms, including artisan cheeses, Australia's southernmost vineyard and a boat cruise past seal colonies and cliffs. Don't miss the little penguins at Bruny Island Neck.

Back on the Tasmanian 'mainland', swing west to funky **Cygnet** for lunch at Lotus Eaters Cafe. Continue north along the scenic Huon River to **Huonville**. Roadside summer fruit stalls – apples, cherries and more – plus lunch at Summer Kitchen Bakery and cider at the Apple Shed are tasty distractions.

Travel south to **Geeveston**. Take to the treetops at **Tahune Forest AirWalk** or go bushwalking in **Hartz Mountains National Park**. Continue south through chilled-out **Dover** to **Hastings Caves and Thermal Springs**, then negotiate the winding, unsealed road to end-of-the-road **Recherche Bay** and **Cockle Creek**.

Plan Your Trip

Walking in Tasmania

Forget the convict history, the food, the architecture... For many, the number one reason to visit Tasmania is to go bushwalking. Brimming with outdoor opportunities, the island's unique wilderness areas pack a whole lot of diversity into a small area. So break out the thermals and the tent and get walking.

Planning

The first thing to consider is whether you're going to walk independently or sign up for a guided experience. Planning and successfully completing one of Tassie's epic trails independently is hugely rewarding. But if you're after a tad more comfort than tents and sleeping mats afford, many of the island's guided walks offer catered food and wine, and actual beds for a good night's sleep.

When to Go

Choosing when to walk means putting some thought into issues such as track popularity, visitor numbers and climate conditions. Bear in mind that Tasmania's notoriously changeable weather delivers plenty of surprises: come prepared for anything. See the 'Before You Walk' section under 'Recreation' on www.parks.tas.gov.au for more info on timing your trek.

Summer

Summer (December to February) offers long days and a higher likelihood of warmer, settled weather (but no guarantees, OK?). But summer is also peak season and popular tracks do get crowded. Try to head off midweek to avoid the crush. An exception is the Overland Track, which has

Best Bushwalks for...

Wildlife

➡ Maria Island for Cape Barren geese, wallabies, pademelons, wombats, echidnas and Tasmanian devils.

➡ Mt William National Park for Forester kangaroos.

Families

➡ Easy 20-minute boardwalk track to Cape Tourville on Freycinet Peninsula.

➡ Creepy Crawly Nature Trail in Southwest National Park – another easy 20-minute detour.

Scenery

➡ Frenchmans Cap (peer over the cliffs if you dare) and Cradle Mountain for views across Tasmania's alpine heartland.

➡ Tasman Peninsula has the scenic Tasman Coastal Trail and the new Three Capes Track.

A Challenge

➡ Federation Peak – arguably Australia's toughest bushwalk.

➡ The rugged South Coast Track: fly into Melaleuca then walk out to Cockle Creek.

instigated a capped booking system and one-way walking to alleviate congestion.

In alpine regions, snow still sometimes falls during summer. Be prepared to sunbake and snowplough on the same day.

Autumn

Mild weather and the gorgeous golden tones of autumn (March to May) are a great time to experience the Tasmanian wilderness. Easter (late March/early April) and Anzac Day (April 25) see higher walker numbers on popular tracks, so plan accordingly.

Winter

Winter (June to August) can be a mixed bag in Tasmania. Crisp, blue-sky mornings offset the very real possibility of snow, especially in the highlands. Days are short and deep snow can make some tracks impassable. Walking in winter is definitely only for the intrepid and very experienced.

Spring

Rain and wind can be the defining characteristics of spring (September to November) in Tasmania. Tracks can be muddy and slippery – add melting snow to the equation and river levels can be at their highest.

Resources

Maps & Track Notes

Tasmap (www.tasmap.tas.gov.au) produces excellent maps, which are available from visitor information centres, outdoor stores and Parks & Wildlife Service (PWS) offices around the state. In Hobart you'll also find them at Service Tasmania (p36) and the Tasmanian Map Centre (p78). Maps can also be ordered online.

Track notes for the Overland Track, Tasman Coastal Trail, Walls of Jerusalem, Freycinet Peninsula Circuit, Frenchmans Cap and South Coast Track are available online from the Parks & Wildlife Service (www.parks.tas.gov.au): click on 'Recreation' then 'Great Walks' and follow the link under 'Great Bushwalks'.

Useful Websites

Check the superb Parks & Wildlife Service website (www.parks.tas.gov.au) for essential pre-departure information: safety hints, equipment checklists, weather information, bushfire updates, track closure notifications, podcasts, track notes and fact sheets. Other online resources include the following:

Bushwalk Australia (www.bushwalk.com) Visit the 'Forum' section for Tasmania for up-to-date trip reports and feedback from local bushwalkers.

Bushwalk Tasmania (www.bushwalktasmania. com) Information on tracks and transport.

TasTrails (www.tastrails.com) More than 70 walking trails around the state with track info and photos.

Books & Brochures

Lonely Planet's *Walking in Australia* has info on some of Tasmania's best (longer) walks. Available free from visitor centres, online and as a mobile-phone app is the Parks & Wildlife Service's excellent brochure, *60 Great Short Walks,* listing the state's best quick ambles – anything from 10 minutes to all day.

Other compilations of walks throughout the state include the following:

A Visitor's Guide to Tasmania's National Parks By Greg Buckman.

120 Walks in Tasmania By Tyrone Thomas; covers short and multi-day walks.

Day Walks Tasmania By John Chapman and Monica Chapman.

South West Tasmania By John Chapman.

Cradle Mountain–Lake St Clair & Walls of Jerusalem National Parks By John Chapman and John Siseman.

Jan Hardy and Bert Elson's short-walk books, covering Hobart, Mt Wellington, Launceston, the northeast and northwest, are also worth hunting down.

Gear & Equipment

You'll find shops specialising in bushwalking gear and outdoor equipment in all the major centres. In Hobart most of these shops congregate on Elizabeth St between Bathurst and Melville Sts. Many shops can also hire gear.

National Park Fees & Track Bookings

Visitors' fees apply to all national parks. If you're planning on doing a lot of bushwalking, purchasing a day pass (per

Top: Mt Ossa (p249)

Bottom: Echidna, Maria Island National Park (p140)

KENICHI HIKI / GETTY IMAGES ©

TASMANIA'S TOP 10 WALKS

Walking is absolutely the best way to see Tasmania's wilderness in its full glory (and it's not a bad way to walk off all that great local food and wine, either). Pack comfy walking shoes and thick socks, and make happy trails. Following are our favourite walks, from 20 minutes to six days in length.

Overland Track (p250) A stunning six-day alpine endeavour through Cradle Mountain–Lake St Clair National Park.

Wineglass Bay (p148) Climb over the saddle and down to Freycinet's famous beach, a super-scenic return walk of around three hours.

Cataract Gorge (p173) Explore Launceston's gorgeous gorge, which cuts into the heart of the city.

Tasman Coastal Trail (p101) Awesome three- to five-day trail along the Tasman Peninsula clifftops. Keep an eye out for migrating whales.

Truganini Track (p57) Hilly, two-hour return climb through sclerophyll bushland between Mt Nelson, behind Hobart, and the southern suburb of Taroona.

Russell Falls (p89) A short jaunt from the car park at Mt Field National Park.

Dove Lake Circuit (p251) A three-hour lake lap at Cradle Mountain–Lake St Clair National Park.

South Coast Track (p259) An 85km monster along the coast in Southwest National Park.

The Nut (p223) Sweat it out on the steep slopes of the Nut in Stanley.

Tahune Forest AirWalk (p123) Take a knee-trembling treetop walk about 1½ hours south of Hobart.

person/vehicle $12/24) each time will soon become an expensive exercise. Instead, buying an eight-week holiday pass (per person/vehicle $30/60) or annual pass (per vehicle $96) might be a smart move. You'll definitely need a holiday or annual pass for any of the multi-day hikes within national parks.

Because of its popularity, from October to May the Overland Track has a limit on the number of walkers, a compulsory north-to-south walking direction and a booking system in place. You'll also have to pay the Overland Track fee (adult/child $200/160) during this period (not applicable June to September). Book online at www.parks.tas.gov.au.

Prior booking of other tracks and walks in Tasmania is not required.

Guided Great Walks

Seven of Tasmania's guided multi-day walks have been handily grouped together for marketing purposes as the **Great Walks of Tasmania** (www.greatwalkstas-mania.com). Together they cover around 300km, traversing rainforest, alpine areas and beautiful coastal scenery.

Bay of Fires Lodge Walk (p163) Four-day luxury walk along this photogenic, rock-strewn stretch of the northeast coast.

Freycinet Experience Walk (p150) Fully catered, lodge-based, four-day stroll down the famous peninsula.

Maria Island Walk (p142) Another four-day option, this time on Maria Island. Nifty hut accommodation.

Cradle Mountain Huts (p252) Six epic days on the Overland Track with hut accommodation.

Tasmanian Expeditions (p257) Tackle the South Coast Track over nine days (with a rest day in the middle).

Tarkine Trails (p229) Six days in the Tarkine Rainforest in the remote northwest.

Tasmanian Expeditions (p211) A six-day 'Walls of Jerusalem Experience', returning to base camp at night.

On the Trail

Tasmanian Weather

In Tasmania (particularly in the west and southwest), a fine day can quickly become cold and stormy at any time of the year. Always carry warm clothing, waterproof gear and a compass. Bring a tent too, rather than relying on finding a bed in a hut – particularly on popular walks such as the Overland Track.

On all extended walks, you must carry extra food in case you have to sit out a few days of bad weather (rather than having to rely on the goodwill of better-prepared hikers). In the worst of circumstances, such lack of preparation puts lives at risk – if the bad weather continues for long enough, everyone suffers.

Tasmanian walks are famous for their mud, so waterproof your boots, wear gaiters and watch where you're putting your feet.

Responsible Bushwalking

To help preserve the ecology and beauty of Tasmania, consider the following when bushwalking.

Code of Ethics

Click on 'Recreation' then 'Leave No Trace' on the Parks & Wildlife Service website (www.parks.tas.gov.au) for info on how to best experience Tasmania's wilderness and leave it as you found it. PWS literature is also available at Service Tasmania and national park visitor information centres around the state.

Safety First

➡ Don't get lost: stick to established trails and avoid cutting corners or taking shortcuts.

➡ Before tackling a long or remote walk, tell someone about your plans and arrange to contact them when you return. Make sure you sign Parks & Wildlife Service registers at the start and finish of your walk.

➡ To avoid becoming separated, keep bushwalking parties small.

Camping & Walking on Private Property

➡ When camping, always use designated campgrounds where possible. When camping away from established sites, try to find a natural clearing in which to pitch your tent.

➡ Always seek permission to camp from landowners.

Rubbish Disposal

➡ Carry all your rubbish out with you; don't burn or bury it.

➡ Don't overlook easily forgotten items (orange peel, cigarette butts, plastic wrappers).

➡ Make an effort to carry out rubbish left by others.

➡ Never bury your rubbish. Digging disturbs soil and ground cover and encourages erosion. Buried rubbish will likely be dug up by animals anyway, and they may be injured or poisoned by it.

➡ Minimise waste by using minimal packaging.

➡ Sanitary napkins, tampons, condoms and toilet paper should be carried out, despite the inconvenience.

Human Waste Disposal

➡ Use toilets where provided.

➡ In the absence of toilets, dig a small hole 15cm deep and at least 100m from any watercourse. Cover waste with soil and a rock.

➡ In snow, dig down to the soil.

➡ Ensure these guidelines are also applied to portable toilet screens/tents if they're being used by a large bushwalking party. Encourage all party members to use a common site.

Washing

➡ Don't use detergents or toothpaste in or near watercourses, even if they are biodegradable.

➡ For personal washing, use biodegradable soap and a water container at least 50m away from any watercourse. Disperse waste water widely to allow soil to absorb it.

➡ Wash cooking utensils 50m from watercourses using a scourer, sand or snow instead of detergent.

Erosion

Hillsides and mountain slopes, especially at high altitudes, are prone to erosion.

➡ If a well-used track passes through a mud patch, walk through the mud so as not to increase the size of the patch.

➡ Avoid removing the plant life that keeps topsoil in place.

➡ Stick to existing tracks and avoid shortcuts.

THE THREE CAPES TRACK

The latest project to consume the hearts, minds and money of the Parks & Wildlife Service is the ambitious 82km Three Capes Track, traversing the majestic clifftops of Cape Raoul, Cape Pillar and Cape Hauy on the Tasman Peninsula. Once construction is complete, walkers will be able to stay in hut accommodation en route. A commercial guided walk is also expected to be operating. The trail is slated to open in late 2015 – see www.parks. tas.gov.au for updates.

Fires & Low-Impact Cooking

Don't depend on open fires, as the collection of firewood in popular bushwalking areas causes rapid deforestation. Bring your own fuel stove instead. Other considerations:

➡ National parks are fuel-stove-only areas.

➡ Cook on a lightweight kerosene, alcohol or Shellite (white gas) stove. Avoid those powered by disposable butane gas canisters.

➡ Boil all water for 10 minutes before drinking, or use water-purifying tablets.

➡ If you're walking with a group, supply stoves for the whole team. In alpine areas, ensure group members wear adequate clothing so that fires aren't necessary for warmth.

➡ Fires may be acceptable below the treeline in areas that get very few visitors. If you do light a fire, use an existing fireplace and only dead, fallen firewood. Leave some wood for the next walker as a courtesy.

➡ Ensure you fully extinguish fires after use. Spread embers and flood them with water.

➡ On days of total fire ban, don't light any fire whatsoever, including fuel stoves.

Wildlife Conservation

➡ Hunting is illegal in all Tasmanian national parks.

➡ Don't attempt to exterminate animals in huts. In wilderness areas, they're likely to be protected species.

➡ Leaving food scraps around encourages wildlife to hang around camps. Place gear out of reach and tie packs to rafters or trees.

➡ Feeding wildlife can lead to unbalanced populations, disease and animals becoming dependent on handouts.

➡ Don't bring pets into national parks.

Bushwalking Safety
Bushfires & Blizzards

Bushfires are an annual reality in Tasmania. In hot, dry and windy weather, be extremely careful with any naked flame and don't throw cigarette butts out of car windows. On a total-fire-ban day it's illegal to use even a camping stove in the open.

When a total fire ban is in place (common from November onwards), delay your hike until the weather improves. Stay tuned to updates from the **Tasmania Fire Service** (www.fire.tas.gov.au). If you're out in the bush and you see smoke, even a long way away, take it seriously – bushfires move very quickly and change direction with the wind. Go to the nearest open space, downhill if possible. A forested ridge, on the other hand, is the most dangerous place to be.

At the other end of the scale, blizzards can occur in Tasmania's mountains at any time of year. Bushwalkers should be prepared for such freezing eventualities, particularly in remote areas. Take thermals and jackets, plus windproof and waterproof garments. Carry a high-quality tent suitable for snow camping, and enough food for two extra days, in case you get snowed in.

Hypothermia & Animal Hazards

Hypothermia is a significant risk in Tasmania, especially during winter. Strong winds produce high chill factors that can result in hypothermia even in moderate temperatures. Early signs include the inability to perform fine movements (such as doing up buttons), shivering and a bad case of the 'umbles' (fumbles, mumbles, grumbles and stumbles). Key elements of treatment include moving out of the cold, changing out of wet gear into dry, windproof, waterproof clothes, adding insulation and providing fuel (water and carbohydrates). Shivering is a good thing – it builds internal temperature. In severe hypothermia, shivering actually stops: this is a medical emergency requiring rapid evacuation in addition to the above measures.

This is Australia, so there are also things that can bite, suck, sting and generally ruin your hike (see p300).

Plan Your Trip

Outdoor Adventures

If Tasmania were a person, it would be very much the 'outdoors type'. The bushwalks here are among Australia's best, while white-water rafting on the Franklin River is charged with environmental grandeur. Abseiling and rock climbing are thrill-a-minute adventures, while cycling and sea kayaking are magical ways to explore the state.

On the Water

Sea Kayaking

Sea kayaking hot spots include Hobart, where you can explore the suburban waterline and docks with an on-the-water fish-and-chip feast; the D'Entrecasteaux Channel south of Hobart; the Tasman Peninsula; Coles Bay on the east coast; and the remote waterways of Bathurst Harbour and Port Davey on the south coast.

Key operators include Roaring 40s Kayaking (p61) in Hobart and Freycinet Adventures (p150).

Online, the Parks & Wildlife Service website (www.parks.tas.gov.au) has tips on minimal-impact sea kayaking.

Rafting

Tasmania is famed for white-knuckle white-water rafting on the Franklin River. Other rivers offering rapid thrills include the Derwent (upstream from Hobart), the Picton (southwest of Hobart) and the Mersey in the north.

Check out the Parks & Wildlife Service website (www.parks.tas.gov.au) for rafting operator listings and lots of solid (or rather, liquid) advice – click on 'Recreation' then 'Other Activities'. The Discover Tasmania (p294) website also lists operators.

Best Activities for...

Families

➡ Swimming at Seven Mile Beach or Boat Harbour Beach.

➡ Winter snow action at Ben Lomond National Park.

Daredevils

➡ Abseiling down the 140m-high wall of the Gordon Dam.

➡ Careering down the slopes of Mt Wellington on a mountain bike.

Taking it Easy

➡ Cruising the Gordon River on a yacht.

➡ Casting a fly across the Central Highland's trout-filled lakes.

Getting Wet

➡ Rafting the Franklin River, a classic 10-day river run.

➡ Diving through underwater kelp forests off the Tasman Peninsula.

Surfing

Tasmania has dozens of kickin' surf breaks, but the water is damn cold – pack an iron will and a thick steamer wetsuit.

Where to Surf

Close to Hobart, the most reliable spots are Clifton Beach and Goats Beach (unsigned) en route to South Arm, and Park Beach near Sorell. Eaglehawk Neck on the Tasman Peninsula is also worth checking out. The southern beaches on Bruny Island – particularly Cloudy Bay – offer consistent swells.

The east coast from Bicheno north to St Helens has solid beach breaks when conditions are working. Binalong Bay, at the southern end of the Bay of Fires, is an accessible option; Ironhouse Point is more hard-core; and Spring and Shelly Beaches near Orford have consistent breaks.

Further north, King Island cops some big Bass Strait swells, while Marrawah on the west coast is famous for its towering waves. Australia's heaviest wave, the utterly gnarly Shipstern Bluff off Tasman Peninsula, isn't recommended for anyone other than serious pros.

Island Surf School (p99) offers lessons at Park Beach.

TOP TASSIE BEACHES

Pack your swimsuit, brace yourself for a cold-water collision, and jump right in!

Binalong Bay (p163) Binalong time since you had a dip? Head for this crescent of sand north of St Helens.

Boat Harbour Beach (p221) The drive down the steep access road offers postcard-perfect beach views.

Seven Mile Beach (p82) Safe swimming, rolling dunes and an occasional point break near Hobart.

Fortescue Bay (p103) A little slice of heaven, complete with low-key camping ground.

Trousers Point (p169) Take your trousers off at this magnificent Flinders Island beach.

Resources

Check out the following for surf reports.

Magic Seaweed (www.magicseaweed.com)

Surfing Tasmania (www.surfingaustralia.com/tas)

Tassie Surf (www.tassiesurf.com)

Swimming

The east coast has plenty of sheltered, white-sand beaches offering excellent swimming, although the water is (to understate it) rather cold. There are also sheltered suburban beaches in Hobart, including Bellerive and Sandy Bay, but the water here can often be a little soupy – things get clearer further south at Taroona, Kingston and Blackmans Bay, or east at Seven Mile Beach.

In the north, Bass Strait beaches such as Sisters Beach and Boat Harbour Beach are great spots for a quick ocean dip. On the west coast, the surf can be ferocious and the beaches aren't patrolled – play it safe.

Canoeing

For a sedate paddle, try the Arthur and Pieman Rivers in the northwest, and Ansons River and Coles Bay on the east coast. You can rent canoes at Arthur River, Corinna and Coles Bay. The Huon, Weld, Leven and North Esk Rivers also attract their fair share of canoes.

Sailing

The D'Entrecasteaux Channel and Huon River south of Hobart are deep, wide and handsome places to set sail, with more inlets and harbours than you could swing a boom at. Fleets of white sails often dot Hobart's Derwent River in summer – many locals own yachts and consider an afternoon sailing on the estuary to be Hobart's greatest perk.

Of course, when the annual Sydney to Hobart Yacht Race (p64) winds up in Hobart just before New Year's Eve, the whole state goes yacht crazy. Check out the big ocean-going maxi-yachts as they bump and sway at their moorings around Sullivans Cove.

Top: Binalong Bay
(p163)

Bottom: Surfing, King
Island (p231)

SEAN DAVEY / GETTY IMAGES ©

Yacht Hire & Moorings

For casual berths in Hobart (overnight or weekly), contact the **Royal Yacht Club of Tasmania** (☎03-6223 4599; www.ryct.org.au) in Sandy Bay. North of the Tasman Bridge you can anchor in Cornelian Bay or New Town Bay. There's also a lovely marina at Kettering, south of Hobart.

Experienced sailors can hire a yacht from **Yachting Holidays** (☎0417 550 879; www.yachtingholidays.com.au), based in Hobart. Charter of a six-berth vessel costs around $750 per day over summer, with reduced rates for long rentals or in the off-peak (April to November) period.

A useful publication is *Cruising Southern Tasmania* ($38.50), available online from Tasmap (p28).

Scuba Diving & Snorkelling

National Geographic once claimed that Tasmania offered the 'most accessible underwater wilderness in the world'. You may well find yourself in agreement. Visibility ranges from 12m in summer to 40m in winter, with temperate waters offering unique biodiversity.

Where to Dive

There are excellent underwater opportunities around Rocky Cape in the north, on the east coast and around the shipwrecks off King and Flinders Islands. At Tinderbox near Hobart and off Maria Island there are marked underwater snorkelling trails. There's also an artificial dive site created by the scuttling of the *Troy D* off the west coast of Maria Island: contact the **Tasmanian Scuba Diving Club** (www.tsdc.org.au) for info.

Gear Hire & Dive Lessons

Contact the following operators if you want to learn to breathe underwater.

Bay of Fires Dive (p163) On the east coast.

Bicheno Dive Centre (p154) On the east coast.

Eaglehawk Dive Centre (p101) On the Tasman Peninsula.

Flinders Island Dive (p169) On Flinders Island.

Scuba Centre (p221) At Wynyard in the north.

Ocean Fishing

Saltwater rod fishing is allowed year-round without a permit, but size restrictions and bag limits apply. If you're diving for abalone, rock lobsters or scallops, or fishing with a net, recreational sea-fishing licences are required. These are available from **Service Tasmania** (Map p54; ☎1300 135 513; www.service.tas.gov.au; 134 Macquarie St; ◷8.15am-5pm Mon-Fri) in Hobart, or online from the **Department of Primary Industries, Parks, Water & Environment** (www.dpiw.tas.gov.au).

Eaglehawk Neck on the Tasman Peninsula and St Helens on the east coast are good spots for fishing-boat charters. Online, **Tasfish** (www.tasfish.com) is a wealth of fishy info and has back issues of the *Tasmanian Fishing & Boating News* available as downloads.

Trout Fishing

Brown trout were introduced into Tasmania's Plenty River in 1866, and into Lake Sorell in 1867. Innumerable lakes and rivers have subsequently been stocked and trout have thrived. Let's go fishing!

Where to Fish

The Central Highlands are home to the state's best-known spots for brown and rainbow trout: Arthurs Lake, Great Lake, Little Pine Lagoon, Western Lakes (including Lake St Clair), Lake Sorell and the Lake Pedder impoundment. On some parts of Great Lake you're only allowed to use artificial lures, and you're not allowed to fish any of the streams flowing into Great Lake.

Resources & Equipment

Bone up on Tassie trout with a copy of *Tasmanian Trout Waters* by Greg French. Also worth a look is the two-monthly *Tasmanian Fishing & Boating News*, available online at Tasfish (p36).

In Hobart, buy equipment and licences at Spot On Fishing Tackle (p78).

Fly-fishing Lessons

Tasmanian trout can be difficult to catch. They're fickle about what they eat, and the right lures are needed for the right river, lake, season, weather... Check out

Rod & Fly Tasmania (p134) or Trout Guides & Lodges Tasmania (p296) for info on guides, lessons and fishing trips.

Licences & Costs

A licence is required to fish Tasmania's inland waters, and there are bag, season and size limits on most fish.

An annual licence runs for 12 months from 1 August to 31 July; short-term licences are available for periods of 28 days, seven days and 48 hours. Costs vary from $22 for 48 hours to $72.50 for the full season. Licences are available from the Inland Fisheries Service (p296), Service Tasmania (p36), fishing stores and some visitor information centres.

In general, inland waters open for fishing on the Saturday closest to 1 August and close on the Sunday nearest 30 April. The best fishing is between October and April.

On the Land

Cycle Touring

Cycling is a terrific way to tour Tasmania and engage with the island landscapes, especially on the dry east coast. To cycle between Hobart and Launceston along either coast, allow between 10 and 14 days. For a two-wheeled 'lap of the map', give yourself 18 to 28 days.

Short- and long-term bike rental is available in Hobart and Launceston. Cycling tour operators include Green Island Tours (p160) and Tasmanian Expeditions (p310).

Resources

Bicycle Network Tasmania (www.biketas.org.au) Cycling blog and links to route descriptions, online maps and publications – click on 'Resources' then 'Maps and Routes'.

Discover Tasmania (p294) Download the *Self Guided Cycle Touring in Tasmania* PDF, or ask for it at the Hobart visitor information centre.

Where to Ride: Tasmania By Andrew Bain. details 45 rides with maps, altitude profiles and difficulty ratings. Available online at www.bicyclingaustralia.com.au.

TASMANIAN TRAIL

The **Tasmanian Trail** (www.tasmaniantrail.com.au) is a 480km multi-use route from Devonport to Dover, geared towards walkers, horse riders and mountain bikers. Most of the trail is on forestry or fire trails and country roads. It passes farms, forests and towns en route, with camping spots every 30km or so (and lots of opportunities to sleep in a real bed!). All the information you need to tackle some or all of the trail is in the *Tasmanian Trail Guide Book*, available online as a digital file ($24). As a rough guide, mountain bikers should allow around eight days to complete the trail; walkers around 25 days. Have fun!

Mountain Biking

There are plenty of fire trails and off-the-beaten-track routes around Tasmania to explore. Dedicated trails include the **Glenorchy MTB Park** (www.gcc.tas.gov.au) north of Hobart and the new mountain-bike park at Hollybank Treetops Adventure (p193) north of Launceston.

On the competition front, check out January's four-day, 140km **Wildside Mountain Bike Race** (www.wildsidemtb.com) on the west coast. There's also the multisport **Freycinet Challenge** (www.freycinetchallenge.com.au) held every October. The 2015 and 2016 **Australian Cross Country Marathon Mountain Bike Championships** (www.mtba.asn.au) will be happening in Derby in the northeast.

Tours

An essential part of any visit to Hobart should be a knobbly, two-wheeled Mt Wellington Descent (p60). Beyond the capital, Mountain Bike Tasmania (p176) and Wild Bike Tours (p62) run excellent tours around the state.

Resources

Parks & Wildlife Service (p302) Mountain-biking code of conduct for low-impact biking.

Tassie Trails (www.tassietrails.org) Online guide to all things MTB in Tasmania.

Ride Tassie (www.ridetassie.com) Comprehensive guide to Tassie's mountain-bike trails.

Tasmanian Trail (p37) Guide to this blockbuster 480km multi-use trail from Devonport to Dover.

Caving

Tasmania's limestone karst caves are among the most impressive in Australia. The Mole Creek and Gunns Plains caves in the north and Hastings Caves in the southeast are open to the public daily, with troglodytic cave tours.

Rock Climbing & Abseiling

Rock climbing and abseiling are alive and well in Tasmania. There are some awesome cliffs for climbing, particularly along the sunny east coast. The Organ Pipes on Mt Wellington above Hobart, the Mt Killiecrankie cliffs on Flinders Island and Launceston's Cataract Gorge also offer brilliant climbing on solid rock. The soaring coastal cliffs on the Tasman Peninsula are rock-climbing nirvana – especially the legendary Totem Pole and Candlestick dolerite stacks – but they're impossible to access if there's any kind of ocean swell.

See the Discover Tasmania website (www.discovertasmania.com) for climbing-trip and course listings, including Tasmanian Expeditions (p310) and **Rock Climbing Adventures Tasmania** (☎0438 087 477; www.rcat.com.au). Click on 'What to Do' then 'Outdoors and Adventure'.

Abseiling around the state doesn't get much better than dangling your way down the 140m-high face of the Gordon Dam near Strathgordon: contact Aardvark Adventures (p258).

Skiing

There are two petite ski resorts in Tasmania: Ben Lomond (p199), 55km southeast of Launceston, and Mt Mawson (p90) in Mt Field National Park, 80km northwest of Hobart. Both offer cheaper (though much less developed) ski facilities than mainland resorts. The ski season usually runs from July to mid-September, but snowfalls tend to be patchy and unreliable.

See www.ski.com.au/reports/australia/tas for snow conditions. For gear hire, contact Skigia (p78) in Hobart or Ben Lomond Snow Sports (p199).

Plan Your Trip

Travel with Children

As any parent will tell you, getting from A to B is the hardest part of travelling with children. Fortunately, in Tasmania A is never very far from B. This will leave your family feeling unhurried, stress-free and ready to enjoy the state's beaches, rivers, forests and wildlife parks.

Tasmania for Kids

Tasmania is naturally active, with plenty of fun times and exercise opportunities for children (sometimes all at once). Cruise past coastal scenery to spy on seals and dolphins, or paddle a kayak around Hobart's docks. Explore the forest canopy, or ride a mountain bike down Mt Wellington.

On the gentler side are riverbank bike paths and feeding times at Tassie's excellent wildlife parks. And when the kids have hiked, biked and kayaked all day, treat them to superfresh local fruit from a roadside stall, or some al fresco fish and chips.

Accommodation

Many motels and better-equipped caravan parks can supply cots. Caravan parks also often have playgrounds, sandpits, trampolines, games rooms, swimming pools and hectares of grass on which to run around.

Top-end, and some midrange, hotels are well versed in the needs of guests with children. Some may also have in-house children's videos and child-minding services. B&Bs, on the other hand, often market themselves as blissfully child free.

Eating Out with Children

Dining with kids in Tasmania rarely causes any hassles. If you sidestep the flashier restaurants, children are generally

Best Regions for Kids

Hobart & Around

A musical education: live Friday-night tunes at Salamanca Arts Centre followed by Saturday's Salamanca Market buskers. Other highlights include harbourside fish and chips, the Tasmanian Museum & Art Gallery and Mt Wellington for mountain biking and winter snowball throwing.

The Southeast

Check out Bruny Island's wild coastline by boat. Don't miss the Tahune Forest AirWalk, Hastings Caves and Thermal Springs and the Ida Bay Railway.

The East Coast

Brilliant beaches, Coles Bay kayaking, hungry Tasmanian devils at East Coast Natureworld and Bicheno's cute penguins.

Launceston & Around

Curious critters: City Park's Japanese macaques and the odd little residents at Beauty Point's Seahorse World and Platypus House. Defy gravity with the Cataract Gorge chairlift or some Cable Hang Gliding.

welcomed, particularly at Asian, Greek and Italian eateries. Cafes are kid-friendly and you'll see families getting in early for dinner in pub dining rooms. Most places can supply high chairs.

Dedicated kids menus are common, but selections are usually uninspiring (ham-and-pineapple pizza, fish fingers, chicken nuggets etc). If a restaurant doesn't have a kids menu, find something on the regular menu and ask the kitchen to adapt it. It's usually fine to bring toddler food in with you.

If the sun is shining, there are plenty of picnic spots around the state, many with free or coin-operated barbecues. During summer, Tassie is also a great place to buy fresh fruit at roadside stalls.

Breastfeeding & Nappy Changing

Most Tasmanians are relaxed about public breastfeeding and nappy changing: wrestling with a nappy in the open boot of a car is a common sight! Alternatively, Hobart and most major towns have public rooms where parents can go to feed their baby or change a nappy; ask at local visitor centres or city councils. Items such as infant formula and disposable nappies are widely available.

Babysitting

In Hobart contact the Mobile Nanny Service (p63); or check out the statewide listings on www.babysittersrus.com.au.

Admission Fees & Discounts

Child concessions (and family rates) often apply for accommodation, tours, museum admission and bus transport, with discounts as high as 50% of the adult rate.

Nearly all tourist attractions offer kids' prices, with kids under four or five years of age often admitted free. However, the definition of 'child' can vary from under 12 to under 18 years. Accommodation concessions generally apply to children under 12 years sharing the same room as adults. On the major airlines, infants up to three years of age travel free (provided they don't occupy a seat).

Children's Highlights

Getting Active

Tarkine Forest Adventures (p227) Slip down a 110m-long slide into a deep-forest sinkhole.

Tahune Forest AirWalk (p123) Make like a possum in the treetops, 20m above the ground.

Mt Wellington Descent (p60) Awesome downhill mountain-bike run from the summit to the Hobart waterfront.

Hollybank Treetops Adventure (p193) Swing through the trees with the greatest of ease.

Killiecrankie Enterprises (p169) Fossick for 'diamonds' (well, semi-precious topaz).

Meeting the Locals

Maria Island National Park (p140) Close-up encounters with wallabies, echidnas, honking Cape Barren geese and maybe even a Tasmanian devil.

Bonorong Wildlife Centre (p83) A whole bunch of beasts, not far from Hobart. The emphasis is on conservation and education.

Bicheno Penguin Tours (p154) Watch the waddling locals (no, not retirees) come home to roost.

Seahorse World (p188) On the waterfront at Beauty Point. 'Dad, what's a *Hippocampus*?'

DISCOVERY RANGERS

At Tasmania's most popular national parks during summer (usually from the week before Christmas until early February) and over Easter, the Parks & Wildlife Service (p302) runs a fab program of free, family-friendly 'Discovery Ranger' activities: guided walks, spotlight tours, slide shows, quiz nights and games.

National parks that stage these activities include Cradle Mountain–Lake St Clair, Freycinet, Maria Island, Tasman, Mt Field, Narawntapu and South Bruny. Click on 'Learning & Discovery' then 'Education Services' on the PWS website to see what's happening.

East Coast Natureworld (p154) Daily Tasmanian devil feeding sessions.

Messing about in Boats

Bruny Island Cruises (p113) Boat tours of the island's southern coastline, cliffs and caves.

Lady Nelson (p61) Tall-ship sailing on Hobart's Derwent River (just like the olden days).

Freycinet Adventures (p150) Easy-going sea-kayak paddles around sheltered Coles Bay. Sunset tours a bonus.

Huon Jet (p120) Jetboat rides on the otherwise tranquil Huon River in the southeast.

Arthur River Canoe & Boat Hire (p228) Paddle around on the Arthur River in a Canadian canoe.

Beaches & Swimming

Seven Mile Beach (p82) The best safe-swimming beach near Hobart.

Sisters Beach (p222) Sandy stretch and safe swimming in Rocky Cape National Park.

Douglas-Apsley National Park (p157) Take a dip in a deep, dark river waterhole.

Fortescue Bay (p103) If you've made the effort to drive in here, you might as well camp the night. And have a swim.

Cataract Gorge (p173) Cool off in the free outdoor swimming pool at First Basin.

We're Hungry, Mum

Flippers (p71) Fish and chips on Hobart's Constitution Dock. Launceston's equivalent is Fish 'n' Chips (p181) by the river.

Sorell Fruit Farm (p99) Bag your own fruit (cherries, strawberries, apricots, apples etc) on the doorstep of the Tasman Peninsula.

Doo-Lishus Food Caravan (p100) The best curried scallop pies in Tasmania are from this unassuming little food van near Eaglehawk Neck.

Honey Farm (p211) Grab a pot of the sticky stuff in Chudleigh.

House of Anvers (p206) For a quick-fire choc fix near Devonport.

A History Lesson

Historic Ghost Tour (p105) The Port Arthur Historic Site by day is creepy enough, but come back at dusk for extra atmos-fear.

Ida Bay Railway (p310) Historic WWII-era rattler, running 14km through bushland to the beach.

Callington Mill (p129) Oatland's old-time mill is cranking out flour again.

Beaconsfield Mine & Heritage Centre (p189) Hands-on gold-mining displays and plenty of heritage.

Mawson's Huts Replica Museum (p53) Antarctic heritage comes to Hobart.

Planning

Lonely Planet's *Travel with Children* contains buckets of useful information for travel with little 'uns. To aid your planning once you get to Tassie, pick up the free **LetsGoKids** (www.letsgokids.com.au) magazine at visitor information centres for activity ideas, kid-friendly accommodation listings and event discount vouchers.

When to Go

When it comes to family holidays, Tasmania is a winner during summer. Having said that, summer is peak season and school-holiday time: expect pricey accommodation and a lot of booking ahead for transport and accommodation (especially interstate flights, rental cars, the *Spirit of Tasmania* ferry, camping grounds and motels).

If your own kids don't need to be in school, a better bet may be the shoulder months of March and April (sidestepping Easter) and November, when the weather's still good and there's less pressure on the tourism sector. Winter is even better – if you don't mind the cold and aren't into swimming and camping, you'll have the whole place to yourselves!

What to Pack

Tasmania's weather is truly fickle, even in summer, so a diverse wardrobe with lots of layers is recommended. Definitely pack beach gear for your summer holiday, but also throw in a few thermal long-sleeve tops and jackets. A compact beach tent will also be handy, given Tasmania's capricious winds. Don't forget hats and sunglasses – essential for Tasmania's sharp southern rays.

Regions at a Glance

Hobart & Around

Arts Scene
Gourmet Travel
History

Festival Frenzy

On the quiet rim of the world, Hobart hosts some dizzyingly good arts festivals. MONA FOMA and Ten Days on the Island vie for top honours; Dark MOFO is disquieting and brilliant. Between events, Salamanca Place galleries keep the arts brew bubbling.

Eating & Drinking

Get a food-and-wine infusion from Hobart's fab festivals, hip cafes and restaurants, atmospheric pubs and craft-beer bars. Day-trip to the nearby Coal River Valley Wine Region, then finish up with fish and chips at Constitution Dock.

Old Hobart Town

Salamanca Place and tight-knit Battery Point are awash with memories of a challenging past. Huddled under Mt Wellington, Cascade Brewery and the Female Factory shine a light on two very different aspects of early Van Diemen's Land.

p46

Tasman Peninsula & Port Arthur

Activities
History
Wildlife

Exploring the Coast

Experience the Tasman Peninsula's rugged coast in a sea kayak, on a surfboard, on a boat cruise, or on foot along the super-scenic Tasman Coastal Trail. Camping at remote Fortescue Bay is a must.

Port Arthur & Beyond

Port Arthur's compelling mix of melancholia and photogenia is only the starting point for history buffs. Don't miss the underrated Coal Mines Historic Site and the history of the Dogline at Eaglehawk Neck.

Native Critters

Get a good look at a Tasmanian devil at the Tasmanian Devil Conservation Park (aka Tasmanian Devil Unzoo), then eyeball some seals, dolphins and whales on a sea-salty cruise around Tasman Island.

p97

The Southeast

Gourmet Travel
Wildlife
Natural Landscapes

Roadside Foodie Delights

Throw your schedule out the window and stop off at the southeast's vineyards and roadside fruit stalls. Across on Bruny Island, smoked seafood, fresh oysters, berry pies and handmade cheeses create further delays.

Birds on Bruny Island

Penguins and mutton birds are the immediate stars on Bruny Island, but an in-depth birdwatching excursion will reveal a veritable gaggle of pelagic species. Visit in October for the annual Bruny Island Bird Festival.

Caves, Peaks, Tarns & Springs

Explore the subterranean caverns and geothermal springs of the Hastings Caves and Thermal Springs area, then venture into a wilderness of glacial peaks and tarns in Hartz Mountains National Park.

p108

Midlands & Central Highlands

History
Fishing
Whisky

Heritage Highway

Imagine stage coaches and bushrangers as you rattle into historic towns along the Midland Hwy. Ross Bridge is a sturdy entry point to the town of Ross, and Callington Mill stands out amid Oatlands' fine sandstone buildings.

Trout-Fishing Nirvana

On a misty morning the Central Highlands' elevated lakes and rivers feel otherworldly...and the trout fishing is out of this world, too! Reminisce about the one that didn't get away at a snug lakeside pub.

Super Single Malt

Time for a wee dram? The heritage mill at Bothwell's Nant Distillery is worth a trip in itself. Then you taste Nant's amazing single malt... Detour to Tarraleah and sip into the lodge's cache of 200 single malt whiskies.

p127

The East Coast

Beaches
Gourmet Travel
Wildlife

Sandy Shores

Wineglass Bay and the Bay of Fires get all the press, but equally deserving are Redbill Beach, Spring Beach and Honeymoon Bay. Cool off after a bushwalk, camp behind the dunes or kayak the coast of Freycinet Peninsula.

Picnic Supplies

The east coast is a fertile hunting ground for foodies, with seasonal berries, oysters, chocolate, fresh seafood and wonderfully whiffy cheeses all on offer. Craft beer and excellent wines will also make it onto your beach-picnic menu.

Maria Island Locals

Maria Island National Park offers a mini-selection from Dr Dolittle's contact list: wallabies, pademelons, kangaroos, wombats, echidnas, tiger snakes, Cape Barren geese and a healthy population of Tasmanian devils. Offshore are seals, dolphins and wandering whales.

p137

Launceston & Around

Arts Scene
Architecture
Wine

Arty Events

Festivale is Launceston's annual summer arts festival. The city also hosts events during the Tasmania-wide Ten Days on the Island festival. The Tasmanian Breath of Fresh Air Film Festival and Junction Arts Festival are edgier.

Historic Launceston

Tasmania's second city has a compelling architectural heritage, with grand public buildings and an amazingly well-preserved crop of domestic architecture: Federation, Victorian, art deco, modern...it's all here. Tag onto a guided walking tour for the low-down.

Tamar Valley Wine Region

Tamar Valley vineyards produce world-class cool-climate wines. Our favourites include Ninth Island Vineyard, cascading down a hillside; Velo Wines with its brilliant cafe; and family-friendly Goaty Hill Wines. Who wants to drive?

p171

Devonport & the Northwest

Gourmet Travel
National Parks
Arts Scene

Beer, Chocolate & Whisky

These three major food groups are covered on yet another of Tasmania's excellent food trails. In between sampling the local chocolate, single malt whisky and craft beer, make some room for local smoked salmon, cheeses and fresh berries.

Camping & Caving

Head to the Walls of Jerusalem National Park for superb bushwalking – rug up for some dramatic camping during snow-covered winter. Not far away, turn off your torch and check out the glow-worms at Mole Creek Karst National Park.

Murals, Workshops & Galleries

The historic towns of Sheffield and Deloraine foster funky murals and creative arts cultures, while Burnie's Makers Workshop and Regional Art Gallery continue to push the boundaries of paper making and contemporary Tasmanian art respectively.

p200

Cradle Country & the West

Bushwalking
Kayaking
History

Alpine Heartland

The island's untamed southwest provides endless opportunities for bushwalking – up peaks, traversing tarn shelves and across moorlands. The return hike up Cradle Mountain is a robust eight hours; the Overland Track is a spectacular six- to eight-day epic.

Remote Waterways

Paddle onto mirror-flat Bathurst Harbour in a kayak, or set sail along the isolated Gordon and Pieman Rivers. For an adrenaline hit, a multi-day white-water rafting trip on the Franklin River will redefine your concept of wilderness.

Railways & Historic Towns

Ride the historic West Coast Wilderness Railway through rainforest between Queenstown and Strahan. The towns' differences couldn't be more stark – Queenstown's rugged, unabashed mining ambience versus Strahan's cutesy (but undeniably lovely) harbourside vibes.

p233

On the Road

Hobart & Around

Best Places to Eat

➡ Pilgrim Coffee (p69)

➡ Jackman & McRoss (p72)

➡ Retro Café (p71)

➡ Picnic Basket (p81)

Best Places to Stay

➡ Islington (p68)

➡ Henry Jones Art Hotel (p66)

➡ Alabama Hotel (p64)

➡ Quayle Terrace (p67)

➡ Daisy Bank Cottages (p84)

Why Go?

Australia's second-oldest city and southernmost capital, Hobart dapples the foothills of Mt Wellington, angling down to the slate-grey Derwent River. The town's rich cache of colonial architecture and natural charms are complemented by hip festivals, happening markets and top-notch food and drink.

It's a gorgeous place, but until quite recently Hobart was far from cosmopolitan or self-assured – it's taken a while for Hobartians to feel comfortable in their own skins. Paralleling this shift (or perhaps driving it), the mainland Australian attitude to Hobart has changed from derision to delight: investors now recognise that Tasmania's abundant water, stress-free pace and cool climate are precious commodities.

Not far past the outskirts of town are some great beaches, alpine areas and historic villages. And don't miss MONA, Hobart's dizzyingly good Museum of Old and New Art, which has vehemently stamped Tasmania onto the global cultural map.

When to Go

➡ For a week either side of New Year's Eve, Hobart heaves with sailors, travellers, food festivals and concerts. This is prime-time Hobart, when the old town treads the boards of the world stage.

➡ During the long days of summer – January into February – the time is right for eating, drinking, afternoons at the cricket and maybe even a swim (when the sea around Hobart is warm...almost).

➡ When the southern winter blows in (June to August), catch some Australian Rules football, throw snowballs on Mt Wellington or Mt Field and cosy up by an open fire in a pub. Crowds are down, so take your pick of the waterfront accommodation.

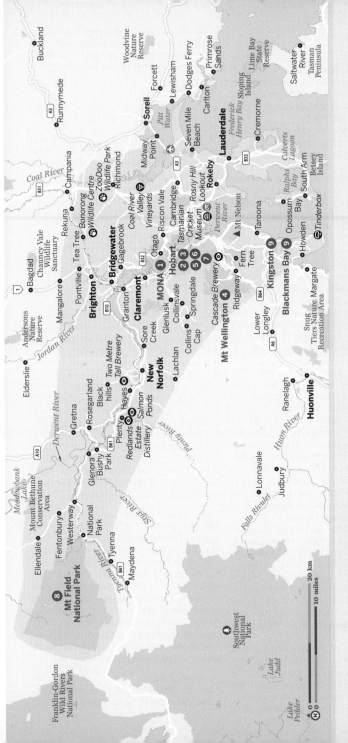

Hobart & Around Highlights

1 Be inspired, turned on, appalled, educated and amused at **MONA** (p57).

2 Lose yourself in the crowds at Hobart's Saturday morning **Salamanca Market** (p53).

3 While away an afternoon exploring historic **Battery Point** (p53).

4 Career down from the summit of Mt Wellington on a **mountain bike** (p60).

5 Sip your way towards the weekend at **Knopwood's Retreat** (p76), Hobart's best pub.

6 Devour fish and chips from **Flippers** (p71) fish punt.

7 See what's cooking along the ever-evolving **North Hobart restaurant strip** (p74).

8 Brace yourself for a cold-water spray at **Russell Falls** (p89) in Mt Field National Park.

9 Splash into the chilly sea south of Hobart at **Kingston** (p81) or **Blackmans Bay** (p82).

HOBART

POP 218,000

No doubt about it, Hobart's future is looking rosy. Tourism is booming and the old town is brimming with new-found self-confidence. Plan on staying a while – you'll need at least a few days to savour the full range of beers flowing from the city's pubs.

Riding high above the city is Mt Wellington, a rugged monolith seemingly made for mountain biking and bushwalking. Down on the waterfront, the cafes, bars and restaurants along Salamanca Pl and in nearby Battery Point showcase the best of Tassie produce. There's more great eating and boozing in cashed-up Sandy Bay and along Elizabeth St in bohemian North Hobart.

History

Hobart's original inhabitants were the seminomadic Mouheneenner band of the Southeast Aboriginal tribe, who called the area Nibberloonne. In 1803 the first European settlers in Van Diemen's Land pitched their tents at Risdon Cove on the Derwent River's eastern shore, which became the site of the first massacre of the Mouheneenner (Risdon Cove was returned to the Aboriginal community by the state government in 1995). The colony relocated a year later to the site of present-day Hobart, where water running off Mt Wellington was plentiful.

When Britain's jails overflowed with sinners in the 1820s, Hobart's isolation loomed as a major selling point. Tens of thousands of convicts were chained into rotting hulks and shipped down to Hobart Town to serve their sentences in vile conditions. In the 1840s, Hobart's sailors, soldiers, whalers and rapscallions boozed and brawled shamelessly in countless harbourside pubs.

With the abolition of convict transportation to Tasmania in 1853, Hobart became marginally more moral and the town came to rely on the apple and wool industries for its fiscal fortitude. In the 20th century Hobart stuttered through the Great Depression and both World Wars, relying on the production of paper, zinc and chocolate and the deep-water Derwent River harbour to sustain it.

It could be argued that the city has only ever partially sobered up – the day Hobart's waterfront is no longer the place to go for a beer will be a sad day indeed – but today's convicts are more likely to be white-collared than bad company at the bar. Skeletons rattle in Hobart's closet – Indigenous Tasmanians and thousands of convicts suffered here – but the city's shimmering beauty and relaxed vibe scare away the ghosts of the past.

⊙ Sights

◉ City Centre

★**Farm Gate Market**   MARKET
(Map p54; www.farmgatemarket.com.au; Bathurst St, btwn Elizabeth & Murray Sts; ⊙9am-1pm Sun) Salamanca Market on the waterfront has been a success for decades, but this hyperactive new foodie street-mart might just give it a run for its money. Trading commences with the ding of a big brass bell at 9am. Elbow your way in for the best buys, or take your time to browse the fruit, veg, honey, wine, baked goods, beer, smoked meats, coffee, nuts, oils, cut flowers and jams... Terrific!

**Penitentiary Chapel
Historic Site**   HISTORIC SITE
(Map p50; ☑03-6231 0911; www.penitentiarychapel.com; cnr Brisbane & Campbell Sts; tours adult/child/family $12/5/25; ⊙tours 10am, 11.30am, 1pm & 2.30pm Sun-Fri, 1pm & 2.30pm Sat) Ruminating over the courtrooms, cells and gallows here, writer TG Ford mused: 'As the Devil was going through Hobart Gaol, he saw a solitary cell; and the Devil was pleased for it gave him a hint, for improving the prisons in hell.' Take the excellent National Trust–run tour here, or the one-hour **Penitentiary Chapel Ghost Tour** (Map p50; ☑03-6231 0911; www.hobartghosts.com; adult/child/family $15/10/50; ⊙8.30pm Mon & Fri) held twice weekly (bookings essential).

Maritime Museum of Tasmania   MUSEUM
(Map p54; ☑03-6234 1427; www.maritimetas.org; 16 Argyle St; adult/child/family $9/5/18; ⊙9am-5pm) Highlighting shipwrecks, boat building, whaling and Hobart's unbreakable bond with the sea, the Maritime Museum of Tasmania has an interesting (if a little static) collection of photos, paintings, models and relics (try to resist ringing the huge brass bell from the *Rhexenor*). Upstairs is the council-run **Carnegie Gallery** (Map p54; ⊙10am-5pm) FREE, exhibiting contemporary Tasmanian art, craft, design and photography.

Parliament House   HISTORIC BUILDING
(Map p56; ☑03-6212 2248; www.parliament.tas.gov.au; Salamanca Pl; ⊙tours 10am & 2pm Mon-

Fri on nonsitting days) FREE Presiding over an oak-studded park adjacent to Salamanca Pl, Tasmania's sandstone Parliament House (1840) was originally a customs house. There's a tunnel under Murray St from Parliament House to the Customs House pub opposite: the official line is that no one knows what it was used for, but we'd hazard a guess... Public 45-minute tours run when parliament isn't sitting.

Theatre Royal   HISTORIC BUILDING
(Map p50; www.theatreroyal.com.au; 29 Campbell St; 1hr tour adult/child $12/10; ☺tours 11am Mon, Wed & Fri) Take a backstage tour of Hobart's prestigious Theatre Royal. Host to bombastic thespians since 1834, and despite a major fire in 1984, it remains Australia's oldest continuously operating theatre.

Hobart Real Tennis Club   HISTORIC BUILDING
(Royal Tennis Club; Map p54; ☑03-6231 1781; www.hobarttennis.com.au; 45 Davey St; ☺9am-6pm Mon-Fri) Dating from 1875, this is one of only five such tennis courts in the southern hemisphere (the others are in Melbourne, Ballarat, Sydney, and Romsey in country Victoria). Real (or 'Royal') tennis is an archaic form of the highly strung game, played in a jaunty four-walled indoor court. Visitors can watch, take a lesson ($50) or hire the court ($40 per hour per two players).

Allport Library &
Museum of Fine Arts   MUSEUM
(Map p54; ☑03-6165 5584; www.linc.tas.gov.au/findus/southern/statewide/allport; 91 Murray St; ☺9.30am-5pm Mon-Fri, to 2pm Sat) FREE The State Library is home to this collection of rare books on the Australia-Pacific region, as well as colonial paintings, antiques, visiting exhibits and a special collection of artworks that get dusted off for display several times a year.

Australian Army
Museum Tasmania   MUSEUM
(Anglesea Barracks; Map p50; ☑03-6237 7160; www.militarymuseumtasmania.org.au; cnr Davey & Byron Sts; adult/family $5/10; ☺9am-1pm Tue-Sat, guided tours 11am Tue) The Anglesea Barracks were built adjacent to Battery Point in 1811. Still used by the army, this is the oldest military establishment in Australia. Inside is a volunteer-staffed museum, which runs 45-minute guided tours of the buildings and grounds on Tuesdays.

HOBART IN...

Two Days

Get your head into history mode with an amble around **Battery Point** (p53) – coffee and cake at **Jackman & McRoss** (p72) is mandatory. Afterwards, wander down Kelly's Steps to **Salamanca Place** (p52), where you can check out the craft shops and galleries or chug a few cool Cascades at **Knopwood's Retreat** (p76), the quintessential Hobart pub. Bone up on Hobart's Antarctic heritage at the **Mawson's Huts Replica Museum** (p53) before a promenade along the Sullivans Cove waterfront and fish and chips for dinner from **Flippers** (p71) fish punt. On a Friday or Saturday night, leave the seagulls to finish off your chips, and sniff out a few single malts at **Lark Distillery** (p53).

On day two recuperate over a big breakfast at **Retro Café** (p71) on Salamanca Pl (if it's a Saturday, **Salamanca Market** (p53) will be pumping), then catch the ferry out to **MONA** (p57) for an afternoon of saucy, subversive, mindful distraction. Come down to earth with dinner and drinks in **North Hobart** (p74) followed by some live music at **Republic Bar & Café** (p77).

Four Days

If you've got a bit more time on your hands, blow out the cobwebs with a mountain-bike ride down **Mt Wellington** (p60) – on a clear day it'll be hard to keep your eyes on the road. Tucked into the foothills of the mountain in South Hobart is the legendary **Cascade Brewery** (p56): take a tour and sip a few beers. Snooze away the afternoon on the sunny lawns of the **Royal Tasmanian Botanical Gardens** (p58), then boot it back into the city for dinner.

Still here? On day four take a photo-worthy day trip to nearby **Richmond** (p82), or to the waterfalls and alpine peaks of **Mt Field National Park** (p89). Wine buffs will find plenty to quaff en route to Richmond in the **Coal River Valley wine region** (p83).

Hobart

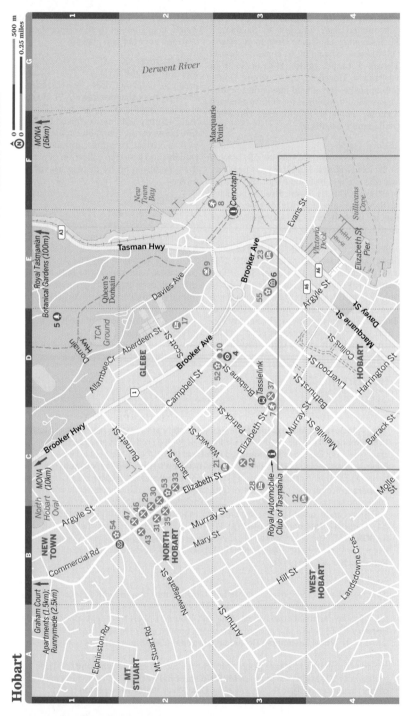

Derwent River

Macquarie Point

New Town Bay

Queen's Domain

TCA Ground

Botanical Gardens (100m);
Royal Tasmanian

MONA
(16km)

Tasman Hwy

Cenotaph

Brooker Ave

Brooker Ave

Davies Ave

Aberdeen St

Scott St

Domain Hwy

Allambee Cr

GLEBE

Campbell St

Brooker Hwy

MONA
(10km)

Burnett St

Patrick St

Warwick St

Tasma St

Elizabeth St

Elizabeth St

North Hobart Oval

Argyle St

NORTH HOBART

Murray St

Mary St

NEW TOWN

Commercial Rd

Newdegate St

MT STUART

Elphinston Rd

Mt Stuart Rd

Arthur St

Graham Court
Apartments (1.5km);
Runnymede (2.5km)

Hill St

WEST HOBART

Landsdowne Cres

Royal Automobile
Club of Tasmania

Molle St

Evans St

Sullivans Cove

Victoria Dock

Elizabeth St Pier

Argyle St

HOBART

Macquarie St

Davey St

Collins St

Liverpool St

Bathurst St

Melville St

Murray St

Harrington St

Barrack St

500 m
0.25 miles

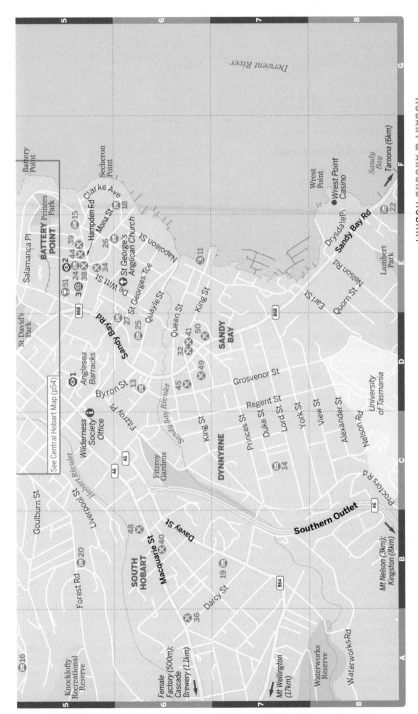

Hobart

◉ **Sights**
1 Anglesea Barracks.................................D5
   Australian Army Museum
   Tasmania ....(see 1)
2 Battery Point.......................................E5
3 Narryna Heritage Museum..................E5
4 Penitentiary Chapel Historic Site D3
5 Queen's Domain....................................D1
6 Theatre Royal.......................................E3

⊕ **Activities, Courses & Tours**
7 Artbikes...D3
8 Derwent Bike Hire..............................F2
9 Hobart Aquatic Centre.........................E2
10 Penitentiary Chapel Ghost Tour...........D3
11 Roaring 40s Kayaking...........................E6

⊜ **Sleeping**
12 Altamont House....................................C3
13 Apartments on Star...............................D6
14 At Eleven – La Petite Maison...............C7
15 Battery Point Boutique
   Accommodation.................................E5
16 Bay View Villas...................................A5
17 Corinda's Cottages..............................D2
18 Grande Vue Private Hotel....................F6
19 Islington..B7
20 Library House......................................B5
21 Lodge on Elizabeth..............................C3
   Montacute......................................(see 3)
22 Motel 429..F8
23 Old Woolstore Apartment Hotel...........E3
24 Prince of Wales Hotel...........................E5
25 Quayle Terrace....................................D6
26 Shipwright's Arms Hotel......................E6
27 St Ives Motel.......................................D6

28 Waratah Hotel......................................C3

⊗ **Eating**
29 All Thai..B2
30 Annapurna..C2
   Berta..(see 29)
31 Burger Haus...B2
32 Don Camillo...D6
33 Elizabeth St Food + Wine.....................C2
34 Environs...E5
35 Fresco Market......................................B2
36 Ginger Brown.......................................A6
37 Island Espresso....................................D3
38 Jackman & McRoss..............................E5
39 Jam Jar Lounge....................................E5
40 Macquarie St Foodstore.......................B6
   Magic Curries................................(see 39)
41 Me Wah..D6
42 Pasha's..C3
43 Raincheck Lounge B2
44 Ristorante Da Angelo...........................E5
45 Solo Pasta & Pizza...............................D6
46 Sweet Envy..B2
47 Vanidol's..B2
48 Vanidol's..B6
49 Woolworths..D6
50 Written on Tea.....................................D6

◉ **Drinking & Nightlife**
51 Preachers...E5

✪ **Entertainment**
52 Brisbane Hotel.....................................D3
53 Republic Bar & Café.............................C2
54 State Cinema B1
55 Theatre Royal......................................E3

◎ Waterfront & Salamanca Place

★ Salamanca Place   HISTORIC SITE
(Map p56; www.salamanca.com.au) This picturesque row of four-storey sandstone warehouses is a classic example of Australian
colonial architecture. Dating back to the
whaling days of the 1830s, Salamanca was
the hub of Hobart's trade and commerce.
By the mid-20th century many of the warehouses had fallen into ruin, before res-
torations began in the 1970s. These days
Salamanca hosts myriad restaurants, cafes,
bars and shops, and the unmissable Saturday morning Salamanca Market.

The development of the quarry behind
the warehouses into Salamanca Sq has bolstered the atmosphere, while at the eastern
end of Salamanca the conversion of four old
wheat silos into plush apartments has also
been a hit.

Operating behind the scenes is a vibrant
and creative arts community. The nonprofit
Salamanca Arts Centre (Map p56; ☏03-
6234 8414; www.salarts.org.au; 77 Salamanca Pl;
⊙shops & galleries 9am-5pm) occupies seven
Salamanca warehouses, home to 75-plus
arts organisations and individuals, including shops, galleries, studios, performing-arts
venues and versatile public spaces. Check
the website for happenings.

To reach Salamanca from Battery Point,
descend the well-weathered Kelly's Steps
(1839), wedged between warehouses halfway along the main block of buildings.

Waterfront   HISTORIC SITE
(Map p54) Hobartians flock to the city's waterfront like seagulls to chips. Centred around
Victoria Dock (a working fishing harbour)
and Constitution Dock (chock-full of floating takeaway-seafood punts), it's a brilliant

place to explore. The obligatory Hobart experience is to sit in the sun, munch some fish and chips and watch the harbour hubbub. If you'd prefer something with a knife and fork, there are some superb restaurants here, too – head for Elizabeth St Pier.

Celebrations surrounding the finish of the annual Sydney to Hobart Yacht Race (p64) also revolve around Constitution Dock at New Year. The fab food festival Taste of Tasmania (p63) is also in full swing around this time. There are so many people around the waterfront, Hobart could be Monaco! The waterfront on New Year's Eve can be both exhilarating and nauseating (depending on how late you stay out).

Hunter St has a row of fine Georgian warehouses, most of which comprised the old Henry Jones IXL jam factory. It's occupied these days by the University of Tasmania's Art School and the uber-swish Henry Jones Art Hotel (p66), both retaining their original heritage facades.

Most of the Hobart waterfront area is built on reclaimed land. When the town was first settled, Davey St marked the shoreline and the Hunter St area was an island used to store food and imported goods. Subsequent projects filled in the shallow waters and created the land upon which the Hunter St and Salamanca Pl warehouses were constructed. On Hunter St itself, markers indicate the position of the original causeway, built in 1820 to link Hunter Island with the long-since-demolished suburb of Wapping.

★ Mawson's Huts
Replica Museum   MUSEUM
(Map p54; www.mawsons-huts-replica.org.au; cnr Morrison & Argyle Sts; adult/child/family $12/4/26; ⊘9am-6pm Oct-Apr, 10am-5pm May-Sep) This excellent new waterfront installation is an exact model of the hut in which Sir Douglas Mawson hunkered down on his 1911–14 Australasian Antarctic Expedition, which set sail from Hobart. Inside it is 100% authentic, right down to the matches, the stove and the bunks. A knowledgeable guide sits at a rustic table, ready to answer your Antarctic enquiries. Entry fees go towards the upkeep of the original hut at Cape Denison in the Antarctic.

Tasmanian Museum & Art Gallery MUSEUM
(Map p54; www.tmag.tas.gov.au; Dunn Pl; ⊘10am-4pm Tue-Sun) FREE Incorporating Hobart's oldest building, the Commissariat Store (1808), this revamped museum features colonial relics and excellent Aboriginal

DON'T MISS

SALAMANCA MARKET

Every Saturday morning since 1972, the open-air Salamanca Market (Map p56; www.salamanca.com.au; ⊘8am-3pm Sat) has lured hippies and craft merchants from the foothills to fill the tree-lined expanses of Salamanca Pl with their stalls. Fresh organic produce, secondhand clothes and books, tacky tourist souvenirs, ceramics and woodwork, cheap sunglasses, antiques, exuberant buskers, quality food and drink… It's all here, but people-watching is the real name of the game. Rain or shine – don't miss it!

and wildlife displays. The gallery curates a collection of Tasmanian colonial art. There are free guided tours at 1pm and 2pm from Wednesday to Sunday (hordes of school kids might be a little less interested in proceedings than you are), plus tours of a historic cottage within the museum grounds at 11am on Wednesdays. There's a cool cafe, too.

Lark Distillery   DISTILLERY
(Map p54; ☑03-6231 9088; www.larkdistillery.com.au; 14 Davey St; tastings per person $15, 3hr whisky tours per person $75; ⊘9am-7pm Sun-Thu, to 10pm Fri & Sat) The Lark Distillery, next door to the visitor information centre, is at the fore of Tasmania's surge into the world of single malt whisky. Enjoy a wee dram via a tasting session, or a longer tour of the distillery that's 20 minutes' drive from the cellar door. On Friday and Saturday nights there's live music from 6pm, plus cheese-and-dip platters and Moo Brew on tap, if you're more of a beer boffin.

◎ Battery Point, Sandy Bay & South Hobart

Battery Point   HISTORIC SITE
(Map p50; www.batterypoint.net) An empty rum bottle's throw from the waterfront, the old maritime village of Battery Point is a tight nest of lanes and 19th-century cottages, packed together like shanghaied landlubbers in a ship's belly. Spend an afternoon exploring: stumble up Kelly's Steps from Salamanca Pl and dogleg into South St, where the red lights once burned night and day. Spin around picturesque Arthur Circus, refuel in the cafes on Hampden Rd, then ogle St George's Anglican Church on Cromwell St.

Central Hobart

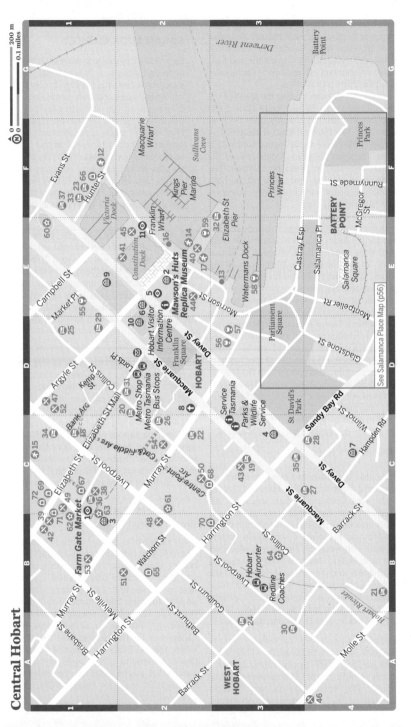

Central Hobart

Battery Point's name derives from the 1818 gun battery that stood on the promontory, protecting Hobart Town from nautical threats both real and imagined. The guns were never used in battle and the only damage they inflicted was on nearby windowpanes when fired during practice.

Architectural styles here reflect the original occupants' varying jobs (and salaries), ranging from one- and two-room fishermen's cottages to the lace-festooned mansions of merchants and master mariners. Most houses are still occupied by Hobartians, and many are now guesthouses where you can stay (usually for a pretty penny) and absorb the village atmosphere. For a fortifying stout, duck into the Shipwright's Arms Hotel (p68).

Salamanca Place

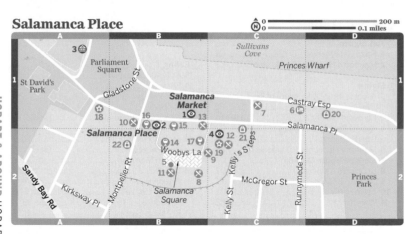

N ⊕ 0 | 200 m
0 | 0.1 miles

Salamanca Place

◎ Top Sights
1 Salamanca Market B1
2 Salamanca Place B1

◎ Sights
3 Parliament House A1
4 Salamanca Arts Centre C2

✪ Activities, Courses & Tours
5 Ghost Tours of Hobart & Battery
  Point B2

⌂ Sleeping
6 Salamanca Wharf Hotel C1

✸ Eating
7 Blue Eye C1
8 Machine Laundry Café B2
9 Mezethes C2
10 Retro Café B1
11 Salamanca Bakehouse B2

Salamanca Fresh ....(see 16)
12 Tricycle Café Bar C2
13 Vietnamese Kitchen B1

◒ Drinking & Nightlife
14 Barcelona B2
15 Jack Greene B1
16 Knopwood's Retreat B1
17 Nant Whisky Bar B2
  Syrup ....(see 16)

◉ Entertainment
18 Irish Murphy's A1
  Peacock Theatre .... (see 4)
19 Salamanca Arts Centre Courtyard C2

◉ Shopping
20 Despard Gallery D1
21 Handmark Gallery C2
22 Wursthaus B2

Cascade Brewery BREWERY
(☏ 03-6224 1117; www.cascadebrewery.com.au; 140 Cascade Rd, South Hobart; adult/family brewery tours $25/65, heritage tours $15/37; ⊙ brewery tours 11am & 12.30pm daily, heritage tours 12.30pm Mon, Wed & Fri) Standing in startling, gothic isolation next to the clean-running Hobart Rivulet, Cascade is Australia's oldest brewery (1832) and still pumps out superb beers. Tours involve plenty of history, with tastings at the end. Note that under-16s aren't permitted on the brewery tour (take the family-friendly Heritage Tour instead), and that brewery machinery doesn't operate on weekends (brewers have weekends, too). Bookings essential. To get here, take bus 44, 46, 47 or 49.

Mt Wellington MOUNTAIN
(Kunanyi; www.wellingtonpark.org.au; Pinnacle Rd, via Fern Tree) Cloaked in winter snow, Mt Wellington (1270m) towers above Hobart like a benevolent overlord. The citizens find reassurance in its constant, solid presence, while outdoorsy types find the space to hike and bike on its leafy flanks. And the view from the top is unbelievable! You can drive all the way to the summit on a sealed road; alternatively, the Hobart Shuttle Bus Company (☏ 0408 341 804; www.hobartshuttlebus.com; tours per adult/child $30/20, transfers per person $20) runs daily two-hour tours to the summit, plus one-way transfers for walkers.

Hacked out of the mountainside during the Great Depression, the summit road winds up from the city through thick temperate forest, opening out to lunar rockscapes at the summit. If you don't have wheels, local buses 48 and 49 stop at Fern Tree halfway up the hill, from where it's a five- to six-hour return walk to the top via Fern Glade Track, Radfords Track, Pinnacle Track and then the steep Zig Zag Track. The Organ Pipes walk from the Chalet (en route to the summit) is a flat track below these amazing cliffs. Download maps at www.wellingtonpark.org.au/maps, or pick up the free *Wellington Park* walk map or detailed *Wellington Park Recreation Map* ($9.90) from the visitor information centre.

Feeling more intrepid? Bomb down the slopes on a mountain bike with Mt Wellington Descent (p60). Don't be deterred if the sky is overcast – often the peak rises above cloud level and looks out over a magic carpet of cotton-topped clouds.

Female Factory　　　HISTORIC SITE

(☑03-6233 6656; www.femalefactory.org.au; 16 Degraves St, South Hobart; adult/child/family admission $5/5/15, tour $15/10/40, 'Her Story' dramatisation $20/12.50/60; ☉9.30am-4pm, tours hourly 10am-3pm, 'Her Story' dramatisation 11am) Finally being recognised as an important historic site (one in four convicts transported to Van Diemen's Land was a woman), this was where Hobart's female convicts were incarcerated. Explore the site under your own steam, or book a guided tour or 'Her Story' dramatisation. It's not far from the Cascade Brewery – combining the two makes an engaging afternoon. To get here by public transport, take bus 44, 46, 47 or 49 and jump off at stop 13.

Narryna Heritage Museum　　MUSEUM

(Map p50; ☑03-6234 2791; www.narryna.com.au; 103 Hampden Rd, Battery Point; adult/child $10/4; ☉10am-4.30pm Tue-Sat, noon-4.30pm Sun) This stately Greek-revival sandstone-fronted mansion (pronounced 'Narinna'), built in 1837, is set in established grounds and contains a treasure trove of domestic colonial artefacts. Not far away is the adjunct Markree House Museum (Map p54; www.tmag.tas.gov.au/visitor_information/markree_museum; 145 Hampden Rd, Battery Point; adult/child $10/4; ☉10.30am-5pm Sat Oct-Apr, tours 10.30am & 2.30pm Tue-Sun), putting a 1920s spin on Hobart domestic life; book a for guided tours.

Mt Nelson　　　VIEWPOINT

(Nelson Rd) The Old Signal Station atop Mt Nelson (352m) provides immaculate views over Hobart and the Derwent estuary. The Mt Nelson semaphore station (established 1811) was once the major link between Hobart and the Port Arthur penal colony further south. To get here, drive up Davey St then take the Southern Outlet towards Kingston and turn left at the top of the hill. Local buses 57, 58, 156 and 158 also come here.

There's a sassy restaurant (p73) beside the signal station, plus barbecues and picnic tables. You can also walk to the top via the 90-minute return Truganini Track, which starts at Cartwright Reserve beside the Channel Hwy in Taroona (p80).

◉ North & West Hobart

★MONA　　　MUSEUM, GALLERY

(Museum of Old & New Art; ☑03-6277 9900; www.mona.net.au; 655 Main Rd, Berriedale; adult/child $20/free, Tasmanian residents free; ☉10am-6pm Wed-Mon Dec & Feb-Apr, 10am-6pm daily Jan, 10am-5pm Wed-Mon May-Nov) Twelve kilometres north of Hobart's city centre, MONA occupies a saucepan-shaped peninsula jutting into the Derwent River. Arrayed across three underground levels, abutting a sheer rock face, the $75-million museum has been described by philanthropist owner David Walsh as 'a subversive adult Disneyland'. Ancient antiquities are showcased next to contemporary works: sexy, provocative, disturbing and deeply engaging. Don't miss it!

HERITAGE BUILDINGS

Hobart's amazing cache of well-cured old buildings makes it exceptional among Australian cities. There are more than 90 buildings classified by the National Trust – 60 of them are on Macquarie and Davey Sts. The intersections of these streets feature a gorgeous sandstone edifice on each corner, including the austere St David's Cathedral (Map p54; www.saint-davids.org.au; 23 Murray St; ☉8.30am-5pm Mon-Fri, 9am-5pm Sat, 8am-7.30pm Sun). Also worth a look is the 1864 Town Hall (Map p54; www.hobartcity.com.au; 50 Macquarie St; ☉8.15am-5.15pm Mon-Fri), taking its architectural prompts from the Palazzo Farnese in Rome.

SYDNEY TO HOBART YACHT RACE

Arguably the world's greatest and most treacherous open-ocean yacht race, the Sydney to Hobart Yacht Race (p64) winds up at Hobart's Constitution Dock some time around New Year's Eve. As the storm-battered maxis limp across the finish line, champagne corks pop and weary sailors turn the town upside down. On New Year's Day, find a sunny spot by the harbour, munch some lunch from the Taste of Tasmania food festival and count spinnakers on the river. New Year's resolutions? What New Year's resolutions?

To get here catch the MONA Roma ferry or shuttle bus from Hobart's Brooke St Pier ($20 return). Book everything online.

Also at MONA is the cellar door for Moorilla (☑03-6277 9960; www.moorilla.com.au; tastings $10, redeemable with purchase; ☉9.30am-5pm Wed-Mon, daily Jan), a winery established here in the 1950s. Duck in for a wine or Moo Brew beer tasting, or have lunch upstairs at the outstanding restaurant, The Source (☑03-6277 9900; www.mona.net.au/mona/restaurant; lunch mains $27-38, dinner degustation from $75; ☉7.30-10am & noon-2pm Wed-Mon, 6pm-late Wed-Sat). You can also catch a summer concert on the lawns, or maybe splash out for a night in the uber-swish Pavilions (p69).

MONA is also the driving force behind Hobart's annual MONA FOMA (p63) arts and music festival, and the disquieting Dark MOFO (p63) winter festival.

Royal Tasmanian Botanical Gardens
GARDENS

(☑03-6236 3057; www.rtbg.tas.gov.au; Lower Domain Rd, Queens Domain; ☉8am-6.30pm Oct-Mar, to 5.30pm Apr & Sep, to 5pm May-Aug) FREE On the eastern side of the Queen's Domain, these small but beguiling gardens hark back to 1818 and feature more than 6000 exotic and native plant species. Picnic on the lawns, check out the Subantarctic Plant House or grab a bite at the Botanical Restaurant, which also houses a gift shop and kiosk. Across from the main entrance is the site of the former Beaumaris Zoo, where the last captive Tasmanian tiger died in 1936.

Queen's Domain
PARK

(www.hobartcity.com.au/recreation/queens_domain) When Hobart was settled, the leafy hill on the city's northern side was the governor's private playground, upon which no houses were to be built. Today the hillock is called the Queen's Domain and is public parkland, strewn with cricket, tennis and athletics centres, the Hobart Aquatic Centre (p61), native grasslands, lookouts and the Royal Tasmanian Botanical Gardens. Pedestrian overpasses on the western side provide easy access to North Hobart.

Moonah Arts Centre Art Gallery
GALLERY

(☑03-6214 7633; www.moonahartscentre.org.au; 23-27 Albert Rd, Moonah; ☉10am-5pm Tue-Fri, to 2pm Sat) FREE Opened in 2015, the new Albert Rd building for this long-running community arts co-op stages everything from Indigenous arts exhibitions and concerts to workshops and special events. Buses departing stop E on Elizabeth St go to groovy Moonah.

Lady Franklin Gallery
GALLERY

(☑03-6228 0076; www.artstas.com.au/our-history/lady-franklin-gallery; Ancanthe Park, 268 Lenah Valley Rd, Lenah Valley; ☉11am-5pm Sat & Sun Nov-Apr, to 4pm Sat & Sun May-Oct) FREE In an exquisitely proportioned colonnaded 1842 sandstone building called Ancanthe (Greek for 'vale of flowers' – enough of a reason to visit alone), the Lady Franklin Gallery displays contemporary work by Tasmanian artists. To get here without your own wheels, take bus 6, 7, 8 or 9.

Runnymede
HISTORIC BUILDING

(☑03-6278 1269; www.nationaltrusttas.org.au; 61 Bay Rd, New Town; adult/child $10/free; ☉10am-4.30pm Tue-Fri, noon-4.30pm Sun) This gracious 1840 sandstone-and-slate residence is 5km north of the city centre in New Town. It was built for Robert Pitcairn, the first lawyer to qualify in Tasmania, and named by a later owner, whaling captain Charles Bayley, after his favourite ship. Visiting is largely a DIY affair: contact the National Trust or check the website for any upcoming tours or events. To get here, take bus 15, 16 or 20.

Cadbury Chocolate Factory
FOOD FACTORY

(☑1800 627 367; www.cadbury.com.au; 100 Cadbury Rd, Claremont; adult/child $4/free; ☉8am-4pm Mon-Fri Nov-Apr, 8.30am-3.30pm Mon-Fri May-Oct) Cadbury no longer runs factory tours (occupational health and safety...sigh), but you can still catch a 30-minute info session (hourly from 9am to 2pm) and invest in some choc products. Driving is the best way to get here or, if you must, take bus 37, 39 or 40.

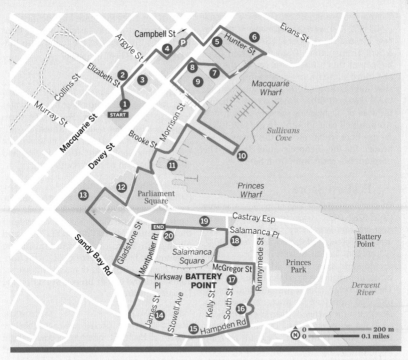

City Walk
Hobart's Harbour & History

START FRANKLIN SQ
END KNOPWOOD'S RETREAT
LENGTH 3KM; THREE HOURS

Launch your expedition at **1** **Franklin Sq** under the statue of Sir John Franklin. Track down Macquarie St past the 1906 sandstone clock tower of the **2** **General Post Office** (p79), the 1864 **3** **Town Hall** (p57) and into the **4** **Tasmanian Museum & Art Gallery** (p53). Navigate across Campbell and Davey Sts to the fishing boats at **5** **Victoria Dock** (p52).

Check out the renovated **6** **Henry Jones Art Hotel** (p66). Formerly the IXL jam factory, it was once Tasmania's largest private employer. Cross the swing bridge and fishtail towards **7** **Mures** (p72) or **8** **Flippers** (p71) for lunch by **9** **Constitution Dock**.

Next stop is the slickly reworked **10** **Elizabeth St Pier** jutting into Sullivans Cove – classy accommodation upstairs, restaurants and bars downstairs. If the tide is out, take the low-road steps around **11** **Watermans Dock**. Cross Morrison St then wander through Parliament Sq in front of **12** **Parliament House** (p48). Resist the photogenic frontage of Salamanca Pl for now, turning right instead to detour through **13** **St David's Park**, the site of Hobart Town's original cemetery, with a picturesque pergola and walls of colonial gravestones. Cut through Salamanca Mews, jag right onto Gladstone St, left onto Kirksway Pl then right onto Montpellier Retreat, arcing uphill into **14** **Battery Point** (p53), Hobart's oldest residential area.

Reconstitute with a coffee and pie at **15** **Jackman & McRoss** (p72), then turn left into Runnymede St to check out **16** **Arthur Circus**, an improbably quaint roundabout lined with eave-free Georgian cottages. Continue down Runnymede St and turn left into McGregor St, casting an eye up well-preserved **17** **South St**. Turn right onto Kelly St and bumble down **18** **Kelly's Steps**, an 1839 sandstone link between Battery Point and the redeveloped warehouses of **19** **Salamanca Place** (p52). Nearby is our favourite Hobart pub, **20** **Knopwood's Retreat** (p76), and a well-earned cold beer.

Tasmanian Transport Museum   MUSEUM
(☑ 03-6272 7721; www.railtasmania.com/ttms; Anfield St, Glenorchy; adult/child $8/4; ☺ 1-4pm Sat & Sun) Trainspotter? Tram fan? Train rides happen at this transport mecca on the first and third Sundays of each month (admission increases to $10/8 per adult/child on these days). At other times, you can mourn the loss of Tasmania's passenger-train network, which called it quits in the mid-1970s. To get here, catch any of the many buses headed for the Glenorchy interchange. The museum is a short walk from here.

⊙ Eastern Shore

Tasmanian Cricket Museum   MUSEUM
(☑ 03-6282 0433; www.crickettas.com.au/blundstone-arena/museum-library; cnr Church & Derwent Sts, Bellerive; adult/child $2/1, tours $10/2; ☺ 10am-3pm Tue-Thu, to noon Fri) Cricket fans should steer a well-directed cover drive towards Blundstone Arena (aka Bellerive Oval). There's a beaut cricket museum and library, plus oval tours (call for times and bookings). Don't miss the corner of the museum dedicated to the achievements of Tasmanian legend Ricky 'Punter' Ponting. There's still no commemoration of David Boon's 52 cans of beer quaffed on a Sydney-to-London flight in 1989. Bus 608 from the city runs past the oval.

Rosny Hill Lookout   VIEWPOINT
(off Riawena Rd, Rosny) For a classic view of Hobart, the Derwent River and the hulking mass of Mt Wellington in the background, drive up to this secret hilltop lookout (not so secret now!). Council thoughtfully lops the tops off any trees that dare impede the view. To get here, cross the Tasman Bridge, head for Rosny, turn right at the lights onto Riawena Rd and follow the signs.

🏃 Activities

Hobart's city beaches look inviting, especially at Bellerive and Sandy Bay, but the water tends to get a bit soupy. For a safe, clean swim, head further south to Kingston (p81) and Blackmans Bay (p82). The most reliable local surfing spots are Clifton Beach and Goats Beach, en route to South Arm.

★ Mt Wellington Descent   CYCLING
(☑ 1800 064 726; www.underdownunder.com. au; adult/child $75/65; ☺ 10am & 1pm daily year-round, plus 4pm Jan & Feb) Take a van ride to the summit of Mt Wellington (1270m), and follow with 22km of downhill cruising on a mountain bike. It's terrific fun, with minimal energy output and maximum views! Tours start and end at Brooke St Pier on the Hobart waterfront.

Hobart Bike Hire   BICYCLE RENTAL
(Map p54; ☑ 0447 556 189; www.hobartbikehire. com.au; 35 Hunter St; bike hire per day/overnight from $25/35; ☺ 9am-5.30pm) Centrally located on Hobart's waterfront, and has lots of ideas for self-guided tours around the city or along the Derwent River to MONA. Electric bikes and tandems also available, and maps and helmets included.

Artbikes   BICYCLE RENTAL
(Map p50; ☑ 03-6165 6666; www.artbikes.com.au; 146 Elizabeth St; ☺ 9am-4.30pm Mon-Fri) More than 140cm tall? You qualify for free city-

---

HOBART'S ANTARCTIC LINKS

Tasmania was the last chunk of Gondwanaland to break free from Antarctica, which is now about 2500km south of Hobart, across the Southern Ocean. As the planet heats up and scientists' eyes are on melting Antarctic ice, Hobart is well placed to become the world's leading Antarctic gateway city, and has become a centre for Antarctic and Southern Ocean science. The Australian Antarctic Division (p81) has its headquarters at suburban Kingston; the CSIRO (Commonwealth Scientific and Industrial Research Organisation) has its Division of Marine Research is in Battery Point; and the sleek new Institute of Antarctic and Southern Ocean Studies building on the waterfront is also home to the Antarctic Climate and Ecosystems Cooperative Research Centre. The Antarctic Division's garish orange research vessel *Aurora Australis* and the CSIRO's boats *Southern Surveyor* and MV *Franklin* often dock at Hobart's wharves.

Don't miss the fascinating Mawson's Huts Replica Museum (p53) near Constitution Dock, which re-creates the famed explorer Douglas Mawson's 100-year-old Antarctic hut in intricate detail. For a sense of Antarctic life, check out the climate-controlled Subantarctic Plant House at Hobart's Royal Tasmanian Botanical Gardens (p58), which re-creates the flora (and soundtrack!) of Tasmania's Macquarie Island, which lay en route to Antarctica.

bike hire from Artbikes. Just bring a credit card and some photo ID, and off you go. If you want to keep the bike overnight it's $22; for a weekend it's $44.

Derwent Bike Hire   BICYCLE RENTAL
(Map p50; ☑ 03-6234 2143, 0428 899 169; www. southcom.com.au/~bikehire; Regatta Grounds Cycleway, Cenotaph; bike hire per 3hr/day/week $15/20/90; ⊙ 10am-4pm Sat & Sun Sep-May, daily Dec-Mar) Mountain bikes and tandems for hire. You can hop on the bike track here and roll all the way to MONA.

Roaring 40s Kayaking   KAYAKING
(Map p50; ☑ 0455 949 777; www.roaring40skayaking.com.au; adult/child $90/50; ⊙ 10am daily year-round, plus 4pm Nov-Apr) Hobart is perhaps at its prettiest when viewed from the water. Take a safe, steady, 2½-hour guided paddle with Roaring 40s, named after the prevailing winds at these latitudes. You'll cruise from Sandy Bay past Battery Point and into the Hobart docks for some fish and chips while you float, before returning to Sandy Bay.

Hobart Aquatic Centre   SWIMMING
(Map p50; ☑ 03-6222 6999; www.hobartcity. com.au/recreation/the_hobart_aquatic_centre; 1 Davies Ave, Queens Domain; adult/child/family $7.50/5/20; ⊙ 6am-9pm Mon-Fri, 8am-6pm Sat & Sun) The Hobart Aquatic Centre offers recreational moisture, even when it's raining. Inside are leisure pools, lap-swimming pools, a spa, a sauna, a steam room, aqua aerobics, and regulation aerobics for landlubbers.

Rockit Climbing   ROCK CLIMBING
(Map p54; ☑ 03-6234 1090; www.rockitclimbing.com.au; 54 Bathurst St; adult/child/family $17/12/50; ⊙ noon-9pm Mon-Fri, to 6pm Sat & Sun) Inside a converted warehouse, Rockit offers world-class climbing walls. Don nifty rubber shoes, chalk up your paws and up you go.

Lady Nelson   SAILING
(Map p54; ☑ 03-6234 3348; www.ladynelson.org. au; Elizabeth St Pier; adult/child $30/10; ⊙ 11am, 1pm & 3pm Sat & Sun Oct-Mar, 11am & 1pm Apr-Sep) Sail around the harbour for 90 minutes on a replica of the surprisingly compact brig, *Lady Nelson*, one of the first colonial ships to sail to Tasmania. Longer trips are occasionally on offer: check the website.

Windeward Bound   SAILING
(Map p54; ☑ 0409 961 327, 0418 120 243; www. windewardbound.com; Elizabeth St Pier; 3hr sail incl lunch adult/child/family $80/35/195; ⊙ hours vary) An elegant replica tall ship with lots of opportunities to get involved with the sailing. Call for sailing times. Also runs occasional eight-day voyages around Port Davey and Recherche Bay (per person $3500).

 Tours

Most cruises and bus and walking tours run daily during summer (December to February), but schedules and prices vary with the season and demand, so call in advance to confirm. Several boat-cruise companies operate from the Brooke St Pier and Watermans Dock area, cruising around the harbour and up and down the river.

Hobart Historic Tours   WALKING TOUR
(☑ 03-6238 4222, 03-6231 4214; www.hobarthistorictours.com.au; adult/child/family $30/14/75) Informative, entertaining 90-minute walking tours of Hobart (3pm Thursday to Saturday and 9.30am Sunday) and historic Battery Point (5pm Wednesday and 1pm Saturday). There's also an Old Hobart Pub Tour (5pm Thursday to Saturday), which sluices through some waterfront watering holes. Reduced winter schedule, and bookings essential.

Gourmania   FOOD TOUR
(☑ 0419 180 113; www.gourmaniafoodtours.com. au; per person from $95) Flavour-filled walking tours around Salamanca Pl and central Hobart, with plenty of opportunities to try local foods and chat to restaurant, cafe and shop owners. A tour of Hobart's best cafes was also mooted at the time of writing.

Louisa's Walk   WALKING TOUR
(☑ 03-6229 8959, 0437 276 417; www.livehistoryhobart.com.au; 2hr tour adult/family $35/90) Engaging tours of Hobart's female convict heritage at the Female Factory (p57), interpreted through 'strolling theatre' with live actors. Tours depart Cascade Brewery at 2pm.

Hobart Historic Cruises   BOAT TOUR
(Map p54; ☑ 03-6223 5893; www.hobarthistoriccruises.com.au; 6 Franklin Wharf; 1hr cruises adult/child/family $20/15/60; ⊙ daily) Chug up or down the Derwent River on cute old ferries. Also runs longer lunch (adult/child/family $30/25/100) and dinner ($49/45/150) cruises travelling both up and down the river. Call for times and bookings.

Red Decker   BUS TOUR
(☑ 03-6236 9116; www.reddecker.com.au; 20-stop pass adult/child/family $30/15/80) Commentated

sightseeing on an old London double-decker bus. Buy a 20-stop, hop-on-hop-off pass (valid for three days), or do the tour as a 90-minute loop. Pay a bit more and add a Cascade Brewery tour (adult/child/family $55/30/140) or Mt Wellington tour ($55/30/130) to the deal.

Herbaceous Tours
FOOD & WINE TOUR

(☑ 0416 970 699; www.herbaceoustours.com.au; half-/full-day tours per person from $65/110) Specialist food and wine tours across Tasmania, including Hobart, the Coal River Valley wine region, D'Entrecasteaux Channel, Bruny Island and the Huon Valley. Look forward to lots of tasty sampling of foodie goodies.

Long Lunch Wine Tour Co
WINERY

(☑ 0409 225 841; www.longlunchtourco.com.au) Time for a wine? Sign up for a full-day minibus tour around some fine southern wineries, including the Coal River Valley wine region and Moorilla at MONA. Lots of tastings and tasty food. Longer tours up the east coast also available.

Tasman Island Cruises
BOAT TOUR

(Map p54; ☑ 03-6234 4270; www.tasmancruises. com.au; Franklin Wharf; full-day tour adult/child $225/155; ☺ 7.45am) Take a bus to Port Arthur for a three-hour eco-cruise around Tasman Island – checking out the astonishing sea cliffs at Cape Pillar, the highest in the southern hemisphere – then exploring the Port Arthur Historic Site and bussing it back to town. Includes morning tea, lunch and Port Arthur admission.

Navigators
BOAT TOUR

(Map p54; ☑ 03-6223 1914; www.navigators.net.au; cruise per person from $159; ☺ 8.15am Fri & Sun Oct-Apr) Slick ships sailing south to the Port Arthur Historic Site on the Tasman Peninsula. Prices include admission, a walking tour and a coach ride back to Hobart.

Wild Bike Tours
MOUNTAIN BIKING

(☑ 0407 797 748; www.wildbiketours.com; half-/full-day tours from $80/195) Adventurous mountain-biking tours through the forests and along lesser-known tracks around Hobart, Mt Wellington and beyond.

Peppermint Bay Cruise
BOAT TOUR

(Map p54; ☑ 1300 137 919; www.peppermintbay. com.au; adult/child from $98/68) A five-hour float from Hobart down the D'Entrecasteaux Channel to the sassy Peppermint Bay development at Woodbridge (once known as Peppermint Bay). Prices include lunch at Peppermint Bay.

Tasmanian Whisky Tours
DISTILLERY TOUR

(☑ 0412 099 933; www.tasmanianwhiskytours.com. au; per person $185; ☺ 9am Wed, Fri & Sun) Tasmanian whisky has been getting plenty of press since Sullivans Cove Whisky won the coveted 'Best Single Malt' gong at the World Whisky Awards in 2014. Take a day tour with this passionate outfit, visiting three or four distilleries and tasting up to 10 top Tassie single malts. Minimum four passengers.

Ghost Tours of Hobart & Battery Point
WALKING TOUR

(Map p50; ☑ 0439 335 696, 03-3933 5696; www. ghosttoursofhobart.com.au; adult/child $25/15) Walking tours oozing ectoplasmic tall tales, departing the Bakehouse in Salamanca Sq at dusk most nights. Bookings essential, and no kids under eight.

Tours Tasmania
GUIDED TOUR

(☑ 1800 777 103; www.tourstas.com.au) Small-group full-day trips from Hobart, including a 'Mt Field, Wildlife & Mt Wellington' tour with lots of walks and waterfalls (adult/concession $125/115). Park fees included; BYO lunch.

Par Avion
SCENIC FLIGHTS

(☑ 03-6248 5390; www.paravion.com.au) Scenic flights above Hobart (30 minutes per person $95) and into the southwest from Cambridge Aerodrome near Hobart Airport. A four-hour Southwest World Heritage Tour, including a boat ride on Bathurst Harbour, costs $320/240 per adult/child. An eight-hour Day in the Wilderness tour costs $420/360, including lunch and a visit to Port Davey.

Rotor-Lift Helicopters
SCENIC FLIGHTS

(☑ 03-6248 4117; www.rotorlift.com.au) Twenty-minute helicopter flights over Hobart and Mt Wellington for $195 – add MONA and a return ferry to the deal for an extra $154. One-hour sightseeing flights over Hobart and the Tasman Peninsula cost $675. Depart Hobart Airport.

Jump Tours
BUS TOUR

(☑ 0422 130 630; www.jumptours.com) Youth- and backpacker-oriented three- and five-day Tassie tours.

Gray Line
BUS TOUR

(☑ 1300 858 687; www.grayline.com.au) City coach tours (from $45/22.50 per adult/child), plus longer tours to destinations including Mt Wellington ($47/23.50), Mt Field National Park ($125/62.50), Bruny Island ($195/140) and the Huon Valley ($160/80).

HOBART FOR CHILDREN

Parents won't break the bank keeping the troops entertained in Hobart. The free Friday-night **Rektango** (p76) music event in the courtyard at the Salamanca Arts Centre is a family-friendly affair, while the street performers, buskers and visual smorgasbord of Saturday's **Salamanca Market** (p53) captivate kids of all ages. There's always something going on around the **waterfront** (p52) – fishing boats chugging in and out of Victoria Dock, yachts tacking in Sullivans Cove...and you can feed the tribe on a budget at the floating fish punts on Constitution Dock.

Rainy-day attractions to satisfy your child (or inner child) include the **Tasmanian Museum & Art Gallery** (p53), the **Maritime Museum of Tasmania** (p48) and the excellent new **Mawson's Huts Replica Museum** (p53).

Hobart is an active kinda town: take a boat cruise up or down the river; assail the heights of **Mt Wellington** (p56) or **Mt Nelson** (p57); hire a bike and explore the cycling paths; or pack the teens into the Kombi and go surfing at **Clifton Beach** (p60). And beyond the edge of town there's a plethora of animal parks, beaches, caves, nature walks and mazes to explore.

If you're in need of a romantic dinner for two, contact the **Mobile Nanny Service** (☑03-6273 3773, 0437 504 064; www.mobilenannyservice.com.au).

⭐ Festivals & Events

MONA FOMA MUSIC, ART
(MOFO; www.mofo.net.au; ☺ Jan) On the grounds of MONA, the wonderfully eclectic Festival of Music & Arts features a high-profile 'Eminent Artist in Residence' (EAR) every year. Previous EARs have included John Cale and Nick Cave. Stirring stuff.

Australian Wooden Boat Festival CULTURAL
(www.australianwoodenboatfestival.com.au; ☺ Feb) This biennial event (odd-numbered years) coincides with the Royal Hobart Regatta. The festival showcases Tasmania's boat-building heritage and maritime traditions. You can almost smell the Huon pine!

Royal Hobart Regatta SPORTS
(www.royalhobartregatta.com; ☺ Feb) Three days of yacht watching and mayhem on the Derwent River. Held annually in mid-February, coinciding with the Australian Wooden Boat Festival every second year.

Ten Days on the Island CULTURAL, ART
(www.tendaysontheisland.com; ☺ late Mar-early Apr) Tasmania's premier cultural festival is a biennial event (odd-numbered years) celebrating Tasmanian arts, music and culture at statewide venues. Expect concerts, exhibitions, dance, film, theatre and workshops.

Savour Tasmania Food Festival FOOD, WINE
(www.savourtasmania.com; ☺ May) Highbrow food and wine events are held around the state, including red-wine weekends, long-table lunches and sundry super-chefs conducting workshops.

Dark MOFO MUSIC, ART
(www.darkmofo.net.au; ☺ Jun) The sinister sister of MONA FOMA, Dark MOFO broods in the half-light of June's winter solstice. Expect live music, installations, readings, film noir and midnight feasts, all tapping into Tasmania's edgy gothic undercurrents.

Festival of Voices MUSIC
(www.festivalofvoices.com; ☺ Jul) Sing to keep the winter chills at bay during this quirky festival, featuring myriad performances, workshops, cabaret and choirs at venues around town.

Royal Hobart Show FAIR
(www.hobartshowground.com.au; ☺ Oct) Enduring rural-meets-urban festival showcasing Tassie's primary industries. Overpriced showbags, hold-on-to-your-lunch rides, carnies and the fecund aromas of nature – you get the picture.

Tasmanian Beerfest BEER
(www.tasmanianbeerfest.com.au; ☺ Nov) More than 200 brews from around Australia and the world, with brewing classes and lots of opportunities for waterfront snacking, foot tapping and imbibing.

★ Taste of Tasmania FOOD, WINE
(www.thetasteoftasmania.com.au; ☺ late Dec-early Jan) On either side of New Year's Eve, this week-long harbourside event is a celebration of Tassie's gastronomic prowess. The

WHALES IN THE DERWENT

In the 1830s Hobartians joked about walking across the Derwent River on the backs of whales, and complained about being kept awake at night by the noise of the ocean giants cavorting in the river. In typical Tasmanian style, the ensuing whaling boom was catastrophic, driving local populations of southern right and humpback whales to near extinction. Though still endangered, the occasional forgiving whale returns to the Derwent during the June–July northbound and October–November southbound migration. If you spy one, call the **Parks & Wildlife Service Whale Hotline** (☏ 0427 942 537).

seafood, wines and cheeses are predictably fab, or branch out into mushrooms, truffles, raspberries... Stalls are a who's who of the Hobart restaurant scene. Live music, too.

Falls Festival MUSIC
(www.fallsfestival.com.au; ⊙ 29 Dec-1 Jan) The Tasmanian version of the Victorian rock festival is a winner! Three nights and four days of live Oz and international tunes (Paul Kelly, Dan Sultan, Cold War Kids, Alt J) at Marion Bay, an hour east of Hobart.

Sydney to Hobart Yacht Race SPORTS
(www.rolexsydneyhobart.com; ⊙ Dec) Maxi-yachts competing in this gruelling annual open-ocean race start arriving in Hobart around 29 December – just in time for New Year's Eve! (Yachties sure can party...)

🛏 Sleeping

The pumping-est areas to stay in Hobart are the waterfront and Salamanca Pl, though prices here are usually sky-high and vacancy rates low. If you're visiting in January, book as far in advance as humanly possible. The CBD has less atmosphere, but most of the backpacker hostels, pubs with accommodation and midrange hotels are here.

To the north of the city centre are suburban North Hobart and New Town, with apartments and B&Bs within walking distance of the North Hobart restaurants. To the south, accommodation in Sandy Bay is surprisingly well priced, but it's a fair hike from town (check that you won't be in for a long walk).

Like the rest of Tasmania, midrange accommodation in Hobart isn't exactly a bargain, but top-end accommodation can be quite reasonable. If your budget stretches to around $200 per night, you can afford something quite special: designer hotels, historic guesthouses and mod waterside apartments.

🏙 City Centre

⭐ **Alabama Hotel** HOTEL $
(Map p54; ☏ 0499 987 698; www.alabamahobart. com.au; level 1, 72 Liverpool St; d/tw from $85/90; ☏) Sweet home Alabama! This old art-deco boozer – once a grim, sticky-carpet lush magnet – has been reborn as a boutique budget hotel. None of the 17 rooms has a bathroom, but the shared facilities are immaculate and plentiful. Decor is funky and colourful with retro-deco flourishes, and there's an all-day bar with a sunny balcony over the street. Cool!

Tassie Backpackers HOSTEL $
(Brunswick Hotel; Map p54; ☏ 03-6234 4981; www.tassiebackpackers.com; 67 Liverpool St; dm $20-30, d/tr with bathroom from $79/85; ☏) While we struggle with the hokey overuse of 'Tassie' nomenclature around the state, it's hard to deny this hostel's merits (Hobart's cheapest beds?). The venerable old Brunswick Hotel (some of the sandstone walls here date back to 1816) now offers plenty of shared spaces, a kitchen and a laundry in a central location. Energetic management also runs the bar downstairs.

Hobart Hostel HOSTEL $
(Map p54; ☏ 1300 252 1922, 03-6234 6122; www. hobarthostel.com; cnr Goulburn & Barrack Sts; dm $26-30, s/d without bathroom $65/73, d & tw with bathroom $85-95; @ ☏) In a former pub (the ever-rockin' Doghouse), Hobart Hostel offers clean, recently redecorated dorms, with good-value en-suite twins and doubles upstairs. Downstairs there are huge red sofas, and well-behaved backpackers going about their business (party somewhere else).

Imperial Hotel Backpackers HOSTEL $
(Map p54; ☏ 03-6223 5215; www.backpackersimperialhobart.com.au; 138 Collins St; dm/s/tw/d from $24/59/82/90; ☏) Right in the middle of the city, in one of Hobart's original hotels (1870), this maze-like hostel has loads of

communal space, an upgraded kitchen, high ceilings and friendly staff, plus extras such as baggage storage and a tour desk. Ask for a sunny north-facing room over Collins St.

Montgomery's Private Hotel & YHA
HOSTEL $

(Map p54; 03-6231 2660; www.montgomerys. com.au; 9 Argyle St; dm from $29, d & tw with/ without bathroom from $140/120, f from $118; @) Attached to a historic pub (lately called the Fluke & Bruce), this simple but clean YHA offers bright, secure accommodation right in the middle of town. Spread over three maze-like levels are dorms of all sizes, including nifty en-suite rooms and family-sized rooms. No parking, but you're walking distance from everything here.

Pickled Frog
HOSTEL $

(Map p54; 03-6234 7977; www.thepickledfrog. com; 281 Liverpool St; dm $23-28, s/d $62/66; P@) Yet another old Hobart pub (the former Bavarian Tavern) turned into a back-packers, this one given a lurid frog-coloured paint job. It's a rambling, chilled-out place with a bar, murals everywhere, parking out the back and Baloo the Alaskan malamute on duty. Skip the rooms with windows opening onto the lightwell.

Waratah Hotel
PUB $

(Map p50; 03-6234 3685; www.thewaratah-hotel.com.au; 272 Murray St; s/d/tr/q from $70/90/130/170; P) Known as 'W Block' to truant students from the nearby college, the Waratah is short on aesthetics but big on live music. The only thing it has in common with its namesake native bloom is its brick colour, but upstairs there are good-value beds and it's a short walk from town and North Hobart. Live bands deafen downstairs: check who's playing before you book.

★Astor Private Hotel
HOTEL $$

(Map p54; 03-6234 6611; www.astorprivatehotel. com.au; 157 Macquarie St; s $79-95, d $93-140, all incl breakfast;) A rambling downtown 1920s charmer, the Astor retains much of its character: stained-glass windows, old furniture, lofty celings (with ceiling roses) and the irrepressible Tildy at the helm. Older-style rooms have shared facilities, which are plentiful, while newer en-suite rooms top the price range. Strict 'No Bogans' policy!

Edinburgh Gallery B&B
B&B $$

(Map p54; 03-6224 9229; www.artaccom.com. au; 211 Macquarie St; r incl breakfast $90-230;

P@) This funky, art-filled boutique hotel puts an eclectic stamp on a 1909 Federation house, just to the west of the CBD. Some rooms share immaculate bathrooms, and all have DVD players and quirky, artsy decor (try for a verandah suite). Continental breakfast (farm honey and jam, yoghurt, cereals and chocolate-chip cookies!) centres around the lovely communal kitchen.

Hotel Collins
HOTEL $$

(Map p54; 03-6226 1111; www.hotelcollins. com.au; 58 Collins St; d $180-275, apt from $385; @) One of Hobart's newest hotels effortlessly shows up other places around town as a little old and weary. A youthful energy at reception flows through all 10 floors of spacious rooms and apartments, some with super views of Mt Wellington's gargantuan bulk. There's also a relaxed cafe-bar downstairs. No parking is the only bummer.

Quest Savoy
HOTEL $$

(Map p54; 03-6220 2300; www.questapart-ments.com.au; 38 Elizabeth St; r $180-329; P@) In a noble converted sandstone bank, the savvy Savoy offers 31 super-duper modern studios – all with kitchenettes and living/dining areas – smack bang in the middle of downtown Hobart. If you're travel weary, there's a day spa downstairs, with a pool and sundry rub/scrub treatments.

Old Woolstore Apartment Hotel
HOTEL $$

(Map p50; 1800 814 676, 03-6235 5355; www. oldwoolstore.com.au; 1 Macquarie St; d from $150, 1/2-bedroom apt from $180/260; P@) Oodles of parking and super-friendly staff are the first things you'll notice at this large, lavish hotel-apartment complex in an area of Hobart known as Wapping in colonial times. You won't notice much wool lying around – it hasn't been a wool store for 100 years. Roomy apartments have kitchens and laundry facilities. Book online for killer discounts.

Hadleys Hotel
HISTORIC HOTEL $$

(Map p54; 03-6237 2999; www.hadleysho-tel.com.au; 34 Murray St; d/f from $160/235; P@) This sumptuous place has clocked up more than 170 years of hospitality in the heart of the CBD. It's acquired plenty of modern embellishments since its colonial beginnings – both good and not so good – but new management has poured several million dollars into restoring its heritage charms. Some rooms are a tad compact, but wasn't everything in 1834?

DAVID BUTTON – HOBART ARCHITECT

David Button is a Hobart architect and all-round Tassie enthusiast, with a penchant for national parks, bushwalking and the good life.

Top Places to See Colonial Architecture

Tasmania has some of Australia's best early colonial architecture. The standouts are the **Port Arthur Historic Site** (p105), **Evandale** (p197) and **Ross** (p130). In Hobart there's **Battery Point** (p53) and the **Penitentiary Chapel Historic Site** (p48). The penitentiary is a bit grim, but it is an intact remnant of early Hobart Town.

Enjoying Tasmania's National Parks

The beaches on the east coast are great, especially around **Freycinet National Park** (p146). **Maria Island National Park** (p140) is great for camping – there are a couple of mountains to climb, lovely beaches and some tranquil, isolated spots. It's also excellent for mountain biking, as it has gravel roads and no cars.

Great Short Walks

In Hobart, walk from the city around Sullivans Cove, through the docks, around Battery Point and down to Sandy Bay. Get a bus to Fern Tree and explore **Mt Wellington** (p56). Bring warm clothing, water and food and allow a day to make a good job of it.

In Tasmania's southeast, walk from **Cockle Creek** (p126) to South Cape Bay. It's a pretty easy two-hour walk each way – some of it along boardwalks – to one of the wildest ocean beaches in the world. The Southern Ocean swell crashes in with huge surf on the edge of coastal rainforest.

Macquarie Manor HISTORIC HOTEL $$
(Map p54; ☑03-6224 4999; www.macmanor.com.au; 172 Macquarie St; r $120-315; 🗟) Plush, high-ceilinged heritage rooms and cooked breakfast buffets are the order of the day at this central, well-groomed, Regency-style guesthouse. Enough chesterfields and mahogany writing desks to fill three gentlemen's clubs. Originally built as a residence for Hobart's first surgeon (1875).

Mantra One APARTMENT $$
(Map p54; ☑03-6221 6000; www.mantra.com.au; 1 Sandy Bay Rd; d from $145; 🅿✳🗟) These spacious and stylish loft apartments, in a staunch old red-brick building, are a short stroll from Salamanca, the city and Battery Point (you probably won't need the sleek kitchenettes). Ask for a room on the building's southern side to negate occasional road noise from busy Davey St.

Central Café & Bar PUB $$
(Map p54; ☑03-6234 4419; www.centralcafebar.com; 73 Collins St; d/tw $120/130; 🅿🗟) Downstairs is a classic Aussie pub with gaming machines, cheap meals and big-screen sports; upstairs are surprisingly decent double en-suite rooms with TVs and hip furniture. You'll struggle to find anywhere more central, so we can't take issue with the name. Parking $15 per day.

Welcome Stranger Hotel PUB $$
(Map p54; ☑03-6223 6655; www.welcome-strangerhotel.com.au; cnr Harrington & Davey Sts; s/d incl breakfast from $105/125; 🅿🗟) Only a discerning eye will appreciate the aesthetic qualities of this modern red-brick pub, but upstairs there are 10 decent pub rooms with en suite, plus a few shared-bathroom options for budget travellers. It's on a noisy intersection, but double glazing does its best. Bend an elbow in the pool hall downstairs.

Waterfront & Salamanca Place

Zero Davey APARTMENT $$
(Map p54; ☑03-6270 1444, 1300 733 422; www.escapesresorts.com.au; 15 Hunter St; 1/2/3-bedroom apt from $185/329/429; 🅿✳🗟) These modern, funky apartments on the edge of Hobart's kinetic waterfront precinct don't garner much external architectural kudos, but inside they're great and the location is primo. Nab one with a balcony for views over Hobart's raffish fishing fleet. Good discounts online.

⭐**Henry Jones Art Hotel** BOUTIQUE HOTEL $$$
(Map p54; ☑03-6210 7700; www.thehenryjones.com; 25 Hunter St; d from $310; 🅿✳@🗟) Super-swish HJs is a beacon of sophistication. In the restored waterfront Henry

Jones IXL jam factory, with remnant bits of jam-making machinery and huge timber beams, it oozes class but is far from snooty (this is Hobart, not Sydney). Modern art enlivens the walls, while facilities and distractions (bar, restaurant, cafe) are world class. Just brilliant.

Sullivans Cove Apartments   APARTMENT $$$
(Map p54; ☑ 03-6234 5063; www.sullivanscoveapartments.com.au; 5/19a Hunter St; 1/2/3-bedroom d apt from $260/320/520, extra person $45; P ✲ 🛜) Exclusive, boutique, luxury, private... All apply to these sassy apartments, dotted around the Hobart waterfront in five locations (check-in for all is at 5/19a Hunter St). Our faves are the hip new architect-designed units inside the charismatic old Gibson's Flour Mill on Morrison St, where the mill's original timber and steel structures are highlighted in the interior design.

Somerset on the Pier   HOTEL $$$
(Map p54; ☑ 03-6220 6600, 1800 766 377; www.somerset.com; Elizabeth St Pier; 1/2-bedroom apt from $295/395; P ✲ @ 🛜) In a definitively Hobart location, on the upper level of the Elizabeth St Pier, this cool complex offers luxe apartments with beaut harbour views and breezy, contemporary design. You'll pay more for a balcony, but with these views you won't need to do any other sightseeing! Limited free parking.

Salamanca Wharf Hotel   APARTMENT $$$
(Map p56; ☑ 03-6224 7007; www.salamancawharfhotel.com; 17a Castray Esplanade, Battery Point; d $225-395, extra person $40; P ✲ 🛜) Filling a slender gap between historic sandstone ordnance stores just east of Salamanca Pl, these 22 slick new one-bedroom apartments offer nifty kitchens, cool art, affable staff and an unbeatable location. Units at the front have balconies; those at the back have baths (take your pick).

🛏 Battery Point, Sandy Bay & South Hobart

Montacute   HOSTEL $
(Map p50; ☑ 03-6212 0474; www.montacute.com.au; 1 Stowell Ave, Battery Point; dm/tw/d from $35/90/100; P 🛜) Getting rave reviews, this new 'boutique bunkhouse' occupies a renovated house in Battery Point. Many Hobart hostels are cheap remodellings of old pubs, but Montacute sets the bar a mile higher, with immaculate rooms and shared bathrooms, nice art, quality linen and mattresses,

and proximity to cafes – all just a 10-minute walk from the city and Salamanca. Nice one!

★ Quayle Terrace   RENTAL HOUSE $$
(Map p50; ☑ 0418 395 543; www.quayleterrace.com.au; 51 Quayle St, Battery Point; d $180-250, extra person $20; P ✲) Tracing the boundary between Battery Point and Sandy Bay, Quayle St features a long run of photogenic terrace houses (ignore the power lines and this could be 1890). Quayle Terrace is one such edifice – a two-storey, two-bedroom, tastefully renovated house with a cosy gas fire and mountain views from the shower (any snow this morning?). Free street parking.

Tree Tops Cascades   RENTAL HOUSE $$
(☑ 03-6223 2839, 0408 323 839; www.treetopscascades.com.au; 165 Strickland Ave, South Hobart; d/q from $150/250, extra person $25; P 🛜) Book ahead for this lovely three-bedroom house (sleeps five) in an idyllic bush setting, 6km from town near Cascade Brewery and several Mt Wellington walks. Built on 5 acres, it has a zoo-full of wildlife about: possums, wallabies, bandicoots and tame kookaburras (which you can feed on the barbecue deck). Buses 44, 46, 47 and 49 run here from the city.

Apartments on Star   APARTMENT $$
(Map p50; ☑ 03-6225 4799, 0400 414 656; www.apartmentsonstar.com.au; 22 Star St, Sandy Bay; 1/2/3-bedroom apt from $190/230/300; P 🛜) This old brick house at the bottom of Star St (the lower floor of which was once home to a Lonely Planet author who shan't be named) now comprises two hip apartments, bolstered by a new adjacent building housing a further two slick units. Cool kitchens, big TVs and quality furnishings...and Sandy Bay's buzzing restaurant scene is metres away.

Motel 429   MOTEL $$
(Map p50; ☑ 03-6225 2511; www.motel429.com.au; 429 Sandy Bay Rd, Sandy Bay; d $130-200; P ✲ @ 🛜) This motel's ongoing facelift has given most rooms (all but six of 33) a sleek designer sheen. The staff are friendly, everything's clean and shipshape, and the restaurants of Sandy Bay are a short drive away. The deluxe rooms are super-comfortable, and Wrest Point Casino is across the road if you're feeling lucky.

St Ives Motel   MOTEL $$
(Map p50; ☑ 03-6221 5555; www.stivesmotel.com.au; 67 St Georges Tce, Battery Point; d from $145, 2-bedroom units from $200; P 🛜)

Within walking distance of Battery Point, Salamanca and the city is this excellent option – a curvalicious '80s building with dozens of rooms, all with kitchens. A recent flash makeover has introduced the property to the 21st century – pleased to meet you. Good last-minute deals online.

At Eleven – La Petite Maison APARTMENT **$$**
(Map p50; ☏03-6223 6573, 0406 125 472; www.ateleven.com.au; 11 Randall St, Sandy Bay; d $190, extra person $40; P@☎) Soak up some Gallic style at this lovely little self-contained house in the cute backstreets of Sandy Bay, just a short stroll from the Sandy Bay shops and restaurants. The little brick-paved courtyard is beaut for breakfast, which is a DIY continental affair. It's a one-bedroom set-up – extra bods can sleep on the sofa bed.

Battery Point Boutique Accommodation APARTMENT **$$**
(Map p50; ☏03-6224 2244, 0422 629 432; www.batterypointaccommodation.com.au; 27-29 Hampden Rd, Battery Point; d $150-225, extra person $35; P☎) Typical colonial midrangery in a block of four salmon-coloured serviced apartments – sleeping three, with full kitchens – in Battery Point's heart (somewhere near the left ventricle). Off-street parking is a bonus, and there are good long-stay rates.

Shipwright's Arms Hotel PUB **$$**
(Map p50; ☏03-6223 5551; www.shipwrightsarms.com.au; 29 Trumpeter St, Battery Point; d $150, s/d without bathroom from $85/90; P) Concealed in the backstreets of Battery Point, 'Shippies' is one of the best old pubs in town. Soak yourself in maritime heritage (and other liquids) at the bar, then repair to your clean, above-board berth upstairs or in the newer en-suited wing. Other bonuses include hefty pub meals and the delight in saying you're staying on Trumpeter St.

Prince of Wales Hotel PUB **$$**
(Map p50; ☏03-6223 6355; www.princeofwaleshotel.net.au; 55 Hampden Rd, Battery Point; r incl breakfast from $115; P☎) A severe 1960s glitch in Battery Point's urban planning (would Charles and Camilla approve?), the POW is nonetheless exquisitely located. It offers basic pub-style rooms in need of an update, though all have en suites. Off-street parking and Moo Brew on tap are two more ticks. Light continental breakfast included.

★**Islington** BOUTIQUE HOTEL **$$$**
(Map p50; ☏03-6220 2123; www.islingtonhotel.com; 321 Davey St, South Hobart; d from $395; P☎) At the top of Hobart's accommodation tree, the classy Islington effortlessly merges heritage architecture with antique furniture, contemporary art and a glorious garden. Service is attentive but understated, with breakfast served in an expansive conservatory. In the evening, wind down with a wine in the guest library, study/music room or drawing room. Exquisite private dinners are also available. Superb.

Grande Vue Private Hotel B&B **$$$**
(Map p50; ☏03-6223 8216; www.grande-vue-hotel.com; 8 Mona St, Battery Point; d $225-285; P☎) 'Vues' from the best rooms at this lovingly restored 1906 mansion take in a broad sweep of Sandy Bay and the Derwent River, or Mt Wellington in the other direction. Sleek new bathrooms and super-friendly service lift Grande Vue above similar B&Bs nearby. Breakfast ($12.50) includes still-warm baked goodies from Jackman & McRoss.

North & West Hobart

Waterfront Lodge MOTEL **$**
(☏03-6228 4748, 1800 060 954; www.hotelsplus.com.au; 153 Risdon Rd, New Town; d $69-160, extra person $30; P☎☒) Overlooking the semi-industrial New Town Bay and the Cornelian Bay Cemetery, 5km north of the centre, this funky 1960s motel has compact, modern units, most with kitchenettes. There's also a guest kitchen. Great value if you don't mind the view or the drive.

Hobart Cabins & Cottages CARAVAN PARK **$**
(☏03-6272 7115; www.hobartcabinscottages.com.au; 19 Goodwood Rd, Glenorchy; powered sites $35, cabins d & f from $110, 3-bedroom house $200; P☎) An unflattering 8km north of the city in Glenorchy, but offers a range of tidy cottages and cabins and a three-bedroom house sleeping up to 10 bods.

Lodge on Elizabeth B&B **$$**
(Map p50; ☏03-6231 3830; www.thelodge.com.au; 249 Elizabeth St; r incl breakfast $165-230; P☎) Built in 1829 this old-timer has been a schoolhouse, a boarding house and a halfway house, but now opens its doors as a value-for-money guesthouse. Rooms are dotted with antiques (not for the modernists) and all have en suites. The self-contained cottage overlooks the tulip-dappled courtyard out the back. Two-night minimum stay.

Bay View Villas MOTEL, APARTMENT **$$**
(Map p50; ☑ 1800 061 505, 03-6234 7611; www.
bayviewvillas.com; 34 Poets Rd, West Hobart; d
$149-219, extra person $20; P 🖥 🖀) A few kilo-
metres up the steep West Hobart slopes
from the city, this family-focused option
offers a games room and an indoor pool (fol-
low the scent of chlorine from reception).
There's a rank of tarted-up motel units out
the front, and 12 stylish one-bedroom units
behind with magical river views.

Graham Court Apartments MOTEL **$$**
(☑ 03-6278 1333, 1800 811 915; www.graham-
court.com.au; 15 Pirie St, New Town; d $135-170,
extra person $29; P 🖥) One of Hobart's
best-value family options, this trim complex of 23 self-contained apartments sits in
established gardens in subdued New Town.
Units range from one to three bedrooms,
and decor ranges from 1990s to the 2000s.
A playground, cots, high chairs and on-call
babysitters make it a solid family choice.
Aim for the red-brick section out the front.

Altamont House APARTMENT **$$$**
(Map p50; ☑ 0409 145 844, 0437 344 932; www.
altamonthouse.com.au; 109 Patrick St, West Hobart;
d $200, extra adult/child $60/30; P 🖵 🖥) Are
there rules about how steep a street can be?
The town planners weren't paying attention
when they laid out Patrick St...but the views
are great! Occupying the ground floor of a
gorgeous old stone-and-slate house, Alta-
mont offers a plush double suite with an ex-
tra room that can be opened up as required.
No sign of the Rolling Stones...

Corinda's Cottages B&B, APARTMENT **$$$**
(Map p50; ☑ 03-6234 1590; www.corindascottag-
es.com.au; 17 Glebe St, Glebe; d incl breakfast from
$250; P 🖵 🖥) Gorgeous Corinda, a reno-
vated Victorian mansion with meticulously
maintained parterre gardens, sits high on
the sunny Glebe hillside a short (steep!)
walk from town. Three self-contained cottages (garden, coach house or servants'
quarters) provide contemporary comforts
with none of the twee, olde-worlde guff in
which too many Tasmanian hotels wallow.
Breakfast is DIY gourmet (eggs, muffins,
fresh coffee etc).

Library House BOUTIQUE HOTEL **$$$**
(Map p50; ☑ 0407 246 633; www.libraryhouse.com.
au; 82 Forest Rd, West Hobart; 4 people $750, extra
person $50; P 🖥) Resting in fine Federation
style on a steep reach of Forest Rd, the exclu-
sive Library House is far from bookish. Five

hip, contemporary suites fill the old house
and an angular new extension, from which
the river views are mesmerising. Pricey for
a couple, but decent value for groups (sleeps
up to eight). Two-night minimum stay.

Pavilions BOUTIQUE HOTEL **$$$**
(☑ 03-6277 9900; www.mona.net.au/mona/accom-
modation/the-pavilions; 655 Main Rd, Berriedale; d
from $490; P 🖵 @ 🖥 🖀) For a slice of luxury,
book a private, uber-chic pavilion at MONA
(p57), 12km north of the city. These mod
self-contained chalets (one- and two-bedroom)
are equipped to the nines, with private
balconies, wine cellars, river views and oh-
so-discreet service. An indoor swimming pool
is an essential aid to relaxation, and MONA is
in your backyard.

🍴 Eating

Hobart's city centre proffers some classy
brunch and lunch venues, but when the
sun sinks behind the mountain, there's not
much going on here. Instead, head for the
waterfront, the epicentre of the city's culinary scene, where there's quality seafood
everywhere you look.

Salamanca Pl is an almost unbroken
string of excellent cafes, bars and restaurants, especially busy during Satur-
day-morning market festivities. Battery
Point's Hampden Rd restaurants are always worth a look, while Elizabeth St in
North Hobart (aka 'NoHo') has evolved
into a diverse collection of cosmopolitan
eateries. The Sandy Bay food scene is also
bubbling along nicely with some quality
budget options, but so far it doesn't have a
cool-sounding nickname. Any ideas?

For Hobart's best pub grub, head to the
New Sydney Hotel (p77), the Shipwright's
Arms Hotel, or the Republic Bar & Café (p77).

🍽 City Centre

⭐ **Pilgrim Coffee** CAFE **$**
(Map p54; ☑ 03-6234 1999; 48 Argyle St; mains $11-
20; ⊗ 7am-5pm Mon-Fri) With exposed bricks,
timber beams and distressed walls, L-shaped
Pilgrim is Hobart's hippest cafe. Expect
wraps, panini and interesting mains (Peruvi-
an spiced alpaca with quinoa and beetroot!),
plus expertly prepared coffee. Fall into con-
versation with the locals at big shared tables. Down a laneway around the back is the
Standard (Map p54; ☑ 03-6234 1999; Hudsons
La; burgers $7-12; ⊗ 11am-10pm daily), a fab burg-
er bar run by the same hipsters.

Small Fry
CAFE $

(Map p54; ☑ 03-6231 1338; www.small-fryhobart. com.au; 129 Bathurst St; mains $6-25; ⊙ 7.30am-3.30pm Mon-Thu, to 9pm Fri, 8.30am-9pm Sat) 🍃 Hip Small Fry is now one of Hobart's best cafe-bars in its own right. Conversation comes naturally at the shared steel counter: sip a glass of wine, some soup or a coffee; talk, listen, laugh, crunch a salad... It's a flexible vibe designed to 'avoid labels'. Love the wooden menu cubes!

Raspberry Fool
CAFE $

(Map p54; ☑ 03-6231 1274; 85 Bathurst St; mains $9-17; ⊙ 7.30am-4pm Mon-Fri, to 2.30pm Sat & Sun) The all-day menu here features dressed-up comfort food with a chef's spin. Try the cheesy leeks on toast with bacon and a fried egg, or the baked eggs with caramelised onion, ham and Gruyère. It gets as busy as a woodpecker when the Farm Gate Market (p48) is happening outside on Sunday mornings. Great coffee, too.

Providore
CAFE, DELI $

(Map p54; ☑ 03-6231 1165; 100 Elizabeth St; mains $3-12; ⊙ 10am-4pm Mon-Sat) A daytime business adjunct to night-time restaurant Ethos, funky Providore conducts trade with moral fortitude, sourcing ethically produced local ingredients. Super salads and awesome sandwiches are the main thrust, plus shelves full of artisan breads, oils, pestos, pastes, honey and cookbooks. There's a great yoghurt and juice bar next door, too.

Criterion Street Café
CAFE $

(Map p54; ☑ 03-6234 5858; www.criterionstcafe. com; 10 Criterion St; mains $6-15; ⊙ 7am-4pm Mon-Fri, 8am-3pm Sat & Sun) It's a short menu on a short street, but Criterion Street Café effortlessly meets the criteria for keeping both breakfast and lunch fans sated, and caffeine fiends buzzing through the day. Try the Spanish omelette or the haloumi salad with brown rice and baby spinach. Beers and wines, too.

Yellow Bernard
CAFE $

(Map p54; ☑ 03-6231 5207; www.yellowbernard. com; 109 Collins St; items from $3; ⊙ 7am-4pm Mon-Fri) With a global selection of interesting blends, Yellow Bernard (great name!) takes its coffee *very* seriously. If you're in a hippie mood, its chai – made with local honey and the cafe's own spice blend – is a perfect way to tune in while wandering Hobart's CBD. Biscuits and corners of cake to go.

R. Takagi Sushi
JAPANESE $

(Map p54; ☑ 03-6234 8524; 155 Liverpool St; sushi from $3; ⊙ 10.30am-5.50pm Mon-Fri, to 4pm Sat, 11.30am-3pm Sun) Hobart's best sushi spot makes the most of Tasmania's great seafood. Udon noodles and miso also make an appearance at this sleek, compact eatery – a favourite of Hobart desk jockeys.

Island Espresso
CAFE $

(Map p50; ☑ 03-6231 3317; 171 Elizabeth St; mains $9-15; ⊙ 8am-4pm Mon-Fri, 9am-2pm Sat; 🛜) Fab little espresso joint in an atmospheric old shopfront, en route from the city to North Hobart. Order the scrambled eggs with chilli and coriander on sourdough and a Hobart-roasted Zimmah coffee and head for the little courtyard at the back.

Sawak Cafe
MALAYSIAN $

(Map p54; ☑ 03-6234 3622; 131 Collins St; mains $8-14; ⊙ 11am-3pm & 5-9pm Mon-Sat) Duck into buzzy Sawak for a well-priced fix of spicy, authentic Malaysian food. Usually full of students on the run from the books, slurping prawn laksas or chewing pork and Chinese cabbage dumplings and *char kway teow* (stir-fried flat noodles).

Westend Pumphouse
CAFE $$

(Map p54; ☑ 03-6234 7339; www.pumphouse.com. au; 105 Murray St; mains $19-38; ⊙ 8.30am-late) An excellent wine list, good coffee and craft beers on tap feature at the versatile, industrial Pumphouse. Smash your first coffee of the morning, then come back later in the day with some friends for shared plates (try the lamb shoulder, cabbage and mustard salad) and a few ales. Check out the milk-container wall!

Ivory Cafe
THAI $$

(Map p54; ☑ 03-6231 6808; 112 Elizabeth St; mains $12-20; ⊙ 11.30am-3pm Mon-Sat, 5-9pm Tue-Sat) Hobart's most popular Thai restaurant is a modest, slender affair, with a long bench seat along one wall and three stools in the front window, which are perfect if you're dining solo. Order the excellent green chicken curry and peer out at Elizabeth St's occasional bustle.

Ethos
MODERN AUSTRALIAN $$$

(Map p54; ☑ 03-6231 1165; www.ethoseatdrink. com; 100 Elizabeth St; 6/8-course menu $75/90; ⊙ 6pm-late Tue-Sat) Hidden in a courtyard down a flagstone alley off Elizabeth St, Ethos rigorously supports local farmers and ethically produced Tasmanian food. The menu

ELIZABETH FLEETWOOD – HOBART HISTORIAN

Elizabeth Fleetwood is one of Hobart's most knowledgeable historians. She provided us with a few lesser-known facts and quirky stories about the city.

A Famous Visitor

Charles Darwin visited Hobart in 1836. It's said that it was his studies of our geology, particularly while walking along the foreshore at Bellerive, and our many curious animal forms, that helped lay the foundations for his theories on evolution.

The Truth about Hobart's Weather

Here's a fact about Hobart that takes many visitors by surprise – of all of Australia's state capitals, only Adelaide gets less rain.

Just One More Beer, OK?

Before the Tasman Bridge was completed, a fellow called Burt was a well-known regular on the trans-Derwent ferry. He liked to have a few beers at the waterfront pubs before catching the ferry home from work. One day he got a bit too enthusiastically into his beer, and only had half the money for his fare. He appealed to the ferryman, saying he knew him well and that he would provide the missing amount the next morning. Halfway across the river, the ferry came to a halt, and the captain announced: 'We've stopped here so Burt can get off. He's only paid for half the journey.'

is very seasonal, with artisan-produced ingredients showcasing whatever's fresh. Servings are on the small side, but the flavours are innovative and delicious. Bookings essential. There's also a moody new **wine bar** downstairs.

✗ Waterfront & Salamanca Place

★ **Retro Café**   CAFE $
(Map p56; ☏ 03-6223 3073; 31 Salamanca Pl; mains $10-18; ⊗ 7am-5pm) So popular it hurts, funky Retro is ground zero for Saturday brunch among the market stalls (or any day, really). Masterful breakfasts, bagels, salads and burgers interweave with laughing staff, chilled-out jazz and the whirr and bang of the coffee machine. A classic Hobart cafe.

Flippers   SEAFOOD $
(Map p54; www.flippersfishandchips.com.au; Constitution Dock; meals $10-24; ⊗ 9.30am-8.30pm) With its voluptuous fish-shaped profile and alluring sea-blue paint job, floating Flippers is a Hobart institution. Not to mention the awesome fish and chips! Fillets of flathead and curls of calamari – straight from the deep blue sea and into the deep fryer. The local seagulls will adore you.

Machine Laundry Café   CAFE $
(Map p56; ☏ 03-6224 9922; 12 Salamanca Sq; mains $7-17; ⊗ 7.30am-5pm Mon-Sat, 8.30am-5pm Sun) Hypnotise yourself watching the tumble dryers spin at this bright retro cafe, where you can wash your dirty clothes ($5) while discreetly adding fresh juice, soup or coffee stains to your clean ones. Don't miss the chilli-infused roti wrap for breakfast.

Tricycle Café Bar   CAFE $
(Map p56; ☏ 03-6223 7228; www.salarts.org.au/portfolio/tricycle; 71 Salamanca Pl; mains $8-15; ⊗ 8.30am-4pm Mon-Sat) This cosy red-painted nook inside the Salamanca Arts Centre (p52) serves up a range of cafe classics (BLTs, toasties, free-range scrambled eggs, salads, house-brewed chai and fair-trade coffee), plus awesome daily specials (braised Wagyu rice bowl with jalapeño cream – wow!). Wines by the glass from the bar.

Vietnamese Kitchen   VIETNAMESE $
(Map p56; ☏ 03-6223 2188; 61 Salamanca Pl; mains $8-16; ⊗ 11am-9.30pm) With slick waterfront eateries closing in on all sides, it's downright refreshing to wander into this cheap, kitsch kitchen with its glowing drinks fridge and plastic-coated photos of steaming soups and stir-fries. Eat in or takeaway.

Salamanca Bakehouse   BAKERY $
(Map p56; ☏ 03-6224 6300; 5/47 Salamanca Sq; items from $3; ⊗ 24hr) Open 24/7, with pies, pastries and rolls to soak up the beer and build a better tomorrow for nocturnal drinkers. The curried scallop pies are great any time of the day (or night).

Salamanca Fresh
SUPERMARKET **$**

(Map p56; ☑ 03-6223 2700; www.salamancafresh. com.au; 41 Salamanca Pl; ⊘ 7am-7pm) Gourmet self-caterers alert: don't miss the fruit, veg, meats and groceries here, plus a suite of Tasmanian wines.

Fish Frenzy
SEAFOOD **$$**

(Map p54; ☑ 03-6231 2134; www.fishfrenzy.com. au; Elizabeth St Pier; mains $14-35; ⊘ 11am-9pm) A casual, waterside fish nook, overflowing with fish fiends and brimming with fish and chips, fishy salads (spicy calamari, smoked salmon and brie) and fish burgers. The eponymous 'Fish Frenzy' ($18) delivers a little bit of everything. Quality can be inconsistent, but good staff and buzzy harbourside vibes compensate. No bookings.

Jam Packed
CAFE **$$**

(Map p54; ☑ 03-6210 7700; www.thehenryjones. com; 27 Hunter St; mains $10-25; ⊘ 7am-5.30pm; 🛜) Inside the excellent Henry Jones Art Hotel (p66), this atmospheric cafe is jam-packed at breakfast time. If you're sporting a hangover of some description, the Texas BBQ beef burger is the perfect reintroduction to civilisation, plus there are all-day breakfasts, beaut cakes and biscuits, and Tasmanian beer and wine if you want to get started again.

Mill on Morrison
SPANISH, MODERN AUSTRALIAN **$$**

(Map p54; ☑ 03-6234 3490; www.themillonmorrison.com.au; 11 Morrison St; tapas $4-16; ⊘ noon-2pm Mon-Fri, 5.30pm-late Mon-Sat) Inside the gorgeously renovated Gibson's City Mill (cast-iron columns, exposed timber ceilings, dark-wood tables and chairs) is this sharp but relaxed tapas restaurant: a bit Spanish, a bit Mexican, a bit Mod Oz. Don't overlook the chargrilled calamari or the cheese and arancini balls. Terrific wines by the glass, from the Coal River Valley to Catalonia.

Mures
SEAFOOD **$$**

(Map p54; ☑ 03-6231 2121; www.mures.com.au; Victoria Dock; mains lower deck $10-25, upper deck $36-45; ⊘ lower deck 7am-late, upper deck 11am-late) Mures and Hobart seafood are synonymous. Downstairs you'll find a fishmonger, sushi bar, ice-cream parlour and the hectic, family-focused **Lower Deck** bistro, serving meals for the masses (fish and chips, salmon burgers, crumbed scallops). The **Upper Deck** is a sassier, bookable affair, with silvery dockside views and à la carte seafood dishes.

Mezethes
GREEK **$$**

(Map p56; ☑ 03-6224 4601; www.mezethes.com.au; Woobys Lane, Hobart; mains $27-36; ⊘ 8am-late) Tried and true Greek dishes and Adonis-like staff come together perfectly at Mezethes. All the classics (moussaka, souvlaki, lamb, fish, saganaki, baklava) plus, in true Hellenic style, a dazzling array of starters. The entrée platter ($32 for two) is hard to beat.

Henry's Harbourside
MODERN AUSTRALIAN **$$$**

(Map p54; ☑ 03-6210 7700; www.thehenryjones. com; 25 Hunter St; breakfast $11-30, dinner mains $30-40; ⊘ 7-10am & 5-9pm) Inside the flash Henry Jones Art Hotel (p66) is this top-flight lobby eatery. It can get pricey in here, but the atmosphere and exquisite mains, starring local meats (Bruny Island pork, Doo Town venison, Cape Grim beef), more than compensate. And the wine list is devastating. Aim for an atrium table.

Blue Eye
SEAFOOD **$$$**

(Map p56; ☑ 03-6223 5297; www.blueeye.net.au; 1 Castray Esplanade; mains $29-45; ⊘ 5-9pm Mon, 11am-9pm Tue-Sat) Ignore the slightly clinical decor and dive into some of Hobart's best seafood. Standouts include scallop and prawn linguine, curried seafood chowder and a terrific seafood pie with dill-and-spinach cream. Moo Brew ale on tap and a Tasmanian-skewed wine list complete a very zesty picture.

🗺 Battery Point, Sandy Bay & South Hobart

★ Jackman & McRoss
BAKERY **$**

(Map p50; ☑ 03-6223 3186; 57-59 Hampden Rd, Battery Point; meals $8-13; ⊘ 7am-6pm Mon-Fri, to 5pm Sat & Sun) Don't bypass this conversational, neighbourhood bakery-cafe, even if it's just to gawk at the display cabinet full of delectable pies, tarts, baguettes and pastries. Early-morning cake and coffee may evolve into a quiche for lunch, or perhaps a blackberry-and-wallaby pie. Staff stay cheery despite being run off their feet. The city branch (Map p54; ☑ 03-6231 0601; 4 Victoria St; ⊘ 7am-4.30pm Mon-Fri) has parallel prices.

Ginger Brown
CAFE **$**

(Map p50; ☑ 03-6223 3531; 464 Macquarie St, South Hobart; mains $10-20; ⊘ 7.30am-4pm Tue-Fri, 8.30am-4pm Sat & Sun; 🖶) When a food business is this well run, the mood infects the entire room: happy staff, happy customers and happy vibes. Try the slow-cooked lamb panini with cornichons and hummus. Very kid- and cyclist-friendly. Last orders 3pm.

Environs
CAFE $

(Map p50; ✐03-6224 3929; www.environs.biz; 38 Waterloo Cres, Battery Point; mains $8-22; ⊘7.30am-4pm Mon-Sat, 8am-4pm Sun) Chipper service combines with mod decor and a shady garden area at the excellent Environs. It's a top spot for a leisurely breakfast before a walk around Battery Point: try the field mushrooms with parmesan. Tasmanian wines and beers buddy-up with lunch options such as duck and orange risotto and a smokin' Wagyu beef burger.

Jam Jar Lounge
CAFE, JAPANESE $

(Map p50; ✐03-6224 1447; www.jamjarlounge. com; 45 Hampden Rd, Battery Point; mains $7-18; ⊘7.30am-3pm Wed & Thu, 7.30am-3pm & 6-10pm Fri, 8am-3pm & 6-10pm Sat & Sun; 🖱) Art-deco style infuses a 19th-century cottage at this friendly cafe-bistro combo. Lose yourself in the labyrinth of nooks and crannies, and break up your Battery Point explorations with classic cafe fare (croissants, coffee, sardines on toast) and Japanese ramen noodle soups. On Friday nights, the big shared tables are awash with locals tucking into Japanese-inspired tapas.

Written on Tea
CHINESE $

(Map p50; ✐03-6223 3298; www.writtenontea. com; 8/236 Sandy Bay Rd, Sandy Bay; mains $11-25; ⊘11.30am-10pm) Excellent steamed dumplings, squid studded with ginger and spring onion, and roast duck feature at this humble suburban eatery delivering the authentic flavours of the owners' Chinese hometown of Nanjing (where the tea leaves must be sizeable).

Macquarie St Foodstore
CAFE $

(Map p50; ✐03-6224 6862; 356 Macquarie St, South Hobart; mains $9-16; ⊘7.30am-3pm Mon-Fri, 8am-3pm Sat & Sun) It's a little way out of the city, but an excursion to the Food Store – a pioneering South Hobart cafe – always rewards. It's an old shopfront full of booths, bookish students, brunching friends and kids mooching under the tables. Chew into a Foodstore Pizza (bacon, chorizo, mozzarella, red peppers) after a visit to the Cascade Brewery.

Woolworths
SUPERMARKET $

(Map p50; ✐03-6281 4806; www.woolworths. com.au; 57 King St, Sandy Bay; ⊘7am-midnight) Gargantuan supermarket in Sandy Bay.

Ristorante Da Angelo
ITALIAN $$

(Map p50; ✐03-6223 7011; www.daangelo.com; 47 Hampden Rd, Battery Point; mains $18-32; ⊘5pm-late) An enduring (and endearing) Italian *ristorante*, Da Angelo presents an impressively long menu of homemade pastas, veal and chicken dishes, calzone and pizzas with 20 different toppings. Colosseum and Carlton Football Club team photos add authenticity. Takeaway, BYO and open late.

Don Camillo
ITALIAN $$

(Map p50; ✐03-6234 1006; www.doncamillores-taurant.com; 5 Magnet Ct, Sandy Bay; mains $23-33; ⊘6-9pm Tue-Sat) Just about the oldest restaurant in Hobart, little Don Camillo has been here forever and is still turning out a tight menu of classic Italian pastas, risottos and meat dishes. Look for the red Vespa parked out the front.

Magic Curries
INDIAN $$

(Map p50; ✐03-6223 4500; www.magiccurries. com.au; 41 Hampden Rd, Battery Point; mains $14-19; ⊘5-9pm; 🖱) There's a photo on the wall here of the Indian cricket team's visit in 2004 – a while ago, we know, but if it's good enough for Anil Kumble, it's good enough for us. Sip a Kingfisher beer in the magically coloured interior and await your face-meltingly hot beef vindaloo. Excellent vegetarian options; takeaway available.

Signal Station Brasserie
MODERN AUSTRALIAN $$

(✐03-6223 3407; www.signalstation.com.au; 700 Nelson Rd, Mt Nelson; mains $22-37; ⊘9am-5pm Mon-Fri, 10am-5pm Sat & Sun) Looking for a romantic lunch spot? Direct your partner towards a window table at this elegant, glass-fronted restaurant with awesome Derwent views, inside Mt Nelson's signalman's house (built in 1897). Try the oven-baked duck breast stuffed with cranberries, orange and walnuts. Friday dinners may or may not be happening – call to check.

Solo Pasta & Pizza
ITALIAN $$

(Map p50; ✐03-6234 9898; www.solopastaand-pizza.com.au; 50b King St, Sandy Bay; mains $12-26; ⊘5-10pm Tue-Sun) The brilliant pastas, pizzas, risottos and calzones at Solo have been drawing hungry hordes for decades. Not that you'd know its age from looking at it: the snazzy glass-fronted room backed by racks of wine is almost futuristic.

Me Wah
CHINESE $$

(Map p50; ✐03-6223 3688; www.mewah.com. au; 16 Magnet Ct, Sandy Bay; mains $19-40;

⊙noon-2.30pm & 6-9.30pm Tue-Sun) From the outside, Me Wah looks just like any suburban shopping-mall joint. But inside it's an elegant confection of chinoiserie, almost bordering on over the top. The food is equally stellar, including terrific ways with seafood and world-famous-in-Hobart yum cha sessions from 11am on weekends.

Beach House   CAFE $$
(✆03-6225 4644; www.beachhouserestaurant. com.au; cnr Sandy Bay Rd & Beach Rd, Lower Sandy Bay; mains $10-24; ⊙7.30am-6pm Mon-Thu & Sat, to 8pm Fri) A rockin' pub in the 1970s, the Beach House is now a classy cafe-bar next to the beach at Lower Sandy Bay. Wander along the sand before retiring for creative seafood, salads and pastas, or sip some Tasmanian wine on the sunny terrace out the front.

Prosser's on the Beach   SEAFOOD $$$
(✆03-6225 2276; www.prossersonthebeach. com; 19 Beach Rd, Lower Sandy Bay; mains $35-38; ⊙noon-2pm Wed-Sun, 6pm-late Mon-Sat) A glass-fronted pavilion by the water in Lower Sandy Bay, classy Prosser's is BIG on seafood: try the Bruny Island oysters with ponzu citrus dressing, or the signature Cajun-spiced fish of the day with mash and citrus butter. It's a taxi ride from town, but worth the trip. Bookings recommended.

✗ North & West Hobart

Watch this space... North Hobart is changing fast, with new bars and restaurants opening all the time.

★Burger Haus   BURGERS $
(Map p50; ✆03-6234 9507; 364a Elizabeth St, North Hobart; mains $10-14; ⊙11.30am-9.30pm Mon-Fri, 11am-9.45pm Sat & Sun) Blaring 1980s rock, big beefy burgers and a little terrace on which to sit, chew and contemplate the moody hues of Mt Wellington...this place has got it all! The Haus Burger (with bacon, onion rings, caramelised pineapple and mustard mayo) reigns supreme.

Pigeon Hole   CAFE $
(Map p54; ✆03-6236 9306; www.pigeonholecafe. com.au; 93 Goulburn St, West Hobart; mains $10-13; ⊙8am-4.30pm Tue-Sat) This funky, friendly cafe is the kind of place every inner-city neighbourhood should have. A serious coffee attitude comes together with cafe food that's definitely a cut above. The freshly

baked panini are the best you'll have, while the baked eggs *en cocotte* (casserole) with serrano ham is an absolute knockout.

Sweet Envy   CAFE $
(Map p50; ✆03-6234 8805; www.sweetenvy. com; 341 Elizabeth St, North Hobart; items $5-10; ⊙8.30am-6pm Tue-Fri, to 5pm Sat) A delicate diversion along North Hobart's restaurant strip, Sweet Envy conjures up gossamer-light macarons, madeleines and cupcakes. Gourmet pies and sausage rolls (try the pork and fennel version) and fantastic ice creams and sorbets, all made on the premises. Grab a scoop of bad-ass black-sesame ice cream and hit the streets.

Fresco Market   SUPERMARKET $
(Map p50; ✆03-6234 2710; 1/346 Elizabeth St, North Hobart; ⊙9am-7.30pm) Self-caterers should find what they need at this boutiquey, black-painted supermarket on the North Hobart strip.

Elizabeth St
Food + Wine   MODERN AUSTRALIAN, DELI $$
(Map p50; ✆03-6231 2626; 285 Elizabeth St, North Hobart; mains $10-20; ⊙8am-6pm Sun-Thu, to 8pm Fri, to 4pm Sat) 🍴 Cafe, providore, wine room – take your pick at this vibrant North Hobart foodie space. Expect excellent breakfasts, big salads and classy mains (try the spicy beef cheek with potato and peperonata), all paired with local wines (except the breakfasts...). Communal tables and shelves crammed with 100% seasonal and sustainable Tasmanian produce.

Raincheck Lounge   CAFE $$
(Map p50; ✆03-6234 5975; www.raincheckslounge. com.au; 392 Elizabeth St, North Hobart; tapas $6-17, mains $9-22; ⊙7am-late Mon-Fri, 8am-late Sat, 8.30am-late Sun) A slice of urban cool, Raincheck's bohemian, quasi-Moroccan room and streetside tables see punters sipping coffee, reconstituting over big breakfasts, and conversing over generous tapas such as broccolini with anchovy crumb and chorizo in peperonata. Great wine list and sassy staff to boot. Perfect before or after a movie at the State Cinema (p77). Nice one.

Vanidol's   ASIAN $$
(Map p50; ✆03-6234 9307; www.va-nidols-north-hobart.com; 353 Elizabeth St, North Hobart; mains $18-30; ⊙5.30-9pm daily; 🖊) A pioneering North Hobart restaurant, Vanidol's has a diverse menu that travels effortlessly

LOCAL KNOWLEDGE

AGRARIAN KITCHEN: COOKING SCHOOL

Rodney Dunn and Séverine Demanet run the Agrarian Kitchen (p88), a highly regarded Tasmanian farm-based cooking school. Classes are led by Rodney, a former food editor of *Australian Gourmet Traveller* magazine and a one-time apprentice to iconic Australian chef Tetsuya Wakuda. Here are the Agrarian Kitchen's recommendations for Hobart-bound foodies.

Hobart's Don't Miss
In North Hobart try **Sweet Envy** (p74), a tiny patisserie with superb pastries and desserts. Its chef, Alistair Wise, used to work at Gordon Ramsay's restaurant at The London in New York.

Coffee & More
Other places we love in Hobart are **Tricycle Café Bar** (p71) and **Pigeon Hole** (p74).

Craft Beer in the Country
The **Two Metre Tall** (p86) brewery in the Derwent Valley near New Norfolk only uses hops and barley grown on its property to make its ales. Apparently it's the only microbrewery in the world to do this. Its on-site Farm Bar is open every Friday night and Sunday afternoon.

around Asia with dishes including spicy Thai beef salad, Nepalese lamb curry and Balinese chicken. Expect a well-thumbed passport full of vegetarian dishes, too. Also in South Hobart (Map p50; ☑03-6224 5986; www.vanidolsouth.com; 361a Macquarie St, South Hobart; mains $20-25; ☺11am-2pm & 5.30-9pm Tue-Sat).

Cornelian Bay
Boathouse MODERN AUSTRALIAN $$
(☑03-6228 9289; www.theboathouse.com. au; Queen's Walk, Cornelian Bay; mains $26-34; ☺noon-2pm daily, 6-8.30pm Mon & Thu-Sat) This stylish, light-filled restaurant-bar occupies a converted beach pavilion on shallow Cornelian Bay (the swimming destination of choice for sweaty Hobartians circa 1900), 3km north of town. On the menu is contemporary cuisine starring quality local produce and delivered with great service. Try the Boathouse chowder.

Annapurna INDIAN $$
(Map p50; ☑03-6236 9500; www.annapurnaindiancuisine.com; 305 Elizabeth St, North Hobart; mains $14-19; ☺noon-3pm Mon-Fri, 5-10pm daily; ☑) It seems like half of Hobart lists Annapurna as their favourite eatery (bookings advised). Northern and southern Indian options are served with absolute proficiency. The *masala dosa* (south Indian crepe filled with curried potato) is a crowd favourite. Takeaways, too.

Berta CAFE $$
(Map p50; ☑03-6234 4844; www.bertahobart. com.au; 323a Elizabeth St, North Hobart; mains $12-29; ☺7.30am-4pm Wed-Fri, 8.30am-2.30pm Sat & Sun) Atmospheric NoHo cafe with perfect people-watching window seats, pressed-tin ceilings, classy cafe fare and a wine list travelling from Tasmania to Tuscany. Kick-start your morning with five-grain porridge with cinnamon crumble; for lunch try the pistachio-crumbed calamari with chickpeas, parsley and harissa mayo.

All Thai THAI $$
(Map p50; ☑03-6234 8113; www.allthai.com. au; 333 Elizabeth St, North Hobart; mains $16-22; ☺5.30-9pm Mon-Thu & Sun, to 9.30pm Fri & Sat) Straight-up, reliable Thai offerings on the North Hobart strip – orange-and-black colour scheme, clattery chairs and a busy vibe. Check the blackboard for daily specials (pray for the stir-fried crispy pork belly in homemade curry paste).

Pasha's TURKISH $$
(Map p50; ☑03-6234 6300; 216 Elizabeth St, North Hobart; mains lunch $10-34, dinner $18-34; ☺11am-late Tue-Sat) More interesting than your average Turkish eatery, Pasha's menu incorporates the expected Ottoman goodies – *pide, dolma, kofte* – plus a few more surprising dishes. Try the *sukuk:* grilled Turkish sausage with garlic yoghurt, tomato and spinach. Takeaway Turkish dips, too.

🍷 Drinking & Nightlife

Hobart's younger drinkers are 10,000 leagues removed from the rum-addled whalers of the past, but the general intentions remain true – drink a bit, relax a lot, and maybe get lucky and take someone home. Salamanca Pl and the waterfront host a slew of pubs and bars with outdoor imbibing on summer evenings and open fires in winter. North Hobart is another solid (or rather, liquid) option.

Other good watering holes include the Shipwright's Arms Hotel (p68), New Sydney Hotel, Republic Bar & Café and Lark Distillery (p53).

★ Knopwood's Retreat   PUB
(Map p56; www.knopwoods.com; 39 Salamanca Pl; ⊙10am-late) Adhere to the 'when in Rome...' dictum and head for 'Knoppies', Hobart's best pub, which has been serving ales to sea-going types since the convict era. For most of the week it's a cosy watering hole with an open fire. On Friday nights, city workers swarm and the crowd spills across the street.

Preachers   BAR
(Map p50; 5 Knopwood St, Battery Point; ⊙noon-late) Grab a retro sofa seat inside, or adjourn to the ramshackle garden bar – in which an old Hobart bus is now full of beer booths – with the hipsters. Lots of Tasmanian craft beers on tap, plus cool staff and a resident ghost. A steady flow of $15 burgers and $12 tapas keeps the beer in check.

Jack Greene   BAR
(Map p56; www.jackgreene.com.au; 47-48 Salamanca Pl, Hobart; ⊙11am-late) The gourmet burgers here cost up to $20 but atmospheric

FRIDAY NIGHT FANDANGO

Some of Hobart's best live tunes get an airing every Friday night at the Salamanca Arts Centre Courtyard (Map p56; www.salarts.org.au/portfolio/rektango; 77 Salamanca Pl; ⊙5.30-7.30pm), just off Woobys Lane. It's a free community event that started in about 2000, with the adopted name 'Rektango', borrowed from a band that sometimes graces the stage. Acts vary from month to month; expect anything from African beats to rockabilly, folk and gypsy-Latino. Drinks essential (sangria in summer, mulled wine in winter); dancing near-essential.

Jack Greene (a European hunting lodge on the run?) is worthwhile if you're a wandering beer fan. Glowing racks of bottled brews fill the fridges, and there are at least 16 beers on tap from around Australia and New Zealand. Occasional acoustic troubadours perch next to the stairs.

IXL Long Bar   BAR
(Map p54; www.thehenryjones.com; 25 Hunter St; ⊙5-10.30pm Mon-Fri, 3pm-late Sat & Sun) Prop yourself at the glowing bar at the Henry Jones Art Hotel (p66) and check out Hobart's fashionistas over a whisky sour. If there are no spare stools at the not-so-long bar, flop onto the leather couches in the lobby. Moo Brew on tap, and live jazz Friday to Sunday.

T-42°   BAR
(Map p54; www.tav42.com.au; Elizabeth St Pier; ⊙7.30am-late Mon-Fri, from 8.30am Sat & Sun) Waterfront T-42° makes a big splash with its food (mains from $13 to $30), but also draws late-week barflies with its minimalist interior, spinnaker-shaped bar and ambient tunes. If you stay out late enough, it also does breakfast.

Lower House   BAR
(Map p54; www.thelowerhouse.com.au; 9/11a Murray St; ⊙noon-late Mon-Sat) Across the road from Parliament House is this hip basement bar, keeping escapee MPs lubricated with top-shelf whisky, cocktails and a massive wine list. Mature crowd and occasional DJs.

Nant Whisky Bar   BAR
(Map p56; www.nant.com.au; 63 Woobys Lane; ⊙noon-midnight Sun-Fri, 10am to midnight Sat) Prop yourself at the bar in this compact, heritage-hued room off Salamanca Pl and see how whisky from the Nant Distillery (p133) in Tasmania's central highlands stacks up next to other peaty drops from around the globe.

Hope & Anchor   PUB
(Map p54; www.hopeandanchor.com.au; 65 Macquarie St; ⊙11am-late) Depending on who you believe (don't listen to the barman at the Fortune of War in Sydney), this is the oldest pub in Australia (1807). The woody interior is lined with nautical knick-knacks. Not a bad spot for a cold Cascade.

Barcelona   BAR
(Map p56; www.barcelonahobart.com; 23 Salamanca Sq; ⊙noon-late Mon-Fri, 9am-late Sat & Sun) Lots of different beers on tap, a slick wine

list and well-priced bistro-style food make this one of Salamanca's most versatile drinking spots. The outdoor tables are perfect for suit-watching during the day, while cheap cocktails and beer steins lure the students on Wednesday nights. DJs Wednesday, Friday and Saturday nights.

Syrup CLUB
(Map p56; 39 Salamanca Pl; ⊙9pm-5am Fri & Sat) Over two floors above Knopwood's Retreat, this is an ace place for late-night drinks and DJs playing to the techno-house crowd. Vale Round Midnight, the blues bar that used to be on the top floor.

Mobius Lounge Bar CLUB, BAR
(Map p54; 7 Despard St; ⊙9pm-4am Wed, 10.30pm-4.30am Fri, 10pm-5am Sat) A pumping, clubby dungeon meets cool lounge bar, tucked in behind the main waterfront area. Occasional name DJs.

Observatory CLUB
(Map p54; www.observatorybar.com.au; level 1, Murray St Pier; ⊙9pm-late Wed, Fri & Sat) Sip a 'Big O' cocktail as you swan between the moody nooks at Observatory. Commercial dance in the main room, urban funk in the lounge. Don't dress down (the bouncers can be picky).

☆ Entertainment

★State Cinema CINEMA
(Map p50; ☑03-6234 6318; www.statecinema.com.au; 375 Elizabeth St, North Hobart; tickets adult/child $18/14; ⊙10am-late) Saved from the wrecking ball in the 1990s, the multiscreen State shows independent and arthouse flicks from local and international film-makers. There's a great cafe and bar on-site, a browse-worthy bookshop and the foodie temptations of North Hobart's restaurants right outside.

Republic Bar & Café LIVE MUSIC
(Map p50; ☑03-6234 6954; www.republicbar.com; 299 Elizabeth St, North Hobart; ⊙11am-late) The Republic is a raucous art-deco pub hosting live music every night (often free entry). It's the number-one live-music pub around town, with an always-interesting line-up, including international acts. Loads of different beers and excellent food – just the kind of place you'd love to call your local.

Brisbane Hotel LIVE MUSIC
(Map p50; 3 Brisbane St; ⊙noon-late Tue-Sat, 3pm-late Sun) The bad old Brisbane has dragged itself up from the pit of old-man, sticky-carpet alcoholism to be reinvented as a progressive live-music venue. This is where anyone doing anything original, offbeat or uncommercial gets a gig: punk, metal, hip-hop and singer-songwriters.

New Sydney Hotel LIVE MUSIC
(Map p54; www.newsydneyhotel.com.au; 87 Bathurst St; ⊙noon-midnight) Low-key folk, jazz, blues and comedy play to a mature crowd Tuesday to Sunday nights (usually free): see the website for gig listings. Great pub food and a terrific beer selection, including an ever-changing array of island microbrews. Irish jam session 2pm Saturdays.

Theatre Royal THEATRE
(Map p50; ☑03-6233 2299, 1800 650 277; www.theatreroyal.com.au; 29 Campbell St; shows $20-60; ⊙box office 9am-5pm Mon-Fri) This venerable old stager is Australia's oldest continuously operating theatre, with actors first cracking the boards here back in 1834. Expect a range of music, ballet, theatre, opera and university revues.

Grand Poobah LIVE MUSIC
(Map p54; 142 Liverpool St; ⊙8pm-1am Wed, 9pm-4.30am Fri & Sat) This versatile bohemian bar doubles as a music venue with everything from live bands to DJs, dance and comedy.

Peacock Theatre THEATRE
(Map p56; ☑03-6234 8414; www.salarts.org.au/portfolio/peacock-theatre; 77 Salamanca Pl; ⊙box office 9am-6pm) This intimate theatre (165 seats) is inside the Salamanca Arts Centre, along with a handful of other small performance spaces. Hosts theatre, dance, music and film.

Irish Murphy's LIVE MUSIC
(Map p56; www.irishmurphys.com.au; 21 Salamanca Pl; ⊙11am-late) Pretty much what you'd expect from any out-of-the-box Irish pub: crowded, lively, affable and dripping with Guinness. Free live music of varying repute from Wednesday to Sunday nights (originals on Wednesdays).

Federation Concert Hall CLASSICAL MUSIC
(Map p54; ☑1800 001 190; www.tso.com.au; 1 Davey St; ⊙box office 9am-5pm Mon-Fri) Welded to the Hotel Grand Chancellor, this concert hall resembles a huge aluminium can leaking insulation from gaps in the panelling. Inside, the Tasmanian Symphony Orchestra does what it does best.

Playhouse Theatre
THEATRE

(Map p54; ☑ 03-6234 1536; www.playhouse.org.au; 106 Bathurst St; tickets from $25; ☺ box office opens 1hr prior to performances) This vintage city theatre is home to the Hobart Repertory Theatre Society (musicals, Shakespeare, kids' plays). Book online.

Village Cinemas
CINEMA

(Map p54; ☑ 1300 555 400; www.villagecinemas.com.au; 181 Collins St; tickets adult/child $17.50/13, Gold Class from $30; ☺ 10am-late) An inner-city multiplex screening mainstream releases. Cheap-arse Tuesday tickets $12.

🛍 Shopping

Head to Salamanca Pl for shops and galleries stocking jewellery, Huon pine knick-knacks, hand-knitted beanies, local cheeses, sauces, jams, fudge and other assorted edibles. The hyperactive Salamanca Market (p53) happens here every Saturday.

The city centre has department stores, and on Elizabeth St, between Melville and Bathurst Sts, there's a swathe of stores catering to the great outdoors. Bathurst St also hosts the excellent Sunday morning Farm Gate Market (p48). There are also some interesting antique stores in the city and around Battery Point.

Fullers Bookshop
BOOKS

(Map p54; www.fullersbookshop.com.au; 131 Collins St; ☺ 8.30am-6pm Mon-Fri, 9am-5pm Sat, 10am-4pm Sun) Hobart's best bookshop has a great range of literature and travel guides, plus regular launches and readings, and a cool cafe in the corner.

Cool Wine
WINE

(Map p54; www.coolwine.com.au; shop 8, MidCity Arcade, Criterion St; ☺ 9.30am-6.30pm Mon-Sat, 10am-2pm Sun) Excellent selection of Tasmanian wine and global craft beers.

Tommy Gun Records
MUSIC, CLOTHING

(Map p54; 127 Elizabeth St; ☺ 10am-5pm Mon-Fri, to 3pm Sat) Head here for all your vinyl, studded-leather wristband and black rock T-shirt requirements.

Wursthaus
FOOD

(Map p56; www.wursthaus.com.au; 1 Montpelier Retreat; ☺ 8am-6pm Mon-Fri, to 5pm Sat, 9am-5pm Sun) Fine-food showcase just off Salamanca Pl selling speciality smallgoods, cheeses, cakes, breads, wines and pre-prepared meals.

Handmark Gallery
ARTS

(Map p56; www.handmark.com.au; 77 Salamanca Pl; ☺ 10am-5pm) Handmark has been here for 30 years, displaying unique ceramics, glass, woodwork and jewellery, plus paintings and sculpture – 100% Tasmanian.

Despard Gallery
ARTS

(Map p56; www.despard-gallery.com.au; 15 Castray Esplanade, Battery Point; ☺ 11am-6pm Mon-Fri, to 5pm Sat, to 4pm Sun) Top-notch contemporary Tasmanian arts – jewellery, canvases, glassware and ceramics – in a lovely old sandstone building.

Art Mob
ARTS

(Map p54; www.artmob.com.au; 29 Hunter St; ☺ 10am-late) Gorgeous Aboriginal fine arts from around Australia have found their way to the Hobart waterfront.

Antiques to Retro
ANTIQUES

(Map p54; www.antiquestoretro.com.au; 128 Bathurst St; ☺ 10am-5pm Mon-Fri, to 4pm Sat) Furniture, vinyl, books, clothes and jewellery, old and not-so-old.

Skigia
SPORTS

(Map p54; www.skigia.com.au; 123 Elizabeth St; ☺ 9.30am-6pm Mon-Fri, to 4pm Sat) Hire skis, snow clothes and chains for your car if you're heading to Mt Mawson or Ben Lomond.

Spot On Fishing Tackle
SPORTS

(Map p54; www.spotonfishing.com.au; 87-91 Harrington St; ☺ 9am-5.30pm Mon-Fri, to 3.45pm Sat) Advice on what's biting where, plus fishing supplies and trout licences (per day/week $22/37).

Tasmanian Map Centre
MAPS

(Map p54; www.map-centre.com.au; 110 Elizabeth St; ☺ 9.30am-5.30pm Mon-Fri, 10.30am-2.30pm Sat) Bushwalking maps, GPS units and travel guides.

ℹ Information

EMERGENCY

Hobart Police Station (☑ 03-6230 2111, nonemergency assistance 13 14 44; www.police.tas.gov.au; 43 Liverpool St; ☺ 24hr) Hobart's main cop shop.

Police, Fire & Ambulance (☑ 000) Emergency only.

INTERNET ACCESS

Ruffcut Records (www.ruffcut-records.com; 35a Elizabeth St; ☺ 8.30am-6pm Mon-Fri, 10am-5pm Sat) Internet terminals and offbeat vinyl.

State Library (www.linc.tas.gov.au; 91 Murray St; ⊙9.30am-6pm Mon-Thu, to 8pm Fri, to 2pm Sat) Free one-hour internet access.

MEDIA

Hobart's long-running newspaper the *Mercury* (www.themercury.com.au; aka 'the Mockery') is handy for discovering what's on where. The Thursday edition lists entertainment options. For gig listings, pick up a copy of the free street-press *Warp* (www.warpmagazine.com.au).

MEDICAL SERVICES

Australian Dental Association Emergency Service (⊘03-6248 1546; www.ada.org.au) Advice for dental emergencies.

City Doctors & Travel Clinic (⊘03-6231 3003; www.citydoctors.com.au; 188 Collins St; ⊙9am-5pm Mon-Fri) General medical appointments and travel immunisations.

My Chemist Salamanca (⊘03-6235 0257; www.mychemist.com.au; 6 Montpelier Retreat, Battery Point; ⊙8.30am-6.30pm Mon-Fri, to 5pm Sat, 10am-4pm Sun) Handy chemist just off Salamanca Pl.

Royal Hobart Hospital (⊘03-6222 8423; www.dhhs.tas.gov.au; 48 Liverpool St; ⊙24hr) Emergency entry on Liverpool St.

Salamanca Medical Centre (⊘03-6223 8181; www.tasmedicarelocal.com.au/providers/salamanca-medical-centre; 5a Gladstone St; ⊙8.30am-4pm Mon-Fri, 10am-3pm Sat, noon-1pm Sun) General medical appointments, just off Salamanca Pl.

MONEY

The major banks all have branches and ATMs around Elizabeth St Mall. There are also ATMs around Salamanca Pl.

POST

General Post Office (GPO; Map p54; www.auspost.com.au; cnr Elizabeth & Macquarie Sts; ⊙8.30am-5.30pm Mon-Fri) Forget about the mail...check out the heritage architecture!

TOURIST INFORMATION

Hobart Visitor Information Centre (Map p54; ⊘03-6238 4222; www.hobarttravelcentre.com.au; cnr Davey & Elizabeth Sts; ⊙9am-5pm daily, extended hours in summer) Information, maps and state-wide tour, transport and accommodation bookings.

Parks & Wildlife Service (Map p54; ⊘1300 827 727, 1300 135 513; www.parks.tas.gov.au; 134 Macquarie St; ⊙9am-5pm Mon-Fri) Information, maps, passes and fact sheets for bushwalking in national parks. Inside the Service Tasmania office.

Royal Automobile Club of Tasmania (RACT; Map p50; ⊘03-6232 6300, roadside assis-

tance 13 11 11; www.ract.com.au; cnr Murray & Patrick Sts, Hobart; ⊙8.45am-5pm Mon-Fri) Maps, road advice and emergency roadside assistance for members (or interstate/international affiliates).

USEFUL WEBSITES

Dwarf (www.thedwarf.com.au) Online gig guide.

Hobart City Council (www.hobartcity.com.au) City-council website: parks, transport and recreation.

Welcome to Hobart (www.welcometohobart.com.au) Official visitors guide.

ⓘ Getting There & Away

AIR

Hobart's 'international' airport has only domestic flights, with services operated by Qantas, Virgin Australia, Jetstar and Tiger Airways (p305).

BUS

There are two main intrastate bus companies operating to/from Hobart, running statewide routes. Check online for fares and timetables.

Redline Coaches (Map p54; ⊘1300 360 000; www.redlinecoaches.com.au; 230 Liverpool St) Buses leave outside the Liverpool St shopfront.

Tassielink (Map p50; ⊘1300 300 520; www.tassielink.com.au; 64 Brisbane St) Until a new bus terminal can be found/built (the lease is up on the old one), Tassielink buses will run from Brisbane St as well as a temporary stop on Elizabeth St, across the road from the Hobart Visitor Information Centre. Call or check online for location updates.

ⓘ Getting Around

TO/FROM THE AIRPORT

Hobart Airport (p304) is at Cambridge, 19km east of the city. A taxi into the city will cost around $42 between 6am and 8pm weekdays, and around $50 at other times.

Hobart Airporter (Map p54; ⊘1300 385 511; www.airporterhobart.com.au; one way/return $18/32) Hotel-door-to-airport services (and the other way around), connecting with all flights. Bookings essential.

BICYCLE

There are a number of bike-hire options around the city (see p60).

BUS

Metro Tasmania (⊘13 22 01; www.metrotas.com.au) operates the local bus network, which is reliable but infrequent outside of business hours. The **Metro Shop** (Map p54; 22 Elizabeth St; ☺ 8am-6pm Mon-Fri) handles ticketing and enquiries: most buses depart from this section of Elizabeth St, or from nearby Franklin Sq.

One-way fares vary with distances ('sections') travelled (from $3 to $6.20). For $5.30 you can buy an unlimited-travel **Day Rover** ticket, valid after 9am from Monday to Friday, and all weekend. Buy one-way tickets from the Metro Shop, the driver (exact change required) or ticket agents (newsagents and post offices). Drivers don't sell Day Rover tickets.

CAR & MOTORCYCLE

Timed, metered parking predominates in the CBD and tourist areas such as Salamanca Pl and the waterfront. For longer-term parking, large CBD garages (clearly signposted) offer inexpensive rates.

The big-boy rental firms have airport desks and city offices. Cheaper local firms offer daily rental rates from as low as $30. Some companies won't allow you to take their cars onto Bruny Island: ask when you book.

AAA Car Rentals (📞 0437 313 314, 03-6231 3313; www.aaacarrentals.com.au; 73 Warwick St; ☺ 9am-5pm Mon-Fri, 10am-2pm Sat & Sun)

AutoRent-Hertz (📞 03-6237 1111, 1300 067 222; www.autorent.com.au; cnr Bathurst & Harrington Sts; ☺ 8am-5pm)

Avis (📞 03-6214 1711; www.avis.com.au; 2/4 Market Pl; ☺ 8am-5.30pm Mon-Fri, to 4pm Sat & Sun)

Bargain Car Rentals (📞 1300 729 230; www.bargaincarrentals.com.au; 173 Harrington St; ☺ 8am-5pm Mon-Fri, 9am-3pm Sat & Sun)

Budget (📞 03-6234 5222, 1300 362 848; www.budget.com.au; 96 Harrington St; ☺ 7.30am-5.30pm Mon-Fri, to 4.30pm Sat, 9am-2pm Sun)

Europcar (📞 03-6231 1077, 1300 131 390; www.europcar.com.au; 112 Harrington St; ☺ 8am-5.30pm Mon-Fri, to 4pm Sat, 8am-2pm Sun)

Rent For Less (📞 1300 883 728, 03-6231 6844; www.rentforless.com.au; 92 Harrington St; ☺ 8am-5pm Mon-Fri, 8.30am-5pm Sat, 9am-1pm Sun)

TAXI

131008 Hobart (📞 13 10 08; www.131008hobart.com) Standard taxis.

Maxi-Taxi Services (📞 13 32 22; www.hobartmaxitaxi.com.au) Wheelchair-accessible vehicles and taxis for groups.

Yellow Cab Co (📞 13 19 24; http://hobart.yellowcab.com.au) Standard cabs (not all of which are yellow).

AROUND HOBART

You won't have to travel too far from Hobart to swap cityscapes for countryside, sandy beaches and historic sites. Reminders of Tasmania's convict history await at Richmond, and the waterfalls, wildlife and short walks at Mt Field National Park make an easy day trip. New Norfolk is a curious place to visit, while Seven Mile Beach and the Channel Hwy suburbs are great for an estuarine escape.

Channel Highway

The convoluted Channel Hwy is the continuation of Sandy Bay Rd, mimicking the D'Entrecasteaux Channel coastline as it flows south. It was once the main southbound road out of Hobart, but was relegated to a pleasant tourist drive once the Southern Outlet (Hwy A6) from Hobart to Kingston opened in 1985. Drive slowly and check out the views, hilltop houses and gardens en route south.

Taroona

POP 2000

Ten kilometres south of Hobart lies the snoozy residential beach suburb Taroona, its name derived from an Aboriginal word meaning 'chiton' (a type of marine mollusc). On the suburb's northern fringe is Truganini Reserve and the bottom end of the 2km **Truganini Track**, which leads up a wooded valley to the old signal station at Mt Nelson (p57). At the southern end of the 'hood, the excellent 3.5km **Alum Cliffs Track** heads off towards Kingston from just below the Shot Tower.

◉ Sights

Shot Tower   HISTORIC BUILDING

(📞 03-6227 8885; www.taroona.tas.au/shot-tower; Channel Hwy; adult/child/family $8/4/20, tearoom meals $5-10; ☺ 9am-5pm Sep-Apr, to 4pm May-Aug, tearoom 10am-4pm) On Taroona's southern fringe stands the Shot Tower, a 48m-high, circular sandstone turret (1870) built to make lead shot for firearms. Molten lead was once dribbled from the top, forming perfect spheres on its way down to a cooling vat of water at the bottom. The river views from atop the 318 steps (correct?) are wondrous. You can also devour a Devonshire tea on the stone rampart outside.

CROWN PRINCESS MARY OF DENMARK (AKA MARY DONALDSON OF TAROONA)

A few Tasmanians have found themselves in the spotlight recently (hooray for Richard Flanagan!) but no one has garnered more international attention than Mary Donaldson, the girl from Taroona, now living a modern-day fairy tale in Europe. Mary was born in Hobart in 1972, the youngest of four children. She attended Taroona High School before graduating from the University of Tasmania (in commerce and law) in 1993. She then moved to Melbourne, worked in advertising, travelled through Europe and the US, then returned to Australia to live in Sydney.

Mary met Denmark's Crown Prince Frederik at the Slip Inn pub in Sydney during the 2000 Olympic Games: the prince was in Oz with the Danish sailing team. The pair sailed into a relationship that sent the paparazzi into a frenzy, until Mary and Fred announced their engagement in 2003. They married in a lavish ceremony in Copenhagen in 2004 with a sea of well-wishers lining the streets, waving Danish and Australian flags. Interest in Tasmania as a holiday destination for the Danes has skyrocketed, and Tassie produce has found a new export market in Denmark.

'Our Mary' is never far from the covers of Danish and Australian gossip mags, as journos dissect every aspect of her life. Is she too thin? How's her Danish coming along? Is she pregnant again? Speaking of which, the real showstoppers of course have been Frederick and Mary's four kids: Prince Christian (born 2005), Princess Isabella (2007) and twins Prince Vincent and Princess Josephine (2011). Give or take a few months, that made it four kiddies under the age of five for Frederick and Mary. No doubt she's getting a bit of help at home, though...

HOBART & AROUND CHANNEL HIGHWAY

✖ Eating

⭐**Picnic Basket**   CAFE **$**
(📱0459 466 057; 176 Channel Hwy; mains $7-17; ⊙7.30am-4pm Mon-Fri, 8am-4pm Sat & Sun) What a find! This funky old petrol-station building has been reworked as an earthy cafe, with giant wooden electrical spools for tables and strawberries and herbs growing in planter boxes – a far remove from its petrochemical past. Chipper staff deliver breakfast burritos, croissants, big salads and homemade muesli with local yoghurt. Wide-awake coffee, too. Winner!

Taroona Lounge Bar   MODERN AUSTRALIAN **$$**
(📱03-6227 8886; 178 Channel Hwy; mains $16-32; ⊙11am-late) The Taroona Lounge Bar is a great detour from Hobart for lunch or dinner. It's a funky reworking of a 1970s pub with killer views, terrific wood-fired pizzas and superior versions of Aussie classics such as tempura-battered fish and chips and Black Angus scotch fillet. Popular on weekends – book in advance.

ℹ Getting There & Away

To get to Taroona from Hobart, take **Metro Tasmania** (📱13 22 01; www.metrotas.com.au) bus 56, 61, 62, 63, 65, 67 or 68 from Franklin Sq ($4.20).

Kingston

POP 13,000

Sprawling Kingston, 12km south of Hobart, is a booming outer suburb. Once a sleepy beach enclave, Kingston changed in the 1980s when the Southern Outlet roadway established a rocket-shot route into town. The beach here is great for a chilly swim on a sunny afternoon.

⊙ Sights

Kingston Beach   BEACH
(Osborne Esplanade) This relaxed swimming and sailing spot has steep wooded cliffs at each end of a long arc of sand. There's a picnic area at the northern end, accessed by a pedestrian bridge over the pollution-prone (and therefore aptly named) Browns River. The 3.5km **Alum Cliffs Track** from near the Shot Tower in Taroona finishes here. Behind the sailing clubhouse at the beach's southern end is a track leading to a secret little swimming cove called **Boronia Beach**.

Australian Antarctic Division   SCIENCE CENTRE
(📱03-6232 3209; www.aad.gov.au; 203 Channel Hwy; ⊙8.30am-5pm Mon-Fri) **FREE** Just south of Kingston is the government HQ responsible for administering Australia's 42% wedge of the frozen continent. Australia has a long

TINDERBOX

Drive through Blackmans Bay and continue 10km to the delightfully named Tinderbox: the views en route are eye-popping, and at Tinderbox itself there is a small beach bordering **Tinderbox Marine Reserve** (www.parks.tas.gov.au). Here you can snorkel along an underwater trail running alongside a sandstone reef, marked with submerged information plates explaining the rich local ecosystem.

Bruny Island is just across the water: locals launch their boats here and skim across to Dennes Point for a beach barbecue. Roaring 40s Kayaking (p61) runs day tours around this coast (adult/child $170/150).

From Tinderbox, continue around the peninsula to Howden and then back to Kingston via the Channel Hwy.

history of exploration and scientific study of Antarctica (p60): it's one of the original 12 nations that ratified the Antarctic Treaty in 1961. Visitors can check out the displays here, which feature Antarctic equipment, clothing and scientific vehicles, plus ecological info and some brilliant photographs. There's a cafe here, too.

Blackmans Bay Beach BEACH
(Ocean Esplanade, Blackmans Bay) About 3km from Kingston, Blackmans Bay has a decent beach and a blowhole. The water is usually quite cold, and there's rarely any surf...but it sure is pretty! If you wander around the cliff base near the blowhole, there's a deep swimming gulch, with waves surging in and out.

✕ Eating & Drinking

Beach CAFE, BAR **$$**
(☏03-6229 7600; www.thebeachrestaurant.com.au; 14 Ocean Esp, Blackmans Bay; mains $16-31; ☺10am-midnight Mon-Fri, 9am-midnight Sat & Sun) The mainstream cafes in Kingston are no great shakes – you're better off driving a few kilometres to the sunny terrace at this angular cafe-bar on Blackmans Bay beach. Wood-fired pizzas, risotto, lamb shanks and pasta are all done with flair. There's a great range of Tasmanian wines and beers, too, if you feel like settling in for the afternoon.

❶ Getting There & Away

To get to Kingston Beach from Hobart ($4.20) take **Metro Tasmania** (☏13 22 01; www.metrotas.com.au) bus 67 or 68 via Taroona, or 74, 84, 86 or 89 via the Southern Outlet. All these services also loop through Blackmans Bay.

By car, as you branch off from the Southern Outlet and approach Kingston continue straight ahead at the first set of lights – this road takes you to the beach. If you're trundling down the Channel Hwy from Taroona, turn left at these lights.

Seven Mile Beach

POP 450

Out near the airport, 15km east of Hobart, is this brilliant, safe swimming beach backed by shacks, a corner store and pine-punctured dunes. When the swell is working, the point break here is magic.

Follow Surf Rd out past the airport runway and around to the left for 2km and you'll come to **Barilla Bay Oyster Farm** (☏03-6248 5458; www.barillabay.com.au; 1388 Tasman Hwy, Cambridge; tours adult/child $17.50/13, mains $28-35; ☺11.30am-2.30pm daily, 5.30-8pm Fri & Sat). Hit the slick restaurant, or grab a dozen shucked oysters ($12) and wash them down with some Oyster Stout. Tours run at 11am on Fridays, from October to March – call for bookings.

To get to Seven Mile Beach, drive towards the airport and follow the signs. Metro Tasmania (p79) buses 665 and 668 also run here.

Richmond & Around

POP 750

Straddling the Coal River 27km northeast of Hobart, historic Richmond was once a strategic military post and convict station on the road to Port Arthur. Riddled with 19th-century buildings, it's arguably Tasmania's premier historic town, but like the Rocks in Sydney and Hahndorf in Adelaide, it's in danger of becoming a parody of itself with no actual 'life', just a passing tourist trade picking over the bones of the colonial past.

That said, Richmond is undeniably picturesque and kids love chasing the ducks around the riverbanks. It's also quite close to the airport – a happy overnight option if you're on an early flight.

See www.richmondvillage.com.au for more information.

⊙ Sights & Activities

Interesting historic buildings abound around the olde towne: check out St John's Church (St Johns Circle), the first Catholic church in Australia (1836); the castellated St Luke's Church of England (cnr Church & Torrens Sts), built 1834; the 1825 courthouse (54 Bridge St); the 1826 post office (36 Bridge St), now a frilly gift shop; and the solid Richmond Arms Hotel (Bridge St), built 1888.

Richmond Bridge   BRIDGE
(Wellington St) This chunky but not inelegant bridge still funnels traffic across the Coal River and is the town's proud centrepiece. Built by convicts in 1823 (making it the oldest road bridge in Australia), it's purportedly haunted by the 'Flagellator of Richmond', George Grover, who died here in 1832.

Bonorong Wildlife Centre   WILDLIFE RESERVE
(📞03-6268 1184; www.bonorong.com.au; 593 Briggs Rd, Brighton; adult/child/family $25/11/65; ⊙9am-5pm) 🐾 This impressive operation is about 17km west of Richmond (or alternatively, signposted off Hwy 1 at Brighton). From Richmond, take Middle Tea Tree Rd, and turn left into Tea Tree Rd after 11km. 'Bonorong' derives from an Aboriginal word meaning 'native companion' – look forward to Tasmanian devils, koalas, wombats, echidnas and quolls. The emphasis here is on conservation, education and the rehabilitation of injured animals.

ZooDoo Wildlife Park   WILDLIFE RESERVE
(📞03-6260 2444; www.zoodoo.com.au; 620 Middle Tea Tree Rd; adult/child $25/13; ⊙9am-5pm) Six kilometres west of Richmond on the road to Brighton (Middle Tea Tree Rd), ZooDoo has 'safari bus' rides, playgrounds, picnic areas and half of Dr Dolittle's appointment book, including tigers, llamas, Tasmanian devils and wallabies. Hungry white lions chow down at regularly scheduled intervals.

Richmond Gaol
Historic Site   HISTORIC BUILDING
(📞03-6260 2127; www.richmondgaol.com.au; 37 Bathurst St; adult/child/family $9/4/22; ⊙9am-5pm) The northern wing of the remarkably well-preserved jail was built in 1825, five years before the penitentiary at Port Arthur, making it Australia's oldest jail. And like Port Arthur, fascinating historic insights abound, but the mood is pretty sombre.

Old Hobart Town
Historical Model Village   HISTORIC SITE
(📞03-6260 2502; www.oldhobarttown.com; 21a Bridge St; adult/family $14/35; ⊙9am-5pm) A painstaking re-creation of Hobart Town in the 1820s, built from the city's original plans – the kids will love it. Admission is a bit steep, but it's actually pretty amazing, with some solid historical insights.

Richmond Park Boat House   BOATING
(📞0401 233 652, 03-6260 1099; www.richmondparkboathouse.com.au; 56 Bridge St; rowboats

---

COAL RIVER VALLEY WINE REGION

Richmond and nearby Cambridge are at the centre of Tasmania's fastest-growing wine region, the Coal River Valley. Some operations here are sophisticated affairs with gourmet restaurants; others are small, family-owned vineyards with cellar doors open by appointment. See www.winesouth.com.au for more info. Here's a few spots to get you started:

Frogmore Creek (📞03-6274 5844; www.frogmorecreek.com.au; 699 Richmond Rd, Cambridge; 4/5/6-course menu $80/95/125, with wine $100/125/160; ⊙10am-5pm, restaurant noon-4pm) Overlooking the Mt Pleasant Observatory, 9km southwest of Richmond, corporate Frogmore Creek has a flashy restaurant serving lunch, along with excellent chardonnay, pinot noir and sticky botrytis riesling. Don't miss *Flawed History,* an in-floor jigsaw by local artist Tom Samek. Restaurant bookings recommended (no kids).

Craigow Vineyard (📞03-6248 5379; www.craigow.com.au; 528 Richmond Rd, Cambridge; ⊙11am-5pm Jan-Mar) Offers tastings in a colonial cottage. Great whites, including riesling, chardonnay and sauvignon blanc. Located opposite Frogmore Creek.

Puddleduck Vineyard (📞03-6260 2301; www.puddleduck.com.au; 992 Richmond Rd, Richmond; ⊙10am-5pm) Small, family-run vineyard producing just 1200 cases per year: shoot for the riesling, pinot noir and 'Bubbleduck' sparkling white. Snaffle a cheese platter ($20), or fire up the barbecues (BYO meat) for lunch by the lake with Lucky the duck.

Richmond

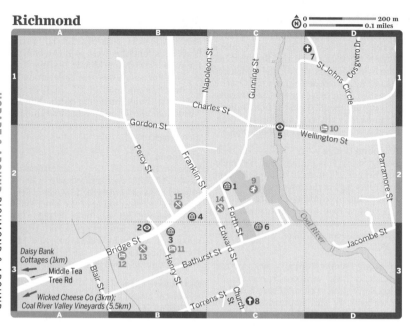

Richmond

⊙ **Sights**
- 1 Courthouse C2
- 2 Old Hobart Town Historical Model
  Village B3
- 3 Post Office B3
- 4 Richmond Arms Hotel B2
- 5 Richmond Bridge C2
- 6 Richmond Gaol Historic Site C3
- 7 St John's Church D1
- 8 St Luke's Church of England C3

🟢 **Activities, Courses & Tours**
- 9 Richmond Park Boat House C2

🛌 **Sleeping**
- 10 Laurel Cottage D2
- 11 Number 3 Henry Street B3
- 12 Richmond Coachmans Rest B3

🍽 **Eating**
- 13 Ashmore on Bridge Street B3
  Richmond Arms Hotel .... (see 4)
- 14 Richmond Bakery C2
- 15 Richmond Wine Centre B2

per 30min $25, bikes per hr $25; ⊙10am-4pm
Wed-Sun) Hire a bike and wheel yourself
around the town, or jump in a little row-
boat down on the river and dodge the local
ducks.

🛏 Sleeping

Barilla Holiday Park   CARAVAN PARK $
(☑03-6248 5453, 1800 465 453; www.barilla.
com.au; 75 Richmond Rd, Cambridge; unpowered/
powered sites $34/40, cabins & units $80-150;
❄@🛜🏊) A decent option for those with
wheels, Barilla is midway between Hobart
(14km) and Richmond (14km). It's close to
the airport, the Coal River Valley wineries
and a couple of good wildlife parks. The
grounds are dotted with well-kept cabins,
plus there's minigolf (oh, how quaint) and
an on-site restaurant serving wood-fired
pizzas.

⭐**Daisy Bank Cottages**   B&B $$
(☑03-6260 2390; www.daisybankcottages.
com.au; 78 Middle Tea Tree Rd; d $150-190) This
place is a rural delight: two spotless, stylish
self-contained units (one with spa) in a con-
verted 1840s sandstone barn on a working
sheep farm. There are loft bedrooms, views
of the Richmond rooftops and plenty of bu-
colic distractions for the kids. The surround-
ing farmland has interpretative walks and
soaring birds of prey. Breakfast provisions
daily. Hard to beat.

Laurel Cottage   RENTAL HOUSE $$
(☑03-6260 2397; www.laurelcottages.com.au;
9 Wellington St; s/d $120/150, extra adult/child

$30/20) Ramshackle two-bedroom, 1830s convict-brick cottage near the Richmond Bridge, with an authentic interior and a wood fire. Self-catering kitchen, with breakfast provisions supplied daily (plus port and chocolate for the other end of the day). Kids welcome.

Richmond Coachmans Rest   MOTEL $$
(☑03-6260 2609; www.richmondcoachmans-rest.com.au; 28 Bridge St; d from $130, bedroom unit from $150) A no-fuss, tidy row of three motel-style units on the main street. Unit 1 is a two-storey, two-bedroom affair; the other two are studio-style doubles. Simple, clean and totally sans colonial frills – what a relief!

Number 3 Henry Street   COTTAGE $$$
(☑03-6260 2847; www.numberthree.com.au; 3 Henry St; d $350, extra person $75; ❋ 🛜) This lovely old house has had its innards extended, reorganised and modernised – it still looks quaint from the street, but out the back things are utterly contemporary. Expect muted hues, plush linen, flash bathrooms (plural) and a private flagstone-entry courtyard. Sleeps four in two bedooms (the upstairs one is built into the roof space – fabulously angular!).

✖ Eating

Richmond Bakery   BAKERY $
(☑03-6260 2628; 50 Bridge St, off Edward St; items $3-8; ☺7.30am-6pm) Pies, pastries, sandwiches, croissants, muffins and cakes – takeaway or munch in the courtyard. If the main street is empty, chances are everyone is in here.

Richmond Wine Centre   MODERN AUSTRALIAN $$
(☑03-6260 2619; www.richmondwinecentre.com.au; 27 Bridge St; mains $22-30; ☺10am-4pm daily, 6-9pm Fri & Sat) Don't be duped by the name: this place dedicates itself to fine food as well as 100% Tasmanian wine. Slink over the daisy-studded lawn to one of the dinky outdoor tables and peruse the menu. Tassie produce reigns supreme.

Ashmore on Bridge Street   CAFE $$
(☑03-6260 2238; www.ashmoreonbridge.com.au; 34 Bridge St; mains $7-20; ☺9am-4.30pm Mon-Fri, to 5pm Sat & Sun, 6-9pm Tue & Wed) Cheery corner food room where the sun streams in through small-paned windows. Order up a big breakfast (pancakes with bacon and maple syrup) and a zingy lunch (Thai-style pork meatballs). The best coffee in town, too. Bookings essential for dinner.

Wicked Cheese Co   CHEESE $$
(☑03-6260 2341; www.wickedcheese.com.au; 1238 Richmond Rd; mains $9-23; ☺10am-4.30pm) In a black-painted barn on the way into Richmond from Hobart, Wicked Cheese is a top spot for cheese tastings (dig that whisky cheddar), a fresh, contemporary lunch (try the hot smoked-trout salad), or takeaway cheesy delights.

Richmond Arms Hotel   PUB FOOD $$
(☑03-6260 2109; www.richmondarmshotel.com.au; 42 Bridge St; mains $19-35; ☺noon-2pm & 6-8pm) This laid-back sandstone pub, popular with day-tripping, moustachioed bikers, has a reliable pub-grub menu (try the pork chops with cider sauce). The streetside tables are where you want to be. There's also motel-style accommodation (doubles from $110) in the renovated stables out the back.

❶ Getting There & Away

BUS
Tassielink (☑1300 653 633; www.tassielink.com.au) runs multiple buses from Hobart to Richmond ($7.60, 45 minutes) weekdays, plus two buses on Saturday and one on Sunday.

Richmond Tourist Bus (☑0408 341 804; www.hobartshuttlebus.com/richmond-village.html; adult/child return $30/20; ☺9am Sun-Fri, 12.15pm daily) runs daily services from Hobart, with three hours to explore Richmond (unguided) before returning. Call for bookings and pickup locations.

CAR
Richmond is a 20-minute drive east of Hobart.

New Norfolk & Around
POP 9000

Cropping up unexpectedly amid the lush, rolling countryside (and heavy industry) of the Derwent Valley is New Norfolk, settled in 1808. Here, 38km north of Hobart, the Derwent River narrows, and black swans rubberneck across the water.

By the 1860s the valley had become a hops-growing hub (hops are used to give beer its bitterness). Through the 20th century, New Norfolk was sculpted (and stigmatised) by two forces – the insane asylum Willow Court and the Boyer newspaper print mill. Hobartians came to view 'Norfick' as

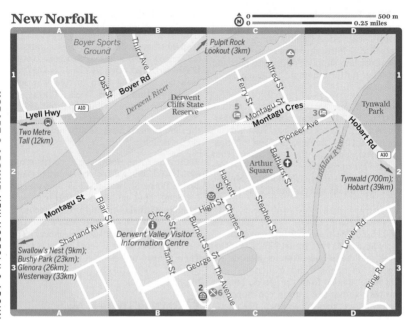

New Norfolk

mainland Australians viewed Hobart: lesser, working class and of vague moral certainty. These days the asylum is gone, and New Norfolk maintains a small-town, riverside sensibility along with eight antiques shops (eight!).

⊙ Sights & Activities

Two Metre Tall   BREWERY
(📞 0400 969 677; www.2mt.com.au; 2862 Lyell Hwy, Hayes; ⊙ noon-10pm Fri, noon-5pm Sun) One of Tassie's best microbreweries (the brewer here ain't short) throws open its gates every Friday and Sunday afternoon. These 'Farm Bar' sessions feature hand-pumped ales and ciders, with barbecues available (BYO snags). Hops and barley are sourced from

Two Metre Tall's own farm in the Derwent Valley. If you'd rather drink than drive, a return bus runs from Hobart ($15 per person, minimum 15 people). You'll find the brewery 12km northwest of New Norfolk, en route to Hamilton.

Pulpit Rock Lookout   VIEWPOINT
(www.newnorfolk.org/~pulpit_rock; Pulpit Rock Rd) For camera-conducive views over New Norfolk and a sweeping Derwent River bend, take the road along the northern side of the river eastward for 1km, then up a steep, unsealed side road to this ace lookout.

Church of St Matthew   CHURCH
(📞 03-6261 2223; www.newnorfolk.org/~st_matthews; 6 Bathurst St; ⊙ service 9.30am Sun) Built in 1823, St Matthew's is Tasmania's oldest church. It's been extensively altered since it first rose from the ground – its best features today are some impressive stained-glass windows.

Willow Court Historic Site   HISTORIC BUILDING
(www.newnorfolk.org/~willow_court; George St; ⊙ daylight hours) FREE Infamous Willow Court dates from the 1820s and once housed invalid convicts before it became a mental institution. In 1968 it had 1000 patients, but by the 1980s asylums began to be phased out

in favour of community-based treatment. In 2000 the asylum finally closed. The stately old buildings are grim but are slowly being repurposed, and now include a motel, the Patchwork Cafe and an eccentric antiques shop.

Tassie Bound   CANOEING

([☑]0417 008 422; www.tassiebound.com.au; per person/family incl lunch $150/550) Take a small-group 3½-hour downstream canoe paddle on the scenic, serene (and sometimes not-so-serene) Derwent River, with lunch on the riverbank. Pick-ups from New Norfolk. Friday twilight paddles with a visit to the Two Metre Tall microbrewery are also available ($99 per person).

[🛏] Sleeping & Eating

New Norfolk Caravan Park   CARAVAN PARK $

([☑]03-6261 1268; www.newnorfolkcaravanpark. com; 1 Esplanade; unpowered/powered sites $22/28, on-site caravans d $50, cabins d $85-95, extra person $10) Shady, poplar-studded grounds on the Derwent River's south bank, with ducks waddling around on the lawns. There are four cabins, all of which have en suites – everyone else uses the spotless amenities blocks.

Tynwald   B&B $$

([☑]03-6261 2667; www.tynwaldtasmania.com.au; 1 Tynwald St; d incl breakfast $165-250; [@][🐾]) Run by a couple of chefs, Tynwald is a beautiful, turreted 1830s mansion overlooking the river, with six antique-stuffed guestrooms, a heated pool, rambling gardens and cooked breakfasts. The **restaurant** (mains $32 to $38, from 6pm nightly) is the best in 'Norfick' – outside guests are welcome, but you'll need to book ahead.

Heimat Chalets   CABIN $$

([☑]03-6261 2843; www.heimatchalets.com; 430 Black Hills Rd, Black Hills; powered sites $45, wagon/chalets d $120/165) About 9km north of town (signposted off Lyell Hwy, west of the bridge) is Heimat, offering kid-friendly accommodation in a rural setting with friendly alpacas and goats. There are two powered, en-suite sites, two self-contained chalets (breakfast provisions included) and a rather wonderful 'gypsy wagon'. Visit from October to December to see Tasmania's cutest lambs. Extra person in chalets $35.

Junction   MOTEL $$

([☑]03-6261 4029; www.junctionmotel.com.au; 50 Pioneer Ave; d $99-125; [🐾]) This refurbished motel has spotless rooms – including a few Asian-themed luxury options – and energetic ex-Sydney and New Zealand owners forging a new life in Tasmania. There's also an on-site **restaurant** (mains from $17 to $28, serving 6pm to 8pm Monday to Friday) for guests.

Old Colony Inn   B&B $$

([☑]03-6261 2731; www.oldcolonyinn.com; 21 Montagu St; d incl breakfast from $110) Set in picture-perfect gardens, the black-and-white-striped Old Colony Inn (1815) has quaint rooms offering just the right mix of heritage and new-century comfort, with neat bathrooms and flat-screen TVs. There's also an on-site **tearoom** and ramshackle rooms full of antiques and portraits (if you're not staying the night, you can have a look around for $2 per person).

Patchwork Cafe   CAFE $

([☑]0417 916 479; www.patchworkcafe.com; George St, Willow Court Historic Site; mains $8-13; [⏰]9am-4pm Mon-Sat, 10am-4pm Sun) Inside the old wooden Willow Court nurses' chapel (flat-packed in England then shipped here) is this beaut little cafe, with sunny outdoor tables and Sunday live-music sessions in summer. Emerging from the kitchen are salmon patties, burgers, lamb-and-aubergine pies, scones and decent coffee. Willow Court's saving grace.

[ℹ] Information

Derwent Valley Visitor Information Centre

([☑]03-6261 3700; www.riversrun.net.au; Circle St; [⏰]10am-4pm) The local info hub handles accommodation bookings and dishes the local low-down.

[ℹ] Getting There & Away

Tassielink ([☑]1300 300 520; www.tassielink. com.au) runs between Hobart and New Norfolk ($8.30, 50 minutes), with buses on Tuesday, Thursday, Friday and Sunday (and every weekday during school terms).

New Norfolk to Mt Field

En route from New Norfolk to Mt Field National Park, the road travels through the historic towns of Plenty, Bushy Park, Glenora and Westerway. The countryside here is utterly photogenic, with long runs of roadside poplar trees, rambling hop fields and old shingle-roof oast houses (used for drying hops). Bushy Park remains the largest hops-producing town in the southern hemisphere, supplying Australian breweries of all sizes.

◉ Sights & Activities

Salmon Ponds   FARM
(☑03-6261 5663; www.salmonponds.com.au; Salmon Ponds Rd, Plenty; adult/child/family $8/6/22; ☺9am-5pm, restaurant 9am-4pm Nov-Apr, 10am-3pm May-Oct) In 1864 rainbow and brown trout were bred for the first time in the southern hemisphere at this hatchery, 9km west of New Norfolk at Plenty. You can feed the fish in the display ponds, visit the hatchery and check out the angling museum. The restaurant (mains $8 to $20) here specialises in sweet and savoury crepes (try the smoked salmon and camembert) plus island wines and serves decent coffee.

Redlands Estate Distillery   DISTILLERY
(☑03-6261 5728; www.redlandsestate.com.au; 759 Glenora Rd, Plenty; tastings & self-guided tours from $10; ☺10am-4pm Thu-Mon) Since Hobart's Sullivans Cove distillery took out the gold medal at the world whisky championships in 2014, Tasmania has gone mad for whisky! This outfit has been distilling since 2012, and by the time you visit, its single malt should be ripe for your appreciation. Check out the gorgeous old Redlands homestead (1819) and gardens while you're here.

🛏 Sleeping

Base Camp Tasmania   CABIN $
(BCT; ☑1300 882 293, 0414 238 458; www.twe.travel; 959 Glenfern Rd, Glenfern; tent per person $15, dm $36, f cabin $120) ✐ It's just 14km west of New Norfolk, but BCT feels a thousand miles from anywhere. A winding mountain dirt road passes spooky shacks and car wrecks before revealing rustic but comfortable dorms and cabins, which share a spotless kitchen and amenities. Expect abundant wildlife. It's the base camp for Tasmanian Wilderness Experiences tours, but casual guests are welcome. Bookings essential.

★Duffy's Country Accommodation   COTTAGE $$
(☑03-6288 1373; www.duffyscountry.com; 49 Clark's Rd, Westerway; d $130-145, extra adult/child $25/15; 🛜) Overlooking a field of raspberry canes are these two immaculate self-contained cottages, one a studio-style cabin for couples, the other a two-bedroom relocated rangers' hut from Mt Field National Park for families. There are also a couple of cute two-bed bunkhouses (one next to each cottage) where you can file the teenagers. Breakfast provisions available. Wallabies a distinct possibility.

Platypus Playground   COTTAGE $$
(☑0413 833 700; www.riverside-cottage.com; 1658 Gordon River Rd, Westerway; d $135-175) ✐ You can't miss this little red shiplap cottage

---

COOKING IN THE COUNTRY

Tasmania is rapidly becoming renowned globally as a destination for passionate, foodie travellers. The state's fruit and vegetables, seafood and meat, and wine and beer are held in high regard by star mainland chefs such as Tetsuya Wakuda, and local chefs are also forging an international reputation. It's the kind of superior produce that any self-respecting home cook would love to get into. Here's your chance!

Agrarian Kitchen (☑03-6261 1099; www.theagrariankitchen.com; 650 Lachlan Rd, Lachlan), located in a 19th-century schoolhouse in the Derwent Valley village of Lachlan, about 45 minutes' drive from Hobart, is Tasmania's first hands-on, farm-based cookery school. The surrounding 5 acres provide sustainable, organically grown vegetables, fruit, berries and herbs. Other ingredients are sourced from local farmers, fishers and artisan producers.

One of the most popular classes is the Agrarian Experience (per person $385), a day-long celebration of the seasons, commencing with choosing the freshest of fruit and veggies in the garden and then cooking up a storm before settling in for lunch with Tasmanian wines and beers from the nearby Two Metre Tall (p86) microbrewery. Other classes specialise in charcuterie and gourmet sausage making, pastries and pasta, bread making and desserts. Brilliant!

If you're travelling in Tasmania's north, Hadspen's Red Feather Inn (p194) also offers cooking classes, inspired by the Slow Food movement.

by the Tyenna River in Westerway. Winning features include a little outdoor deck over the river (spot a platypus or hook a trout) and a little BBQ. Everything's little! The owners make it a priority to minimise guests' environmental impact (ecofriendly toiletries and detergents all the way).

Hamlet Downs   B&B $$

(☑ 03-6288 1212; www.hamletdowns.com; 50 Gully Rd, Fentonbury; d $129-155, extra adult/child $40/30; ☜) Amid rural quiet and spectacular flower beds around 3km northwest of Westerway at Fentonbury, Hamlet Downs is a gracious 1860s homestead transformed into three self-contained apartments. Take a walk down to Fentonbury Creek to look for a platypus. Dinner, bed and breakfast packages also available (from $219). Mt Field is 10km away.

Swallow's Nest   B&B $$$

(☑ 0418 982 150, 03-6286 1144; www.swallows-nestguesthouse.com.au; 1358 Glenora Rd, Plenty; up to 10 people $400; ☜) For a group, or roaming river rats, or a big family, this renovated four-bedroom oast house sits by the Derwent River around 15 minutes from New Norfolk. Over two floors you'll find multiple living areas and bathrooms, an open fire, a laundry and a big communal dinner table. There are swallow's nests in the eaves and resident platypuses in the river.

✕ Eating

Possum Shed   CAFE $

(☑ 03-6288 1364; www.thepossumshed.com.au; 1654 Gordon River Rd, Westerway; mains $11-18; ☺ 9am-4pm Wed-Fri, to 5pm Sat & Sun, daily Dec-Feb) At Westerway, en route to Mt Field, you'll find this brilliant riverside haunt, with outdoor seating, a resident platypus (sightings not guaranteed – you have to be *really* quiet) and locally sourced lunches and snacks (salads, burgers, pancakes, muffins, BLTs). The coffee is good to go.

Mt Field National Park

POP 170 (NATIONAL PARK TOWNSHIP)

Mt Field, 80km northwest of Hobart and 7km beyond Westerway, was declared a national park in 1916. It is famed for its alpine moorlands, lakes, rainforest, waterfalls, walks, skiing and rampant wildlife. It's an accessible day trip from Hobart, or you can bunk down overnight.

✇ Activities

Swing by the visitor information centre for maps and advice on the various walks around the park. Sign the intentions book here if you're heading off on a longer hike.

Short Walks

The park's most touted attraction is the cascading, 40m-high Russell Falls, which is in the valley close to the park entrance. It's an easy 20-minute circuit walk from the car park along a wheelchair-suitable path. From Russell Falls, you can continue past Horseshoe Falls and the Tall Trees Circuit to Lady Barron Falls, a two-hour return walk past mountain ash (the world's tallest flowering plants).

The 15-minute Lyrebird Nature Walk starts 8km up Lake Dobson Rd. It's a pocket-sized introduction to park flora and fauna – great for kids – with numbers along the track corresponding to information in a brochure from the visitor centre.

For kids (and adults!) who don't mind a longer walk, there's the Pandani Grove Nature Walk, which traces the edge of Lake Dobson through magical stands of endemic pandani palms, which grow up to 12m high before toppling over. This walk takes 30 minutes. Park at Lake Dobson car park, 16km from the park entrance.

High-Country Walks

There are some awesome walks at the top of the range, where glaciation has sculpted steep cliffs and bruised deep valleys into what was once a continuous plateau. Shimmering lakes perforate the valley floors, and smaller tarns adorn the ridge tops.

If you're setting out on a walk to the high country, take waterproof gear and warm clothing – the weather is changeable year-round, so check weather and track conditions with the visitor centre before you set out. Walks here include those to Lake Nicholls, Seagers Lookout and Lake Seal Lookout (all two hours return), the Mt Field East Circuit (four to five hours return) and Lake Belcher (five to six hours return).

Tarn Shelf Track

The Tarn Shelf Track is a brilliant walk year-round in clear weather. In summer the temperature is mild, and in autumn deciduous beech trees along the way turn golden. In winter you may need skis or snowshoes. In spring the sound of melting snow trickling beneath the boardwalk enhances the silence.

ℹ WINTER ROAD WARNING

If you're staying in the Lake Dobson cabins, skiing at Mt Mawson or trampling the high-country walks, you'll have to drive the 16km unsealed Lake Dobson Rd. In winter, despite climate change's best efforts, you'll need chains and antifreeze for your car. Hire them in Hobart at Skigia (p78).

Most people walk from the Lake Dobson car park, taking the Urquhart Track to the ski fields, at the top of which is the start of the Tarn Shelf Track. The track is fairly level, with a boardwalk protecting delicate vegetation and keeping walkers out of the mud. Either continue as far as you like along the track and then backtrack, or circle east past Twisted Tarn, Twilight Tarn and Lake Webster, which all up takes five or six hours return from the car park.

Skiing

Skiing was first attempted here on **Mt Mawson** (www.mtmawson.info; skiing adult/child full day $30/15, half-day $20/10, ski tow deposit $10; ⊘10am-4pm Sat & Sun mid-Jul–mid-Sep) in 1922. A low-key resort with clubby huts and rope tows has evolved, and when nature sees fit to offload some snow (infrequently in recent years) it makes a low-key change from the commercial ski fields on mainland Australia. Check the website for snow reports and cams.

There are no ski-equipment hire outlets here; hire ski gear from Skigia (p78) in Hobart.

🛏 Sleeping

There's also accommodation around Westerway, 7km east of the national park.

Mt Field National Park Campground　　　CAMPGROUND $
(☑03-6288 1149; www.parks.tas.gov.au; off Lake Dobson Rd; unpowered/powered sites per 2 adults $16/20, extra adult $7/9, extra child $3/4) Run by the park administration, this self-registration campground is a few hundred metres past the visitor information centre and has adequate facilities (toilets, showers, laundry and free barbecues). No bookings. Site prices are additional to national park entry fees.

Lake Dobson Cabins　　　CABIN $
(☑03-6288 1149; www.parks.tas.gov.au; Lake Dobson Rd; cabins up to 6 people $45) Get back to

your rootsy mountaintop essence at these three simple, six-bed cabins 16km inside Mt Field National Park. All are equipped with mattresses, cold water, wood stove and firewood (there's no power), with a communal outdoor toilet block. BYO gas lamps, cookers, utensils and bedding. Book via the visitor centre or online.

Russell Falls Holiday Cottages　　　COTTAGE $$
(☑03-6288 1198; www.russellfallscottages.com.au; 40 Lake Dobson Rd; d $160-180, 2-bedroom cottage per 4 people $200) These four self-contained cottages are a bit soulless, but they're spotless and in a super location next to the Mt Field National Park entrance.

🍴 Eating

Waterfalls Cafe & Gallery　　　CAFE $
(90 Lake Dobson Rd; mains $7-25; ⊘9am-5pm summer, 10am-3pm winter) Simple eatery inside the visitor information centre, serving up reasonable cafe fare (burgers, nachos, toasted sandwiches and chicken schnitzels).

National Park Hotel　　　PUB FOOD $$
(☑03-6288 1103; www.nationalparkhotel.com.au; Gordon River Rd; mains $14-30; ⊘6-8pm Dec-Feb) A few hundred metres past the park turn-off is this old country pub (1920), cooking up mixed grills, chicken dishes and steaks. The bartender shakes her head and says, 'They love their meat round here...' The bar scenes from the 2011 Willem Dafoe movie *The Hunter* were filmed here.

ℹ Information

The **Mt Field National Park Visitor Information Centre** (☑03-6288 1149; www.parks.tas.gov.au; 66 Lake Dobson Rd; ⊘8.30am-5pm Nov-Apr, 9am-4pm May-Oct) houses the Waterfalls Cafe and displays on the park's origins, and has reams of information on walks and ranger-led activities, held from late December until early February. There are excellent day-use facilities in the park, including barbecues, shelters, lawns and a children's playground.

ℹ Getting There & Away

The drive to Mt Field through the Derwent River Valley and Bushy Park is an absolute stunner, with river rapids, hop fields, old oast houses, rows of poplars and hawthorn hedgerows. There's no public transport to the park, but some Hobart-based tour operators offer Mt Field day trips.

Wine, Wilderness & Wonderful Food

Tasmania is a land of contrasts, laced with social and historical contradictions. It follows, then, that a jaunt into the the island's epic wilderness should be followed by some seriously good food and drink. It's a cycle of effort and reward, effort and reward... How satisfying!

Contents
➡ **Walk on the Wild Side**
➡ **Tasting Tasmania**
➡ **Drinking Down South**

Above: Cascade Brewery (p56)

JULIAN LOVE / GETTY IMAGES ©

1. Mersey River, Overland Track (p250) **2.** Lake Oberon, Southwest National Park (p259) **3.** Bishop and Clerk (p142), Maria Island National Park **4.** Tarkine Wilderness (p229)

2

Walk on the Wild Side

Sign out of civilisation for a few days and head for Tasmania's wild forests, alpine plateaus and empty beaches. Trudge off with a tent and some dried fruit in your backpack, or take things easier on a multiday guided hike with upmarket hut accommodation en route.

The Overland Track

Traversing Cradle Mountain–Lake St Clair National Park, the famous six- to eight-day Overland Track is a challenging procession of craggy peaks, tarn shelves, eucalypt forests and ice-cold lakes. What a week!

Bay of Fires Walk

Give your Tasmanian trek a luxury twist. This four-day/three-night guided hike combines the pristine bays and granite headlands of the northeast with ecolodge accommodation and fine food and wine.

4

South Coast Track

The legendary 85km South Coast Track ain't for beginners: have you got what it takes? Spend a week negotiating the lonesome coastline of Southwest National Park, with nothing between you and Antarctica but thundering ocean waves.

Tarkine Wilderness

The Tarkine is an ancient collusion of rainforests, rugged button-grass plains and wild, windy beaches – the most diverse wilderness area in Tasmania. Tackle a trail independently, or sign up for a guided experience. Either way, come prepared for isolation and capricious weather.

Maria Island National Park

Not far off Tasmania's east coast, Maria Island (pronounced 'Ma-*rye*-ah') is popular with peak baggers, here to scale Mt Maria (711m) and Bishop and Clerk (620m). Closer to sea level, you can see the island on a guided hike with gourmet trimmings.

JULIAN LOVE / GETTY IMAGES ©

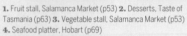

1. Fruit stall, Salamanca Market (p53) **2.** Desserts, Taste of Tasmania (p63) **3.** Vegetable stall, Salamanca Market (p53) **4.** Seafood platter, Hobart (p69)

Tasting Tasmania

Welcome to Australia's finest food destination. Fire your creativity with a cooking class, fill your basket at a farmers market or tour the state's artisan producers. If you'd rather eat without the effort, time your trip to coincide with one of Tassie's fab food festivals.

Cooking Schools

Get crafty in the kitchen at one of Tasmania's cool cooking schools. The Agrarian Kitchen near Hobart has its own organic farm; the Red Feather Inn in Hadspen combines plush accommodation with a slow-food emphasis.

To Market, to Market

Hobart's Salamanca Market is prime local-produce territory, but the new Farm Gate Market in the CBD offers a 100% foodie focus with baked goods, wine, smoked meats, eggs, fruit, veg, honey, beer, coffee, nuts, oils and condiments. Harvest in Launceston is similar, highlighting organic producers and sustainable suppliers.

Food Festivals

Locals love to to blow their culinary trumpet. Fill your innards at the state-wide Savour Tasmania Food Festival, Hobart's long-running Taste of Tasmania, Launceston's Festivale or Huonville's Taste of the Huon festival.

Briny Bounty

Tasmania is an island: it's a no-brainer that the seafood here is awesome! Highlights include fresh-off-the-boat fish in St Helens, oysters from Bruny Island's Get Shucked or the Freycinet Marine Farm, and curls of calamari from Flippers floating fish punt on Hobart's Constitution Dock.

Gourmet Farmer

For onscreen inspiration, check out the excellent SBS television series *Gourmet Farmer*. Ex-food critic Matthew Evans retreats from Sydney to Cygnet to try his hand at organic farming.

Whisky barrels aging at the Lark Distillery (p53)

Drinking Down South

There simply are no reasons not to have a drink in Tasmania. Local cool-climate wines grace the state's menus, and Tasmanian single malt whisky has become a global smash. Meanwhile, the local craft-beer scene is bubbling along nicely.

Top Tassie Drops

The cool-climate Tamar Valley and Pipers River regions north of Launceston are Tasmania's key wine-producing areas. Spend a day vineyard hopping, then fill the car boot with pinot noir, riesling and bottles of bubbles.

Southern Wine Touring

Day-trip east of Hobart to the fast-emerging Coal River Valley wine region for some cellar door action, followed by a classy lunch at Frogmore Creek. Further south you can meet the friendly winemakers at Bruny Island Premium Wines and Dover's St Imre Vineyard.

The Beer Down Here

Tasmanian craft-beer hits include hip Moo Brew pilsner and *hefeweizen,* Iron House lager and real ales from Two Metre Tall and Van Dieman Brewing. Try them all at the Weldborough Hotel in the northeast.

Cascade Brewery

South Hobart's gothic-looking Cascade Brewery has been bottling the good stuff since 1832 – it's Australia's oldest brewery. Take a tour of the workings, then sample its globally acclaimed stouts, ales and lagers.

Make Mine a Double

Wait a minute...this place looks just like the Scottish highlands! Must-visit Tasmanian single malt distilleries include Sullivans Cove, Lark Distillery in Hobart, Nant Distillery in Bothwell, and Hellyers Road Whisky Distillery in Burnie.

Tasman Peninsula & Port Arthur

Best Places to Eat

➡ Doo-Lishus Food Caravan (p100)

➡ Dunalley Waterfront Café & Gallery (p100)

➡ Gabriel's on the Bay (p107)

➡ Lucky Ducks (p103)

Best Places to Stay

➡ Casilda House (p100)

➡ Norfolk Bay Convict Station (p102)

➡ Sea Change Safety Cove (p107)

➡ Larus Waterfront Cottage (p103)

Why Go?

Just an hour from Hobart lie the staggering coastal landscapes, sandy beaches and historic sites of the Tasman Peninsula. Bushwalking, surfing, sea-kayaking, scuba-diving and rock-climbing opportunities abound – all good reasons to extend your visit beyond a hurried day trip from Hobart.

Don't miss visiting the peninsula's legendary 300m-high sea cliffs – the tallest in the southern hemisphere – which will dose you up on natural awe. Most of the cliffs are protected by Tasman National Park, a coastal enclave embracing chunky offshore islands and underwater kelp forests. The cliffs are a safe haven for seabirds, while the fertile waters below throng with seals, dolphins and whales.

Waiting portentously at the end of Arthur Hwy is Port Arthur, the infamous and allegedly escape-proof penal colony dating from the early 19th century. Today kids kick footballs and dads poke sausages on BBQs there, but it's impossible to totally blank out the tragedy of this place, both historically and more recently.

When to Go

➡ Tasman Peninsula weather is at its most reliable from November to March, but from December to February be prepared for crowds at the Port Arthur Historic Site, especially on weekends. Alternatively, visiting Port Arthur during winter (June to August) makes the experience even more confronting, imagining the cold-weather hardships the convicts experienced here.

➡ Fresh fruit fans should visit from December to January, when boughs at the Sorell Fruit Farm hang heavy with ripe varieties.

➡ Tackling the Tasman Peninsula's bushwalking tracks and surf breaks is definitely best done during summer: aim for January to April.

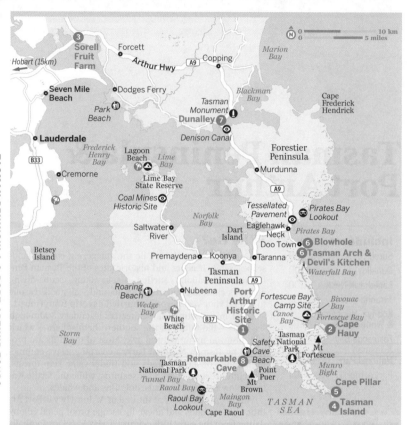

Tasman Peninsula & Port Arthur Highlights

1 Pay your respects to the past, both distant and recent, at the **Port Arthur Historic Site** (p105).

2 Sea kayak around the wild, broken coastline of **Cape Hauy** (p99).

3 Pick raspberries, apricots and silvanberries at the **Sorell Fruit Farm** (p99).

4 Spot seals and dolphins on a cruise around **Tasman Island** (p98).

5 Battle vertigo atop the southern hemisphere's highest sea cliffs at Cape Pillar on the **Tasman Coastal Trail** (p101).

6 Cruise the streets of Doo Town en route to the

Blowhole, Tasman Arch and Devil's Kitchen (p101).

7 Chow down on local seafood at the **Dunalley Waterfront Café & Gallery** (p100).

8 Watch the waves surge in and out of **Remarkable Cave** (p103) south of Port Arthur.

👉 Tours

Tasman Island Cruises   BOAT TOUR

(Pennicott Wilderness Journeys; ☎ 03-6250 2200; www.tasmancruises.com.au; full-day tour adult/child $225/155) Trips depart Hobart and include a three-hour cruise past the Tasman Peninsula's most spectacular coastal scenery and admission to Port Arthur. You can also join the cruise at Port Arthur (6961 Arthur Hwy) and

save a few dollars (adult/child $125/75, not including Port Arthur admission).

Under Down Under   TOUR

(☎ 1800 444 442; www.underdownunder.com.au; per person $110) Guided backpacker-style day trips to Port Arthur via Richmond, including accommodation pick-up, admission fees, a guided walk and a harbour cruise.

Roaring 40s Kayaking KAYAKING
(✍0455 949 777; www.roaring40skayaking.com.
au; day tour $200; ☺Nov-Apr) Roaring 40s con-
ducts epic sea-kayaking day tours around
the Tasman Peninsula, paddling past the
monumental coastline of Cape Hauy. Prices
include equipment, lunch and transfers
from Hobart.

Tours Tasmania TOUR
(✍1800 777 103; www.tourstas.com.au; full-day
tour $120; ☺Sun-Fri) Good-value, small-group
day tours to Port Arthur (including admission fees, walking tour and harbour cruise)
via Richmond, Devil's Kitchen and Tasman
Arch. Backpacker focused.

Navigators CRUISE
(✍03-6223 1914; www.navigators.net.au; Brooke
St Pier, Hobart; full-day tour adult/child $229/204;
☺Oct-Apr) Cruises from Hobart to Port Arthur,
returning on a coach. Includes entrance to
the historic site, morning tea, lunch, a walking tour and a tour of the Isle of the Dead.
Omit the meals and the Isle of the Dead and
the price drops (adult/child $159/128).

Gray Line BUS TOUR
(✍1300 858 687; www.grayline.com.au; full-day
tour adult/child $139/70) Cushy coach tours
ex-Hobart, including a harbour cruise
around the Isle of the Dead, Port Arthur
admission and guided tour, and pit stops at
Tasman Arch and the Devil's Kitchen.

Sorell

POP 2480
Sorell is one of Tasmania's oldest towns,
settled in 1808 primarily to supply locally
processed wheat and flour to the rest of the
colony, but its historic aura has tarnished
over time. These days it's a T-junction service town with more petrol stations and
fast-food joints than anything else...but it remains the gateway to the Tasman Peninsula.

◉ Sights & Activities

A handful of 19th-century buildings are
worth a look. The 1841 **Scots Uniting
Church** (Arthur St) is behind the high school.
Nearby are the **Sorell Barracks** (www.sorell-
barracks.com; 31 Walker St), now colonial accommodation, and the 1829 **Blue Bell Inn**
(26 Somerville St). On the main drag is the
1884 **St George's Anglican Church** (www.
srtanglican.org.au; 16 Gordon St, Sorell), its adjacent graveyard propped with the head-

stones of early settlers. The *Let's Talk About
Sorell* brochure from the visitor information
centre has a map.

Sorell Fruit Farm FARM
(✍03-6265 2744; www.sorellfruitfarm.com; 174
Pawleena Rd; containers from $8.50; ☺8.30am-
5pm Oct-May) Pick your own fruit (15 different
kinds including strawberries, raspberries,
cherries, apricots, peaches, apples and loganberries) at this intensively planted 12½-acre
farm, or grab a bite and a coffee at the cafe
(items $9 to $13). December and January
are the best months for variety, but different fruits are in season at different times –
check the website for a nifty chart. Head east
through Sorell towards Port Arthur; you'll
see Pawleena signposted on your left.

Island Surf School SURFING
(✍0400 830 237, 03-6265 9776; www.islandsurf-
school.com.au; 2hr group lesson per person $40)
Hit the surf with a lesson or two at Park
Beach at Dodges Ferry, not far south of
Sorell. All gear, including wetsuits, is provided. Bookings essential.

🛏 Sleeping

Steele's Island RENTAL HOUSE, COTTAGE $$
(✍03-6265 8077; www.steelesisland.com; via River
St, Carlton Beach; d/house from $100/540, extra
person from $10) Wanna play castaway? This
private headland (accessed over a sandy
causeway via a little bridge) is at the mouth
of the Carlton River, 16km south of Sorell.
On offer is a large beach house sleeping 12,
and two two-bedroom cottages for couples or
small families. It's a terrific spot, with gentle
surf and sunset views across the water.

Cherry Park B&B $$
(✍03-6265 2271; 114 Pawleena Rd; d incl break-
fast $160; @☎) Close to Sorell Fruit Farm,
Cherry Park has three plush rooms with
antique furniture and spacious bathrooms.
There's 7 hectares of encircling space:
bird-filled gardens, an orchard, a compact
vineyard, and sheep bleating on hillsides.
Breakfast includes homemade jams and
free-range eggs.

ℹ Information

Sorell Visitor Information Centre (✍03-
6269 2924; www.tasmanregion.com.au; 16
Gordon St; ☺10am-4pm May-Sep, 9am-5pm
Oct-Apr) For maps and peninsula info. Pick up
the *Tasman – The Essence of Tasmania* booklet,
which covers the peninsula's key sites.

ⓘ Getting There & Away

Tassielink (☑1300 300 520; www.tassielink. com.au) Services down the Tasman Peninsula from Hobart, stopping at Sorell ($7.60, 40 minutes).

Dunalley

POP 275

The thickly timbered Forestier Peninsula – the precursor peninsula you'll cross en route to the Tasman Peninsula – is connected to mainland Tasmanian soil by the isthmus town of Dunalley. Much of the area was ravaged by bushfires in 2013 – are the hillsides green again? At Dunalley itself, the Denison Canal (1905) bisects the isthmus, providing a short cut for small boats.

🛏 Sleeping & Eating

★**Casilda House** B&B $$
(☑03-6253 5265; www.casildahouse.com.au; 18 Imlay St; s/d $120/140, extra person $30; 🛜) Built in 1880, this waterfront heritage cottage (old fashioned, but not too chintzy) is a short stroll from the Dunalley Waterfront Café & Gallery. Homemade bread and biscuits, cooked breakfasts and free fishing gear will help you sink deeper into Dunalley's laconic lifestyle. Fire up the barbecue, or use the shared kitchen if you're in self-catering mode. Sleeps seven.

Dunalley Fish Market SEAFOOD $
(☑03-6253 5428; 11 Fulham Rd; mains $10-25; ⊙9am-6pm) Grab some takeaway fish and chips, settle beside the canal and commune with the local seagulls. Oysters and lobsters also make an appearance in season. What's cooking depends entirely on what the local boats have caught that day, so the menu can be a bit hit and miss.

★**Dunalley Waterfront Café & Gallery** CAFE $$
(☑03-6253 5122; www.dunalleywaterfrontcafe. com; 4 Imlay St; mains $13-37; ⊙9am-5pm daily & 6-9pm Fri & Sat) With its broad outdoor deck and views across the water, this bright, airy cafe is Dunalley's cultural and culinary epicentre. The menu ranges from seafood pie with Gruyère gratin to a pulled-pork sandwich with fennel slaw and chilli aioli. Homemade cakes, brilliant coffee and Tasmanian wines are further excuses to linger. The funky gallery showcases local artists.

ⓘ Getting There & Away

Tassielink (☑1300 300 520; www.tassielink. com.au) Tasman Peninsula services to Dunalley from Hobart ($14, one hour).

Eaglehawk Neck

POP 340

Eaglehawk Neck is the second isthmus you'll cross heading south to Port Arthur, this one connecting the Forestier Peninsula to the Tasman Peninsula. Its historical importance harks back to the convict days, when the 100m-wide Neck had a row of ornery dogs chained across it to prevent convicts from escaping – the infamous Dogline. Timber platforms were also built in narrow Eaglehawk Bay to the west, and stocked with yet more ferocious dogs to prevent convicts from wading around the Dogline. To discourage swimming, rumours were circulated that the waters were shark infested – the occasional white pointer does indeed shimmy through these waters, but 'infested' is an overstatement. Remarkably, despite these measures, several convicts made successful bids for freedom.

WORTH A TRIP

DOO TOWN

No one is really sure how it all started, but the raggedy collection of fishing shacks at Doo Town (3km south of Eaglehawk Neck on the way to the Blowhole) all contain the word 'Doo' in their names. There's the sexy 'Doo Me', the approving 'We Doo', the Beatles-esque 'Love Me Doo', and (our favourite) the melancholic 'Doo Write'. We doo hope the new breed of architecturally adventurous beach houses here maintain the tradition.

At the Blowhole car park, the **Doo-Lishus Food Caravan** (Blowhole Rd, Doo Town; snacks $5-15; ⊙8.30am-6pm) dishes up fresh berry smoothies, beaut fish and chips and the best curried scallop pies in Tasmania (we should know – we conducted a comprehensive survey).

◉ Sights

Pirates Bay Lookout VIEWPOINT
(Pirates Bay Dr) As you approach Eaglehawk Neck from the north, turn east onto Pirates Bay Dr for eye-popping views across Pirates Bay, the Neck and the jagged coastline to the south.

**Blowhole, Tasman Arch &
Devil's Kitchen** LANDMARK
(off Blowhole Rd) For a close-up look at the spectacular coastline south of the Neck, follow the signs to the Blowhole, Tasman Arch (a cavern-like natural bridge) and Devil's Kitchen (a rugged 60m-deep cleft). Watch out for sporadic bursts at the Blowhole, and keep behind the fences at the other sites – the cliff edges do decay. On the road to the Blowhole, look for the signposted 4km gravel road leading to Waterfall Bay, which has further camera-conducive views.

**Eaglehawk Neck
Historic Site** HISTORIC SITE, MUSEUM
(☑ 03-6214 8100; www.parks.tas.gov.au; Arthur Hwy; ⊙ 24hr, museum 9am-3.30pm) **FREE** Down on the isthmus, the only remaining structure from the convict days is the Officers Quarters Museum (1832) – the oldest wooden military building in Australia. Inside is a series of rooms loaded with historical info, covering the Dogline, escapee prisoners and the erudite bushranger Martin Cash.

Tessellated Pavement LANDMARK
(Pirates Bay Dr) At the northern end of Pirates Bay is a rocky coastal terrace that has eroded into what looks like tiled paving. At low tide you can walk along the foreshore to Clydes Island, where there are several graves and wicked coastline panoramas down to Cape Hauy.

☆ Activities

Waterfall Bluff WALKING
(off Blowhole Rd) From the car park at Waterfall Bay, take the 1½-hour return hike to Waterfall Bluff. Much of the walk is through a forest of tall, slender trees that somewhat obscure the view, but the track stays close to the water and there are plenty of places to stop and gawp from the clifftops. Continue to the bluff itself before returning to the part of the walk that takes you down past the falls.

Tasman Coastal Trail WALKING
(www.parks.tas.gov.au/recreation/tracknotes/tasman.html; off Blowhole Rd) Waterfall Bay is the gateway to this trail that heads into Tasman National Park. The track climbs over Tatnells Hill (two hours) then follows the coast to Bivouac Bay (six hours) and Fortescue Bay (eight hours), then extends out to Cape Hauy and on to Cape Pillar. Allow five to six days for the full return trip.

At the time of writing, parts of the track were being upgraded to form the epic new **Three Capes Track**, encompassing Cape Raoul, Cape Pillar and Cape Hauy. Check the website for updates.

Eaglehawk Dive Centre DIVING
(☑ 03-6250 3566; www.eaglehawkdive.com.au; 178 Pirates Bay Dr) Runs underwater explorations (sea caves, giant kelp forests, a sea-lion colony and shipwrecks) and a range of PADI courses. A one-day introduction to diving costs $310 (no experience necessary). Two boat dives per person with/without gear is $200/115. It also provides Hobart pick-ups and basic accommodation for divers (dorm/double $25/80).

Personalised Sea Charters FISHING
(☑ 03-6250 3370; seachart@bigpond.com; 322 Blowhole Rd; per person half/full day from $120/200) Small-group game, deep-sea, reef or bay fishing trips from Eaglehawk Neck. All gear supplied.

⌂ Sleeping

**Lufra Hotel &
Apartments** HOTEL, APARTMENT **$$**
(☑ 03-6250 3262; www.lufrahotel.com; 380 Pirates Bay Dr; hotel d/tw/f from $90/90/170, 1-/2-bedroom units from $160/230) This chowder-coloured old naughty-weekender is something of an icon in this neck of the woods (neck of the Neck?), with million-dollar views over Pirates Bay. The owners are progressively renovating the modest rooms in the original building, or there are newer self-contained one- and two-bedroom units off to one side. The downstairs cafe-bistro plates up pub classics (mains $14 to $25).

ℹ Getting There & Away

Tassielink (☑ 1300 300 520; www.tassielink.com.au) Buses from Hobart to Eaglehawk Neck ($21, 1½ hours).

TASMAN PENINSULA & PORT ARTHUR EAGLEHAWK NECK

Taranna

POP 280

Taranna is a small town strung out along the shores of Norfolk Bay about 10km north of Port Arthur, its name coming from an Aboriginal word meaning 'hunting ground'. Historically important, it was once the terminus for Australia's first railway, which ran here from Long Bay near Port Arthur. This public transport was powered by convicts, who pushed the carriages uphill, then jumped aboard for the downhill run. Not far offshore, **Dart Island** was used as a semaphore station to relay messages from Port Arthur to Hobart. Today, the waters near the island are used for oyster farming.

◉ Sights

Tasmanian Devil Conservation Park   WILDLIFE RESERVE
(☑ 1800 641 641; www.tasmaniandevilpark.com; 5990 Arthur Hwy; adult/child/family $33/18/79; ⊙ 9am-5pm) Taranna's main attraction is this wildlife reserve, in the process of rebranding itself as the **Tasmanian Devil Unzoo** when we visited. The native habitat here is rampant with wildlife – native hens, wallabies, quolls, eagles, wattlebirds, pademelons and, of course, Tasmanian devils, which you can see being fed every hour. Walking trails extend to 2.5km. See the website for updates.

⌂ Sleeping

Taranna Cottages   CABIN $
(☑ 03-6250 3436; www.tarannacottages.com.au; 19 Nubeena Rd; unpowered sites $20, d $95-125, extra adult/child $24/12) This value-for-money enterprise at the southern end of Taranna features self-contained accommodation in two neat-as-a-pin apple-pickers' cottages relocated from the Huon Valley, and a railway building from the Midlands. It's a quiet bush setting, with open fires and breakfast provisions (free-range eggs, homemade jams) for a few dollars extra. A pioneer **museum/cafe** was set to open just after we visited.

Norfolk Bay Convict Station   B&B $$
(☑ 03-6250 3487; www.convictstation.com; 5862 Arthur Hwy; d incl breakfast $160-180; 🖭) Once the convict railway's port terminus (as well as the first pub on the Tasman Peninsula and the local post office), this gorgeous old place (1838) is now an endearing B&B. Eclectic rooms come with homemade buffet breakfasts (cooked $10 extra), complimen-tary port, and fishing gear and a dinghy for hire. The owners are a mine of knowledge on local history.

Abs by the Bay   MOTEL $$
(☑ 0488 998 227; www.absbythebay.com; 5730 Arthur Hwy; s/d/f from $115/125/135) Abalone? Abdominals? We suspect it's the former, although the water-view deck at the best of these three brown-brick units affords the opportunity to relax the latter after a busy day's sightseeing. Flexible configurations can accommodate families, couples and singles with ease.

❶ Getting There & Away

Tassielink (☑ 1300 300 520; www.tassielink. com.au) Buses from Hobart stop at Taranna ($21, 1¾ hours) en route to Port Arthur.

Koonya, Nubeena & White Beach

Just past Taranna is the Nubeena Rd turnoff, depositing you 6km later in diminutive Koonya (population 100). Originally called 'Cascades', 400 convicts once toiled on the farms here, but there's not a whole lot of shakin' going on these days.

About 12km further along is Nubeena (population 490), the largest town on the peninsula, fanned out along the shore of Wedge Bay. It's much more low-key than Port Arthur – it's really just an easygoing holiday destination for locals – but if all the other accommodation on the peninsula is booked out (trust us, it happens), you might be able to find a bed here. There's also a supermarket, plus a couple of good options for eating.

The main things to do around town are swimming and chilling out on nearby White Beach (population 280), or fishing from the jetty or foreshore. Down a side road 3km south of town is some energetic walking to **Tunnel Bay** (five hours return), **Raoul Bay Lookout** (two hours return) and the exquisitely named **Cape Raoul** (five hours return). To the north is **Roaring Beach**, which gets wicked surf, but isn't safe for swimming.

⌂ Sleeping & Eating

White Beach Tourist Park   CARAVAN PARK $
(☑ 03-6250 2142; www.whitebeachtouristpark. com.au; 128 White Beach Rd, White Beach; unpowered sites $22-28, powered sites $28-36, cabins

---

DON'T MISS

REMARKABLE CAVE

About 5km south of Port Arthur is Remarkable Cave, a long tunnel eroded from the base of a collapsed gully, under a cliff and out to sea. The waves surge through the tunnel and fill the gully with sea spray. A boardwalk and stairs provide access to a metal viewing platform above the gully, a few minutes' amble from the car park. Believe it or not, hardcore surfers brave the cave, paddling out through the opening to surf the offshore reefs beyond.

You can also follow the coast east from the car park to **Maingon Blowhole** (one hour return) or further on to **Mt Brown** (four hours return), from which there are magical views.

$95-140) This beachfront park rests in quiet splendour south of Nubeena. Facilities include laundry, shop, playground and barbecue areas with impossibly well-manicured lawns. Ask about local walks (though you'll probably only get as far as the beach).

Parson's Bay Retreat MOTEL $
(Tasman Ecovillage; ☑ 03-6250 2000; www.parsonsbayretreat.com.au; 1583 Nubeena Rd, Nubeena; d/f from $88/138, 2-bedroom apt $158; ☎ ☒) 🅿 A good option for families and eco-warriors, this eccentric place offers comfortable motel-style units, many of which are full of WWOOFers (Willing Workers on Organic Farms) who spend their days tending the surrounding veggie patches. On-site restaurant The Hub (mains $15 to $26, open 11am to 8pm) maintains the social vibes, with curries, soups and burgers at communal tables.

★**Larus Waterfront Cottage** RENTAL HOUSE $$
(☑ 0457 758 711; www.larus.com.au; 576 White Beach Rd, White Beach; d $145-200) Contemporary design, a marine colour scheme, audacious views and all mod-cons (big-screen TV, gas cooking, flash barbecue) equate to a great Tasman Peninsula bolthole. It's in a quiet spot with just a narrow strip of scrub between you and the sea. You'll be spending a lot of time sitting, sipping and admiring the sunset from the wraparound deck. Sleeps four.

Harpers on the Beach B&B $$
(☑ 03-6250 2933; www.harpersonthebeach.com.au; 8 Harpers Pl, White Beach; d $160-240, cottage $160-220; ☎) 'On the beach' means exactly that at this classy B&B. After dark there's good food and wine to be had, with a wood-fired oven, organic veggie garden and restaurant-quality dinners ($49). Elegant rooms are decked out in muted tones and have ocean-facing decks. The adjoining woody cottage is a lovely reminder of sleepy beach holidays in days gone by.

★**Lucky Ducks** CAFE $$
(☑ 03-6250 2777; 1665 Main Rd, Nubeena; mains $11-32; ☉ 9.30am-4pm Sat-Wed) With huge picture windows, this bright waterfront food room is perfect for coffee and cake, a beer, a glass of wine…or all of them in sequence. Other options include excellent gourmet pies, urbane tarts, filo rolls and a chicken, chorizo and bacon terrine. The huge farmer's lunch with marinated mushrooms is also recommended for non-rural types.

ℹ Getting There & Away

Tassielink (☑ 1300 300 520; www.tassielink.com.au) Tassielink will take you from Hobart to Nubeena ($25, two hours) via Koonya.

Fortescue Bay & Tasman National Park

Sequestered 12km down a gravel road from the highway (the turn-off is halfway between Taranna and Port Arthur) is becalmed Fortescue Bay, with a sweeping sandy arc backed by thickly forested slopes. The sheltered bay was one of the semaphore-station sites used during the convict period to relay messages to and from Eaglehawk Neck. Early last century a timber mill was in operation, and the boilers and jetty ruins are still visible near Mill Creek, plus the remains of tramways used to collect the timber. The mill closed in 1952.

Fortescue Bay is one of the main access points for **Tasman National Park** (☑ 03-6250 3497; www.parks.tas.gov.au; person/vehicle per day $12/24), encompassing the territory around Cape Raoul, Cape Hauy, Cape Pillar, Tasman Island and up the rugged coast

WORTH A TRIP

COAL MINES HISTORIC SITE & LIME BAY STATE RESERVE

At Premaydena, take the signposted turn-off (the C431) 13km northwest to Saltwater River and the restored ruins at the **Coal Mines Historic Site** (☑1800 659 101; www.parks.tas.gov.au; Coal Mine Rd, via Saltwater River; ☺dawn-dusk) **FREE**, a powerful reminder of the colonial past. Excavated in 1833, the coal mines were used to punish the worst of the convicts, who worked here in abominable conditions. The poorly managed mining operation wasn't economically viable, and in 1848 it was sold to private enterprise. Within 10 years it was abandoned. Some buildings were demolished; fire and weather put paid to the rest.

These days the site is managed by the Port Arthur Historic Site Management Authority. A low-key contrast to Port Arthur, the old mines are interesting to wander around, following a trail of interpretative panels. You can snoop around the well-preserved solitary confinement cells, which are torturously small and dark. If you want to stay nearby, **Tigerbay Retreat** (☑0414 851 962; www.tigerbayretreat.com.au; 719 & 724 Saltwater River Rd, Saltwater River; d from $190) comprises two historic homes – the Surgeons Cottage and Semaphore House – both charismatic convict-era houses, lovingly restored and with plenty of beds.

Continuing past the coal mines you'll reach **Lime Bay State Reserve** (www.parks.tas.gov.au; Coal Mines Rd, Lime Bay) **FREE**, a beautiful area aflutter with rare birds and butterflies, and with some lazy coastal walks. From Lime Bay, the 2½-hour return journey to Lagoon Beach is an untaxing amble. To the north, along a sandy track, there's basic bush **camping** (unpowered sites $13) with pit toilets. BYO water and fuel stoves.

north to Eaglehawk Neck. Offshore, dolphins, seals, penguins and whales are regular passers-by.

🏃 Activities

Apart from swimming and bumming around on the beach, most people come here to launch fishing boats or do some bushwalking.

Several walking tracks kick off at Fortescue Bay. Heading north, a solid track traces the shoreline to **Canoe Bay** (two hours return) and **Bivouac Bay** (four hours return), continuing all the way to the Devil's Kitchen car park at **Eaglehawk Neck** (10 hours oneway). To the east, a track meanders out to **Cape Hauy** (four to five hours return) – a well-used path leading out to sea cliffs with sensational views of the famous **Candlestick** and **Totem Pole** sea stacks. To get into some rainforest, follow the same track towards Cape Hauy, then take the steep side track to **Mt Fortescue** (six to seven hours return). Another track extends all the way to **Cape Pillar** near Tasman Island, where the sea cliffs are 300m high – the highest in the southern hemisphere. You'll need two to three days return to knock off the Cape Pillar track. The new **Three Capes Track**, linking Cape Raoul, Cape Pillar and Cape Hauy,

was being built at the time of writing; check the park's website for updates.

For detailed track notes, see Lonely Planet's *Walking in Australia*.

🛏 Sleeping

Fortescue Bay Camp Site CAMPGROUND $
(☑03-6250 2433; www.parks.tas.gov.au; Fortescue Rd, Fortescue Bay; unpowered sites $26) Dream the night away to the sound of gentle surf. There are no powered sites and showers are cold, but fireplaces and gas BBQs compensate. National park fees apply in addition to camping fees. Book ahead during summer and BYO supplies.

Port Arthur

POP 250

In 1830 Governor Arthur chose beautiful Port Arthur on the Tasman Peninsula to confine prisoners who had committed further crimes in the colony. It was a 'natural penitentiary' – the peninsula is connected to the mainland by Eaglehawk Neck, a strip of land less than 100m wide, where ferocious guard dogs and tales of shark-infested waters deterred escape.

Between 1830 and 1877, 12,500 convicts did hard, brutal prison time at Port Arthur. For most it was hell on earth, but those who behaved often enjoyed better conditions than they'd endured in England and Ireland. Port Arthur became the hub of a network of penal stations on the peninsula, its fine buildings sustaining thriving convict-labour industries, including timber milling, shipbuilding, coal mining, shoemaking, and brick and nail production.

Australia's first railway literally 'ran' the 7km between Norfolk Bay at Taranna and Long Bay near Port Arthur: convicts pushed the carriages along the tracks. A semaphore telegraph system allowed speedy communication between Port Arthur, other peninsula outstations and Hobart. Convict farms provided fresh vegetables, a boys' prison was built at Point Puer to reform and educate juvenile convicts, and a church was erected.

Despite its redemption as a major tourist site, Port Arthur is a sombre place. Don't come here expecting to remain unaffected by what you see. There's a sadness here that's undeniable, and a Gothic pall of woe that can cloud your senses on even the sunniest of days. Compounding this, in April 1996 a young gunman fired bullets indiscriminately at the community, murdering 35 people and injuring 37 more. After burning down a guesthouse, he was finally captured and remains imprisoned north of Hobart.

◎ Sights

Port Arthur Historic Site   HISTORIC SITE
(☑ 03-6251 2310; www.portarthur.org.au; Arthur Hwy; adult/child/family from $37/17/90; ☺ tours & buildings 9am-5pm, grounds 9am-dusk) This amazing World Heritage convict site is one of Tasmania's big-ticket tourist attractions. There are dozens of structures here, best interpreted via a guided tour. The museum was originally an asylum, and the Separate Prison was built to punish prisoners through isolation and sensory deprivation. The 1836 church burned down in 1884, and the penitentiary was originally a granary. The shell of the Broad Arrow Café, scene of many of the 1996 shootings, has been preserved with a memorial garden around it.

Inside the main visitor centre is a cafe, Felons Bistro (p107) and a gift shop (which stocks some interesting convict-focused publications). Downstairs is an interpretative gallery where you can follow the convicts' journey from England to Tasmania. Buggy transport around the site can be arranged for people with restricted mobility – ask at the information counter. The ferry plying the harbour is also wheelchair accessible.

☞ Tours

Leaving regularly from the visitor centre, the 40-minute Port Arthur Historic Site guided tour is included in the admission price. It's an excellent introduction to the site, visiting all the old buildings. Also included in the ticket price is a 25-minute harbour cruise (with commentary) past Point Puer and the Isle of the Dead. When you buy your ticket you'll be told the times of the next tour and cruise.

The following tours cost a little bit extra, but are highly recommended. Bookings essential.

Isle of the Dead Cemetery Tour   TOUR
(adult/child/family $15/8/35) A detailed guided tour through Port Arthur's old burial ground on a spooky island in the harbour.

Point Puer Boys' Prison Tour   TOUR
(adult/child/family $15/8/35) This tour visits the first reformatory in the British Empire built for juvenile male convicts (aged nine to 18).

Historic Ghost Tour   TOUR
(adult/child/family $25/15/65) This 90-minute, lantern-lit tour leaves from the visitor centre nightly at dusk (rain or shine), visiting a number of historic buildings, with guides relating ghoulish occurrences. Bookings essential. Leave the little kids at home.

ⓘ PORT ARTHUR ADMISSION PASSES

The Port Arthur Site Entry Pass includes admission to the site, a guided tour and a harbour cruise, and is valid for daytime entry for two consecutive days. Optional tours to Isle of the Dead and Point Puer Boys' Prison can be added to the pass. An After Dark Pass ($69) gets you onto the Historic Ghost Tour and snares you a two-course meal at Felons Bistro (p107).

It's possible to prebook passes and tours at www.portarthur.org.au or phone ☑ 03-6251 2310 – recommended during summer and school holidays.

Port Arthur

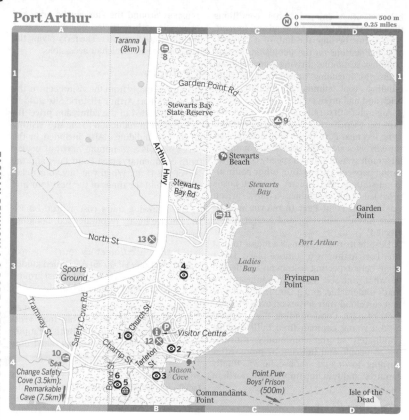

TASMAN PENINSULA & PORT ARTHUR PORT ARTHUR

Port Arthur

◉ Sights

◈ Activities, Courses & Tours

🛏 Sleeping

⊗ Eating

🛏 Sleeping

Given the glittering status of Port Arthur in the Tasmanian tourism sector, it's surprising to find limited quality accommodation or dining offerings down here. Bland, dated motel units and cheesy B&Bs prevail, with a few notable exceptions. If you're driving, consider staying in Taranna or around Koonya and Nubeena.

Port Arthur Holiday Park　　CARAVAN PARK **$**
(🖉1800 620 708, 03-6250 2340; www.portar-thurhp.com.au; Garden Point Rd; dm $25, unpowered/powered/en-suite sites $28/33/43; cabins from $120; ❋ 🐾) Spacious and with plenty of greenery and sing-song bird life, this park is 2km before Port Arthur, not far from a sheltered beach. Facilities are abundant, including a camp kitchen, wood BBQs, petrol pump and shop. The best (and only) budget option around these latitudes.

Sea Change Safety Cove
B&B **$$**

(📋 0438 502 719, 03-6250 2719; www.safetycove.com; 425 Safety Cove Rd, Safety Cove; d $180-240, extra adult/child $40/20; 🐾) Whichever way you look from this guesthouse, 4km south of Port Arthur, there are fantastic views – misty cliffs, sea-wracked Safety Cove Beach or scrubby bushland. There are a couple of B&B rooms inside the house plus a self-contained unit downstairs that sleeps five. Outside, camellia-filled gardens roll down to a beaut deck overlooking the beach (G&Ts anyone?).

Stewarts Bay Lodge
RESORT **$$**

(📋 03-6250 2888; www.stewartsbaylodge.com.au; 6955 Arthur Hwy; cabins/units d from $159/219, 2-bedroom $260/319, 3-bedroom cabin $360; 🌸🐾) Arrayed around a gorgeous hidden cove – seemingly made for swimming and kayaking – Stewarts Bay Lodge combines older, rustic log cabins with newer deluxe units, some with private spa baths. Modern kitchens are great for making the most of good local produce, but you'll probably spend more time in the sleek Gabriel's on the Bay restaurant.

Port Arthur Villas
MOTEL **$$**

(📋 1800 815 775, 03-6250 2239; www.portarthurvillas.com.au; 52 Safety Cove Rd; d $180-310; 🌸🐾) This place has tidy self-contained units sleeping up to four, horseshoeing around the garden and outdoor barbecue area. Externally it's all faux-Victorian lace and brickwork, but inside things are a little more stylish, with mod bathrooms and kitchenettes. Walking distance to the historic site. Cheaper for multi-night stays.

Fox & Hounds Inn
MOTEL **$$**

(📋 03-6250 2217; www.foxandhounds.com.au; 6789 Arthur Hwy; d $135-175, extra person $20) Ye olde mock Tudor! Still, the motel doubles are affordable (especially in winter) and it's just seconds from the historic site. You can also get a bang-up pub dinner (mains $20 to $30, serving 5.30pm to 8pm) here amid the faux splendour of old Blighty. The two-bedroom apartments sleep five and are a pragmatic choice for nomadic families.

🍴 Eating

There are a couple of daytime food options at the historic site: the **Museum Coffee Shop** in the Old Asylum and the hectic **Port Café** inside the visitor centre.

Gabriel's on the Bay
MODERN AUSTRALIAN **$$**

(📋 03-6250 2771; www.stewartsbaylodge.com.au; Stewarts Bay Lodge, 6955 Arthur Hwy; mains lunch $18-35, dinner $28-35; ⏱8-10am & noon-2pm daily, 5.30-8.30pm Thu-Mon; 🐾) Housed in a modern glass-and-wood pavilion with water views, Gabe's showcases local produce with Eaglehawk Neck oysters, Tasman Peninsula salmon burgers and Tasmanian scotch fillet with sweet-potato mash, braised leeks and red wine jus. Definitely worth a detour if you're overnighting anywhere nearby. Bookings recommended.

Felons Bistro
MODERN AUSTRALIAN **$$**

(📋 1800 659 101; www.portarthur.org.au; Port Arthur Historic Site; mains $23-32; ⏱5pm-late) Swing into a wing of the visitor centre at the historic site and shackle dinner at Felons onto the nocturnal ghost tour. Upmarket, creative dinners with a seafood bias reinforce Felons' catchy slogan, 'dine with conviction'. Hungry carnivores should try Cape Grim braised beef cheek or the grilled Doo Town venison with Tasmanian ginseng. Reservations advised.

Port Arthur Centre
CAFE, DELI **$$**

(📋 03-6250 2555; 6962 Arthur Hwy; mains $10-20; ⏱8am-5pm) The old Eucalypt Cafe was in the process of rebranding as the Port Arthur Centre when we visited. It remains a versatile spot for robust breakfasts and lunches (try the chilli burger or the pumpkin soup) and Port Arthur's best coffee. The on-site shop sells locally made handicrafts, basic groceries and gourmet produce.

ℹ️ Getting There & Away

Tassielink (📋 1300 300 520; www.tassielink.com.au) Tassielink runs a weekday afternoon bus from Hobart to Port Arthur ($25, 2¼ hours) during school terms, reducing to Monday, Wednesday and Friday afternoons during school holidays, plus a morning bus on Saturday and an afternoon bus on Sunday. Buses stop at the main towns en route.

The Southeast

Best Places to Eat

➡ Get Shucked Oyster Farm (p115)

➡ Lotus Eaters Cafe (p118)

➡ Summer Kitchen Bakery (p121)

➡ Peppermint Bay (p118)

➡ Post>Office 6985 (p125)

Best Places to Stay

➡ Peppermint Ridge Retreat (p117)

➡ 43 Degrees (p113)

➡ Cherryview (p118)

➡ Huon Bush Retreats (p120)

➡ Jetty House (p125)

Why Go?

Still harbours and misty valleys – Tasmania's southeast has much to offer. The apple-producing heartland of the Apple Isle, this fertile area now also produces cherries, apricots, Atlantic salmon, wines, mushrooms and cheeses. The wide, tea-coloured Huon River remains the region's lifeblood. Courtesy of these southern latitudes and myriad waterways, the southeast is also known for its rainbows.

As you head south the fruity hillsides of the Huon Valley give way to the sparkling inlets of the D'Entrecasteaux Channel, with Bruny Island awaiting enticingly offshore. Hartz Mountains National Park is not far inland and, further south, the epic South Coast Track kicks off at magnificent Recherche Bay.

All sounding a bit French? French explorers Bruni d'Entrecasteaux and Nicolas Baudin charted much of the region's coastline in the 1790s and early 1800s, a good decade before the Brits hoisted the Union Jack at Risdon Cove near Hobart in 1803.

When to Go

➡ Peckish? Summer – from December to March – is definitely the time to visit the southeast. The Huon Valley harvest is in, and roadside stalls are jam-packed with fresh produce, including juicy cherries and crisp apples.

➡ The cool southern waters around Bruny Island are much more inviting in the summer sunshine. Alternatively, birdwatching fans should wing it here in October for the annual Bruny Island Bird Festival.

➡ January is the time to be in funky-hippie Cygnet for the annual Cygnet Folk Festival.

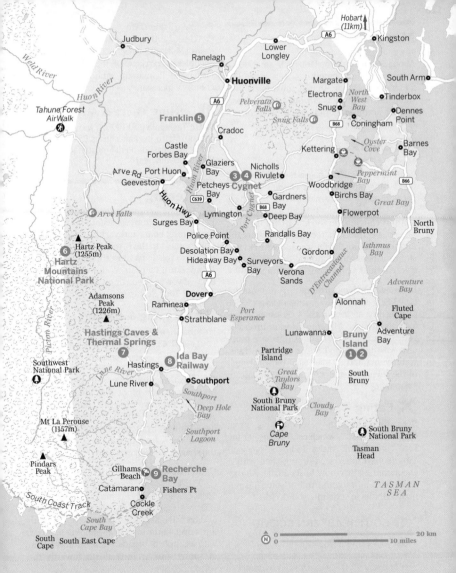

The Southeast Highlights

1. Drop out of mobile-phone reception on **Bruny Island** (p111) for a couple of days.

2. Explore Bruny Island's ragged southern coastline with **Bruny Island Cruises** (p113).

3. Pick up a bag of the Huon Valley's finest at a **roadside apple stall** (p121) around Cygnet.

4. Tune in to the twang and stomp of the **Cygnet Folk Festival** (p118).

5. Smell the sweet scent of a Huon pine hull at Franklin's **Wooden Boat Centre** (p120).

6. Smile at your reflection in an alpine moorland tarn at **Hartz Mountains National Park** (p123).

7. Spelunk into the subterranean gloom at **Hastings Caves and Thermal Springs** (p125).

8. Ride the **Ida Bay Railway** (p126), Australia's southernmost railway.

9. Imagine French explorers and their tall ships anchored in **Recherche Bay** (p117).

Margate

POP 1370

About 23km south of Hobart is small-town Margate, which sometimes feels more like a suburb of Hobart than a town in its own right. There are a few curious pit stops here, but for accommodation you'll be better off further south.

◉ Sights

Margate Train   TRAIN
(☑ 03-6267 1667; 1567 Channel Hwy; ⊙ 9am-5pm)
FREE Margate Train is a chance for train geeks to gawk at Tasmania's last passenger train – the good ol' Tasman Ltd – which stopped chugging in the late 1970s. It stands idly on a redundant section of track by the highway just north of town, and houses craft shops, a bookshop, antique dealers, a pancake cafe and a providore for picnic supplies.

Inverawe Native Gardens   GARDENS
(☑ 03-6267 2020; www.inverawe.com.au; 1565 Channel Hwy; adult/child $12/4; ⊙ 9am-6pm Sep-May) Behind the Margate Train is Inverawe Native Gardens, a private, 9.5-hectare property with landscaped native gardens, trails, water views and 80 species of blow-through birds, including the 12 species endemic to Tasmania.

✖ Eating

Brookfield Margate   CAFE $
(☑ 03-6267 2880; www.brookfieldmargate.com; 1640 Channel Hwy; mains $6-18; ⊙ 9am-5pm) This 1930s timber seed-drying shed with a chequered history now hosts a cafe. All-day breakfasts, a bratwurst roll or some Tasmanian Valhalla ice cream – you decide.

> ### ⓘ SOUTHEASTERN SCENIC
> ....
> Get your camera, your phone, or just your eyeballs ready – the southeast is super-scenic! The views from the Channel Hwy between Hobart and Woodbridge via Taroona, Kingston, Margate and Kettering are terrific. The road continuing from Woodbridge to Gardners Bay en route to Cygnet is also a real show-stopper. If you've got a spare hour up your sleeve, the longer route from Woodbridge to Cygnet through snoozy Verona Sands passes close to the shoreline. The riverside road from Cygnet to Cradoc (p119) is also worth a drive.

Pancake Train Café   CAFE $$
(☑ 03-6267 1120; www.pancaketrain.com.au; mains $14-24; ⊙ 9am-5pm) This flapjack shack occupies a carriage of the Margate Train. Order the Tasmanian salmon version with creamy caper sauce.

ⓘ Getting There & Away

Metro Tasmania (☑ 13 22 01; www.metrotas. com.au) Metro Tasmania buses 65 and 92–98 run from Hobart through Kingston to Margate ($6.10, 30 minutes).

Kettering

POP 990

Photogenic Kettering's sedate harbour shelters fishing boats and yachts in Oyster Cove Marina, next to the Bruny Island ferry terminal. Most folks just blow through en route to Bruny, but it's a pretty spot to pause for half a day if you've been running yourself ragged on your Tour de Tassie.

⌖ Sleeping & Eating

Herons Rise Vineyard   COTTAGE $$
(☑ 03-6267 4339; www.heronsrise.com.au; 1000 Saddle Rd; d with/without breakfast from $165/140, extra person $30) Just north of town, Herons Rise has three upmarket self-contained cottages set among pinot noir vines. All three have log fires: we especially like the roomy apartment above the barn (good for families). Dinners by arrangement; breakfast optional. The whole operation is overseen by the shaggy, four-legged Toby.

Oyster Cove Inn   PUB FOOD $$
(☑ 03-6267 4446; www.kettering.tas.au/entity/ oyster-cove-inn; 1 Ferry Rd; mains $13-35; ⊙ noon-1.30pm & 5.30-7.30pm Sun-Wed, noon-1.30pm & 5.30-8pm Thu-Sat) This tarted-up monolith lords over Kettering's boat-bobbing harbour, with a couple of broad deck areas and a span of sunny grass rolling down towards the water. The short-but-sweet menu of pub favourites (also tarted-up) might lure you into the bistro from the busy bar.

ⓘ Information

Bruny d'Entrecasteaux Visitor Information Centre (☑ 03-6267 4494; www.brunyisland. org.au; 81 Ferry Rd; ⊙ 9am-5pm) The local visitor centre is at the ferry terminal – it's the best place for info on accommodation and services on Bruny Island, including walking maps and driving advice. There's a cafe here, too.

THE SOUTHEAST MARGATE

❶ Getting There & Away

Metro Tasmania (☑13 22 01; www.metrotas. com.au) Buses 94–97 run from Hobart to Kettering ($8, 50 minutes) via Kingston and Margate.

Bruny Island

POP 600

Bruny Island is almost two islands, joined by a narrow, 5km-long sandy isthmus called the Neck. Renowned for its wildlife (little penguins, echidnas, mutton birds), it's a windswept, sparsely populated isle, blown by ocean rains in the south and dry and beachy in the north. Access is via a short car-ferry chug from Kettering.

Bruny's coastal scenery is magical. There are countless swimming and surf beaches, plus good sea and freshwater fishing. South Bruny offers the steep, forested South Bruny National Park, which has some beaut walking tracks, especially around Labillardiere Peninsula and Fluted Cape.

Tourism is becoming increasingly important to the island's economy but remains fairly low-key. There are (as yet) no homogenized resorts, just plenty of interesting cottages and houses, most self-contained. Too many visitors try unsuccessfully to cram their Bruny experience into one day. If you can handle the peace and quiet, definitely stay a few days. It's the kind of place that takes hold slowly, then tends not to let go.

South Bruny has two general stores – at Adventure Bay (☑03-6293 1119; 712 Main Rd, Adventure Bay; ⊙9am-5pm) and Alonnah (☑03-6293 1040; 3 William Carte Dr, Alonnah; ⊙9am-5pm) – with Eftpos facilities, takeaway food and limited provisions. Adventure Bay has petrol and an ATM. There are no stores on North Bruny.

History

The island was spied by Abel Tasman's beady eyes in 1642, and between 1770 and 1790 was visited by Furneaux, Cook, Bligh and Cox. It was named after Rear Admiral Bruni d'Entrecasteaux, who explored the area in 1792. Strangely, confusion reigned about the spelling – in 1918 it was changed from Bruni to Bruny.

Nuenonne Aboriginals called the island Lunawanna-Alonnah, a name given contemporary recognition (albeit broken in two) as the titles of two island settlements. Among their numbers was Truganini, daughter of Mangana, chief of the Nuenonne. Truganini left Bruny in the 1830s to accompany George Robinson on his infamous statewide journey to win the trust of all the Tasmanian Aboriginals. Many of Bruny's landmarks, including Mt Mangana, are named after the isle's original inhabitants.

The island has endured several commercial ventures. Sandstone was mined here and used for the post office and Houses of Parliament in Melbourne, and coal was also mined. Both industries gradually declined due to lofty transport costs. Only farming, aquaculture and forestry have had long-term viability.

◎ Sights & Activities

South Bruny National Park   NATIONAL PARK
(☑03-6293 1419; www.parks.tas.gov.au; car/person per day $24/12) There's terrific bushwalking here. At **Fluted Cape**, east of Adventure Bay, an easy trail winds out to the old whaling station at **Grass Point** (1½ hours return). From here follow the shore to **Penguin Island**, accessible at low tide, or complete the more difficult **cape circuit** (2½ hours return).

The park's southwestern portion comprises the **Labillardiere Peninsula**, featuring jagged coastal scenery and a lighthouse. Walks here range from leisurely beach meanderings to a seven-hour circuit of the entire peninsula.

Bruny Island Neck   NATURE RESERVE, VIEWPOINT
(www.brunyisland.org.au/about-bruny-island/the-neck) Park halfway across the isthmus – aka the Neck – between North and South Bruny and climb the 279 steps (correct?) to the **Truganini Memorial** for broad views of both ends of the island. Another timber walkway crosses the Neck to the beach on the other side. Keep to the boardwalk in this area: mutton birds and little (fairy) penguins nest here. Your best chance of seeing the penguins is at dusk in the warmer months.

Bligh Museum of Pacific Exploration   MUSEUM
(☑03-6293 1117; www.southcom.com.au/~-jontan/index.html; 876 Main Rd, Adventure Bay; adult/child/family $4/2/10; ⊙10am-4pm) This curio-crammed museum details the local exploits of explorers Bligh, Cook, Furneaux, Baudin and, of course, Bruni d'Entrecasteaux. The engaging collection includes maps, charts and manuscripts, many of them originals or 1st editions.

Bruny Island

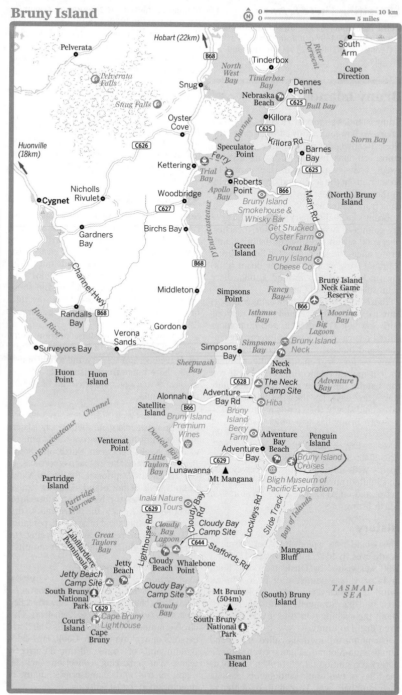

0 _____ 10 km
0 _____ 5 miles

Pelverata

Hobart (22km)

B68

Tinderbox

South Arm

Cape Direction

Pelverata Falls

North West Bay

Tinderbox Bay

Dennes Point

Snug

Nebraska Beach

C625

Bull Bay

Snug Falls

Oyster Cove

Killora

C625

Killora Rd

Storm Bay

Huonville (18km)

C626

Speculator Point

Ferry

Barnes Bay

Kettering

Trial Bay

C625

Roberts Point

B866

Cygnet

Nicholls Rivulet

Woodbridge

Apollo Bay

Bruny Island Smokehouse & Whisky Bar

(North) Bruny Island

Main Rd

C627

D'Entrecasteaux

Get Shucked Oyster Farm

Birchs Bay

Gardners Bay

Green Island

Great Bay

Bruny Island Cheese Co

B68

Bruny Island Neck Game Reserve

Middleton

Simpsons Point

Fancy Bay

B866

Moorina Bay

Channel Hwy

Isthmus Bay

Big Lagoon

Huon River

Randalls Bay

B68

Gordon

Verona Sands

Simpsons Bay

Simpsons Bay

Bruny Island Neck

Surveyors Bay

Neck Beach

Huon Point

Huon Island

Sheepwash Bay

C628

The Neck Camp Site

Adventure Bay

Alonnah

Adventure Bay Rd

Hiba

Satellite Island

B866

Bruny Island Premium Wines

Bruny Island Berry Farm

Adventure Bay Beach

Penguin Island

D'Entrecasteaux Channel

Daniels Bay

Ventenat Point

Adventure Bay

Bruny Island Cruises

Partridge Island

Little Taylors Bay

Lunawanna

C629

Mt Mangana

Bligh Museum of Pacific Exploration

Partridge Narrows

Inala Nature Tours

C629

Cloudy Bay Rd

Lockleys Rd

Bay of Islands

Great Taylors Bay

Cloudy Bay Lagoon

Cloudy Bay Camp Site

C644

Staffords Rd

Slide Track

Mangana Bluff

Labillardiere Peninsula

Jetty Beach

Cloudy Beach

Whalebone Point

TASMAN SEA

Jetty Beach Camp Site

South Bruny National Park

Cloudy Bay Camp Site

Mt Bruny (504m)

(South) Bruny Island

C629

Cloudy Bay

Courts Island

Cape Bruny Lighthouse

Cape Bruny

South Bruny National Park

Tasman Head

Cape Bruny Lighthouse　　LIGHTHOUSE
(www.brunyisland.net.au/Cape_Bruny/Lightstation/lighthouse.html; Lighthouse Rd, South Bruny; ⊘reserve 10am-4pm) Worth visiting is the 1836, 13m-high stone lighthouse – Australia's second-oldest – on South Bruny, designed by colonial architect John Lee Archer. You can check out the inside of the lighthouse on tours with Bruny Island Safaris or Bruny Island Traveller, or just wander around the surrounding reserve.

Court House History Room　　MUSEUM
(☑03-6260 6366; www.brunyisland.net.au/Alonnah/historyroom.html; 3893 Main ˙Rd, Alonnah; ⊘10am-3pm) FREE At the council offices in Alonnah is this wee, volunteer-run museum (in an old court house) displaying newspaper clippings, photos and records of the island community's past, plus info on walks and attractions around Bruny Island.

☞ Tours

Bruny Island Cruises　　BOAT TOUR
(Pennicott Wilderness Journeys; ☑03-6234 4270; www.brunycruises.com.au; adult/child/family $125/75/390) This highly recommended three-hour tour of the island's awesome southeast coastline takes in rookeries, seal colonies, bays, caves and towering sea cliffs. Trips depart Adventure Bay jetty at 11am daily, with an extra 2pm cruise in summer. You can also take the tour as a full-day trip from Hobart (adult/child $195/140, including lunch) or from Kettering (adult/child $140/90).

Bruny Island Traveller　　TOUR
(Pennicott Wilderness Journeys; ☑03-6234 4270; www.brunyislandtraveller.com.au; adult/child $195/170) Operated by the same folks who run Bruny Island Cruises, this is a full-day tour ex-Hobart for landlubbers who don't fancy the idea of too much time in a boat. The itinerary includes beaches, wildlife, Bruny Island Cheese Co, Cape Bruny Lighthouse and lunch at Bruny Island Premium Wines. Prices include transfers, ferry crossings, lunch and national park fees.

Inala Nature Tours　　WALKING, 4WD
(☑03-6293 1217; www.inalabruny.com.au; 320 Cloudy Bay Rd, South Bruny) These highly regarded walking and 4WD tours of the island (from three hours to three days) zoom in on flora and fauna. The tour leader is a botanist, zoologist and conservationist, and her 200-hectare property is home to almost

140 bird species, including all 12 endemic Tasmanian species. There are also two farm cottages to rent (double $220).

Inala has been instrumental in establishing the annual **Bruny Island Bird Festival** (www.bien.org.au), a three-day celebration of all things avian in late October.

Bruny Island Safaris　　TOUR
(☑0437 499 795; www.brunyislandsafaris.com.au; per person $149) Full-day tours departing Hobart, focusing on Bruny's history and landscapes. Look forward to opportunities to sample the island's culinary bounty, including oysters, salmon, cheese, wine and berries, and a look inside the old Cape Bruny Lighthouse.

🛏 Sleeping

Self-contained cottages abound on Bruny, and most of them are suitable for midsized groups or families and offer economical weekly rates (if generally pricey for shorter stays, and mostly without wi-fi). Adventure Bay has the lion's share of accommodation, but there are also places at Alonnah, and at Barnes Bay and Dennes Point (pronounced 'Denz') on North Bruny.

Bookings are essential – owners/managers and their keys aren't always easily located. The Bruny d'Entrecasteaux Visitor Information Centre in Kettering is a good starting point. For online bookings see www.brunyisland.net.au and www.brunyisland.com.

Bruny's cheapest beds are the bush camp sites within South Bruny National Park at **Jetty Beach** and **Cloudy Bay**. These sites are free, but national park fees apply. There's also a free camp site outside the national park at **Neck Beach**. All sites have pit toilets and fireplaces. BYO firewood and water.

Captain Cook Caravan Park　　CARAVAN PARK $
(☑03-6293 1128; www.captaincookpark.com; 786 Main Rd, Adventure Bay; unpowered/powered sites $25/30, on-site vans/cabins d $70/140; ✱) Across the road from the beach in Adventure Bay, this park could do with a few trees but has decent facilities, including some swish new one-bedroom cabins with little decks out the front. The new owners are tidying things up.

★ 43 Degrees　　APARTMENT $$
(☑03-6293 1018; www.43degrees.com.au; 948 Adventure Bay Rd, Adventure Bay; d/apt $190/240, extra person $40) 🌿 At 43 degrees south

latitude, the accommodation here neatly bookends Adventure Bay beach: there are three nifty, roll-roofed studios (sleeping two) at the western end; and two similarly styled apartments (sleeping four) at the eastern end near the jetty. Double-glazing keeps the heat out/in, depending on the season. Ask about package deals with Bruny Island Cruises (p113).

Morella Island Retreats RENTAL HOUSE **$$**
(☑ 03-6293 1131; www.morella-island.com; 46 Adventure Bay Rd, Adventure Bay; d $180-250, extra person $25) These unique, arty cottages are 6km north of Adventure Bay. There are a couple of retreats for couples (we love 'the Cockpit') and a family-sized holiday house. All are self-contained, with design and decor best described as 'classic castaway'. Prices drop by $30 for stays longer than one night. The Hothouse Cafe is here, too.

Bruny Beach House RENTAL HOUSE **$$**
(☑ 0419 315 626; www.brunybeachhouse.com; 91 Nebraska Rd, Dennes Point; d $155, extra person $25) High above the sandy sliver of Nebraska Beach on North Bruny is this good-value, woody beach house sleeping four. It's got all the requisite facilities, a wood heater and a north-facing deck on which to sip and scan. BYO supplies. Two-night minimum stay.

Eversley RENTAL HOUSE **$$**
(☑ 0409 973 033, 03-6293 1088; www.brunyislandvillas.com; 4435 Main Rd, Lunawanna; d from $190) Surrounded by lawns in a bucolic setting, this modern two-bedroom house is operated by the adjacent Bruny Island Premium Wines. Classy decor, nice linen and high-end appliances prove the operators are as particular about their accommodation as they are about their pinot.

Mickeys Bay Holiday Cottage RENTAL HOUSE **$$**
(☑ 03-6293 1481; www.mickeysbay.com; 736 Lighthouse Rd, Lunawanna; d $140, extra adult/child $25/10) About 12km south of Lunawanna, en route to the lighthouse, is this self-contained, four-bedroom house featuring lots of creative carpentry and timber work. It has a hip, modern design, with polished floorboards, handmade furniture, a BBQ, a private beach, and even an adventure playground! Perfect for families.

Lumeah RENTAL HOUSE **$$**
(☑ 03-6293 1265, 0419 870 341; www.lumeah-island.com.au; Adventure Bay Rd, Adventure Bay; d $155, extra person $30) Lumeah, an Adventure Bay sawmiller's cottage knocked up 120-something years ago, offers accommodation perfect for groups or families. It has three bedrooms and two bathrooms (sleeping nine) and is fully self-contained, 50m from the beach. It also has a BBQ area, spa and casual craft gallery out the front. Two-night minimum stay.

Explorers' Cottages COTTAGE **$$**
(☑ 03-6293 1271; www.brunyisland.com/accommodation; 20 Lighthouse Rd, Lunawanna; d $195, extra person $25) Just south of Lunawanna, on the way to the lighthouse, this row of motel-style self-contained cottages (sleeping four) falls on the unremarkable side of the ledger, but the units are reasonable value for a family and come with log fires, board games and decks. We found a combination of crackers and two-day-old bread went down well with the resident ducks.

★**All Angels**
Church House RENTAL HOUSE **$$$**
(☑ 03-6293 1271; www.brunyisland.com/accommodation; 4561 Main Rd, Lunawanna; d from $235) Your prayers have been answered with this restored 1912 church near Daniels Bay, now rental accommodation with three bedrooms and a soaring-ceiling open-plan lounge. Fire up the BBQ in the sheltered garden, eat al fresco on the picnic table or dine inside at the huge shared table. Sleeps five.

Wainui RENTAL HOUSE **$$$**
(☑ 1300 889 557, 03-6293 2096; 87 Main Rd, Dennes Point; d $240, extra person $40; ✳) Spacious, open-plan living and super views are thrust to the fore at this mod house at Dennes Point. Design-wise it's all corrugated-iron cladding, polished boards, Roman blinds and downlights. Fire up the BBQ and make the most of the vista. The name means 'big water' in New Zealand's Maori language. Sleeps six; minimum two-night stay.

St Clairs Cottage RENTAL HOUSE **$$$**
(☑ 03-6293 1300; www.stclairs.com; Lighthouse Rd, Lunawanna; d $250; ☎) Surrounded by shady bushland on the road to the lighthouse (just past the Explorers' Cottages) is this unpretentious, getaway cottage for two. Look forward to a lazy hammock, water glimpses through the trees, a little spa at the end of the deck and cooked-breakfast provisions (dinner by arrangement). And wi-fi!

Tree House RENTAL HOUSE $$$
(☑0405 192 892, 03-6265 7528; www.thetree-house.com.au; 66 Matthew Flinders Dr, Alonnah; d $205, extra person $30) Up on tree-stump stilts on a hillside above Alonnah, this is a good-lookin', open-plan place overlooking the agriculturally named Sheep Wash Bay. Inside are two bedrooms, all the mod cons and super views. The price drops for stays of two nights or more.

✖ Eating

Bruny Island has some great food producers serving up to visitors.

Penguin Cafe CAFE $
(☑03-6293 1352; 710 Main Rd, Adventure Bay; mains $5-12; ☺9am-3pm, extended summer hours) Located next to the Adventure Bay store, the eccentric little Penguin Cafe serves up simple homemade burgers, fish and chips, egg-and-bacon rolls, amazing curried scallop pies and muffins baked inside coffee cups.

Jetty Cafe CAFE $$
(☑03-6260 6245; www.jettycafebrunyisland.com; 18 Main Rd, Dennes Point; lunch $15-20, dinner $28-30; ☺10am-9pm Thu-Sun) Part cafe-restaurant, part providore, part local art gallery – the stylish Jetty Cafe (designed by ace architect John Wardle) is a great addition to Bruny's dining scene. Duck in for a coffee, or book for lunch or Friday-night fish and chips – seasonal menus showcase local produce. Phone ahead as opening hours tend to sway in the sea breeze.

Hothouse Cafe CAFE $$
(☑03-6293 1131; www.morella-island.com/hothouse.htm; 46 Adventure Bay Rd, Adventure Bay; mains $11-18; ☺9am-5pm; ☑) The cafe at Morella Island Retreats occupies a converted curvy-roof hothouse (sit inside on a sunny day and you'll start to sprout). Isthmus views and flappy bird life distract you from the menu of interesting snacks and mains, including gourmet burgers, vegetable frittatas and seafood chowder. Also a top spot for a drink.

THE SOUTHEAST BRUNY ISLAND

BRUNY ISLAND ON A PLATE

Bruny island has a growing reputation for top-quality food and wine. Here's a rundown of the best Bruny foodie experiences to get you started.

Bruny Island Smokehouse & Whisky Bar (☑03-6260 6344; 360 Lennon Rd, North Bruny; mains from $30; ☺9.30am-5.30pm Sep-May, to 4.30pm Jun-Aug) The old Bruny Island Smokehouse has expanded its repertoire and is now a tasting room for every whisky distillery in the state. Gourmet platters, smoked meats and seafood chowder are also on offer. Don't blame us if you miss the last ferry back to Kettering...

Bruny Island Cheese Co (☑03-6260 6353; www.brunyislandcheese.com.au; 1087 Main Rd, Great Bay; meals $10-24; ☺10am-5pm) Hankering for a quivering sliver of cheese? Head to the Bruny Island Cheese Co, where Kiwi cheesemaker Nick Haddow draws inspiration from time spent working and travelling in France, Spain, Italy and the UK. Artisan bread, wood-fired pizzas, zippy coffee and local wines also available.

Get Shucked Oyster Farm (☑0428 606 250; www.getshucked.com.au; 1735 Main Rd, Great Bay; 12 oysters from $12; ☺9.30am-6.30pm, reduced winter hours) Get Shucked cultivates the 'fuel for love' in chilly Great Bay. Visit the tasting room and wolf down a briny dozen with lemon juice and Tabasco and a cold flute of Jansz bubbles. Shucking brilliant.

Bruny Island Premium Wines (☑03-6293 1008, 0409 973 033; www.brunyislandwine.com; 4391 Main Rd, Lunawanna; ☺11am-4pm) If you're working up a thirst, swing into the cellar door at Australia's most southerly vineyard. Pinot noir and chardonnay rule the roost; burgers, platters and meaty mains also available.

Bruny Island Berry Farm (☑03-6293 1055; www.brunyislandberryfarm.com.au; 550 Adventure Bay Rd, Adventure Bay; mains $10-15; ☺10am-5pm Oct-Apr) Pick a punnet of strawberries, blackberries or boysenberries, or enjoy the farm's juicy output with ice cream, scones or pancakes.

Hiba (☑03-6293 1456; www.hiba.com.au; 53 Adventure Bay Rd, Adventure Bay; ☺10am-4pm) A smart little roadside providore selling silky-smooth fudge.

Hotel Bruny
PUB FOOD **$$**

(📞 03-6293 1148; www.hotelbruny.com; 3959 Main Rd, Alonnah; mains $18-25; ⏲ 11am-late) Bruny's only pub is an unassuming affair in Alonnah – the architectural cousin of an Idaho roadhouse – with a few outdoor water-view seats and an all-day menu heavy on local seafood and grills. Live bands monthly.

ℹ Information

Mobile-phone coverage on Bruny Island is limited to Telstra, and even that's patchy. Your best bet will be to park yourself on Adventure Bay beach and point your mobile device at the sky.

Bruny d'Entrecasteaux Visitor Information Centre (📞 03-6267 4494; www.brunyisland.org.au; 81 Ferry Rd, Kettering; ⏲ 9am-5pm) At the ferry terminal in Kettering. Accommodation bookings and info on walks, camping and driving. You can also buy South Bruny National Park passes here (per vehicle/person per day $24/12).

Online Access Centre (📞 03-6293 2036; www.linc.tas.gov.au; School Rd, Alonnah; ⏲ 9am-noon & 1-4pm Mon-Wed, 1-4pm Thu & Fri) At Alonnah's school (signposted).

ℹ Getting There & Away

Bruny Island Ferry (📞 03-6273 6725; www.brunyislandferry.com.au; Ferry Rd, Kettering; car return $30-35, motorcycle/bike/foot passenger $5/5/free) The double-decker *Mirambeena* shuttles cars and passengers from Kettering to Roberts Point on North Bruny. There are at least 10 services daily each way (a 20-minute trip). The first ferry leaves Kettering at 6.35am (7.45am Sunday); the last one leaves at 6.30pm (7.30pm Friday). The first ferry from Bruny sails at 7am (8.25am Sunday); the last one leaves at 7pm (7.50pm Friday).

> ### ℹ BRUNY ISLAND FERRY
>
> Note that the timetable for the Bruny Island Ferry does vary occasionally – double-check departure times. Buy your return ticket (cash only) from the drive-up ticket booth at Kettering. There are no such formalities on the way back – just queue up and drive on.
>
> On summer weekends and over Christmas and Easter there are often long queues waiting to board the ferry, despite extra sailings. You'll likely spend a significant chunk of the day queuing for the ferry at either end. Our advice: make it an overnighter rather than a day trip.

ℹ Getting Around

You'll need your own wheels to get around – there are no buses. A bicycle is a great option, but be prepared for long rides between outposts of civilisation. Bruny has some narrow, winding gravel roads, the slippery, log-truck-infested road over Mt Mangana being the prime case in point. Not all car-rental companies are cool with this concept.

Woodbridge & Around
POP 450

Established in 1874 as Peppermint Bay (after the area's peppermint gums), Woodbridge was eventually renamed by a landowner nostalgic for his old home in England. It's a quiet village sitting squarely on the tourist trail, thanks to the sexy Peppermint Bay development, which has consumed the old Woodbridge pub.

◎ Sights

Grandvewe Cheeses
FARM, FOOD

(📞 03-6267 4099; www.grandvewe.com.au; 59 Devlyns Rd, Birchs Bay; tastings free; ⏲ 10am-5pm Sep-Jun, to 4pm Jul & Aug) About 3km south of Peppermint Bay is this top stop for foodies. Grandvewe Cheeses churns out organic cheese from sheep's milk. Snack on a cheese platter for lunch (the pecorino and blue are perfection) and nose into some pinot noir from local wineries.

Hartzview Vineyard
WINERY

(📞 03-6295 1623; www.hartzview.com.au; 70 Dillons Rd, Gardners Bay; tastings $2, refunded with purchase; ⏲ 10am-5pm) Hartzview is located 8km up the hill from Woodbridge (or 11km from Cygnet), off the road to Gardners Bay. On offer for your palate's pleasure are fruit liqueurs, peppery pinot noir and smooth mead. Lunch here is also a goer with gourmet pies, focaccias, smoked quiches and cheese platters (mains $14 to $18). There's also accommodation if you need to have a little lie-down.

☞ Tours

Peppermint Bay Cruises
BOAT TOUR

(📞 1300 137 919; www.peppermintbay.com.au; adult/child from $98/68) A five-hour cruise from the Hobart waterfront down the D'Entrecasteaux Channel to Woodbridge, including lunch at Peppermint Bay.

FRENCH CONNECTIONS

A decade ago it seemed that Tasmania's pristine deep south was about to change for the worse. In 2004 the Tasmanian government gave private landowners permission to log the forests of the northeast peninsula of Recherche Bay – a decision that stirred up controversy in Tasmania and as far away as France.

In 1792 two French ships under the command of explorer Bruni d'Entrecasteaux, *La Recherche* and *L'Espérance,* anchored in a harbour near Tasmania's southernmost point and called it Recherche Bay. More than a decade before British settlers arrived in Tasmania, the French met the Lyluquonny Aboriginals here and were carrying out the first significant scientific studies on the continent. There are two heritage sites at Recherche Bay with protected status (relics of the French observatory and garden, not accessible to the public), but the explorers' journals record them venturing far into the bush. With the government's announcement, historians, scientists and conservationists became concerned that the area earmarked for clear-felling was home to yet more sites of historical interest to both Australia and France. Needless to say, tensions between the anti- and pro-logging groups escalated – the prospect of the kinds of protests that took place in Tasmania when the Franklin River was under threat in the mid-1980s loomed large.

Fortunately, in 2006 the landowners agreed to sell the northeast peninsula to the Tasmanian Land Conservancy and it's now protected as a significant site. For more background check out www.tasland.org.au/permanent/recherchebay.

🛏 Sleeping & Eating

★ **Peppermint Ridge Retreat**   RENTAL HOUSE **$$**
(☑03-6267 4192; www.peppermintridge.com.au; 290 Woodbridge Hill Rd; d $160-230, extra person $35) 🍴 Two amazing handmade straw-bale-and-stone studios, complete with composting toilets, recycled timbers, spa baths, lofty ceilings and brilliant D'Entrecasteaux Channel and Bruny Island views. Each sleeps five, with breakfast supplies included. 'Hippie-savvy' best describes proceedings.

Hartzview Vineyard   RENTAL HOUSE **$$**
(☑03-6295 1623; www.hartzview.com.au; 70 Dillons Rd, Gardners Bay; d $180-250, extra adult/child $50/25) This hilltop vineyard has a fully equipped three-bedroom house (just a bit chintzy) behind the cellar door, with an open fire and room for seven slumberers. Breakfast provisions and views over Gardners Bay seal the deal. Dinners by arrangement. Cheaper for multi-night stays.

Telopea   APARTMENT **$$**
(☑03-6267 4565; www.telopea-accommodation.com.au; 144 Pullens Rd; d $140, extra person $30) A good base for exploring the southeast, Telopea is a modest rural property with two wheelchair-accessible, self-contained brick units on offer. Pull up a pew on the shared deck near the main house and eyeball Bruny Island. Breakfast provisions for the first morning included. Pullens Rd intersects with the Channel Hwy on the northern outskirts of Woodbridge.

Satellite Island   RENTAL HOUSE **$$$**
(☑0400 336 444; www.satelliteisland.com.au; Satellite Island, via Alonnah or Middleton; d/extra person from $950/450) An island, off an island, off an island... Adrift in the D'Entrecasteaux Channel, this amazing private-island lodge (boatshed-chic) offers self-contained accommodation for up to 15 castaways. Kayaks and fishing rods for distraction; walking trails and oyster-clad rocks for exploring. Private-boat access from Alonnah on Bruny Island or Middleton on the Tasmanian 'mainland'. Two-night minimum (though you'll want to stay longer).

Woodbridge Hill Hideaway   CABIN **$$$**
(☑0457 714 325; www.woodbridgehillhideaway.com.au; 369 Woodbridge Hill Rd; d $300; 🛜🚻) These flash self-contained cabins pitch themselves towards the 'seduction and indulgence' sector (a little too heavily, pehaps). But they really are something special, with spectacular D'Entrecasteaux Channel and Bruny Island views and rustic-but-chic design. Local artwork, recycled timber, handmade stained-glass and granite bathrooms add up to a classy package. Heated indoor pool, too.

Fleurtys   CAFE **$$**
(☑03-6267-4078; www.fleurtys.com.au; 3866 Channel Hwy, Birchs Bay; ◷11am-4pm Thu-Sun)

Not far south of Woodbridge is Fleurtys (named after a convict sawmiller) – a cool little glass-fronted providore in the trees where you can take a bushwalk, inspect the essential-oil distillery and stock up on homemade jam, vinegar, honey, chutney, herbs, fudge and oils. The cafe is great for lunch (mains $12 to $22).

Peppermint Bay MODERN AUSTRALIAN **$$**
(☑03-6267 4088; www.peppermintbay.com.au; 3435 Channel Hwy; mains $16-35; ⊙noon-3pm & 5.30-8.30pm) On a mesmeric D'Entrecasteaux Channel inlet, jaunty Peppermint Bay has a bottle department selling local beers and wines and a cool, contemporary bar/bistro, open all day for coffee (or a drink) and for lunch and dinner daily. The emphasis is squarely on local produce, with seafood, fruits, meats, cheeses and other ingredients from just down the road. Bookings advised.

❶ Getting There & Away

Metro Tasmania (☑13 22 01; www.metrotas. com.au) Buses 94–97 run from Hobart to Woodbridge ($10.50, one hour) via Margate and Kettering.

Cygnet

POP 1460

Groovy Cygnet was originally named Port de Cygne Noir (Port of the Black Swan) by Bruni d'Entrecasteaux, after the big noir birds that cruise around the bay. Youthfully reincarnated as Cygnet (a baby swan), the town has evolved into a dreadlocked, artsy enclave, while still functioning as a major fruit-producing centre. Weathered farmers and banjo-carrying hippies chat amiably in the main street and prop up the bars of the town's pubs. To the south, the **Randalls Bay** and **Verona Sands** beaches aren't far away.

January's hippie-happy **Cygnet Folk Festival** (www.cygnetfolkfestival.org; tickets per day/weekend from $70/130) is three days of words, music and dance, attracting talent such as Jeff Lang and Monique Brumby. Along similarly earthy lines, the **Cygnet Market** (www.cygnetmarket.com.au; Town Hall, 14 Mary St; ⊙10am-2pm) happens on the first and third Sunday of the month. The town's other claim to fame is **Pagan Cider** (www.pagancider.com.au), the Cygnet-brewed 'champagne of ciders' that's made its way into the taps of pubs around the state.

For a window into Cygnet's soul, the little **Cygnet Living History Museum** (☑03-6295 1602; 37 Mary St; admission by donation; ⊙10am-3pm Mon-Thu, 12.30-3pm Fri-Sun) is a quaint history room next to the church on the main street, stuffed full of old photos, documents and curios. Check out the fantastic old apple-crate labels from the 1930s.

🛏 Sleeping

Commercial Hotel PUB **$**
(☑03-6295 1296; 2 Mary St; s/d without bathroom $65/85; ⊛) Upstairs at the rambling 1884 Commercial Hotel (aka 'the bottom pub') are decent pub rooms, recently dolled up and with little TVs, fridges and new beds. Downstairs, a laconic crew of locals drink at the bar and hit the bistro for robust steak dinners (mains $10 to $28, serving noon to 2pm and 6pm to 8pm).

Cygnet Hotel PUB **$**
(☑03-6295 1267; cygnettophotel@bigpond.com; 77 Mary St; s/d without bathroom $45/80, d with bathroom $88; ⊛) A handsome, red-brick heritage pub (the 'top pub') on the upper slopes of Cygnet's main drag. Rooms are heritage chic and pubby, and downstairs in the bar you can grab a cold Cascade and a porterhouse steak with curried scallop sauce (mains $18 to $21, serving noon to 2pm and 6pm to 8pm Wednesday to Sunday).

Cygnet Holiday Park CAMPGROUND **$**
(☑03-6295 1267, 0418 532 160; cygnettophotel@ bigpond.com; 3 Mary St; unpowered sites $17) A bog-basic camping ground across the road from (and managed by) the Cygnet Hotel. It's essentially just a grassy paddock by the town creek: don't expect any games rooms or solar-heated pools.

★**Cherryview** COTTAGE **$$**
(☑03-6295 0569; www.cherryview.com.au; 90 Supplices Rd; d $130-160) Backed by a tall stand of eucalypts on 10 quiet hectares, this self-contained studio is a beauty. It's a simple, stylish affair, overlooking a valley with the Hartz Mountains beyond. Love the antique-door bedhead! Your GPS might freak out: is it Supplice Rd or Supplices Rd? Either way, it's 4km north of Cygnet's bright lights.

🍽 Eating

★**Lotus Eaters Cafe** CAFE **$**
(☑03-6295 1996; www.thelotuseaterscafe.com.au; 10 Mary St; mains $10-25; ⊙9am-4pm Thu-Mon; ☑) This mighty-fine hippie cafe has rustic decor that belies real culinary savvy: expect

CYGNET COAST ROAD

If you're not in a rush, don't miss the scenic coast road (C639) between Cradoc and Cygnet. The more direct route along the Channel Hwy (B68) is about 7km (this is the route for **roadside apple stalls**), but the coastal route is a lazy, meandering 27km past Petcheys Bay and Glaziers Bay.

One kilometre from the Cradoc junction, on a north-facing bank of the Huon River, is the egalitarian **Panorama Vineyard** (☑03-6266 3409; www.panoramavineyard.com. au; 1848 Cygnet Coast Rd, Cradoc; tastings free; ☺10am-5pm Wed-Mon). Stick your nose into some pinot noir, chardonnay, merlot, riesling and an unusual white port.

An impressive place to stay at Glaziers Bay is **Riverside** (☑03-6295 1952; www.huon-riverside.com.au; 35 Graces Rd, Glaziers Bay; d $250, extra adult/child $55/35), a luxe contemporary abode (good for two couples) with Huon views from wide verandahs. Fresh flowers, quality linen and homemade breakfast provisions seal the deal. Minimum three-night stay: look forward to slowing the holiday tempo right down.

terrific eggy breakfasts, curries and soups, with a rigorous focus on the seasonal, the organic, the free-range and the local. Superlative homemade cakes, almond croissants and coffee.

School House Coffee Shop CAFE $
(☑0425 732 466; 23a Mary St; mains $7-22; ☺8am-3pm Tue-Fri, 9am-3pm Sat) With geranium-filled window boxes, this modest little coffee shop fills out an 1860s school building just off the main drag. The breakfast menu evolves into Turkish-bread sandwiches, pastas, burgers, wraps, soups and cakes later in the day. Occasional Friday dinners and live music.

❶ Getting There & Away

Metro Tasmania (☑13 22 01; www.metrotas. com.au) Bus 98 rocks in/out of Cygnet from Hobart via Kingston and Margate ($10.50, 80 minutes). Once daily each way, Monday to Friday only.

Tassielink (☑1300 300 520; www.tassielink. com.au) Buses to Cygnet from Hobart via Huonville ($12.50, two hours). Twice daily each way Monday to Friday; three times daily Saturday and Sunday.

Huonville & Around

POP 2540

The biggest town in the southeast, agrarian Huonville flanks the Huon River 35km south of Hobart, not far from some lovely vineyards and small villages. Having made its name as Tasmania's apple-growing powerhouse, it remains a functional, working town – low on charm but with all the services you need.

The Huon and Kermandie Rivers were named after Huon d'Kermandec, second in command to explorer Bruni d'Entrecasteaux. Prior to that, the area was known by the local Aboriginal people as Tahune-Linah. The region was originally steeped in tall forests, and timber milling quickly became a major industry, focusing on the coveted softwood Huon pine. The initial plundering of Huon pine groves nearly wiped the tree out, as it's extremely slow growing. Today, only immature trees survive along the river. Once the forest was levelled, apple trees were planted and the orchard industry blossomed – it's still the region's primary money-spinner.

The Huon Hwy traces the Huon River south, passing the settlements of Franklin, Castle Forbes Bay and Port Huon. These were once important shipping ports for apples, but nowadays the old wharves and packing sheds are decaying like old fruit. Strung-out Franklin (population 1110) is the oldest town in the Huon Valley. The wide, reedy riverscape here is one of Australia's best rowing courses.

◎ Sights & Activities

★ **Apple Shed** MUSEUM
(☑03-6266 4345; www.williesmiths.com.au; 2064 Main Rd, Grove; gold coin donation; ☺10am-6pm) At Grove, 6km north of Huonville, this revamped cafe/providore/museum is home to Willie Smith's Organic Apple Cider, at the fore of the cider wave that's been sweeping Australia's pubs and bars of late. Swing by for a coffee, a cheese plate, meals (mains $7 to $24), a cider tasting paddle ($12), or a more purposeful 1.89L 'growler' of Willie Smith's Bone Dry. The museum zooms in on

Huonville's appley heritage, with old cider presses and an amazing wall of different apple varieties.

Live music and extended opening hours on Friday nights.

Wooden Boat Centre
MUSEUM

(☑03-6266 3586; www.woodenboatcentre.com; 3341 Huon Hwy, Franklin; adult/child/family $9/3/20; ☺9am-5pm) This engaging, sea-centric spot incorporates the School of Wooden Boatbuilding, a unique institution running accredited courses (from one to seven weeks) in traditional boat building, using Tasmanian timbers. Stick your head in the door to learn all about it, watch boats being cobbled together and catch a whiff of Huon pine.

Home Hill Wines
WINERY

(☑03-6264 1200; www.homehillwines.com.au; 38 Nairn St, Ranelagh; tastings free; ☺10am-5pm) In Ranelagh, 3km west of Huonville, is this super-stylish winery – all rammed-earth and corrugated iron – which has been collecting trophies for its pinot noir, chardonnay and dessert wines. There's also a sassy restaurant here.

Huon Valley Horsetrekking
HORSE RIDING

(☑03-6266 0343; www.horsehavenfarmstay.com; 179 Judds Creek Rd, Judbury; 2hr/half-day rides per person from $90/170) Take a ride through the Huon Valley bushland about 13km from Huonville at Judbury. There's also cottage accommodation (doubles from $130, extra adult/child from $15/10). A cooked farm breakfast is $16.

Huon Jet
BOATING

(☑03-6264 1838; www.huonjet.com; Esplanade, Huonville; adult/child $80/58; ☺9am-5pm Oct-Apr, 10am-4pm May-Sep) Jet boating? That's so '80s... Still, these frenetic, 35-minute rides are a great way to see the river up close. Bookings recommended.

☞ Tours

Under Down Under
TOUR

(☑1800 444 442; www.underdownunder.com.au; per person $115) Small-group day tours of the deep south from Hobart, taking in the Apple Shed at Grove, Hastings Caves (with a swim!), Cockle Creek and Recherche Bay en route.

Yukon Tours
SAILING

(☑0447 972 342, 0498 578 535; www.yukon-tours.com.au; Franklin Marina, Franklin; tours adult/child/family $45/25/120) Take a 90-minute sailing cruise on the flat, deep Huon River aboard the 1930 *Yukon*. The ship was dredged from the bottom of a harbour near Copenhagen in 2004, restored and then sailed to Tasmania.

Gray Line
BUS TOUR

(☑1300 858 687; www.grayline.com.au; tours adult/child $160/80) Huon Valley day tours ex-Hobart visiting Huonville, Franklin, Geeveston and the Tahune Forest AirWalk.

⛱ Sleeping

Huon Valley Caravan Park
CARAVAN PARK $

(☑0438 304 383; www.huonvalleycaravanpark.com.au; 177 Wilmot Rd, Huonville; unpowered/powered sites $30/34) At the junction of the Huon and Mountain Rivers is this grassy patch, filling a budget-shaped gap in the local accommodation market. There are no cabins here (yet), but there's a brand new camp kitchen with a pizza oven and tidy amenities.

★ Huon Bush Retreats
CABIN $$

(☑03-6264 2233; www.huonbushretreats.com; 300 Browns Rd, Ranelagh; unpowered sites $30, tepees/cabins d $145/295) ✿ This private, wildlife-friendly retreat dapples the flanks of not-miserable Mt Misery. On site are five modern, self-contained cabins, luxury tepees, tent and campervan sites, plus 5km of walking tracks and a fantastic BBQ camp kitchen. Superb blue wrens flit through the branches. Check the website for directions – it's 12km from Huonville (beware: steep dirt road!).

Whispering Spirit Holiday Cottages
RENTAL HOUSE $$

(☑03-6266 3341; www.whisperingspirit.com.au; 253 Swamp Rd, Franklin; d $95-140) We're not convinced a spirit can actually whisper, but we get what these guys are trying to say. The homey self-contained cottage and fantastic two-bedroom, crimson straw-bale unit definitely have soul! Cheaper rates for longer stays. Miniature ponies and raspberry canes on site for everyone's inner child.

Kermandie Hotel
PUB $$

(☑03-6297 1052; www.kermandie.com.au; 4518 Huon Hwy, Port Huon; s/d/tw/f from $90/120/140/190) Having a real crack at keeping itself contemporary, the old highway-side Kermandie (1932) at Port Huon has 11 tastefully refurbished bedrooms upstairs, all with bathroom. The best ones have views across the road to the river and marina. Downstairs you can grab a meal in the **bar** (mains $15 to $28) or **bistro** (mains $28 to $35).

Cottage on Main   RENTAL HOUSE **$$**
(☑03-6266 3040; www.cottageonmain.com; 3420 Huon Hwy, Franklin; d $140, extra person $30; ❋🐾) Two-bedroom Cottage on Main is indeed on the main street, right in the middle of Franklin and sleeping up to six. Simple, affordable and with a reasonably inoffensive serve of chintz.

Donalea B&B   B&B **$$**
(☑03-6297 1021; www.donalea.com.au; 9 Crowthers Rd, Castle Forbes Bay; d/apt $140/180, extra person $30) A B&B with welcoming hosts, river views, a petal-filled garden and twittering birds. All rather English, really. Donalea has two bright rooms (one with spa), a spacious four-berth apartment and a guest lounge with a log fire.

✗ Eating

★**Summer Kitchen Bakery**   BAKERY, CAFE **$**
(☑03-6264 3388; 1 Marguerite St, Ranelagh; items $4-7; ⊘7.30am-4pm Tue-Fri, 8am-4pm Sat) Locals come from miles around just for a loaf of bread from this excellent little bakery, on a street corner in Ranelagh a few kilometres out of Huonville. Organic wood-fired sourdough, sprouted-rye sourdough, organic beef-and-wallaby pies, pastries and the best coffee in the Huon. Nice one.

DS Coffee House Cafe & Internet Lounge   CAFE **$**
(☑03-6264 1226; www.dscoffeehousecafe.com. au; 12 Main Rd, Huonville; mains $7-14; ⊘7am-5pm Mon-Fri, 9am-5pm Sat & Sun; 🐾) Hands down Huonville's most interesting cafe (despite the mealy-mouthed name), with funky retro furniture and uni-student vibes. All-day breakfasts, sourdough sandwiches, daily soup specials, myriad *Mona Lisa* portraits and Huonville's best coffee all feature. Also has internet terminals and wi-fi.

Aqua Grill   SEAFOOD, CAFE **$**
(☑03-6266 3368; 3419 Huon Hwy, Franklin; meals $7-20; ⊘11.30am-8pm) Excellent takeaway or dine-in fish and chips and other marine snacks (try the curried-scallop crepe with white wine and cream sauce). The sweet-potato cakes and tempura mushrooms are also mighty fine. On the liquid front, there's good coffee and well-chosen beers and wines.

FAST FOOD

All along the Huon Valley roadsides, particularly the B68 between Huonville and Cygnet, you can pull over and buy farm-fresh produce from makeshift (or sometimes sophisticated, illuminated and refrigerated) **roadside apple stalls**. These usually take the form of tin sheds out the front of farms, stocked with bags of whatever is in season: pears, apricots, peaches, blueberries, blackberries, raspberries, boysenberries, strawberries, potatoes, peas, beans and, of course, apples. It's an honesty system – grab your bag, drop some coins in the box and drive off brimming with vitamin C.

Petty Sessions   CAFE **$$**
(☑03-6266 3488; www.pettysessions.com.au; 3445 Huon Hwy, Franklin; mains $19-32; ⊘9am-4pm & 5.30-8pm Mon-Fri, 9am-8pm Sat & Sun) A picket fence and garden blooms encircle this likeable cafe, inside an 1860 court house. Head for the deck and order classic cafe fare (salads, BLTs, grilled Huon River salmon and seafood fettuccine) – or try the house special: abalone chowder.

Home Hill Wines   MODERN AUSTRALIAN **$$$**
(☑03-6264 1200; www.homehillwines.com.au; 38 Nairn St, Ranelagh; mains $35; ⊘noon-3pm daily, 6-8pm Fri & Sat) Home Hill Wines has a fab restaurant in a slick-looking rammed-earth building with pasture views. The seasonal menu offers select Tasmanian produce: Bothwell goat's cheese, Huon Valley mushrooms and King Island cream, as well as morning and afternoon tea. And don't forget the wine!

ℹ Information

DS Coffee House Cafe & Internet Lounge
(☑03-6264 1226; www.dscoffeehousecafe. com.au; 12 Main Rd, Huonville; ⊘7am-5pm Mon-Fri, 9am-5pm Sat & Sun; 🐾) Internet terminals and wi-fi access.

Huon Valley Visitor Information Centre
(☑03-6264 0326; www.huontrail.org.au; 2273 Huon Hwy, Huonville; ⊘9am-5pm) Southeast tourist information on the way into town from Hobart.

Parks & Wildlife Service (☑03-6121 7026; www.parks.tas.gov.au; 22 Main Rd, Huonville; ⊘10am-4pm Mon-Fri) Main-street office. Sells national parks passes.

DEEP SOUTH FOODIE EXPERIENCES

Tasmania's southeast is emerging as a real gourmet hotspot. Here are some of our favourite deep-south eating encounters. See www.huontrail.org.au to download handy seasonal food-trail brochures.

Roadside apple stalls Munch the quintessential Tasmanian apple, fresh from the stalls between Huonville and Cygnet.

Taste of the Huon (www.tasteofthehuon.com) Visit the Ranelagh showgrounds in mid-March for this annual showcase of Huon Valley produce.

Wine tasting Sip a late-afternoon pinot noir or two at Home Hill Wines (p120), Hartzview Vineyard (p116) or Panorama Vineyard (p119).

Grandvewe Cheeses (p116) Sniff out some peppery pecorino and smooth Sapphire Blue cheese; south of Woodbridge.

Get Shucked Oyster Farm (p115) Get hot and bothered after a few oysters on Bruny Island.

Peppermint Bay (p118) Wind down from a lazy lunch at this fabulous restaurant in Woodbridge.

Lotus Eaters Cafe (p118) Swing into surprising Cygnet for some of Tasmania's best cafe food.

Bruny Island Smokehouse & Whisky Bar (p115) Knock back a few fiery Tasmanian whiskies.

❶ Getting There & Away

Tassielink (☑ 1300 300 520; www.tassielink. com.au) Regular daily buses from Hobart to Huonville ($10.50, one hour) via Ranelagh ($10.50, 50 minutes) and continuing to Franklin ($10.50, 70 minutes) and beyond.

Geeveston

POP 1430

A rugged timber town, Geeveston is 31km south of Huonville. It's a utiltarian sort of place without much of a tourist angle, but offers accommodation close to the Hartz Mountains and Tahune Forest AirWalk.

Geeveston was founded in the mid-19th century by the Geeves family, whose descendants still have fingers in lots of local pies. In the 1980s the town was the epicentre of an intense battle over logging the Farmhouse Creek forests. At the height of the controversy, some conservationists spent weeks living in the tops of 80m-tall eucalypts to prevent them being felled. The conservation movement ultimately won: Farmhouse Creek is now protected from logging.

◉ Sights

Southern Design Centre   GALLERY
(☑ 03-6297 0039; 11 School Rd; ☺ 10am-4pm Sun-Fri) A curiosity-arousing place to browse for local crafts (ceramics, paintings, knits) or grab a quick coffee. The Tasmanian timber furniture here fills the space with an amazing woody fragrance. Also sells Hastings Caves passes.

Forest & Heritage Centre   MUSEUM
(☑ 03-6297 1836; www.visitgeeveston.com.au; 15 Church St; ☺ 9am-5pm) FREE In the town centre, this wood-lined building houses displays delving into the forestry heritage of the area. It's also the town's unofficial visitor information centre and sells Tahune Forest AirWalk tickets.

🛏 Sleeping & Eating

Cambridge House   B&B $$
(☑ 03-6297 1561; www.cambridgehouse.com.au; 2 School Rd; d with/without bathroom incl breakfast $140/115) This photogenic 1870s B&B – cottagey but not kitsch – offers three bedrooms upstairs with shared facilities (good for families), and two downstairs en-suite rooms. The timber staircase and Baltic pine ceilings are wonders. If you're quiet you might spy a platypus in the creek at the bottom of the garden. Cooked breakfast.

Bears Went Over the Mountain   B&B $$
(☑ 03-6297 0110; www.bearsoverthemountain. com; 2 Church St; d $120; 🐾) Right in the middle of town, Bears has three en-suite rooms,

polished floorboards, lofty ceilings, leadlight windows and breakfast in the adjacent tea rooms. Free wi-fi, too.

Masaaki's Sushi   JAPANESE $
(☑0408 712 340; 20b Church St; sushi $8-20; ☺11.30am-6.30pm Fri &Sat) What a surprise! Tasmania's best sushi – including fresh Tasmanian wasabi – is in sleepy Geeveston. Opening hours are disappointingly limited, but you'll also find Masaaki and his outstanding sushi at Hobart's Sunday morning Farm Gate Market (p48).

ⓘ Getting There & Away

Tassielink (☑1300 300 520; www.tassielink. com.au) Regular daily buses from Hobart to Geeveston ($14, 80 minutes) via Huonville.

Arve Road & Around

The sealed Arve Rd, constructed to extract timber from the local forests, trucks west from Geeveston through rugged, tall-timber country to the Hartz Mountains, the Tahune Forest Reserve and the Tahune Forest AirWalk.

◉ Sights & Activities

Tahune Forest Reserve   NATURE RESERVE
(www.parks.tas.gov.au; Arve Rd) About 29km west of Geeveston is the Tahune Forest Reserve, its name derived from Tahune-Linah, the Aboriginal name for the area around the Huon and Kermandie Rivers. There are plenty of picnic spots here and limited free unpowered campervan spots (no tents).

Arve Road Walks   WALKING
(Arve Rd) A map from the Forest & Heritage Centre in Geeveston details easy short walks along the Arve Rd. At the **Arve River picnic area** there's free (unofficial) camping and a ferny forest walk (10 minutes return). **Big Tree Lookout** is a sub-five-minute walk leading to a timber platform beside a giant 87m-high swamp gum. **Keogh's Creek Walk** is a 15-minute streamside circuit. **West Creek Lookout** offers views from a bridge extending out from the top of an old tree stump.

Tahune Forest AirWalk   WALKING
(☑1300 720 507; www.adventureforests.com. au; Tahune Forest Reserve, Arve Rd; adult/child/family $26/13/52; ☺9am-5pm Oct-Mar, 10am-4pm Apr-Sep) Tahune Forest has 600m of wheelchair-accessible steel walkways suspended 20m above the forest floor. One 24m cantilevered section is designed to sway disconcertingly with approaching footsteps. Vertigo? Ground-level walks include a 20-minute riverside stroll through stands of young Huon pine. There's also a **cafe** (mains $10 to $30) and lodge **accommodation** (dorm/double/family $47/95/115).

Eagle Hang Glider   ADVENTURE TOUR
(☑1300 720 507; www.tahuneairwalk.com. au; Tahune Forest Reserve, Arve Rd; adult/child $15/13.50; ☺9am-5pm Nov-Mar, 9am-4pm Sep-Apr) Near the AirWalk, wannabe birds of prey are strapped into a hang-glider, which in turn is latched to a 250m-long cable 50m above the Huon River and forest. Fly my pretties! Minimum/maximum weight 25/100kg.

Hartz Mountains National Park

If you prefer your wilderness a little less pre-packaged than the Tahune Forest Reserve, head for **Hartz Mountains National Park** (☑03-6264 8460; www.parks.tas.gov.au; vehicle/person per day $24/12). A century ago, the Hartz plateau was a logging hotspot, and stocks of small varnished gums were harvested for eucalyptus oil, which was distilled in Hobart for medicinal applications. Eventually the area was declared a national park, and in 1989 became part of the Tasmanian Wilderness World Heritage Area.

The 65-sq-km national park is only 84km from Hobart – within striking distance for weekend walkers and day trippers. The park is renowned for its jagged peaks, glacial tarns, gorges and bleak alpine moorlands, where fragile cushion-plant communities hunker down in the cold, misty airs. Rapid weather changes bluster through: even day walkers should bring waterproofs and warm clothing.

There are some great hikes and isolated, sit-and-ponder-your-existence viewpoints in the park. **Waratah Lookout**, 24km from Geeveston, is an easy five-minute shuffle from the road. Other well-surfaced short walks include **Arve Falls** (20 minutes return) and **Lake Osborne** (40 minutes return). The steeper **Lake Esperance** walk (1½ hours return) takes you through beautiful high country. You'll need to be fairly fit and experienced to tackle the steep, rougher track that leads to **Hartz Peak** (1254m; four hours return), which is poorly marked beyond Hartz Pass (two hours return).

There's no camping within the park – just basic day facilities, including toilets, shelters, picnic tables and barbecues. See the website for details. Access is via the Arve Road from Geeveston: the last 10.5km is unsealed and sometimes snowed under.

Dover

POP 770

A Port Esperance fishing town with a beach and a pier (but sadly no pub – it burned down in 2013), Dover is a chilled-out spot to while away a few deep-south days. The town was originally called Port Esperance after a ship in Bruni d'Entrecasteaux's fleet, but that moniker now only applies to the bay. The bay's three small islands are called Faith, Hope and Charity.

In the 19th century this was timber territory. Huon pine and local hardwoods were milled and shipped from here (and also from nearby Strathblane and Raminea), heading to China, India and Germany for use as railway sleepers. Today the major industries are fruit growing and aquaculture, with Atlantic salmon reared here then exported throughout Asia.

If you're heading further south, buy petrol and food supplies here. Before you leave, pay a visit to St Imre Vineyard (☑ 03-6298 1781; www.stimrevineyard.com.au; 6902 Huon Hwy, Dover; tastings free; ☉ 10am-5pm) 🍷. Bottling pinot noir, chardonnay, pinot gris and the robust 'Tiger Blood', this compact hillside vineyard has a fabulous timber tasting room, built by the Hungarian owner. Crumpuss the cat is on duty.

🛏 Sleeping & Eating

Dover Beachside Tourist Park   CARVAN PARK $
(☑ 03-6298 1301; www.dovercaravanpark.com. au; 27 Kent Beach Rd; unpowered/powered sites $22.50/35, cabins from $95; ☎) Opposite the sandy shore and new kids' playground, this decent southern set-up features grassy expanses, trim cabins and a chatty cockatoo in reception (don't take any of his lip).

Far South Wilderness Lodge   RENTAL HOUSE $$
(☑ 03-6298 1922; www.farsouthwilderness.com.au; 247 Narrows Rd, Strathblane; d $160, extra adult/child $25/5) On the Esperance River, 5km south of Dover, Far South is a self-contained lodge in a bush setting, sleeping up to 10 (two doubles upstairs, six singles downstairs, two bathrooms). There's heaps of wildlife around (kookaburras ahoy), a BBQ on the deck and a cosy heater for cold nights.

Ashdowns of Dover   B&B $$
(☑ 0417 746 437; www.ashdownsofdover.com.au; 6957 Huon Hwy; d $140, extra person $25; ☎) Forget about the white cliffs; Ashdowns of Dover is a far more welcoming prospect. Three cosy en-suite rooms in this 1950 timber house come with Asian and African thematic touches, full cooked breakfasts and a field full of sheep to observe out the back. The kids can collect eggs from the resident chooks.

Driftwood Holiday Cottages   RENTAL HOUSE $$
(☑ 1800 353 983; www.driftwoodcottages.com. au; 51 Bay View Rd; d $145-290) These mod, self-contained studio units huddle by the beach road; further up the hill are two newer studios. Sit on your verandah, sip something chilly and watch fisherfolk pulling oars on Port Esperance. Driftwood manages other local accommodation too, including the private, open-plan Tides Reach (sleeps six); Beach Front, a heritage sand-side cottage (sleeps four); and lavish Peninsula.

Smuggler's Rest   MOTEL, APARTMENT $$
(☑ 0425 816 398, 03-6298 1396; www.smugglers-rest.com.au; 56 Station Rd; d $110-140, 2-bedroom apt $140-160; ☀ ☎) Externally this terracotta-coloured place channels downtown Santa Fe. Inside are tidy self-contained studios and two-bedroom family units. The owners have bikes, fishing rods and old golf clubs for guest to play with, and there's a free laundry and a BBQ out the back. Check out the rhododendrons!

Peninsula   RENTAL HOUSE $$$
(☑ 03-6298 1441, 1800 353 983; www.peninsula-tas.com.au; Blubber Head Rd; d $550, extra bedroom $150; ☎) Poised on a private peninsula, this stately 19th-century farmhouse is now a thoroughly 21st-century luxury retreat. Asian-chic design infuses the three bedrooms (sleeps six), while the elegant kitchen is packed with enough fine food and wine for a couple of days. At dusk, pademelons, wallabies and echidnas patrol the grounds. Sorry, no kids. Managed by Driftwood Holiday Cottages.

HASTINGS CAVES & THERMAL SPRINGS

Signposted 5km inland from the Huon Hwy about 15km south of Dover (just past the Southport turn off) is the entrance to the amazing **Hastings Caves & Thermal Springs** (☑ 03-6298 3209; www.parks.tas.gov.au/reserves/hastings; 754 Hastings Caves Rd, Hastings ; caves & pool adult/child/family $21/15/60, pool only $5/2/12; ☺ 9am-5pm Jan, 10am-4pm Feb-Apr, 10.30am-3.30pm May-Sep, 10am-3.30pm Oct-Dec). The only way to explore the caves (which are within the Hastings Caves State Reserve) is on a guided tour. Buy tickets at the visitor centre. Tours leave roughly hourly, but times vary throughout the year: call or check the website for specifics. Admission includes a 45-minute tour of the amazing dolomite **Newdegate Cave**, plus entry to the **thermal swimming pool** behind the visitor centre, filled with 28°C water from thermal springs. The wheelchair-friendly **Hot Springs Trail** does a big loop from the pool area, taking 20 minutes to navigate (the pool is also wheelchair accessible).

There's a decent **cafe** (mains $10 to $20) at the visitor centre, which also sells barbecue packs and picnic hampers.

From the visitor centre, the cave entrance is a further 5km drive. No public transport runs out this way.

★ **Post>Office 6985** SEAFOOD, PIZZA $$
(☑ 03-6298 1905; 6985 Huon Hwy; mains $15-30; ☺ noon-2.30pm Wed-Sun & 6-8pm Thu-Sun Sep-May, 4-8pm Thu-Sat Jun-Aug) Leonard Cohen and alt-country on the stereo, cool decor, foodie magazines... And that's before you get to the menu, which features local seafood and wood-fired pizzas (try the scallop, caramelised onion and pancetta version). An evening here will probably have you asking your accommodation if you can stay an extra night. Sterling beer and wine list, too.

❶ Information

Online Access Centre (☑ 03-6298 1552; www.linc.tas.gov.au; Old School, Main Rd; ☺ 10am-2pm Mon-Fri) Near the Post>Office 6985 restaurant.

❶ Getting There & Away

Tassielink (☑ 1300 300 520; www.tassielink.com.au) Buses from Hobart to Dover ($21, 1¾ hours) run via Huonville and Geeveston. Three times daily, Monday to Friday, in each direction.

Southport

POP 280

Originally Southport was called Baie des Moules (Bay of Mussels), one of several names it's had over the years. Many travellers don't take the 2km detour off the main road to visit the town, but it's a worthy diversion if only to stay in its B&Bs, which make good use of the waterside slopes.

Unfortunately, public transport won't get you here.

Known as **Burying Ground Point**, the bluff south of town was once a convict cemetery; it's now a public reserve. There's also a **memorial** to the 1835 shipwreck of the *King George III* in which 35 people drowned.

🛏 Sleeping & Eating

Southport Hotel & Caravan Park CARAVAN PARK $
(☑ 03-6298 3144; www.southportcaravanpark.com.au; 8777 Huon Hwy; unpowered/powered sites $18/28, cabins/motel d $69/120) This sprawling, faux-colonial pub, general store, petrol station and caravan park is Southport's cultural and commercial core. The weary can bunk down for the night in the caravan park or adjacent motel units, while the hungry can resolve the problem in the **dining room** (mains $18 to $27, serving noon to 2pm and 6pm to 8pm).

★ **Jetty House** B&B $$
(☑ 03-6298 3139; www.southportjettyhouse.com; 8848 Huon Hwy; s/d incl breakfast $120/170, extra person $30; 🐾) Perfect for your post–South Coast Track recovery, this family-run guest house near the wharf is a rustic, verandah-encircled homestead built in 1875 for the sawmill boss. Rates include full cooked breakfast and afternoon tea. Open fires, intersting art, the total absence of doilies and the friendly feline attentions of Pushkin complete the package. Dinner by arrangement; cheaper rates for longer stays.

Southern Forest COTTAGE **$$**
(☑ 03-6298 3306; www.southernforest.com.au; 30 Jager Rd; d $130, extra person $30) Up the hill opposite the pub is this hospitable self-contained cottage, sleeping six bods in two bedrooms. Surrounded by bushland brimming with native birds (80 species!), it's super-private, with plenty of warm timber and zero floral excess. Breakfast provisions include beaut homemade jam and bread.

Lune River

A few kilometres southwest of Hastings Caves is diminutive Lune River, home to Australia's southernmost railway. The **Ida Bay Railway** (☑ 0428 383 262, 03-6298 3110; www.idabayrailway.com.au; 328 Lune River Rd; adult/child/family $30/15/75; ⊙ 9am-5pm) tracks a scenic 14km, 1½-hour narrow-gauge course through native bush to Deep Hole Bay: take a picnic lunch and explore the beach, then catch a later train back to Lune River. Trains depart Lune River at 9.30am, 11.30am, 1.30pm and 3.30pm October to April, and 10am, noon and 2pm May to September. Additional Friday twilight trains leave at 5.30pm in summer (no 9.30am train on these days). There's a *cafe* (mains $5 to $15) at the Lune River end of the line serving cakes, sandwiches, burgers and bacon and eggs.

Cockle Creek

Australia's most southerly drive is the 19km gravel stretch from Ida Bay past the soft-lulling waves of Recherche Bay to Cockle Creek. A grand grid of streets was once planned for Cockle Creek, but dwindling coal seams and whale numbers poured cold water on that idea.

This is epic country, studded with craggy, clouded mountains, sigh-inducing beaches and (best of all) hardly any people – perfect for camping and bushwalking. The challenging **South Coast Track** starts (or ends) here, taking you through to Melaleuca in the **Southwest National Park** (www.parks.tas.gov.au; vehicle/person per day $24/12). Combined with the **Port Davey Track** you can walk all the way to Lake Pedder. Shorter walks from Cockle Creek include ambles along the shoreline to the lighthouse at **Fishers Point** (two hours return), and a section of the South Coast Track to **South Cape Bay** (four hours return). National park entry fees apply to all these walks; self-register at Cockle Creek.

There are some brilliant free **campgrounds** along Recherche Bay, including at Gilhams Beach, just before Catamaran. You can also camp for free at Cockle Creek itself, but national park fees apply as soon as you cross the bridge. Bring all your own provisions, including fuel or gas stoves. There are pit toilets (no showers) and some tank water (boil before drinking).

❶ Getting There & Away

Contact **Evans Coaches** (☑ 03-6297 1335; www.evanscoaches.com.au) to see if it's running the Geeveston–Cockle Creek route when you want it to be. Otherwise, BYO wheels.

Midlands & Central Highlands

Best Places to Eat

➡ Ross Village Bakery (p131)

➡ Red Bridge Cafe & Providore (p132)

➡ Zeps (p132)

➡ Highlander Restaurant (p136)

Best Places to Stay

➡ Blossom's Cottage (p129)

➡ Cherry Villa (p136)

➡ Tarraleah Lodge (p136)

Why Go?

Baked, straw-coloured plains, hawthorn hedgerows, rows of poplars, roadside mansions...Tasmania's Midlands have a distinct English-countryside feel. This is old-school Tasmania, tracing the route between Hobart and Launceston hammered out by convict gangs in the early 1800s. As the road rolled itself out, sandstone garrison towns and pastoral properties appeared: the Midlands soon became the food factory of Van Diemen's Land.

The current course of the Midland Hwy has strayed from its original path – a few meandering detours are required to explore the old towns with their Georgian main streets, antique shops and country pubs.

The underpopulated, undertouristed Central Highlands feature subalpine moorlands and trout-filled lakes. On the highlands' southern fringe is the Derwent Valley, a fecund fold studded with vineyards, hop fields, orchards and old oast houses (for drying hops). If you thumbed through a dictionary looking for the definition of 'sleepy backwater', it would say 'See Derwent Valley towns'.

When to Go

➡ The Midlands and the Central Highlands are definitely at their best from December to March, with warm, settled weather and extended opening hours.

➡ Through the winter months (June to August), snow is quite common around the Central Highlands. A wee dram of local single malt whisky will keep the chills at bay on a cold highland night.

➡ If you're keen on checking out the heritage architecture around Ross and Oatlands, shoot for the shoulder months – October, November, April and May – when accommodation owners crank up the discounts.

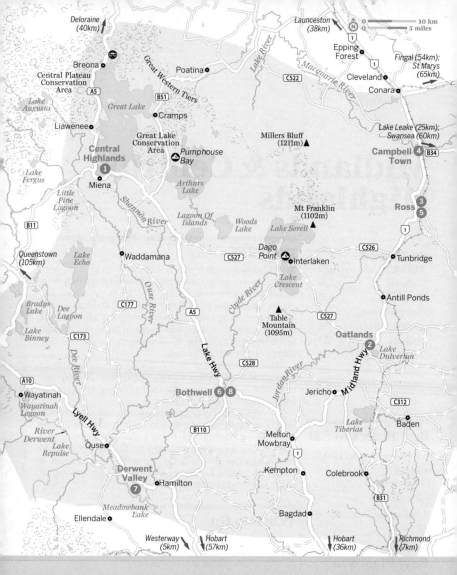

Midlands & Central Highlands Highlights

① Arc a fly across a highland stream and **snare a trout** (p134) in the Central Highlands.

② Ascend the steps inside Oatlands' heritage **Callington Mill** (p129).

③ Look for the carving of Jorgen Jorgenson, former king of Iceland, on the **Ross Bridge** (p130).

④ Read the heinous convict histories in the red bricks along the main street of **Campbell Town** (p132).

⑤ Question your moral direction at the **Four Corners of Ross** (p130).

⑥ Nose your way into a whisky tasting at the **Nant Distillery** (p133) in Bothwell.

⑦ Wander through sandstone villages and old hydroelectric towns in the **Derwent Valley** (p135)

⑧ Make par on Australia's oldest golf course, **Ratho Farm** (p134).

MIDLANDS

Hobart was founded in 1804 and Launceston in 1805. By 1807 the need for a land link between the two settlements prompted surveyor Charles Grimes to map an appropriate route. The road was constructed by convict gangs, and by 1821 was suitable for horses and carriages. Two years later a mail cart operated between the two towns, which became Tasmania's first coach service. The main towns on this road were established in the 1820s as garrisons for prisoners and guards, protecting travellers from the menace of bushrangers.

Online, see www.heritagehighway.com.au.

🛈 Getting Around

Redline (☑1300 360 000; www.tasredline.com.au) buses power between Hobart and Launceston ($41.50, 2½ hours) two to four times daily, via Oatlands, Ross and Campbell Town. **Tassielink** (☑1300 300 520; www.tassielink.com.au) plies the same route as an express service, so doesn't stop at the Midlands towns.

Oatlands

POP 860

Oatlands contains Australia's largest single collection of Georgian architecture. On the stately main street alone (which feels like a film set) there are 87 historic buildings.

The town's site was chosen in 1821 as one of four military posts on the Hobart–George Town road, but it was slow to develop. In 1832 an optimistic town surveyor marked out 80km of streets on the assumption Oatlands would become the Midlands' capital. Many folks made the town home in the 1830s, erecting solid buildings with the help of former convicts and soldiers who were skilled carpenters and stonemasons.

👁 Sights & Activities

Callington Mill   HISTORIC BUILDING
(☑03-6254 1212; www.callingtonmill.com.au; 1 Mill Lane; tours adult/child/family $15/8/40; ☺9am-5pm) ✎ Spinning above the Oatlands rooftops, the Callington Mill was built in 1837 and ground flour until 1891. After decades of neglect, with the innards collecting pigeon poo and the stonework crumbling, it's been fully restored and is once again producing high-grade organic flour. It's an amazing piece of engineering, fully explained on guided tours leaving hourly from 10am to 3pm. The town's visitor information centre is here, too.

History Room   MUSEUM
(☑03-6254 1111; cnr High St & Esplanade; ☺10.30am-4pm Mon, Wed, Fri & Sun) FREE At the northern end of town, fronted by an old petrol pump that don't pump no more, this old garage is full of photos, relics and sundry historical knick-knacks. It's volunteer-run so hours may vary.

🛏 Sleeping

There's free **camping** (three-night maximum) in the picnic area beside Lake Dulverton, at the northern end of the Esplanade. There are toilets and barbecues here.

Blossom's Cottage   B&B $$
(☑03-6254 1516; www.blossomscottageoatlands.com.au; 116 High St; d incl breakfast $110; 🐾) In a self-contained garden studio, Blossom's is bright and cheerful, with a cast-iron bed, blackwood timber floors, leadlight windows, a small kitchenette and a couple of easy chairs under a silver birch. Great value. Fullsome breakfast basket provided.

Oatlands Lodge   B&B $$
(☑03-6254 1444; www.oatlandslodge.com; 92 High St; s/d incl breakfast $100/120) Warm and welcoming in two-storey, hen-pecked sandstone splendour, Oatlands Lodge (1837) is a classy B&B option. Rates include a huge breakfast spread and lots of chat with the affable owners.

Waverley Cottages   RENTAL HOUSE $$
(☑0408 125 049; www.waverleycottages.com; d $190, extra person $25) These two cottages are self-contained and fully equipped. The old-dame Amelia Cottage (104 High St) sleeps 10 people in quirky attic bedrooms. The newer and vaguely funky Forget-me-not Cottage (17 Dulverton St), directly behind Amelia, sleeps four.

🍴 Eating

TKO Bakery Cafe   BAKERY, CAFE $
(Kentish Hotel; ☑03-6254 1119; www.viewtasmania.com.au/kentishhotel; 60 High St; items $5-15; ☺cafe 8am-5pm, pub noon-late) Hanging off the side of the old Kentish Hotel, TKO delivers total-knockout steak sandwiches, steak-and-bacon pies, soups and scallop pies (either curried or creamy). There are usually a few locals sipping frothies at the bar next door, which does evening pizzas ($12 to $17, serving 6pm to 8pm).

Woodfired Bakery Cafe BAKERY, CAFE **$**

(☑ 0418 551 546; www.naturespath.com.au; 106 High St; mains $10-16; ☺ 10am-4pm Wed-Mon) The newest eatery in town (they were still putting the signs up when we visited), this upbeat outfit splits its attention between selling natural olive-oil soaps and quality cafe fare, such as breakfast burritos, soups, toasted panini and buttermilk pancakes. Saturday-night pizzas were also looking like a distinct possibility.

Casaveen CAFE **$**

(☑ 03-6254 0044; www.casaveen.com.au; 44 High St; mains $10-15; ☺ 9am-4pm Mon-Fri, 11am-4pm Sat & Sun) Part of the Casaveen knitwear centre at the southern end of town, this bright garden cafe is fronted by a flagstone courtyard and plates up panini, baguettes and gourmet pies. There are regular soup and salad specials, plus 'high tea' sessions ($27) on Sunday and Wednesday from 1pm to 4pm.

❶ Information

Oatlands Visitor Information Centre (☑ 03-6254 1212; www.heritagehighwaytasmania.com.au; Callington Mill, 1 Mill Lane; ☺ 9am-5pm) Proffers general info and handles accommodation bookings. Pick up the free handouts: *Welcome to Oatlands,* which includes self-guided town-tour directions; *Lake Dulverton Walkway Guide,* for explorations around the lake; and guides to the town's old military and supreme court precincts.

❶ Getting There & Away

Redline (☑ 1300 360 000; www.tasredline.com.au) Buses to Hobart ($22, 1¼ hours) and Launceston ($25, 1¼ hours).

Ross

POP 420

Another tidy (nay, immaculate) Midlands town, Ross is 120km north of Hobart. Established in 1812 to protect Hobart–Launceston travellers from bushrangers, Ross became an important coach-staging post at the centre of Tasmania's burgeoning wool industry and, before the famous Ross Bridge was built in 1836, a fording point across the Macquarie River.

These days Ross' elm-lined streets are awash in colonial charm. Plenty of tourist accommodation keeps the town bubbling along.

Sights

Ross Bridge BRIDGE

(Bridge St) The oft-photographed 1836 Ross Bridge is the third-oldest bridge in Australia. Its graceful arches were designed by colonial architect John Lee Archer, and it was built by two convict stonemasons, Messrs Colbeck and Herbert, who were granted pardons for their efforts. Herbert chiselled the 186 intricate carvings decorating the arches, including Celtic symbols, animals and the faces of notable people (including Governor Arthur and Anglo-Danish convict Jorgen Jorgenson, the farcical ex-king of Iceland). At night the bridge is lit up – the carvings shimmer with spooky shadows.

Ross Female Factory MUSEUM

(www.parks.tas.gov.au; cnr Bond & Portugal Sts; ☺ site 9am-5pm, cottage 9.30am-4.30pm Mon-Fri & 1-4pm Sat & Sun) **FREE** This barren site was one of Tasmania's two female convict prisons (the other was in Hobart, p57). Only one cottage remains, full of interesting historical info, but archaeological excavations among the sunburnt stubble are under way. Descriptive panels provide insight into the hard lives these women led. Pick up the *Ross Female Factory* brochure from the visitor centre, then walk along the track from the top of Church St to get here.

Nearby is the wind-blown **Old Ross Burial Ground**, with headstones carved by the same stonemasons who worked on the bridge.

Four Corners of Ross LANDMARK

(cnr Church & Bridge Sts) The crossroads in the middle of town is the Four Corners of Ross, potentially leading your soul in one of four directions: temptation (represented by the Man O'Ross Hotel), salvation (the Catholic Church), re-creation (the town hall) or damnation (the old jail).

Other notable historic edifices include the 1832 **Scotch Thistle Inn** (Church St), now a private residence; the 1830 **barracks** (Bridge St), restored by the National Trust and also a private residence; the **Uniting Church** (Church St), dating from 1885; **St John's Anglican Church** (cnr Church & Badajos Sts), knocked up in 1868; and the **post office** (26 Church St), opened in 1896 and still going strong.

Tasmanian Wool Centre MUSEUM

(☑ 03-6381 5466; www.taswoolcentre.com.au; 48 Church St; ☺ 9.30am-4.30pm Mon-Fri, 10am-4pm

Sat & Sun) This place houses a sheep-centric museum, the town visitor information centre and a craft shop. The museum focuses on convict times and the Australian wool industry, with hands-on samples of wool to feel (so thick and greasy!) and woolly audio-visual displays.

🛌 Sleeping

Ross Caravan Park CARAVAN PARK $
(🗹 03-6381 5224; www.rossmotel.com.au; Bridge St; unpowered/powered sites $24/32, cabins s/d $50/70; 🔊) An appealing patch of green near Ross Bridge on the banks of the fish-filled Macquarie River. Utilitarian, sandstone, barracks-style cabins sleep two to four people (with cooking facilities) and are the cheapest accommodation in town. Bathrooms are shared; BYO linen. Reception is at the Ross Motel.

Stone Cottage RENTAL HOUSE $$
(🗹 03-6381 5444; www.stonecottageross.com.au; 4 Church St; d $120, extra adult/child $20/10; ✳🔊) One of the town's best options for families is indeed made of stone (amazingly detailed!), with a truckload of kids' toys and DVDs and an expansive garden with established fruit trees. The country kitchen with a long wooden table is perfect for lazy lunches and dinners. Sleeps seven.

Ross Bakery Inn GUESTHOUSE, RENTAL HOUSE $$
(🗹 03-6381 5246; www.rossbakery.com.au; 15 Church St; tr/s/d from $85/120/150, 3-bedroom cottage d $165, extra person $20, all incl breakfast; 🔊) Wake up to breakfast fresh from a vintage wood-fired oven when you stay in this 1830s coaching house, adjacent to the Ross Village Bakery. Small, cosy rooms are enhanced by a guest lounge with an open fire and complimentary bakery breakfasts.

In the attic is a backpacker-style triple; the three-bedroom cottage is just down the street.

Country Style Cabin COTTAGE $$
(🗹 03-6381 5453; tspot@bigpond.com; 13-17 Bridge St; d from $99) How refreshing: a modern alternative to the heritage styling of most accommodation options in Ross. Enjoying a bucolic backstreet outlook, this wood-lined cottage has a mod bathroom and an open-plan lounge with a DVD player and piles of magazines for rainy days.

Ross Motel MOTEL $$
(🗹 03-6381 5224; www.rossmotel.com.au; 2 High St; d/f incl breakfast from $135/195; 🔊) The independently owned Ross Motel offers spick-and-span Georgian-style cottage units (reasonably inoffensive reproductions), each with microwave, fridge and TV. Family units sleep four. Quiet and central, with breakfast provisions included for your first morning.

Ross B&B B&B $$
(🗹 0417 522 354, 03-6381 5354; www.rossaccommodation.com.au; 12 Church St; B&B d $110-140, cottages d $170-180; 🔊) Choose from two en-suite rooms in a 1927 abode, or a two-bedroom retreat in a separate wing, among plenty of peachy colours and a garden setting with warbling birds. This organisation also manages a few other carefully restored, self-contained cottages dotted around Ross: see the website for details.

🍴 Eating

Ross Village Bakery BAKERY $
(🗹 03-6381 5246; www.rossbakery.com.au; 15 Church St; items $3-20; ⊙ 8.30am-4.30pm) Overdose on savoury carbs, pies, astonishingly tall vanilla slices and Saturday-night wood-fired pizzas in summer, plus virtuous soups

---

KEMPTON & ANTHONY FENN KEMP

Strung-out **Kempton** (population 360), about 50km north of Hobart and bypassed by the main highway, was founded in 1838, making it one of the state's earliest settlements. Originally known as Green Ponds, it was later renamed after one-time resident and notorious rabble-rouser Anthony Fenn Kemp.

Kemp was a charismatic dude: one-half egotistical bankrupt with scant moral fibre, one-half progressive patriot who was critical in Tasmania's evolution from convict dump to independent colony. Fleeing debts in England, he became a dedicated pastoralist, merchant and political sabre rattler. Never far from controversy, he made as many friends as enemies, and left behind more than a dozen children – a fact that has seen him dubbed the 'Father of Tasmania'. For a critical (and comical) look at Kemp's exploits, read Nicholas Shakespeare's excellent *In Tasmania*.

and salads of all kinds. The owners get up at 4am every day to light the 1860 wood oven.

Tasmanian Scallop Pie Company CAFE $
(Bakery 31; ☑ 03-6381 5422; www.tasmanianscalloppiecompany.com.au; 31 Church St; pies $5-7, mains $9-15; ⊗ 7am-5pm) Ross is a fair way from the coast, but reserve cynicism and wolf down an excellent curried scallop pie for lunch. All-day breakfasts and agricultural mains (lamb's fry, rissoles with peas and mash, vegetable soup) also available.

Man O'Ross Hotel PUB FOOD $$
(☑ 03-6381 5445; www.manoross.com; 35 Church St; mains $19-30; ⊗ noon-2pm & 6-8pm; ☎) Dinner options in Ross are scant, but the town's heritage pub offers an old-school pub menu, including beer-battered east-coast flathead, homemade rissoles with chips and veg, chicken Kiev and roast o' the day. There's a beaut beer garden out the back that's all raised decks and brollies.

❶ Information

Ross Visitor Information Centre (☑ 03-6381 5466; www.visitross.com.au; 48 Church St; ⊗ 9am-5pm) Inside the Tasmanian Wool Centre. If you've got a group of eight or more, the centre runs guided town tours (per person $5, bookings essential).

❶ Getting There & Around

Redline (☑ 1300 360 000; www.tasredline.com.au) Rolls out of Ross towards Hobart ($31, 1½ hours) and Launceston ($14, one hour).

Campbell Town
POP 990

Campbell Town, 12km north of Ross, is another former garrison and convict settlement. Unlike in Oatlands and Ross, the Midlands Hwy still trucks right on through town, making it a handy pit stop. Along High St, rows of red bricks set into the footpath detail the crimes, sentences and arrival dates of convicts such as Ephram Brain and English Corney, sent here for crimes as various as stealing potatoes, bigamy and murder.

After convict transportation ended, Campbell Town's first white settlers were Irish timber workers who spoke Gaelic and had a particularly debauched reputation. Today, Campbell Town is ground zero for Tasmania's cattle- and sheep-farming

industries. The annual **Campbell Town Show** (www.campbelltownshow.com.au), held in May, is the oldest country show in Australia (since 1839).

◎ Sights & Activities

Campbell Town Museum MUSEUM
(☑ 03-6381 1503; Town Hall, 75 High St; ⊗ 10am-3pm Mon-Fri) FREE The curio-strewn, volunteer-run museum features histories of characters such as John Batman and Martin Cash (a local bushranger) and sundry old artefacts such as an amazing 1930s film projector, once used by the Bye brothers, who screened Saturday-night movies here in the 1930s.

Red Bridge BRIDGE
(High St) The convict-built bridge across the Elizabeth River here was completed in 1838, making it almost as venerable as the Ross Bridge. Locals call it the Red Bridge because it was built from more than 1.5 million red bricks, baked on site.

Other notable heritage structures around town include the 1835 **St Luke's Church of England** (High St); the 1840 **Campbell Town Inn** (100 High St); the 1834 **Fox Hunters Return** (132 High St); the 1847 **Grange** (High St), a mansion now used as a conference centre; and the 1878 **old school** (Hamilton St) in the current school's grounds.

🛏 Sleeping & Eating

Red Bridge Cafe & Providore CAFE $
(☑ 03-6381 1169; 137 High St; items $4-13; ⊗ 7.30am-4pm Mon, Wed & Thu, to 5pm Fri, 8am-5pm Sat & Sun; ☎) At the southern end of town, near the Red Bridge, a former brewery has been transformed into a funky dining room with shared wooden tables and a providore packed with beaut Tasmanian food, wine and beer. Fab cakes, quiches, tarts and gourmet pies make this an essential stop, whether you're heading north or south.

Zeps CAFE $$
(☑ 03-6381 1344; 92 High St; meals $12-27; ⊗ 7am-8pm Mon-Fri, 8am-8pm Sat & Sun) A top refuelling spot is the hyperactive Zeps, serving brekky, panini, pasta, fat pies and good coffee throughout the day, plus impressive pizzas and more substantial mains in the evening (this ain't no blow-through truck stop). It's also handy if you're staying in Ross and have exhausted the local nocturnal options.

LAKE LEAKE

The secondary B34 road from Campbell Town heads east through the excellent fishing and bushwalking area around Lake Leake (33km from Campbell Town) to Swansea (69km) on the east coast.

Shimmering Lake Leake itself is punctuated by ghostly tree stumps and is encircled by holiday shacks. For passersby there's the rough-and-tumble, shingle-covered Lake Leake Inn (☑03-6381 1329; www.lakeleakeinn.com.au; 340 Lake Leake Rd; s/d $40/80), which also does meals (mains $18 to $30, noon to 2pm and 6pm to 8pm daily).

Explore further east to the Meetus Falls and Lost Falls forest reserves. Meetus Falls is the pick of the two: it's 10km from the signposted turn off and has a sheltered BBQ area.

If you're into trout fishing, Currawong Lakes (☑03-6381 1148; www.currawonglakes. com.au; 1204 Long Marsh Rd; d from $190) is a private trout fishery 12km west of the Lake Leake turn off. The property offers trout-filled lakes, a handful of good-quality self-contained cabins, equipment hire and fly fishing (no licence required). Call for current prices.

ℹ Information

Campbell Town Visitor Information Centre (☑03-6381 1353; www.campbelltowntasmania.com; Town Hall, 75 High St; ⊙10am-3pm Mon-Sat) Local info, plus the Campbell Town Museum. The centre is volunteer-run so hours may vary. Pick up the *Campbell Town – Historic Heart of Tasmania* brochure which plots sundry historic edifices on a map.

Book Cellar (www.bookcellar.com.au; 132 High St; ⊙10am-4pm) In a vaulted cellar of what was once a coaching inn, then a B&B, and built with convict labour in 1833, is the unexpected Book Cellar, specialising in Tasmanian tomes.

ℹ Getting There & Away

Redline (☑1300 360 000; www.tasredline. com.au) Buses from Campbell Town head to Hobart ($31, 1¾ hours) and Launceston ($14, 50 minutes).

CENTRAL HIGHLANDS

The people-free Central Highlands area is spiked with steep mountains and perforated with glacial lakes, waterfalls, abundant wildlife and unusual flora, including the ancient pencil pine. The plateau's northwestern sector is part of the Tasmanian Wilderness World Heritage Area. The region is also known for its world-class trout fishing and for its socially divisive hydroelectric schemes, which have seen the damming of rivers, the creation of artificial lakes, the building of power stations and the construction of massive pipelines arcing over rough terrain like giant metal worms. If you want to see the developments first-hand, check out the active Tungatinah, Tarraleah and Liapootah power stations on the extensive Derwent scheme between Queenstown and Hobart.

On the western edge of the Central Plateau is the Walls of Jerusalem National Park, a perennial favourite of bushwalkers and cross-country skiers. Experienced bushwalkers can hike across the Central Plateau into 'the Walls' and also into Cradle Mountain–Lake St Clair National Park.

Online, see www.centralhighlands.tas.gov. au/tourism.

Bothwell

POP 390

Encircling a village green, Bothwell is a becalmed historic town 74km north of Hobart in the Clyde River valley. Its Scottish heritage runs deep: the town has adopted tartan street signs. Bothwell is best known for its proximity to trout heaven, but the town also lays claim to Australia's oldest golf course, Ratho Farm. Worthy eating and accommodation options are thin on the ground: make it a day trip rather than an overnighter.

◉ Sights & Activities

Nant Distillery DISTILLERY
(☑1800 746 453, 03-6259 5790; www.nant.com. au; 254 Nant Lane; tastings & tours $15; ⊙10am-4.45pm, tours 11am & 3pm) A key component of Bothwell's mini-Scotland ambience is this distillery, where superb single malt whisky is crafted in an 1820s flour mill. The modern art and cutting-edge architecture of the restaurant (mains $28 to $34, serving

noon to 3pm) contrasts beautifully with older structures, including the estate's original convict-built homestead. Book ahead for tours.

Australasian Golf Museum MUSEUM
(☑ 03-6259 4033; www.ausgolfmuseum.com; Market Pl; adult/child $4/2; ⊙10am-4pm Sep-May, 11am-3pm Jun-Aug) In the same building as the visitor centre, this museum celebrates golf achievements Down Under. There's a miniature putting green where you can try out old-style clubs, and a stupendous selection of collectable, golf-themed Jim Beam bourbon decanters (sadly, empty).

Thorpe Farm FARM
(☑ 03-6259 5678, 0418 216 780; 189 Dennistoun Rd) Thorpe Farm produces sensational goat's-milk cheese under the Tasmanian Highland Cheese label. The farm also makes wasabi and stone-ground flour. Visits by appointment only; call ahead for directions.

Ratho Farm GOLF
(☑ 0497 644 916, 03-6259 5553; www.rathofarm.com; 2122 Highland Lakes Rd; 9/18 holes $20/35, club hire $15; ⊙8am-dusk) Australia's oldest golf course was rolled out of the dust in 1822 by the Scottish settlers who built Bothwell. It's an eccentric course: watch out for sheep, hedges and hay bales. A major redevelopment was underway when we visited – check the website for new accommodation info.

ℹ **Information**

Bothwell Visitor Information Centre (☑ 03-6259 5503; www.centralhighlands.tas.gov.au; Market Pl; ⊙10am-4pm) Pick up the free *Browse Historic Bothwell* leaflet and check out the wee map, marked with locations of historic buildings.

 ℹ **Getting There & Away**

There's no public transport to Bothwell: BYO wheels.

Lake Country

Levelling out at 1050m above sea level on the Central Plateau, **Great Lake** is the largest natural freshwater lake in Australia. In 1870 brown trout were released into the lake and it soon became a fishing fantasia. Rainbow trout were added in 1910 and also thrived. Trout have now penetrated most of the streams across the plateau.

In the seminal days of hydroelectric ambition, a small Great Lake dam was constructed to raise water levels near Miena. Great Lake is linked to nearby Arthurs Lake by canals, and a pumping station supplies water to the Poatina power station on its northeastern shore.

Public transport services to the area are nonexistent.

🏃 **Activities**

There's brilliant **trout fishing** right across the Central Plateau, with good access to most of the larger lakes. Great Lake, Lake Sorell, Arthurs Lake and Little Pine Lagoon are all popular haunts. The plateau itself actually contains of thousands of lakes; many are tiny, but most still contain trout.

SHOUT ABOUT TROUT

Catching brown and rainbow trout in the Lake Country should be as easy as getting your feet wet – but you still need to be in the right place at the right time, and fly fishing takes skill! There are also restrictions on fish size, daily catch allocations and the types of tackle permitted in various areas in different seasons: the **Inland Fisheries Service** (www.ifs.tas.gov.au) offers priceless advice.

Live bait (impaling a grasshopper, grub or worm on a hook) is tried and true, but bait fishing is banned in most inland Tasmanian waters – it's too effective to give the fish a sporting chance! Artificial lures and flies are more acceptable, coming in myriad shapes, sizes, weights and colours: 'Cobra' wobbler might work for you in lakes, or a 'Celta' in streams.

In the Lake Country, always bring warm, waterproof clothing, even in summer (snow happens). Engaging a professional guide for lessons, or taking a guided trip, is a stellar idea: try **Rod & Fly Tasmania** (www.rodandfly.com.au) or **Trout Guides & Lodges Tasmania** (p296). And don't forget your fishing licence – pick one up from **Spot On Fishing Tackle** (p78) in Hobart.

🛏 Sleeping & Eating

Campers can try the basic camping ground at **Dago Point** (☑ 03-6263 5133; www.central-highlands.tas.gov.au; unpowered sites adult/child $4/2) beside Lake Sorell. A better bet for families is the camping ground on Arthurs Lake at **Pumphouse Bay** (☑ 0439 503 211; www.centralhighlands.tas.gov.au; unpowered sites adult/child/family $4/2/10), which has better facilities, including hot showers. Campers self-register at both sites. BYO supplies; boil your tap water.

Great Lake Hotel PUB $
(☑ 03-6259 8163; www.greatlakehotel.com.au; 3096 Marlborough Hwy, Miena; dm $35, cabins s/d $50/70, units d/f from $105/150) From Miena, take the turn off to Bronte Park and you'll soon come across this small-town pub, offering accommodation from bog-basic anglers' cabins with shared facilities to self-contained motel-style units. The meaty meals in the **bar** (mains $16 to $30, serving noon to 2pm and 6pm to 8pm) will reduce vegetarians to tears. 'Go bush or go home!' is its motto: who are we to argue?

Central Highlands Lodge HOTEL $$
(☑ 03-6259 8179; www.centralhighlandslodge.com.au; Haddens Bay, Miena; d/f from $115/135) On the southern outskirts of Miena, this jaunty, rough-sawn timber lodge offers clean, comfortable cabins. The lodge **restaurant** (mains $19 to $30, serving noon to 2pm and 6pm to 8pm) is a great place to rejuvenate with a cold beer and a hot meal – venison hot pot, trout, salmon and quail have the authentic tinge of the encircling wilderness.

ℹ Information

For lake and bushwalking info, try the **Parks & Wildlife Great Western Tiers Field Centre** (☑ 03-6363 5133; www.parks.tas.gov.au) or the Bothwell Visitor Information Centre.

DERWENT VALLEY

Lake St Clair is the headwaters of the Derwent River, which flows southeast towards Hobart through the fertile Derwent Valley. From New Norfolk (p85), north of Hobart, the Lyell Hwy largely mimics the flow of the Derwent to the Central Plateau, continuing past Derwent Bridge west to Queenstown.

BLACK BOBS

You won't find it on any maps, but somewhere in the upper Derwent Valley was once the notorious town of Black Bobs. Tasmania has only recently shaken off its 'two-headed Tasmanian' tag, a throwaway insult used by mainlanders who viewed Tasmanians as hopeless inbreds wading through the shallow end of the gene pool. Isolated in the backwoods for decades, Black Bobs was allegedly rife with cousin-love – a place of evil, depraved men and their questionable spouses, existing in unnatural harmony. It seems Black Bobs has been lost to myth and history – no one's really sure where it was, or it if ever actually existed – but keep an ear out for lonesome banjos on the back roads while you're passing through...

Hamilton
POP 150

National Trust–classified Hamilton was planned with great expectations. Settled in 1808 – the same year New Norfolk was established – it was a mid-19th-century boom town. By 1835 it had 800 residents, who were well watered by 11 hotels and two breweries. Grids of streets were surveyed, but the dry local soils defeated many farmers. The town stagnated and several buildings were eventually removed.

These days, historic sandstone buildings adorn the main street, with photo-worthy views of mountain ranges and peaks to the west. The Lyell Hwy rolls through town, calling itself Franklin Pl along this short stretch.

⊙ Sights & Activities

Hamilton Heritage Centre MUSEUM
(☑ 03-6286 3381; Tarleton St; adult/child $1/0.50; ⊙noon-3pm Tue Dec-Feb) Hamilton's history gets an overview in the little Hamilton Heritage Centre, set up in an 1835 cottage that was once part of a larger jail. Ridiculously limited opening hours might stop you from getting in the door (call to see if the situation has improved).

TARRALEAH

Midway between Hobart and Queenstown, **Tarraleah** (☑03-6289 0111; www.tarraleah. com) – pronounced 'Tarra-*lee*-uh'; population 10 – is a surreal place. It was built in the 1920s and '30s as a residential village for hydroelectric workers, and at its peak had a population of hundreds, complete with police station, town hall, shops, church, golf course and 100 houses. Once the hydro work dried up, the village declined and the population plummeted. Hydro sold off most of the houses for removal in the 1990s and then put the remainder of the village up for sale. In 2002 Tarraleah was purchased by a family from Queensland ('The Family that Bought a Town', as the tabloids tagged them). They poured buckets of cash into the place, then sold the whole shebang to private interests who've spent further millions.

Today, Tarraleah makes a handy pit stop between Hobart and the west coast, with comfortable accommodation and a swathe of wilderness activities. It still feels like a ghost town if you visit outside peak season, but history is palpable here, and even in the mists of July it's curiously engaging. Activities include mountain biking, bushwalking, golf, birdwatching, fishing, kayaking and squash. More passive types can submit to the pleasures of the lodge's cliff-top spa, or cooking lessons focusing on local produce.

Accommodation traverses the budgetary terrain, from the **Highland Caravan Park** (unpowered sites $10-23, powered sites $36, cabin d $100) to rooms in the **Scholars House** (d from $135); self-contained one- to three-bedroom **cottages** (2-4 people from $220, extra person $30); and ritzy rooms in the luxury art deco **Tarraleah Lodge** (d incl breakfast from $310). On the food front there's dinner and drinks in the **Highlander Restaurant** (mains $25-38; ⊘5-8pm), and breakfast, lunch and good coffee in the casual **Teez Café** (mains $6-15; ⊘8am-3pm).

Tassielink buses (☑1300 300 520; www.tassielink.com.au) stop here on request on Tuesday, Thursday, Friday and Sunday (and every weekday during school terms) from Hobart ($28, two hours) and Strahan ($50, five hours).

Curringa Farm FARM
(☑03-6286 3332.; www.curringafarm.com.au; 5831 Lyell Hwy; tours per person from $60; ⊘10am-4pm Sep-Apr) Take a fascinating tour of the locally owned, 300-hectare, working Curringa Farm, 3km west of Hamilton. The owners aim to strike a balance between business and sustainability, an approach applied to the 3000 sheep plus poppies, oats and cabbage seed farmed here. There's also **accommodation** (double $225, extra person $45) in four secluded spa cottages.

🛏 Sleeping & Eating

Hamilton Camping Facilities CAMPGROUND $
(☑0428 741 909, 03-6286 3202; River St; unpowered sites per vehicle $5) No-frills camping on a grassy river flat near Hamilton's old pub, with a BBQ hut, toilets, showers and a laundry across the street.

Cherry Villa B&B $$
(☑03-6286 3418; 12 Arthur St; d incl breakfast $130, extra person $45) The 1835 Cherry Villa offers three attractive heritage rooms amid buzzy-bee rose gardens. Straight out of an architectural textbook, it's a classically symmetrical Georgian house, with twin dormer windows and chimneys. Dinners by arrangement. Steep stairs!

Jackson's Emporium CAFE $
(☑03-6286 3232; www.jacksonsemporium.com.au; 13 Franklin Pl; mains $5-15; ⊘9am-9pm, to 8pm Jun-Aug) Enterprising Jackson's (an emporium since the 1850s) offers up locally sourced cafe fare (quiches, burgers, chilli con carne, soups), plus desserts, wine and beer, in its rustic shopfront. Ask about heritage accommodation options: **McCauley's Cottage** (double $305, extra person $35) and the four-bedroom **Bonnie Brae Lodge** (double $265, extra adult/child $35/20). McCauley's sleeps seven, Bonnie Brae sleeps 10.

ℹ Getting There & Away

Tassielink (☑1300 300 520; www.tassielink.com.au) Runs between Hobart and Hamilton ($14.80, two hours), with daily buses on Tuesday, Thursday, Friday and Sunday (and every weekday during school terms).

The East Coast

Best Places to Eat

➡ Pasini's (p156)

➡ Freycinet Marine Farm (p152)

➡ Purple Possum Wholefoods (p158)

➡ Moresco Restaurant (p164)

➡ Bridport Café (p168)

Best Places to Stay

➡ Schouten House (p144)

➡ Eagle Peaks (p151)

➡ Piermont (p145)

➡ Scamander Sanctuary Caravan Park (p159)

➡ Weldborough Hotel (p164)

Why Go?

White-blond sand, gin-clear water, high blue skies...now strip off and plunge in! But don't think about it for too long – water temperatures here can leave you breathless.

Tasmania's east coast is sea-salted and rejuvenating – a land of quiet bays and sandy shores, punctuated by granite headlands splashed with flaming orange lichen. The whole coast is fringed with forests, national parks and farmland.

Tasmania's west coast cops all the rain – by the time the clouds make it out here they're virtually empty! No surprise, then, that this is prime holiday terrain for Tasmanians, with plenty of opportunities to hike, bike, kayak, surf, dive and fish – set up your beachside camp and get into it. At the end of the day, fish and chips on the beach is a sure-fire winner. Or, if luxury is more your thing, you'll find hip lodges and top-flight eateries aplenty.

When to Go

➡ Picture-postcard east coast images conjure up visions of high summer, but in truth those clear photographers' dream days are often in winter: be open-minded about when you visit.

➡ The whole coast comes alive in summer. A relaxed vacation vibe prevails, but popular spots get busy and accommodation prices surge. Conversely, in the dead of winter (June to August) many east coast beach towns are half-asleep and empty.

➡ From March to April the sea is at its warmest, and you might have a beach all to yourself.

The East Coast Highlights

1 Sweat it out on the track to **Wineglass Bay** (p148)...then cooling off in the sea once you get there.

2 Bump into wombats and wallabies at **Maria Island National Park** (p140).

3 Reel in a deep-sea monster – or at least catch your dinner – at **St Helens** (p159).

4 Drink your way around Tasmania with craft brews at the **Weldborough Hotel** (p164).

5 Camp under whispering she-oaks at **Mt William National Park** (p164).

6 Paddle a kayak on mirror-calm Ansons River on the **Bay of Fires Lodge Walk** (p163).

7 Dunk your head under the waves at **Binalong Bay** (p163).

8 Quaff the afternoon away at the **east coast wineries** (p143).

9 Beachcomb for Killiecrankie diamonds on **Flinders Island** (p168).

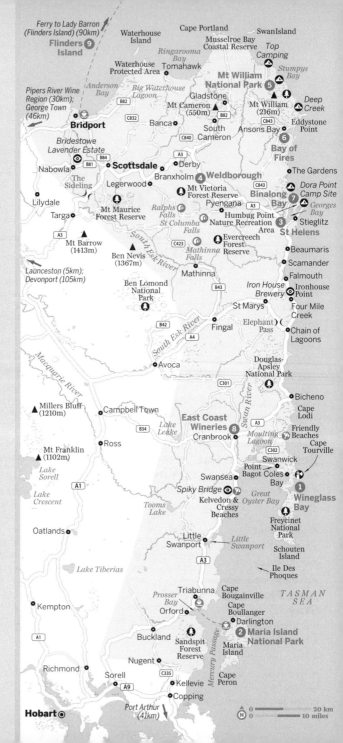

Orford

POP 520

Seaside Orford was once a port for the east-coast whaling fleet and the convict and military settlement on Maria Island, just across Mercury Passage. These days, Orford is a holiday hamlet where Hobartians have their seaside 'shacks' and spend summer holidays on the sand.

The Prosser River flows through **Paradise Gorge** as it heads towards the town, and is often mirror-calm with perfect reflections. On the north side of the river is a convict-built road that once ran all the way to Hobart; it's now a riverside **walking track**. Another coastal track (5km) leads from Raspins Beach, along Shelly Beach, around the Luther Point cliffs and onto photogenic **Spring Beach**, which has improbably clear water and, if the surf gods are smiling, decent waves. The track passes a convict-era **quarry** that coughed out sandstone for buildings in Hobart and Melbourne.

The fish are biting in the Prosser River – ideal for messing about in boats. There's also diving offshore, particularly around the scuppered **Troy D**, which has provided an artificial reef that has attracted plenty of underwater residents. Contact the **Tasmanian Scuba Diving Club** (www.tsdc.org.au) for access info.

Just off the highway, opposite the service station, is **Darlington Vineyard** (☑03-6257 1630; www.darlingtonvineyard.com.au; 63 Holkham Ct; ⊙10am-5pm Fri-Mon, daily in summer), the most southerly of the east-coast wineries, producing quaffable riesling. The simple cellar door is open for tastings and sales.

🛏 Sleeping & Eating

Sanda House   B&B **$$**

(☑03-6257 1527; www.orfordsandahouse.com.au; 33 Walpole St; d $139-159, extra person $30; 🛜) A colonial B&B in Orford's oldest house, a photogenic 1840s stone cottage (actually, some sections date back to 1825!) surrounded by lovingly tended gardens on the south side of the river. Continental breakfasts are served fireside in the dining room (love those stewed fruits). Four rooms, all with bathroom.

Nosh   RENTAL HOUSE **$$$**

(☑0419 117 613; www.noshholiday.com.au; 2 Happy Valley Rd, Spring Beach; up to 6 people $320) 🍽 *Star Wars'* Tatooine meets ecofriendly at this holiday home that looks like it was sculpted from white clay and filled with designer furniture. Just up the hill from Spring Beach, it sleeps up to six comfortably. Pour a glass of wine, kick back on the upstairs deck and ogle the views towards Maria Island.

Loft   APARTMENT **$$$**

(☑03-6257 1539; www.gatewaycafeorford.com.au; 1 Charles St; d $240, extra person $30; ✳🛜) Above the Gateway Cafe is this hip new apartment, sleeping up to seven in two bedrooms (great for families). Everything has a contemporary sheen, from the nifty bathroom tiling to the big stainless-steel fridge to the large sunny deck overlooking the river. Two-night minimum stay.

Gateway Cafe   CAFE **$**

(☑03-6257 1539; www.gatewaycafeorford.com.au; 1 Charles St; mains $7-21; ⊙7.30am-4pm; 🛜) This cafe does bang-up breakfasts, then serves other filling stuff throughout the day: pies, wraps, sausage rolls, vegetable frittata, biscuits and slices. The salt-and-pepper squid is so fresh it's wriggling. Wailing Robert Palmer and outdoor seats.

Scorchers by the River   CAFE, PIZZA **$$**

(☑03-6257 1033; www.scorcherspizzacafe.com.au; 1 Esplanade; mains $25-29; ⊙11am-8pm Fri-Mon, 4-8pm Tue) Scorchers gets big ticks for superior eat-in or takeaway wood-fired pizzas, served all day, of which the garlic prawn and Spring Bay seafood disc tops the list. There's also lasagne, salads and a long list of Tasmanian wines by the glass or bottle (go on, upsize – you're on holiday).

❶ Getting There & Away

Tassielink (☑1300 300 520; www.tassielink.com.au) Buses stop here en route to Swansea ($10.50, one hour), and run south to Hobart ($17, 1½ hours).

Triabunna

POP 900

Triabunna, 8km north of Orford, sits on an inlet of Spring Bay and shelters a small cray- and scallop-fishing fleet. There's an old pub here and the Triabunna Visitor Information Centre (p140), but not much else of interest to tourists other then the fact that this is the jumping-off point for magical Maria Island. East Coast Cruises (p142) runs ecotours to the island, visiting the Ile des Phoques seal colony, the island's Painted Cliffs, and the old convict settlement at Darlington.

THE EAST COAST ORFORD

🛏 Sleeping & Eating

Triabunna Cabin & Caravan Park　　　　　CARAVAN PARK **$**
(✎ 03-6257 3575; www.mariagateway.com; 4 Vicary St; unpowered/powered sites from $27/30, on-site vans/cabins/d from $70/88/125; 🐾) This small-but-progressive compound, opposite the school, has all the usual caravan-park facilities, as well as a couple of en-suite double rooms in the front of a lovely old house.

Tandara Hotel Motel　　　　　MOTEL **$$**
(✎ 03-6257 3333; info@tandaramotorinn.com. au; 17 Tasman Hwy; d $135; 🐾) This low-slung, highway-side, red-brick tavern has a few motel rooms out the back (25 of them, to be precise), which have been given a lick of paint and a new lease on life. Smash down a few aces on the on-site tennis courts. No meals.

Gallery Artspaces Cafe　　　　　CAFE **$**
(✎ 03-6257 3311; www.galleryartspaces.com; 7 Vicary St; mains $7-25; ⊙ 8.30am-4pm) Light lunches, snacks and great coffees are produced by the chef-hatted (no, not Michelin-hatted) crew here, and are served among the art pieces and stuff for sale (candles, knits, jewellery, leather goods, packaged gourmet goodies and secondhand books) in the gallery.

Fish Van　　　　　SEAFOOD **$**
(✎ 0407 552 847; Esplanade West; mains $4-11; ⊙ 11am-7pm) Gobble some east-coast fish and chips from this marina-side caravan. It cooks up boat-fresh flathead, trevalla, barracouta and flake along with mountains of chips. Burgers and steak sangers, too.

ℹ Information

Triabunna Visitor Information Centre (✎ 03-6257 4772; www.tasmaniaseastcoast.com.au;

Charles St; ⊙ 9am-5pm Oct-Apr, 10am-4pm May-Sep) Local information plus Maria Island ferry tickets and penitentiary accommodation bookings.

ℹ Getting There & Away

Tassielink (✎ 1300 300 520; www.tassielink. com.au) Tassielink coaches from Hobart ($21, 1¾ hours) stop at the visitor information centre.

Maria Island National Park

Captivating Maria Island (pronounced 'Ma-rye-ah'), with its jagged peaks, rises up like a fairy-tale castle across Mercury Passage, which separates it from the mainland. It's a carefree, car-free haven – a top spot for walking, wildlife-watching, cycling, camping and reading a book on the beach.

Maria is laced with impressive scenery: curious cliffs, fern-draped forests, squeaky-sand beaches and azure seas. Forester kangaroos, wombats and wallabies wander around; grey-plumed Cape Barren geese honk about on the grasslands; and an insurance population of Tasmanian devils has been released and is thriving. Below the water there's also lots to see, with good snorkelling and diving in the clear, shallow marine reserve.

In 1972 Maria became a national park, as much for its history as for its natural assets, and Darlington is now also a Unesco World Heritage Site.

The island doesn't have any shops: BYO food and gear.

History

Maria Island has seen various incarnations as a penal settlement, an industrial site and

---

THE SAGA OF THE TRIABUNNA MILL

The old Triabunna woodchip mill has been in the news of late. Millionaire Tasmanian conservationists Jan Cameron (co-founder of Kathmandu) and Graeme Wood (founder of Wotif.com) purchased the mill in 2011, handing over $10 million to controversial (and now defunct) timber company Gunns Ltd. Cameron and Wood shut the mill down, effectively choking the state's woodchip industry by denying access to the only deep-water port on the east coast.

Furore and confusion ensued. How could these millionaires jeopardise the state's economy like this? Should the state government compulsorily acquire the mill to free up the port? What would become of Triabunna without the mill?

After a wrecking crew put paid to the mill's machinations, most locals resigned themselves to its closure and now seem to want to move on. Wood has been making murmurs about 'Spring Bay Mill', a multimillion-dollar redevelopment of the site as a tourist destination to rival MONA in Hobart. Watch this space...

Northern Maria Island

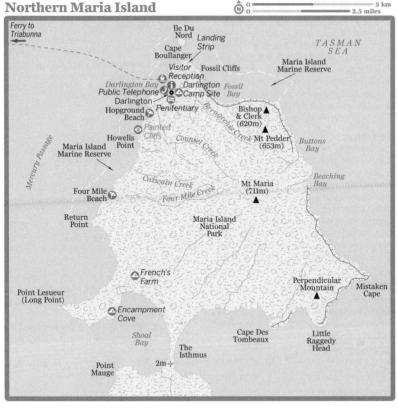

a farming community. The island was originally home to the Oyster Bay community of Tasmanian Aboriginals, who called it Toarra Marra Monah. They lived primarily on shellfish, and made the crossing to the mainland in bark canoes.

Dutch explorer Abel Tasman landed here in 1642, and named the island in honour of Anthony van Diemen's wife. The island became Tasmania's second penal settlement in 1821 and, for the next 10 years, the convicts were set to work developing it. Many of the surviving buildings, such as the commissariat store (1825) and the penitentiary (1830), are from this era. By the early 1830s Maria Island was becoming too expensive to be viable, so the convicts were shipped back to settlements on the Tasmanian mainland. For the next 10 years, the island was the domain of whalers, farmers and smugglers.

In 1842 Darlington reopened as a probation station and a road was built to a second settlement at Long Point (Point Lesueur). At one stage there were about 600 convicts on Maria, but when convict transportation to Tasmania slowed, numbers dwindled and Darlington was again closed in 1850.

With the arrival of enterprising Italian businessman Diego Bernacchi in 1884, Maria Island began a new era. Darlington's buildings were renovated and structures such as the Coffee Palace (1888) were added. The town of 260 people was renamed San Diego. Over the next 40 years a cement factory and wine and silk-growing industries were developed. This industrial era ended with the advent of the Great Depression, and by the 1940s the island reverted to farming.

In the 1960s the government bought the properties on the island and reintroduced animals such as Forester kangaroos, Bennett's wallabies and Cape Barren geese, which had been wiped out since European occupation.

◉ Sights & Activities

Lucky twitchers might spot the endangered forty-spotted pardalote, or perhaps the aptly named swift parrot. You'll certainly see Cape Barren geese waddling around (and depositing their dietary byproducts on) the lawns at Darlington. Meandering wombats and grazing wallabies are also a common sight. Keep an eye out for echidnas and nocturnal Tasmanian devils on forest tracks.

Darlington   HISTORIC SITE

The township of Darlington is where you'll start your time on the island. Close to the ferry jetty are some amazing old **silos** (good for some monastic chanting inside) and the historic **commissariat store**, now the national park visitor centre. Through an avenue of gnarled macrocarpa trees, lies the **penitentiary**, which once housed convicts (now bunkhouse-style accommodation) as well as the restored **Coffee Palace** and **mess hall**.

Painted Cliffs   LANDMARK

From Darlington it's a one-hour return walk to the Painted Cliffs, at the southern end of Hopground Beach. From the beach you can clamber along the sculpted sandstone cliffs, stained with iron oxide in a kaleidoscope of colours. We suggest a visit in the late afternoon when the sun paints the cliffs a fiery orange.

Mountain Biking   MOUNTAIN BIKING

With well-maintained tracks, dirt roads and no cars, Maria is a fantastic place for mountain biking. You can bring a car on the ferry ($10 return), or hire bikes from the ferry company ($20 per day). Ask about the best trails at visitor reception on the island.

Fossil Cliffs, Bishop and
Clerk & Mt Maria   WALKING

From Darlington, there's a two-hour loop walk to the Fossil Cliffs and the old brickworks. If you have more time (four hours return from Darlington), climb **Bishop and Clerk** (620m) for a bird's-eye view while you eat your packed lunch on the exposed, rocky summit. **Mt Maria** (711m) is the island's highest point; it's a seven-hour return hike through the eucalypt forests from Darlington, with brilliant views over the island's isthmus from the top.

Maria Island
Marine Reserve   DIVING, SNORKELLING

(www.parks.tas.gov.au) The seas from Return Point to Bishop and Clerk are a designated marine reserve – no fishing allowed, including in the Darlington area. The reserve encompasses the giant kelp forests and caves around Fossil Bay – excellent for diving and snorkelling. Other good snorkelling spots include the ferry pier and Painted Cliffs. Bring a wetsuit if you want to stay submerged for more than five minutes!

☞ Tours

Maria Island Walk   WALKING

(☑03-6234 2999; www.mariaislandwalk.com.au; per person $2350) Blisters, soggy tents and two-minute noodles? Redefine your concept of bushwalking on this luxury guided four-day hike through Maria's best bits. The first two nights are spent at secluded bush camps, with the third at the historic former home of Diego Bernacchi in Darlington. Price includes amazing food, fine Tasmanian wines, accommodation, park fees and transport from Hobart.

East Coast Cruises   BOAT TOUR

(☑03-6257 1300; www.eastcoastcruises.com.au; tours adult/child from $175/65) See Maria Island's amazing Fossil Cliffs and Painted Cliffs from the water, then check out some seals and sea caves at Iles des Phoques, north of the island. You can even jump in and snorkel with the seals! Another option is to circumnavigate the island, with a stop at Darlington.

🛏 Sleeping

Darlington Camp Site   CAMPGROUND $

(www.parks.tas.gov.au; unpowered sites s/d/f $7/13/16, extra adult/child $5/2.50) There are unpowered sites at Darlington (fees apply, but no bookings required), plus free sites at **French's Farm** and **Encampment Cove** three to four hours' walk from the ferry pier. There are BBQs, toilets and showers ($1) at Darlington. Fires are allowed in designated fireplaces (often banned in summer). French's Farm and Encampment Cove have limited tank water – bring your own.

Penitentiary   LODGE $

(☑03-6256 4772; www.tasmaniaseastcoast.com.au; dm/d/f $15/44/50, extra adult/child $10/5) The brick penitentiary once housed the island's convicts. These days it's simple, sensible accommodation, with six-bunk rooms, shared bathrooms and coin-operated showers ($1). BYO linen, lighting (there's no electricity), food, cooking gear and ability to dismiss the possibility of ghosts. It's often full of school groups, so plan ahead.

DON'T MISS

EAST COAST WINERIES

Along the Tasman Hwy north of Swansea is a string of terrific wineries, the producers here making the most of sunny east-coast days and cool nights. From south to north:

Milton Vineyard (✆03-6257 8298; www.miltonvineyard.com.au; 14635 Tasman Hwy, Swansea; ⊙10am-5pm) Milton is 13km north of Swansea, with tastings in an old weatherboard pavilion presiding over the vines. Sip some sparkling rosé and enjoy a cheese platter by the lake

Spring Vale Wines (✆03-6257 8208; www.springvalewines.com; 130 Spring Vale Rd, Cranbrook; ⊙11am-4pm) Down a long driveway in Cranbrook, 15km north of Swansea, this winery is on land owned by the same family since 1875. The cellar door is housed in an 1842 stable. Don't miss the pinot gris.

Gala Estate Vineyard (✆0408 681 014; www.galaestate.com.au; 14891 Tasman Hwy, Cranbrook; ⊙10am-4pm Sep-May) A funky little cellar door right on the main road through Cranbrook. Stop by for some pinot gris, a few walnuts and a ploughman's lunch.

Devil's Corner (✆03-6257 8881; www.brownbrothers.com.au; Sherbourne Rd, Apslawn; ⊙10am-5pm) Just past the Great Oyster Bay lookout, Devil's Corner is one of Tasmania's largest vineyards, run by the estimable Brown Brothers company. The mod cellar door here overlooks Moulting Lagoon, beyond which is Freycinet Peninsula.

Freycinet Vineyard (✆03-6257 8574; www.freycinetvineyard.com.au; 15919 Tasman Hwy, Apslawn; ⊙10am-5pm) The Bull family has been growing grapes 'neath the east-coast sun since 1980 – it was the first vineyard on the coast. The vibe at the cellar door is agricultural, not flashy – we like it! Super sauvignon blanc.

ℹ Information

Buy your national parks passes at the Triabunna Visitor Information Centre (p140) before you get to the ferry, or at visitor reception once you get to Maria.

Public Telephone Outside the Darlington rangers' station. For an emergency within office hours, call ✆03-6257 1420; outside office hours call ✆000.

Visitor Reception (✆03-6257 1420; www. parks.tas.gov.au; ⊙daylight hours) In the old commissariat store; buy national park passes, pay camping fees, and get bushwalking and cycling information.

ℹ Getting There & Away

Maria Island Ferry (✆0419 746 668; www. mariaislandferry.com.au; adult/child return $35/25, bike/kayak $10/20) Twice-daily service from December to April between Triabunna and Darlington, with Friday-to-Monday services in other months. It also offers bike hire (per day $20). The ferry fits 40 bums on seats, although at the time of writing a newer/larger/faster/better ferry was being investigated.

Par Avion (✆03-6248 5390; www.paravion. com.au; full-day tour adult/child $400/360) You can land on the grass airstrip near Darlington by light plane. Talk to Par Avion, which visits Maria on a fly-cruise package.

Swansea

POP 780

Unhurried Swansea graces the western shore of sheltered Great Oyster Bay, with sweeping views across the water to the peaks of the Freycinet Peninsula. Founded in 1820 as 'Great Swanport', Swansea also delivers some interesting historic buildings and a museum.

The town's revival since the doldrums of the 1980s has paralleled the boom in tourism across the state, though it manages to retain a laid-back holiday vibe. There are plenty of enticements for visitors in and around town, including myriad accommodation options, beaches, restaurants, cafes and some impressive wineries to the north. Swansea gets busy as a beaver (or perhaps a platypus?) in summer, so book ahead.

◎ Sights & Activities

East Coast Heritage Museum   MUSEUM
(✆03-6256 5072; www.eastcoastheritage.org. au; 22 Franklin St; ⊙10am-4pm) **FREE** Inside Swansea's original schoolhouse – now also home to the Swansea Visitor Information Centre – this engaging little museum covers Aboriginal artefacts, colonial history and east-coast surfing safaris in the 1960s. Old Dr Story looks like he could use a shot from his medicine still...

Spiky Bridge LANDMARK

About 7km south of town is the rather amazing Spiky Bridge, built by convicts in the early 1840s using thousands of local fieldstones. The main east-coast road used to truck right across it, but these days it's set beside the highway. Nearby **Kelvedon Beach** and **Cressy Beach** have deep golden sand and rarely a footprint.

Bark Mill Museum MUSEUM

(☎03-6257 8094; www.barkmilltavern.com.au; 96 Tasman Hwy; adult/child/family $10/6/23; ⊙9am-4pm) Out the back of the Bark Mill Tavern, this museum explains the processing of black wattle bark to obtain tannin for tanning leathers. The mill was one of the few industries that operated in Swansea through the Great Depression and helped keep the town afloat. There's also a display on early French exploration along Tasmania's east coast.

Loontitetermairrelehoiner Walk WALKING

(Foreshore) This trail skirts the headland between Waterloo Beach and the Esplanade, passing a mutton bird (short-tailed shearwater) rookery. During breeding season (September to April) the adult birds return at dusk after feeding at sea. Allow 30 to 50 minutes to loop around the trail (you'll need at least that long to figure out how to pronounce it – it's named after the Aboriginal community that lived in the area).

🛏 Sleeping

Swansea Backpackers HOSTEL $

(☎03-6257 8650; www.swanseabackpackers.com.au; 98 Tasman Hwy; unpowered & powered sites $18, dm/d/tr/q from $31/81/81/87; 🐾) This hip backpackers, next door to the Bark Mill, was purpose-built a few years ago, and is still looking sharp. Inside are smart, spacious public areas and a shiny stainless-steel kitchen. Rooms surround a shady deck and are clean and shipshape. The bar is right next door.

Swansea Holiday Park CARAVAN PARK $

(☎03-6257 8148; www.swansea-holiday.com.au; 2 Bridge St; powered sites $30-35, cabins d $80-130; 🐾🏊) A neat, family-friendly park close to Schouten Beach. There's not much space between cabins and not many trees, but kids get a kick out of the games room, playground and solar-heated pool. There's also a camp kitchen and BBQs for when dinnertime rolls around.

★**Schouten House** B&B $$

(☎03-6257 8564; www.schoutenhouse.com.au; 1 Waterloo Rd; d incl breakfast $160-200) This brick-and-sandstone 1844 mansion was built by convicts, and was the centre of 'Great Swanport' before the action shifted a little to the north. Decorated in simple, masculine Georgian style (no frills), its huge rooms now house antique beds and bathrooms. The history-buff owners do a mean pancake breakfast, and have perfected the art of making shortbread.

Swansea Beach Chalets CABIN $$

(☎03-6257 8177; www.swanseachalets.com.au; 27 Shaw St; d $180-240, extra adult/child $20/10; ❇🐾🏊) These 20 chic, self-contained, grey-and-blue chalets are just steps from Jubilee Beach. The best ones have amazing 180-degree water vistas – high, wide and handsome. There's also a BBQ pavilion, a games room and an outdoor pool if the beach doesn't do it for you.

Hamptons on the Bay CABIN $$

(☎0412 203 743; www.hamptonsonthebay.com.au; 12164 Tasman Hwy, Rocky Hills; d $180-220) This former Japanese restaurant complex has been reborn as tasteful clifftop cabin accommodation, with black-painted floorboards, top-of-the-line beds and sunrise views over Freycinet Peninsula. Sea eagles circle overhead, whales and dolphins cavort offshore and there's a private rocky beach at the bottom of the cliffs. It's 12km south of Swansea.

Meredith House B&B $$

(☎03-6257 8119; www.meredithhouse.com.au; 15 Noyes St; d $160-220, extra adult/child $50/25; 🐾) This noble house on the hill above Swansea has been a B&B for 100 years – plenty of time to perfect the formula! Book a room inside the 1853 house (open fires, antiques, old photographs), or a more modern room in the adjacent mews, with little kitchenettes hidden in cupboards. Cooked breakfasts are served on the verandah if it's not too windy.

Wagner's Cottages COTTAGE $$

(☎03-6257 8494, 0419 882 726; www.wagnerscottages.com; 13182 Tasman Hwy; d $180-270; ❇🐾) Wagner's Cottages entails four stone cottages in cottage gardens a couple of kilometres south of town. Cottagey, yes, but they're characterful and eccentric, variously with open fires, loft bedrooms and freestone walling. Breakfast is a DIY affair, featuring fresh eggs from resident chooks and just-out-of-the-oven bread.

Swansea

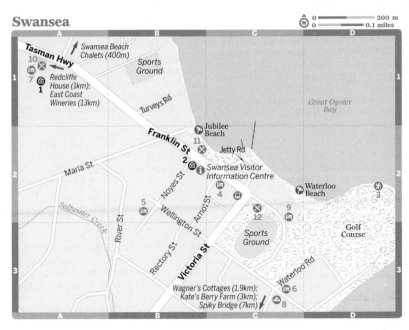

Freycinet Waters   B&B $$

(☑03-6257 8080; www.freycinetwaters.com.au; 16 Franklin St; s/d/apt from $120/140/160; ☎) This brightly decorated,1935 weatherboard house on the main street has friendly hosts and sunny rooms. The breakfast room (also sunny) has water views, and there's a self-contained apartment out the back with its own deck and entrance. No kids under 16.

Redcliffe House   B&B $$

(☑03-6257 8557; www.redcliffehouse.com.au; 13569 Tasman Hwy; d incl breakfast $140-185; ☎) This restored, two-storey heritage farmhouse, built in 1835, is just north of town on the banks of the Meredith River. The five guest rooms have various bedding and bathroom configurations (no kids in some) and are decked out in rustic style. If you're feeling sociable, there's a snug guest lounge with a decanter of port awaiting decanting.

Swansea Waterloo Inn   MOTEL $$

(☑03-6257 8577; www.swanseawaterlooinn.com. au; 1a Franklin St; d & f $115-175) You can't miss this clunky red-brick block on the beach as the road bends through Swansea. It's an aesthetic poke in the eye, but some of the rooms have close-up sea views and it's definitely at the affordable end of the Swansea accommodation spectrum.

Swansea

◎ **Sights**
1 Bark Mill Museum A1
2 East Coast Heritage Museum B2

◉ **Activities, Courses & Tours**
3 Loontitetermairrelehoiner Walk D2

◎ **Sleeping**
4 Freycinet Waters.................................C2
5 Meredith House B2
6 Schouten House C3
7 Swansea Backpackers A1
8 Swansea Holiday Park C3
9 Swansea Waterloo Inn C2

◎ **Eating**
10 Bark Mill Tavern & Bakery A1
11 Saltshaker..B2
12 Ugly Duck Out C2

★ **Piermont**   CABIN $$$

(☑03-6257 8131; www.piermont.com.au; 12990 Tasman Hwy; d $235-355; ☎☒) Down a hawthorn-hedged driveway, 10km south of Swansea, these 21 stylish stone cabins array out from an old farmhouse close to the sea. Each has a fireplace and a spa. There's also a pool, tennis court, bikes for hire, sea kayaks and a restaurant that's been getting positive press. Big on weddings (book ahead).

Rocky Hills Retreat   RENTAL HOUSE $$$
(☑1300 361 136, 0428 250 399; www.rockyhills-retreat.com.au; 11901 Tasman Hwy, Rocky Hills; d $500-600; ☜) About 15km south of Swansea, this architect-designed hideaway overlooking Oyster Bay bills itself as having mastered the 'gentle art of light'. It's 2km up a driveway on bush acreage – no-one else within miles. The design is mighty fine, the views are jaw-dropping and the fridge is deliciously stocked.

Avalon Coastal Retreat   RENTAL HOUSE $$$
(☑1300 361 136, 0428 250 399; www.avaloncoast-alretreat.com.au; 11922 Tasman Hwy, Rocky Hills; up to 6 adults incl breakfast $900-1000; ☜) What a beauty! Like something out of a James Bond movie – all glass and steel and endless ocean views – this is possibly the most luxurious beach house in Tasmania. The kitchen and cellar are well stocked and the beach is nearby – though you'll hardly want to leave the house. It's 14km south of Swansea.

✖ Eating

Kate's Berry Farm   CAFE $
(www.katesberryfarm.com; 12 Addison St; meals $10-14; ☺9.30am-4.30pm) Sit under the wisteria-draped pergola at Kate's (3km south of Swansea) and decide which handmade berry incarnation suits your mood: berry ice creams, jams, sauces, chocolates, waffles, pancakes or pies (go for anything with raspberries involved). Great coffee and 'potted' pies (think beef and burgundy or pork and chorizo), too. Look for the signs off the Tasman Hwy.

Ugly Duck Out   CAFE, MODERN AUSTRALIAN $$
(☑03-6257 8850; www.theuglyduckout.com.au; 2 Franklin St; mains $12-32; ☺8.30am-8pm) 🍃 The meaning of the name seems lost on everybody, but this little shore-side diner is one of the best places to eat around here. Burgers, salads, curries, pastas, grills, rolls...locally sourced, homemade, biodegradable and sustainable all the way. Try the wallaby sausage sandwich. The owner loves a chat.

Saltshaker   CAFE, MODERN AUSTRALIAN $$
(☑03-6257 8488; www.saltshakerrestaurant.com.au; 11a Franklin St; mains lunch $18-27, dinner $20-39; ☺noon-2pm & 5.30pm-late, cafe 8.30am-9pm, to 4pm Jun-Aug) Ebullient Saltshaker gets the urban vote in Swansea. This bright, chic, waterfront spot serves fresh lunches and classy dinners that are big on local seafood (try the crab pasta with spinach, red pep-

per and white-wine-and-dill sauce). There's a wine list as long as your afternoon, and a takeaway cafe (mains $6 to $12) next door.

Bark Mill Tavern & Bakery   CAFE, PUB FOOD $$
(☑03-6257 8094; www.barkmilltavern.com.au; 96 Tasman Hwy; mains bakery $4-12, tavern $14-36; ☺bakery 6am-4pm, tavern noon-2pm & 5.30-8pm) The Bark Mill has two foodie faces: a busy bakery-cafe and a pubby tavern, both doing a roaring trade (to the exclusion of many other businesses in town, it seems). The bakery serves cooked breakfasts, stuffed rolls, sweet temptations and good coffee; the tavern does pizzas and voluminous mains (try the sweet-and-sour pork).

Piermont   MODERN AUSTRALIAN $$$
(☑03-6257 8131; www.piermont.com.au; 12990 Tasman Hwy; mains $32-38, degustation with/without wine $150/120; ☺6-8pm, closed Aug) There are swoon-worthy Great Oyster Bay views from Piermont, 10km south of Swansea, but focus on your plate. It's an 'award-winning' restaurant (aren't they all?) – and in this case we can see why someone might have bestowed a medal. The kitchen works magic with all things local and fresh, and the five-course degustation menu is a knockout.

❶ Information

Online Access Centre (☑03-6257 8806; www.linc.tas.gov.au; Franklin St; ☺10am-1pm Mon & Fri, to 3pm Tue-Thu) Adjacent to the town's primary school.

Swansea Visitor Information Centre (☑03-6256 5072; www.tasmaniaseastcoast.com.au; 22 Franklin St; ☺9am-5pm; ☜) In the old school building on the corner of Noyes St (sharing space with the East Coast Heritage Museum).

❶ Getting There & Away

Tassielink (☑1300 300 520; www.tassielink.com.au) Buses to/from Hobart ($30, 2¼ hours) and Bicheno ($8.50, 50 minutes), stopping at Swansea Corner Store (cnr Franklin St and Tasman Hwy).

Coles Bay & Freycinet National Park

POP 310

Coles Bay township sits on a sweep of sand at the foot of the dramatic pink-granite peaks of the Hazards. It's a laid-back holiday town with plenty of accommodation (though book well ahead in summer) and some active tour

Coles Bay

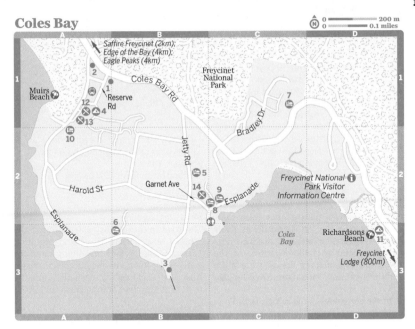

options. The sublime Freycinet National Park is the reason everyone is here: a wild domain of sugar-white beaches and gin-clear water. In the coastal heath and forests, wildflowers and native critters hold sway.

The park encompasses the whole of the peninsula south of Coles Bay, including Schouten Island to the south, and a stretch of coastal scrub around the Friendly Beaches further north. The park's big-ticket sight is the gorgeous goblet of Wineglass Bay. Take the steep hike up to the saddle and grab your photo opportunity, or continue down to the sand on the other side for a (decidedly cool) dip in the sea.

History

The first folks to live around Coles Bay and the Freycinet Peninsula were the Oyster Bay Aboriginal community. Their diet was rich in the abundant shellfish of the bay, and there are shell middens as evidence of this all over the peninsula.

Dutch explorer Abel Tasman visited in 1642 and named Schouten Island. In 1802 Baudin's French expedition explored and named Freycinet Peninsula. When subsequent expeditions spied seals lounging around on the rocks, sealers arrived from Sydney to plunder them.

Coles Bay

✦ Activities, Courses & Tours
1 All4Adventure	....	A1
2 Freycinet Adventures	....	A1
3 Wineglass Bay Cruises	....	B3

🛏 Sleeping
4 BIG4 Iluka on Freycinet Holiday Park	....	A1
5 Coles Bay Retreat	....	B2
6 Freycinet Getaway	....	B3
7 Freycinet Haven	....	C1
8 Freycinet Rentals	....	C2
9 Freycinet Sanctuary	....	C2
10 Hubie's Hideaway	....	A2
11 Richardsons Beach	....	D3

🍴 Eating
12 Coles Bay Express	....	A1
Freycinet Cafe & Bakery	....	(see 12)
13 Iluka Tavern	....	A1
14 Tombolo Freycinet	....	B2

A whale 'fishery' was established at Parsons Cove at the foot of the Hazards in 1824 – the area is still known as the Fisheries. Here southern right whales that were hunted on their migration down the peninsula were processed; the sparkling waters and blond sands became polluted with rotting whale remains. The station was closed by the 1840s.

WINEGLASS BAY

Wineglass Bay's perfect arc of talc-white sand fringed with clear waters makes it a regular on lists of 'World's Top 10 Beaches'. But visiting Wineglass is no lazy day at the beach. Getting here involves a steep, sweaty hike.

To reach the bay on foot is at least a half-day expedition, with 800 steep steps each way. If you only climb to the viewpoint over the bay, your Wineglass Bay wineglass will likely be overflowing with a horde of other camera clickers.

To beat the crowds, visit early and trudge right down to the bay on the other side of the viewpoint. On the way back, take the shady Isthmus Track from the beach then follow the coastal track along the west side of the peninsula back to the car park (about four hours). Take water, food and sun protection – and have a swim!

If this sort of physical exertion fills you with fear and loathing, you can swoop over the bay on a scenic flight, or cruise in by boat.

Coles Bay was named after Silas Cole, who arrived in the 1830s and burnt shells from Aboriginal middens to produce lime for the mortar to build Swansea. In the 1920s the first holiday homes were built, and the area has been a much-loved holiday 'hood ever since.

In the early days of the colony, both Freycinet Peninsula and Schouten Island were farmed, but in 1906 both became game reserves. In 1916 Freycinet shared the honour with Mt Field in becoming Tasmania's first national park; Schouten Island was added in 1977. The Friendly Beaches were added to the park in 1992.

◉ Sights

For all national park walks, remember to get a parks pass. For longer walks, sign in (and out) at the car-park registration booth.

Friendly Beaches   BEACH
This windswept ocean beach is signposted from the main road about 26km north of Coles Bay. A five-minute walk leads from the car park to a vantage point over tumbling surf and an abandoned stretch of sand.

Cape Tourville   LANDMARK
There's an easy 20-minute circuit here for eye-popping panoramas of the peninsula's eastern coastline. You can even get a wheelchair or a pram along here. Also here is **Cape Tourville Lighthouse**, which is totally spectacular when the sun cracks a smile over the horizon at dawn.

Honeymoon Bay   BAY
Tiny Honeymoon Bay – a short walk from Freycinet Lodge – comes into its own at sunset when the lichen-covered rocks light up a deep umber.

Moulting Lagoon   LANDMARK
The road into Coles Bay skirts around the estuary of the Swan River and Moulting Lagoon, an important breeding ground for waterbirds. Residents include black swans, Australian shelducks, greenshanks...and the oysters at Freycinet Marine Farm (p152)!

Sleepy Bay   BAY
A beautiful granite-framed cove 10 minutes from the Cape Tourville Rd.

Bluestone Bay & Whitewater Wall LANDMARK
There's challenging climbing, views and a quiet camp site at Whitewater Wall. You may need a 4WD to reach it, but many 2WDs make it in (not your hire car!). Take your camera on the short walk to Bluestone Bay. Near Cape Tourville.

🏃 Activities

★**Wineglass Bay Walk**   WALKING
This route is deservedly one of the most popular walks in Tasmania. Make the steep climb to the **Wineglass Bay Lookout** (1½ hours return) for a super view over the bay and peninsula. If you want to hear the beach squeak beneath your feet, the steep descent from the lookout to the bay takes another 30 minutes, making the out-and-back trip from the car park 2½ to three hours.

Freycinet Peninsula Circuit   WALKING
This is a three-day, 30km trek around the peninsula, from Hazards Beach south to Cooks Beach (with optional extension to Bryans Beach) then across the peninsula over a heathland plateau before descending to Wineglass Bay. Consult the Freycinet National Park Visitor Information Centre (p153) for advice and maps, and check out Lonely Planet's *Walking in Australia*.

Freycinet Peninsula National Park

N
0 —————————————— 2 km
0 —————————————— 1 mile

Picnic Island

Coles Bay

See Coles Bay Map (p147)

Cape Tourville

Cape Tourville Lighthouse

Richardsons Creek

Richardson's Bistro
Bay

Freycinet Lodge

Sleepy Bay

Honeymoon Bay
Parsons Cove

P

Mt Parsons (331m)

Mt Amos (454m)

Mt Dove (485m)

Wineglass Bay Lookout

Mt Amos

Mt Mayson (415m)

Hazards Beach Track

Isthmus Track

Wineglass Bay

Fleurieu Point

Lemana Lookout

Promise Rock

Hazards Beach

Refuge Island

Hazards Lagoon

Wineglass Bay Camp Site

Lemon Rock

Cape Forestier

Promise Bay

Freycinet National Park

Graham Creek

Hazards Beach Camp Site

Lone Rock Ridge

Half Lemon Rock

TASMAN SEA

Freycinet Peninsula Circuit

Laguna Creek

Indigo Creek

Barrel O'The Cliff

Lulof Rock

Mt Graham (579m)

Freycinet Peninsula Circuit

Mt Freycinet (620m)

Regleeta Creek

Freycinet Peninsula

Eastern Creek

Caltris Creek

Gates Bluff

Cooks Beach

Weatherhead Point

Botanical Creek

East Freycinet Saddle

Gates Gulch

Cooks Beach Camp Site

Freycinet National Park

Jimmy's Rivulet

Bryans Beach Track

Bryans Lagoon

Bryans Beach

Bryans Beach Camp Site

Baldys Bluff

TASMAN SEA

Cape Degerando

Passage Rock

Mt Amos WALKING

If your thighs are up to the challenge, make the trek to see the killer views from this summit (454m; three hours return), one of the Hazards peaks. Dangerously slippery in wet weather.

Tours

Freycinet Experience Walk WALKING

(☑03-6223 7565, 1800 506 003; www.freycinet.com.au; adult/child $2350/2000; ☺Nov-Apr) ⬤ For those who like their wilderness more mild, less wild, Freycinet Experience Walk offers a four-day, fully catered exploration of the peninsula. Walkers return each evening to the secluded, environmentally attuned Friendly Beaches Lodge for superb meals, local wine, hot showers and comfortable beds. The walk covers around 37km.

Freycinet Adventures KAYAKING

(☑03-6257 0500; www.freycinetadventures.com.au; 2 Freycinet Dr, Coles Bay; tour per person $95; ☺tours 8.30am Oct-Apr, 9am May-Sep) View the peninsula from the sheltered waters around Coles Bay on these terrific three-hour paddles. There are also daily twilight tours, setting off three hours before sunset. No experience necessary. Kayak hire is also available ($55 per person per day, including safety gear).

Wineglass Bay Cruises BOAT TOUR

(☑03-6257 0355; www.wineglassbaycruises.com; Jetty Rd, Coles Bay; adult/child $130/85; ☺tours 10am Sep-May) Sedate, four-hour cruises from Coles Bay to Wineglass Bay, including champagne, oysters and nibbles. The boat chugs around the southern end of the peninsula, passing Hazards Beach and Schouten Island. You're likely to see dolphins, sea eagles, seals, penguins and perhaps even migrating whales in the right season. Book ahead.

Wineglass Bay Day Tour BUS TOUR

(☑0407 778 308, 03-6265 7722; www.wineglassbaytours.com.au; adult/child $105/60) Full-day minibus tours to the gorgeous goblet, departing Hobart at 7.45am and getting back around 7pm. You'll walk into Wineglass Bay, and also see Spiky Bridge, Cape Tourville and Honeymoon Bay.

Long Lunch Tour Co BUS TOUR

(☑0409 225 841; www.longlunchtourco.com.au; tour $145) Now this is a great idea! A full-day east coast gastronomic adventure departing Coles Bay and ducking into Freycinet Marine Farm, three east coast wineries and Kate's Berry Farm.

All4Adventure ADVENTURE SPORTS

(☑03-6257 0018; www.all4adventure.com.au; 1 Reserve Rd, Coles Bay; adult/child 2hr $139/89, half-day $239/129) Get off the beaten track into parts of the national park few others access on these quad-bike tours. Tours depart at 1pm daily (with 30 minutes' training beforehand), plus 4.30pm November to March. Half-day tours to the Friendly Beaches area depart 8am daily. Bring your driver's licence.

Freycinet Air SCENIC FLIGHTS

(☑03-6375 1694; www.freycinetair.com.au; 30/45min flight from $110/150) Scenic fixed-wing swoops over the peninsula, plus longer flights as far afield as Maria Island. The airfield is close to Friendly Beaches, signposted off the main road.

Sleeping

Richardsons Beach CAMPGROUND $

(☑03-6256 7000; www.parks.tas.gov.au; unpowered/powered sites from $13/16) These camp sites are seriously popular. From late December to mid-February and at Easter, site allocation is via a ballot system: download the form and submit it by 31 July. Outside the ballot period, book via the Freycinet National Park Visitor Information Centre (p153). National park entry fees apply.

BIG4 Iluka on Freycinet Holiday Park CARAVAN PARK, HOSTEL $

(☑1800 786 512, 03-6257 0115; www.big4.com.au; end of Reserve Rd; unpowered sites $30, powered sites $36-40, hostel dm/d $30/78, cabins & units d $100-185; ☎) Iluka is a big, rambling park that's been here forever and is an unfaltering favourite with local holidaymakers – book well ahead. The backpackers section is managed by YHA; there are six four-bed dorms, a double and a predictably decent kitchen. The local shop, bakery and tavern are a short stroll down the hill.

Freycinet Sanctuary RENTAL HOUSE $$

(☑03-6257 0320; www.freycinetsanctuary.com.au; 9 East Esplanade; d from $170) These two hillside holiday houses – one with two bedrooms, one with one – are just how Australian beach shacks should be: simple, unpretentious, bright and breezy. Throw in decks with water views and you've got a winning combo. The pine-lined one-bedroom unit is further up the slope and has a loftier outlook.

Freycinet Rentals RENTAL HOUSE $$

(☑03-6257 0320; www.freycinetrentals.com; 5 East Esplanade; cottages $170-250) This is your hub for renting (mostly older-style, affordable) holiday houses and beach 'shacks' in and around Coles Bay. Prices swing wildly between summer and winter, and minimum stays apply for long weekends and Christmas holidays. One option, **81 On Freycinet**, has heaps of charm – the stone-and-timber house has three bedrooms, a spiral staircase and Hazards views (double $180).

Freycinet Getaway   APARTMENT $$
(☑ 0411 383 047, 0418 578 701; www.freycinetgetaway.com; 97 Esplanade; d $135-215, extra person $25) Freycinet Getaway is actually two separate, two-bedroom apartments – one upstairs, one downstairs – in a big timber beach house decked out in better-than-beach-house style (polished floorboards, natty red-and-white colour schemes). Apartment 2 has a wood heater for winter and kickin' views of the Hazards any time of year, interrupted only by the odd power line.

Hubie's Hideaway   RENTAL HOUSE $$
(☑ 0427 570 344; www.nauticabutnice.com.au/hubies-hideaway; 33 Esplanade; d $160, extra adult/child $25/10; ❄) At this two-bedroom, self-contained timber cabin with jasmine curling around the gutters, you'll fall asleep to the sound of the sea. It's close to the shop, bakery and pub (the trifecta!) and sleeps up to seven.

Coles Bay Retreat   RENTAL HOUSE $$
(☑ 0418 132 538, 03-8660 2446; www.colesbayretreat.com; 29 Jetty Rd; cottage/house d $130/210, extra person $35) There's a modest cottage and a flashier three-bedroom house here, with close-up Hazards views. The house is a bit '90s in style (glass bricks, terracotta tiles, wicker chairs, royal-blue steelwork, lurid linen), but the location is primo.

★ Eagle Peaks   APARTMENT $$$
(☑ 03-6257 0444, 0419 101 847; www.eaglepeaks.com.au; 11-13 Oyster Bay Ct; d $275-425, beach

house $295-445, extra person $50; ❄ ☎) These two beautiful Tasmanian-oak and rammed-earth studios are 4km north of Coles Bay. Each unit has its own kitchenette, timber deck and comfortable king-size bed. The immaculate Beach House is here, too, sleeping four. All guests have access to BBQs; eat outside as wattlebirds dart in and out of the foliage. The property is a five-minute walk to Sandpiper Beach.

Saffire Freycinet   RESORT $$$
(☑ 1800 723 347, 03-6256 7888; www.saffire-freycinet.com.au; 2352 Coles Bay Rd; d incl meals from $1800; ❄ @ ☎) Saffire is an architectural, gastronomic and wallet-slimming marvel that sets the bar for top-notch Tasmanian hospitality. There are 20 luxe suites here. The curvilicious main building houses a swanky restaurant, self-serve bar, library, art gallery and spa. There's also a menu of activity options, many included in the price.

Freycinet Haven   RENTAL HOUSE $$$
(☑ 03-6428 3486, 0419 139 927; www.freycinethaven.com.au; 91 Freycinet Dr; d from $225, extra person $25; ❄) This is about as close as holiday houses get to the national park. The elevated, ash-coloured, new four-bedroom house sits unobtrusively among the trees, with a fab BBQ deck out the front. Sleeps up to eight. Stylish in a very Australian kind of way.

Edge of the Bay   RESORT $$$
(☑ 03-6257 0102; www.edgeofthebay.com.au; 2308 Main Rd; d $218-360, extra person $30; ☎) Away from the main holiday hubbub, right on the beach about 4km north of Coles Bay, this small resort dances to the beat of its own drum. It has keenly decorated waterside suites, great staff and cottages sleeping five. Once you've woken up, there are mountain bikes, dinghies and tennis courts for guests to serve-and-volley on. There's also an excellent restaurant.

THE EAST COAST COLES BAY & FREYCINET NATIONAL PARK

ℹ FREE CAMPING AT FREYCINET

Inside Freycinet National Park, beyond the main Richardsons Beach camp sites near Coles Bay, there are free walk-in camp sites at Wineglass Bay, Hazards Beach (both two to three hours' walk from the car park), Cooks Beach (4½ hours) and Bryans Beach (5½ hours). Further north, there are two basic camp sites with pit toilets at Friendly Beaches. All of these camp sites are free, but national park entry fees apply. The park is a fuel-stove-only area – campfires are not permitted. There's limited water availability at camp sites: check with a ranger before stomping into the undergrowth.

Outside the national park there's free bush camping at the River & Rocks site at Moulting Lagoon. To get here, drive 8km north of Coles Bay, turn left onto the unsealed River & Rocks Rd, then left again at the T-junction. BYO water (and wine).

LOCAL KNOWLEDGE

TIM WARREN: OUTDOOR GUIDE

I've been coming to the east coast since I was a kid. Now as a bushwalking and kayaking guide, I spend a lot of time in nature here. Because the national parks here are so heavily visited, sustainable practices in the outdoors are more important than almost anywhere. There's so much bush and so many beaches, and not many rangers to oversee it, so it's up to the visitor to know how to be sustainably responsible in the outdoors.

Must Do

Always talk to park staff before you go on a bushwalk. On the east coast there are a lot of seasonal changes that affect where it's best to go – sustainably – at a certain time of year.

Don't Forget

Always scrub your boots with water before entering a national park on the east coast. There's a big problem with the root-rot fungus *Phytophthora cinnamomi* which can devastate vegetation, and it's transmitted very easily by contaminated soil on boots.

Don't Walk There

Always walk below the high-tide mark on beaches. Several endangered bird species nest – almost invisibly – among seaweed just above the high-tide mark. You wouldn't know if you trod on a nest. And stick to tracks: it's easy to trample things. Walking on mosses and small plants can have a really big impact.

Biggest No-No

Feeding wildlife or throwing food scraps into the bush. It can kill an animal.

Freycinet Eco Retreat   APARTMENT $$$
(☑ 0408 504 414, 03-6257 0300; www.mtpaul.com; d incl breakfast from $360, shack d from $200; 🖝) Beat a retreat up Mt Paul, north of Coles Bay, where two carefully crafted ecolodges offer super peninsula vistas, and resident wildlife are your only neighbours. This is a magic spot – you'll want to stay for days. Gay friendly, wheelchair accessible and eco-certified. It also has the older-style 'Saltwater Shack' with Friendly Beaches views. No kids.

Freycinet Lodge   RESORT $$$
(☑ 1800 236 420, 03-6256 7222; www.freycinetlodge.com.au; Coles Bay Rd, Freycinet National Park; d from $220, extra adult/child $65/35) Pioneering Freycinet Lodge is in an amazing location, completely surrounded by the national park at the end of Richardsons Beach (we doubt the planners would let anyone build here these days!). Classy cabin accommodation is scattered through bushland, linked to the main lodge building by boardwalks. Staff happily direct you between guided activities, bikes, the tennis court, bar and restaurants.

🍴 Eating

Freycinet Cafe & Bakery   BAKERY, CAFE $
(☑ 03-6257 0272; 2 Esplanade; items $6-15; ⊗ 8am-4pm; 🖝) This bakery has fuelled many a Freycinet walking epic. Pick up pies, cakes and sandwiches, or lurch into an all-day breakfast after a night at the tavern next door. Unexpected interlopers such as Thai beef salad and freshly squeezed juices also make an appearance.

Coles Bay Express   SUPERMARKET $
(☑ 03-6257 0383; 31 Esplanade; ⊗ 8am-6pm) General store and newsagency. Has an ATM and sells petrol and holiday essentials: fishing rods, sunscreen, tackle, bait, buckets...

★ Freycinet Marine Farm   SEAFOOD $$
(☑ 03-6257 0140; www.freycinetmarinefarm.com; 1784 Coles Bay Rd; plates $15-25; ⊗ 9am-5pm Sep-May, 10am-4pm Jun, 11am-4pm Jul & Aug) Super-popular Freycinet Marine Farm grows huge, succulent oysters ($15 a dozen) in the tidal waters of Moulting Lagoon. Also for your consideration are mussels, rock lobsters, scallops and abalone. Sit on the deck, sip some chardonnay and dig into your seafood picnic, as fresh as Freycinet.

Tombolo Freycinet   CAFE, PIZZA $$
(☑ 03-6257 0124; 6 Garnet Ave; mains $16-24; ⊗ 8.30am-4pm Mon & Tue, to 8.30pm Wed-Sun) Local wines and seafood, wood-fired pizzas and the best coffee in town (Villino, roasted in Hobart), all served on a trim little deck overlooking the main street. Ooh look – poached pear and frangipane tarts!

Iluka Tavern PUB FOOD **$$**
(☑03-6257 0429; 31 Esplanade; mains $8-28; ⊙noon-3pm & 5.30-8pm; ☎) This amiable boozer gets packed to the gills with tourists and locals. The pub nosh is top shelf – in between the reef 'n' beef and the chicken parmigiana you'll find things such as Cambodian seafood curry and seafood linguine. Two pool tables – bar or bistro, take your pick.

Richardson's Bistro MODERN AUSTRALIAN **$$**
(☑03-6256 7222; www.freycinetlodge.com.au; Freycinet Lodge; mains $20-24; ⊙10am-5.30pm) There's nothing fancy about this casual dining option at Freycinet Lodge, but the bistro food (burgers, antipasto plates, steamed mussels, sticky-date pudding) is decent.

Edge MODERN AUSTRALIAN **$$$**
(☑03-6257 0102; www.edgeofthebay.com.au; 2308 Main Rd, Edge of the Bay; mains $25-39; ⊙6-8pm) Head to the Edge of the Bay resort early to snare a window seat for dinner. The chefs serve up fresh east-coast produce with prodigious amounts of seafood. Try the lobster pasta, stripy trumpeter risotto, or the pan-fried 'fish of the moment' on vegetable bouillabaisse. Super service and a simple but sophisticated vibe.

Bay MODERN AUSTRALIAN **$$$**
(☑03-6256 7222; www.freycinetlodge.com.au; Freycinet Lodge; mains $32-42; ⊙6-9.30pm) When the sun goes down over Great Oyster Bay, Freycinet Lodge wheels out the fine dining. Expect delicacies such as farm rabbit with pancetta and white-bean cassoulet, or a seafood platter for two with everything out of the bay (great oysters indeed!). There's a Tasmania-heavy wine list to boot. Bookings mandatory.

❶ Information

Coles Bay is 31km from the Tasman Hwy turn-off. Traverse this stretch slowly between dusk and dawn to avoid hitting any wildlife on the road.
Freycinet National Park Visitor Information Centre (☑03-6256 7000; www.parks.tas.gov.au; Freycinet Dr; ⊙8am-5pm Nov-Apr, 9am-4pm May-Oct) At the park entrance; get your parks passes here. Ask about free ranger-led activities December to February.

❶ Getting There & Away

Bicheno Coach Service (☑0419 570 293, 03-6257 0293; www.freycinetconnections.com.au) runs buses from Bicheno to Coles Bay ($11.50, 45 minutes) then on to the national park walking tracks ($14.50, 50 minutes). These buses con-

nect with **Tassielink** (www.tassielink.com.au) east coast buses from Hobart ($34, three hours) at the Coles Bay turn-off. From the turn-off into Coles Bay, it's $9 (30 minutes). In Coles Bay, buses depart from in front of the Iluka Tavern.

❶ Getting Around

It's 7km from Coles Bay to the car park where most of the national park walks begin. Bicheno Coach Service does the 10-minute trip twice each weekday and once on Saturday and Sunday (one-way/return $6/10); bookings essential.

Bicheno

POP 750

Unlike upmarket Swansea and Coles Bay, Bicheno (pronounced 'Bish-uh-no') is still a functioning fishing port. With brilliant ocean views and lovely beaches, it's madly popular with holidaymakers, but it never sold its soul to the Tourism Devil and remains rough-edged and unwashed. A busy fishing fleet still comes home to harbour in the Gulch with pots of lobsters and scaly loot. Food and accommodation prices here will seem realistic if you're heading north from Freycinet. You'll still need to book ahead in summer.

European settlement began here when whalers and sealers came to the Gulch in 1803. The town became known as Waubs Bay Harbour, after an Aboriginal woman, Waubedebar, rescued two drowning men when their boat was wrecked offshore. After her death in 1832, the settlement bore her name until the 1840s when it was renamed to honour James Ebenezer Bicheno, once colonial secretary of Van Diemen's Land.

◎ Sights & Activities

★ **Bicheno Motorcycle Museum** MUSEUM
(☑03-6375 1485; www.bichenomotorcyclemuseum.com; 33 Burgess St; adult/child $9/free; ⊙9am-5pm, closed Sun Jun-Aug) Andrew Quin got his first Honda at four years of age, and since then he's been hooked on motorbikes. You don't have to be an aficionado, though, to visit his wonderful little museum out the back of his bike-repair shop. It's all shiny chrome and enamel under the bright lights here, with 60 immaculately restored bikes on display, including the rare Noriel 4 Café Racer – the only one of its kind in the world.

Diamond Island ISLAND
(Redbill Beach, off Gordon St) Off the northern end of Redbill Beach is this photogenic

granite outcrop, connected to the mainland via a short, semi-submerged, sandy isthmus, which you can wade across. Time your expedition with low tide or you might end up chest-deep in the waves trying to get back!

East Coast Natureworld   ZOO
(☑ 03-6375 1311; www.natureworld.com.au; 18356 Tasman Hwy; adult/child/family $22/10.50/56; ☺ 9am-5pm) About 7km north of Bicheno, this wildlife park is overrun with native and non-native wildlife, including Tasmanian devils, wallabies, quolls, snakes, wombats and enormous roos. There are devil feedings daily at 10am, 12.30pm and 3.30pm, and a devil house where you can see these little demons up close. There's a cafe here, too.

Waubs Beach   BEACH
A fairly safe ocean beach for swimming on calm days.

Redbill Beach   BEACH
Often has good beach breaks – there's usually a surf carnival here in January.

Foreshore Footway   WALKING
This 3km seaside stroll extends from **Red-bill Beach** to the **Blowhole** via **Waubede-bar's Grave** and the **Gulch**. When the sea is angry (or just a bit annoyed), huge columns of foamy seawater spurt spectacularly into the air at the Blowhole. Don't get too close: even on calm days you can be unexpectedly drenched. Return along the path up **Whalers Hill**, which offers broad views over town. In whaling days, passing sea giants were spotted from here.

Bicheno Dive Centre   DIVING
(☑ 03-6375 1138; www.bichenodive.com.au; 2 Scuba Ct; ☺ 9am-5pm) The clear waters off Bicheno offer brilliant temperate-water diving. This crew visits dive sites mainly in the nearby **Governor Island Marine Reserve**. One-day charters, including equipment and one/two boat dives, cost $140/160. A guided shore dive with equipment is $120. There's also budget accommodation here for divers.

☞ Tours

Bicheno Penguin Tours   BIRDWATCHING
(☑ 03-6375 1333; www.bichenopenguintours.com.au; Tasman Hwy; adult/child $30/15; ☺ dusk nightly) Bicheno is one of the top spots in Tasmania to see penguins. Spy them on these one-hour dusk tours as they waddle back to their burrows. Expect a sincere, pure nature experience: no cafes or souvenirs (and no

photography allowed). Departure times vary year-round, depending on when dusk falls. Bookings essential.

Bicheno's Glass Bottom Boat   BOAT TOUR
(☑ 03-6375 1294, 0407 812 217; bichenoglassbottomboat@activ8.net.au; Esplanade, the Gulch; adult/child $20/5; ☺ 10am, noon & 2pm) This 40-minute trip will give you a watery perspective on Bicheno's submarine wonders. Tours run October to May from the Gulch, weather permitting (bookings advised in January).

🛏 Sleeping

Bicheno Backpackers   HOSTEL $
(☑ 03-6375 1651; www.bichenobackpackers.com; 11 Morrison St; dm $28-31, d $75-95; ☎) This congenial backpackers has dorms spread across two mural-painted buildings, plus the Shack, a 12-berth house a block away on Foster St (set up as six doubles). The communal kitchen is the place to be. There's also free luggage storage, and the friendly owners can help with bookings.

Bicheno East Coast Holiday Park   CARAVAN PARK $
(☑ 03-6375 1999; www.bichenoholidaypark.com.au; 4 Champ St; unpowered/powered sites $25/33, units/cabins from $95/138, extra person $25; ☎) This neat, decent park with plenty of grass (not many trees) is right in the middle of town and has BBQs, a camp kitchen, laundry facilities and a kids' playground. Cabins sleep up to seven. If you're slumming it in the back of a campervan, showers are available for non-stayers ($5).

Bicheno Hideaway   CABIN $$
(☑ 03-6375 1312; www.bichenohideaway.com; 179 Harveys Farm Rd; d from $155, extra person $25) A scatter of architecturally interesting chalets in wildlife-rich bushland a few kilometres south of town, close to the sea and with show-stopping views. Tune your ears into the raucous bird life (including a peacock wandering around), or browse the herb garden for edibles. Minimum stays apply, depending on the cabin and the season.

Anchlia Waterfront Cottage   APARTMENT $$
(☑ 03-6375 1005; www.anchliawaterfront.com.au; 2 Murray St; d from $145, extra person $30; ❄ ☎) Anchlia is one big house – vaguely Swiss-looking, vaguely '80s – divided into two separate self-contained cottages (one sleeps five, one sleeps three), set among gum trees right by the sea (the Foreshore Footway

Bicheno

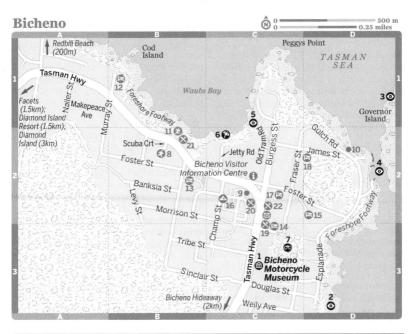

0 ____ 500 m
0 ____ 0.25 miles

tracks right past). If you're in luck you might spy penguins gambolling in the garden.

Bicheno by the Bay　　　　CABIN $$
(☑ 03-6375 1171; www.bichenobythebay.com.au; cnr Foster & Fraser Sts; 1/2/3/4-bedroom cabins from $160/190/260/360, motel d from $120; ❊ ☎) There are 19 cabins and five motel rooms in a bushy setting here, the biggest sleeping 10. The sea-view cabins are the pick of the bunch. Facilities include an outdoor heated pool, a tennis court, a communal fire pit, a kids' pirate-boat playground and

a duck-filled lake with a few canoes ('only accidental swimming permitted').

Beachfront at Bicheno　　　　MOTEL $$
(☑ 03-6375 1111; www.beachfrontbicheno.com.au; Tasman Hwy; d $125-170; ❊ ☎) There are renovated ocean-facing rooms with balconies and snazzy bathrooms here, or unrenovated rooms out the back – sans views and a tad weary, but with baths and tsunami-like showers. The **tavern** is Bicheno's take on a pub, with footy on the telly and big meals (mains $18 to $30, noon to 2pm and 6pm to 8pm).

Sandpiper Ocean Cottages COTTAGE **$$**
(☑ 03-6375 1122; www.sandpipercottages.com.au; 18546 Tasman Hwy, Denison Beach; d $145-300, extra adult/child $30/15; 🐾) These simple, secluded cottages and the smart Beach House are 8km north of Bicheno in the dunes behind Denison Beach. All have BBQs and decks for admiring the surrounding wilds. Less admirable are the kooky 'Tassie icon' sculptures dotted around the garden...

Aurora Beach Cottage RENTAL HOUSE **$$$**
(☑ 03-6375 1774; www.aurorabeachcottage.com.au; 31 Pedder St, Seymour; 1/2/3/4 people $230/230/310/375) For total seclusion, marvellous Aurora Beach Cottage is a great option. It's a timber-and-stone house 18km north of Bicheno at Seymour, set in the dunes behind a wide span of empty sand. Sit out on the deck and watch the waves, or look for messages in bottles along the shore. Breakfast provisions on request; no kids under 12.

Diamond Island Resort RESORT **$$$**
(☑ 03-6375 0100; www.diamondisland.com.au; 69 Tasman Hwy; d $250-510; 🐾🏊) About 2km north of Bicheno, this complex of 27 sun-soaked apartments is surrounded by lawns and has winning views north along the coast. There's private beach access, or a swimming pool if you'd rather have chlorine than salt in your hair. Wander over to namesake Diamond Island itself when the tide is low. On-site Facets restaurant, and free penguin tours for guests.

Windows on Bicheno B&B **$$$**
(☑ 03-6375 2010; www.windowsonbicheno.com.au; 13 James St; d incl breakfast $250-350) This sparkling B&B has two plush, stylish suites on the top floor, furnished and managed with vigorous attention to detail. Spot whales from the balcony, sink into a leather sofa or your king-size bed, or wallow in a deep spa bath for two. It's pricey for Bicheno, but top quality all the way. Serious breakfasts, too.

✖ Eating

Sir Loin Breier DELI **$**
(☑ 03-6375 1182; 57 Burgess St; items $5-20; ⊙ 8.30am-5.30pm Mon-Fri, 9am-4pm Sat) This superior butcher's shop has an amazing range of deli items, so stock up for picnics. The shop brims with cooked local crayfish, smoked trout, oysters, gourmet pies, cheeses, dips, terrines, soups, east coast beer and wine and awesome smoked-quail sausages. Divine. Open Sundays in January.

Blue Edge Bakery BAKERY **$**
(☑ 03-6375 1972; 55 Burgess St; items $3-15; ⊙ 6am-4pm) Blue Edge does servicable sandwiches, pies, Cornish pasties, cakes and salads in a room all a-waft with the aromas of freshly baked bread. The chicken and camembert pie will right your rudder. Cooked breakfasts to boot.

★ Pasini's CAFE **$$**
(☑ 03-6375 1076; 70 Burgess St; mains $10-17; ⊙ 9am-8pm Tue-Sat, 9am-3pm Sun) This impressive outfit does Italian staples such as antipasto plates, wood-fired pizzas and lasagne – but oh, *so much* better than most. The breakfasts border on artisanal, the pastas and gnocchi are homemade and the coffees ('Ooomph' brand, roasted in Hobart) are richly delicious. Takeaways, east coast beers and wines and sumptuous sandwiches also make the cut. What a winner!

Facets MODERN AUSTRALIAN **$$**
(☑ 03-6375 0100; www.diamondisland.com.au; 69 Tasman Hwy; mains from $24; ⊙ 5.30-8.30pm) Facets restaurant at Diamond Island Resort has a taut, nautical vibe and serves up equally well-composed fare. Have an aperitif on the deck and check out the sunset, before a feast of fresh seafood. Bonus: if you have dinner here you can go on the resort's penguin tour for free. Bookings advised.

Sea Life Centre Restaurant SEAFOOD **$$**
(☑ 03-6375 1121; www.sealifecentre.com.au; 1 Tasman Hwy; mains $15-37; ⊙ 10am-9pm) The best thing about this place – an '80s aquarium successfully reincarnated as a restaurant – is the view over the startlingly blue waters of Waubs Bay (if you're here in November or December you might even spy a whale or two). The crayfish and seafood chowder get the thumbs up from locals.

❶ Information

Bicheno Visitor Information Centre (☑ 03-6256 5072; www.tasmaniaseastcoast.com.au; 41b Foster St; ⊙ 9am-5pm Oct-Apr, 10am-4pm May-Sep) Assists with local information and accommodation bookings.

Online Access Centre (☑ 03-6375 1892; www.linc.tas.gov.au; Burgess St; ⊙ 9.30am-3.30pm Mon-Fri) Local library with computer and internet access; behind the public loos at the oval.

❶ Getting There & Away

Bicheno Coach Service (☑ 03-6257 0293, 0419 570 293; www.freycinetconnections.com.au) From Bicheno to Coles Bay ($11.50, 45 minutes) and the start of the walks in Freycinet National Park ($14.50, 50 minutes).

Calow's Coaches (☑ 0400 570 036, 03-6376 2161; www.calowscoaches.com.au) From Bicheno north to St Helens ($14, two hours) and Launceston ($36, three to four hours).

Tassielink (☑ 1300 300 520; www.tassielink. com.au) Hobart to Bicheno ($38, three to four hours).

Douglas-Apsley National Park

This stretch of intact dry eucalypt forest is typical of the environment that blanketed much of the east coast before European settlement. The area was declared a national park in 1989 after a public campaign against the woodchipping of local forests.

Douglas-Apsley (☑ 03-6359 2217; www.parks.tas.gov.au; person/vehicle per day $12/24) is often overlooked, but it's an impressive park, with rocky peaks, waterfalls, abundant bird and animal life and a river gorge with deep swimming holes – and best of all, you won't encounter the midsummer hordes that swarm over Freycinet.

Access to the park is on gravel roads. From the south, turn west off the highway 4km north of Bicheno and follow the signposted road for 7km to the car park. There's a basic camp site here (free, but national park entry fees apply) with a pit toilet, and you can hurl yourself into **Apsley Waterhole** to cool off.

At the time of writing, road access to the northern end of the park was restricted due to dangerous road conditions on the forestry E-road; until things improve it's a 5km walk in from Thompsons Marshes. Note that open fires are banned in the park from October to April; cook on a fuel stove instead.

🎋 Activities

From Apsley Waterhole, a three- to four-hour return walk leads to gorgeous **Apsley Gorge**.

At the park's northern end is the walk to **Heritage and Leeaberra Falls**, which takes five to seven hours return (plus the walk in along the E-road). There's camping near the falls.

For experienced bushwalkers, the major walk is the three-day **Leeaberra Track**. The walk must be done from north to south to prevent the spread of the *Phytophthora* plant disease present in the south. There's not much adequate drinking water on this walk – carry your own. Note that water from the Apsley River should be boiled for three minutes before you can drink it.

St Marys

POP 800

St Marys is an unhurried little village in the Mt Nicholas range, encircled by forests and cattle farms. Visit for the small-town vibes and the craggy heights around town, which you can climb for wicked views over the area.

The top of **South Sister** (832m), towering over German Town Rd 6km north of town, is a 10-minute walk from the car park. To get to **St Patricks Head** (683m) turn down Irishtown Rd, just east of town. This long, steep, 90-minute (one-way) climb, with some cables and a ladder, is a real challenge, but at the top there's a stellar vista along the coast.

You can also explore the local bush on horseback: give **Mariton House** (☑ 03-6372 2059; www.maritonhouse.com; 1 Irishtown Rd) a call and ask about trail rides close to town and beach rides further afield.

🛏 Sleeping

St Marys Recreation Ground CAMPGROUND $ (Harefield Rd, off Gray Rd) There are free grassy unpowered sites, toilets and showers next to the town oval. It's a right turn after the rivulet off Gray Rd (A4), heading out of town towards Elephant Pass.

St Marys Hotel PUB $ (☑ 03-6372 2181; www.stmaryshotel.com.au; 48 Main St; s/d/tw/f $55/70/75/110) There's accommodation upstairs at this 1910 pub in the middle of town; ask for one of the handsome, newly renovated rooms. It also does huge pub meals (mains $15 to $30, serving noon to 2pm and 6pm to 8pm) downstairs. 'You don't see too much plate', says one well-fed local.

★ Addlestone House B&B $$ (☑ 03-6372 2783, 0412 425 666; www.addlestonehouse.com.au; 19 Gray Rd; s/d incl breakfast

---

ℹ CYCLING ELEPHANT PASS

Cyclists riding over **Elephant Pass** to/from St Marys beware: the road is steep, narrow and winding, and drivers tend to get *really* impatient trying to negotiate their way around two-wheelers.

FINGAL VALLEY

To escape the east-coast tourist tirade, detour west from St Marys on the A4 and drive through the beautiful, rolling countryside of the Fingal Valley.

Sleepy Fingal (population 370), 21km west of St Marys, was one of the larger agricultural settlements from the early days of the colony and has some sturdy 19th-century buildings on the main street. The kooky **Fingal Valley Festival** (www.fingalvalleyfestival.com.au) happens here in March, including the World Roof Bolting and World Coal Shovelling Championships.

For some amazing tree-scapes, check out the **Evercreech Forest Reserve**, 34km north of Fingal near Mathinna. A 20-minute circuit walk through blackwood and myrtle delivers you to the **White Knights**, a group of the world's tallest white gums (*Eucalyptus viminalis*); the loftiest boughs here reach 91m. You can also visit **Mathinna Falls** (follow signs from the Mathinna junction on the B43), an impressive 80m-high, four-tier waterfall. There's a 30-minute return stroll to the base of the falls.

Online, see www.fingalvalley.com.au.

$140/165; @ 🛜) This immaculate, 100-year-old B&B (transported here a while ago from nearby Mathinna) is as good as they get. The rooms are beautifully decorated, there's a snug guest lounge, and the host is a charming gent. Highly recommended, indeed the best place to stay in this neck of the woods.

St Marys Seaview Farm FARMSTAY $$
(✆03-6372 2341; www.seaviewfarm.net; 686 Germantown Rd; d/cottage $125/280) 'Seaview' is correct: the coastal panoramas from this working beef and blueberry farm, 500m above sea level, are unbelievable! It's the kind of place you'll want to stop and stay a while. Book an en-suite double, or the cottage sleeps seven. BYO food, but leave the kids (under 12) at home.

✘ Eating

★**Purple Possum Wholefoods** CAFE $
(✆03-6372 2655; www.purplepossum.com.au; 5 Story St; mains $7-13; ⊙ to 2.30pm Sat; 🛜 🍴) ✿ An unexpected find in a little country town, this chipper wholefoods cafe serves excellent homemade soups, vegetarian wraps, fabulous coffee, cakes and slices. There are also vats of nuts, chocolates and spices, and a DIY peanut butter grinder. You'll regret it forever if you don't try the rhubarb cake.

Mt Elephant Fudge CAFE $
(✆03-6372 2787; 7 Story St; items from $4; ⊙10am-4pm Wed-Sun) Got a sweet tooth? Or a whole mouth full of them? Don't miss this little fudge factory, selling the sticky stuff in 10 different flavours. Also sells handmade chocolates, Belgian hot chocolate, smoothies, sundaes and cheesecake. Pack your dental floss.

Mt Elephant Pancake Barn CAFE $$
(✆03-6372 2263; www.mountelephantpancakes.com.au; 824 Mt Elephant Pass Rd; pancakes $8-23; ⊙8am-5.30pm, reduced winter hours) This rustic hilltop place, 9km south of town on the highway to Bicheno, is a bit of an institution. Some say it's overrated and overpriced, but the smoked salmon and camembert version sure hits the spot. Cash only.

ℹ Getting There & Away

Calows Coaches (✆0400 570 036, 03-6376 2161; www.calowscoaches.com.au) Stops at St Marys on its way between Launceston ($31, two hours) and St Helens ($7, 40 minutes).

Scamander & Beaumaris

POP 1010 (COMBINED)

Unfazed by life, Scamander and Beaumaris probably aren't much of an attraction in themselves, but they do have beautiful, long, white-sand beaches where the surf rolls in and you feel like you can wander forever. There's reliable surf around Four Mile Creek, while fisher-folk can toss in a line for bream from the old bridge over the Scamander River, or catch trout further upstream. Shelley Point, just north of town, has rock pools to explore and shells to collect.

◉ Sights

★**Iron House Brewery** BREWERY
(✆0409 308 824, 03-6372 2228; www.ironhouse.com.au; 21554 Tasman Hwy, White Sands Estate, Four Mile Creek; tastings $5, refundable with purchase; ⊙11.30am-7.30pm, reduced winter hours) Has all this beach time left you thirsty?

Quench yourself 16km south of Scamander at Iron House, a craft brewery producing flavoursome pale ale, lager, wheat beer, stout, pilsner and porter. The brewery is part of White Sands Estate – a fancy accommodation set-up – but beer is why you're here. Sample the good stuff and grab some lunch at the **BrewHaus** (mains $18 to $25).

🛏 Sleeping & Eating

★**Scamander Sanctuary**
Caravan Park CARAVAN PARK $
(☑03-6372 5311; www.scamandersanctuarycaravanpark.com.au; Curtis Dr, Scamander; unpowered/powered sites $20/37, safari tents from $120, linen per person $10; ☺Nov-Apr) Just south of Scamander township is this affable caravan park, with dune and bush camp sites and quirky canvas safari tents (sleeping seven) on stilts above the ground, each with a kitchen, bathroom and little deck. It's a short walk to the surf beach, or into town for a beer and a bite.

Pelican Sands APARTMENT $$
(☑03-6372 5231; www.pelicansandsscamander.com.au; 157 Scamander Ave, Scamander; d $100-150, f $160-210; 🛜🏊) If you want to stay on the waterfront, you can't get much closer than this. The six top-notch, motel-style, self-contained units have been tastefully renovated.

Scamander Beach Resort HOTEL $$
(☑03-6372 5255; www.scamanderbeach.com.au; 158 Tasman Hwy, Scamander; d $120-140, f $175; 🛜🏊) Though it's Soviet bloc-ish from the outside, this hotel has a lovely lounge interior and the newly renovated rooms are really decent – most have sea views. The in-house **restaurant** (mains $22 to $29, open 6pm to 8pm Monday to Saturday) does regulation pub-style classics.

Eureka Farm CAFE $
(☑03-6372 5500; www.eurekafarm.com.au; 89 Upper Scamander Rd, Scamander; mains $8-15; ☺8am-6pm Oct-Jun, 10am-4pm Jul-Sep) A couple of kilometres south of Scamander is a sign pointing towards this fruitarian's paradise. Try a smoked-salmon omelette for breakfast, or get stuck into the all-day fruit wonders: berry crepes, fruit pies, ice creams, smoothies, summer puddings and an amazing choc-raspberry pavlova.

Pelican's Bill Bistro MODERN AUSTRALIAN $$
(☑03-6372 5657; 157 Scamander Ave, Scamander; mains $23-27; ☺10am-late) Next door to Pelican Sands accommodation, the Pelican's Bill is full of tip-top seafood, steak, pasta and chicken dishes. Try the 12-hour-cooked Cape Grim beef cheek with honey beetroots. Takeaways and good coffee, too.

St Helens
POP 2180
On the broad, protected sweep of Georges Bay, St Helens began life as a whaling and sealing settlement in the 1830s. Soon the 'swanners' came to plunder, harvesting the bay's black swans for their downy underfeathers. By the 1850s the town was a permanent farming settlement, which swelled in 1874 when tin was discovered nearby. Today, St Helens is a pragmatic sort of town, harbouring the state's largest fishing fleet. This equates to plenty for anglers to get excited about; charter boats will take you out to where the big game fish play. For landlubbers there are plenty of places to eat, sleep and unwind, and good beaches nearby.

🏃 Activities

Fishing
If you are at all into game fishing, then St Helens – Tasmania's ocean-fishing capital – is the place to catch the big one that didn't get away (or a small one closer to land). Call charter operators for prices and bookings.

Zulu Fishing Charterz FISHING
(☑0407 046 571, 0487 351 408; www.zulucharterz.com) Chase the big fish out on the deep blue sea.

Gone Fishing Charters FISHING
(☑0419 353 041, 03-6376 1553; www.breamfishing.com.au) Hook a bream or two on a close-to-shore fishing trip with a local guide.

Bushwalking
Both sides of the entrance to Georges Bay are state reserves and are laced with easy walking tracks. A good track circles around **St Helens Point** (one hour return) – take St Helens Point Rd to access it. Also on St Helens Point are the impressive **Peron Dunes**.

On the north side of Georges Bay, off Binalong Bay Rd, is the **Humbug Point Nature Recreation Area** (☑03-6357 2108; www.parks.tas.gov.au). Within this park, **Skeleton Bay** and **Dora Point** are prime destinations on well-marked tracks. Ask at the St Helens Visitor Information Centre for a walking map and track notes.

St Helens

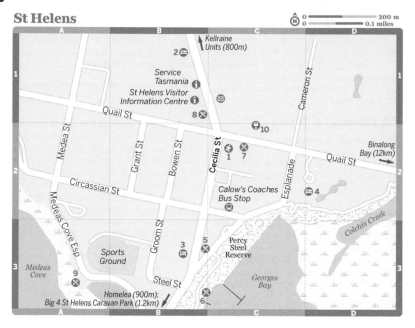

St Helens

🟢 Activities, Courses & Tours
1 East Lines..C2

🛏 Sleeping
2 Artnor Lodge B1
3 St Helens Backpackers B3
4 Tidal Waters Resort D2

❌ Eating
5 Bayside Inn Bistro..............................B3
6 Blue Shed Restaurant B3
7 Lifebuoy Cafe C2
8 Mohr & Smith B1
9 Salty Seas A3

🟢 Drinking & Nightlife
10 Crossroads Bar C2

Swimming & Water Sports
Because it's set on a muddy, tidal bay, St Helens' beaches aren't too flash for swimming. The beaches at **Stieglitz** (7km away at St Helens Point) and at Humbug Point Nature Recreation Area (p159) are better options, though the surf can be a bit dicey. **East Lines** (☑ 03-6376 1720; www.eastlines.wordpress.com; 28 Cecilia St; ⊙ 9am-5pm Mon-Fri, 10am-2pm Sat & Sun Dec-Feb) hires equipment (surfboards, wetsuits and fishing rods) and has bikes for rent ($5/15/25 per hour/four hours/day).

☞ Tours

Green Island Tours   CYCLING
(☑ 03-6376 3080; www.cycling-tasmania.com; 7-day tour $1090-1790, 11-day tour $1790-3580) Mosey along the east coast by bike – with all the tricky logistics taken care of – on seven-day St Helens to Hobart and 11-day Launceston to Hobart (via the east coast) trips, including transfers, national park fees, breakfasts, lunches and accommodation in varying levels of luxury. Bike hire sans tour also available.

🛏 Sleeping

**Humbug Point Nature
Recreation Area**   CAMPGROUND $
(☑ 03-6357 2108; www.parks.tas.gov.au; off Binalong Bay Rd) There are free camp sites in bushland 8km north of St Helens in Humbug Point Nature Recreation Area, en route to Binalong Bay. The camping area is a further 5km into the reserve, at Dora Point.

BIG4 St Helens Holiday Park CARAVAN PARK $
(☑ 03-6376 1290; www.sthelenscp.com.au; 2 Penelope St; unpowered/powered sites from $35/37, cabins & villas d $95-225, extra person $22; ❄🔊✈) This park rolls itself across a green hillside 1.5km south of town and has plenty of family-centric amenities (games

room, jumping pillow, playground, swimming pool). Shoot for one of the smart row of blue-and-cream villas running up the hill. Decent camp kitchen.

St Helens Backpackers HOSTEL $
(☑03-6376 2017; www.sthelensbackpackers.com.au; 9 Cecilia St; dm $27-30, d with/without bathroom $80/65; ☎) Spick and span, laid-back and spacious – this main-street hostel has a 'flashpacker' section upstairs (good for families) and a couple of dorms out the back with super-chunky handmade timber bunks. Hang out on the deck or ponder the amazing wall of beer-bottle labels (not that this is a party place – keep it down after dark).

Kellraine Units APARTMENT $
(☑03-6376 1169; www.kellraineunits.com.au; 72 Tully St; d $85, extra adult/child $40/20; @☎) On the way out of town heading north, these deeply old-school, self-contained brick units (one with wheelchair access) are roomy and great value, if stylistically lost in another era. The owners are incredibly friendly and unjaded (attitudes also seemingly from another era).

Homelea MOTEL, COTTAGE $$
(☑03-6376 1601; www.homeleasthelens.com.au; 16 & 22 Tasman Hwy; d $95-177, cottage $189, extra adult/child $25/18; ☎) On the way into town from the south, it's hard to know what to make of homely Homelea – a renovated '70s motel with lurid colours splashed everywhere (the linen, the walls outside, the walls inside...). Motel units are roomy and have kitchens, or there's a spa cottage down the street (sleeps six).

Artnor Lodge MOTEL $$
(☑03-6376 1234; www.artnorlodge.com.au; 71 Cecilia St; d $90-130) Just off St Helen's leafy main street, this neat, peaceful little motel complex extends from the back of a 1940 house. Clean budget rooms share bathrooms, or there are two renovated en-suite rooms and an en-suite studio at the back of the garden. Check out the Wild West BBQ pavilion!

Tidal Waters Resort RESORT $$
(☑1800 833 980, 03-6376 1999; www.tidalwaters.com.au; 1 Quail St; d $165-260, extra person $30; ☎☎☎) On the tidal lagoon at Georges Bay, this rangy, corporate complex has 60 rather generic rooms and echoingly large public areas. There's a **restaurant** (mains $23 to $32, open for breakfast, lunch and dinner), a swimming pool, and a deck for summer wines right on the water's edge.

Bed in the Treetops B&B B&B $$$
(☑03-6376 1318; www.bedinthetreetops.com.au; 701 Binalong Bay Rd; s $220-310, d $250-310, extra person $70, all incl breakfast; ☎) Some 7km out of St Helens en route to Binalong Bay, take the (steep!) drive up and up through the trees to reach this secluded, stylish timber home. There are two plush apartments, tastefully furnished and with private decks, spas and verdant views. Rates include afternoon tea or pre-dinner drinks, and a cooked breakfast.

Eating & Drinking

Lifebuoy Cafe CAFE $
(☑0439 761 371; 29 Quail St; mains $8-14; ⊙7.30am-4pm Mon-Sat) This secretive, bookish little coffee joint is tucked in behind an eccentric antiques shop off the main drag. Reliable coffee and homemade soups are what you're here for, plus salmon burgers, waffles, eggs Benedict and good ol' country scones.

Salty Seas SEAFOOD $
(☑0428 509 591, 03-6376 1252; 18 Medeas Cove Esplanade; takeaways from $10; ⊙noon-5pm Mon-Fri, 10am-2pm Sat) There's a hint of the bayou about this fish shack, up on stilts above the muddy reaches of Medeas Cove. Crayfish is the speciality – pick one right out of the tank – or there are oysters, mussels and fish fresh off the boat.

Mohr & Smith CAFE, MODERN AUSTRALIAN $$
(☑03-6376 2039; 55/59 Cecilia St; mains breakfast & lunch $10-22, dinner mains $22-30; ⊙8am-4.30pm Sun-Wed, to 8pm Thu-Sat) A classy urban nook with a sunny front terrace, snug open-fire lounge area and chilled tunes, M&S would feel right at home on Salamanca Pl in Hobart. Order a pulled-pork quesadilla or some baked eggs with avocado, cheese and chorizo for breakfast and see what the day brings. Good for an evening drink, too.

Blue Shed Restaurant SEAFOOD $$
(☑03-6376 1170; www.blueshedrestaurant.com.au; 1 Marina Pde; mains $29-30, takeaways $10-18; ⊙restaurant noon-2pm & 6-8pm, takeaways 10am-7.30pm Mon-Fri, from 11.30am Sat & Sun) This classy harbourside eatery does wonders with seafood. Start with a spicy oyster shooter then move on to the signature crispy squid, or maybe the grilled rock lobster with herb and mascarpone butter. Pork, chicken and beef dishes for the non-piscatorial. There's a takeaway outlet on the side called **Captain's Catch**, with the same winning menu since 1994.

WORTH A TRIP

THE GREEN FIELDS OF PYENGANA

About 26km west of St Helens, the turn-off to tiny Pyengana ('Pie-en-ga-na' – an Aboriginal word describing the meeting of two rivers) leads to an impossibly emerald-green valley with some interesting diversions.

In the 1890s European pioneers noted the area's high rainfall and brought in dairy cattle, which thrived. Exporting milk from this isolated valley was impractical, but once converted into cheese and butter the produce could survive the slow journey to market.

Today, cheese is still produced using century-old recipes at the **Pyengana Dairy Company** (☑03-6373 6157; www.pyenganadairy.com.au; St Columba Falls Rd; ⊙9am-5pm Sep-May, 10am-4pm Jun-Aug; tastings free, cafe mains $11-22). Taste and purchase cheddars in myriad flavours at the Holy Cow Café, then settle in for dairy delights like ploughman's lunch, cheese on toast, milkshakes and rich ice cream (try the pepperberry version, flavoured with berries from the nearby Blue Tier plateau).

Pyengana's **Pub in the Paddock** (☑03-6373 6121; www.pubinthepaddock.com.au; St Columba Falls Rd; s/d/tw $60/80/90, mains $14-30; ⊙10.30am-late) is dubiously famed for Priscilla, Princess of the Paddock, the beer-imbibing pig. But it's also worth a visit for its old-time country atmosphere and home-cooked meals. The simple pub rooms are fine if you're just looking for a bed; you'll wake up to pasture views and country sounds.

Further into the valley you'll find **St Columba Falls**, taking a spectacular 90m plunge off the hillside – particularly impressive after rain. An easy 20-minute walk from the car park leads to a platform at its base. There's more vertical water at **Ralphs Falls** – take the signed turn-off to the right shortly before St Columba Falls. There's a 20-minute return walk, or a 50-minute circuit, taking in the falls here, with sweeping views across astoundingly green farmland.

Bayside Inn Bistro PUB FOOD $$
(☑03-6376 1466; www.baysideinn.com.au; 2 Cecilia St; mains $16-38; ⊙8-10am, noon-2pm & 6-8pm) A big, crowd-pleasing menu is on offer at the local pub, with the usual meat and fish dishes (roasts, seafood pasta, schnitzels, steaks, fish and chips), but also crayfish (in season) and a few vegetarian options. Terrific outdoor terrace overlooking the bay.

Crossroads Bar BAR
(☑03-6376 1011; www.crossroadswinebar.com.au; 5/34 Quail St; bar food $10-15; ⊙3pm-late Wed-Fri, 6pm-late Sat, 1pm-late Sun; 🛜) Named after the Robert Johnson blues classic, this surprising find is one of the east coast's only regular live-music venues: there's blues, country and rock gigs most Friday nights. On other evenings, the owners usually fire up some music DVDs to complement a few cold ones (sports-free zone here). Open daily in summer.

ℹ Information

Online Access Centre (☑03-6376 1116; www. linc.tas.gov.au; St Helens Library, 61 Cecilia St; ⊙9am-5pm Mon-Fri, 10am-noon Sat & Sun; 🛜) Internet access at the town's library.

Service Tasmania (☑1300 135 513; www.service.tas.gov.au; 65 Cecilia St; ⊙10am-4.30pm Mon-Fri) Sells national parks passes.

St Helens Visitor Information Centre (☑03-6376 1744; www.tasmaniaseastcoast.com.au; 61 Cecilia St; ⊙9am-5pm) Just off the main street behind the library. Sells national parks passes. The town's history is recorded through memorabilia and photographs.

ℹ Getting There & Away

Calow's Coaches (☑0400 570 036, 03-6376 2161; www.calowscoaches.com.au) runs from Launceston to St Helens ($33, three hours) via Fingal, St Marys and Scamander, connecting with **Tassielink** (☑1300 300 520; www.tassielink. com.au) buses at Conara, on the Midlands Hwy, for the run to Hobart ($56, four hours). Calow's also runs from St Helens to Bicheno ($14, two hours).

Bay of Fires

The Bay of Fires is a 29km-long sweep of powder-white sand and crystal-clear seas that's been called one of the most beautiful beaches in the world. To refer to the Bay of Fires as a single beach, though, is a mistake: it's actually a string of superb beaches, punctuated by lagoons and rocky headlands, backed by coastal heath and bush. There are gulches full of crayfish and abalone, and superb diving in the bay's clear waters.

The ocean beaches offer some good surf, but are prone to rips, so check conditions with locals, or plunge into one of the tiny rock-protected coves.

There's no road that runs the length of the bay. The C850 heads out of St Helens to the gorgeous beachside holiday settlement of Binalong Bay, which marks the southern end of the bay. The road (C848) continues north to the holiday houses at the Gardens, but stops here. There are some beaut bush-camping sites behind the dunes along this stretch; **Swimcart Beach** and **Cosy Corner** are the most popular and have pit toilets. **Seatons Cove** and **Sloop Beach** are generally quieter, while **Grants Lagoon** is close to Binalong Bay. BYO water and firewood.

The bay's northern end is reached via the gravel C843, which leads to **Ansons Bay** and then Mt William National Park. Ansons Bay is a quiet holiday hamlet that's big on fishing, boating and swimming. If you have a kayak, Ansons River Lagoon is perfect for sheltered paddling, while Policemans Point has free camping. There are no petrol stations or shops at Ansons Bay – fill up at either St Helens or Gladstone.

Eddystone Point, just north of Ansons Bay, within Mt William National Park, marks the Bay of Fires' northern extremity. Since 1889 the 37m-high granite tower of **Eddystone Point Lighthouse** (www.lighthouses. org.au) has warned ships off this rocky shoreline. The complex, which includes historic lighthouse keepers' cottages, is worth a look. There's bush camping at nearby Deep Creek.

👉 Tours

Bay of Fires Lodge Walk   WALKING
(📞 03-6392 2211; www.bayoffires.com.au; tour from $2250; 🕐 Oct-May) A four-day, three-night guided adventure. A maximum of 10 guests beachcomb the coastline, led by knowledgable guides. The first night is spent at a secluded tented beach camp, with the next two at the sublime Bay of Fires Lodge. Based here for day three, you can kayak on Ansons River or just laze around in the sun, working up an appetite for dinner. Fine food and wine included. Magic!

Binalong Bay

POP 210

Curling around a sheltered sandy inlet 11km north of St Helens, Binalong Bay is the only permanent settlement in the Bay of Fires. It was first used by fishermen and farmers around 1900, but no-one (no-one white, that is) actually lived here until the 1940s. Now, this quiet spot is a beachy holiday town. There's not much here – the beach, a restaurant and a hillside dotted with pricey holiday houses – but this is precisely why everyone loves it.

There's good surf in and around the bay, and great swimming on calm days. Snorkellers head to **Binalong Gulch**, where they can pick up abalone (with a licence). This is also one of the best spots in Tasmania for diving: the elusive weedy sea dragon often hangs out here. **Bay of Fires Dive** (📞 03-6376 8335, 0419 372 342; www.bayoffiresdive.com.au; 291 Gardens Rd) rents out scuba equipment, snorkelling gear and wetsuits, and runs boat dives and sub-aqua training (introductory scuba session $175).

🛏 Sleeping & Eating

Bay of Fires Character Cottages   RENTAL HOUSE **$$**
(📞 03-6376 8262; www.bayoffirescottages.com.au; 66-74 Main Rd; d $180-230; ❄ 📶) These five well-kitted-out cottages have a million-dollar location overlooking the bay. Interspersed with native scrub, all have mesmerising views in which you can lose yourself as you prod the BBQ on your deck. There are full kitchen and laundry facilities in each unit.

Arthouse Tasmania   RENTAL HOUSE **$$$**
(📞 0457 750 035; www.arthousetasmania.com.au; 61 Lyall Rd; 4 people from $500; 📶) Lasso some like-minded amigos and book this architect-designed beach house, with polished floorboards, granite benchtops and a wide curvy deck backed by a phalanx of sliding doors. About 50m away is a classic Bay of Fires scene: white sand, rocks studded with orange lichen, and gently rolling waves. Sleeps four; no kids under 12.

Bay of Fires Retreat   RENTAL HOUSE **$$$**
(📞 0419 319 131; www.stayz.com.au; Jeanneret Beach; d $220-240, extra person $10) Twenty minutes' stroll along the beach from Binalong Bay (or via a walking track around Grants Lagoon), this breezy, private beach house sleeps up to six in classy surroundings, with Tasmanian art on the walls. Two-night minimum stay.

Point Break   RENTAL HOUSE **$$$**
(📞 03-6331 1224; www.pointbreakbinalong.com; 20 Beven Heights; d $220, extra person $40; ❄) All timber floors, high ceilings, roofs shaped

like rolling waves, and bright, nautical white interiors, this stylish holiday house is a place to chill with friends after a day in the surf. It has every possible mod con, and sleeps up to eight. Multiple deck areas invite a leisurely approach to the day.

★ **Moresco**
Restaurant   CAFE, MODERN AUSTRALIAN **$$**
(✉ 03-6376 8131; www.morescorestaurant.com.au; 64 Main Rd; mains breakfast $11-24, lunch & dinner $22-39; ☺ 7.30am-9pm daily, closed Mon Jun-Aug) Binalong Bay's only business means business: a fantastic food room overlooking the water, serving top-flight meals all day. Roll in for some Huon Valley mushrooms on toast with Tasmanian truffle oil for breakfast, hit the surf, then come back for Moulting Bay oysters and Bass Strait calamari with spicy tomato relish for dinner. Great coffee and even greater wine list.

Mt William National Park

The little-known, isolated **Mt William National Park** (✉ 03-6376 1550; www.parks.tas.gov.au; person/vehicle per day $12/24, camping s/d/f $13/13/16, extra adult/child $5/2.50) brings together long sandy beaches, low ridges and coastal heathlands; visit during spring or early summer when the wildflowers are at their bloomin' best. The highest point, **Mt William** (1½-hour return walk), stands only 216m tall, yet projects your gaze over land and sea. The area was declared a national park in 1973, primarily to protect Tasmania's remaining Forester (eastern grey) kangaroos, which were nearly wiped out by disease in the 1950s and '60s (they've been breeding themselves silly ever since). Activities on offer in the area include birdwatching and wildlife-spotting, fishing, swimming, surfing and diving.

Aboriginal habitation of the area is illustrated by the **large shell midden** at Musselroe Point, and many others across the region. To the south, the lighthouse at **Eddystone Point** is clearly visible, its night-time beam a beacon to ships entering dangerous Banks Strait, between the Furneaux Group and mainland Tasmania.

There's beachside **camping** under the she-oaks at Stumpys Bay, at Top Camp near Musselroe Bay and beside tannin-stained Deep Creek in the park's south. All sites have pit toilets, but no drinking water. Fires are allowed in designated fire spots; BYO firewood and heed fire restrictions. Pay camp-ing fees on-site: pay park fees at the kiosk on the northern access road or, if approaching from the south, buy a pass from Service Tasmania (p162) in St Helens or the St Helens Visitor Infomation Centre (p162).

❶ Getting There & Away

The northern end of Mt William National Park is 17km from Gladstone on gravel roads; the southern end is 60km from St Helens (also gravel) – these two towns are the closest petrol stops. From Bridport, take the road towards Tomahawk and continue to Gladstone. Be careful driving at night – these roads are rife with wildlife.

Weldborough & the Blue Tier
POP 50

As the Tasman Hwy approaches Weldborough Pass – an arabesque cutting famously popular with motorcyclists – it traces a high ridge with vistas of surrounding forests and mountains. Near the top, the **Weldborough Pass Rainforest Walk** is a 15-minute interpretative circuit through moss-covered myrtle rainforest.

Tiny Weldborough is almost a ghost town these days, compared with the busy settlement it must have been in the thick of the 1800s northeast tin rush. In mining days Weldborough had 800 inhabitants, many of whom were Chinese.

The hub of town life remains the characterful **Weldborough Hotel** (✉ 03-6354 2223; www.weldborough.com.au; 12 Main Rd; unpowered/powered sites $15/30, s/tw/d/f $70/82/98/125; ☺ 11.30am-late Tue-Sun), an excellent lunchtime stop or overnighter. If you're a beer boffin, you shouldn't miss this place – it's an informal cellar door for every craft brewery in Tasmania! The kitchen delivers excellent food (mains $20 to $30, serving noon to 2pm and 6pm to 7.30pm Tuesday to Sunday) and there are comfortable pub rooms if you've had too many ales to drive anywhere else. There are also verdant camp sites, hot showers, and a BBQ out the back.

You could base yourself in Welborough for a day or two to do some hiking or mountain biking around the gorgeous **Blue Tier Forest Reserve**, where rainforest walks wander past overgrown mining ruins. The mountain bike trails here are developing an enviable reputation among cyclists in the know. Pick up a map at the St Helens or Scottsdale visitor information centres.

Derby & Around

POP 210

Derby (pronounced 'Dur-bee') is a rather forlorn little town in the Ringarooma River valley. If you're driving from Weldborough, check out the gigantic trout mural splashed across the cliffs near the bridge into town.

One hundred years ago Derby was a thriving mining centre, springing up when tin was discovered here in 1874. At its boom-time height, the town numbered 3000 souls. In 1929, after heavy rain, a mining dam burst in Derby and 14 people died in the resulting flood. The mines closed for five years after this tragedy. They reopened in 1935, but closed again after WWII, causing an exodus.

Today Derby is pinning its hopes of a sustained community revival on the 2015 and 2016 Australian Cross Country Marathon Mountain Bike Championships, which will bring thousands of thirsty/hungry/tired two-wheelers into town.

◉ Sights

Tin Dragon Interpretation
Centre & Cafe   MUSEUM
(Tin Centre; ☑03-6354 1062; www.trailofthetindragon.com.au/derby; Main St; adult/child/family $12/6/30; ⊙9am-5pm, reduced winter hours) Derby's tin-mining heritage is on display in this architecturally impressive museum. The centrepiece is its multimedia presentation, 'Small Town, Big History', documenting the life and times of miners and mining in the northeast's tin-mining boom days. The cafe (items $4 to $15) does reasonable coffee and homemade cakes, slices, nachos and souvlakis. Call ahead in winter to ensure it's open.

Derby Schoolhouse Museum   MUSEUM
(53 Main St; ⊙11am-3pm Mar-Nov, 10am-4pm Dec-Feb) **FREE** In the 1897 school building adjacent to the Tin Dragon Interpretation Centre & Cafe, there's a display on the social history of Derby as opposed to its mining past, including some amazing old photos. Opening hours can vary (volunteer staffing).

★☆ Festivals & Events

For info on the 2015 and 2016 Australian Cross Country Marathon Mountain Bike Championships, see www.mtba.asn.au.

Derby River Derby   BOAT RACE
(www.nerivorsfestival.com.au) Derby gets up to 10,000 visitors in late October for the annual Derby River Derby, part of the North East Rivers Festival. Around 500 competitors in all sorts of homemade inflatable craft race down a 5km river course. The primary goal is not so much to win, but to sabotage your neighbours' vessels and be the last one afloat.

⌖ Sleeping & Eating

There's not much accommodation in Derby – Branxholm, 7km west, is a better bet. At a pinch there's free short-term camping in **Derby Park** by the Ringarooma River, with unpowered sites, a toilet block, a BBQ hut and an au naturel dunk in the river.

Cloverlea Gardens Bed & Breakfast B&B $$
(☑03-6354 6370; pbduffy7@hotmail.com; 27 Legerwood Lane, Branxholm; s & d incl breakfast $100) This little B&B occupies a small self-contained studio room behind a gracious 1910 farmhouse at Branxholm – arguably the best accommodation option in or around Derby. The glorious camellia-filled gardens

---

TRAIL OF THE TIN DRAGON

Tin was discovered in Tasmania's northeast in the late 1800s, attracting thousands of miners. Many came from the goldfields of Victoria, and many were Chinese. At its peak, the Chinese community in and around Derby, Weldborough and Moorina numbered 1000. Documenting this Chinese mining heritage is the tourist route called the Trail of the Tin Dragon.

The trail runs between Launceston and St Helens, with its centrepiece, the Tin Dragon Interpretation Centre and Cafe in Derby. Key sites with interpretation panels crop up along the route, including those at **Moorina** and **Branxholm**. Chinese miners also congregated for recreation at **Weldborough**, where there was once a Daoist temple (or 'joss house'), now in the **Queen Victoria Museum and Art Gallery** (p173) in Launceston. There are also Chinese mining artefacts on display at **St Helens** in the visitor information centre.

Locals are cynical about the trail's success. Make your own mind up: pick up a trail brochure at the Scottsdale or St Helens visitor information centres, or check out www.trailofthetindragon.com.au.

THE EAST COAST DERBY & AROUND

WORTH A TRIP

LEGERWOOD CHAINSAW SCULPTURES

When the small town of Legerwood was forced to lop the gigantic trees along its main street – planted to commemorate its WWI soldiers – it came up with a novel idea. It commissioned chainsaw sculptor Eddie Freeman to carve dramatically posed figures of the soldiers (and other significant local personages) from the tree stumps that remained. For a quick look, detour off the A3 to/from St Helens, 24kms south of Scottsdale, onto the C423, signed to Legerwood and Ringarooma.

are reason enough to visit. Breakfast provisions included.

Tin Dragon Trail Cottages   COTTAGE **$$**
(☑03-6354 6210, 0407 501 137; www.tindragontrailcottages.com.au; 3 Cox's Lane, Branxholm; d $150-220) ✎ These five neat, sustainably built cottages sit near the Ringarooma River on a property that has an interesting story to tell from the Chinese mining past. Two interpretative walks here follow some of the original (now dry) mining races built by Chinese miners. More contemporary is the amazing 'micro-hydro' station the owners have built, powering the whole property.

Cobbler's Cottage   RENTAL HOUSE **$$**
(☑03-6354 2145; 63 Main St; d $150, extra person $20) This old self-contained miner's cottage is rustic and low-key, but if you're just looking for a bed en route to/from somewhere else, it's a sound option. It's managed by Federal Tavern, just up the street. Sleeps six.

Painted Art Cafe   CAFE **$**
(☑03-6354 2407; 62 Main St; mains $6-16; ◷9am-4pm Mon-Thu & Sun, to 7pm Fri & Sat) All-day cooked breakfasts, pizzas, toasties, burgers and coffee are the go at this art-spangled, main-street cafe, one of Derby's finite eating options. Pick a pizza from the list (the 'Painted Art Fury' packs a chilli punch) or design your own.

❶ Getting There & Away

Sainty's North East Bus Service (☑0400 791 076, 0437 469 186; www.saintysnortheastbusservice.com.au) Runs between Launceston and Derby ($21, 2½ hours) once daily (Monday to Friday) in each direction.

Scottsdale & Around

POP 2470

Scottsdale planted itself on the rich agricultural soils of Tasmania's northeast in the 1850s. It's an industrious, pocket-sized town that looks out to the rolling hills that surround it. Poppies, forestry and potatoes are the town's raison d'être. If you're passing through in summer, don't miss the amazing purple haze of lavender at nearby Nabowla.

◉ Sights

Bridestowe Lavender Estate   FARM
(☑03-6352 8182; www.bridestowelavender.com.au; 296 Gillespies Rd, Nabowla; ◷9am-5pm) **FREE** Near Nabowla, 22km west of Scottsdale, is the turn-off to the largest lavender farm in the southern hemisphere, producing lavender oil for the perfume industry. The purple fields in flowering season (mid-December to late January) are unforgettable. There's also a **cafe** and **gift shop** that sells all things lavender.

Sideling   LOOKOUT
(Tasman Hwy) The road from Scottsdale to Launceston crosses a pass called the Sideling (about 15km south of Scottsdale). Outfitted with toilets, picnic tables and killer views as far as Flinders Island on a clear day, it makes a great break from the wiggly road.

🛏 Sleeping & Eating

Lords Hotel   PUB **$**
(☑03-6352 2319; www.lordshotel.com.au; 2 King St; s/d/tw/f $50/70/80/110) Lords has been lording it over Scottsdale since 1911 and still pulls in the punters for hefty pub meals (mains $16 to $25, serving noon to 2pm and 6pm to 8pm). Upstairs are 15 basic pub rooms with shared facilities.

Willow Lodge   B&B **$$**
(☑03-6352 2552; www.willowlodge.net.au; 119 King St; s $120, d $135-165, extra person $30, all incl breakfast; 🐾) This endearing Federation-era (1881) B&B is presented with absolute attention to detail. Bright, colourful rooms overlook garden blooms, and the owners intoxicate guests with after-dinner liqueurs (best consumed in the hot tub). Dinners by arrangement. Two attic rooms and a heated lap pool were on the drawing board when we visited.

Bella Villa   RENTAL HOUSE **$$**
(☑0428 137 286; www.bellecottage.com.au; 83 King St; d from $150, extra person $20; ❄) There

are two spacious units here: one has two bedrooms sleeping up to five, the other has one bedroom and sleeps three. They're neat, contemporary and stylish and both have full kitchens, or it's a short walk to the pub. Breakfast provisions included.

Beulah   B&B **$$**
(✐03-6352 3723; www.beulaheritage.com; 9 King St; s/d incl breakfast from $110/135; ☎) This appealing 1878 home has three rooms decked out in heritage style. There's also a little shop downstairs that's cornered the global market in rhubarb jam. Ease into a chair by the fire in the guest lounge, sip a complimentary port and chew the fat (or rather, the rhubarb) with the affable owner.

Anabel's of Scottsdale   MOTEL **$$**
(✐03-6352 3277, restaurant 0437 358 124; www.anabelsofscottsdale.com.au; 46 King St; s/d/f from $110/130/160) Anabel's is a National Trust–classified home with accommodation in a wing of motel-style units (some with cooking facilities) off to one side. They're a bit '90s style-wise, but they're roomy and overlook a garden full of huge rhododendrons. There's also a French-inspired **restaurant** (mains $18 to $33, serving 6pm to 8pm Thursday to Saturday).

Cottage Bakery   BAKERY **$**
(✐03-6352 2273; 9 Victoria St; items $4-9; ☺9am-5pm Mon-Fri, 7am-2pm Sat) Duck into this famously good bakery to pick up picnic fodder. It also does a mighty fine curried scallop pie (get in early before they sell out).

Scottsdale Steakout   CAFE **$$**
(✐03-6352 2248; 15 King St; mains $9-24; ☺9am-8pm Mon-Sat) This little cafe-restaurant ain't fancy, but it's a real local stalwart, with breakfast until 11am and bistro meals all day. There are steaks and hamburgers, seafood, schnitzels and the odd vegetarian option. There's a takeaway booth next door.

ℹ Information

Scottsdale Visitor Information Centre
(✐03-6352 6520; www.northeasttasmania.com.au; 4 Alfred St; ☺9am-5pm; ☎) Get the local info inside an 1889 courthouse.

ℹ Getting There & Away

Sainty's North East Bus Service (✐0437 469 186; www.saintysnortheastbusservice.com.au) Runs between Launceston and Scottsdale ($13, one hour) once daily in each direction, Monday to Friday.

Bridport
POP 1720

This well-entrenched, snoozy holiday town squats on the shores of Anderson Bay. Just 85km from Launceston, it's popular with sea-seeking weekenders, with safe swimming beaches and good fishing. There's also trout fishing in nearby lakes and dams. Meanwhile, golfers come from across the globe to play on the two (two!) world-class courses here. Bridport is also the launching point for the boat to Flinders Island.

⊙ Sights & Activities

Bridport Wildflower Reserve   NATURE RESERVE
(www.parks.tas.gov.au; off Richard St) FREE Bridport is big on native orchids, which flower from September to December. At this scrubby, 50-hectare reserve – part of the Granite Point Conservation Area, 2km past the caravan park – you might spot an endangered juniper wattle, or maybe a threatened eastern barred bandicoot, spotted-tail quoll or wedge-tailed eagle.

Bridport Walking Track   WALKING
(www.bridportwalkingtrack.com) Feel like stretching your legs? Hoof it along this scenic 11km circuit around town, passing beaches, forests, riverbanks and the Bridport Wildflower Reserve. If you really push it, you can do the loop in a couple of hours. Download a map online.

Barnbougle   GOLF
(✐03-6356 0094; www.barnbougle.com.au; 425 Waterhouse Rd; 9/18 holes $77/109, club hire from $35; ☺7am-dusk Mon-Fri, 6.30am-dusk Sat & Sun) Who would have thought two of Australia's top-10 public golf courses would be in this remote location, 5km east of Bridport? The Dunes is a challenging par-71 links in rolling sand dunes right on the edge of Bass Strait; Lost Farm is an adjacent 20-hole links 4km down the road. There's accommodation and a restaurant here too, plus a day spa at Lost Farm.

☞ Tours

Kookaburra Ridge Quad Bike Tours   ADVENTURE SPORTS
(✐0409 656 213, 03-6356 1391; www.kookaburraridgequadbiketours.com; 238 Boddingtons Rd; 90min tour per adult/child $80/40; ☺tours 10am, 1pm & 3.30pm) Just the thing for the hoon in everyone: quad-bike tours over the pastures, gullies and hidden bush tracks outside

Bridport. You don't need a licence, but you must be over 16 to drive. Under 16s travel half price as passengers – no under eights.

🛏️ Sleeping & Eating

Bridport Seaside Lodge   HOSTEL $

(☑️03-6356 1585; www.bridportseasidelodge.com; 47 Main St; dm $28, d $55-75) There are great water views from this bright, clean, friendly hostel that feels more like a beach house than a backpackers. You can hire bikes and canoes, or char something on the BBQ on the deck.

Bridport Holiday Park   CARAVAN PARK $

(☑️03-6356 1227; www.bridportholidaypark.com. au; Bentley St; unpowered/powered sites $24/34) Strung out for 1.3km along the foreshore, this must be Tasmania's longest caravan park. There are BBQs, a kids' playground and a tennis court nearby, and the Bridport Walking Track trucks right by. Fills up quickly in summer: book ahead.

Barnbougle   COTTAGE $$

(☑️03-6356 0094; www.barnbougle.com.au; 425 Waterhouse Rd; s/d $160/190, extra person $20) Arcing along the dunes at Barnbougle golf course is a tightly spaced row of 22 self-contained timber cottages with little decks, each sleeping up to eight. Sip something Tasmanian at the bar, or sate your golf-induced appetite at the **restaurant** (mains $17 to $33, serving noon till late). Adjacent Lost Farm has 50 slick hotel rooms (single/double from $170/190).

Bridport Bay Inn   MOTEL, APARTMENT $$

(☑️03-6356 1238; www.bridportbayinn.com.au; 105 Main St; d/villas from $105/135, extra adult/child $15/10; ❄️) There's a U-shaped collation of older-style motel units out the back of this tavern, plus smart new self-contained villas (a better choice) not far away. The **restaurant** plates up fresh, locally caught seafood, roasts and wood-fired pizzas (mains $18 to $30, serving noon to 2pm and 5.30pm to 8pm daily).

Platypus Park
Country Retreat   APARTMENT, COTTAGE $$

(☑️03-6356 1873; www.platypuspark.com.au; 20 Ada St; d/apt from $110/120; 📶) In a quiet spot beside the Brid River, a short drive out of town, Platypus Park has a range of cottagey cottages and doubles, overseen by the friendly owners – fifth-generation Tasmanians who can tell you all about the 'hood. There's trout fishing in dams nearby.

Bridport Resort   RESORT $$

(☑️03-6356 1789; www.bridportresort.com. au; 35 Main St; d $140, 1/2/3-bedroom villas $180/260/340; 📶) A low-key little complex set in bushland across the road from the sea, this place has a range of nifty rolled-roof cabins (some of which have been sold off to private residents, confusing the corporate vibe a little). May well be called 'Bridport Residential Villas' by the time you read this. Good winter rates.

★ Bridport Café   CAFE $$

(☑️03-6356 0057; 97 Main St; mains $15-26; ⏱️9am-4pm) With a broad deck, an eclectic scatter of tables and chairs, and a crochet-clad tree out the front, this cafe on the main drag is a real gem. Sidle in for fish and chips, a vegetarian breakfast taco, some Indian chickpea-and-vegetable dahl, or a bowl of seafood chowder. Live music Sunday afternoons, and Tasmanian beers and wines aplenty. Open for dinner in summer.

ℹ️ Getting There & Away

Furneaux Freight (p170) operates a slow boat to Flinders Island from Bridport.

Sainty's North East Bus Service (☑️0437 469 186; www.saintysnortheastbusservice.com.au) Runs from Bridport to Launceston ($20, two hours) via Scottsdale once daily in each direction, Monday to Friday.

Flinders Island

POP 900

'Mountains in the Sea' is how Flinders Island describes itself – and that's exactly what Flinders and the other 51 islands of the Furneaux Group are. Scattered into Bass Strait off Tasmania's eastern tip, they're all that remains of the land bridge that connected Tasmania with mainland Australia 10,000 years ago.

Flinders had a lawless early history as the domain of sealers. These pirates slaughtered thousands of seals, lured ships onto the island's rocks with lanterns and kidnapped local Aboriginal women to claim as 'wives', taking many to Kangaroo Island in South Australia where Tasmanian Indigenous lineage can still be traced. Mainland Tasmanian Aboriginals also suffered here: between 1829 and 1834, 135 Indigenous people were transported to Wybalenna to be 'civilised and educated'. After 14 years, only 47 survived.

Today, sparsely populated and naturally gorgeous, Flinders is a rural community that lives mostly from fishing and agriculture. For visitors there's great bushwalking, wildlife spotting, fishing, kayaking, snorkelling, diving and safe swimming in its curvaceous bays. Or you can spend a few leisurely hours combing the beaches for elusive Killikrancie diamonds and nautilus shells.

Sights

Wybalenna Historic Site HISTORIC SITE
(www.visitflindersisland.com.au/places/wybalenna; Port Davies Rd, Emita; daylight hours) FREE A few piles of bricks, the chapel and cemetery are all that remain of this settlement built to 'care for' relocated mainland Tasmanian Aboriginal people. Eighty-seven people died here from poor food, disease and despair. The site is on Aboriginal land: be respectful.

Furneaux Museum MUSEUM
(03-6359 2010; www.visitflindersisland.com.au/places/furneaux-museum; 8 Fowlers Rd, Emita; adult/child $4/free; 1-5pm Sat-Thu late Dec-Apr, 1-4pm Sat & Sun May-Nov) The grounds around the Furneaux Museum are strewn with whalebones, blubber pots and rusty wrecks. Inside are Aboriginal artefacts (including beautiful shell necklaces), plus sealing, sailing and mutton-bird industry relics.

Mt Tanner LANDMARK
(off Palana Rd, Killiecrankie) Drive to the top of Mt Tanner (331m) to see the island laid out like a treasure map below (just ignore the ugly communications tower).

Unavale Vineyard VINEYARD
(03-6359 3632, 0427 593 631; www.unavale.com.au; 10 Badger Corner Rd, Lady Barron) The island's only vineyard produces a decent sauvignon blanc. Everything is done on-site, right down to the labels. Roll up for a tasting at the cellar door – call first to make sure someone is around.

Activities

There's great **bushwalking** on Flinders. The highlight is a well-signposted track to the peak of **Mt Strzelecki** (756m, five hours return) for awe-inspiring views. At the disarmingly named **Trousers Point** there's a terrific 1.9km coastal circuit walk. Keen for more? Source a copy of *A Walking Guide to Flinders Island and Cape Barren Island* by Doreen Lovegrove and Steve Summers, or *Walks of Flinders Island* by Ken Martin.

It's easy to find your own private beach for **swimming**. A local secret is the **Docks** below Mt Killicrankie, where granite boulders protect white-sand coves. **Trousers Point Beach** is the classic Flinders swimming spot, with picnic tables, BBQs, toilets and unpowered camp sites under the she-oaks; national park entry fees (person/vehicle per day $12/24) apply here.

Fishing possibilities around Flinders abound. BYO gear, or book a charter with **Flinders Island Adventures** (03-6359 4507; www.flindersisland.com.au; 2 days per person $675), which also runs land-based tours. There's also great diving in the clear waters here: talk to **Flinders Island Dive** (0428 598 529, 03-6359 8429; www.flindersislanddive.com.au; 22 Wireless Station Rd, Emita).

The elusive Killiecrankie 'diamond' is actually semiprecious topaz. **Killiecrankie Enterprises** (03-6359 2130; www.killiecrankieenterprises.com.au; 7 Lagoon Rd, Whitemark; 9.30am-4.30pm Mon-Fri, to 12.30pm Sat) hires shovels ($2) and sieves ($2), and can advise where to fossick.

For rocks on a much larger scale, the granite faces of Mt Killiecrankie (319m) offer challenging **rock climbing**. There's also a climbable 200m granite wall on Mt Strzelecki.

Sleeping

The **Department of Parks, Wildlife and Heritage** (03-6359 2217; www.parks.tas.gov.au) operates a handful of free camp sites around the island, mostly with toilets and BBQs. North East River, Lillies Beach and Trousers Point are the best of the bunch (though national park entry fees – 24 hours per vehicle/person $24/12 – apply at Trousers Point).

Interstate Hotel PUB $
(03-6359 2114; www.interstatehotel.com.au; Patrick St, Whitemark; s $60-70, d $90-120) Expect clean, comfortable rooms, the pricier ones with en suites (otherwise it's a short walk down the hall to shared bathrooms), above this old Federation pub. A big cooked breakfast is included. Pub meals kick in later in the day (mains $12 to $30, noon to 1.30pm and 6pm to 7.30pm Monday to Saturday).

Green Valley Homestead RENTAL HOUSE $$
(03-6359 6509; www.flinderislandaccommodation.com.au; Butterfactory Rd, Whitemark; d $150, extra person $25) Two faultlessly pretty properties: the swish Green Valley Homestead close to Whitemark (sleeps six); and Echo Hills Retreat (doubles from $120, extra person

$20, sleeps eight) a short drive east at Lackrana. Set in rural paddocks with views and plentiful peace. Two-night minimum stay.

Lemana   RENTAL HOUSE **$$**
(☑03-6359 6507; www.lemana.com.au; Port Davies Rd, Emita; d $195, extra person $40) A handsome new beach house, sleeping up to six, that's beautifully equipped and only minutes' stroll from Emita Beach. No kids under 12. Breakfast provisions for your first morning included.

Furneaux Tavern   MOTEL **$$**
(☑03-6359 3521; www.furneauxtavern.com.au; 11 Franklin Pde, Lady Barron; s/d/f from $90/120/150; ☎) Timber-panelled motel cabins with wraparound decks, set in native gardens. The fish-focussed Shearwater Restaurant is here, too, and you can bend an elbow over the pool table in the bar.

Lady Barron Holiday Home   RENTAL HOUSE **$$**
(☑03-6359 3555; www.ladybarron.com; 31 Franklin Pde, Lady Barron; d $130, extra person $25) A homely, renovated 1940s place with three bedrooms (sleeping up to six). Good for families. Have a look in the veggie garden and see what's sprouting.

Flinders Island Cabin Park   CABIN **$$**
(☑03-6359 2188; www.flindersislandcp. au; 1 Bluff Rd, Flinders Island Airport; s/d/f $90/100/145) Near the airport are these busily managed and recently renovated cabins, plus car and campervan hire. Mountain bikes, kayaks and fishing gear also available. Ask about car-and-cabin package deals.

✖ Eating

Deep Bite Cafe   CAFE **$**
(☑03-6359 8499; www.deepbitecafe.com.au; 527 Killiecrankie Rd, Killiecrankie; mains $9-25; ⊘9am-9pm late Dec-Apr; ☎) Close to the beach at Killiecrankie, this summer-only pavilion is a cafe by day and restaurant by night. The views from the deck are beaut and the seafood is super. Ring to confirm opening hours before you make the trip. There's a general store here, too.

Flinders Island Bakery   BAKERY **$**
(☑03-6359 2105; 4 Lagoon Rd, Whitemark; items $4-8; ⊘7am-4pm Mon-Fri) Divine wallaby and red-wine pie (or chicken and corn, if you're not into eating the natives). Good coffee, sandwiches and sausage rolls, too. Open weekends in summer.

Shearwater Restaurant   PUB FOOD **$$**
(☑03-6359 3521; www.furneauxtavern.com.au; Furneaux Tavern, 11 Franklin Pde, Lady Barron; mains $16-33; ⊘noon-1.30pm & 6-7.30pm) Excellent pub bistro food, with an unsurprising and entirely pleasing seafood bent. Don't be late.

❶ Information

The island has no ATMs, but there's a Westpac bank agency in Whitemark and most businesses have Eftpos facilities for cash withdrawals.

Flinders Island Visitor Information Centre (☑03-6359 5002; www.visitflindersisland. com.au; 4 Davies St, Whitemark; ⊘9am-5pm Mon-Fri) The main hub for island advice.

Online Access Centre (☑03-6359 2151; www.linc.tas.gov.au; 2 Davies St, Whitemark; ⊘5-7pm Tue, 10am-1pm & 1.30-5pm Wed-Fri) Internet access at Flinders Island Library.

Post Office (☑03-6359 2020; 7 Patrick St, Whitemark; ⊘9am-5pm Mon-Fri) The island's main post office; there's another at Lady Barron.

Service Tasmania (☑1300 135 513; www. servicetasmania.tas.gov.au; 2 Lagoon Rd, Whitemark; ⊘11am-3pm Mon-Wed, noon-4pm Thu & Fri) Walking track advice and national park passes.

❶ Getting There & Away

Flinders Island Travel (☑1800 674 719; www. flindersislandtravel.com.au) Offers package deals (flights, accommodation and car rental).

Furneaux Freight (☑03-6356 1753; www.furneauxfreight.com.au; Main St, Bridport; adult/child/car return $140/90/550) Operates a Bridport–Lady Barron car ferry. The trip takes eight hours. Bookings essential.

Sharp Airlines (☑1300 556 694; www. sharpairlines.com) Flies between Melbourne (Essendon Airport) and Flinders Island Airport at Whitemark (one-way $245), and between Launceston and Flinders Island (one-way $181).

❶ Getting Around

Many island roads are unsealed – take care when driving. Don't drive after dusk unless you really have to: the native wildlife has suicidal tendencies.

Flinders Island Car Hire (☑03-6359 2168; www.ficr.com.au; 21 Memana Rd, Whitemark) has vehicles from $75 per day. Flinders Island Cabin Park rents out budget cars from $40 per day and campervans from $120 per day (three-day minimum). Both operators can meet you at the airport.

Flinders Island Airport Shuttle (☑0415 505 655, 03-6359 2168; www.visitflindersisland. com.au/getting-around) does precisely what its name suggests, with prices per person from $10.

Launceston & Around

Best Places to Eat

➡ Stillwater (p182)

➡ Blue Café Bar (p182)

➡ Sweetbrew (p181)

➡ River Cafe (p190)

➡ Home of the Artisan (p197)

Best Places to Stay

➡ Two Four Two (p181)

➡ Fresh on Charles (p180)

➡ Red Feather Inn (p194)

➡ Wesleyan Chapel (p198)

➡ Trig (p193)

Why Go?

It's hard to imagine a pocket-sized city more appealing than Launceston. 'Lonnie', as the locals call it, is certainly large enough for some urban buzz, but little enough for country congeniality. The city effortlessly melds the historic with the contemporary, bolstered by bright arts and food scenes. Surrounded by bush, amazing Cataract Gorge brings the wilds into the heart of town.

Launceston is cradled by rolling hills, with craggy peaks on the horizon. Just outside the city, the gently beautiful Tamar Valley unfolds – a broad estuary channelling the sea breeze. The vine-covered hillsides and fertile soils here nurture famous wines and produce. Where the river meets the sea you'll find penguins, lighthouses and Tasmania's earliest European settlement.

The historic towns to the the south and west of the city offer stately homes, heritage streetscapes and buckets of small-town charm.

When to Go

➡ In summer (December to February) Launceston gets giddy with flowering parks, festivals and long, still evenings by the river.

➡ March is vintage time in the Tamar Valley: the vineyards hum with pickers and pruners, then turn golden brown for autumn.

➡ Launceston winters (June to August) are still, sunny and crisp: the frosted peaks nearby are ripe for snowman construction and maybe even some skiing.

➡ October delivers a return to budding green, and Cataract Gorge pumps with white water and crazed kayakers.

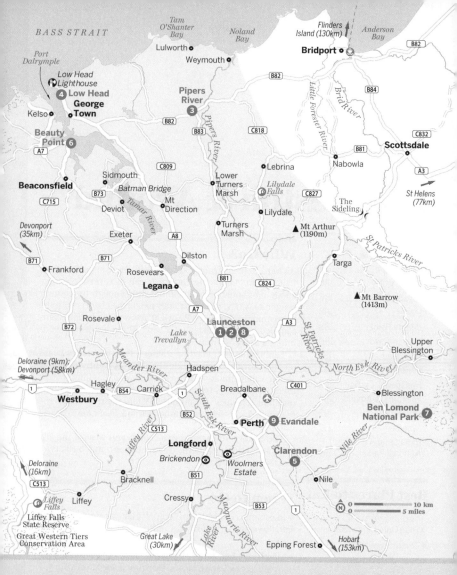

Launceston & Around Highlights

① Walk, swim, eat or just chill out at Launceston's **Cataract Gorge** (p173).

② Check out Launceston from the water with **Tamar River Cruises** (p177).

③ Wobble between cellar doors in the **Pipers River Wine Region** (p192).

④ Watch the penguins come home from sea at dusk with **Low Head Penguin Tours** (p191).

⑤ Pretend you're in *Gone with the Wind* at Tasmania's grandest colonial home, **Clarendon** (p197).

⑥ Befriend the critters at Beauty Point's **Seahorse World** (p188).

⑦ Swoop down the ski slopes at lofty **Ben Lomond National Park** (p199).

⑧ Catch a live band and quaff a few pints at Launceston's **Royal Oak Hotel** (p184).

⑨ Holler at the speeding cyclists in Evandale's **National Penny Farthing Championships** (p198).

LAUNCESTON

POP 106.200

Tasmania's second city has forever been locked in rivalry with big-smoke Hobart to the south. Launcestonians argue their architecture is more elegant, their parks more beautiful, their surrounding hills more verdant – and even their food scene just downright zestier. And on many of these points it's hard to argue.

It might have something to do with the recent rebuilding of the city's museums, and with an influx of students and creative types to the University of Tasmania. Art and design are big here, and there's a new respect for the city's fabulous cache of heritage buildings.

Or perhaps it's the recent success of its food and wine scene that's transformed the city. Launceston punches well above its weight in epicurean excellence, and the ambrosial wines of the Tamar Valley garner international respect.

Launceston has also become a sporty, outdoorsy city of late. Get up early and you'll see squads of Lycra-clad cyclists, rowers on the river, swimmers funnelling into Tasmania's best pool and joggers traversing the city's crown jewel – gorgeous Cataract Gorge.

History

George Bass and Matthew Flinders were the first Europeans to spy Launceston's Tamar River when they sailed in here on their 1798 voyage of discovery. The area's first white settlement was established in 1804, when the British, intent on beating the French in claiming the island, built a military post at George Town. Not long after, an expedition scouted south and found the present-day site of Launceston, naming it for the English town in Cornwall – although the Tasmanian version came to be pronounced 'Lon-sess-ton', rather than the traditional 'Lawnston'.

Early Launceston was both a port and a military headquarters. By 1827 it already had a population of 2000, and was shipping wool and wheat from the surrounding districts. By the 1850s the town was Tasmania's second major centre and was proclaimed a municipality. In 1871 tin was discovered at Mt Bischoff, which further cemented Launceston's fortunes as a trading hub. A decade later it opened its own stock exchange. In the 20th century the city was an important service town for the rich agricultural region that surrounds it, and more recently a university town.

⊙ Sights

★ **Cataract Gorge** PARK
(Map p174; ☑ 03-6331 5915; www.launcestoncataractgorge.com.au; via Cataract Walk, Trevallyn; chairlift one way adult/child $12/8, return $15/10; ☺ 24hr) A 10-minute wander west of the city centre is magnificent Cataract Gorge. The bushland, cliffs and ice-cold South Esk River here feel a million miles from town. At First Basin there's a free outdoor **swimming pool** (November to March), the world's longest single-span **chairlift** (9am to 5.30pm), summer concerts, huge European trees and sociable peacocks. Eating options include a cafe, kiosk and the sassy Gorge Restaurant (p182). The whole shebang is impressively floodlit at night.

Two walking tracks straddle the gorgeous gorge (Cataract Walk is level; the Zig Zag Track is steep), leading from Kings Bridge up to First Basin. You can also drive to the First Basin car park – follow the signs from York St to Hillside Cres, Brougham St and Basin Rd.

Just upstream from First Basin is the **Alexandra Suspension Bridge**. Another walking track (45 minutes one way) leads further up the gorge to Second Basin and further still to **Duck Reach**, the earliest municipal hydroelectric power station in Australia (1895).

★ **Queen Victoria**
Museum & Art Gallery MUSEUM, GALLERY
(QVMAG; Map p178; ☑ 03-6323 3777; www.qvmag.tas.gov.au; 2 Wellington St; ☺ 10am-4pm) **FREE** Launceston's brilliant QVMAG spreads itself over two locations: the meticulously restored **art gallery** (colonial painting and decorative arts) on the edge of Royal Park; and the natural, social and technology-focused collections at the **museum** at the **Inveresk Railyards** (Map p178; 2 Invermay Rd, Invermay; ☺ 10am-4pm, planetarium shows noon & 2pm Tue-Fri, 2pm & 3pm Sat) **FREE**. The buildings themselves are half the attraction, particularly the Inveresk site, which was Launceston's rail hub until not so long ago. Learn about black holes at the **planetarium** (adult/child/family $6/4/16), or fill a stomach hole at the **cafe**.

Boag's Brewery BREWERY
(Map p178; ☑ 03-6332 6300; www.boags.com.au; 39 William St; tours adult/child $30/15; ☺ tours 11am, 1pm & 3pm) James Boag's beer has been brewed on William St since 1881. See the amber alchemy in action on 90-minute

Launceston

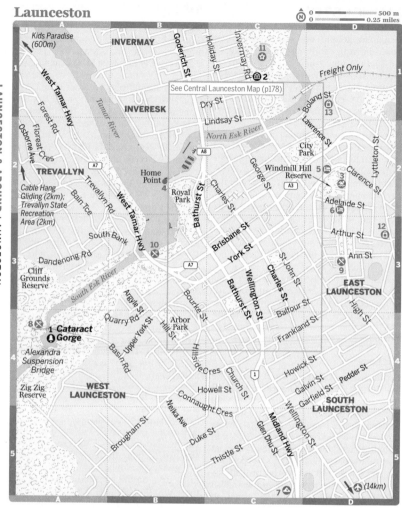

See Central Launceston Map (p178)

tours with tastings afterwards. The free on-site museum sheds further light on brewing history (old TV ads, beer labels and photographs aplenty). Tour bookings essential. Extra tours December to March.

City Park PARK
(Map p178; www.launceston.tas.gov.au; cnr Tamar & Cimtiere Sts; ☉ daylight hours) Expansive City Park has enormous oak and plane trees, an elegant fountain, a glass conservatory, a Victorian bandstand and a playground and mini-train for kids. Peer into your gene pool at the glass-walled **Japanese macaque**

enclosure (8am to 4pm April to September, to 4.30pm October to March), a gift from Japanese sister-city Ikeda.

Design Centre Tasmania GALLERY
(Map p178; ☑ 03-6331 5506; www.designtasmania. com.au; cnr Brisbane & Tamar Sts; ☉ 9.30am-5.30pm Mon-Fri, 10am-4pm Sat & Sun) FREE On the fringe of City Park, this heritage church hall houses a shop/gallery selling beautiful handmade Tasmanian crafts. Next door is the excellent **Design Tasmania Wood Collection** (entry by donation), showcasing local timber furniture design – more sassafras,

Launceston

Huon pine and myrtle than you can poke a stick at. Reduced winter hours.

National Automobile
Museum of Tasmania   MUSEUM
(Map p178; ☑03-6334 8888; www.namt.com.au; 86 Cimitiere St; adult/child/family $13/7/32.50; ☺9am-5pm Sep-May, 10am-4pm Jun-Aug) Revheads get all revved up over the displays here – one of Australia's slickest presentations of classic and historic cars and motorbikes, all privately owned. The saucy 1969 Corvette Stingray will burn tyre tracks into your retinas.

Tramway Museum   MUSEUM
(Map p174; ☑03-6334 8334; www.ltms.org.au; 2 Invermay Rd, Invermay; adult/child $5/2; ☺10am-4pm Wed & Fri-Sun) Launceston had trams until 1952, when the rails were ripped up and the carriages sold off. Now you can trundle in the lustrously restored No 29, on a little track that runs out past Aurora Stadium. The stories of what happened to all the old carriages are nerdishly fascinating.

Princes Square   PARK
(Map p178; www.launceston.tas.gov.au; btwn Charles & St John Sts) All shady oaks, cooing pigeons and snoozing students, Princes Sq

once hosted military drills, public hangings and rowdy political meetings. The bronze fountain here was purchased at the 1855 Paris Exhibition. There's also a statue of the top-hatted Dr William Russ Pugh, the first surgeon in the southern hemisphere to use general anaesthetic.

Old Umbrella Shop   HISTORIC BUILDING
(Map p178; ☑03-6331 9248; www.nationaltrust. org.au; 60 George St; ☺9am-5pm Mon-Fri, to noon Sat) **FREE** Launcestonians once kept dry under the umbrellas made here by R Shott & Sons. Now the shop stands as a rare example of an intact early-20th-century store, complete with its original till and blackwood display cases.

Tasmania Zoo   ZOO
(☑03-6396 6100; www.tasmaniazoo.com.au; 1166 Ecclestone Rd, Riverside; adult/child $25/12; ☺8am-4.30pm) There are more than 80 species of feathered, furred and finned critters – native and non native – at this laid-back wildlife park. This is your chance to see some Tasmanian devils, which you can watch snarling over meaty meals at 10.30am, 1pm and 3pm. To get here, take the West Tamar Hwy (A7) out of Launceston and turn onto Ecclestone Rd (C734) just north of Riverside (about a 15km drive).

Franklin House   HISTORIC BUILDING
(☑03-6344 7824; www.nationaltrust.org.au/tas/ franklinhouse; 413 Hobart Rd, Youngtown; adult/ child $10/free; ☺9am-5pm Mon-Sat, noon-4pm Sun) Just south of the city, Franklin House is one of Launceston's most fetching Georgian homes. Built in 1838 by reformed convict and savvy businessman Britton Jones, it's now fully restored, furnished and managed by the National Trust. Reduced winter hours.

Trevallyn State Recreation Area   PARK
(☑03-6336 5391; www.parks.tas.gov.au; Reatta Rd, Trevallyn; ☺8am-dusk) **FREE** Artificial Lake Trevallyn, on the South Esk River (Tasmania's longest river) above Cataract Gorge, is a favourite spot with the locals. Take a picnic and have a splash in the shallows on a warm day. There are also walking trails, a bike track, archery and equestrian clubs and Cable Hang Gliding (p176) on offer.

To get here, follow Paterson St west (after crossing Kings Bridge it becomes Trevallyn Rd and then Gorge Rd), turn right into Bald Hill Rd, left into Veulalee Ave and veer left into Reatta Rd to the reserve.

TOP FIVE LAUNCESTON BUILDINGS

Launceston has an amazingly well-preserved collation of heritage architecture, across all eras and styles. It probably has something to do with the state's notoriously slow economy – there's just never been enough cash around to knock things down and build something worse! Take a wander around suburban Trevallyn and Windmill Hill to sticky-beak at some beautifully crafted private homes, and keep your eyes open in the city for these notable public edifices.

Launceston City Council (Map p178; ☑03-6323 3000; www.launceston.tas.gov.au; Town Hall, 18-28 St John St; ⊙8.30am-5pm Mon-Fri) publishes a map called *Launceston Heritage Walks*, which takes in these landmarks and more. Pick one up from the Town Hall or download it from the website.

Albert Hall (Map p178; ☑03-6331 4616; www.launceston.tas.gov.au; 45 Tamar St; ⊙by arrangement) An underutilised, steep-roofed Launceston landmark (now a convention venue), built in 1891 in classical Victorian style. Inside the Great Hall is the Brindley Organ, Australia's largest pre-1860 organ.

Town Hall (Map p178; ☑03-6323 3000; www.launceston.tas.gov.au; 18-28 St John St; ⊙8.30am-5pm Mon-Fri) Erected in 1864 with soaring neoclassical columns. 'Progress with Prudence' says the coat of arms – duck inside to the council offices and see how they're going with that.

Custom House (Map p178; ☑03-6332 3600; www.customs.gov.au; 89 Esplanade) Has a magnificent 1885 neoclassical facade reflecting Launceston's 19th-century prosperity. Currently offices are not open to the public...wouldn't it make a brilliant boutique hotel?

Holyman House (Map p178; cnr Brisbane & George Sts) Built in 1936, and a fine example of interwar art deco. Four levels of deco detailing surround sundry offices. The future-thinking Holyman transport empire has long since left the building.

Henty House (Map p178; ☑1300 13 55 131; www.service.tas.gov.au; 1 Civic Sq; ⊙8.30am-4.30pm Mon-Fri) Tasmania's finest example of raw concrete brutalist architecture, built in 1983. It's big, it's ballsy, it's beautifully ugly.

🏃 Activities

Mountain Bike Tasmania MOUNTAIN BIKING (☑0447 712 638; www.mountainbiketasmania.com.au) Runs guided rides along the North Esk River ($100), through the Trevallyn State Recreation Area ($120) and down the slopes of Ben Lomond ($225) – a downhill rush shedding 1050m in altitude as fast as you can say 'Marzocchi shocks'.

Tasmanian Expeditions ROCK CLIMBING (☑1300 666 856, 03-6331 9000; www.tasmanianexpeditions.com.au) Rock-climbing adventures on the dolerite cliffs of Cataract Gorge. It offers half-day ($250 per person, $150 per person for two or more climbers) and full-day ($400 per person, $225 for two or more) climbs. No experience necessary for half-day trips (but you'll need it for a full day). All gear included.

Launceston Aquatic SWIMMING (Map p174; ☑03-6323 3636; www.launceston-aquatic.com.au; 18a High St; adult/child/family $7/5/18.50; ⊙6am-8pm Mon-Fri, 8am-6pm Sat & Sun) Follow the sniff of chlorine up steep Windmill Hill, with its lush lawns and roof-top views, to Launceston's aquatic centre. There are several pools inside and out, slides, a fitness centre, a watery playground for kids and a rather salubrious cafe.

Cable Hang Gliding ADVENTURE SPORTS (☑0419 311 198; www.cablehanggliding.com.au; Reatta Rd, Trevallyn State Recreation Area, Trevallyn; adult/child/tandems $20/15/30; ⊙10am-5pm daily Dec-Apr, Sat & Sun during May-Nov school holidays) Make like a condor with a spot of cable hang-gliding in the Trevallyn State Recreation Area. You'll hurtle over the edge of a cliff and glide down a 200m-long cable, suspended under wide wings. Stomach-in-your-mouth stuff. Head west along Paterson St and from King's Bridge follow the signs.

Kids Paradise PLAYGROUND (☑03-6334 0055; www.kidsparadise.net.au; 1 Waterfront Dr, Riverside; adult/child $12/9; ⊙9am-4pm Tue-Thu & Sun, to 8.30pm Fri & Sat; 🚼) On rainy days this is the place to let the bairns loose. There are three floors for inducing rapturous exhaustion, with a pirate playground, interactive rooms and giant inflatables for bouncing all over, plus an array of Wiis, Xboxes and Playstations for little-screen tragics. Open daily during school holidays.

👉 Tours

Tamar River Cruises   BOAT TOUR
(Map p174; ☑03-6334 9900; www.tamarriver-cruises.com.au; Home Point Pde) To check out Launceston from the water, hop aboard the 1890s-style *Lady Launceston* for a 50-minute exploration of Cataract Gorge and the riverfront (adult/child/family $29/12/70). Longer morning and after-noon cruises (2½ hours, adult/child/family $79/35/179) on the *Tamar Odyssey* take you downstream to Rosevears and back.

Launceston Historic Walks   WALKING TOUR
(Map p178; ☑03-6331 2213; www.1842.com.au/launceston-historic-walks; per person $15; ☺4pm Mon, 10am Tue-Sat) Get your historical bearings with a 1½-hour walking journey through the Georgian, Victorian and mod-ern architecture of the city. Walks depart from the '1842' building, on the corner of St John and Cimitiere Sts.

Valleybrook Wine Tours   WINERY
(☑0400 037 250, 03-6334 0586; www.valleybrook.com.au; half-/full-day tours from $100/150) Full-day vino tours visiting six Tamar Valley cel-lar doors. Morning/afternoon tours visiting four wineries also available. Pick-up/drop-off at your accommodation.

Tasmanian Safaris   ADVENTURE TOUR
(www.tasafari.com.au; 3/5-day tours from $650/1295) Offers multi-day, all-inclusive, eco-certified 4WD tours ex-Launceston, heading to Hobart via the east coast. There's bushwalking, bush camping and lots of wil-derness. Canoe trips also available.

Walks on the Wildside   WILDLIFE WATCHING
(☑03-6331 0916; www.walksonthewildside.com.au; per person $75; ☺5.30pm Mon, Wed & Fri) Small-group evening wildlife spotting trips to Narawntapu National Park, near the mouth of the Tamar River (about an hour away). Cradle Mountain and Bay of Fires trips also available.

Launceston City Ghost Tours   WALKING TOUR
(Map p178; ☑0421 819 373; www.launcestoncityghosttours.com; adult/child/family $25/15/55; ☺dusk) Just after sunset, get spooked on a 90-minute wander around the city's

back alleys. Tours depart at dusk from the **Royal Oak Hotel** (☑6331 5346; 14 Brisbane St) – where Cyril is the resident ghost. Book-ings essential, and departure time varies throughout the year. Not for little kids.

Launceston City Explorer   BUS TOUR
(☑03-6326 1555; tours adult/child $65/33) Run by Rexy's Tours, these three-hour city-highlight bus jaunts give good bang for your buck (though they're a tad mainstream).

✪ Festivals & Events

Festivale   FOOD, ART
(www.festivale.com.au; ☺Feb) Three festive days in City Park, with eating, drinking, arts and live bands (usually of the washed-up-but-still-touring variety). Tasmanian food and wine get an appropriate airing.

Launceston Cup   SPORTS
(www.tsrc.com.au; ☺Feb) The pinnacle event of the Tasmanian Summer Racing Carni-val. Much champagne, hat wearing and well-presented fillies.

Junction Arts Festival   ART
(www.junctionartsfestival.com.au; ☺Sep) Five days of offbeat and interesting arts perfor-mances, installations, gigs and nocturnal brouhahas.

Royal Launceston Show   FAIR
(www.launcestonshowground.com.au; ☺Oct) Think fairy floss, bumper cars, pedigree bulls and carnies in need of cosmetic dentistry.

Tasmanian Breath of Fresh Air Film Festival   FILM
(BOFA; www.bofa.com.au; ☺Nov) At Inveresk Park screens flicker with the art house, the independent, the innovative – films to in-spire thought and change. What a BOFA!

🛏 Sleeping

Arthouse Backpacker Hostel   HOSTEL $
(Map p178; ☑03-6333 0222, 1800 041 135; www.arthousehostel.com.au; 20 Lindsay St, Invermay; dm $23-27, s/d $57/67; @🛜) 🚲 In the old Espla-nade Hotel (1881), Arthouse is our favourite Launceston hostel: airy dorms (love the attic rooms); a welcoming sitting room with huge TV, a handsome upstairs balcony (and bell tower) for shooting the breeze, and a BBQ courtyard out the back. It's also Australia's first carbon-neutral backpackers (recycling, tree planting and worm farms ahoy!). Bike and camping-gear hire available.

Central Launceston

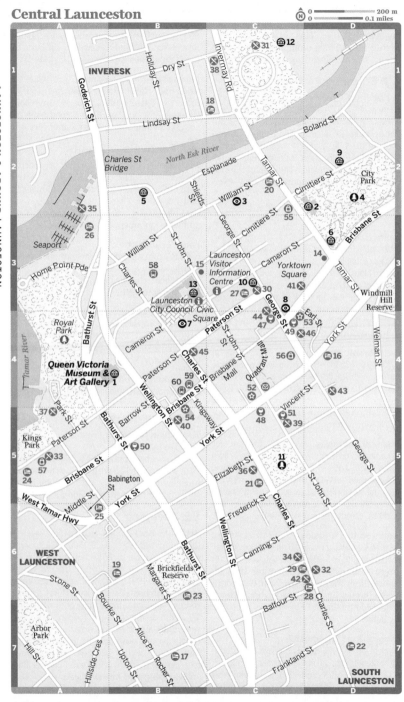

0   200 m
0   0.1 miles

INVERESK

Dry St
Holiday St
Goderich St
Lindsay St
Invermay Rd

31
38
12
18

North Esk River
Charles St Bridge
Esplanade
Shields St
William St
Tamar St
Boland St

35
26
Seaport

5
20
3

9
Cimitiere St
City Park
2
4
55
6
Brisbane St

Home Point Pde
William St
St John St
George St
Cimitiere St
Cameron St

58
15
Launceston Visitor Information Centre
13
Launceston City Council
Yorktown Square
14

Royal Park
Charles St
10
27
30
41
8

7
Civic Square
Paterson St
44
47
49
53
46
Earl St
York St

Windmill Hill Reserve
Weiman St

Queen Victoria Museum & Art Gallery 1

Tamar River
Bathurst St
Cameron St
Paterson St
Charles St
45
Brisbane St
Quadrant Mall
56
16

60
59
52
43
Vincent St

37
Park St
Barrow St
Wellington St
54
40
Kingsway
48
51
39

Kings Park
33
57
24
Paterson St
Bathurst St
50
York St

Babington St
Middle St
West Tamar Hwy
25
York St

Elizabeth St
36
21
11
St John St
George St

WEST LAUNCESTON
19
Stone St
Margaret St
Bathurst St
Brickfields Reserve
23
Canning St
Wellington St
Charles St
34
29
32
42
28
Balfour St

Arbor Park
Hill St
Hillside Cres
Upton St
Bourke St
Alice Pl
Rocher St
17
Frankland St
22

SOUTH LAUNCESTON

Central Launceston

◎ Top Sights
1 Queen Victoria Museum & Art
 Gallery B4

◎ Sights
2 Albert Hall D2
3 Boag's Brewery C2
4 City Park D2
5 Custom House B2
6 Design Centre Tasmania D3
7 Henty House B4
8 Holyman House C3
9 National Automobile Museum of
 Tasmania D2
10 Old Umbrella Shop C3
11 Princes Square C5
12 Queen Victoria Museum C1
13 Town Hall B3

◎ Activities, Courses & Tours
14 Launceston City Ghost Tours D3
15 Launceston Historic Walks B3

◎ Sleeping
16 41 on York D4
17 Alice's Cottages & Spa Hideaways B7
18 Arthouse Backpacker Hostel C1
19 Auldington B6
20 Clarion Hotel City Park Grand C2
21 Fresh on Charles C5
22 Hotel Charles D7
23 Launceston Backpackers B6
24 Leisure Inn Penny Royal Hotel &
 Apartments A5
25 Old Bakery Inn A6
26 Peppers Seaport Hotel A3
27 Quest Launceston Serviced
 Apartments C3
28 Sportsmans Hall Hotel D6
29 Two Four Two C6

◎ Eating
30 Black Cow Bistro C3
31 Blue Café Bar C1
32 Burger Got Soul D6

33 Cataract on Patterson A5
34 Elaia C6
35 Fish 'n' Chips A2
 Fresh on Charles .... (see 21)
36 Garden of Vegan C5
37 Hallam's Waterfront A5
38 Me Wah C1
39 Milkbar C5
40 Monty's Food Hall B5
 Mud .... (see 26)
41 Novaro's C3
42 Pasta Merchant D6
43 Pickled Evenings D4
44 Pierre's C3
 Sportsmans Hall Hotel .... (see 28)
45 Star of Siam B4
46 Sweetbrew C4

◎ Drinking & Nightlife
47 Alchemy Bar & Restaurant C4
48 Bakers Lane C5
49 Dickens Ciderhouse C4
50 Irish B5
 Royal Oak Hotel .... (see 14)
51 Saint John C5

◎ Entertainment
52 Hotel New York C4
53 Princess Theatre C4
54 Village Cinemas B5

◎ Shopping
55 Harvest C2
56 Paddy Pallin C4
57 Pinot Shop A5

◎ Transport
 Calow's Coaches .... (see 58)
58 Cornwall Square Transit Centre B3
59 Lee's Coaches B4
60 Manions' Coaches B4
 Redline Coaches .... (see 58)
 Sainty's North East Bus
 Service .... (see 58)
 Tassielink .... (see 58)

Sportsmans Hall Hotel PUB **$**
(Map p178; ☑03-6331 3968; www.sportieshotel.
com.au; cnr Charles & Balfour Sts; s $55, d with/
without bathroom $80/70; [P][🖳]) On hip Charles
St, 'Sportiés' is a bit of a local institution. It's
been done up recently and the rooms are
pretty good: three have bathrooms and others have their own private bathrooms down
the hallway. Ask for a room away from the
bar on a Friday or Saturday night (live bands).

Launceston Backpackers HOSTEL **$**
(Map p178; ☑03-6334 2327; www.launceston-
backpackers.com.au; 103 Canning St; dm/s/tw/tr

$24/52/56/75, d with/without bathroom $67/58;
[P][🖳]) This large Federation house has been
gutted to make way for a cavernous backpackers. It's in a leafy spot looking over
Brickfields Reserve, but it's not the most inspiring hostel in which you'll ever stay. Still,
there are hardly any hostels in Launceston
these days, so take what you can get. Rooms
are clean and bright.

Treasure Island Caravan Park CARAVAN PARK **$**
(Map p174; ☑03-6344 2600; www.treasureisland-
tasmania.com.au; 94 Glen Dhu St, South Launceston; unpowered/powered sites $27/32, on-site

LAUNCESTON & AROUND FOR CHILDREN

City Park (p174) Squeal at/with the Japanese macaques.

Cataract Gorge (p173) Float through the air on the chairlift.

Kids Paradise (p176) Burn off excess carbs with some creative play.

Seahorse World (p188) Check out the weird and wonderful critters.

Beaconsfield Mine & Heritage Centre (p189) Dig up a golden past.

caravans $60, cabins $90-100; P) The closest camping to the city centre – about 2.5km to the south – but it's right on the highway and pretty noisy. OK as a last resort. The business was rebranding when we visited, so it might be called something else when you arrive.

★**Fresh on Charles**   APARTMENT **$$**
(Map p178; ☑ 03-6331 4299; www.freshoncharles. com.au; 178 Charles St; d $120-150; 🛜) Take the stairs up from Fresh on Charles (p182) to these two excellent self-contained apartments with polished concrete floors. They're retro, minimal, brilliantly central and great value for money. The pricier unit faces off with the boughs of Princes Sq across the road. Free street parking out the front after dark.

Hi George   B&B **$$**
(Map p174; ☑ 03-6331 2144; www.higeorge.com.au; 64 York St; d incl breakfast from $130; P 🛜) Somewhat confusingly, Hi George isn't on George St. You'll have to wander up York St if you want to say hello. And if you do, you'll find six simple, tasteful en-suite rooms in an appealing 1880 brick house, with no fiddly bits to collect dust. Cooked breakfast included.

Quest Launceston Serviced Apartments   APARTMENT **$$**
(Map p178; ☑ 03-6333 3555; www.questlaunceston. com.au; 16 Paterson St; d from $159, 2-bedroom apt from $249; P 🌢 @ 🛜) Occupying the beautifully restored Murray Building in the heart of town, these 43 apartments are everything you could want in an upmarket home away from home: spacious, comfortable, fully self-contained and decorated with pizzazz.

Auldington   BOUTIQUE HOTEL **$$**
(Map p178; ☑ 03-6331 2050; www.auldington.com. au; 110 Frederick St; d from $129, 2-bedroom apt

from $252; P 🛜) This small boutique hotel has a historic exterior – all earnest brown brick with lacy wrought-iron balconies – that belies the funky internal fit-out. Right in the middle of town yet convent-quiet, it has great city views and the kind of amiable service you just don't get in the larger hotels.

Kurrajong House   B&B **$$**
(Map p174; ☑ 03-6331 6655; www.kurrajonghouse. com.au; cnr High & Adelaide Sts; d/cottage from $155/175; P 🛜) Angling for a mature clientele (over 21s only), this quiet 1887 B&B has a just-like-home-but-much-smarter vibe. Outside are blooming roses and a self-contained cottage set up for longer stays. The mile-a-minute Scottish host serves impressive cooked breakfasts in the bright conservatory.

Alice's Cottages & Spa Hideaways   COTTAGE **$$**
(Map p178; ☑ 03-6334 2231; www.alicescottages. com.au; 121-129 Balfour St; d $170-230; P 🌢 🛜) Alice bills itself as the place for 'wickedly wonderful romantic retreats'. Why not? There's a row of four self-contained 1850s workers' cottages out the back (aka 'The Shambles'), and two sumptuous B&B units out the front. Charm to burn in a quiet, city-fringe location.

Clarion Hotel City Park Grand   HOTEL **$$**
(Map p178; ☑ 03-6331 7633; www.cityparkgrand. com.au; 22 Tamar St; d from $165, 1/2-bedroom apt from $185/230; P 🌢 🛜) This old stager is having an identity crisis: it's just got too many names (is it the City Park Grand Clarion Hotel? No? Maybe the Clarion City Park Hotel Grand?). It remains a good central option regardless, spread over two lovely old city buildings. Big with the corporate sector and full as a boot when the AFL football is on.

Old Bakery Inn   HOTEL **$$**
(Map p178; ☑ 03-6331 7900; www.oldbakeryinn. com.au; cnr York & Margaret Sts; d $90-140, f $145-165; P 🌢) You can almost smell the bread in the ovens that are still a feature of this 135-year-old inn. The 24 rooms are all different – some have fireplaces, some have four-poster beds, some have amazing old ceiling roses – but they're all shipshape (if a little twee). Close to the city, the waterfront and Cataract Gorge.

Leisure Inn Penny Royal Hotel & Apartments   HOTEL **$$**
(Map p178; ☑ 03-6335 6600; www.leisureinn-pennyroyal.com.au; 147 Paterson St; d/tr from $135/181, 2-bedroom apt from $191; P 🛜) The

oldest part of this hotel complex was originally a coaching inn in Tasmania's Midlands, and was moved here brick by painstaking brick. Rooms come in sundry configurations, the ones with most character retaining their original chunky wooden beams.

★ **Two Four Two** APARTMENT $$$
(Map p178; ☑ 03-6331 9242; www.twofourtwo. com.au; 242 Charles St; d incl breakfast from $250; ☎) Now *this* is a cool renovation! Furniture maker Alan has channelled his craft into four self-contained town houses, each with blackwood, myrtle or Tasmanian-oak detailing. Stainless-steel kitchens, coffee machines, private courtyards and spa baths complete the experience.

Hotel Charles HOTEL $$$
(Map p178; ☑ 03-6337 4100; www.hotelcharles. com.au; 287 Charles St; d from $220; P❋@☎) Launceston's hippest hotel was once a dreary hospital. The entrance ramps and sliding doors still feel like you should be arriving in an ambulance, but inside the Charles is all light and bright, with snappy decor, intelligent service and a stylish restaurant. Cheaper rooms are a squeeze; pay a bit more for a studio. All rooms have kitchenettes.

41 on York APARTMENT $$$
(Map p178; ☑ 0419 113 371; www.41onyork. com.au; 5/41 York St; 1/2/3-bedroom apt from $290/320/380; P❋☎) Craving a bit of private luxury? This swanky downtowner fits the bill. It's a flexible set up, with three bedrooms, three bathrooms, a gorgeous Huonpine kitchen stocked with Tasmanian wines and provisions, and a BBQ deck.

Peppers Seaport Hotel HOTEL $$$
(Map p178; ☑ 03-6345 3333; www.peppers. com.au/seaport; 28 Seaport Blvd; d $200-400, 2-bedroom apt $280-550; P❋☎) Right on the waterfront in the Seaport development, this glam hotel wins points for natural timbers, classy bathrooms, muted tones and good linen to sleep in/on. River-view rooms will cost you a bit more. Big with business bods.

✖ Eating

★ **Sweetbrew** CAFE $
(Map p178; ☑ 03-6333 0443; 93a George St; mains $4-10; ⊗ 7am-5pm Mon-Fri, 8am-3pm Sat, 9am-2pm Sun) 'Melbourne is just a suburb of Launceston,' says the barista at this new cafe. If his coffee is anything to go by, he's not wrong because the sweet brew here is definitely Melbourne-worthy, as are the pastries, ba-

guettes, quiches and classy tarts on the counter. Dig the little booth room out the back!

Le Café CAFE $
(Map p174; ☑ 03-6334 8887; 39 Ann St, East Launceston; mains $8-16; ⊗ 8.30am-5pm Mon-Fri, to 4pm Sat) Crowded with conversations, this Frenchy little number faces onto St Georges Sq on top of the hill in East Launceston. Beyond the beautiful old shopfront (stained glass, art-deco tiles) you'll find fresh juices, cakes, tarts, chicken-and-pumpkin pie, happy staff and kickin' coffee. *Trés bon.*

Pasta Merchant ITALIAN $
(Map p178; ☑ 03-6334 7077; 248b Charles St; mains $9-15; ⊗ 8.30am-9pm Mon-Fri, 9am-9pm Sat) Look forward to wonderful fresh pasta with authentic sauces, all made on-site at this little Charles St nook. Try the unbeatable spinach-and-ricotta ravioli with pesto. It also serves panini, pizza and improbably good gelati. Takeaway pasta and sauces, too.

Fish 'n' Chips FISH & CHIPS $
(Map p178; ☑ 03-6331 1999; 30 Seaport Blvd; mains $7-17; ⊗ 11am-midnight; ⊛) The late-afternoon sun on the upmarket riverfront deck here makes for a memorable meal. Seafood cooked fresh to order, plus salads, antipasto platters and wines by the glass. Kid friendly, too.

Milkbar CAFE $
(Map p178; ☑ 0457 762 378; www.themilkbarcafe. com.au; 139 St John St; mains $8-12; ⊗ 8am-4.30pm Mon-Fri; ☎) ✐ Sixties retro cool and 21st-century hipster chic collide at Milkbar, which serves excellent coffee, huge milkshakes (the chai-flavoured one is a liquid meal in itself) and homestyle baking and sandwiches, all as local and sustainable as possible. There's a little shop section showcasing vintage-inspired crafts. Shame it's not open weekends!

Burger Got Soul BURGERS $
(Map p178; ☑ 03-6334 5204; www.burgergotsoul. com; 243 Charles St; burgers $11-18; ⊗ 11am-9pm; ☎✐) Everyone will tell you these are the best burgers in Launceston. They're healthy, too: lean, preservative-free meat and low-sugar bread, plus gluten-free and veggie burgers for noncarnivores. Downside: you might die of hunger while you wait on a busy night.

Monty's Food Hall ASIAN $
(Map p178; cnr Brisbane & Wellington sts; mains $10-15; ⊗ 10am-9.30pm) Good-value Asian

eats, including Thai, Indian, Chinese, Malaysian... If you've been travelling the lesser-populated corners of the state and need a laksa fix, you've come to the right place.

★ **Stillwater** MODERN AUSTRALIAN $$
(Map p174; ☑ 03-6331 4153; www.stillwater.net.au; 2 Bridge Rd, Ritchie's Mill; breakfast $12-23, lunch & dinner mains $29-35; ⊗ 8.30am-3.30pm daily, 6pm-late Tue-Sat; ✍) Still waters run deep here – deep into the realm of outstanding service and excellent Mod Oz, that is. Beside the Tamar, in the renovated Ritchie's Flour Mill (parts of which date back to 1832), Stillwater does laid-back breakfasts and relaxed lunches...then puts on the ritz for dinner. The best restaurant in Launceston, hands down. The wine cellar also runs deep.

Blue Café Bar CAFE $$
(Map p178; ☑ 03-6334 3133; www.bluecafebar.com.au; Inveresk Railyards, Invermay; mains $15-30; ⊗ 8am-4pm Sun-Thu, til late Fri & Sat, closed evenings Jul & Aug) ✍ In a converted chunky-concrete power station next to the Tasmanian College of the Arts, this cool cafe serves awesome coffee and creative local, organic dishes to architecture students on the run from the books. Go for the Reuben pizza, with Wagyu, pastrami, Gruyère, sauerkraut and horseradish.

Elaia CAFE $$
(Map p178; ☑ 03-6331 3307; www.elaia.com.au; 240 Charles St; mains $11-30; ⊗ 7.30am-8pm Mon-Sat, to 3.30pm Sun; ☎) Elaia – Charles St's pioneering cafe. Here's a list of everything you need to know: pizzas, pastas, risottos, salads, all-day breakfasts, alt-country tunes, hip tattooed staff, wrap-around bench seats, live music Friday nights and colourful footpath tables. Hard to beat.

Cataract on Patterson STEAKHOUSE $$
(Map p178; ☑ 03-6331 4446; www.cataractonpaterson.com.au; 135 Paterson St; mains $26-38; ⊗ noon-2pm Fri & Sun, 5pm-late daily) Peer through your cataracts into this cool steakhouse down near Cataract Gorge – a mod-industrial space serving tender slabs of Great Southern Pinnacle beef. Not now for cow? Chicken, pork and lamb dishes also make the grade, plus a token vegetarian lasagne if you feel like being the odd one out.

Pickled Evenings INDIAN $$
(Map p178; ☑ 03-6331 0110; www.pickledevenings.com.au; 135 George St; mains $17-22; ⊗ 5.30-9.30pm Tue-Sun; ✍) Pickled evenings and holidays go hand in hand, but a visit to this excellent Indian restaurant will not (necessarily) involve excessive drinking. What you're here for are the curries, which are generous, spicy and sublime. Good vegetarian options, and takeaways available.

Hallam's Waterfront SEAFOOD $$
(Map p178; ☑ 03-6334 0554; www.hallamswaterfront.com.au; 13 Park St; mains $24-36; ⊗ 11.30am-2.30pm & 6pm-late Mon-Sat) This place conjures up nautical vibes – like the inside of a very spacious yacht – with friendly service and super-fresh seafood, particularly crayfish. The seafood platter ($98 for two people) gets the big thumbs up. Actual yachts bob and sway in the marina outside.

Sportsmans Hall Hotel PUB FOOD $$
(Map p178; ☑ 03-6331 3968; www.sportieshotel.com.au; cnr Charles & Balfour Sts; mains $22-41; ⊗ 11am-3pm Fri, 9am-3pm Sat & Sun, 6-8pm Tue-Sat) The restaurant at the Sportsmans Hall Hotel serves really impressive bistro gear: thick beef sausages with creamy mash; pork rib-eye with caramelised apple; lemon-pepper flathead with fetta and walnuts. Leave room for wicked desserts. There's accommodation (p179) upstairs, too.

Pierre's FRENCH $$
(Map p178; ☑ 03-6331 6835; www.pierres.net.au; 88 George St; mains lunch $18-29, dinner $28-38; ⊗ 11am-late Tue-Fri, 8am-late Sat) Pierre's is a Launceston institution (since 1956). Coolly dressed in dark leather with subdued lighting, it offers a tight menu of long-time classics (steak tartare with dijon mustard, cognac and fries) and – some say – the best coffee in Launceston. Dishes are expertly paired with local wines. *Oui, oui!*

Fresh on Charles CAFE $$
(Map p178; ☑ 03-6331 4299; www.freshoncharles.com.au; 178 Charles St; mains $10-22, shared plates $35-65; ⊗ 8.30am-3pm Sat-Thu, 8.30am-late Fri; ☎✍) ✍ Retro-arty Fresh offers an all-vegetarian/vegan menu that's both delicious and environmentally aware ('food that remembers where it comes from'). Rock up for an energising breakfast, or linger over lunch, coffee and cake in between. Organic all the way, and gluten free aplenty. There's terrific apartment accommodation (p180) upstairs.

Gorge Restaurant MODERN AUSTRALIAN $$
(Map p174; ☑ 03-6331 3330; www.launcestoncataractgorge.com.au/gorgerestaurant.html; Cataract

---

LOCAL KNOWLEDGE

KIM SEAGRAM: LAUNCESTON RESTAURATEUR

A good food culture follows good wine – it just goes hand in hand. That's how the local restaurant industry began. The wine styles that are grown here complement the amazing fresh produce that's available: sparkling wine and oysters, sauvignon blanc and crayfish, pinot noir and rabbit...they're a marriage made in heaven. Then came the coffee culture, following the Italian model, and once you've got your coffee organised, you get your breads sorted. We've got a few wood-fired bread ovens from the late 1800s still around here. And the climate here suits a food culture, too – we grow olives, make olive oil and produce all sorts of wonderful fruit and veg. How could this not be foodie heaven?

Top Food Experience

The cooking school at the **Red Feather Inn** (p194) at Hadspen, where you learn to treat quality produce with the respect it deserves, and then get to eat the amazing results.

Best Cafe

Blue Café Bar at the Inveresk Railyards precinct for brilliant coffees and arty ambience.

Top Drop

The Arras sparkling from **Bay of Fires Wines** (p192).

Must Try

The first fresh cherries of the season...exquisite.

Gorge; mains lunch from $22, dinner $30-39; ⊘noon-2.30pm daily, 6.30pm-late Tue-Sat) It's worth eating here for the beautiful setting alone, especially when sitting outside in summer and watching the peacocks strut. Walk off your eye-fillet steak with red-onion marmalade on the walk back to town through Cataract Gorge. Super-romantic at night.

Me Wah CHINESE $$
(Map p178; ☑03-6331 1308; www.mewah.com. au; 39-41 Invermay Rd, Invermay; mains $24-36; ⊘11.30am-2.30pm Tue-Sun, 5-9pm Sun-Thu, 5-10.30pm Fri & Sat) Launceston's best Chinese restaurant serves old-fashioned faves as well as innovative new-fangled dishes, leaning heavily on fresh Tasmanian seafood. The slow-braised blacklip abalone with shiitake mushrooms entrée ($45) may blow your budget – but might also blow your mind.

Garden of Vegan VEGETARIAN $$
(Map p178; ☑0421 928 041; 3/166 Charles St; mains $13-17; ⊘11am-3pm Mon-Fri, 5-8pm Wed-Fri; ☑) Get your veg face on at this new Charles St cafe, which plates up brilliant laksas, noodles, salads, soups and stews. And if you don't do dairy, gluten, sugar, soy or nuts either (what's left?), this is the place for you. Retro pressed-tin chairs and chunky outdoor tables with knee blankets for chilly Launceston morns.

Star of Siam THAI $$
(Map p178; ☑03-6331 2786; www.starofsiam. com.au; cnr Paterson & Charles Sts; mains $11-26; ⊘noon-2.30pm Tue-Fri, 5pm-late daily) Launceston's best Thai joint does generous, value-for-money Thai staples, as well as at least 10 more adventurous chef's specials, which you won't find anywhere else (chilli quails, anyone?).

Black Cow Bistro STEAKHOUSE $$$
(Map p178; ☑03-6331 9333; www.blackcowbistro. com.au; 70 George St; dinner mains $35-47; ⊘noon-2.30pm Fri, 5.30pm-late daily) This high-class bistro/steakhouse specialises in Tasmanian free-range, grass-fed, artificial-hormone-free beef. It offers six different cuts and claims to be the best steakhouse in Tassie, which, judging by the restaurant's runaway success, can't be too far wrong. Go the Cape Grim eye fillet with truffled Béarnaise sauce. Worth every cent.

Mud MODERN AUSTRALIAN $$$
(Map p178; ☑03-6334 5066; www.mudbar.com. au; 28 Seaport Blvd; mains lunch $24-29, dinner $35-48; ⊘11am-late) This hip bar-restaurant is the pick of the eateries in the moneyed Seaport enclave. Hang out with a beer at the bar then migrate to your table for superior Asian-inspired fare (Vietnamese sugar-cooked pork belly, soy-roasted duck,

ginger-rubbed salmon). Views of the crews from the North Esk Rowing Club gliding past.

Novaro's
ITALIAN $$$

(Map p178; ☑03-6334 5589; www.novaros.com; 28 Brisbane St; mains $30-40; ⊙5.30-9.30pm Wed-Sat) Set in an unremarkable terrace house on an unremarkable stretch of Brisbane St, Novaro's does truly remarkable Italian. It's known for its excellent service and a down-to-earth atmosphere as much as for its food. Book ahead – it gets packed, even on weeknights.

🍷 Drinking & Nightlife

★Royal Oak Hotel
PUB

(Map p178; ☑03-6331 5346; 14 Brisbane St; ⊙noon-late) Launceston's best pub. We really don't need to expand on this fact, but it's hard not to – brilliant beers on tap, open-mic nights (last Wednesday of the month), live music Wednesday to Sunday and ballsy 1970s rock on the stereo. If you're too old to be a hipster, but still feel culturally valid, this is the place for you.

★Saint John
BAR

(Map p178; ☑0424 175 147; 133 St John St; ⊙noon-midnight Tue-Sun) Hipsters rejoice! Bearded barmen pour craft beers from the taps here, the huge beer menu behind them listing your options in exhaustive detail. Out the back is an unexpected little food van, plating up Philly cheese steaks and lamb burgers that you can eat in the bar. The perfect symbiosis!

Bakers Lane
BAR

(Map p178; ☑03-6334 2414; 81 York St; ⊙11.30am-late Tue-Fri, 3pm-late Sat & Sun) Literally a day old when we visited, we're fans of this bar more for what it represents than what it achieved in its first 24 hours. Launceston is in *dire need* of more small bars: we just pray this one endures. Cool kids, live acoustic acts, cocktails, craft beer and late-night conversations – what can possibly go wrong?

Dickens Ciderhouse
BAR

(Map p178; ☑03-6334 8915; www.dickenscider.com.au/ciderhouse; 63a Brisbane St; ⊙5pm-late Mon-Fri, 4pm-late Sat & Sun) We weren't going to review this cider bar because of the name (really, so crass...). But then we learned the owners' surname is actually Dickens – so all is forgiven (almost). It's one of Launceston's precious few small bars, with rustic wood panelling straight from an apple packing shed.

Irish
PUB

(Map p178; ☑03-6331 4440; www.theirish1835.com.au; 211 Brisbane St; ⊙4pm-late Mon & Tue, 2pm-late Wed & Thu, noon-late Fri-Sun) This low-lit watering hole is trying hard to push the hackneyed old Irish pub concept somewhere closer to today. They've kept some of the good bits in the process, incuding live music every night (usually free) and a mighty fine beef-and-Guinness pie.

Alchemy Bar & Restaurant
BAR

(Map p178; ☑03-6331 2526; www.alchemylaunceston.com.au; 90 George St; ⊙11am-late) One of Lonnie's oldest pubs was recently reborn as a new-century bar-cafe combo. Launceston has a few of these mainstream all-things-to-all-people operations, but Alchemy stands out with live bands, DJs, craft beer and tapas. The footpath tables go off on a warm summer evening.

☆ Entertainment

Princess Theatre
THEATRE

(Map p178; ☑03-6323 3666; www.theatrenorth.com.au; 57 Brisbane St; ⊙box office 9am-5pm Mon-Fri, 10am-1pm Sat) Built in 1911 and incorporating the smaller Earl Arts Centre out the back, the old Princess stages an eclectic schedule of drama, dance and comedy, drawing acts from across Tasmania and the mainland.

Aurora Stadium
SPECTATOR SPORT

(Map p174; ☑03-6323 3383; www.aurorastadiumlaunceston.com.au; Invermay Rd, Invermay; tickets adult/child from $25/15) If you're in town during football season (April to August), see the big men fly – Melbourne-based AFL team Hawthorn plays a handful of home games each season at Aurora Stadium. 'BAAAAAALL!!!'

Hotel New York
LIVE MUSIC

(Map p178; www.hotelnewyork.net.au; 122 York St; ⊙4pm-late Wed, Fri & Sat) This clubby pub with international pretensions hosts a steady stream of DJs and local and interstate rock acts (not too many from NYC). Cover charges (from $10) usually apply.

Village Cinemas
CINEMA

(Map p178; ☑1300 866 843; www.villagecinemas.com.au; 163 Brisbane St; tickets adult/child $17.50/13) Escape your present reality with Hollywood blockbusters and the saliva-stirring aroma of popcorn.

Shopping

Harvest MARKET
(Map p178; ☑0417 352 780; www.harvestmarket.
org.au; Cimitiere St car park; ⊗8.30am-12.30pm
Sat) Excellent weekly gathering of organic producers and sustainable suppliers from
around northern and western Tasmania.
Craft beer, artisan baked goods, cheese and
salmon all feature heavily.

Mill Providore & Gallery FOOD
(Map p174; ☑03-6331 0777; www.millprovidore.
com.au; 2 Bridge Rd; ⊗9.30am-5.30pm Mon-Fri,
9am-5.30pm Sat, to 4pm Sun) Above Stillwater
restaurant you'll find this most excellent
treasure trove of good things for the home,
kitchen, stomach and soul. There are shelves
full of of books, food and wine (and books
about food and wine), a brilliant deli section
and a community gallery area.

Alps & Amici FOOD
(Map p174; ☑03-6331 1777; www.alpsandamici.
com; 52 Abbott St, East Launceston; ⊗7.30am-
6.30pm Mon-Fri, 8am-2pm Sun) Super-chef
Daniel Alps has set up this smart providore
where you can buy his restaurant-quality
meals to take home and adore. Classy cakes,
cheeses, meats and seafood, the freshest
fruit and veg, and Tasmanian beer and wine
also available. Good coffee, too.

Pinot Shop WINE
(Map p178; ☑03-6331 3977; www.pinotshop.com;
135 Paterson St; ⊗10am-6pm Mon-Sat) The future of Tasmanian wine may be sparkling
whites, but pinot noir is where it's at today.
This boutique bottle shop specialises in
the latter, plus premium international and
'big-island' (ie Australian mainland) vintag-
es. Australia-wide freight available.

Paddy Pallin OUTDOOR EQUIPMENT
(Map p178; ☑03-6331 4240; www.paddypallin.
com.au; 110 George St; ⊗9am-5.30pm Mon-Fri, to
4pm Sat, 10am-2pm Sun) Sells (and hires out)
all the gear you need for your camping epic.
Named after a legendary bushwalker.

Information

Cyber King (☑03-6334 2802; 113 George St;
⊗9.30am-7pm Mon-Fri, to 4.30pm Sat & Sun)
Internet access.
Launceston General Hospital (☑03-6348
7111; www.dhhs.tas.gov.au; 287-289 Charles St;
⊗24hr) 24-hour accident and emergency.
Launceston Visitor Information Centre (Map
p178; ☑03-6336 3133, 1800 651 827; www.
visitlauncestontamar.com.au; 68-72 Cameron
St; ⊗9am-5pm Mon-Fri, to 1pm Sat & Sun)
Everything you ever wanted to know about
Launceston, but were afraid to ask.
Main Post Office (GPO; Map p178; ☑13 13 18;
68-72 Cameron St; ⊗8.30am-5.30pm Mon-Fri,
9am-12.30pm Sat) Inside a fab 1880s red-brick
building.

Getting There & Away

AIR
There are regular flights between Launceston
and Melbourne, Sydney and Brisbane, connect-
ing with other Australian cities.
Jetstar (www.jetstar.com) Flights to Brisbane,
Sydney and Melbourne.
Qantas (www.qantas.com.au) Direct flights to
Melbourne, Sydney and Brisbane.
Virgin Australia (www.virginaustralia.com)
Direct flights to Melbourne and Sydney.

BUS
The depot for most services is the **Cornwall
Square Transit Centre** (Map p178; 200 Cim-
itiere St).
Calow's Coaches (Map p178; ☑03-6376 2161,
0400 570 036; www.calowscoaches.com)
Services the east coast (St Marys, St Helens,
Bicheno) from Launceston.
Lee's Coaches (Map p178; ☑03-6334 7979;
www.leescoaches.com) Services the East
Tamar Valley region from Launceston. Buses
stop on Brisbane St.
Manions' Coaches (Map p178; ☑03-6383
1221; www.manionscoaches.com.au; 168 Brisbane St) Services the West Tamar Valley region
from Launceston. Buses stop on Brisbane St.
Redline Coaches (Map p178; ☑1300 360 000;
www.tasredline.com.au) From Launceston west
to Westbury, Deloraine, Devonport, Burnie and
Stanley, and south to Hobart. Plenty of stops
in between.
Sainty's North East Bus Service (Map
p178; ☑0400 791 076, 0437 469 186; www.
saintysnortheastbusservice.com.au) Buses
between Launceston and Lilydale, Scottsdale,
Derby and Bridport.
Tassielink (Map p178; ☑1300 300 520; www.
tassielink.com.au) West coast buses via Devonport and Cradle Mountain, and an express
service from the Devonport ferry terminal
to Hobart via Launceston. Also runs from
Launceston to Evandale and Longford.

CAR
The major car-rental firms have desks at the
airport.
Avis (☑03-6324 1500; www.avis.com.au; Hotel
Grand Chancellor, 29 Cameron St; ⊗8am-
5.30pm Mon-Fri, to 4pm Sat & Sun)

Budget (☑03-6331 5422; www.budget.com.au; 76 Frederick St; ⊙8am-5pm Mon-Fri, 9am-1pm Sat & Sun)

Europcar (☑03-6331 8200; www.europcar.com.au; 80 Tamar St; ⊙8am-5.30pm Mon-Fri, to noon Sat & Sun)

Hertz (☑03-6335 1111; www.hertz.com.au; 58 Paterson St; ⊙8am-5pm Mon-Fri)

Rent For Less (☑03-6391 9182, 1300 883 739; www.rentforless.com.au; 153 St John St; ⊙8am-5pm Mon-Fri, 8.30am-5pm Sat, 9am-1pm Sun)

Thrifty (☑03-6333 0911; www.thrifty.com.au; 2-10 Tamar St; ⊙8am-5pm Mon-Fri, to noon Sat)

❶ Getting Around

TO/FROM THE AIRPORT

Launceston Airport (p304) is 15km south of the city, on the road to Evandale. **Launceston Airporter** (☑1300 38 55 22; www.airporter-launceston.com.au; adult/child $18/14) shuttle bus runs door-to-door services. A taxi into the city costs about $35.

BICYCLE

Arthouse Backpacker Hostel (p177) rents out decent bikes for $15 per day.

Artbikes (☑03-6331 5506; www.artbikes.com.au; Design Centre Tasmania, cnr Brisbane & Tamar Sts; ⊙9.30am-5.30pm Mon-Fri, 10am-4pm Sat & Sun) Free city-bike hire from the Design Centre Tasmania. Bring a credit card and photo ID. Overnight hire costs $22; for a weekend it's $44.

BUS

Free Tiger Bus (☑03-6323 3000; www.launceston.tas.gov.au) Runs from Inveresk to Princes Park, Windmill Hill and back to Inveresk every 30 minutes between 10am and 3.30pm Monday to Friday.

Metro Tasmania (☑13 22 01; www.metrotas.com.au) Runs Launceston's suburban bus network. One-way fares vary with distances ('sections') travelled (from $3 to $6.20). A Day Rover pass ($5.30) allows unlimited travel after 9am. Buses depart from the two blocks of St John St between Paterson and York Sts. Many routes don't operate in the evenings or on Sundays.

TAMAR VALLEY

Funnelling 64km north from Launceston towards Bass Strait, the Tamar River and the valley that cradles it are fringed with reed beds and emerald hills. The wide, tidal river is often glassy calm. On the river's eastern bank is Launceston's ocean port, Bell Bay, near George Town. The western bank sustains a string of laid-back country towns.

The Batman Bridge unites the Tamar's two shores near Deviot.

The Tamar Valley and the nearby Pipers River region are also key Tasmanian wine-producing areas – the premium cool-climate drops bottled here have been swilled at the tables of royalty. Most of the wineries here are marketed under the banner of the **Tamar Valley Wine Route** (www.tamarvalleywineroute.com.au). Pick up a self-drive guide from the Launceston Visitor Information Centre (p185), download a map, or take a guided tour.

Legana & Rosevears

POP 3990 (COMBINED)

These two hubs offer the first pit stops heading north out of Launceston along the West Tamar Hwy (A7) – they're almost suburbs of Launceston, they're so darn proximal. Legana is right on the highway; Rosevears adheres to narrow Rosevears Dr, running along the water past moored yachts and swaying reed beds.

◉ Sights & Activities

Tamar Island Wetlands   NATURE RESERVE
(☑03-6327 3964; www.parks.tas.gov.au; West Tamar Hwy, Legana; adult/child/family $3/2/6; ⊙daylight hours) A 10-minute drive north of Launceston, this wetland reserve has a 2km wheelchair-friendly boardwalk running through it, strategically positioned so you can ogle the resident birds. The island itself has BBQs and an elevated bird hide. Scan the reedy swamp alongside the boardwalk for frogs, skinks and the occasional copperhead snake.

Vélo Wines   WINERY
(☑03-6330 3677; www.velowines.com.au; 755 West Tamar Hwy, Legana; ⊙cellar door 10am-5pm Wed-Sun, restaurant 12.30-3.30pm Wed-Sun & 6pm-late Fri & Sat) Vélo Wines was founded by former Olympic and Tour de France cyclist Michael Wilson (*velo* is French for bicycle). Try the reserve chardonnay or the surprising cool-climate shiraz. The **cafe** (mains $20 to $35) here is super-popular – so popular that it runs a shuttle bus from Launceston on Friday and Saturday nights. Winning pizzas and gnocchi.

Ninth Island Vineyard   WINERY
(☑03-6330 2388; www.kreglingerwineestates.com; 95 Rosevears Dr, Rosevears; ⊙10am-5pm) Even if you're no wine buff, drop into glo-

Tamar Valley

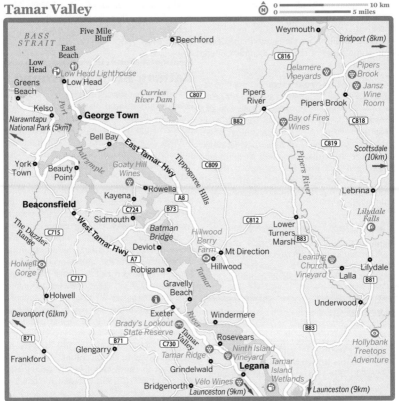

rious Ninth Island. The vine views are achingly beautiful, especially when the grape leaves burn with autumn hues. Super sauvignon blanc.

Tamar Ridge
WINERY

(☏03-6330 0300; www.tamarridge.com.au; 1a Waldhorn Dr, Rosevears; ☉10am-5pm) Tamar Ridge produces some of Tasmania's best sparkling whites and pinots. Sip some at the counter, choose a bottle then hit the terrace for a platter (terrine, salmon or cheese, $20 to $25). The kids can spin hula hoops on the lawn, or scrawl on the blackboard wall.

Brady's Lookout State Reserve
NATURE RESERVE

(www.parks.tas.gov.au; Brady's Lookout Rd, Rosevears; ☉24hr) FREE From Rosevears Dr take Brady's Lookout Rd and follow the signs to this reserve. Nefarious bushranger Matthew Brady used the rocky outcrop here to spy prospective victims on the road below

(so the views are pretty good). Brady was known as the 'Gentleman Bushranger' for his impeccable mid-theft manners.

🛏 Sleeping & Eating

Launceston Holiday Park
CARAVAN PARK $

(☏03-6330 1714; www.launcestonholidaypark. com.au; 711 West Tamar Hwy, Legana; unpowered/ powered sites from $24/30, cabins d budget $70-115, deluxe $90-120; @🛜) While you mightn't come to this highway-rumbling park specifically for a holiday, it's still a passable option, just 11km from Launceston, if your bank balance has seen better days. There's camping under the trees, grassy caravan spots and a range of cabins, from bog-basic to deluxe-spa.

Viewenmore Villa
APARTMENT $$

(☏0428 914 059; www.viewenmorevilla.com; 321 Rosevears Dr, Rosevears; d $120-140, extra person $20) This immaculate little hexagonal villa is up a steep drive just past Rosevears Waterfront Tavern heading north. There are sensational views, a full kitchen and it's pin-neat and comfortable. Hang out on the deck, char something on the BBQ, or crack open one of the day's wine buys.

Rosevears Waterfront Tavern PUB FOOD $$ (☑ 03-6394 4074; www.rosevearstavern.com. au; 215 Rosevears Dr, Rosevears; mains $25-29; ☺ noon-3pm daily, 6-9pm Wed-Sat) Built in 1831 Rosevears Waterfront Tavern offers pub-grub faves (burgers, chicken parmigiana) and more up-tempo fare such as lamb-leg rogan josh and grilled tiger prawn pizza. The river views are wild, and the beer terrace is pumping. Live music most Sunday afternoons.

❶ Getting There & Away

Manions' Coaches (☑ 03-6383 1221; www. manionscoaches.com.au) Monday to Saturday buses from Launceston to Legana ($4, 10 minutes) and Rosevears ($8, 25 minutes).

Exeter

POP 810

The land around little Exeter is predomi-nantly orchard and farming country. The **Tamar Visitor Information Centre** (☑ 1800 637 989, 03-6394 4454; www.visitlauncestontamar. com.au; 81 West Tamar Hwy; ☺ 8.30am-5pm Mon-Fri, 9am-5pm Sat & Sun) has the skinny on local highlights, not the least of which is the eter-nally busy **Exeter Bakery** (☑ 03-6394 4069; 104 Main Rd; items $3-9; ☺ 7am-5pm Mon-Fri, 8am-3pm Sat, 9am-3pm Sun). The century-old wood-fired oven here produces all manner of pies – from seafood to egg-and-bacon to Thai massaman and glistening custard. Also on offer are cakes, breads, slices, tarts, ham-and-cheese croissants and filled rolls to go.

South of Exeter, Gravelly Beach Rd will take you to Robigana (derived from the Ab-original word for swans), where the road crosses the Supply River. From here there's a marked walking track (one hour return) beside the Tamar River to **Paper Beach**.

Also on Gravelly Beach Rd is the **View** (☑ 0434 200 3000434 200 300; 279 Gravelly Beach Rd, Gravelly Beach; d $120-140), a hip two-person B&B studio next to a mechanic's workshop. The breakfast hamper is stuffed with fruit, eggs, bread, jams, cereals and coffee, which you can cobble together in the little kitchen in the corner. And indeed, the view is awesome!

Manions' Coaches (☑ 03-6383 1221; www.manionscoaches.com.au) runs here from Launceston ($8, 20 minutes) from Monday to Saturday.

Batman Bridge & Around

Spanning the Tamar River, the **Batman Bridge** (pronounced 'Batm'n', as opposed to Gotham's caped crusader) opened in 1968 as one of the world's first cable-stayed truss bridges. The jaunty design resulted not so much from creative inspiration as from foun-dation problems. The Tamar's eastern shore offered poor support for a hefty bridge, so it holds up just a minor part of the span. Most of the bridge is actually supported by the 100m-tall west tower that leans out over the river. There are great views from the east side.

Arcing underneath the bridge on the western shore is a road leading to little **Sidmouth**. Here the much-loved local in-stitution is **Auld Kirk** (West Tamar Presbyterian Church; ☑ 03-6330 3702; www.westtamarpres-byterianchurch.org.au; 50 Auld Kirk Rd, Sidmouth; ☺ services 10am Sun) – which means 'old church' – built in 1843 from 'freestone' by convict and free labour. Proceed north on the C724 to the Auburn Rd junction at Kayena. Turning left on Auburn Rd, contin-ue along to the family-friendly **Goaty Hill Wines** (☑ 1300 819 997; www.goatyhill.com; 530 Auburn Rd, Kayena; ☺ 10am-5pm Aug-May, by ap-pointment Jun & Jul), best known for top-notch riesling and pinots gris and noir. Acoustic troubadors strum on the deck in summer, and impromptu cricket matches happen on the lawns.

Beauty Point

POP 1210

While the surrounding hillsides and river-scapes are certainly beautiful, the name of this strung-out town actually derives from pulchritude of the bovine variety: a now-im-mortalised bullock called Beauty. There are a couple of winning places to stay here, plus a beaut riverside cafe.

◉ Sights

Seahorse World AQUARIUM (☑ 03-6383 4111; www.seahorseworld.com.au; 200 Flinders St, Inspection Head Wharf, Beauty Point; adult/child/family $22/9/54; ☺ 9.30am-4pm Dec-Apr, 10am-3pm May-Nov) At coo-inducing Sea-horse World, cute seahorses are hatched and

WORTH A TRIP

THE BEACONSFIELD MINE

Little Beaconsfield (population 1200), set in apple-growing country, has had two big moments in the spotlight. The first was when gold was discovered here in 1877; the second was in 2006 when a mine collapse killed one miner and trapped two others in a cage 1km underground.

After an exhaustive two-week rescue operation that made global headlines (further sensationalised by the heart-attack death of a TV reporter on the surface), the two miners emerged to a media feeding frenzy. Magnates quaffed beer at the pub; rock stars flew in to perform; Dave Grohl wrote a song; Oprah was mentioned... Weathering the storm, the miners signed lucrative deals for their story, but to everyone's great disappointment they turned out to be regular blokes. Oprah never called. Tony Wright's *Bad Ground: Inside the Beaconsfield Mine Rescue* is the definitive account of the tragedy.

Now that the hype has died down, Beaconsfield is the same as it ever was: a slightly shabby town presiding over what was historically one of the richest small gold mines in Australia. The **Beaconsfield Mine and Heritage Centre** (☑ 03-6383 1473; www.beaconsfieldheritage.com.au; West St, Beaconsfield; adult/child/family $12/4/30; ⊙ 9.30am-4.30pm) has hands-on interactive exhibits, including old mining machinery, a waterwheel, a mine-rescue exhibition and an interactive high-tech mine hologram that seems to take you right down into the mine. The working mine headshaft is right behind the museum. To save a few dollars, buy a three-attraction **Tamar Triple Pass** (adult/family $50/136) to the Mine and Heritage Centre and the Platypus House and Seahorse World in Beauty Point.

Nine kilometres south of Beaconsfield is **Holwell Gorge** reserve, with giant trees and three waterfalls. The walking track linking the southern and northern gorge entrances takes around two hours one way.

Manions' Coaches (☑ 03-6383 1221; www.manionscoaches.com.au) runs between Launceston and Beaconsfield ($10, 80 minutes) from Monday to Saturday.

raised to supply aquariums worldwide. Access is via 45-minute guided tours, which run on the hour and take you into the world of the *Hippocampus abdominalis* (pot-bellied seahorse). There's a bit of a **cafe** here, too.

The three-attraction **Tamar Triple Pass** (adult/family $50/136) gets you into Seahorse World, Platypus House and the Beaconsfield Mine & Heritage Centre.

Platypus House   ZOO
(☑ 03-6383 4884; www.platypushouse.com.au; 200 Flinders St, Inspection Head Wharf, Beauty Point; adult/child/family $23/9/55; ⊙ 9.30am-3.30pm) In the wharf shed opposite Seahorse World, Platypus House put the world's only two monotremes – the platypus and the echidna – on display for your viewing pleasure. Platypuses gambol in glass-sided tanks and transparent 'burrows', while in the echidna room you can walk among these trundling creatures as guides dish out scientific facts. Tours run hourly.

🛏 Sleeping & Eating

Beauty Point Tourist Park   CARAVAN PARK $
(☑ 03-6383 4536; www.beautypointtouristpark.com.au; 36 West Arm Rd; powered sites $33, cabins

$99-199; ☎) There's easy-going camping on plush pastures by the water here, plus tidy, well-equipped cabins. A tennis court and river swimming will keep you busy if you've finished your book.

⭐**Tamar Cove**   MOTEL $$
(☑ 03-6383 4375; www.tamarcove.com; 4421 Main Rd; d $119-150, 2-bedroom apt $149; ☎ ☒) What a winning little hillside enclave! Nine stylishly done up motel rooms front well-manicured gardens with a solar-heated pool. The **restaurant** (mains $15 to $30, serving 8am until late) gets rave reviews, too – don't go past the house-special seafood chowder. Free wifi. Good one!

Beauty Point Cottages   B&B $$
(☑ 03-6383 4556; www.beautypointcottages.com.au; 14 Flinders St; d $160-195; ☎) Book yourself into the large guestroom in this noble 1880s house (with your own bathroom and entrance), or lodge yourself in one of two contemporary self-contained spa studios in the garden. The studios have sunrise views over the river, and there's a little path at the bottom of the daisy-spotted garden leading down to the water.

Pomona Spa Cottages COTTAGE $$$
(☑ 03-6383 4073; www.pomonaspacottages.com.
au; 77 Flinders St; d from $220, extra person $40)
Woah – déjà vu! These three self-contained
spa cottages are exact replicas of the main
house further down the driveway, painted
up in a Federation colour scheme of cream,
mustard, red and forest green. On the side
of each one is a little pointy-roofed rotunda
with a BBQ deck and, naturally, great views.

★**River Cafe** CAFE, MODERN AUSTRALIAN $$
(☑ 03-6383 4099; www.therivercafe.com.au; 225
Flinders St; mains $8-30; ⊙ 11am-late; 🛜) On
sunny days at the River Cafe the windows
fold right back and the water feels so close
you could touch it. The menu tempts with
fresh local fare – the Tasmanian eye fillet is
sublime – and the coffe is just about perfect,
too. Takeaway pizzas, free wi-fi and Tamar
Valley wines all the way.

❶ Getting There & Away

Manions' Coaches (☑ 03-6383 1221; www.
manionscoaches.com.au) Runs between
Launceston and Beauty Point ($10, one hour)
Monday to Saturday.

George Town

POP 4310

George Town stands sentinel on the Tamar
River's eastern shore, close to where it empties into Bass Strait. The town was founded in 1804 by Lieutenant Colonel Paterson
as part of the British attempt to stave off
settlement by the French, who had been
reconnoitring the area. The town's older
buildings date from the 1830s and 1840s,
when it prospered as the port linking Tasmania with Victoria. Though today it's perhaps not the most instantly appealing of
towns, it maintains a salty maritime feel and
has a couple of attractions worth your time.

◉ Sights

Bass & Flinders Centre MUSEUM
(☑ 03-6382 3792; www.bassandflinders.org.au;
8 Elizabeth St, George Town; adult/child/family
$10/4/24; ⊙ 9am-4pm) Undoubtedly the high-
light of a visit to George Town, this small museum houses a red-sailed replica of the *Norfolk*, the little yacht used by Bass and Flinders
for their 1897 circumnavigation of Van Diemen's Land. There are other old wooden
boats here, too – it's altogether a rather fabulous collection. Reduced winter hours.

Hillwood Berry Farm FARM
(☑ 03-6394 8180; www.hillwoodberryfarm.com.
au; 105 Hillwood Rd, Hillwood; ⊙ 9am-5pm daily
late Oct-Feb, 10am-5pm Wed-Sun Mar) Hillwood
burgeons with berries in summer. Pick your
own strawberries, raspberries, loganberries,
blackcurrants, redcurrants and blueberries
and then beeline to the **cafe** (mains $8 to
$16) for a berry sundae, a slice of berry-swirl
cheesecake or a coffee. It's just off the East
Tamar Hwy, 22km south of George Town.

George Town Heritage Trail HISTORIC BUILDINGS
(☑ 03-6382 1700; www.provincialtamar.com.
au) **FREE** Sick of modern living? Ask at the
visitor centre for a map detailing this trail,
which takes you on foot through George
Town's history, starting at the **Old Watch
House** on Macquarie St.

🛏 Sleeping & Eating

Pier Hotel Motel HOTEL, MOTEL $$
(☑ 03-6382 1300; www.pierhotel.com.au; 5 Eliza-
beth St; d $110-260; 🛜) There's a wing of qui-
et motel rooms out the back and renovated
pub rooms upstairs here, but the star attrac-
tion is the **bistro** (mains $14-33; ⊙ noon-2pm
& 6-8pm), which serves excellent pizzas, por-
terhouse steaks, salads and surf 'n' turf with
an awesome sweet-chilli béchamel sauce.
Fold-back doors open towards the water in
warm weather.

Peppers York Cove HOTEL, APARTMENT $$
(☑ 03-6382 9900; www.peppers.com.au/york-cove;
2 Ferry Blvd; d $170-250, 2/3-bedroom apt from
$270/300; ⊙ restaurant 7-10am daily, noon-3pm
Tue-Sun, 6-8pm Mon-Sat; 🛜🏊) This corporate
waterfront resort is making waves on the
Tamar. There are upmarket hotel rooms and
apartments, and the funky bar-restaurant
(lunch and dinner mains $24 to $35) does
contemporary cafe food and excellent coffee.

Oven Bakery BAKERY, CAFE $
(☑ 03-6382 2560; 95 Macquarie St; items $4-10;
⊙ 7am-4pm Mon-Fri, to 2pm Sat) This buzzy
bakehouse is the best place in town for a coffee, but most folks breeze through to pick up
takeaway pies, pasties, sandwiches, laming-
tons and bodacious slabs of caramel slice.

❶ Information

George Town Visitor Information Centre
(☑ 03-6382 1700; www.provincialtamar.com.
au; 92-96 Main Rd; ⊙ 9am-5pm) On the main
road as you enter from the south. Bike hire per
half-/full day is $15/20.

NARAWNTAPU NATIONAL PARK

On the other side of the Tamar River mouth from Low Head, and about 20km east of Devonport, **Narawntapu National Park** (☑03-6428 6277; www.parks.tas.gov.au; vehicle/person per day \$24/12; ⏱ranger station 9am-4pm Dec-Apr, to 3pm May-Nov) is a reserve of coastal heath, dunes and bushland that's astoundingly abundant in wildlife (it's been called 'Tasmania's Serengeti'). Visit just on dusk and you'll see Forester kangaroos, foraging wombats, wallabies and pademelons. It used to be called Asbestos Range National Park, but park management thought the name was deterring people from visiting. Go figure...

The park can be accessed at two points near the small coastal settlement of Greens Beach (via the C721), or via the main entrance at Springlawn off the B71 near Port Sorell, where there's a **ranger station**. Rangers run guided walks and activities from here in summer. If you're entering the park from the Greens Beach side, self-register on entry.

Horse riding is allowed and the park has corrals and a 26km trail; ask at the ranger station. **Bakers Beach** is the safest swimming spot around here.

There are some great walking trails in the park. You can hike round **Badger Head** in about six to eight hours (via Copper Cove), while **Archers Knob** (114m; two hours return) has good views of Bakers Beach. The one-hour **Springlawn Nature Trail** includes a boardwalk over wetlands to a bird hide. The beach from Griffiths Point to Bakers Point is good for beachcombing and sunset watching.

The park has four self-registration **camp sites** (unpowered sites per 2 people/family \$13/16, powered sites \$16/22, extra adult/child from \$5/2.50). There are powered sites that campervans can access at **Springlawn**, plus unpowered sites at **Koybaa**, **Bakers Point** and the **Horse Yards**. There are tables and toilets at all sites. Firewood is sometimes provided, but there's not always reliable water: check with rangers before setting off or bring your own.

❶ Getting There & Away

Lee's Coaches (☑03-6334 7979; www.leescoaches.com) Services George Town from Launceston (\$14, one hour), continuing to Low Head. Travels once daily in each direction Monday to Saturday only; bookings required.

Low Head

POP 450

Low Head and George Town are barely divided – you won't notice leaving one before arriving in the other. Historic Low Head is in a spectacular setting though, looking out over the swirling – and treacherous – waters of the Tamar as it empties into the sea. There's good surf at **East Beach** on Bass Strait, and safe swimming away from the river mouth at beaches around the head.

◉ Sights & Activities

Low Head Pilot Station Museum HISTORIC SITE, MUSEUM
(☑03-6382 2826; www.lowheadpilotstation.com; 399 Low Head Rd; adult/child/family \$5/3/15; ⏱10am-4pm) Helping ships navigate into the treacherous mouth of the Tamar River, whitewashed Low Head Pilot Station is Australia's oldest (1805) and houses an interesting maritime museum cluttered with historical displays and mandatory rusty anchors. There's a cafe and accommodation (p192), too.

Low Head Lighthouse LIGHTHOUSE
(☑03-6382 2826; www.lowheadpilotstation.com; end of Low Head Rd; ⏱grounds 9am-6pm Sep-May, to 5pm Jun-Aug) **FREE** On the end of Low Head itself, this 1888 lighthouse (designed by colonial architect John Lee Archer) is a great spot to watch the torrent of the Tamar spilling into Bass Strait. On Sunday at noon the foghorn sounds with an ear-splitting bellow.

Low Head Penguin Tours BIRDWATCHING
(☑0418 361 860; http://penguintours.lowhead.com; end of Low Head Rd; adult/child \$18/10; ⏱dusk) Check out the little penguins that live around the Low Head Lighthouse. Tours leave nightly at dusk from a signposted spot beside Low Head Rd just south of the lighthouse. Cash only; bookings advised.

⎈ Sleeping & Eating

Low Head Tourist Park CARAVAN PARK \$
(☑03-6382 1573; www.lowheadtouristpark.com.au; 136 Low Head Rd; unpowered sites \$15-20, powered sites \$24-30, en-suite sites \$34-40, dm \$28, on-site caravans \$60-80, cabins \$95-115, cottages

DON'T MISS

PIPERS RIVER WINE REGION

Don't miss a long afternoon wobbling between cellar doors in the Pipers River Region, an easy day trip north of Launceston. Online, see www.tamarvalleywineroute.com.au.

Pipers Brook (☑03-6382 7527; www.pipersbrook.com.au; 1216 Pipers Brook Rd, Pipers Brook; tastings free, cafe mains $14-25; ⊙10am-5pm, cafe 10am-3pm) The region's most famous vineyard. Try Pipers Brook, Ninth Island and Krieglinger wines in an architecturally innovative building. There's also a cafe, which serves a changing menu of light snacks and a delectable tasting plate.

Jansz Wine Room (☑03-6382 7066; www.jansz.com.au; 1216b Pipers Brook Rd, Pipers Brook; ⊙10am-4.30pm) Next door to Pipers Brook, savvy Jansz (named after explorer Abel Jansz Tasman) makes fine sparkling wine, aka 'Méthode Tasmanoise' (ha ha). A cheese platter plus two flutes of the sparking stuff is $30.

Bay of Fires Wines (☑03-6382 7622; www.bayoffireswines.com.au; 40 Baxters Rd, Pipers River; ⊙10am-5pm Sep-May, 11am-4pm Jun-Aug) About 3km south of the main Pipers River T-intersection, Bay of Fires Wines is the home of prestigious Arras sparkling and easy-drinking whites and pinots. There's a touch of Cape Cod about the cellar-door design. Tasting platters $32.

Delamere Vineyards (☑03-6382 7190; www.delamerevineyards.com.au; 4238 Bridport Rd, Pipers Brook; ⊙10am-5pm) Affable, family-run Delamere is the antithesis of the big-ticket wineries around here. It's a small set-up, with everything grown, produced and bottled on site. Superb rosé, sparkling white and pinot noir.

$120-140) There are two sections – old and new – to this strangely treeless riverside park. Price ranges reflect the variations between the two. Dorm beds are in a converted caravan with an annex. Book one of the new timber-lined cabins and settle in for a sunset spectacular.

Low Head Pilot Station COTTAGE $$
(☑03-6382 2826; www.lowheadpilotstation.com; 399 Low Head Rd; cottages sleeping 2/5/6/8/9 $180/210/210/250/300) Low Head's historic pilot station precinct offers a range of nine very smartly refurbished, self-contained, waterfront cottages for up to nine people. Great for families; the kids will get into the maritime mood and wait with flapping ears for the foghorn boom from the lighthouse (midday on Sundays).

Coxwain's Cottage Café CAFE $$
(☑03-6382 2826; www.lowheadpilotstation.com; 399 Low Head Rd, Low Head Pilot Station; mains $6-20; ⊙10am-5pm Jun-Nov, 9am-5pm Dec-May) The best (only) place to eat in Low Head is this excellent cafe in an 1847 cottage at the Low Head Pilot Station. Offerings include homemade pies (try the lamb-and-veggie version), quiches, toasted sandwiches and hearty soups in winter – plus Pipers River wines and fine espresso.

❶ Getting There & Away

Lee's Coaches (☑03-6334 7979; www.leescoaches.com) Buses between Launceston and Low Head ($15, 1¼ hours) via George Town, once daily in each direction Monday to Saturday. Bookings required.

Lilydale & Around

POP 660

Quiet Lilydale is little more than a main street with a few stores and services – and some brightly painted utility poles. Stock up on picnic goods at National Trust–listed 1888 **Bardenhagen's General Store** (1965 Main Rd; ⊙7am-7pm Mon-Fri, to 6pm Sat, 8am-6pm Sun), then drive 3km north of town for the short walk to **Lilydale Falls**. If you're feeling more energetic, propel yourself up **Mt Arthur** (1188m; five to seven hours return), which looms above the town.

❍ Sights & Activities

Leaning Church Vineyard WINERY
(☑03-6395 4447; www.leaningchurch.com.au; 76 Brooks Rd, Lalla; ⊙10am-5pm Oct-Apr) Visit to funky Leaning Church for excellent sparkling wine and pinots. Linger over a cheese platter ($25 for two people), or rock up for the eye-fillet steak BBQ every Sunday ($30 per person).

Hollybank Treetops
Adventure
ADVENTURE SPORTS

(📋 03-6395 1390; www.treetopsadventure.com.au; 66 Hollybank Rd, Underwood; adult/child $120/85; ⊘ 9am-5pm) High adventure at Hollybank, about 7km south of Lilydale. Harnessed to a cable-mounted swing seat, you'll skim through the treetops at vertigo-inducing heights in the care of an experienced guide, who (if you're listening) will provide interpretative insights on the surrounding forest. There are short walks and picnic spots for non-adventurers, and a brilliant new **mountain bike park** here, too.

🛌 Sleeping & Eating

There's free casual **camping** (unpowered sites plus a toilet block and BBQ hut) next to the Lilydale Falls car park.

Cherry Top & Eagle Park   FARMSTAY $$
(📋 03-6395 1167; www.cherrytop.com.au; 81 Lalla Rd; d from $120) 🖋 Experience farm charms at this sustainably minded property that grows most of its own food. Share a yarn around the firepit; collect chook eggs; dig in the veggie patch; or have an unofficial cup of tea in the unofficial tearooms. It's about 1km out of town: take the C822 and follow the signs.

★ Trig   COTTAGE $$$
(📋 03-6395 2073; www.thetrig.com.au; 345 Mountain Rd; d $250) 🖋 A superb little architect-designed cabin, 3km up a dirt road on the sheep-studded slopes of broody Mt Arthur. There's a guitar to strum, an outdoor bath on the deck, arty furniture, Alps & Amici (p185) meals in the freezer and views that just won't quit. Powered by solar (and hydro!) setups on-site. Can we stay another night?

Lilydale Larder   CAFE $$
(📋 03-6395 1230; www.lilydalelarder.com.au; 1983 Main Rd; mains $15-21; ⊘ 9.30am-5pm Sat-Thu, to 8pm Fri) The bad old Lilydale Tavern has been reborn as a cool providore, cafe and wine room. Settle into a Larder Burger; sip Tasmanian wine and whisky; and check out the local craft. Good coffee, plus live music every now and then.

❶ Getting There & Away

Sainty's North East Bus Service (📋 0437 469 186; www.saintysnortheastbusservice. com.au) Runs once daily, Monday to Friday, between Launceston and Lilydale ($8, 30 minutes) in each direction, continuing either to Bridport or Derby.

SOUTH OF LAUNCESTON

Hadspen & Carrick
POP HADSPEN 2070; CARRICK 870

Just 15km and 19km southwest of Launceston respectively, historic Hadspen and Carrick are endearing old hamlets with a few interesting diversions if you're pulling off the highway.

⊙ Sights & Activities

Entally Estate   HISTORIC BUILDING
(📋 03-6393 6201; www.entally.com.au; Entally Rd, Hadspen; adult/child/family $10/8/25; ⊘ 10am-4pm) Built in 1819 by shipping entrepreneur Thomas Haydock Reibey, Entally is one of Tasmania's oldest – and loveliest – country homesteads, painting a vivid picture of the affluent rural life back in the day. Have a look around the house then roll out a picnic rug under avenues of English trees. Interesting fact for the day: Mary Reibey, Thomas' mum, is on the Australian $20 note.

Carrick Mill   HISTORIC BUILDING
(67 Meander Valley Rd, Carrick) On the main road through Carrick is the amazing four-storey Carrick Mill, bulit in 1846. The mill's original waterwheel is still functional (in theory), but a string of failed hospitality businesses here has stopped it spinning (for now...). Anyone want to buy a historic Tasmanian stone flour mill, going cheap?

Archer's Folly   RUIN
(6 Church St, Carrick) On the hill behind historic Carrick Mill are the crumbling ruins of an 1847 mansion, known as Archer's Folly. Standing in gorgeous gothic isolation, it was once a grand merchant's home, but burned down in 1978.

Tasmanian Copper &
Metal Art Gallery   GALLERY
(📋 03-6393 6440; www.tascoppermetalart.com; 8 Church St, Carrick; ⊘ 10am-4pm Mon-Fri) This quirky art gallery is an Aladdin's Cave of imaginative handmade metalwork airbrushed in lurid colours. It's located next to the stone ruins of Archer's Folly.

🛌 Sleeping & Eating

Hawthorn Villa Stables   B&B $$
(📋 0427 936 150, 03-6393 6150; www.hawthornvilla.com.au; cnr Meander Valley Rd & Church St, Carrick; d $160-170, extra adult/child $35/25, breakfast $20; ❄🛜) In the manicured gardens of a

historic house are these four mud-brick, slate-roofed cottages with little kitchens. Bright white linen and extra-thick bath towels add a plush overlay to proceedings, while breakfast is a hamper for two with free-range eggs and fresh garden herbs for your morning omelette.

★ Red Feather Inn   BOUTIQUE HOTEL $$$
(☑ 03-6393 6506; www.redfeatherinn. au; 42 Main St, Hadspen; d/q incl breakfast from $250/450; ✲) The unreservedly gorgeous 1852 Red Feather Inn is a magical boutique hotel and cooking school, lifted from the pages of a chic magazine. Rooms range from attic doubles to a cottage sleeping 10. Full-day cooking classes (from $195) happen in the country kitchen, which also services the restaurant (three courses from $90), open to the public on Friday and Saturday nights.

Carrick Inn   PUB FOOD $$
(☑ 03-6393 6143; www.greatwesterntiers.net.au/bars/carrick/carrick-inn; 1 Meander Valley Rd, Carrick; mains $17-26; ⊙noon-2pm & 6-8pm) This inn has been in the hospitality business since 1833 – plenty of time to perfect the art of pub grub in the Sammy Cox Bistro. Steaks, lamb shanks, roast duck and scallops ahoy.

🛈 Getting There & Away

Metro Tasmania (☑ 13 22 01; www.metrotas. com.au) Bus 78 runs from Launceston to Hadspen ($4.50, 30 minutes). Monday to Saturday only. No Carrick service.

Westbury & Around

POP 2110

This languid country town, with its tree-lined avenues, common and village green, has a feast of historic buildings and a decidedly English vibe.

Between Carrick and Westbury is the village of Hagley, where Quamby Estate – an 1828 Anglo-Indian-style homestead that has been converted into swanky accommodation – is the star attraction.

💿 Sights & Activities

Pearn's Steam World   MUSEUM
(☑ 03-6393 1414; www.pearnssteamworld.org.au; 65 Meander Valley Rd; adult/child $10/5; ⊙9am-4pm Oct-Jun, 10am-3pm Jul-Sep) Pearn's Steam World comprises two huge vaulted sheds filled with (allegedly) the world's largest collection of antique steam engines and relics.

If your timing's good the little steam passenger train will be doing laps of the complex.

Westbury Maze   MAZE
(☑ 03-6393 1840; 10 Meander Valley Rd; adult/child/family $6.50/5.50/22; ⊙10am-5pm Dec-May, to 4pm Jun-Nov) Lose the kids among the 3000-plant privet hedges of Westbury Maze, then recover in the tearoom.

Vintage Tractor Shed Museum   MUSEUM
(☑ 03-6393 1167; www.greatwesterntiers.net.au/attractions/westbury/vintage-tractor-shed-museum; 5 Veterans Row; adult/child $5/free; ⊙9am-4pm) Oil your engine at the Vintage Tractor Shed Museum, an informal assembly of farmyard sheds full of rusty old trundlers, dating from 1916 to 1952. There are also 600 scale models of tractors here – a real shrine to these beasts of the field.

John Temple Gallery   GALLERY
(☑ 03-6393 1666; www.johntemplegallery.com. au; 103 Meander Valley Rd; ⊙10am-5pm Sep-May, to 4pm Jun-Aug) FREE Exhibits inspiring, large-format landscape photographs by this top Tasmanian photographer. Sometimes closed if John is out on a field trip: call ahead or check the website.

🛏 Sleeping

Gingerbread Cottages   RENTAL HOUSE $$
(☑ 03-6393 1140; www.westburycottages.com.au; 52 William St; d $170-190, extra adult/child $30/20; ☎) It's worth staying in Westbury just for these five little self-contained cottages, decked out with antiques and snug country vibes. The affable owners even bring you freshly baked cake for afternoon tea. Our fave is the sweet 1860 Apple Tree Cottage.

Fitzpatricks Inn   INN $$
(☑ 03-6393 1153; www.fitzpatricksinn.com.au; 56 Meander Valley Rd; d incl breakfast from $110) This grand 1833 inn retains its historic vibes, despite the extensive renovations that were nearing completion when we visited (check out the handmade nails in the old floorboards!). There are seven en-suite rooms: three upstairs in the main building and four out the back. There's also a restaurant (mains from $30), open to the public for lunch and dinner.

Quamby Estate   BOUTIQUE HOTEL $$$
(☑ 03-6392 2235; www.quambyestate.com.au; 1145 Westwood Rd, Hagley; d $199-346, breakfast $15-20, dinner 2/3 courses $60/75; ☎) Follow the looong hawthorn-hedged driveway to this

classy country-house hotel, built in 1828. Ten stylish en-suite rooms are uniquely furnished, merging antique with contemporary style. Inside are two sitting rooms and a **restaurant** serving breakfast and dinner. Outside are acres of lawns, mature trees, tennis courts and a golf course. Prices dip to $99 for standard rooms in deepest, darkest winter.

✗ Eating

Andy's Bakery   BAKERY $
(☑ 03-6393 1846; www.andystasmania.com; 45 Meander Valley Rd; items $3-25; ⊙ 7am-5.30pm; 🛜) Roadside Andy's is a bit of an icon around these parts, with a big rep for pies, steak sandwiches and gelati. A steak-and-pepper pie followed by a scoop of baked cheesecake sorbet will max out your daily calorie allowance. Extended summer hours.

Westbury Hotel   PUB FOOD $$
(☑ 03-6393 1151; 107 Meander Valley Rd; mains $15-30; ⊙ noon-2pm & 6-8pm) Mainstream pub meals on the main street: roasts, chicken Kiev and a chicken parmigiana that's up there with the best of them.

ℹ Getting There & Away

Redline (☑ 1300 360 000; www.tasredline. com.au) Daily buses between Launceston and Westbury ($11.50, 35 minutes).

Liffey Valley

This lush valley at the foot of the Great Western Tiers (Kooperona Niara or 'Mountains of the Spirits') is famously the spiritual home of conservationist and politician Dr Bob Brown. The natural centrepiece is **Liffey Falls State Reserve**, 34km southwest of Carrick, is **Liffey Falls**. There are two approaches to the falls, which are actually four separate cascades. From the upstream car park (reached by a steep, winding road) it's a 45-minute return walk on a well-marked track. You can also follow the river upstream on foot from the Gulf Rd picnic area; allow two to three hours return. The area has some mighty fine fishing, too – feisty brown and rainbow trout inhabit the waterways.

Longford

POP 3760

Longford was founded in 1807 when free landholding farmers were moved to Van Diemen's Land from Norfolk Island. It's one

TALL POPPIES

As you explore Tasmania's northern agricultural heartlands, you'll likely come across fields of purple poppies, their heads bobbing in the breeze. Nearly half of the world's legal poppy crop is grown in Tasmania – an industry worth $100 million a year. The opiate alkaloids used in painkillers and other medicines are extracted at the sprawling Tasmanian Alkaloids plant near Westbury.

The growing and harvesting of poppies in Tasmania is strictly controlled by the state government and the Poppy Advisory and Control Board. Never try to jump the fence into a poppy field – access is illegal and most are protected by electric fences. Believe the warning signs on fences, too: the unrefined sap from opium poppies is toxic and will more likely send you to the afterlife than give you any kind of high.

of the few Tasmanian towns not established by convicts.

Longford is also known for something quite different: the town's stint as host to the Australian Grand Prix from 1953 to 1968. The **Country Club Hotel** (☑ 03-6391 3141; 19 Wellington St; ⊙ 11am-late) is a shrine to this racy past, with photos and paraphernalia spangling the walls.

There are also two amazing historic estates nearby, established by the Archer family in the colony's early days. Both **Woolmers Estate** and **Brickendon** are now Unesco World Heritage Sites. They're firmly on the 'must-see' list when you're visiting this neck o' the woods.

◉ Sights & Activities

Longford spreads itself out around Memorial Park, and is known for architectural gems such as the **Christ Church** (☑ 03-6391 2982; www.christchurchlongford.com.au; cnr William & Wellington Sts; ⊙ services 9am Sun), the **Town Hall** (☑ 03-6397 7303; 67 Wellington St) and the **Queen's Arms Hotel** (☑ 03-6391 1130; 69 Wellington St).

Woolmers Estate   HISTORIC SITE
(☑ 03-6391 2230; www.woolmers.com.au; Woolmers Lane; tours adult/child/family $20/7/45; ⊙ 9.30am-4.30pm) The homestead at Woolmers dates from 1819 and, along with nearby

Brickendon, it's one of the 11 Unescso World Heritage Australian Convict Sites. Admission is via guided tours, which run at 10am, 11.15am, 12.30pm, 2pm and 3.30pm. Wandering through the antique-filled rooms you'll feel like you've fallen backwards into another century. There's also a heritage rose garden here – 2 hectares of headily scented blooms on the banks of the Macquarie River. Accommodation also available.

Brickendon   HISTORIC SITE
(☑ 03-6391 1383; www.brickendon.com.au; Woolmers Lane; adult/child/family $12.50/5/38; ⊙ 9.30am-5pm Oct-May, to 4pm Jun-Sep) World Heritage–listed Brickendon – one of the 11 Unesco World Heritage Australian Convict Sites – was established in 1824. The homestead is still occupied by by the Archer family, so you can't see inside, but you can explore the gorgeous old gardens and the farm village, and take the 2.8km Brickendon Walk. There's animal feeding for the kids, trout biting in the river and accommodation also on offer.

★★ Festivals & Events

Blessing of the Harvest Festival   FAIR
(www.longfordharvest.com; ⊙ Mar) Harking back to feudal times in the Mother Country, Longford's Harvest Festival brings a street parade and country-fair stalls.

Longford Revival Festival   SPORTS
(www.longfordfestival.com.au; ⊙ Mar) This festival celebrates the halcyon days of motor racing at Longford – featuring some of the original cars that burned rubber here, as well as newer specimens. Demonstrations of raw speed along a section of road known as the 'Flying Mile' steal the show.

🛏 Sleeping

Longford Riverside Caravan Park   CARAVAN PARK $
(☑ 03-6391 1470; www.longfordriversidecaravanpark.com; 2a Archer St; unpowered/powered sites $28/34, on-site caravans & cabins d $85-110; 🛜) Down on the grassy, shady verges of the Macquarie River, this caravan park offers affordable cabins and caravans, decent amenities blocks and the occasional passing trout just begging to be hooked.

Racecourse Inn   INN $$
(☑ 03-6391 2352; www.racecourseinn.com; 114 Marlborough St, Longford; d incl breakfast $180-225; 🛜) Expect a warm welcome at this restored Georgian coach inn (1840) at the far end of town. The five spacious en-suite rooms are antiquey but not over the top (the upstairs ones have interesting ceiling lines), while breakfasts are distinctly gourmet: think eggs Benedict, eggs with smoked salmon, and berries and fruits from the property.

Brickendon   COTTAGE $$
(☑ 03-6391 1383; www.brickendon.com.au; Woolmers Lane; d from $185, extra person $45) Historic Brickendon has two well-equipped 1830s cottages – built by convicts to house the estate's coachman and gardener – and three newer self-contained farm cottages with old-style trimmings. Staying here is entirely atmospheric – a mainline into Tasmania's colonial heritage. Cottages sleep two to seven.

Woolmers Estate   COTTAGE $$
(☑ 03-6391 2230; www.woolmers.com.au; Woolmers Lane; d from $145, extra adult/child $35/30) History buff? These seven little self-contained estate cottages, built to house servants and free settlers in the 1840s when Woolmers was really humming with activity,

---

FLANAGAN WINS THE BOOKER!

Tasmanian author Richard Flanagan – born in Longford in 1961 and descended from Thomas Flanagan, a convict transported to Van Diemen's Land for stealing food – has published six novels since 1994 (one every three years – impressive!). Thematically, Flanagan skirts around the frayed edges of Tasmanian history, both black and white. The disturbing imagery and noir realities he conjures are soaked in place, pain and portent. His 2013 novel *The Narrow Road to the Deep North* concerns Dorrigo Evans, a survivor of the construction of the Burma Railway. Overseen by occupying Japanese forces in 1943, the railway's construction claimed the lives of thousands of Burmese civilians and Allied prisoners of war and scarred its survivors irrevocably, including Flanagan's father. The novel swept Flanagan to global prominence in 2014 when it won the Man Booker Prize, awarded to the year's best original English-language novel published in the UK.

now shelter visitors to Woolmers Estate. The Rose Garden Cottage is improbably quaint.

Longford Boutique Accommodation B&B $$
(☑03-6391 2126; www.longfordboutique.com; 6 Marlborough St; d incl breakfast $165-195; ☎) Just off the main street, this National Trust–listed bank (1865) is now a boutique B&B. Luxe benefits include port and chocolates, fluffy bathrobes, a wood fire and a DVD library. There are three rooms in the main building, and a cottage out the back sleeping four (good for families).

✖ Eating

JJ's Bakery & Old Mill Café BAKERY $
(☑03-6391 2364; www.jjsbakery.com; 52 Wellington St; items $4-23; ☺7am-5pm) This bakehouse inside the Old Emerald Flour Mill is always busy. It does great pizzas, bruschettas, pies, quiches and a mighty fine chocolate-mud muffin, all made on-site. Myriad trophies sit on top of the bread shelves.

★**Home of the Artisan** CAFE $$
(☑03-6391 2042; 15 Wellington St, Longford; mains lunch $18-22, dinner $38-45; ☺9am-4.30pm Mon-Wed & Fri, to 8pm Thu) Longford's best cafe is an earthy, value-for-money eatery in an 1860 shopfront (a former chemist). Fresh herbs and vegetables from the garden out the back find their way into terrifc salads, plus there are super homemade cakes, muffins and great coffee. Thursday-night dinners feature rustic country mains. Providore shelves, affordable wines and takeaway sauces and chutneys, too.

ⓘ Information

Online Access Centre (☑03-6391 1696; www.linc.tas.gov.au; Lyttleton St; ☺11am-5pm Mon & Wed, to 6pm Tue & Thu, to 7pm Fri) At the Longford library.

ⓘ Getting There & Away

Tassielink (☑1300 300 520; www.tassielink.com.au) Monday to Saturday buses between Launceston and Longford ($7.50, 50 minutes) via Evandale.

Evandale

POP 1410

Walk down the main street in Evandale and you'll feel like you've time-warped back a century...precisely why the entire town is National Trust listed. It's a ridiculously photogenic place, and a few hours wandering the quiet streets, browsing the galleries and hanging out at the cafes is time well spent. The highlight of the year is February's National Penny Farthing Championships (p198), when two-wheel warriors race around the town's streets at alarming velocities.

Evandale is also close to Launceston Airport: it's a doable option for accommodation if you've got an early flight.

⊙ Sights & Activities

Clarendon HISTORIC BUILDING
(☑03-6398 6220; www.nationaltrust.org.au/tas/clarendon; 234 Clarendon Station Rd; adult/child $15/free; ☺10am-4pm Sep-Jun) South of town via Nile Rd is stately, two-storey Clarendon. Built in 1838 in neoclassical style, it looks like it's stepped straight out of *Gone with the Wind;* it was long the grandest house in the colony. Take a self-guided tour of the home, which is graced with antiques, and the seven park-like hectares of gardens on the South Esk River. Also here is the Australian Fly Fishing Museum.

Evandale Market MARKET
(☑03-6391 9191; Falls Park, Logan Rd; ☺8am-1.30pm Sun) An exuberant mix of happy locals selling fresh fruit and veg, kids pony rides (and occasionally a mini train), food vans and stalls selling crafts and bric-a-brac.

Australian Fly Fishing Museum MUSEUM
(☑03-6398 6220; www.affm.net.au; Clarendon, 234 Clarendon Station Rd; admission $5; ☺10am-4pm Mon-Sat, noon-4pm Sun) 'Tis a noble art, fly fishing. Not to mention actually tying the flies so they look like something a trout might want to eat. This new museum has a beaut collection of rods, reels and flies. Think of it as a value-added experience when you're visiting Clarendon.

Water Tower HISTORIC BUILDING
(cnr High St & Cambock Lane W) As you enter town from the north you'll see this castle-like red-brick water tower (1896), which encloses a convict-dug tunnel designed to supply water to the town. There's still 80,000L inside, maintaining pressure on the walls so they don't collapse.

St Andrews Uniting (Presbyterian) Church CHURCH
(☑03-6344 1293; www.evandaletasmania.com; 9 High St; ☺service 11am Sun) This historic church on High St, with its sturdy Doric columns and a classical bell tower, opened for

worship in 1839. It's a much-admired example of Greek revival architecture.

St Andrews Anglican Church CHURCH
(☑ 03-6391 8371; www.anglicantas.org.au; 6 High St; ☺ service 10am Sun) Also on High St, the 'other' St Andrews, with its soaring spire, first opened in 1837. Faulty foundations meant it had to be rebuilt from the ground up not long after, and it was rededicated in 1871.

✪ Festivals & Events

Evandale Village Fair & National Penny Farthing Championships SPORTS
(www.evandalevillagefair.com; ☺ Feb) During the village fair Evandale comes out to play. There are breakneck penny-farthing races, a market, clowns and pipe bands parading the streets. There's also a 'Slow Race' for the penny farthings (last bike over the line wins – it's actually really difficult to ride these bad boys slowly!).

Glover Art Prize ART
(www.johnglover.com.au; ☺ Mar) During the March long weekend each year, the historic pavilion in Falls Park hosts an exhibition of finalists' works in the Glover Art Prize competition, Australia's richest. It's a feast of contemporary landscape art that's not to be missed.

🛏 Sleeping

Prince of Wales Hotel PUB $
(☑ 03-6391 8381; www.evandaletasmania.com/prince-of-wales-hotel.html; cnr High & Collins Sts; dm/d/f $30/90/110) Evandale has two pubs, and this one is probably the best bet for accommodation, despite being 180 years old. Upstairs are decent pub-style rooms with bathrooms and new TVs; downstairs the beer garden is an actual garden (what a rarety!). The **bistro** (mains $10 to $30; serving noon to 2pm and 6pm to 8pm) does great pizzas.

Wesleyan Chapel COTTAGE $$
(☑ 03-6331 9337; www.windmillhilllodge.com.au; 28 Russell St; d incl breakfast from $150) Built in 1836, this tiny brick chapel has since been used variously as a druids hall, an RSL hall and a scout hall. Now it's stylish, self-contained accommodation for two, right on the main street. Check out the old steel tie rods running through the lofty ceiling space, holding the external walls together.

Grandma's House COTTAGE $$
(☑ 0408 295 387; www.grandmashouse.com.au; 10 Rodgers Lane; d $130-170, extra person $50; ☎)

This four-bedroom house (sleeps five) occupies the leafy gardens of historic Marlborough House in the centre of town. There's a wisteria-draped verandah with a BBQ out the back, and you have the run of the extensive gardens. Reduced rates for longer stays.

Arendon Cottage COTTAGE $$
(☑ 0428 353 430, 03-6391 8520; www.evandaletasmania.com/arendon-cottage-boutique-accommodation.html; 30 Russell St; d incl breakfast $130-160, extra person $25; ❄ ☎) A lovely little self-contained 1840s cottage at the quiet end of the main street. Its pure Georgian proportions were redeemed after the owners rebuilt the original roof shape a few years ago. Two bedrooms; sleeps four. Full kitchen and laundry. The owners live in the house out the back, so no parties now, y'hear?

🍴 Eating

Vitalogy CAFE $
(☑ 0437 840 035; 1/14 Russell St; mains $9-25; ☺ 9.30am-4pm Wed-Fri, 10am-4pm Sat, 9am-4pm Sun) One for the Pearl Jam fans (what a great album that was...), this cool little eatery does delicious cafe fare using plenty of fresh local produce. Order the pumpkin soup with cornbread, the triple-cheese-and-herb omelette, or a brick of deluxe beef lasagne. The best coffee in town, too.

Ingleside Bakery Cafe CAFE $
(☑ 03-6391 8682; 4 Russell St; meals $6-22; ☺ 8.30am-5pm Mon-Fri, to 4.30pm Sat & Sun) Sit in the flowery walled courtyard or under the high ceiling inside this former council chambers (1867), where fresh-baked aromas waft from the wood oven. Expect delectable pies and pasties, a gap-filling swagman's lunch and all manner of sweet treats. The providore shelves are packed.

Clarendon Arms Hotel PUB FOOD $$
(☑ 03-6391 8181; 11 Russell St; mains $12-26; ☺ noon-2pm & 6-8pm) The old Clarendon oozes atmosphere, the woody bar permanently propped up by locals. The country menu is studded with the likes of beef-and-Guinness pie, roast of the day and crumbed lamb cutlets with mash. A turkey gobbles around on the grass in the beer garden out the back.

ⓘ Information

Evandale Visitor Information Centre (☑ 03-6391 8128; www.evandaletasmania.com; 18 High St; ☺ 9.30am-4.30pm) Local info and accommodation bookings. Stocks the *Evandale*

Heritage Walk pamphlet ($3), detailing the town's historic riches. The **history room** here has displays on local painter John Glover and decorated WWI soldier Harry Murray. Both are commemorated with statues on Russell St: Glover, 18 stone and club footed; Murray hurling a grenade.

❶ Getting There & Away

Tassielink (☑1300 300 520; www.tassielink. com.au) Monday to Saturday buses between Launceston and Evandale ($6.50, 30 minutes) continue to Longford.

Ben Lomond National Park

The 181-sq-km **Ben Lomond National Park** (☑03-6336 5312; www.parks.tas.gov.au; vehicle/ person per day $24/12) takes in the whole of the Ben Lomond massif: a craggy alpine plateau some 14km long by 6km wide. The plateau reaches heights of 1300m and its peaks are above 1500m. Legges Tor (1573m) is the second-highest peak in Tasmania (after the 1617m Mt Ossa) and in fine weather affords amazing 360-degree views. A classic Ben Lomond image is a jumbled landscape of scree slopes and dolerite columns (often with rock climbers attached).

🏃 Activities

Skiing

Ben Lomond is also Tasmania's Aspen – well, not quite, but when the snow does fall the lifts grind into action and you can ski here. The snow can be fickle, but the ski season generally runs from early July to mid-September. Two 'snow guns' top up the natural snow. Full-day ski-lift passes cost $55/30 per adult/child, while half-day passes cost $38/20. Under sixes and over 65s ride free! There are three T-bars and four poma lifts. For snow reports and cams, see www.ski.com.au/reports/australia/tas/ benlomond.

Ben Lomond Snow Sports (☑03-6390 6185; www.skibenlomond.com.au; Ben Lomond Rd, Ben Lomond National Park; ☉9am-4.30pm in season) runs a kiosk selling takeaway fare and a shop doing ski, snowboard and toboggan rental, and associated gear. Skis, boots, poles and a lesson cost $85/70 per adult/child; just skis, boots and poles costs $55/40.

National park entry fees apply to access the snowfields.

Bushwalking

The park is magnificent in summer, with great bushwalking and a riot of alpine flowers. It's a two-hour walk each way to **Legges Tor** from Carr Villa, about halfway up the mountain. You can also climb to the top along marked tracks from the alpine village on the plateau, which takes about 30 minutes each way.

If you're happy to go off track, you can walk across the plateau in almost any direction. This is easy enough in fine weather but not recommended without complete visibility. Unless you're well equipped, walking south of the ski village isn't advised. All walkers and cross-country skiers should register at the self-registration booth at the alpine village.

🛏 Sleeping & Eating

There's a small **camping** area 1km along from the national park entrance: six unpowered sites with flushing toilets, drinking water and super views. National park entry fees apply.

Ben Lomond Alpine Hotel   LODGE **$$**
(☑03-6390 6199; www.northerntasmania.com.au/ accommodation/ben-lomond-alpine-hotel; Alpine Village, Ben Lomond Rd; d $150-250) There's accommodation year-round here at Tasmania's highest pub. There are cosily heated en-suite rooms and – snow permitting – you can ski right to the door. There's also a **restaurant** (mains $16 to $32) where you can replenish your skiing or hiking energies.

❶ Getting There & Away

There's no public transport to the mountain, so driving is your only option. At a pinch **Northern Taxis** (☑0419 745 837) might take you there (it's 90 minutes from Launceston).

Note that the road up to the plateau is unsealed and includes Jacob's Ladder, a sensationally steep climb with six white-knuckle hairpin bends and no safety barriers. During the snow season, chains are standard issue – hire them from Skigia (p78) in Hobart or **Autobarn** (Map p174; ☑03-6334 5601; www.autobarn. com.au/stores/launceston; 6 Innes St; ☉8am-5.30pm Mon-Fri, 9am-5pm Sat, 9am-4pm Sun) in Launceston (around $40 per day, plus $60 deposit). Don't forget antifreeze.

Ben Lomond Snow Sports runs a shuttle bus ($15 per person each way) from the rangers station, 1km from the national park entry booth. Call for pick-ups.

Devonport & the Northwest

Best Places to Eat

➡ Mrs Jones (p205)

➡ Renaessance (p217)

➡ Xanders (p225)

➡ Drift Cafe Restaurant (p205)

➡ Deli Central (p215)

Best Places to Stay

➡ @VDL (p224)

➡ Corinna Wilderness Experience (p231)

➡ Madsen (p216)

➡ Ikon Hotel (p219)

➡ Forest Walks Lodge (p208)

Why Go?

Tasmania's northwest is the island in a nutshell – wild and untramelled in places, quietly sophisticated just about everywhere else. In the far northwest in particular, there are so many candidates for the title of Tasmania's most remote corner, from the dense and ancient rainforests of the Tarkine wilderness to remote beaches swept by the cleanest air on earth. Here also are some of the best places in Australia to see platypuses and penguins, enjoy fabulous beaches and then sleep the night in charming towns where the past sits lightly upon their shoulders. Best of all, the sense of exploring one of the world's last unspoiled corners will linger long after you leave.

When to Go

➡ The northwest blooms in spring and summer: fields of purple poppies, multicoloured tulips, fragrant rainforest leatherwood. There's fresh crayfish, penguin watching, and music and craft festivals, and you can camp beachside, ready for the perfect surf break.

➡ Visit in winter to experience the full power of the Roaring Forties. Locals batten down the hatches for the longest, darkest nights, when the area is exhilaratingly wild and wind-lashed. You'll get a warm welcome, but call ahead: some things close completely – or open less frequently – in winter.

Devonport

POP 22,770

Devonport is the Tasmanian base for the *Spirit of Tasmania I* and *II,* the red-and-white ferries that connect the island state with the mainland. It's quite an evocative sight when, after three deep blasts of the horn, they cruise past the end of the main street to begin their voyage north. The ferry gone, Devonport slips back into obscurity. Most visitors do indeed get off the ferry, jump in their cars and leave Devonport behind. Before you do so, remember to take advantage of Devonport's location: walk along the Mersey and up to the **Mersey Bluff Lighthouse** for unmissable views over the coastline and Bass Strait.

◎ Sights & Activities

Penguin-watching season runs from August to March.

★**Bass Strait Maritime Centre**   MUSEUM

(✐03-6424 7100; www.bassstraitmaritimecentre.com.au; 6 Gloucester Ave; adult/child/family $10/5/25; ⊙10am-5pm) This museum is in the former harbourmaster's residence (c 1920) and pilot station near the foreshore. It has an extensive collection of flags and other maritime paraphernalia, including a superb set of models covering the ages of sail and steam through to the present passenger ferries.

★**Home Hill**   HISTORIC BUILDING

(✐03-6424 8055; www.nationaltrusttas.org.au; 77 Middle Rd; adult/child/concession $10/free/8; ⊙guided tours 2pm Wed-Sun, other times by appointment) This was the residence of Joseph Lyons (Australia's only Tasmanian prime minister; 1932–39) and his wife, Dame Enid Lyons, and their 12 children. Built in 1916, the handsome white home contains some fascinating personal family effects, many of which touch on the couple's prolific public life.

Don River Railway   MUSEUM

(✐03-6424 6335; www.donriverrailway.com.au; Forth Main Rd; adult/child/family $18/13/40; ⊙9am-5pm) You don't have to be a trainspotter to love this collection of locomotives and brightly painted rolling stock. The entry price includes a half-hour ride in a diesel train (on the hour from 10am to 4pm), and you can hop on the puffing steam train on Sundays and public holidays.

To get here, drive west of Devonport along the Bass Hwy then take the B19 exit towards Don, Devonport and Spreyton. The railway is 4.5km from the centre of Devonport.

Devonport Regional Gallery   GALLERY

(✐03-6424 8296; www.devonportgallery.com; 45-47 Stewart St; ⊙10am-5pm Mon-Fri, noon-5pm Sat, 1-5pm Sun) This excellent gallery houses predominantly 20th-century Tasmanian paintings, and contemporary art by local and mainland artists, plus ceramics and glasswork.

Pandemonium   AMUSEMENT PARK

(✐03-6424 1333; www.pandemoniumtas.com.au; 62-64 North Fenton St; admission from $10; ⊙9.30am-4pm Tue-Sun) This is *the* place in Devonport where kids can let off steam. It's an indoor play centre with a giant jungle gym, jumping castles and slides (for kids up to 11 years of age), laser skirmish (eight years and up), rock climbing (six and up) and the hands-on scientific displays of the Imaginarium Science Centre. There's a cafe to collapse in when you're done.

☞ Tours

Murray's Day Out   BUS TOUR

(✐03 64252439; www.murraysdayout.com.au; day trips per person from $150) To be shown some of Tasmania by an entirely passionate and charming Tasmanian, consider taking one of these tours. Murray offers 'service with humour' in his comfortable van (seating up to seven). Go all the way west to Marrawah, drop in on Cradle Mountain, or just tootle around the country lanes near Devonport.

🛏 Sleeping

Mersey Bluff Caravan Park   CARAVAN PARK $

(✐03-6424 8655; www.merseybluff.com.au; 41 Bluff Rd; unpowered sites per person $13, powered sites per 2 adults $33, on-site caravans d $40-80) In a seaside setting on Mersey Bluff, this pleasantly green park is just steps from the beach. There's a campers' kitchen, BBQ facilities and a playground nearby, and the park's close to the facilities of the new Mersey Bluff development.

Tasman Backpackers   HOSTEL $

(✐03-6423 2335; www.tasmanbackpackers.com.au; 114 Tasman St; dm $20-23, tw/d $50/52; P@☎) This hostel was once a sprawling nurses' quarters, but it's now a friendly place to stay and has an international feel. The en-suite doubles all have TVs and DVD players and there are (free) movies in the lounge most nights. The hostel offers free ferry and

Devonport & the Northwest Highlights

1 Walk a heritage trail then climb the Nut for fabulous views in **Stanley** (p222).

2 Search for platypuses in the Mersey River south of **Latrobe** (p207).

3 Go beyond the paved road, deep into the Tarkine rainforest at **Corinna** (p230).

4 Admire one of Tasmania's prettiest beaches at **Boat Harbour Beach** (p221).

5 Marvel at limestone cave formations, lit by glowworms, at **Mole Creek Karst National Park** (p210).

6 Hike through gnarled pencil pine forests at gorgeous **Walls of Jerusalem National Park** (p211).

7 Watch penguins come ashore after braving Bass Strait near **Penguin** (p216).

8 Look out into eternity, or catch a Roaring Forties wave, at **Marrawah** (p227).

9 Learn about the open-air gallery of Sheffield by taking one of the **Mural Audio Tours** (p213).

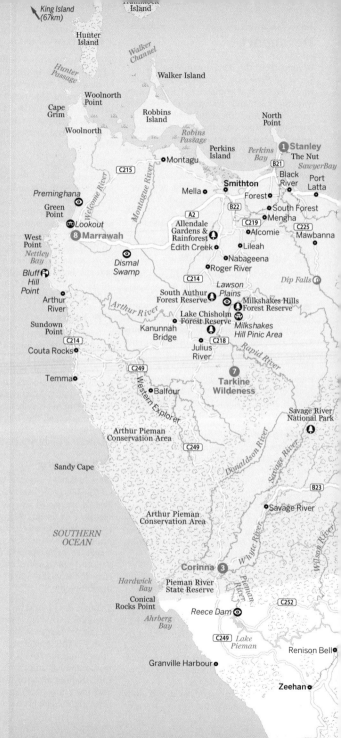

Spirit of Tasmania ferries
to/from Melbourne
(approx. 10 hours
or 360km)

0   20 km
N
0   10 miles

BASS STRAIT

Rocky
Cape
Rocky Cape
National Park
Sisters Beach
Boat Harbour Beach
4 Boat Harbour
Table Cape
Fossil Bluff
Sisters
Creek
Myalla
Wynyard
Detention
Falls
C229
A2 Somerset
Milabena
B26 Burnie
Heybridge
Sulphur Creek
Lillico Beach
Penguin
Watching
Narawntapu
National
Point   Park
Sorell
Yolla
Penguin
7
1 Ulverstone Turners
Ridgley Beach
Dial Range Gawler Forth Devonport
Riana Wings B17 B16
Wildlife Eugenana
Park Spreyton Latrobe Harford
Hawley Beach
Shearwater
Port Sorell
B74
Wesley Vale
Hampshire
Gunns Plain Warrawee
2 Forest
Reserve
B71
Greens
Beach
(34km)
Hellyer Gorge
State Reserve
B18
St Valentines
Peak (1106m)
Gunns
Plains
Caves
Leven Valley
Vineyard & Gallery
Barrington
Lake
Barrington
Railton
B14
B13
1
Guildford
Leven
Canyon
Nietta
South
Nietta
Wilmot
Sheffield
9
Elizabeth
Town
Waratah
Black
Bluff
(1339m)
Winterbrook
Falls
Tasmazia
Mt Roland
(1234m)
Moltema
Weetah
B54
Deloraine
A5
Lake
Lea
Moina
Gowrie Park
O'Neills Creek
Reserve
Trowunna
Wildlife
Park
A10
Lake
Cethana
Mt Claude
(1034m)
Alum Cliffs
Gorge
Mole
Creek Chudleigh
Caveside
41° South
Aquaculture
C123
King Solomons Cave
Marakoopa
Cave
Baldocks
Cave
Honeycomb
Caves
Quamby Bluff
Forest Reserve
Meander
C171
Mole Creek Karst
National Park
Cradle Valley
Cradle
Mountain
(1545m)
Dove Lake
Lake
Parangana
Cradle Mountain-
Lake St Claire
National Park
Devils
Gullet
Meander
Forest Reserve
Meander
Falls
Lake
Mackintosh
Central Plateau
Conservation Area
Lake
Rowallan
Lake
Rosebery
Tullah Mt Farrell
Rosebery
Mt Murchison
(1275m)
Mt Jerusalem
(1458m)
6 Walls of Jerusalem
National Park
Williamson
Hellyer River
Flowerdale River
Cam River
Emu River
Blythe River
Leven River
River Forth
River Forth
Robinson River
5
B17
A10

Devonport

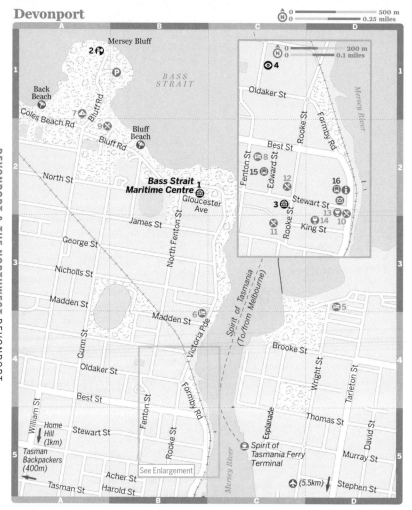

bus-station pick-ups, and can make tour and bus bookings.

Staff also do placements for harvesting and fruit-picking jobs.

Cameo Cottage RENTAL HOUSE **$$**
(☑03-6427 0991, 0439 658 503; www.devonport-bedandbreakfast.com; 27 Victoria Pde; d $165, extra adult/child $35/25; ℗) Tucked away in a quiet backstreets this two-bedroom cottage was built in 1914 but has been beautifully redecorated. It's got a well-equipped kitchen, a cosy lounge, a laundry and a quiet garden with BBQ facilities.

Quality Hotel Gateway HOTEL **$$**
(☑03-6424 4922; www.gatewayinn.com.au; 16 Fenton St; d from $136; ℗❋@☎) Contemporary rooms, recently renovated, catch the eye here, three short blocks back from the waterfront. It lacks the personal touch of a B&B, but the quality is excellent. It has an on-site restaurant as well.

Alice Beside the Sea APARTMENT **$$**
(☑03-6427 8605; www.alicebesidethesea.com; 1 Wright St; d $115-180) Located close to the ferry terminals, this compact B&B offers comfortable, two-bedroom, self-contained accommo-

Devonport

dation across the road from the beach and near to supermarkets. It's pet friendly, too.

✕ Eating

★ **Drift Cafe Restaurant**   CAFE **$$**
(☑ 03-6424 4695; www.driftdevonport.com; 41 Bluff Rd; mains $22-28, burgers $8-16; ⊙ 10am-late Wed-Sun, to 4pm Mon & Tue) Part of the new surf-club complex out on the Mersey Bluff road, this place segues effortlessly from classy to casual. Tasmanian craft beers, gourmet burgers and a sea breeze – what more could you ask for? There's also a fine menu of everything from Tassie salmon to sweet-potato and chickpea curry, plus occasional Greek and Thai inflections. It opens later in summer.

★ **Laneway**   CAFE **$$**
(www.lane-way.com.au; 2/38 Steele St; mains $11-20; ⊙ 7.30am-4pm) Filling a former bakery, we reckon Laneway is one of Tassie's best cafes. Hip waitstaff deliver robust brekkies, including smashed avocado with poached eggs and pancetta, and the sunny, heritage space also functions as a deli showcasing local beer, wine and artisan produce. Evening events with special dinner menus are sometimes scheduled, so pop by to see what's on.

Tapas Lounge Bar   CAFE **$$**
(www.tapasloungebar.com; 97a Rooke St Mall; tapas $10-14, mains $17-24; ⊙ 5-10pm Wed, to midnight Thu, to 2am Fri, to 4am Sat, food 5-9pm Wed-Sat) This cool new place, upstairs in the Rooke St Mall, is all done up in black leather. It has funky music and, people say, the best eating in Devonport. The tempting tapas-style menu also has options for kids. After 9pm it morphs into a bar for over-25s, with live music Thursday to Saturday – check its online gig guide.

Formby Hotel   PUB FOOD **$$**
(Central Restaurant; 82 Formby Rd; mains $20-33; ⊙ noon-2.30pm & 6-9pm Mon-Sat, 8am-2.30pm Sun) The refurbished dining room offers bistro meals, including pizza, pastas, salads, steaks (we liked the Roaring Forties eye fillet) and seafood. There are excellent fresh juices and smoothies at the cafe-bar, and coffee and cakes between mealtimes.

★ **Mrs Jones**   MODERN AUSTRALIAN **$$$**
(☑ 03-6423 3881; www.mrsjonesrbl.com.au; 41 Bluff Rd; mains $29-40; ⊙ noon-late) When they closed the much-loved Wild Cafe along the coast in Penguin to open Mrs Jones, it was definitely Penguin's loss but Devonport's gain. Upstairs in the swish new surf-club development, Mrs Jones has stunning decor (Tasmanian oak tables and leather sofas, and an open kitchen) and exceptional food, with a commitment to local produce.

Menus change with the seasons, but the slow-braised lamb shoulder in cinnamon and all-spice, and the aromatic coconut duck curry, both caught our eye when we passed through.

🍷 Drinking & Nightlife

Central at the Formby   BAR
(82 Formby Rd; ⊙ 2pm-late) Locals regard this as Devonport's best bar. It's decked out with leather sofas and laid-back cool, and the concertina windows open onto the river on warm nights. There are live bands Friday and Saturday, while Sunday afternoon sees acoustic sessions and a more sophisticated crowd.

House Niteclub   CLUB
(☑ 03-6424 7851; www.housenc.com.au; 18-22 King St; admission $6-12; ⊙ 10pm-late Thu-Sat) You're not exactly spoiled for clubbing choice in Devonport, and House (no secret what kind of music they like...) draws a young and boisterous crowd for live bands and Saturday-night DJs.

ℹ Information

Devonport Visitor Information Centre
(☑1800 649 514, 03-6424 4466; www.devon-porttasmania.travel; 92 Formby Rd; ⊙7.30am-5pm) Across the river from the ferry terminal, the info centre opens to meet ferry arrivals. Free baggage storage available.

ℹ Getting There & Away

AIR

QantasLink (☑13 13 13; www.qantas.com.au) Regular flights to Melbourne.

BOAT

Spirit of Tasmania (☑1800 634 906; www.spiritoftasmania.com.au; ⊙ customer contact centre 8am-8.30pm Mon-Sat, 9am-8pm Sun) ferries sail between Station Pier in Melbourne and the ferry terminal on the Esplanade in East Devonport.

BUS

In addition to longer-haul intercity services, Merseylink operates local buses between Devonport and Latrobe ($4.20, 25 minutes) from Devonport's Rooke St interchange.

Redline Coaches (☑1300 360 000; www.tasredline.com.au) Redline Coaches stop at 9 Edward St and the *Spirit of Tasmania* terminal in Devonport. There's a Launceston to Devonport ($25.40, 2½ hours) service, via Deloraine and Latrobe. Other services include Ulverstone ($6.50, 25 minutes), Penguin ($8.50, 40 minutes) and Burnie ($11.20, one hour).

Tassielink (☑1300 300 520; www.tassielink.com.au) Tassielink buses stop at the visitor centre and at the *Spirit of Tasmania* terminal. Services from Devonport include Launceston ($25.50, 70 minutes), Sheffield ($5.60, 40

minutes), Gowrie Park ($10.20, 55 minutes), Cradle Mountain ($42.40, two hours), Queenstown ($56.20, four hours) and Strahan ($66.80, five hours).

CAR

All of the major car-rental companies have offices at the ferry terminal and/or airport.

ℹ Getting Around

The ferry across the Mersey that connected the ferry terminal with the CBD ceased operation in mid-2014. Ask at the visitor centre or on board the *Spirit of Tasmania* in case it has restarted.

TO/FROM THE AIRPORT

The **Devonport Airport & Spirit Shuttle** (☑1300 659 878) runs between the airport, the ferry terminal, the visitor centre and your accommodation ($15). There's also a service to Launceston Airport ($50). Bookings essential.

Combined Taxi (☑03-6424 1431) will carry you from the airport to the centre of town for $20 to $25.

BUS

Devonport has an extensive internal bus network run by **Merseylink** (☑03-6427 7626; www.merseylink.com.au). The most useful service connects the ferry terminal (on the Mersey's east bank) with the CBD (adult $3).

Latrobe

POP 3350

Ten kilometres south of Devonport, Latrobe was once a busy shipping port on the Mersey River. Today it remains an attractive, historic town, with heritage buildings housing cafes

---

WORTH A TRIP

FOODIE DETOURS FROM LATROBE

House of Anvers (☑03-6426 2958; www.anvers-chocolate.com.au; 9025 Bass Hwy; ⊙7am-7pm) A chocolate factory and a museum of chocolate with a range of sweet treats: fudges, truffles and the most amazing chocolate-orange slices. The line between exhibition and hard sell is blurred at times, but why care? You can also come here for breakfast. The complex is approximately 3km from Latrobe, in the direction of Devonport.

Cherry Shed (☑03-6426 2411; www.thecherryshed.com.au; cnr Gilbert St & Bass Hwy; ⊙9.30am-5pm) As the name suggests, this place is all about local cherries. There's an onsite cafe (where even the burgers come with cherry relish) and an information room, with the likes of cherry ice cream, cherry liqueurs and cherry chutney for sale. It's at the Bass Hwy entrance to Latrobe.

Spreyton Cider Co (☑03-6427 2125; www.spreytonciderco.com.au; cnr Sheffield & Melrose Rds, Spreyton; ⊙noon-5pm) Around 7km west of Latrobe along the C146, Spreyton Cider Co produces some of Tasmania's best-loved ciders. Visit its cellar door for tastings of the five different varieties – it's hard to leave without buying any.

and antique shops – there are 75 National Trust–registered buildings on the main street alone. In true Tasmanian style, Latrobe is the home of woodchopping *and* one of the best places in Australia to see platypuses.

◉ Sights

Australian Axeman's Hall of Fame   MUSEUM
(☑ 03-6426 2099; www.axemanscomplex.com.au; 1 Bells Pde; ◎ 9am-5pm) FREE One of those engaging rural museums that could only be in Australia, this impressive complex honours the legendary axemen of the northwest. Most of the displays centre around competitive woodchopping and an examination of sustainable forestry. Also here is the Platypus Interpretation Centre, which sheds light on the breeding life and habits of this shy monotreme that's often spotted in the Mersey River just over the road.

There's also a cafe for light meals. A Tasmanian Makers Market is held here every Sunday and Thursday.

Sherwood Hall   HISTORIC BUILDING
(☑ 03-6426 2888; Bells Pde; adult/child $2/free; ◎ 10am-2pm Tue & Thu, 1-5pm Sat, Sun & public holidays) This historic cottage was built by a remarkable pioneer couple, ex-convict Thomas Johnson and wife, Dolly Dalrymple Briggs, who was of Aboriginal and English descent.

Warrawee Forest Reserve   WILDLIFE RESERVE
(◎ 9am-dusk) This beautiful 229-hectare reserve, centred on the Mersey River south of Latrobe, is named after a local Aboriginal word meaning 'plenty' and it's not difficult to see why – platypus sightings are *almost* guaranteed here. You could come and try your luck on your own, but we recommend taking a Platypus Spotting Tour. The riverine forest here also shelters the shy Tasmanian bettong. Some of the walking trails are wheelchair accessible.

Court House Museum   MUSEUM
(113 Gilbert St; adult/child $2/free; ◎ 1-4pm Tue-Fri) There's a rich photographic display of the area's history here, next to the post office in the centre of town.

🏃 Activities

Platypus-Spotting Tours   TOUR
(☑ 03-6426 1774, 03-6421 4699; adult/child $10/free; ◎ 8am & 4pm) Two-hour tours to look for platypuses in the Warrawee Forest Reserve leave from the Latrobe Visitor Centre daily.

SEEING PLATYPUSES AT LATROBE

Latrobe markets itself – with as much justification as hyperbole, it must be said – as the 'Platypus Capital of the World'. There are several good platypus-related visitor opportunities.

➡ Platypus Interpretation Centre, Australian Axeman's Hall of Fame

➡ Warrawee Forest Reserve

➡ Platypus-Spotting Tours

Glimpses may be fleeting (with a platypus surfacing for just a few seconds) or significantly longer, but the chances of seeing *something* are extremely high. Advance bookings are essential.

✿ Festivals & Events

Henley-on-the-Mersey Carnival   SPORTS
(◎ 26 Jan) Held on Australia Day at Bells Pde, site of the town's former docks.

Latrobe Chocolate Winterfest   FOOD
(www.chocolatewinterfest.com.au; ◎ Aug) This winter festival celebrates all things chocolate.

Latrobe Wheel Race   SPORTS
(◎ 26 Dec) Boxing Day bicycle race, attracting professional riders from around Australia.

🛌 Sleeping & Eating

House of Anvers and the Cherry Shed (see boxed text opposite), just outside Latrobe, both have decent cafe-restaurants.

Lucas Hotel   PUB $$
(☑ 03-6426 1101; www.lucashotellatrobe.com.au; 46 Gilbert St; s/d $110/120, without bathroom $85/95, with spa $125/140; P) This restored pub has comfortable, upmarket rooms with the kind of quietly classic look that works so well in an old-style pub atmosphere. There's good food (mains $13 to $29, serving noon to 2pm and 6pm to 8pm) on offer in an elegant dining room. It also has a kids menu and some wickedly good desserts.

Lucinda   B&B $$
(☑ 03-6426 2285; www.lucindabnb.com.au; 17 Forth St; s/d from $100/115; P 🖥) Lucinda provides handsome accommodation in a quintessentially Latrobe setting – a National Trust–classified home, set in park-like grounds. A couple of its heritage rooms have

spectacularly intricate moulded ceilings: see if you can spot the one red rose in the plasterwork as you lie in your four-poster bed.

Five Figs Cafe CAFE $
(☑ 03-6426 3165; 98 Gilbert St; mains $7-16; ☺ 9am-3.30pm Tue-Sat) This reasonable country cafe serves up all manner of Aussie staples, including pizza, burgers and occasional Middle Eastern or Thai dishes.

ⓘ Information

Latrobe Visitor Centre (☑ 6421 4699; www.latrobetasmania.com.au; 1 Bells Pde; ☺ 9am-5pm, reduced winter hours) At the Axeman's Hall of Fame.

Deloraine

POP 2333

At the foot of the Great Western Tiers, Deloraine has wonderful views at every turn. In the town itself, Georgian and Victorian buildings, ornate with wrought-iron tracery, crowd the main street, which leads to green parkland on the banks of the Meander River. The town has a vibrant, artsy feel, with several cool little eateries, some bohemian boutiques and secondhand shops.

◉ Sights

★ **Deloraine Museum** MUSEUM
(YARNS: Artwork in Silk; ☑ 03-6362 3471; www.yarnsartworkinsilk.com; 98-100 Emu Bay Rd; adult/child/family $8/2/18; ☺ 9am-5pm) The centrepiece of this museum is an exquisite four-panel, quilted and appliquéd depiction of the Meander Valley through a year of seasonal change. It's an astoundingly detailed piece of work that was a labour of love for 300 creative local men and women. Each of the four panels entailed 2500 hours of labour, and the whole project took three years to complete. It's now housed in a purpose-built auditorium, where you can witness a presentation explaining the work.

41° South Tasmania FARM
(☑ 03-6362 4130; www.41southtasmania.com; 323 Montana Rd; ☺ 9am-5pm Nov-Mar, to 4pm Apr-Oct) 🍃 **FREE** At this interesting farm, salmon are reared in raised tanks and a wetland is used as a natural biofilter. This no-waste, no-chemical method of fish farming is the cleanest way of raising fish – and also makes for superb smoked salmon, which you can taste (free) and buy in the tasting room, or lunch on in the cafe. Optional self-guided walks (adult/child/family $10/5/25) take you through the wetlands.

The farm is 6km out of town towards Mole Creek (signed down Montana Rd).

🏃 Activities

Dominating the southern skyline are the **Great Western Tiers** (their Aboriginal name is Kooparoona Niara, 'Mountain of the Spirits'). The **Meander Forest Reserve** is the most popular starting point for walks here. From the swing bridge over the Meander River – where there are bowers of man ferns and tall trees – you can walk to **Split Rock Falls**. This route takes about three hours return, or you can walk to **Meander Falls** – five to six hours return.

Other good walking destinations on the Great Western Tiers include **Projection Bluff** (two hours return), **Quamby Bluff** (five hours return) and **Mother Cummings Peak** (three to five hours return). Ask at the visitor centre for walking information.

✯ Festivals & Events

Tasmanian Craft Fair FAIR
(www.tascraftfair.com.au; adult/child $15/7, weekend pass $25/10; ☺ Nov) Deloraine's strong artistic community oversees this impressive four-day fair, held annually. Up to 30,000 people visit hundreds of craft stalls around town.

⎘ Sleeping

Deloraine Hotel PUB $
(☑ 03-6362 2022; www.delorainehotel.com.au; Emu Bay Rd; s without bathroom $40, d with bathroom $80-120) This 1848 pub is veritably draped in wrought-iron lace, and its once-pubbish interior recently had a cool, contemporary makeover. The simple rooms upstairs have also been given a stylish, if unpretentious, overhaul.

★ **Forest Walks Lodge** LODGE $$
(☑ 03-6369 5150; www.forestwalkslodge.com; Jackeys Marsh; s/d/f incl breakfast from $140/160/170) Set in a lovely rural area, this fabulous place gets consistently good reviews. The rooms are spacious, filled with warm colours, sprinkled lightly with tasteful local crafts and artwork, and yet are smart and contemporary in the quality of the furnishings.

Make a reservation for a fine three-course evening meal, then take a guided walk through the forests of the Great Western Tiers. Bliss.

FOODIE DETOURS FROM DELORAINE

Ashgrove Farm Cheese (☑03-6368 1105; www.ashgrovecheese.com.au; 6173 Bass Hwy, Elizabeth Town; ☺7.30am-5pm, cheesemaking 9am-4pm Mon-Fri) Journey 15km north of Deloraine to Elizabeth Town to find this award-winning cheese factory. You can watch the cheeses being made on weekdays and then sample the fine results in the tasting room/providore. The milk bar serves pies and platters, and milkshakes and ice creams aplenty.

Christmas Hills Raspberry Farm Cafe (www.raspberryfarmcafe.com; Christmas Hills Rd, Elizabeth Town; mains $11-20; ☺7am-5pm) There are 16 acres of raspberries grown here, and you can see them in all their glory before indulging in everything raspberry at the lakeside cafe. Think raspberry sundaes piled high with the ruby-coloured fruits, homemade raspberry ice cream, raspberry waffles, baked raspberry cheesecake, pavlovas, smoothies and even a shocking-pink raspberry latte. The farm is on the Bass Hwy, 8km north of Deloraine.

★**Bluestone Grainstore** B&B $$
(☑03-6362 4722; www.bluestonegrainstore.com.au; 14 Parsonage St; d incl breakfast $165-180; ☜) ✿
A 150-year-old warehouse has been renovated with great style here: think whitewashed stone walls, crisp linen, leather bedheads, deep oval bathtubs and funky touches such as origami flowers. There's even a mini-cinema and films to choose from. Breakfasts draw on local produce – organic where possible.

Blake's Manor APARTMENT $$
(☑03-6362 4724; www.blakesmanor.com; 18 West Goderich St; d $149-229) Wow, what an amazing job has been done on these two self-contained suites, attached to Georgian Blake's Manor. They're wonderfully ornate in period style, with velvet drapes, plush antiques and Persian rugs – and yet both have kitchenettes and contemporary bathrooms. Breakfast provisions, port, cheese and nibbles are laid on.

✖ Eating

Deloraine Deli DELI, CAFE $$
(☑03-6362 2127; 81 Emu Bay Rd; mains $11-21; ☺8.30am-5pm Mon-Fri, to 2.30pm Sat) A fine place for late-morning baguettes, bagels and focaccias, with a variety of tasty fillings. Its coffee is superb, and it does dairy- and gluten-free meals, too.

Empire Hotel & Thai Restaurant THAI $$
(☑03-6362 2100; 19 Emu Bay Rd; mains $19-29; ☺noon-2.30pm & 6-9pm) There's the usual Aussie bar here, and then – a surprising find in Deloraine – a really excellent Thai restaurant. Try the duck curry, its signature dish.

❶ Information

Great Western Tiers Visitor Information Centre (☑03-6362 5280; www.greatwesterntiers. net.au; 98-100 Emu Bay Rd; ☺8am-6pm Mon-Fri & 9am-5pm Sat & Sun Jan-Mar, 9am-5pm daily Apr, May & Sep-Dec, 9am-5pm Mon-Fri & 9.30am-4.30pm Sat & Sun Jun-Aug) Shares premises with the Deloraine Museum.

❶ Getting There & Away

Redline Coaches (☑03-6336 1446, 1300 360 000; www.redlinecoaches.com.au) Buses to Launceston ($14.30, 45 minutes).
Tassielink (☑03-6230 8900, 1300 300 520; www.tassielink.com.au) Buses to Cradle Mountain ($61.50, three hours) and Strahan (with transfer in Queenstown; $85.40, 6½ hours).

Mole Creek

POP 230

Pretty Mole Creek, around 23km west of Deloraine, is a tiny rural town with beautiful mountain views and a couple of good places to stay and eat. It's also a great jumping-off point for the nearby national parks, which around here means caving and bushwalking. There's a good chance of seeing platypuses in the town's waterways – keep an eye out just after sunrise and just before sunset.

❂ Sights & Activities

Devils Gullet VIEWPOINT
Those with transport should head for the Great Western Tiers. The only road that actually reaches the top of the plateau is the gravel road to Lake Mackenzie. Follow this road to Devils Gullet, where there's a 40-minute-return walk to a platform bolted to the top of a dramatic gorge: looking over the edge isn't for the faint-hearted.

Alum Cliffs Gorge VIEWPOINT
A one-hour-return walk along a sloping spur takes you to an impressive lookout. Alum Cliffs (or Tulampanga, as it's known to the

tribal custodians, the Pallittorre people) is a sacred celebration place where tribes met for corroborees.

🍴 Sleeping & Eating

Mole Creek Hotel PUB **$**
(☑03-6363 1102; www.molecreekhotel.com; Main Rd; r $90-150) This pub was built in 1907 and has excellent rooms upstairs, some with good views, although the furnishings may be a little twee for some tastes. The **restaurant** (mains $11 to $28) does meaty meals, such as lamb shanks in red wine and rosemary sauce, while the Tiger Bar has a life-size model of the Tasmanian tiger and a collage of tiger-sighting articles from the local paper. Ask about the bushwalker's transport run from here to Walls of Jerusalem National Park.

★**Mole Creek Guest House & Cafe** B&B **$$**
(☑03-6363 1399; www.molecreekgh.com.au; 100 Pioneer Dr; s/d incl breakfast from $115/130; @🛜) 🍴 This place is a real find. There are beautifully renovated, spacious rooms and a little private cinema upstairs. Downstairs, the **cafe** (mains $16-32; ☺8am-8pm) serves excellent food all day, from hearty walkers' breakfasts to scrumptious homemade quiche at lunch, and fantastic steaks at dinner.

Blackwood Park Cottages COTTAGE **$$**
(☑03-6363 1208; www.blackwoodparkcottages. com; 445 Mersey Hill Rd; d $160-220) There are two lovely self-contained cottages here, set among well-maintained gardens, with views to the surrounding mountains. There's handcrafted furniture and heated floors, and breakfast consists of homemade bread, muffins, fresh coffee and free-range eggs. It's well signed off a side road on the Deloraine side of Mole Creek.

🛍 Shopping

R Stephens FOOD
(☑03-6363 1170; www.leatherwoodhoney.com.au; 25 Pioneer Dr; ☺9am-4pm Mon-Fri) Tasmania's wonderful Leatherwood honey is sold here. Tours of the honey-extraction plant are no longer available.

ℹ Information

Parks & Wildlife Visitor Centre (☑03-6363 1487, 03-6363 5133; www.parks.tas.gov.au; ☺9am-5pm Tue-Fri) The Parks and Wildlife visitor centre can help with info on bushwalking in the area (particularly at the Walls of Jerusalem) and visiting the nearby caves.

Mole Creek Karst National Park

Welcome to one of Tasmania's more unusual national parks. The clue to the appeal of **Mole Creek Karst National Park** (☑tour bookings 03-6363 5182; www.parks.tas.gov.au) lies in the name – the word 'karst' refers to the scenery characteristic of a limestone region, including caves and underground streams. The Mole Creek area contains over 300 known caves and sinkholes, including public caves, which you can tour, and wild caves, which are strictly for experienced cavers.

⊙ Sights & Activities

Public Caves
There are two public caves, both of which are kept at a constant 9°C: wear warm clothes and good walking shoes.

Marakoopa Cave CAVE
The name Marakoopa derives from an Aboriginal word meaning 'handsome' – which this cave surely is, with its delicate stalactites and stalagmites, glowworms, sparkling crystals and reflective pools. Two tours are available here. The easy **Underground Rivers and Glowworms Tour** (adult/child $19/9.50; ☺10am, noon, 2pm & 4pm Oct-May, no 4pm tour Jun-Sep) is for all ages. The **Great Cathedral and Glowworms Tour** (adult/child $19/9.50; ☺11am, 1pm & 3pm) is more challenging, with a stairway ascent to the vast cavern known as Great Cathedral.

King Solomons Cave CAVE
(adult/child $19/9.50; ☺hourly departures 10.30am-4.30pm Dec-Apr, 11.30am-3.30pm May-Nov) Tours of this compact cave will show you lavish colours and formations. Entry to King Solomons Cave is payable only by credit card or Eftpos – no cash. If you don't have a card, cash payments for entry to both caves can be made at the ticket office in Marakoopa, 11km away.

Wild Caves
Cyclops, **Honeycomb** and **Baldocks** are among the better-known wild caves in the Mole Creek area that are without steps or ladders. The best way to explore these and other wild caves is on one of the excursions offered by **Wild Cave Tours** (☑03-6367 8142; www.wildcavetours.com; 165 Fernlea Rd, Caveside); they're not for children under 14. The guide, Debbie, is an environmental scientist and her love of the caves really shines through. She'll

show you a host of endangered species. Book ahead and bring spare clothing and a towel.

❶ Information

Mole Creek Caves Ticket Office (🖉03-6363 5182; www.molecreek.info; 330 Mayberry Rd, Mayberry) Tour tickets are available at the Mole Creek Caves ticket office, close to the Marakoopa Cave entrance.

❶ Getting There & Away

There is no public transport to the caves. If driving, take the B12 from Mole Creek, where the turn off for Marakoopa Cave is 4km west of the town. King Solomons Cave is 15km west of Mole Creek along the B12.

Walls of Jerusalem National Park

The **Walls of Jerusalem National Park** (www.parks.tas.gov.au; per person/vehicle per day $12/24) is one of Tasmania's most beautiful parks. It's a glacier-scoured landscape of spectacularly craggy dolerite peaks, alpine tarns and forests of ancient pines. The park adjoins the lake-spangled wilderness of the Central Plateau and is part of the Tasmanian Wilderness World Heritage Area. Several walking tracks lead through it, and also join the park with hikes in Cradle Mountain–Lake St Clair National Park.

🏃 Activities

The most popular walk here is the full-day trek to the 'Walls' themselves. A steep path leads up from the car park on Mersey Forest Rd to **Trappers Hut** (two hours return), **Solomon's Jewels** (four hours return) and through **Herod's Gate** to **Lake Salome** (six to eight hours return) and **Damascus Gate** (nine hours return). If you plan to visit historic **Dixon's Kingdom Hut** and the hauntingly beautiful pencil-pine forests that surround it (10 hours return from the car park), or climb to the top of **Mt Jerusalem** (12 hours return), it's better to camp overnight. There are tent platforms and a composting toilet at **Wild Dog Creek**.

You'll need to be prepared for harsh weather conditions: it snows a substantial amount here, and not only in winter. Walks across the park are described in *Cradle Mountain Lake St Clair and Walls of Jerusalem National Parks* by John Chapman and John Siseman, and in Lonely Planet's *Walking in Australia*.

WORTH A TRIP

HONEY FARM

At Chudleigh's **Honey Farm** (🖉03-6363 6160; www.thehoneyfarm.com.au; 39 Sorell St, Chudleigh; ⊙9am-5pm Sun-Fri Oct-Mar, 9am-5pm Sun-Thu & 9am-4pm Fri Apr-Sep) you can get sticky fingers lingering over the free tastings of some of its 50-plus different types of honey, or sample some of the superb honey ice cream. In the shop you can browse through all things bees and honey – from beeswax boot polish to propolis supplements, honeycomb and cuddly bee toys. Less cuddly – but much more fascinating – are the 1000 bees you can watch hard at work in a glass-walled hive.

Tasmanian Expeditions   WALKING
(🖉03-6331 9000, 1300 666 856; www.tasmanianexpeditions.com.au) Tasmanian Expeditions conducts a six-day Walls of Jerusalem trip ($1695), taking in the park's highlights as well as some of the more out-of-the-way spots.

❶ Getting There & Away

The park is reached from Mole Creek by taking Mersey Forest Rd to Lake Rowallan. The last 11km is on well-maintained gravel roads.

Gowrie Park

At the foot of Mt Roland, just 14km from Sheffield, Gowrie Park makes an excellent base for mountain walks or a rural retreat. There are walks to the summits of Mts Roland (1234m), Vandyke (1084m) and Claude (1034m) and shorter walks in the shady forests of the lower slopes, such as the pleasant meander through the bush at O'Neills Creek Reserve. Bird lovers take note: 94 species have been recorded in the Mt Roland area.

🏃 Activities

The sharp comb of rock that's the dramatic backdrop to the rural views here is **Mt Roland**. It looks spectacularly difficult, but is easily climbed by confident walkers. Access is from the village of Claude Rd. Turn off at Kings Rd and head south for about 1.5km to the start of the track (about 6.5km, 3½ hours return). There's an easier track from near Gowrie Park. Turn off the main road near the sports ground and travel 2km to the trailhead (10km, four hours return).

🛏 Sleeping & Eating

Silver Ridge Wilderness Retreat   CABIN $$
(☑03-6491 1727; www.silverridgeretreat.com.au; 46 Rysavy Rd; s $65, d $150-190, extra person $25; ✖) At the foot of Mt Roland, these pine-clad cottages are about as peaceful as you can get, and have fantastic mountain views. You can soak in the heated indoor pool, climb mountains, watch the birds and the beasts, or go horse riding on Mustang Sally, Misty or Mac.

**Gowrie Park
Wilderness Village**   CABIN, CARAVAN PARK $$
(☑03-6491 1385; www.gowriepark.com.au; 1447 Claude Rd; unpowered/powered sites $16/30, dm/d $35/110) There are neat but basic self-contained cabins here sleeping up to six, plus bunk rooms and caravan/camping sites. Tracks lead right from the grounds to nearby peaks. The highlight here, though, has to be **Weindorfers Restaurant** (☑0422 042 576; mains $12-28; ⊙noon-2pm & 7-9pm), which has a wonderful log-cabin ambience, especially when the fire is roaring, and serves hearty, post-bushwalking fare.

Lake Barrington

Beautiful Lake Barrington (created by the Mersey-Forth hydroelectric scheme in 1969) stretches for 20km between steep, green banks.

◉ Sights & Activities

The lake's calm waters host international-standard water-sports competitions and the recreation area has an **adventure playground**, BBQs, picnic spots and an easy

---

WORTH A TRIP

TROWUNNA WILDLIFE PARK

About 5km east of Mole Creek on the B12 road, and 2km west of Chudleigh, is the first-rate **Trowunna Wildlife Park** (☑03-6363 6162; www.trowunna.com.au; adult/child/family $22/12/60; ⊙9am-5pm, guided tours 11am, 1pm & 3pm), which specialises in Tasmanian devils, wombats and koalas, as well as birds. There's an informative tour, during which you get to pat, feed or even hold some of the wildlife. Don't miss the interactive Devil Education and Research Centre.

---

two-hour **rainforest walk**. The amazing 84m-high **Devil's Gate Dam**, which holds the waters back, is engineered to be one of the thinnest concrete dams in the world. There are viewing areas where you can get quite close.

Tasmazia   AMUSEMENT PARK
(☑03-6491 1934; www.tasmazia.com.au; 500 Staverton Rd; adult/child $25/12.50; ⊙10am-4pm Apr-Nov, to 5pm Dec-Mar) Close to the lake is Tasmazia. Kids love the whimsical complex of hedge mazes, the Village of Lower Crackpot (a colourful miniature village) and a lavender farm. Look out for Nancy the Witch, who appears to have crashed her broomstick, or the sword in the stone. If you can retrieve it, King Arthur–style, you win this whole fanciful kingdom for yourself.

Highland Trails Horse Riding   HORSE RIDING
(☑03-6491 1533, 0417 145 497; 1030 Staverton Rd; per hr $45) Highland Trails Horse Riding can take you on horseback into the foothills of nearby mountains. Rides range from one hour to several days.

🛏 Sleeping & Eating

Carinya Farm Holiday Retreat   CABIN $$
(☑03-6491 1593; www.carinyafarm.com.au; 63 Staverton Rd; d $105-140) Carinya Farm Holiday Retreat has pine-lined, loft-bedroom chalets overlooking peaceful farmland and Mt Roland. There's a kids cubby and friendly farm animals to view.

Kentisbury Country House   COTTAGE $$$
(☑03-6491 2090; www.kentisburycountryhouse.com; 42 Luttrells Rd, Kentish Park; d $250) Beautiful self-catering Kentisbury Country House is close to Lake Barrington's western shore and set in magnificently green pasture with sublime views.

★**Eagle's Nest Retreat**   LODGE $$$
(☑03-6491 1511; www.eaglesnestretreat.com.au; d $420-620) Surely the best panoramas around Lake Barrington are to be had at Eagle's Nest Retreat, two amazingly opulent holiday houses with wall-high glass framing incredible Mt Roland views.

ℹ Getting There & Away

Lake Barrington's eastern and southern shores are easily accessible from Sheffield. For the western shore, take the C132 south from the coast near Forth.

FOODIE DETOURS FROM LAKE BARRINGTON

Barringwood Park Vineyard (☑03-6492 3140; www.barringwoodpark.com.au; 60 Gillams Rd, Lower Barrington; ⊙11am-5pm Wed-Sun, closed Aug) Lovers of fine food and wine should visit Barringwood Park Vineyard, which has tastings and cellar-door sales of handcrafted cool-climate wines. You can savour a gourmet platter with your vino on the deck and be awed by glorious views over the Don River Valley towards Bass Strait.

Wilmot Hills Vineyard (www.wilmothills.com; 407 Back Rd, Wilmot; ⊙10am-6pm Thu-Tue) On the western side of Lake Barrington, just north of the village of Wilmot, is this winery-distillery. At Wilmot Hills Vineyard you can try a fine pinot noir, the 'Highland White' (a müller-thurgau and gewürztraminer blend) and apple cider. But there's also a delicious range of spirits distilled here – calvados, kirsch, raspberry schnapps, grappa and basilica – and you get to peek in at the winemaking and distilling operations.

Sheffield

POP 1108

In the 1980s Sheffield was a typical small Tasmanian town in the doldrums of rural decline. That was until some astute townsfolk came up with an idea that had been applied to the small town of Chemainus in Canada, with some surprisingly wonderful results. The plan was to paint large murals on walls around town, depicting scenes from the district's pioneer days. Sheffield is now a veritable outdoor art gallery, with more than 50 fantastic large-scale murals and an annual painting festival to produce more.

◉ Sights & Activities

Kentish Museum MUSEUM
(☑03-6491 1861; 93 Main St; admission by donation; ⊙10am-noon & 1-4pm Mon, Wed & Thu, 1-3pm Tue, 10am-3pm Fri) Here there's all sorts of historic clutter on display: an early telephone exchange, old organs, military paraphernalia and the world's first automatic petrol pump, invented by a local Sheffield boy. It has a genealogy research service, which costs $22 per hour.

Mural House GALLERY
(☑03-6491 1784; www.muralhouse.com.au; 100 High St; adult/child $2/0.50; ⊙1-5pm Tue, Thu, Sat & Sun) This odd little attraction contains interpretations of art of various Indigenous cultures in the form of internal wall murals. You may be better off with the outdoor art in town, but if you want to actually buy some art, you can do so here.

★ Mural Audio Tours WALKING
Grab a headset ($9) from the visitor centre and take a thoroughly informative audio tour of Sheffield's outdoor art. The tour takes about 90 minutes (though you can keep the headset all day) and guides you past about 20 of the town's best murals. It also leads you through the Working Art Space (www.traksheffield.blogspot.com.au; 2 Albert St; ⊙11am-3pm, reduced winter hours), where you can see local artists at work.

Mural highlights of the tour include *Stillness and Warmth*, which features Gustav Weindorfer of Cradle Mountain fame; *Butlers Mail Coach 1910*, a huge, magnificent depiction of a coach and horses against the backdrop of Mt Roland; and *Cradle Mountain Beauty*, a wide panorama of Cradle Mountain in snow. Spot the park ranger carrying a bathtub to one of the Overland

Redwater Creek Steam Rail HISTORIC RAILWAY
(☑03-6491 1613; www.redwater.org.au; cnr Main & Spring Sts; adult/child $5/3; ⊙11am-4pm 1st weekend of month) Departing from the original Sheffield train station at the eastern end of town, the steam rail offers rides on locomotives running on a narrow-gauge track one weekend a month and on some public holidays. Train buffs will ooh and aah at the rare A Krauss 10 locomotive – for everyone else, it's a fun family day out.

✸ Festivals & Events

SteamFest CULTURAL
(www.steamfesttasmania.org.au; ⊙Mar) SteamFest is a grand three-day occasion on the March long weekend that's a true celebration of steam and bygone days, and a must (not just for trainspotters). The tractor-pulling competitions are a hoot!

Muralfest ART
(www.muralfest.com.au; ⊙late Mar-early Apr) Sheffield's celebration of outdoor art is held each year. It's a massive paint-off – a theme is set

and artists from all over Australia descend upon the town to compete for a cash prize, with another nine murals added to the town's walls. Book accommodation well ahead.

🛏 Sleeping

There's free overnight **caravan and camp-ervan parking** (with water and toilets – no showers) next to the recreation centre on Albert St. You can use showers at the visitor centre (three minutes for $1).

Sheffield Country Motor Inn   MOTEL $
(☑ 03-6491 1800; www.sheffieldmotorinn.com.au; 49-53 Main St; motel s/d from $90/95, apt d $130-170) There are neat and well-equipped motel rooms here, one with three bedrooms. Some of the town's best murals are immediately adjacent.

Glencoe Rural Retreat   B&B $$
(☑ 03-6492 3267; www.glencoeruralretreat.com. au; 1468 Sheffield Rd, Barrington; d $175-210; 🐾) Just north of Sheffield, on the B14 at Barrington, this gorgeous property, owned by celebrated French chef Remi Bancal, is making a great name for itself. You can stay in its romantic and eminently stylish rooms (no kids under 12) and you mustn't miss the superb three-course dinners ($65), available by prior arrangement.

Sheffield Cabins   CABIN $$
(☑ 03-6491 2176; www.sheffieldcabins.com.au; 1 Pioneer Cres; d $100-105, extra adult/child $15/10) These are simple, clean, self-contained cabins, close to the visitor centre: you can't beat what you get for the price. They're pet friendly, too.

WORTH A TRIP

SEVEN SHEDS

In the small town of Railton, 12km northeast of Sheffield, brewer and beer connoisseur Willie Simpson has turned a passion for home brewing into one of Tasmania's best boutique breweries. **Seven Sheds** (☑ 03-6496 1139; www. sevensheds.com; 22 Crockers St, Railton; ⊘ 11am-3pm Wed-Sun May-Jul, to 5pm Wed-Sun Sep-Apr, closed Aug) was opened in 2008 as a brewery, meadery and hop gardens, and you can pop in to taste its range of Kentish ale, melomel and a fabulous dry mead. You can also tour its microbrewing operation.

Kentish Hills Retreat   MOTEL $$
(☑ 03-6491 2484; www.kentishhills.com.au; 2 West Nook Rd; d $124-154, extra person $30; @) In a quiet location just west of town, with superb views of Mt Roland, Kentish Hills has a range of accommodation, from double rooms to an apartment sleeping up to six. It's more motel than hotel in style, but there are good facilities, including spas, minibars, queen-size beds and a guest laundry.

🍴 Eating

⭐ **Blacksmith Gallery Cafe**   CAFE $
(☑ 03-6491 1887; www.fridaynitemusic.org; 63 Main St; mains $9-18; ⊘ 8.30am-5pm) This friendly, arty cafe boasts of having the best coffee in Sheffield – and it may just be right. With its retro decor, funky music and roaring wood stove on cold days, it's a great place to hang out, have a slap-up breakfast, lazy lunch (the quiche is excellent), or coffee and cake in between. There's a rollicking folk-singing night the last Friday of every month.

Bossimi's Bakery   BAKERY $
(☑ 03-6491 1298; 44 Main St; ⊘ 7am-3pm Mon-Fri) This bakery does the industry proud, with lots of speciality pastries, cakes and bread. It gets very busy when the coach tours come through.

Sheffield Hotel   PUB FOOD $$
(☑ 03-6491 1130; 38 Main St; mains $11-25; ⊘ noon-9pm) This pub offers the usual counter-meal options and has a lively local atmosphere.

ℹ Information

Kentish Visitor Information Centre (☑ 03-6491 1036; www.sheffieldcradleinfo.com.au; 5 Pioneer Cres; ⊘ 9am-5pm) Supplies information on the Kentish region and makes accommodation and tour bookings.

ℹ Getting There & Away

Tassielink (www.tassielink.com.au) buses stop directly outside the visitor centre. Services to/from Sheffield include Launceston ($31.20, two hours), Devonport ($5.60, 40 minutes), Cradle Mountain ($27.60, 70 minutes) and Strahan ($60.30, five hours).

Ulverstone

POP 12,110

Quiet little Ulverstone sits around the mouth of the Leven River and has a pleasantly old-fashioned rural-town feel: you could be forgiven for thinking you've stepped back 30

THE ULVERSTONE & PENGUIN HINTERLAND

The Coast to Canyon Circuit begins in Ulverstone or Penguin. From Ulverstone drive to Penguin along the picturesque coast road, then delve south to Riana. From Riana, a scenic drive brings you to the Woodhouse Lookout, for views over the Leven Valley. More winding road leads to Wings Wildlife Park (www.wingswildlife.com.au; 137 Winduss St, Gunns Plains; adult/child $20/10; ☺10am-4pm), which has an eclectic collection of creatures.

Close by are Gunns Plains Caves (www.gunnsplainscaves.com.au; adult/child $12/6; ☺guided tours 10am, 11am, noon, 1.30pm, 2.30pm & 3.30pm), filled with magical limestone formations and glowworms. Guided tours involve some clambering and ladder work. Back on the B17, you can complete the circuit to Ulverstone or take the C127 and C125 to the Leven Canyon. On the C124 at Gunns Plains is Leven Valley Vineyard & Gallery (☎03-6429 1186; 321 Raymond Rd, Gunns Plains; ☺10am-5pm), a boutique vineyard where you can taste and buy wine and browse fine art. Signposted just off the road near the vineyard are lower and upper Preston Falls, all cascading water and primeval man ferns.

Continue via Nietta to Leven Canyon. A 20-minute return walk leads to the sensational gorge-top lookout, a sky platform peering 300m down to the Leven River below. There's modern B&B accommodation, a tearoom and you can visit the gorgeous gardens (adults $5) at Kaydale Lodge (☎03-6429 1293; www.kaydalelodge.com.au; 250 Loongana Rd, Nietta).

DEVONPORT & THE NORTHWEST ULVERSTONE

years. The commanding feature in town (at the intersection of Reibey St and Alexandra Rd) is the imposing Shrine of Remembrance, built in 1953.

🛏 Sleeping & Eating

★Ulverstone River Retreat   APARTMENT $$
(☎03-6425 2999; www.ulverstoneriverretreat.com. au; 37 Lobster Creek Rd; d $150-185) Watch kingfishers from your front deck, fish and kayak in the river, or just soak up the birdsong and peace. This gorgeous riverside spot offers a smart upstairs apartment and a separate villa, both with decks out front and BBQ facilities. There are kayaks and fishing gear and river swimming when the tide's in. It's next to Ulverstone golf course, 4km from town.

Boscobel   B&B $$
(☎03-6425 1727; http://boscobelofulverstone. com.au; 27 South Rd; s $105-115, d $130-170; 🛜🐾) Boscobel has comfortable, old-fashioned accommodation in a National Trust–listed home that's reminiscent of a grandmother's house in the best possible sense, although the frilly floral decor won't be to everyone's taste. It's set in beautiful gardens and there's a heated indoor pool in summer.

★Deli Central   CAFE $
(48b Victoria St; meals $11-19; ☺8am-4pm Mon-Fri, to 3pm Sat & Sun) What a find – when you can find it (ask for the car park off Edward St, behind Thai Delight). Ulverstone's best food is here – wonderful breakfasts or dishes such as rosemary and garlic-infused lamb rump for lunch: check the specials board. The food is organic and locally grown as far as possible. Stock up for picnics at the impressive deli counter.

Pedro's the Restaurant   SEAFOOD $$
(☎03-6425 6663; www.pedrostherestaurant.com. au; Wharf Rd; lunch $15-27.50, dinner $25.50-33; ☺noon-late) Grab a table right by the water at this eatery perched on the banks of the Leven River, and savour tastes of the sea as the sun goes down. What a view! The paradise seafood platter for two (lunch/dinner $119/135) is the most popular offering here. Pedro's Takeaway (mains $6-15; ☺11am-7pm), for fish and chips, is next door.

ℹ Information

Ulverstone Visitor Information Centre (☎03-6425 2839; www.centralcoast.tas.gov.au; 13 Alexandra Rd; ☺9am-5pm Sep-May, 10am-4pm Jun-Aug) A striking piece of architecture and a treasure trove of local knowledge.

ℹ Getting There & Away

Metro (☎03-6431 3822, 13 22 01; www.metro-tas.com.au) Metro operates local buses to Burnie ($6.20) from the corner of King Edward and Reibey Sts.

Redline Coaches (www.tasredline.com.au) Buses arrive at and depart from Alexandra Rd, outside the IGA supermarket near the war-memorial clock. Departures include Burnie ($8.50, 30 minutes) and Devonport ($6.50, 20 minutes).

Penguin

POP 3159

Penguin feels like one of those pretty little English seaside towns where it's all ice cream, buckets and spades, and the occasional sneaky breeze as you brave it out on the beach. But there's one very un-English thing about this place: penguins! The world's smallest penguin *(Eudyptula minor)* comes ashore here during its breeding season, and even if you don't see any of them in the feather, you can get acquainted with model penguins around town.

● Sights

Collect the brochure *Discover Penguin on Foot* from the visitor information centre to guide your steps around town.

Penguin Market   MARKET
(☉ 9am-3.30pm Sun) The popular undercover Penguin Market takes place every Sunday off Arnold St. Stalls sell local produce, art and crafts, gifts and collectables, but the gourmet food stalls aren't what they used to be.

🏃 Activities

One of Tasmania's most rewarding multiday walks takes you from Penguin down to Cradle Mountain. The 80km **Penguin Cradle Trail** crosses the Dial Range, and takes in

---

WHERE TO SEE PENGUINS

True to its name, Penguin is a base for the little (or fairy) penguins that nightly come ashore from mid-September or October to March or April. There are three places to see them:

Lalico Beach The largest breeding colony arrives here around sunset, 22km east of Penguin. There's a viewing platform and, on most nights in season, there's a park ranger in residence to answer any questions. Contact the **Parks & Wildlife Office** (☑ 6464 3018; parks.tas.gov.au; Short St) in Ulverstone or Penguin's visitor information centre for more details.

Sulphur Creek A smaller colony comes ashore here (4km west of Penguin).

West Beach Located in Burnie (19km west of Penguin), behind the Makers' Workshop.

Leven Canyon and Black Bluff en route to Cradle Mountain. The website of the North West Walking Club (www.nwwc.org.au) has a route description and map.

🛏 Sleeping

Happy Backpacker   PUB $
(Neptune Grand Hotel; ☑ 03-6437 2406; www.thehappybackpacker.com.au; 84 Main Rd; dm/d without bathroom from $25/65; P 🛜) This friendly pub has basic but fairly modern accommodation. Rooms have sinks, but toilets and showers are shared. The dining room serves cheap staples such as chicken parmigiana as well as a few Thai and seafood dishes.

Inglenook by the Sea   B&B $$
(☑ 03-6435 4134; www.inglenook.com.au; 360 Preservation Dr, Sulphur Creek; d $120-140, extra adult/child $40/30; 🛜) On the coast road towards Burnie, 5km from the centre of Penguin, is welcoming Inglenook. There are three rooms here, kitted out in crisply ironed linens. One room has lovely sea views, one has a spa, and the other has a second bunk room attached for travelling families. The friendly hosts whip up a delicious locally sourced breakfast.

52 Main   APARTMENT $$
(☑ 03-6437 1052; 52mainpenguin@gmail.com; 52 Main Rd; d apt with mountain/sea view $180/220, extra person $40; P ❄) Above the cafe of the same name, and run by the same superfriendly people, these modern apartments are enormous, lovingly maintained and supremely comfortable. Decor is modern, the location ideal and families will feel right at home.

★ Madsen   BOUTIQUE HOTEL $$$
(☑ 0438 373 456, 03-6437 2588; www.themadsen.com; 64 Main St; d $165-300, f $220; @ 🛜) This boutique hotel is housed in a grand former bank building across the road from the water. Some of the rooms have great views of Bass Strait. Decorated in good taste, with a touch of the antique and a good measure of contemporary cool, this is a particularly pleasurable place to stay. Book the new penthouse suite for the ultimate luxury.

🍴 Eating

Plunys   THAI $
(☑ 03-6437 2830; 9 Arnold St; mains $13-15; ☉ 5-9pm Wed-Sun) Decent Thai restaurant a block back from the main street (turn at the Neptune Hotel) that mixes things up a little for

dinner. Service can be slow but it's friendly and the soups in particular are a great order.

★ **Renaessance** CAFE $$
(☑0409 723 771; 95 Main Rd; mains $12-25; ☻9am-5pm Mon-Thu & Sat, to 6pm Fri, 10am-4pm Sun) A slice of sophistication along the main street, Renaessance does salads, sandwiches, dips and great coffee. The back terrace, with its Bass Strait views, is arguably the best place to nurse a coffee or glass of wine in town.

52 Main CAFE $$
(☑03-6437 1052; 52 Main Rd; mains $15-25; ☻10am-4pm Wed-Sat, noon-4pm Sun) This charming cafe near the western end of the Penguin waterfront does fabulous fresh seafood, good breakfasts and excellent cakes.

Casablanca MODERN AUSTRALIAN $$$
(☑03-6437 1621; Preservation Dr; lunch mains $15-38, dinner mains $29-40; ☻noon-2.30pm & 6-9pm Wed-Fri, noon-2.30pm Sat, 10am-2.30pm Sun) What a surprising find, set in the brick block of the Penguin Lifesaving Club, overlooking Preservation Bay. The eclectic fine-dining menu is served with beautiful sea views.

❶ Information

Penguin Visitor Information Centre (☑03-6437 1421; 78 Main Rd; ☻9am-4pm Mon-Fri & 9am-3.30pm Sat & Sun Oct-Mar, 9.30am-3.30pm Mon-Fri, 9am-12.30pm Sat & 9am-3.30pm Sun Apr-Sep) Staffed by volunteers, the friendly Penguin visitor centre has information about finding penguins and other local attractions.

❶ Getting There & Away

Metro (☑03-6431 3822, 13 22 01; www.metrotas.com.au) Metro runs regular local buses from Burnie to Penguin ($6.20, 15 minutes). The main stop is at the (now defunct) Penguin station on Crescent St.
Redline (www.tasredline.com.au) Redline buses go from Penguin to Burnie ($6.50, 15 minutes) and Devonport ($8.50, 40 minutes) as part of their northwest-coast runs.

Burnie

POP 19,819

Long dismissed as Tasmania's ugly duckling, once-industrial Burnie is busily reinventing itself as a 'City of Makers', referring both to its heavy manufacturing past and its present creative flair. The amazing new Makers' Workshop is Burnie's showcase tourist attraction and should be your first stop when you

OLIVES

Around 7km south of Ulverstone along the B15, **Cradle Coast Olives** (☑03-6425 3449; http://cradlecoastolives.com.au; 574 Castra Rd, Abbotsham; ☻10am-4pm Sun-Fri), an award-winning producer of extra virgin olive oils has cellar-door tasting and sales every day except Saturday – it's worth ringing ahead to check it's open. Wander through the olive grove and watch the olive press in action from May to July.

visit. Watch also for penguins coming ashore from September or October until February.

⊙ Sights & Activities

Burnie has some impressive civic and domestic architecture that you can view on two **Federation walking trails**. The city is also renowned for its art-deco buildings, and you can see these on the **Art Deco Trail**. Ask at the visitor information counter in the Makers' Workshop for interpretative maps of all three walks.

★ **Makers' Workshop** MUSEUM
(☑03-6430 5831; www.discoverburnie.net; 2 Bass Hwy; ☻9am-5pm) Part museum, part arts centre, this dramatic new structure dominates the western end of Burnie's main beach. It's a fabulous place to get acquainted with this city's creative heart. You'll notice the life-size **paper people** in odd corners of the workshop's cavernous contemporary interior. These are the work of **Creative Paper** (☑03-6430 5830; tours adult/child $15/8; ☻tours 9.15am-4.30pm), Burnie's handmade-paper producers. Its tours take you through the production process of making paper from such unusual raw materials as kangaroo poo, apple pulp and rainforest leaves.

There are also **makers' studios** stationed throughout the centre, where you can watch local producers at work on handicrafts from jewellery to violins, ceramics to glass, felt to papier mâché. In the shop you can buy some of the products produced, and there's a **cafe**.

Hellyers Road Distillery DISTILLERY
(☑03-6433 0439; www.hellyersroaddistillery.com.au; 153 Old Surrey Rd; tours $18; ☻10am-4.30pm) Hellyers Road is one of Tasmania's most respected makers of whisky. You can tour the distillery to see how its golden single malt is

Burnie

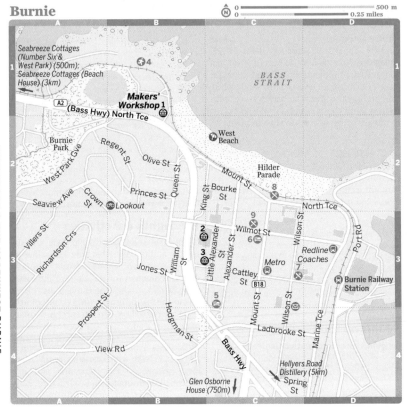

made, and afterwards take a tasting of whisky, whisky cream or Southern Lights vodka, which is also made here (nips $2 to $4).

To get here from Marine Tce/Bass Hwy, turn south onto Mount St (B18), following signs for Upper Burnie and Queenstown. Turn left onto Old Surrey Rd (C112) and follow signs to the distillery.

Burnie Regional Art Gallery GALLERY
(☑03-6430 5875; www.burniearts.net; Burnie Arts & Function Centre, 77-79 Wilmot St; ☺10am-4.30pm Mon-Fri, 1.30-4.30pm Sat & Sun) **FREE** This art gallery has excellent exhibitions of contemporary Tasmanian artworks, including fine prints by some of Australia's most prominent artists such as Sidney Nolan and Brett Whiteley.

Burnie Regional Museum MUSEUM
(☑03-6430 5746; www.burnieregionalmuseum. net; Little Alexander St; adult/child $6.50/2.50; ☺10am-4.30pm Mon-Fri) This absorbing muse-um is a re-creation of a 1900s village streetscape – including blacksmith, wash house, stagecoach depot and bootmaker – complete with appropriate soundtrack.

★**Burnie Penguin Centre** BIRDWATCHING
(☑0437 436 803) **FREE** A boardwalk on Burnie's foreshore leads from Hilder Pde to the western end of West Beach, close to the Makers' Workshop, where there's a spot for watching penguins. From October to March you can take a free **Penguin Interpretation Tour** about one hour after dusk as the penguins emerge from the sea and waddle back to their burrows. Volunteer wildlife guides are present to talk about the penguins and their habits.

🛏 Sleeping

Burnie Oceanview CARAVAN PARK $
(☑03-6431 1925; www.burniebeachaccommodation.com.au; 253 Bass Hwy; unpowered/powered

Burnie

⊙ Top Sights
1 Makers' Workshop B1

⊙ Sights
2 Burnie Regional Art Gallery B3
3 Burnie Regional Museum B3

⊕ Activities, Courses & Tours
4 Burnie Penguin Centre B1

▣ Sleeping
5 Apartments Down Town C3
6 Ikon Hotel C3

⊗ Eating
7 Another Mother C3
8 Bayviews C2
Fish Frenzy .... (see 8)
Hot Mother Lounge .... (see 7)
9 Rialto Gallery Restaurant C3

▣ Shopping
The Cheese Shop .... (see 1)

ⓘ Information
Visitor Information Centre .... (see 1)

---

sites d $24/30, dm $25, on-site caravans d $55, cabins & units d $95-139; @ ☒) Located 4km west of the city centre, this park has backpacker rooms, some grassy camp sites at the property's rear, caravans with kitchenettes and a range of cabins. The indoor heated pool is the best attraction.

★ **Ikon Hotel**   BOUTIQUE HOTEL **$$**
(☑03-6432 4566; www.ikonhotel.com.au; 22 Mount St; d $185-220; ❋ ☎) Boutique hotel chic comes to Burnie at the centrally located Ikon Hotel. The building's heritage exterior is complemented by sleek and (extremely) spacious modern suites with leather furniture and compact kitchenettes. Interesting modern and retro art adorns the walls; the bathrooms are huge; and the rooms are bright and airy.

Seabreeze Cottages   RENTAL HOUSE **$$**
(☑0439 353 491; www.seabreezecottages.com.au; s $160-185, d $175-185) These cottages just west of the city centre may just be Burnie's best. There's the cool, contemporary Beach House (243 Bass Hwy, Cooee), just a stroll across the road from the beach; West Park (14 Paraka St); and cute Number Six (6 Mollison St), both an easy 10-minute walk to town. All are kitted out with modern, chic decor – Number Six has a jukebox and all. We love them!

Glen Osborne House   B&B **$$**
(☑03-6431 9866; www.glenosbornehouse.com.au; 9 Aileen Cres; d $175) It may be set in the suburban hills in Burnie's south (off B18, or Mount St), but there's nothing suburban about this grand establishment. It provides high-standard hospitality in a lavish, National Trust–listed 1885 Victorian house with well-tended gardens. The rate includes a home-style cooked breakfast.

Apartments Down Town   APARTMENT **$$**
(☑03-6432 3219; www.apartmentsdowntown.com.au; 52 Alexander St; d $145-190) Burnie is big on art deco, and this 1937 building is deco through and through. It has been thoroughly modernised to house spacious and well-equipped two- and three-bedroom serviced apartments. Beware: the apartments at the rear of the building may suffer highway noise.

✕ Eating

Another Mother   CAFE **$**
(☑03-6431 8000; 14 Cattley St; mains $9-16; ◷8am-3pm Mon-Fri; ☑) A cute, vibrant eatery with bright red walls, eclectic furniture and local photography for decoration, Another Mother offers wholesome, predominantly vegetarian (and some meaty) dishes crafted from local produce – organic where possible. It serves an exceptional pumpkin-and-cashew burger with yoghurt and chilli. Its sister establishment is **Hot Mother Lounge** (70 Wilson St; ◷7am-3pm Mon-Fri), which serves equally good wraps, bakes, soups and takeaways.

★ **Bayviews**   MODERN AUSTRALIAN **$$**
(☑03-6431 7999; www.bayviewsrestaurant.com.au; 1st fl, 2 Marine Tce; lunch $12-24, dinner $33-39; ◷noon-late Thu-Sat, 5pm-late Mon-Wed) ☑ This upmarket establishment is right on the beach and serves a brief menu of excellent fine-dining dishes, from local free-range pork to the region's amazing grass-fed beef and terrific seafood. The wraparound views are sublime.

Rialto Gallery Restaurant   ITALIAN **$$**
(46 Wilmot St; mains $12-26; ◷noon-2.30pm & 6-9pm Mon-Fri, 6-9pm Sat) It's no wonder this restaurant is such a well-loved Burnie institution – it's been doing a roaring trade for 28 years with its mouth-watering Italian fare. Dishes include tortellini in butter and sage, meltingly delicious ravioli with a pungent four-cheese sauce and fine wood-oven pizzas.

Fish Frenzy
SEAFOOD $$

(☑03-6432 1111; 2 Marine Tce; meals $15-35; ☺11am-9pm) This gourmet fish 'n' chippery does all the usual takes on the seaside favourite, and also offers healthy options such as grilled fish with Greek salad.

🛍 Shopping

The Cheese Shop
FOOD

(☑03-6430 5889; 2 Bass Hwy; ☺9am-5pm) Inside the Makers' Workshop, this cheese-tasting centre and shop has a range of creamy bries and camemberts; hard, crumbly cheddars; and intense blue cheeses to try and buy.

ℹ Information

Visitor Information Centre (☑03-6430 5831; www.discoverburnie.net; 2 Bass Hwy; ☺9am-5pm) In the Makers' Workshop.

ℹ Getting There & Away

AIR

Burnie/Wynyard airport (known as either Burnie or Wynyard airport) is at Wynyard, 20km northwest of Burnie.

Regional Express Airlines (REX; www.regionalexpress.com.au) Burnie-to-Melbourne flights.

Sharp Airlines (☑1300 556 694; www.sharpairlines.com) Flights between Burnie and King Island.

BUS

Metro (☑03-6431 3822, 13 22 01; www.metrotas.com.au) Regular local buses to Penguin, Ulverstone and Wynyard ($6.20 each), departing from bus stops on Cattley St, beside Harris Scarfe department store.

Redline Coaches (☑1300 360 000; www.tasredline.com.au) Redline Coaches stop on Wilmot St, opposite the Metro Cinemas. Useful destinations include Launceston ($39.30, 2½ hours) and Smithton ($24, 1½ hours).

Wynyard & Around

POP 5061

Arranged around the wooded banks of the sinuous Inglis River, Wynyard is a quiet little town that's a service centre for all the surrounding agriculture. It's sheltered from wild westerly weather by prominent Table Cape and Fossil Bluff and has a pleasant, sedate air. On its doorstep are unpeopled beaches, wind-blasted lighthouses and an amazing spring display of tulips that spread like a giant coloured bar code across the rich red soils of Table Cape.

👁 Sights

Wonders of Wynyard
MUSEUM

(Ransley Veteran Ford Collection; adult/child $8/4.50; ☺9am-5pm) Adjacent to the Wynyard visitor centre is the Wonders of Wynyard, a veteran-car collection owned and restored by a Wynyard local. Park your Holden around the corner and visit the rotating collection of at least 15 ancient Ford cars and motorbikes. The showpiece is a 1903 Model A Ford, one of only two in the world.

Table Cape
LANDMARK

An extinct volcano, Table Cape has an otherworldly feel to it. To reach the summit, take the minor road (C234) 4km northwest out of Wynyard, and drive to the **lighthouse** (☑03-6442 3241; ☺11am-3.30pm), which began its seaside vigil in 1888. Although actual opening hours can be erratic, if it's open you can climb the spiral stairs inside and walk around the light at the top for suitably sensational views over Bass Strait. Tours were no longer running at time of research – check at the visitor information centre in Wynyard.

Table Cape Tulip Farm
FARM

(☑03-6442 2012; 363 Lighthous e Rd; ☺10am-4.30pm late Sep–mid-Oct) The v olcanic, chocolate-red soils of the cap e are extraordinarily fertile and it's just the spot to grow tulips. There's a mesmerising array of colour at Table Cape Tulip Farm when the bulbs are in flower in October. A Tulip Festival is held usually on the first weekend of October. From March to August you can buy bu lbs in the farm's shop.

Fossil Bluff
LANDMARK

Three kilometres west of the town centre is 275-million-year-old Fossil Bluff. It was created by an ancient tidewater glacier and is rich in fossils, including the remains of prehistoric whales and the oldest marsupial fossil found in Australia. The species was named *Wynyardia bassiana* in honour of the town. At low tide, walk around the base of the bluff and fossick for fossils. Ask at the visitor centre for the geological guide, *Looking for Fossils*.

🏃 Activities

South of Wynyard, the hills of the Oldina State Forest Reserve offer a short (30- to 45-minute) nature walk known as the **Noel Jago Walk** beside Blackfish Creek. The route passes under man ferns and eucalypts. There are reputed to be platypuses in the creek.

Scuba Centre   DIVING

(☑03-6442 2247; www.levenscubaclub.com.au; 62 Old Bass Hwy; ☺8.30am-4.30pm Mon-Sat) The experienced guides at this centre can take you out on dives in Wynyard Bay and at beautiful Boat Harbour.

🛏 Sleeping & Eating

Beach Retreat Tourist Park   CARAVAN PARK $

(☑03-6442 1998; www.beachretreattouristpark.com.au; 30b Old Bass Hwy; powered sites d $35, backpacker s/d $45/70, cabins & units from $100) This has to be one of the prettiest caravan parks anywhere. It's in a peaceful spot right by the beach, in grounds that are meticulously manicured and pleasingly green. The backpackers accommodation is in simple double rooms – none of that dorm-sleeping nonsense here. There's a well-equipped kitchen to share.

Wharf Hotel   PUB $

(☑03-6442 2344; www.wharfhotelwynyard.com.au; 10 Goldie St; s/d $65/85, bistro mains $20-34; ☺5.30-9pm daily) The Wharf has clean, pleasant and reasonably priced rooms upstairs. Some have baths (baths!) and look out over the peaceful Inglis River. Downstairs the bistro serves excellent steaks and seafood – try the carpet bag eye fillet, a steak stuffed with oysters.

Waterfront Wynyard   MOTEL $$

(☑03-6442 2351; www.waterfrontwynyard.com; 1 Goldie St; d $125, extra person $15; P☎) As motels go, this one is particularly satisfying. As the name implies, the place is slap bang on the water and has clean, stylish rooms with extras such as wi-fi. It's a pleasant and quiet place to stay.

Splash   CAFE $$

(☑03-6442 5333; 30a Old Bass Hwy; mains $8-18; ☺8.30am-4pm Sun-Thu, to 10pm Fri & Sat) This beachy cafe is presided over by a friendly Scottish chef who delivers interesting meals with a strong focus on seafood. Occasional themed dinners on a Friday night attract punters from around the northwestern coast, and Splash's sandy outdoor tables are a good spot for some informal fish and chips. The cafe is located on the main road before you reach Wynyard.

Bruce's Cafe   BISTRO $$

(☑03-6442 4113; www.brucescafe.com.au; 145 Old Bass Highway; mains $9-18; ☺8.30am-4pm Tue-Fri, 9am-3pm Sat & Sun) Bruce's gets consistently good reviews from travellers for its warm, inviting atmosphere and light meals such as the slow-cooked Moroccan lamb wrap or the open steak sandwich that comes with Tassie camembert and chilli jam.

ℹ Information

Wynyard Visitor Information Centre (☑03-6443 8330; www.visitwaratahwynyard.com.au; 8 Exhibition Link; ☺9am-5pm Aug-Apr, 10am-4pm May-Jul) Ask here for the brochure *Scenic Walks of Wynyard and the Surrounding Districts* if you're keen to get out and about on foot.

ℹ Getting There & Away

AIR

The Burnie/Wynyard airport (often listed as Burnie airport) is just one block from Wynyard's main street. Rex connects Wynyard to Melbourne, while Sharp Airlines flies to/from King Island.

BUS

Metro buses from Burnie to Wynyard ($5.50) stop on Jackson St.

Boat Harbour Beach
POP 429

Were it not for the weather, this could be paradise. Picture-perfect Boat Harbour has the kind of blond-sand beach and sapphire-blue waters that make you feel like you've taken a wrong turn off the Bass Hwy and ended up somewhere in the Caribbean. The usually calm seas are perfect for kids, and it's a low-key, family-friendly place.

🛏 Sleeping & Eating

Azzure Holiday Houses   RENTAL HOUSE $$

(☑0430 066 312, 03-6445 1155; www.azzure-beachhouses.com.au; 263 Port Rd; 4/6-bed house from $280/410; ☎) It's all contemporary style at the beach houses in this complex. There's every convenience you could imagine: DVD-CD players, wi-fi, air-conditioning, and swanky kitchens, and walls are hung with contemporary art. There's an on-site health spa in the pipeline, too.

Harbourside B&B   B&B $$

(☑0400 595 036, 0400 595 066; www.harboursidebnb.com.au; 237 Port Rd; d incl breakfast from $195) This cute B&B is more a contemporary private apartment with great water views. There are sensational vistas right from your bed, plus a spa and private decks.

Sunny Sands Holiday Unit RENTAL HOUSE **$$**
(✆03-6442 2578; www.sunnysands.com.au; 285
Port Rd; d $150-170) This well thought out
self-contained unit has balconies to relax on
and wide views of the sea.

Paradise House RENTAL HOUSE **$$$**
(✆03-6435 7718, 0437 350 090; www.paradise-
house.com.au; 22 Azzure Beach Houses, 263 Port
Rd; d $270; ☎) This supersmart beach house
is part of a new complex and has absolutely top-notch accommodation in three bedrooms. The trendy living areas have mod
cons, including free wi-fi. Bikes, fishing gear,
surfboards and boogie boards come free.

Harvest & Cater CAFE **$$**
(✆0458 775 889; 1 Port Rd; mains $15-30; ⊙9am-
5pm Mon & Tue, to 6.30pm Wed-Sun) Attached to
the surf-club building, Harvest & Cater is a
breezy beachfront cafe that serves up fresh
seafood – everything from oysters to blue-
eyed cod with mushroom arancini.

ⓘ Getting There & Away
The daily Redline (p220) bus service from
Burnie will drop you at the turn off to Boat Har-
bour (3km) or Sisters Beach (8km) for $6.50. If
driving from Wynyard, the best route is to follow
the C234 northwest – there are some great views
of the cliffs and rocky coast along this road.

Rocky Cape National Park
Tasmania's smallest national park, stretch-
ing 12km along Bass Strait's shoreline,
was known to Aboriginal Tasmanians as
Tangdimmaa and has great significance to
the Rar.rer.loi.he.ner people, who made their
homes in the sea caves here 8000 years be-
fore European occupation.

Inland the park is made up of coastal
heathland and rare *Banksia serrata* forests.
The rolling green hills are splashed bright
with wildflowers in the spring and summer
months. There's good swimming in the park
at Sisters Beach, Forwards Beach and An-
niversary Bay. Sisters Beach has an 8km
stretch of bleached-blond sand, picnic tables
and a shelter. Close by is Sisters Beach village,
reached via the C233 from Boat Harbour.

On Rocky Cape itself, you can drive out to
a lighthouse with fine Bass Strait views.

🏃 Activities
From Sisters Beach, the walk to Wet Cave,
Lee Archer Cave and Banksia Grove takes
45 minutes (one way). To reach the start, fol-

low the signs to the boat ramp. You can con-
tinue further along the coast to Anniversary
Point (three hours return). It's also possible
to follow the coast to Rocky Cape and return
along the Inland Track (eight hours return).

From the western end of the park, at
Rocky Cape Rd (accessed from a separate
entrance off the Bass Hwy, west of the turn-
off to Sisters Beach), you can walk to two
large Aboriginal caves, South Cave and
North Cave, the latter off the road to the
lighthouse. The caves are significant Aborig-
inal sites, so visitors are encouraged *not* to
enter them. There's also a good circuit of the
cape itself – allow 2½ hours.

🛏 Sleeping
Sisters Beach House RENTAL HOUSE **$$$**
(✆03-8774 2305; www.sistersbeachhouse.com.au;
Irby Blvd; d $200) This traditional Tassie beach
'shack' was built in 1969, but has been coolly
done up inside in laid-back, eclectic beach-
house style. It's just across the road from the
white sands and clear waters of Sisters Beach.

Stanley
POP 481
Get this far west in Tasmania and you begin
to feel it. There's a whiff of something in the
air that feels distinctly like the very end of the
world. Gorgeous little Stanley exudes more
than a trace of this frontier, life-on-the edge
ambience. The town is a scatter of brightly
painted cottages, sheltering in the lee of an
ancient volcano, the Nut. In Stanley's harbour bobs a fleet of fishing boats, piled high
with cray pots and orange buoys, but beyond
this shelter the ocean is often whipped into
whitecaps. Stroll through town on a fine day
and you may not feel that underlying edgi-
ness that comes from being on the world's
rim, but when the Roaring Forties blast
through, you'll feel it sure enough, and that's
part of the excitement of being here.

In late 2014 Stanley turned Hollywood,
being used as part of the movie set for the
historical drama, *The Light Between Oceans.*

⊙ Sights & Activities
Under the Nut – Stanley Heritage Walk,
available from the visitor information centre, takes in 14 of Stanley's more beautiful
and/or interesting historic buildings; the
booklet contains detailed notes on each.
Check out www.stanleyheritagewalk.com.au
for more information.

The Nut LANDMARK
This striking 152m-high volcanic rock formation can be seen for many kilometres around Stanley. It's a steep 20-minute climb to the top – worth it for the views – or take the chairlift (adult one way/return $9/15, child $6/10; ⊙9.30am-5pm Oct-May, 10am-4pm Jun-Sep). The best lookout is a five-minute walk to the south of the chairlift, and you can also take a 35-minute walk (2km) on a path around the top.

In summer, watch for short-tailed shearwaters (mutton birds) returning to their burrows at dusk after a day's foraging at sea.

Seaquarium AQUARIUM
(☑03-6458 2052; www.stanleyseaquarium.com; 6 Wharf Rd, Fisherman's Dock; adult/child/family $12/6/30; ⊙10am-4pm) Providing an interesting display of marine life, Seaquarium is a fun and educational place to bring the kids. We love the touchy-feely tank.

Highfield HISTORIC BUILDING
(☑03-6458 1100; www.historic-highfield.com.au; Green Hills Rd; adult/child/family $12/6/30; ⊙9.30am-4.30pm daily Sep-May, Mon-Fri Jun-Aug) This homestead, 2km north of town, was built in 1835 for the chief agent of the Van Diemen's Land Company. It's an exceptional example of domestic architecture of the Regency period in Tasmania. You can tour the house and outbuildings, including stables, grain stores, workers' cottages and the chapel.

Van Diemen's Land Company Store HISTORIC BUILDING
(16 Wharf Rd) This bluestone warehouse on the seafront dates from 1844, and while it once held bales of wool for export, it now houses an exclusive boutique hotel, @VDL (p224).

Ford's Store HISTORIC BUILDING
(15 Wharf Rd) Near the wharf is this particularly fine old bluestone store, first used for grain storage and then as a bacon factory. It's believed to have been built in 1859 from stones brought here as ship's ballast. Today it's home to Stanley's on the Bay (p225) restaurant.

Joe Lyons Cottage HISTORIC SITE
(☑0408 063 571; 14 Alexander Tce; admission by donation; ⊙10am-4pm) The birthplace of prime minister Joseph Lyons (b 1879).

Tours

Stanley Seal Cruises BOAT TOUR
(☑0419 550 134, 03-6458 1294; www.stanley-sealcruises.com.au; Fisherman's Dock; adult/child over 5yr/child under 5 $55/18/10; ⊙Sep–mid-Jun) These excellent 75-minute cruises take you to see up to 500 Australian fur seals sunning themselves on Bull Rock on the Bass Strait coast. Departures are at 10am and 3pm from September to April, and at 10am in May and June, sea conditions permitting – book ahead to make sure they're running. Stanley Seal Cruises also does offshore fishing charters.

Sleeping

Stanley Hotel HOTEL $
(☑1800 222 397, 03-6458 1161; www.stanleytasmania.com.au; 19 Church St; s/d without bathroom $50/70, d with bathroom from $109) This historic pub has a rabbit warren of rooms. They're brightly painted and truly delightful – this has to be some of the nicest pub accommodation around. The shared bathrooms are superclean and the staff are superfriendly. You can sit out on the upstairs verandah and spy down on the Stanley streetscape. It also runs the six self-catering Abbeys Cottages (d incl breakfast $135-240).

Stanley Cabin & Tourist Park CARAVAN PARK $
(☑03-6458 1266; www.stanleycabinpark.com.au; Wharf Rd; unpowered/powered sites per 2 people $25/30, dm $26, cabins d $90-110; 🐾) With wide views of Sawyer Bay in one direction and the Nut on the other, this park is in a spectacular spot. There are waterfront camp sites, neat cabins and a backpacker hostel comprising six twin rooms. Linen is supplied, but it's BYO towels.

Ark Stanley BOUTIQUE HOTEL $$
(☑0421 695 224; www.thearkstanley.com.au; 18 Wharf Rd; d $140-300) Polished wooden floors, wrought-iron furnishings, luxury linens, goose-down duvets...this place, with its individually styled rooms, takes attention to detail to a whole new level. Fine views are to be had from some of the rooms and the service is discreet but attentive.

Stanley Seaview Inn MOTEL $$
(☑03-6458 1300; www.stanleyseaviewinn.com.au; 58 Dovecote Rd; d $130-210; 🐾) This welcoming option has a selection of motel rooms and self-contained accommodation with million-dollar views of the Nut and township. To get here from Stanley's centre, leave town on Main Rd and bear left onto Dovecote Rd. The motel is situated on a sharp corner, 1.7km from the town centre.

Stanley

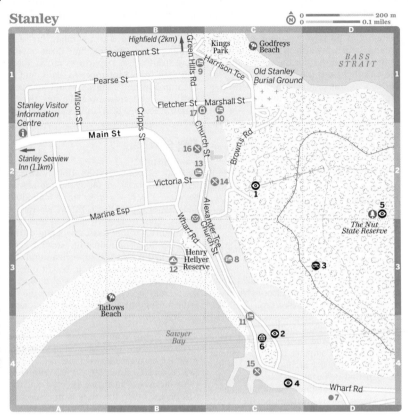

★ @VDL   BOUTIQUE HOTEL $$$
(☎0437 070 222, 03-6458 2032; www.atvdlstan-ley.com.au; 16 Wharf Rd; d $175-255; ☎) What's been done within the bluestone walls of this 1840s warehouse is quite incredible. This ultra-hip boutique hotel has two suites and a self-contained loft apartment. Everything's top class, from the bedding to the artworks on the walls. The same people run a sister property, @The Base (32 Alexander Tce; d $115-140), which is a heritage house divided into two similarly stylish suites.

★ Horizon Deluxe
Apartments   APARTMENT $$$
(☎0448 251 115; www.horizonapartments.com.au; Dovecote Rd; d $340; ☎) These luxurious hill-top apartments are kitted out with spas, sur-round sound, luxury toiletries, fluffy robes and touch-of-a-button climate control. Choc-olate truffles and personal bar are provided. To get here from Stanley, take Main Rd out

of town, and turn left onto Dovecote Rd. It's approximately 2km from the town centre.

@The Beach Stanley   RENTAL HOUSE $$$
(☎0418 119 165; www.thebeach-stanley.com.au; 3 Harrison Tce; d $180-300; P ❀ ☎) Stunning modern interiors inhabit three two-bedroom heritage cottages at this fine place over on the Bass Strait side of Stanley. The views can be superlative, and Sam and Louise are wel-coming hosts.

✖ Eating

Moby Dicks Breakfast Bar   CAFE $
(☎03-6458 1414; 5 Church St; mains $8-16; ⊙7am-noon) Tuck into an enormous breakfast here before you go out and battle the wild west winds – try a cooked-egg breakfast with the lot or waffles with maple syrup...yum.

Stanley Hotel   PUB FOOD $$
(19 Church St; mains $16-39; ⊙10am-9pm) This pub serves bistro fare, including year-round

Stanley

fresh seafood – crayfish in season – and servings the size of the Nut itself. Leave room for the tempting desserts.

★ **Xanders**   MODERN AUSTRALIAN **$$$**
(☑03-6458 1111; 25 Church St; mains $28-42; ⊗6-9pm Wed-Sun) Stanley's best fine-dining restaurant is set in an old house on the main street with views back and front. The menu has an accent on fish and seafood, but Xanders also serves the area's excellent beef and specials such as duck and tandoori-rubbed rack of lamb. There's a good kids menu, too.

★ **Cable Station Restaurant**   MODERN AUSTRALIAN **$$$**
(☑03-6458 1312; www.oldcablestation.com.au; 435 Greenhills Rd, West Beach; 1/2-course lunch $35/45, 2/3-course dinner $59/69) This is a truly sophisticated dining option, offering fine food in the salubrious surrounds of the Cable Station. Don't miss the wood-oven roasted Stanley crayfish or the delectable Black River lamb.

Stanley's on the Bay   MODERN AUSTRALIAN **$$$**
(☑03-6458 1404; 15 Wharf Rd; mains $23-41; ⊗6-9pm Mon-Sat Sep-Jun) Set inside the historic Ford's Store, this fine-dining establish-

ment specialises in steak and seafood. The wonderful seafood platter for two ($100) overflows with local scallops, oysters, fish, octopus and salmon.

🛍 Shopping

★ **Providore 24**   FOOD & WINE
(☑03-6458 1323; www.providore24.com.au; 24 Church St) Some of the finest cheeses, oils, wines and other edible goodies that Tasmania has to offer fill this classy gourmet food store at the top of the main street. It also sells gift baskets as well as clothing, bags, jewellery and other accessories.

ℹ Information

Stanley Visitor Information Centre (☑03-6458 1330, 1300 138 229; www.stanley.com.au; 45 Main Rd; ⊗9.30am-5pm Oct-May, 10am-4pm Jun-Sep) Mine of information on Stanley and surrounding areas. Pick up the *Take on the Edge* brochure for extensive coverage of the far northwest.

ℹ Getting There & Away

Redline Coaches (www.tasredline.com.au) Buses stop at the visitor centre en route to/from Burnie ($21.10, 75 minutes) and Smithton ($6.10, 25 minutes)

Smithton

POP 3240
On a 22km stretch of rugged coast west of Stanley, inland Smithton sprawls along the banks of the Duck River and is a service centre for local beef and dairy farming and vegetable cropping. Forestry has always been big here, and timber milling is still one of the biggest industries in town.

⊙ Sights

Circular Head Heritage Centre   MUSEUM
(☑03-6452 4800; cnr Nelson & King Sts; adult/child $2/1; ⊗10.30am-2.30pm Tue & Thu) For insights into Smithton's pioneer days, visit the volunteer-run Circular Head Heritage Centre. Aside from some old photos, the most fascinating exhibit is the skeleton of the mysterious, giant-wombat-like *Zygomaturus tasmanicum*.

Woolnorth   FARM
Sprawling across the northwestern tip of Tasmania, 25km from Smithton, is the 220-sq-km cattle and sheep property of Woolnorth, still a holding of the Van

WORTH A TRIP

HEAVENLY GARDENS

As you head south on the B22 out of Smithton, just 3km north of Edith Creek you'll come upon **Allendale Gardens & Rainforest** (☑03-6456 4216; www.allendalegardens.com.au; adult/child $10/3.50; ⊙9am-5pm Oct-Apr). This place is truly a wonder of green-fingered creativity, and it's the life's work and passion of Max and Lorraine Cross, who nurture it. You can wander through an incredible variety of trees and flowering plants – there's the glorious birch walk, a spectacular dahlia-and-rose garden, a wisteria pergola, spring blossoms, autumn colours and a panoply of trees, from Himalayan spruces to redwoods, tulip trees and the exquisite Chinese dove tree. Allen Creek ripples its way through the gardens, crossed by six bridges.

There's also a peaceful stand of rainforest where you can admire towering old-growth stringybarks, spot a rare creeping fern and perhaps see platypuses in the creek. You should then indulge in tea, scones and cream in the teahouse, with lashings of Max's homemade raspberry and blackberry jams.

Diemen's Land company two centuries after it began. Today it's also home to enormous wind turbines that harness the power of the Roaring Forties. You can view them up close with **Woolnorth Tours** (☑03-6452 1493; www.woolnorthtours.com), which offers informative half-day tours (adult/child $90/50).

The tours visit Cape Grim, the Woolnorth property and a shipwreck off Woolnorth Point, weather permitting. Take deep lungfuls of the air here: the Baseline Air Pollution Station off Cape Grim declares this to be the cleanest air in the world.

🧭 Tours

Tall Timbers Adventure Tours   ADVENTURE TOUR
(☑1800 628 476, 03-6452 2755; www.talltimbershotel.com.au; Scotchtown Rd) From September to May, Tall Timbers offers 4WD adventure tours to the Tarkine Wilderness ($250 with gourmet lunch, minimum two people, or $105 without lunch, minimum four people). It also runs mine tours, Aboriginal heritage tours and helicopter sightseeing in several variations. Flight options include 30 minutes ($495), 45 minutes ($730) and one hour ($960).

Costs are for a minimum of two and maximum of five people. From October to February or March there are also evening penguin tours ($40 including dinner).

🛏 Sleeping & Eating

Island View Spa Cottage   COTTAGE $$
(☑0418 595 314; 70 Cantara Rd; d $160-180, extra adult/child $40/10) This is a real delight of a place, set in peaceful waterfront bushland only 2km from town. You can hang out on the sunny deck, soak in the luxurious out-

door spa and spot abundant wildlife as the sun goes down over the nearby Bass Strait islands. This beautiful house sleeps up to five.

Tall Timbers   HOTEL $$
(☑1800 628 476, 03-6452 2755; www.talltimbershotel.com.au; Scotchtown Rd; d $145-180, apt from $175; 🐾🛏) Some 2km south of Smithton, Tall Timbers has an impressive portico of massive timber beams and a reception area under an amazing timber cathedral ceiling. The rooms are comfortable, the lakeside apartments are outstanding and a reliable **bistro** (mains $25 to $44, noon to 2pm and 6pm to 9pm) prepares decent dishes (steaks are the speciality) and has a well-equipped playroom for kids.

Time Out on Emmett   CAFE $
(61 Emmett St; mains $6-14; ⊙7.30am-5.30pm Mon-Fri, to 2.30pm Sat) This is a must for a meal or snack when you're in Smithton. It serves imaginative salads, rolls and wraps, lasagne, frittatas, sweet treats – and fabulous coffee. Try its crayfish, or scallop pies baked using local recipes passed down through generations.

❶ Getting There & Away

Redline Coaches (☑03-6336 1446, 1300 360 000; www.redlinecoaches.com.au) Redline Coaches head to Burnie ($24, 1½ hours) from Smith St, opposite the police station.

Around Smithton

There are ancient, dripping rainforests and tannin-brown rivers in the Tarkine south of Smithton, which you can get into the heart of via the **South Arthur Forest Drive**.

Activities

Tarkine Forest Adventures ADVENTURE SPORTS (☑03-6456 7138; www.dismalswamptasmania. com.au; 26,059 Bass Hwy; adult/child $20/10; ☉9am-5pm Dec & Jan, 10am-4pm Feb-Nov) Thirty kilometres southwest of Smithton (just off the A2) is this forest adventure centre, formerly known as Dismal Swamp. There's a 110m-long slide that provides a thrilling descent into a blackwood-forested sinkhole – sliders must be over eight years of age and at least 90cm tall. It also has a cafe, an interpretation centre and boardwalks on the forest floor.

Three **mountain-bike tracks**, graded from 'family' to 'expert', let you get out into it on two wheels. Bring your own bike.

Marrawah

POP 371

Untamed, unspoilt Marrawah is a domain of vast ocean beaches, mind-blowing sunsets and green, rural hills. The power of the ocean here is astounding, and the wild beaches, rocky coves and headlands have changed little since they were the homeland of Tasmania's first people. This coast is abundant with signs of Aboriginal Tasmania – and somehow there's a feeling of lonely emptiness, as if these original custodians have only just left the land.

It's vast ocean waves that Marrawah is best known for today. Sometimes the Southern Ocean throws up the remains of long-forgotten shipwrecks here – things tumble in on waves that sometimes reach more than 10m in length. Experienced surfers and windsurfers also come here for the challenging breaks.

The **general store** (800 Comeback Rd; ☉7.30am-7pm Mon-Fri, 8am-7.30pm Sat & Sun) sells supplies and petrol and is an agent for Australia Post and Commonwealth Bank. Fill up on fuel here if you're planning to take the Western Explorer to Corinna, as there's no other petrol outlet until Zeehan or Waratah, about 200km away.

Activities

There's a lengthy beach walk from **Bluff Hill Point** to **West Point** (four hours one way) and a coastal walk from **Bluff Hill Point** to the mouth of the **Arthur River** (two hours one way). There's also a highly scenic walk north along the beach from **Green Point** to **Preminghana** (around three hours return).

Sleeping & Eating

Camping is possible for free at beautiful Green Point, where there are toilets, water and an outdoor cold shower. You must pitch your tent by the toilets back from the beach, not on the foreshore.

Ann Bay Cabins CABIN $$
(☑03-6457 1361, 0428 548 760; 99 Green Point Rd; d from $150) These two cosy wooden cabins are just the place to hang out and get away from it all. You can sit on the deck and admire the views, or luxuriate in the deep spa bath, with bathing essentials and choccies supplied.

Marrawah Beach House RENTAL HOUSE $$
(☑03-6457 1285; www.marrawahbeachhouse.com. au; d from $160) This secluded place is brightly decorated with starfish and seashells, and has unrivalled views. The friendly owners set it up with fresh flowers and sometimes local honey before you arrive. Sleeps up to four. It's just up the hill from Green Point Beach.

Marrawah Tavern TAVERN $$
(☑03-6457 1102; Comeback Rd; mains $15-33; ☉noon-10pm Mon-Wed, to midnight Thu-Sat, to 9pm Sun) You can get a good meal and a drink at this casual country pub. Choices include steak sandwiches, prawns, roasts, beef 'n' reef and whole local flounders.

Getting There & Away

Marrawah lies 50km west of Smithton along a good sealed road.

MARRAWAH'S SURF BREAKS

The annual West Coast Classic surfing competition is regularly decided at Marrawah in March, as is a round of the state's windsurfing championships. The area has a number of surfing spots.

Green Point 2km from the town centre. Has an impressive break in southerly conditions.

Nettley Bay Along the road from Green Point.

Lighthouse Beach At West Point, south of Marrawah. Has good surfing in an easterly. Take the left-hand branches of the road from the turn-off on the C214.

Bluff Hill Point Great reef surfing in easterly conditions. The surf beach is to the right of the lighthouse off Bluff Hill Point Rd.

TASMANIAN ABORIGINAL SITES

The far northwest of Tasmania has been home to the Tasmanian Aboriginal Tarkininer people for more than 35,000 years. Evidence of their habitation is clearly visible along much of the Tarkine coast, and experts call this one of the most important archaeological regions in the world.

There's a significant Aboriginal site along the road to Arthur River at West Point. Beyond the township at Sundown Point is a site containing several dozen mudstone slabs engraved with mainly circular motifs. The Arthur Pieman Conservation Area, further south, has a particularly dense concentration of middens and, slightly further afield, there are also several important cave sites at Rocky Cape National Park.

Arguably the most significant site on the west coast is 7km north of Marrawah at Preminghana (formerly known as Mt Cameron West). At the northern end of the beach are low-lying slabs of rock with geometric carvings (or petroglyphs) dating back two millennia. Also in this area are hut depressions, stone tools, seal-hunting hides, tool quarries and middens. Natural links with Tasmanian Aboriginal culture here include boobialla, honeysuckle and tea-tree clusters – plants used to prepare food and traditional medicines.

Preminghana was returned to the Aboriginal people in 1995 – you can't visit the area independently. If you'd like to be authoritatively guided around this and other significant Aboriginal sites, contact the **Tasmanian Aboriginal Land and Sea Council** (TALSC; ☑ 03-6231 0288; 4 Lefroy St, North Hobart), which keeps a list of heritage officers who can accompany you.

Arthur River

There are only a few hardy souls who call Arthur River their full-time home – the rest of the population is made up of 'shackies' and fishers who love the wild remoteness of the country around here. This is the end of Tasmania, the end of the paved road and the starting point for many a fine adventure.

◎ Sights & Activities

Gardiner Point, signposted off the main road on the southern side of Arthur River, is Tasmania's official **Edge of the World**: the sea here stretches uninterrupted all the way to Argentina. There's a plaque at the point – a great place to take those leaning-into-the-wind, world's-end photos.

The town **kiosk**, opposite the ranger station, has limited supplies, takeaways and fishing-rod hire (half/full day $15/25). There's a small **general store** on the south side of the river where you can book river cruises.

Arthur River Canoe & Boat Hire   BOATING
(☑ 03-6457 1312; 1429 Arthur River Rd; ⊙ 9am-5pm) Explore the amazing river and rainforest with watercraft hired here. This place offers information on river conditions and storage for your gear, and hires single and double Canadian canoes (per hour $12 to $16, per day $50 to $75). It also rents out aluminium dinghies with outboards (per hour/day $30/175).

Even better, it'll help you organise a downriver canoe trip from Kanunnah Bridge (two-day trip) or the Tayatea Bridge site (four-day trip). It'll meet you at the launching site with boats and river gear, and drive your car back to Arthur River (for a $100 fee).

☞ Tours

Arthur River Cruises   BOAT TOUR
(☑ 03-6457 1158; www.arthurrivercruises.com.au; adult/child $95/10; ⊙ 10am Sep-May) The reflections on the Arthur River have to be seen to be believed, and you can get out among them on board the MV *George Robinson*, operated by Arthur River Cruises. On the five-hour, 28km round trip into the rainforest, you'll see sea eagles and kingfishers, stroll in the rainforest and enjoy a BBQ lunch.

AR Reflections River Cruises   BOAT TOUR
(☑ 03-6457 1288; www.arthurriver.com.au; adult/child $95/48; ⊙ 10.15am) The attractive MV *Reflections* departs daily for a 5½-hour return trip to Warra Landing, where you get a guided rainforest walk and gourmet lunch.

🛏 Sleeping & Eating

The Parks and Wildlife Service at Arthur River manages three camping areas: **Seaside Manuka Campground**, just north of Arthur River; **Peppermint Campground** in Arthur River itself; and **Prickly Wattle** along the road to Couta Rocks. All have unpowered sites ($13 for two people, $5/free per extra adult/child) with taps, cold showers and toilets. None of these camp sites have bins: take your rubbish out with you.

Most accommodation options have a barbecue area, and the Arthur River Tavern does counter meals.

Arthur River Cabin Park CAMPGROUND $
(📋 03-6457 1212; www.arthurrivercabinpark.com; 1239 Arthur River Rd; unpowered/powered sites per 2 people $27/30, s/d from $70/80) There are hot showers and a laundry for all stayers at this neat park, and the spick-and-span cabins are amazingly good value. Various wildlife – including devils – visits in the evening.

⭐**Arthur Riverfront &
Sea Lodge** RENTAL HOUSE $$
(📋 0418 595 314; 22 Gardiner St; d $135-185) This smart new house can be rented as two separate apartments (one two-bedroom, one three-bedroom) or opened up into one big house, sleeping up to 12. It's absolutely on the waterfront and well equipped with spacious living areas, wood stoves, expansive decks and amazing river and Southern Ocean views. One child stays for free.

**Arthur River Sunset
Holiday Villas** RENTAL HOUSE $$
(📋 03-6438 1316; www.sunsetholidayvillas.com; d $115) Simple-yet-comfortable modern homes make for a good Arthur River bolthole. Wildlife, birdwatching and 4WD tours are all possible.

🛈 **Information**

Ranger Station (📋 03-6457 1225; www.parks. tas.gov.au) There's a Parks & Wildlife Service ranger station on the northern side of the river, where you can get camping information and permits for off-road vehicles.

Tarkine Wilderness

The Tarkine is a 4470-sq-km stretch of wild country between the Arthur River in the north and the Pieman River in the south. It's a globally significant ecosystem that encompasses the largest intact area of temperate rainforest in the southern hemisphere, tall eucalyptus forests, endless horizons of buttongrass plains, savage ocean beaches, sand dunes and extensive coastal heathland. It's also believed to be one of the oldest rainforests in Australia, and is home to several endangered species and extensive, ancient archaeological sites. Because of its remoteness, ferocious weather and isolation, the Tarkine survived almost untouched by modernity well into the 20th century.

👉 **Tours**

⭐**Tarkine Trails** WALKING
(📋 0405 255 537, 03-6223 5320; www.tarkinetrail. com.au) Tarkine Trails can take you on a number of different adventures if you want to get really remote on foot. Trips include the full-forest-immersion six-day Tarkine Trail ($1849 per person), four-day Tarkine Rainforest Walk ($1699) or the six-day Tarkine Coast Trail ($1849) from Pieman Heads to Sandy Cape.

The Tarkine Rainforest Walk consists of day walks from the exclusive and deliciously remote Tiger Ridge Base Camp, where you sleep in a comfortable safari-tent-style standing camp and marvel at the surrounding giant tree ferns from the lodge's cantilevered verandah.

Tasmanian Expeditions ADVENTURE TOUR
(📋 03-6331 9000, 1300 666 856; www.tasmanianexpeditions.com.au; trips $1995) Tasmanian

DEVONPORT & THE NORTHWEST TARKINE WILDERNESS

SAVE THE TARKINE?

The Tarkine first entered the national psyche through the controversial construction of the 'Road to Nowhere' – now called the Western Explorer – in 1995, and conservation groups have been seeking full protection for it ever since. In 2005 the federal government protected 730 sq km of the Tarkine's unique myrtle-rich rainforest. In 2009 the area received a National Heritage emergency listing when faced with the threat of more road building. Two years later, following the historic Statement of Principles agreement between Tasmanian forestry and conservation groups, a further 700 sq km of Tarkine forest was to be protected from logging. Whether the agreement will hold remains in doubt. Conservation groups still call for a Tarkine National Park to be added to the remote Savage River National Park, as parts of the Tarkine remain vulnerable to mining, off-road driving and arson. You can read more about the work of the Tarkine National Coalition, which has been instrumental in the long-running campaign to protect the area, at www.tarkine.org.

Expeditions offers different Tarkine experiences, with hiking, canoeing and photographic instruction all part of the possible mix.

🛏 Sleeping & Eating

⭐ **Tarkine Wilderness Lodge** LODGE **$$$**
(☎ 03-6445 9184; www.tarkinelodge.com.au; d from $410; P) 🚗 In the forests behind Rocky Cape National Park, the outstanding new Tarkine Wilderness Lodge offers luxury accommodation and a host of activities for getting out into the forest. Lunch ($20) and dinner ($50) are of a similarly high standard.

ℹ Information

Tarkine Interpretation Centre (☎ 03-6439 7100; www.discoverthetarkine.com.au; Athenaeum Hall, Smith St, Waratah; ⊙10am-2pm Wed-Sun) Informative displays about the Tarkine's natural history and environmental battles, as well as a few brochures.

Western Explorer & Arthur Pieman Conservation Area

The Western Explorer (C249) is probably Tasmania's most excitingly remote road journey. It delves deep into the buttongrass wilderness of the Arthur Pieman Conservation Area of the western Tarkine. Dubbed the 'Road to Nowhere', it was controversially upgraded from a barely-there 4WD track into a wide gravel road in 1995 to the dismay of conservationists, who saw it as opening this vulnerable wilderness to damage and exploitation.

Despite its troubled beginnings, the road is now a well-established means of traversing this rugged part of Tasmania, and it's an unmissable journey if you're in the region. Road conditions vary from season to season. Although it's regularly negotiated by vehicles without 4WD, it's remote, unsealed and at times rough and rocky. Some of the steepest hills now have paved sections, but there are many others where there's potential to skid on a treacherous surface: drive with great care. Don't drive the road at night or in bad weather. For an up-to-date assessment on road conditions, ask at the Parks & Wildlife Service ranger station (p229) in Arthur River. Fill up your car at Marrawah if you're travelling south, or at Zeehan, Tullah or Waratah if heading north: there's no petrol in between.

The 1000-sq-km Arthur Pieman Conservation Area takes in the remote fishing settlement of **Temma**, the mining ghost town of **Balfour**, magnificent beaches such as **Sandy Cape Beach**, the rugged **Norfolk Range**, the **Thornton** and **Interview Rivers** and savage **Pieman Heads**. The Tarkine's wild beaches are feared for their vehicle-swallowing quicksand.

Corinna & the Pieman River

In rip-roaring gold-rush days Corinna was a humming town with two hotels, a post office, plenty of shops and a population that numbered 2500 souls. That's hard to believe now when you pull up on the forested edge of the Pieman, turn off your car's engine and absorb the unbelievable forest peace.

Less than a decade ago, the owners of what remains transformed Corinna into a deep-forest wilderness experience that offers a sense of adventure and immersion in the rainforest without forsaking too many comforts. That said, there's no mobile-phone reception and no TV: the most prevalent sound is birdsong. Wallabies, pademelons, wombats and other wildlife are commonly sighted here.

🏃 Activities

Corinna is the trailhead for some fabulous **bushwalking** from short strolls to more serious rainforest undertakings. Possibilities include **Mt Donaldson** (four hours return), **Philosopher's Falls** (four hours return) and **Whyte River** (two hours). The latter can offer good platypus spotting around dusk.

Also on offer are **canoe** and **kayak** paddles on the Pieman (per hour/half day/full day $10/40/70), **fishing** (rod hire half day/full day $10/20) and **boat trips** (adult/child $50/25) to Lovers' Falls, where you can be dropped with a picnic hamper to sigh at the beauty of it all. For details on all these activities, ask at the reception of Corinna Wilderness Experience.

Pieman River Cruises BOAT TOUR
(☎ 03-6446 1170; adult/child $90/51; ⊙10am) While in Corinna you can't miss the Pieman River Cruise, a pleasingly rustic alternative to the crowded Gordon River cruises out of Strahan. The tour on the historic MV *Arcadia II* lasts 4½ hours and heads downstream to where the Pieman River meets the Southern Ocean. A packed lunch is included and you've time to walk out to the remote beach before returning to Corinna. Book well ahead.

🛏 Sleeping & Eating

★ **Corinna Wilderness
Experience** COTTAGE $$$
(📞03-6446 1170; www.corinna.com.au; camp
sites per 2 people $20, cottages d $200-250,
f $250) Corinna has a collection of new
self-contained timber eco-cottages, as well as
some older-style houses. The newer cottages
are modern and rather lovely inside, and the
rainforest starts right at your back door.

The pub has a well-stocked bar while the
restaurant (mains $14 to $38, serving noon
to 2pm and 6pm to 8pm) serves up dishes
such as steak sandwiches for lunch, and
two or three excellent mains (such as steak
or salmon) for dinner. Picnic hampers and
BBQ packs are also available for order.

❶ Getting There & Away

You can approach Corinna from Somerset, just
west of Burnie, via the Murchison Hwy through
magnificent Hellyer Gorge (perfect for picnic
stops). After Waratah, the C247 is sealed as far
as Savage River, whereafter it's 26km of un-
sealed, but well-maintained gravel that's almost
always passable in a 2WD. If you're taking the
C249 Western Explorer Road, it's an unsealed
109km to Arthur River.

Fatman Vehicle Barge (📞03-6446 1170; mo-
torbike/car/caravan $10/20/25; ⊙9am-5pm
Apr-Sep, to 7pm Oct-Mar) The cable-driven Fat-
man vehicle barge plying the Pieman River at
Corinna allows you to travel from Corinna down
to Zeehan and Strahan. There's a 9m-long, 6.5-
tonne limit on vehicles.

Waratah

POP 248

Waratah is the gateway to the Tarkine Wil-
derness if you're heading to Corinna, and it
was here, in 1936, that the (presumed) last
Tasmanian tiger was trapped. Although it's a
pretty little lakeside town sliced through by
Happy Valley gorge and its cascading water-
fall, there's little to detain you – it's a place
to gather information at the Tarkine Inter-
pretation Centre and stock up on fuel and
supplies before leaving the civilised world
behind.

If you need to stay the night, try the
attractive **O'Connor Hall Guesthouse**
(📞03-6439 1472; 2 Smith St; d $120-165), with
its wrought-iron tracery and four-poster
beds. It's on the main road (B23) through
town. **Bischoff Hotel** (📞03-6439 1188; Main
St; mains $10-19; ⊙noon-8pm) offers counter
meals for lunch and dinner.

King Island

POP 1565

A skinny sliver of land 64km long and 27km
wide, King Island (or 'KI', as locals call it)
is a laid-back place where everyone knows
everyone and life is mighty relaxed. The
island's green pastures famously produce a
rich dairy bounty and its surrounding seas
supply fabulously fresh seafood.

Locals dry kelp to extract its goodies and
tend lighthouses, four of which guard the
rocky coastline. They also surf: KI has some
of the most consistently good surf anywhere.
As a visitor your hardest decision of the day
might be which secluded cove to have all to
yourself, which surf beach to go to for the per-
fect break, or how much more of that amaz-
ing King Island cheese you can consume.

◉ Sights

King Island Dairy DAIRY
(📞1800 677 852, 03-6462 0947; www.kidairy.com.
au; 869 North Rd; ⊙noon-4pm Sun-Fri) Low-key
but top-quality, King Island Dairy's From-
agerie is 8km north of Currie (just beyond
the airport). Taste its award-winning bries,
cheddars and feisty blues, and then stock
up in its shop on cheeses that are budget
priced – only here – to fuel your King Island
exploring. Its cream is sinfully delicious.

Cape Wickham HISTORIC SITE
You can drive right up to the tallest **light-
house** in the southern hemisphere at
Cape Wickham, on KI's northern tip. This
48m-high tower was built in 1861 after sev-
eral ships had been wrecked on the island's
treacherous coastline. Most famous of all
King Island shipwrecks is the *Cataraqui*
(1845), Australia's worst civil maritime dis-
aster, with the loss of 400 lives.

Currie Lighthouse LIGHTHOUSE
(📞0439 705 610; adult/child $15/7.50; ⊙tours
3.30pm Wed & Sat) This lighthouse was built in
1880 in response to numerous shipwrecks.
There are two more lighthouses at **Stokes
Point** and **Naracoopa**.

King Island Museum MUSEUM
(Lighthouse St, Currie; adult/child $5/1; ⊙2-4pm,
closed Jul & Aug) There's information on light-
keeping, shipwrecks and monuments here
and also in the *King Island Maritime Trail:
Shipwrecks & Safe Havens* booklet, which
you can pick up wherever visitor informa-
tion is available.

Kelp Industries' Visitor Centre
MUSEUM

(89 Netherby Rd, Currie; ⊙8am-5pm Mon-Fri) Come here to find out why you see tractors gathering kelp on KI's beaches. Glimpse the huge straps of bull kelp being air dried here. It's exported to factories in Scotland and Norway, which extract alginates for use in products such as sauces, lotions and detergents.

Calcified Forest
NATURE RESERVE

From Currie, head south to the Seal Rocks Reserve (off South Rd). A 30-minute return stroll takes you to a viewing platform to survey the fossilised stumps of rainforest trees.

🏃 Activities

King Island is one of Australia's premier surfing destinations – *Surfing Life* magazine has voted the break at Martha Lavinia as one of the top 10 waves in the world.

Surf and freshwater fishing almost guarantee a good catch, and you can swim at many of the island's unpopulated beaches (beware rips and currents) and freshwater lagoons. Bring your own gear for the legendary snorkelling and diving here.

For hiking, pick up a map from King Island Tourism and go independently, or take a guided walk with King Island Wilderness Walks (☑0400 858 339; Lighthouse St, Currie).

You don't even need to get out on foot for wildlife spotting on KI: it's just about everywhere you look. There are rufus and Bennett's wallabies, pademelons, snakes, echidnas and platypuses, and you may even glimpse seals. The island has 78 bird species and, on summer evenings, little penguins come ashore around the Grassy breakwater.

🛏 Sleeping

Bass Cabins & Campground
CAMPGROUND $

(☑03-6462 1260; 5 Fraser Rd; camp site per person $14, d cabin from $85) There are a few camp spots here, with bathroom facilities adjacent, and two two-bedroom cabins. The campground is 1.5km from the centre of Currie.

★Portside Links
APARTMENT, B&B $$

(☑03-6461 1134; www.portsidelinks.com.au; Grassy Harbour Rd; d apt $170) This fantastic accommodation is the best place to stay on KI. There are two stylish and well-equipped self-catering apartments here as well as a B&B room in the owners' home. It's a short stroll to pretty Grassy Harbour and Sand Blow Beach. Penguins nest nearby. There's a minimum two-night stay, but prices drop the longer you stay.

King Island Accommodation Cottages
RENTAL HOUSE $$

(☑1800 612 269; www.kingislandaccommodationcottages.com.au; 125 Esplanade, Naracoopa; 1/2-bedroom cottage from $120/130) Right on the coast and beautifully maintained, these lovely quiet cottages are an excellent choice.

🍴 Eating

KI is foodie heaven. Must trys include KI cheese and dairy products, but also crayfish in season (November to August), oysters, crabs, grass-fed beef, free-range pork and game. Don't forget to find some Cloud Juice, KI's pure bottled rainwater. There are two supermarkets in Currie and a store in Grassy.

King Island Bakery
BAKERY $

(☑03-6462 1337; 5 Main St, Currie; snacks $5-18; ⊙breakfast & lunch daily, dinner Fri) Best pies for miles.

Boomerang by the Sea
MODERN AUSTRALIAN $$$

(☑03-6462 1288; www.boomerangbythesea.com.au; Golf Club Rd; mains $29-42; ⊙6-9pm Mon-Sat) Arguably the best place to eat on the island, this has wraparound views and a fine menu that's big on seafood.

ℹ Information

ATMs are located at the corner of Main and Edward Sts in Currie, and at KI Foodworks Supermarket, also in Currie.

King Island Tourism (☑03-6462 1355; www.kingisland.org.au; 5 George St, Currie) Ask about the *King Island Grazing Trails* map, which details historical, natural and cultural walks around the island. King Island Tourism's website is an excellent pre-trip planning resource.

ℹ Getting There & Away

King Island Airlines (☑03-9580 3777; www.kingislandair.com.au) Melbourne Moorabbin to King Island twice daily.

Regional Express (☑13 17 13; www.regionalexpress.com.au) Melbourne Tullamarine to King Island.

Sharp Airlines (☑1300 55 66 94; www.sharpairlines.com) Connects King Island to Burnie and Launceston twice daily.

ℹ Getting Around

King Island Car Rental (☑03-6462 1282, 1800 777 282; kicars2@bigpond.com; 2 Meech St, Currie) Per day from around $73.

P&A Car Rental (☑03-6462 1603; 1 Netherby Rd) Per day from around $80.

Cradle Country & the West

Why Go?

If you imagined Tasmania as a land of soaring alpine peaks and dreamy, untouched wilderness, then you've imagined this part of the state. Welcome to the island's wild west, a land of endless ocean beaches, ancient mossy rainforests, tannin-tinted rivers, glacier-sculpted mountains and boundless horizons, where you feel like the only soul on earth. This is Tasmania's vast outdoor playground, where your options for adventure are varied and plentiful. Come here for the toughest multi-day hikes (or gentle rainforest wanders); come to shoot rapids on untamed rivers (or cruise mirror-calm waters); and come to kayak into some of the last untouched temperate wilderness on earth (or fly over it all in a light plane). Get out into the wilds independently, or come with a guided group, but whatever you do, get out there.

Best Places to Eat

➡ Linda Valley Cafe (p247)
➡ Risby Cove (p243)
➡ Highland Restaurant (p254)
➡ Empire Hotel (p247)

When to Go

➡ This whole region buzzes in the warmest months (December to March). It may be busy, but the long days give you more time in the outdoors, and visitor services operate at full tilt.

➡ Tasmania's alpine heart can be gorgeously ice-encrusted in winter (June to August). Fewer souls get out bushwalking now, and even the most-trodden tracks are hushed. If you're equipped and keen for a frosty – even snowy – highland adventure, it's a great time to visit.

➡ The southwest returns to remotest isolation in the cold months (May to September): this is when ferocious western gales arrive...and few visitors dare.

Best Places to Stay

➡ Cradle Mountain Highlanders Cottages (p253)
➡ Franklin Manor (p242)
➡ Wheelhouse Apartments (p242)
➡ Cradle Mountain Lodge (p254)
➡ Penghana (p246)

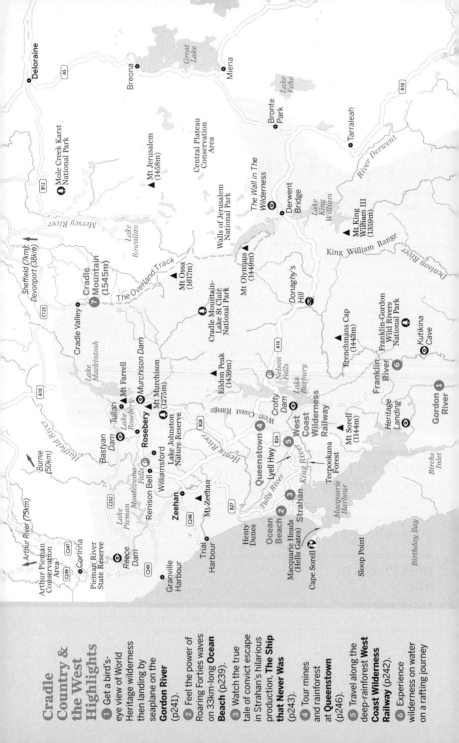

Cradle Country & the West Highlights

❶ Get a bird's-eye view of World Heritage wilderness then landing by seaplane on the **Gordon River** (p241).

❷ Feel the power of Roaring Forties waves on 33km-long **Ocean Beach** (p239).

❸ Watch the true tale of convict escape in Strahan's hilarious production, **The Ship that Never Was** (p243).

❹ Tour mines and rainforest at **Queenstown** (p246).

❺ Travel along the deep-rainforest **West Coast Wilderness Railway** (p242).

❻ Experience wilderness on water on a rafting journey

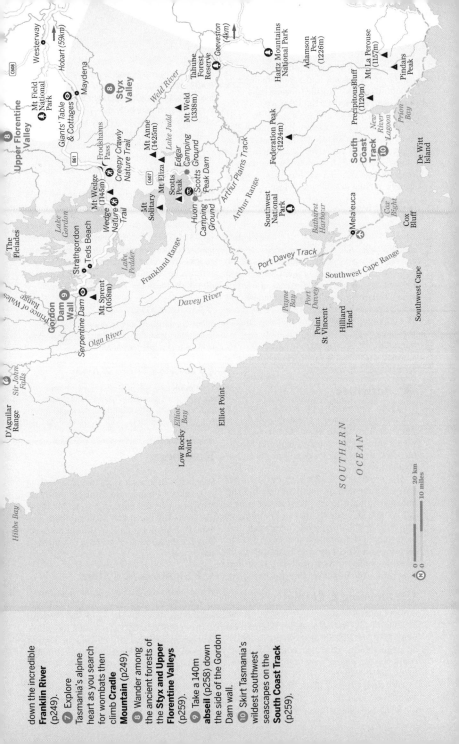

down the incredible **Franklin River** (p249).

⑦ Explore Tasmania's alpine heart as you search for wombats then climb **Cradle Mountain** (p249).

⑧ Wander among the ancient forests of the **Styx and Upper Florentine Valleys** (p259).

⑨ Take a 140m **abseil** (p258) down the side of the Gordon Dam wall.

⑩ Skirt Tasmania's wildest southwest seascapes on the **South Coast Track** (p259).

Tullah

POP 192

A quiet place offering accommodation, excellent trout fishing and some challenging mountain walks, the little town of Tullah has long been isolated in the rainforests of the West Coast Range, and is wrapped by deep, tannin-brown rivers. Indeed, the name Tullah comes from an Aboriginal word meaning 'meeting of two rivers' and the town is almost an island. It shelters in the nape of majestic Mts Farrell and Murchison, and the waters of Lake Rosebery lap close.

◉ Sights

Wee Georgie Wood
Steam Railway   HISTORIC SITE
(📞0417 142 724; www.weegeorgiewood.com.
au; Murchison Hwy; adult/child/family $7/3/14;
⊙10am-4pm 1st Sun, last Sat & last Sun of month
Oct-Jun) To commemorate the days of steam –
when Tullah's only link to the outside world
was by train – local residents have restored
Wee Georgie Wood Steam Railway, one of
the narrow-gauge steam locomotives that
operated on the town's original railway
through the hills and rainforest. The journey
takes around 25 minutes.

🏃 Activities

There are several **scenic drives** from Tullah, alongside hydroelectric dams and lakes. They include **Reece Dam, Anthony Rd** (a scenic shortcut to Queenstown) and **Mackintosh Dam Rd**. Ask for details at the Tullah Wilderness Gallery.

The area's best **walks** include 712m **Mt Farrell** (three to four hours return) and the tallest mountain in the West Coast range, 1275m **Mt Murchison** (six hours return). The folks at Tullah Lakeside Lodge can provide walking information and may be able to guide you. There are also beautiful, short lakeside walks starting near the jetty and boat ramp. You might see platypuses at play.

🛏 Sleeping & Eating

Tullah Lakeside Lodge   HOTEL, CABIN $$
(📞03-6473 4121; www.tullahlakesidelodge.com.au;
Farrell St; d $78-199) Set in ex-hydro-workers'
accommodation, this lake-edge hotel has
comfortable rooms, from budget doubles
to spa suites with lake views. The lodge has
kayaks (free for two hours for most room
categories; half/full day $30/50) and fishing gear, and can arrange guided hikes. The

restaurant (mains $18 to $30, last dinner orders 7.30pm) has glorious lake views and fine steaks and salmon.

Tullah Wilderness Gallery   APARTMENT, CAFE $$
(📞03-6473 4141; 1 Murchison Hwy; d $80-110,
mains $8-20; ⊙9.30am-midnight, reduced hours in
winter; 🛜) The friendly cafe-pub here serves
all-day breakfasts and hearty mountain fare,
such as lasagne and schnitzel, as well as
burgers and sandwiches to eat in or takeaway. You can browse the attached gallery
for art created from local wood, or hope for
some live music in the pub. There are also
two cosy self-contained apartments; book
well in advance.

Tullah Village Café   CAFE $
(📞03-6473 4377; Farrell St; meals $7-16; ⊙10am-
8pm) You can get cooked all-day breakfasts,
snack takeaways, decent hamburgers,
schnitzels, and fish and chips here. It also
does kids' meals.

ℹ Information

Tullah Wilderness Gallery has a few brochures and the locals who work here are usually keen to help visitors with information.

ℹ Getting There & Away

Tassielink (📞1300 300 520; www.tassielink.com.au) Services to/from Queenstown ($22.60, 80 minutes), Strahan ($33.20, 2¾ hours) and Devonport ($33.50, 3¼ hours).

Rosebery

POP 922

Rosebery's best asset is its beautiful setting in a valley of temperate rainforest with Mt Murchison to the east, imposing Mt Black (950m) to the north and Mt Read (with Tasmania's highest rainfall) to the south. Rosebery itself gets an average 3.5m of rain each year.

◉ Sights & Activities

The picnic area at the southern entrance to town is the start of a short (10-minute) walk along the Stitt River and over Park Rd to pretty **Stitt Falls**. Then there's incredible **Montezuma Falls**, 104m tall and the highest in Tasmania, that plume down a rainforest cliff. Head out of Rosebery towards Strahan and follow signs to the falls, 2km south of town. At the end of the road is Williamsford, the site of an abandoned mining town. From here an easy three-hour return walk leads to the falls. You can venture out onto the narrow swing bridge suspended over the yawning chasm for a great view.

👉 Tours

Hay's Adventure Tours OUTDOORS, FISHING
(📞 03-6473 1247) Hay's is the only operator allowed into Lake Johnston Nature Reserve, near Rosebery, to see an extraordinary 10,000-year-old stand of Huon pines. Departure is usually around 11am in summer (on request – 24 hours notice needed) and in winter, whenever the fog lifts. Hay's also offers trout-fishing tours on Mackintosh, Rosebery and Murchison Lakes near Tullah. All gear is supplied.

✨ Festivals & Events

Rosebery Festival CULTURAL
In February (and even as late as early April) each year, Rosebery comes alive with this folk festival. There's live music, horse rides, a puppet theatre, food stalls, fireworks and, of course, that old Tassie favourite: woodchopping.

🛏 Sleeping & Eating

Rosebery Cabin &
Tourist Park CARAVAN PARK $
(📞 03-6473 1366; www.westcoastcabins.com.au; 1 Park Rd; unpowered/powered sites $23/28, cabins d $65-100) This park is surrounded by hills and has grassy camp sites, a gravel caravan area, and basic cabins. It's so shady it can get quite cool once the sun drops below the treeline.

★Mount Black Lodge HOTEL $$
(📞 03-6473 1039; www.mountblacklodge.com; Hospital Rd; d $125-140; 🅿) This rustic little lodge, set in award-winning gardens, is a real pleasure. It's run by friendly owners and looks towards Mt Murchison and Mt Read, so ask for a mountain-view room (extra adult/child $30/15). There's a cosy lounge where you can stay warm by the wood heater.

The on-site Blue Moon Restaurant (mains $25-36; ⊘ 6-8.30pm) serves excellent home-cooked food.

Ol' Jacks Café & Gallery CAFE $
(📞 03-6473 3097; 32 Agnes St; mains $5-16; ⊘ 10am-3pm Tue-Sat) What an asset to Rosebery! You can't miss out on a stop here. It serves delicious, healthy food – focaccias, wraps, a good range of salads, gluten-free cakes, daily blackboard specials and hands-down the best coffee on the west coast – in relaxed surroundings. It's big on using Tasmanian produce – organic where possible.

Hang out on the sofas, peruse the art gallery and let the small ones get into the toys in the kids' corner.

❶ Getting There & Away

Tassielink (www.tassielink.com.au) Services to Launceston ($55.60, 5¼ hours) and Strahan ($30.70, 2½ hours) stop at Mackrell's Milkbar on Agnes St.

Zeehan
POP 728
For Zeehan, as for much of the west coast, the big thing in town has always been mining. In 1882 Frank Long discovered silver and lead on the banks of Pea Soup Creek. In no time Zeehan became known as Silver City, with a population of 10,000 people, 27 pubs, the famous Gaiety Grand theatre (seating 1000 people) and even its own stock exchange.

How times have changed. Cycles of boom and bust continue to dominate the town's fortunes, and rumours of mines reopening ebb and flow with the years. If you're just passing through, Zeehan now has that hushed one-horse-town feel – a handful of worthwhile attractions aside – where you half expect to see tumbleweed rolling down the main street.

◉ Sights

★West Coast Heritage Centre MUSEUM
(📞 03-6471 6225; www.westcoastheritagecentre-zeehan.com.au; 114 Main St; adult/child/family combined ticket with Gaiety Grand $12/10/25; ⊘ 9am-5pm) This excellent museum is in the 1894 School of Mines building and is one of the best regional mining museums in the nation. The ground floor features a world-class mineral display, including samples of bright-orange crocoite, Tasmania's official mineral emblem and only found in this area. Upstairs there's a fascinating photographic history of the west coast.

---

❶ WARNING
If walking off marked tracks in the bush close to Zeehan or at Trial Harbour, beware of abandoned mine shafts hidden by vegetation.

To one side of the museum is an exhibit of steam locomotives and carriages from the early west-coast railways.

Gaiety Grand   HISTORIC BUILDING
(Main St; adult/child/family combined ticket with West Coast Heritage Centre $12/10/25; ⊘9am-5pm) The Gaiety was one of the biggest, most modern theatres in the world when it opened in February 1898. To mark the opening, a troupe of 60 was brought to town from Melbourne and played to 1000 spectators every night for a week. Even Dame Nellie Melba performed here. The theatre has recently been beautifully restored to its former glory – complete with gorgeous red velvet drapes – and hosts occasional ballet and orchestra touring performances.

What a bonus it must have been for the miners to be able to move between the pub and the theatre through connecting doors.

Spray Tunnel   HISTORIC SITE
This 100m-long railway tunnel was constructed as part of silver-mining operations in 1904. You can now walk through it to spy the remains of the Spray Silver Mine on the other side. Head down Fowler St from Main St and park at the golf club, from where you'll have to walk a short distance to access the tunnel.

★ Festivals & Events

Zeehan Gem & Mineral Fair   FAIR
(www.zeehangemandmineralfair.com; ⊘Nov) Each year the town comes alive with a festival featuring gems, jewellery, minerals, crystals and fossils for sale or simply for wondering at. It also has fossicking-related activities, including gem panning and crystal hunts.

🛏 Sleeping & Eating

Hotel Cecil   PUB $
(✐03-6471 6137; Main St; s $60, d with/without bathroom $80/70, cottages $110-150) Characterful Hotel Cecil has pub rooms upstairs that come with their own ghost, Maud – the owners will tell you her story. If you're wary of otherworldly happenings, you might prefer the innocuous self-contained miners' cottages outside. You can eat at Maud's Restaurant (mains $18-33, ⊘noon-9pm Mon-Sat). Its 400g Angus rib-eye steak is tops.

Heemskirk Motor Hotel   MOTEL $$
(✐03-6471 6107; www.heemskirkmotorhotel.com.au; Main St; d $100-150) At the eastern entrance to town, this motel won't win any architectural-design awards, but it does have large, clean motel rooms and the Abel Tasman Bistro (mains $15-34; ⊘noon-2.30pm & 6-8.30pm), which serves Aussie and international fare.

Coffee Stop   CAFE $
(110 Main St; mains $5-16; ⊘10am-3pm Mon-Sat) The light meals here include quiche, soups and sandwiches, and there are decent fish-and-chip takeaways. It also sells little ornaments made of west-coast minerals.

ℹ Information

Visitor information is available at the West Coast Heritage Centre (p237).
Online Access Centre (Zeehan Library, Main St; ⊘2-4.30pm Mon & Thu, 3-7pm Wed, 11am-1pm Fri, 10am-noon Sat) Internet access in Zeehan's library.

ℹ Getting There & Away

Tassielink (www.tassielink.com.au) Bus services stop at Coffee Stop, on the main street, en route to/from Launceston ($64.50, five hours) and Strahan ($20.80, two hours).

Strahan
POP 660

The *Chicago Tribune* newspaper once dubbed Strahan 'the best little town in the world' and we know what it meant. With its perfect location, nestled between the waters of Macquarie Harbour and the rainforest, it has faultless natural assets. Add to that the restored pioneer buildings – the cutesy shops, hotels and cottages crowding up the slope from the compact waterfront – and you've got a scene that could work as a Disney film set. These days it's more sugary sweet than wild west, but it works as a gateway town because of the unbelievable beauty that surrounds it.

⦿ Sights

West Coast Reflections   MUSEUM
(Esplanade; ⊘10am-6pm summer, noon-5pm winter) FREE This is the museum section of the Strahan visitor centre. It houses a creative and thought-provoking display on the history of the west coast, including a refreshingly blunt appraisal of the region's environmental disappointments and achievements, including the Franklin River Blockade (p248).

Strahan

Strahan

⊙ Sights
1 Water Tower Hill D1
2 West Coast Reflections C2

⊕ Activities, Courses & Tours
Bonnet Island Experience ....(see 3)
3 Gordon River Cruises C2
4 Strahan Seaplanes & Helicopters C2
5 West Coast Yacht Charters C2
6 World Heritage Cruises C2

⊜ Sleeping
7 Crays B2
8 Discovery Holiday Parks Strahan A2
9 Franklin Manor D2
10 Gordon Gateway D3
11 Ormiston House B2
12 Strahan Backpackers A2

13 Strahan Bungalows A1
14 Strahan Village C2
15 Wheelhouse Apartments B3

⊗ Eating
16 Banjo's C2
17 Hamer's Hotel C2
18 Regatta Point Tavern C4
19 Risby Cove D2

⊕ Entertainment
Hamer's Hotel ....(see 17)
The Ship that Never Was ....(see 2)

⊕ Shopping
Cove Gallery ....(see 19)
20 Wilderness Woodworks C3

Ocean Beach　　　　　　　　　BEACH
Six kilometres from town is Ocean Beach, awesome as much for its 33km length as for

the strength of the surf that pounds it. This stretch of sand and sea runs uninterrupted from Trial Harbour in the north to Macquarie

Heads in the south – and is *the* place to watch the orange orb of the sun melt into the sea. The water is treacherous: don't swim.

The dunes behind the beach become a **mutton bird rookery** from October, when the birds return from their 15,000km winter migration. They stay until April, providing an evening spectacle as they return to their nests at dusk.

Cape Sorell Lighthouse   LIGHTHOUSE

The 45m-high lighthouse, at the harbour's southern head, is purportedly the second-highest in Australia. You'll need a boat to cross the heads, unless you can find an accommodating fisher to take you over. A return walk of two to three hours along a vehicle track from the jetty at Macquarie Heads leads to the lighthouse.

Hogarth Falls   WATERFALL

This is a pleasant 50-minute return walk through the rainforest beside platypus-inhabited Botanical Creek. The track starts at People's Park, off the Esplanade opposite Risby Cove.

Water Tower Hill   VIEWPOINT

There's a lookout over the town here, accessed by following Esk St, beside the Strahan Village booking office. It's less than 1km from the Esplanade.

Tours

A Gordon River cruise is what most visitors come to do, and the dense rainforest that lines the riverbank, and the sense of peace in these trackless wilds, is something you'll never forget.

You can cruise the Gordon on a large, fancy catamaran in the company of a crowd of fellow river admirers (with plenty of comforts laid on), or be a bit more adventurous and visit with a small group by sailing boat. All cruises cross vast Macquarie Harbour before entering the mouth of the Gordon and proceeding to Heritage Landing for a rainforest walk. Most cruises visit Sarah Island, site of Van Diemen's Land's most infamously cruel penal colony, as well as Macquarie Heads and Hells Gates (the narrow harbour entrance). If you visit under sail, you can sneak a little further up the river than other cruise vessels are allowed to go, to beautiful Sir John Falls.

★ World Heritage Cruises   BOAT TOUR

(🖥 03-6471 7174; www.worldheritagecruises.com. au; Esplanade; adult $105-150, child $50-80, family $260-340; ⊙9am mid-Aug–mid-Jul) This business is run by the Grining family, who have been taking visitors to the Gordon since 1896 and are Strahan's true river experts. You can join the Grinings aboard their new low-wash, environmentally sensitive catamaran, the *Eagle,* for a cruise through Macquarie Harbour out through Hells Gates, to Sarah Island and up the Gordon River.

Prices vary depending on whether you take a window seat (premium, or gold if on the upper deck) or one in the centre of the boat (standard). All prices include a buffet meal. If you're travelling as a family, World Heritage Cruises is the best choice as the kids can go up and visit the captain at no extra cost. There may be an additional afternoon departure in the height of summer, or no service at all in the depths of winter.

HARBOURS, DUNES & WEST-COAST BACKBLOCKS

To experience the west coast in the raw, visit the tiny wave-lashed settlements of **Trial Harbour** and **Granville Harbour**. Directly west of Zeehan the gravel C248 leads to the former. This was Zeehan's port and is now a ragged collection of holiday shacks and the odd permanent home. There are coastal walks here, good fishing and great free camping in the vicinity – but no shops or facilities. The local **history room** (opening times vary) gives an insight into the early days, including tales of the ships that came in and colourful local identities.

Further north, tiny Granville Harbour (reached via the gravel Granville Harbour Rd off the paved C249) is one of the best spots in Tasmania for crayfish. The C249 (which becomes gravel as you head north) also leads to peaceful **Corinna**, which is the jumping-off point for the Pieman River Cruise and the Western Explorer road.

A more accessible beach alternative lies 14km along the road from Strahan to Zeehan: the spectacular **Henty Dunes**, a series of 30m-high sugar-fine sand dunes backing Ocean Beach (p239). From the picnic area take the 1½-hour return walk through the dunes and out to Ocean Beach; remember to carry drinking water.

Gordon River Cruises BOAT TOUR
(☑ 03-6471 4300; www.gordonrivercruises.com.au; Esplanade; adult $105-220, child $52-220, f $260-334) Run by the Royal Automobile Club of Tasmania (which seems to own half of Strahan), the *Lady Jane Franklin II* departs Strahan at 8.30am and returns at 2.15pm, en route exploring Macquarie Harbour, Sarah Island and the Gordon River as far as Heritage Landing.

Prices vary depending on where you are on the boat – the upper deck is an exclusive wine-and-dine experience.

★ **West Coast Yacht Charters** BOAT TOUR
(☑ 03-6471 7422; www.westcoastyachtcharters.com.au; Esplanade; ☺ Oct Apr) If you'd like your Gordon River experience with a little adventure (and fewer people), then sailing on *Stormbreaker* is the way to go. There's a 2½- to three-hour kayaking and fishing cruise that departs on demand most days at noon and/or 5pm (adult/child $90/50). There's also an overnight trip up the Gordon River (adult/child $380/190), with a visit to Sarah Island and meals included.

The only cruise licensed to get a full 35km up the Gordon as far as magical Sir John Falls is *Stormbreaker*'s River Rafter Collection Trip (adult/child $320/190), which departs Strahan at 1pm and returns at noon the next day. You'll hear tales of rafting the west's wild rivers as you cruise back to Strahan. On all trips you can do some fishing and take a short paddle in a sea kayak.

Strahan Seaplanes & Helicopters SCENIC FLIGHTS
(☑ 03-6471 7718; www.strahanseaplanesandhelicopters.com.au; Strahan Wharf; ☺ 8.30am-5pm Sep-May) You can't help but be excited when you hear the distinctive buzz of a seaplane: it speaks of adventure and remoteness. Strahan Seaplanes can take you on an 80-minute flight (adult/child aged three to 11 from $225/155) over Ocean Beach and Macquarie Harbour, landing on the Gordon River at Sir John Falls. There's also a 65-minute flight over Cradle Mountain and Lake St Clair (adult/child from $255/175).

Helicopter possibilities include Teepookana Huon pine forest with hair-raising low flying over the King River (one hour; adult/child from $225/155); Hells Gates and Macquarie Harbour (15 minutes; $130/95); and a flight over the West Coast Range ($225/155), including a landing on the spectacular summit of Mt Jukes (1168m).

★ **Bonnet Island Experience** BOAT TOUR
(☑ 03-6471 4300; Strahan Activity Centre, Esplanade; adult/child/family $95/40/220) This trip takes you to tiny Bonnet Island at the mouth of Macquarie Harbour where you can watch short-tailed shearwaters (mutton birds) and penguins come ashore and hear stories of the remote lighthouse here and its early keepers. Departure is at dusk, which varies through the year. Bookings can be made at the Strahan Activity Centre (p244). Children under five not allowed.

🛏 Sleeping

Discovery Holiday Parks Strahan CARAVAN PARK $
(☑ 1800 454 292, 03-6471 7468; www.discovery-holidayparks.com.au; cnr Andrew & Innes Sts; unpowered sites $22-35, powered sites $30-45, cabins $109-169; @) Right on Strahan's West Beach, this neat and friendly park has good facilities, including a camp kitchen, barbecues and a kids' playground.

Macquarie Heads CAMPGROUND $
(unpowered sites $7) Camping is possible at a basic site at Macquarie Heads, 15km southwest of Strahan – follow the signs to Ocean Beach and see the caretaker. There are pit toilets and water, but no showers or kitchen facilities.

Strahan Backpackers HOSTEL $
(☑ 03-6471 7255; www.strahanbackpackers.com.au; 43 Harvey St; unpowered sites per 2 people $20, dm $27-30, d from $65, cabins from $75; P@🖟) In an attractive bush setting 15 minutes' walk from the town centre, with plain bunks and doubles, and cute A-frame cabins. There's a kitchen block, a laundry and a games room.

★ **Gordon Gateway** APARTMENT $$
(☑ 03-6471 7165, 1300 134 425; www.gordongateway.com.au; Grining St; d $79-140) On the hillside on the way to Regatta Point, this place has motel-like studio units and larger A-frame chalets, most with sweeping water and township views.

West Coast Yacht Charters YACHT $$
(☑ 03-6471 7422; www.westcoastyachtcharters.com.au; Esplanade; dm adult/child $60/30, d $120) If you're hankering to sleep in a floating bunk on a wharf-moored yacht, this is a great option. Because the yacht is used for charters, it has late check-in and early check-out (be prepared to check in after 5pm and disembark before 9am). The yacht

THE WEST COAST WILDERNESS RAILWAY

Love the romance of the days of steam? The old wood-lined carriages with shiny brass trimmings, the breathy puffing of steam engines and the evocative, echoing train whistle? Then hop on board and make the breathtaking 35km rainforest rail journey aboard the **West Coast Wilderness Railway** (☑03-6471 0100; www.wcwr.com.au) between Strahan and Queenstown.

When it was first built in 1896, this train and its route through torturously remote country was a marvel of engineering. It clings to the steep-sided gorge of the (once-polluted, now-recovering) King River, passing through dense myrtle rainforest over 40 bridges and on gradients that few other rolling stock could handle. The railway was the lifeblood of the Mt Lyell Mining & Railway Co in Queenstown, connecting it for ore and people haulage to the port of Teepookana on the King River, and later with Strahan. The original railway closed in 1963.

Since it was reopened as a tourist railway, it's had a chequered run, and only reopened again in 2014 after a period of closure thanks to the prohibitive cost of keeping the line open through such difficult country.

Ride options on offer (expect reduced services in winter months):

Rack & Gorge Departs Queenstown at 9am, loops through the King River Gorge and returns at 1pm Wednesday to Sunday (adult/child/family $89/30/195).

River & Rainforest Departs Strahan at 2pm Wednesday to Friday, skirts the harbour, enters the rainforest and then returns to Strahan at 5.30pm after crossing many of the route's spectacular bridges (adult/child/family $89/30/195).

Queenstown Explorer Departs Strahan at 9am on Monday and Tuesday, running the railway's full length through gorge and rainforest to Queenstown (where there's a one-hour stop), before returning to Strahan at 5.30pm (adult/child/family $95/40/220).

isn't moored every night, so book ahead. Prices include continental breakfast.

Strahan Bungalows APARTMENT $$
(☑03-6471 7268; www.strahanbungalows.com.au; cnr Andrew & Harvey Sts; d $90-180) Decorated with a nautical theme, these award-winning bungalows are bright, light and friendly, and are equipped with everything you need for a self-contained stay. They're close to the beach and the golf course, and less than 15 minutes' walk from the centre of town.

Strahan Village HOTEL $$
(☑1800 628 286, 03-6471 4200; www.strahanvillage.com.au; d from $119) Much of the accommodation in the centre of town belongs to Strahan Village, and ranges from water-level heritage cottages to decent hotel rooms with views. Make sure you know exactly what you're reserving.

Crays COTTAGE $$
(☑0419 300 994, 03-6471 7422; www.thecraysaccommodation.com; 11 Innes St; d $130-220; P 🛜) The Crays has two self-contained units on Innes St and six new bright, roomy cottages at 59 Esplanade, opposite Risby Cove. Only some have views. Guests who stay three nights are rewarded with a succulent Tasmanian crayfish on the house, and there are reduced prices for cruises with West Coast Yacht Charters (p241).

★**Franklin Manor** BOUTIQUE HOTEL $$$
(☑03-6471 7311; www.franklinmanor.com.au; Esplanade; d $175-250; P 🛜) This beautiful historic home is the top spot to stay in Strahan. Set in well-tended gardens just back from the waterfront, it's now an elegant boutique guesthouse with refined rooms, fine dining and equally fine service. There's a legendary wine cellar and a Tasmanian produce room where you can taste and buy local delicacies.

★**Wheelhouse Apartments** RENTAL HOUSE $$$
(☑03-6471 7777; www.wheelhouseapartments.com.au; 4 Frazer St; d $220-320; P ❄) Talk about a room with a view! Perched up high above the harbour, these smart and luxurious houses are designed to feel like you're on the bridge of a ship at sea and have seamless walls of glass to give you jaw-droppingly good views over Macquarie Harbour.

The best spot in Strahan for water panoramas and peaceful seclusion, and also wheelchair accessible.

Ormiston House B&B $$$
(☑03-6471 7077; www.ormistonhouse.com.au;
Esplanade; d $200-270) This stunning 1899
mansion was built by Frederick Ormis-
ton, Strahan's founder, and offers stately
yet relaxed B&B accommodation in five
antique-filled rooms. Well-tended gardens
and a friendly welcome add to a fine, classy
package.

✖ Eating

Banjo's BAKERY $
(Esplanade; light meals from $5; ☺6am-6pm,
hours vary in winter) This central bakery, next
to Hamer's Hotel, serves reasonable break-
fasts and all-day light meals, sandwiches,
pies and pastries.

★ Risby Cove MODERN AUSTRALIAN $$
(☑03-6471 7572; www.risbycove.com.au; Espla-
nade; mains $22-38; ☺6-9pm) People come
from all over to dine at the Cove, a quietly sophisticated place just across the water
from the town centre. The menu features
fancy dishes such as roast Tamar Valley
duck, and there's always fresh Macquarie
Harbour ocean trout. There's a good kids
menu, too. The views over the water are
sensational.

Hamer's Hotel PUB FOOD $$
(☑03-6471 4335; Esplanade; mains lunch $12-23,
dinner $19-32; ☺noon-2.30pm & 6-10pm) This
done-up historic pub is where most tourists
go to eat in Strahan. It serves a varied menu
of excellent pub fare – try the Macquarie
Harbour ocean trout or the huge eye-fillet
steaks. It's often packed in summer, and it
doesn't take bookings, so get here early for
meals.

Regatta Point Tavern PUB FOOD $$
(Esplanade; mains $16-29; ☺bar noon-10pm,
meals noon-2pm & 6-8pm) If you want to eat
with the locals, away from the glitz, make
your way to this down-to-earth pub near
the railway terminus 2km around the bay
from Strahan's centre. There are the usual
steaks and burgers, as well as good fresh
fish. Check out the crayfish mornay – in
season – if you're after something fancy. It
serves good kids meals, too.

View 42° MODERN AUSTRALIAN $$$
(☑03-6471 4200; www.strahanvillage.com.au;
buffet adult/child $53/26.50; ☺6-9pm Sep-May)
This buffet restaurant concentrates on fresh
local seafood and fabulous views out over
the town and Macquarie Harbour.

☆ Entertainment

★The Ship that Never Was THEATRE
(☑03-6471 7700; www.roundearth.com.au/
ship; Esplanade; adult/concession/student/child
$20/15/10/2; ☺5.30pm Sep-May) Every night
for the past two decades, a small theatre
company has retold one of western Tasma-
nia's more picaresque tales in an artfully
converted space next to the Strahan visitor
centre. This unmissable 90-minute produc-
tion is hilarious, entertaining fun for all age
groups.

With a versatile cast of two, some cleverly
conceived props and much audience partic-
ipation, the play tells the story of convicts
who escaped from Sarah Island in 1834 by
hijacking a ship they were building. There's
sometimes an additional curtain call at
8.30pm in January.

Hamer's Hotel LIVE MUSIC
(Esplanade) This pub *occasionally* stag-
es live-music entertainment. Ask at the
Strahan Village reception.

🛍 Shopping

Wilderness Woodworks SOUVENIRS
(☑03-6471 7244; www.wildernesswoodworks.com.
au; Esplanade; ☺8.30am-5pm) Here you can
see Huon pine, sassafras and myrtle being
turned, and then buy the end results – main-
ly kitchen knick-knacks, platters and orna-
mental objects.

Cove Gallery CRAFTS
(☑03-6471 7572; Esplanade; ☺8am-6pm sum-
mer, to 5pm winter) Strahan exhibits more of
its creative side here at Risby Cove, with
fine woodworking, paintings and crafts to
browse and buy.

ℹ Information

Online Access Centre (Esplanade; ☺12.30-
4.30pm Tue, 10am-1pm Wed, 2-5pm Thu) Free
internet access in the library, housed in the
Customs House.

ℹ PARKING IN STRAHAN

Cruise passengers (and anyone else)
can park for free at the visitor centre
car park (on the concrete only), and
can also park alongside Wilderness
Woodworks ($3 all day). Spaces in front
of the main shopping area have 30- to
60-minute time limits; parking fines do
happen here.

CRADLE COUNTRY & THE WEST STRAHAN

Parks & Wildlife Service (☑03-6471 6020; ⊙9am-5pm Mon-Fri) Located in the Customs House building, adjacent to the library – though not open as many hours as it advertises.

Strahan Activity Centre (☑1800 084 620, 03-6471 4300; www.puretasmania.com.au; Esplanade; ⊙hours vary) Although it may have some useful general information, the Strahan Activity Centre is a private company that exists to steer you onto its own cruises (Gordon River Cruises). Usefully, it does act as the Strahan booking agent for the Bonnet Island Experience and the West Coast Wilderness Railway.

Strahan Visitor Centre (☑03-6472 6800; www.westernwilderness.com.au; Esplanade; ⊙10am-6.30pm Oct-Apr, noon-5pm May-Sep) Informative tourist information on Strahan and much of western Tasmania.

❶ Getting There & Around

Bicycles are rented out by the Strahan Activity Centre for $40 per day.

Strahan Taxis (☑0417 516 071) Strahan Taxis can run you to surrounding attractions such as Ocean Beach (around $20 each way, not including waiting time) and Henty Dunes ($25 each way, waiting time extra) and does hotel pickups and drop-offs for the morning river-cruise departures.

Tassielink (☑1300 300 520; www.tassielink.com.au) Services arrive at, and depart from, the visitor centre. Destinations include Launceston ($85.40, seven hours), Hobart ($78.20, 7½ hours) and Queenstown ($10.60, 45 minutes).

WORTH A TRIP

MT JUKES RD

To begin one of the region's more scenic drives, head south out of Queenstown along Conlan St to Mt Jukes Rd (22km one-way), which will take you to side roads leading to sections of the West Coast Wilderness Railway (p242). Further along this scenic road (9km south of town) is **Newall Creek**, where a platform provides access to a patch of superb King Billy and Huon pine rainforest. The bitumen section of the road ends at Lake Burbury (p246), a hydroelectric dam that can be seen to magnificent effect from a lookout on the descent to its shores.

Queenstown

POP 1975

Most of western Tasmania is green. Queenstown is orange or red. The winding descent into Queenstown from the Lyell Hwy is unforgettable for its moonscape of bare, dusty hills and eroded gullies, where once there was rainforest. The area is the clearest testimony anywhere to the scarification of the west coast's environment by mining. Copper was discovered here in the 1890s and mining has continued ever since, but today pollution is closely monitored and sulphur emissions controlled.

The town itself retains its authentic, rough-and-ready pioneer feel. When we last visited, the mine had closed, numerous businesses across the town centre were boarded up and apocalyptic rumours of permanent decline were on the rise. That said, they're a hardy lot out here, Queenstown's tourism star is on the rise and the optimists among the locals were convinced the mine would reopen. Whatever happens, this is a town like no other in Tasmania.

◉ Sights

★**Iron Blow**   VIEWPOINT
On top of Gormanston Hill on the Lyell Hwy, just before the final descent along hairpin bends into Queenstown, is a sealed side road leading to an utterly spectacular lookout over the geological wound of Iron Blow. This decommissioned open-cut mine, where Queenstown's illustrious mining career began, is awesomely deep and is now filled with emerald water. You can get an eagle's-eye view from the new 'springboard' walkway projecting out into thin air above the mine pit.

★**LARQ Gallery**   GALLERY
(☑0407 527 330; www.landscapeartresearchqueenstown.wordpress.com; 8 Hunter St; ⊙2-6pm Tue-Sat mid-Jan–mid-Jun) FREE Run by internationally renowned Tasmanian artist Raymond Arnold, Landscape Art Research Queenstown is a wonderful gallery that runs exhibitions by local and visiting artists, and community workshops in printmaking and painting. Its mission is to nurture a breed of art that's inspired by the powerful natural landscapes of the west coast. It's an excellent institution and definitely worth visiting. If it's not open, ask at the tourist office.

Queenstown

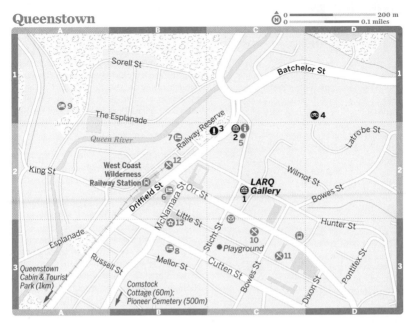

Eric Thomas Galley Museum   MUSEUM

(☏03-6471 1483; 1 Driffield St; adult/child/family $6/4/13; ⊙9.30am-5.30pm Mon-Fri, 12.30-5pm Sat & Sun Oct-Apr, reduced winter hours) This museum started life as the Imperial Hotel in 1898 and now houses an extensive photographic collection, with wonderfully idiosyncratic captions, showing the people and places of Tasmania's west coast, including an exposé of the 1912 Mt Lyell mining disaster, which claimed 42 lives. There's also a clutter of old memorabilia, household items, and clothing, right down to grandma's undies!

Miner's Siding   MONUMENT

Opposite the museum, on the site of the original train station, is the Miner's Siding, a public monument featuring a giant mining drill, a water race and sculptures that commemorate the area's mining heritage. The locomotive that was once parked here is now restored as part of the West Coast Wilderness Railway (p242).

Spion Kop Lookout   VIEWPOINT

Follow Hunter St uphill, turn left onto Bowes St, then do a sharp left onto Latrobe St to a small car park, from where a short, steep track leads to the summit of Spion Kop (named by soldiers after a battle in the Boer War). The rhododendron-lined track

Queenstown

◎ Top Sights

1 LARQ Gallery C2

◎ Sights

2 Eric Thomas Galley Museum C2
3 Miner's Siding.......................................C2
4 Spion Kop Lookout D1

◎ Activities, Courses & Tours

5 Queenstown Heritage Tours C2

◎ Sleeping

6 Empire Hotel...B2
7 Greengate on Central..........................B2
8 Mt Lyell Anchorage.............................B3
9 Penghana A1

◎ Eating

10 Café Serenade......................................C3
    Empire Hotel..................................(see 6)
11 Maloney's Restaurant C3
12 Tracks Cafe...B2

◎ Entertainment

13 Paragon Theatre B3

features a rail adit near the car park, and the top of the hill has a pithead on it. The panoramic views of town are excellent, particularly at sunset, when the bare hills are flaming orange.

WORTH A TRIP

LAKE BURBURY

Heading south out of Queenstown along Conlan St to Mt Jukes Rd for about 15 minutes, you'll come to the end of the bitumen road that leads to Lake Burbury. Built as a large hydroelectric source, the dam's construction here flooded 6km of the old Lyell Hwy. The lake is surrounded by the Princess River Conservation Area, and the scenery around it is magnificent – especially when there's snow on the nearby peaks.

There are impressive vistas from the attractive shoreline **campground** (unpowered sites for 2 people $7) just east of Bradshaw Bridge. Here there's also a public picnic area with sheltered electric barbecues and a children's playground. Fishers say the trout in Lake Burbury make for some of the best fishing in Tasmania.

Pioneer Cemetery   CEMETERY
(Conlan St) Queenstown's story is told in this intriguing old cemetery with more than 500 graves and some fascinating inscriptions on the crumbling headstones.

🧭 Tours

★**Queenstown Heritage Tours**   MINE TOUR
(Mt Lyell Mine Tours; ☑ 0407 049 612; www.queenstownheritagetours.com) The 'Lake Margaret Historic Hydropower' tour (adult/child $45/30) takes you into an early 20th-century hydroelectric power plant, and the 'Mt Lyell Underground Mine Tour' (adult $80) takes you inside the copper mine. But the real charmer is 'Lost Mines, Ancient Pines' (adult/child $80/40), which takes in some old copper and gold mines, a commercial sawmill and a stand of rainforest.

🛏 Sleeping

Empire Hotel   PUB $
(☑ 03-6471 1699; www.empirehotel.net.au; 2 Orr St; s with shared bathroom $45, d with shared/private bathroom $70/90) The rooms here aren't as magnificent as the imposing blackwood staircase, which is a National Trust–listed treasure, but they've a certain jaded pub charm and are generally kept clean.

Queenstown Cabin & Tourist Park   CARAVAN PARK $
(☑ 03-6471 1332; www.westcoastcabins.com.au; 17 Grafton St; unpowered/powered sites $7/30, on-site vans per 2 people $75, cabins per 2 people $90-115) You have to drive through run-down suburbs to get here, and though this basic, rather depressing, park is set on gravel, it does have a small grassy camping area. Seeing the best in a grim situation – that's the Queenstown spirit...

★**Penghana**   B&B $$
(☑ 03-6471 2560; www.penghana.com.au; 32 Esplanade; s $135-150, d $150-175, all incl breakfast; 🅿🛜) This National Trust–listed mansion was built in 1898 for the first general manager of the Mt Lyell Mining & Railway Co and, as befits its managerial stature, is located on a hill above town amid a beautiful garden with a rare number of trees. There's comfortably old-fashioned B&B accommodation here. The house includes a billiards room and a grand dining room for enjoying hearty breakfasts, and evening meals by arrangement.

★**Mt Lyell Anchorage**   B&B $$
(☑ 03-6471 1900; www.mtlyellanchorage.com; 17 Cutten St; d incl breakfast $160-170; 🅿🛜) Though you wouldn't guess from the outside, this 1890s weatherboard home has been completely transformed into a wonderful little guesthouse with quality beds, linen and luxuriously deep carpets. Two of the spacious rooms have smart bathrooms (the others have private facilities across the hall), and there's a shared kitchen and a comfortable lounge with wood fire.

There are also two self-contained apartments ($200 for up to four people, $240 for up to six). Breakfast provisions are included for all.

Comstock Cottage   B&B $$
(☑ 03-6471 1200; www.comstock.com.au; 45 McNamara St; s/d from $120/140; 🅿❄) Gorgeous heritage rooms with stately, classic decor dominate this two-bedroom cottage. Think four-poster beds, antique fireplaces and old photographs on the walls.

Greengate on Central   APARTMENT $$
(☑ 03-6471 1144; 7 Railway Reserve; apt 2/4 people $110/170; 🅿) With shady verandahs, these meticulously tidy, quiet apartments have polished boards and are fully self-contained.

They're just a hop and skip from the train station. Great value for money.

Eating

★ Empire Hotel   MODERN AUSTRALIAN **$$**
(☑03-6471 1699; www.empirehotel.net.au; 2 Orr St; mains lunch $12, dinner $17-30; ☺bar 11am-10pm, lunch noon-2pm, dinner 5.30-8pm) This old miners' pub has survived the ages and includes an atmospheric heritage dining room serving a changing menu of hearty pub standards, including roasts, pastas and fine steaks and ribs. Try the apple and pork rissoles or the Beef Tower, a grilled steak piled high with veggies.

Café Serenade   CAFE **$$**
(40 Orr St; mains $11-18; ☺8.30am-4pm; ☑) This is the best cafe in Queenstown. The food is deliciously homemade from scratch and includes yummy soups, toasted sourdough sandwiches, salads and good vegetarian options, as well as hearty roasts and curries. The curried scallop pies are the speciality. It also does gluten-free and dairy-free sweet treats, and the coffee is excellent.

Tracks Cafe   CAFE **$$**
(Queenstown Station, Driffield St; mains $13-21; ☺8am-3pm) Tracks serves smooth, creamy coffee and cafe staples such as gourmet pies and sandwiches, as well as cakes. You can also sit alfresco on the train platform itself.

Maloney's Restaurant   BISTRO **$$**
(☑03-6471 1866; 54-58 Orr St; mains $17-34; ☺6-9pm Mon-Sat) Who would expect such good food in an otherwise unremarkable small-town motel? It's quite sophisticated fare here, all cooked fresh to order. Try the seafood platter or Maloney's chicken stuffed with camembert and sundried tomatoes. It does a great sticky date pudding, too.

☆ Entertainment

Paragon Theatre   CINEMA
(www.theparagon.com.au; 1 McNamara St) This amazingly refurbished art-deco theatre shows some Hollywood and art-house films, as well as a revolving program of short films about the west coast and Queenstown. You can take your coffee or a glass of vino (and popcorn, of course) into the theatre, where seating is in deep leather couches.

It's worth a look inside even if you aren't going to watch a film.

❶ Information

Parks & Wildlife Service (☑03-6471 2511; westcoast@parks.tas.gov.au; Penghana Rd; ☺8.30-9.30am) Get advice here on nearby walking tracks and buy national park passes. Rafters take note: if you intend to use the Mt McCall Rd 4WD track from the southern end of Lake Burbury to access the Franklin River, ask the ranger for a free permit and a gate key. Ring and book the key prior to coming to Queenstown.

The office is located just out of the town centre, on Penghana Rd (which becomes the Lyell Hwy/A10 to Strahan).

Queenstown Visitor Centre (☑03-6471 1483; 1-7 Driffield St; ☺9.30am-5.30pm Mon-Fri, 12.30-5pm Sat & Sun Oct-Apr, reduced winter hours) In the Eric Thomas Galley Museum and run by volunteers, so opening hours can vary.

❶ Getting There & Away

Tassielink (www.tassielink.com.au) Buses arrive at, and depart from, the milk bar at 65 Orr St. The two main routes go to Hobart ($67.60, six hours) and Launceston ($74.80, 5½ hours); the latter goes via Strahan ($10.60, 45 minutes).

CRADLE COUNTRY & THE WEST QUEENSTOWN

WORTH A TRIP

LINDA VALLEY CAFE

In mining boom days, hundreds of people lived in the hills just west of Queenstown. Today there are just four residents in Linda Valley...and one unexpected gem. About 5km west of Queenstown is the much-lauded **Linda Valley Cafe** (☑03-6471 3082; 1 Lyell Hwy, Linda Valley, Gormanston; mains $32-38; ☺10am-8pm Oct-Apr, reduced hours May-Sep), which locals swear serves some of the best food on the west coast.

The cafe offers contemporary, delicious dining in unpretentious surrounds. Expect dishes such as slow-roasted pork belly and lemon pepper squid, as well as special liqueur coffees and beautiful homemade cakes. There's free camping for tents and RVs out the back.

Franklin-Gordon Wild Rivers National Park

The lifeblood of this awesome park are the wild, pristine rivers that twist their way through the infinitely rugged landscapes and give the national park its name. The park is part of the Tasmanian Wilderness World Heritage Area and encompasses the catchments of the Franklin, Olga and Gordon Rivers. It was proclaimed in 1981 after the failed campaign to stop the flooding of precious Lake Pedder under the Pedder-Gordon hydroelectric dam scheme.

The national park's most significant peak is Frenchmans Cap (1443m), with a white-quartzite top that can be seen from the west coast and from the Lyell Hwy. The mountain was formed by glacial action and has Tasmania's highest cliff face.

The park also contains a number of unique plant species and major Aboriginal sites. The most significant is Kutikina Cave, where over 50,000 artefacts have been found, dating from the cave's 5000-year-long occupation between 14,000 and 20,000 years ago. The only way to reach the cave, which is on Aboriginal land in remote forest, is by rafting down the Franklin River.

Activities

For adventures in this region, you'll need Tasmap's 1:100,000 *Olga* and *Franklin* and 1:25,000 *Loddon* maps, available from the Tasmanian Map Centre (p78) and Service Tasmania (p36) in Hobart.

Collingwood River is the usual put-in point for rafting the Franklin River, of which the Collingwood is a tributary. You can camp for free here; there are pit toilets and fireplaces.

Walking

Much of the park consists of deep river gorges and impenetrable rainforest, but the Lyell Hwy traverses its northern end. Along this road are a number of signposted features of note, including a few short walks that you can take to see just what this park is all about.

Donaghy's Hill, located 4km east of the bridge over the Collingwood River, is accessed on a 40-minute return walk. Rising above the junction of the Collingwood and Franklin Rivers, it has spectacular views of the Franklin and of Frenchmans Cap.

From the picnic ground where the highway crosses the Franklin River, a 25-minute return nature trail has been marked through the forest. Six kilometres further

THE FRANKLIN RIVER BLOCKADE

The Franklin-Gordon Wild Rivers National Park is probably best known as the site of Australia's biggest ever environmental battle, the Franklin River Blockade, which drew national and international attention and was ultimately successful in saving the wilderness from further dams.

The battle to save the lower Gordon and Franklin Rivers was played out in Tasmania in the early 1980s. Despite national park status and then World Heritage nomination, dam-building plans by the then Hydro Electric Commission (HEC) continued. In the aftermath of Lake Pedder's flooding, public opinion on the matter was clear – when a 1981 referendum asked Tasmanians to decide between two different dam schemes, 46% of voters scribbled 'No Dams' across their ballot papers. When the World Heritage Committee eventually announced the area's World Heritage listing and expressed concern over the proposed dam, the new state premier attempted to have the listing withdrawn.

Dam construction began in 1982 and protesters from all over Tasmania set off from Strahan to stage what became known as the 'Franklin River Blockade'. Press pictures from the time show flotillas of blow-up dinghies stretched across the river, blocking the HEC boats' access to the dam work site. Despite the peaceful protests, the Tasmanian government passed special laws allowing protesters to be arrested, fined and jailed. In the summer of 1982–83, 1400 people were arrested in a confrontation so intense it received international news coverage.

The Franklin River became a major issue in the 1983 federal election, which was won partly on a 'No Dams' promise by the incoming Australian Labor Party, which then fully implemented the Franklin and Gordon Rivers' World Heritage assignation, wholly protecting the rivers and forests.

east is the start of the three- to four-day return walk to **Frenchmans Cap**. There are two shelter huts along the way (though you should carry a tent) and the infamous Sodden Loddons mud is now a thing of the past, with a recent rerouting of the track around the Loddon Valley making this a far more accessible (and clean) walk. The Tassielink Hobart–Strahan service stops on request at the beginning of this walk. You can also do the walk as a guided six-day trip ($1695) with **Tasmanian Expeditions** (☑1300 666 856; www.tasmanianexpeditions.com.au).

There's an easy 20-minute return walk through rainforest to 35m-high **Nelson Falls** just east of Lake Burbury, at the bottom of Victoria Pass. Signs beside the track highlight common plants of the area.

Rafting

Rafting the Franklin River is about as wild and thrilling a journey as it's possible to make in Tasmania. This is really extreme adventure and a world-class rafting experience. Skilled rafters can tackle it independently if they're fully equipped and prepared, but for anyone who's less than completely river savvy (and that's about 90% of all Franklin rafters), there are tour companies offering complete rafting packages. If you go with an independent group you must contact the park rangers at the **Queenstown Parks & Wildlife Service** (☑03-6471 2511; Penghana Rd) for current information on permits, regulations and environmental considerations. You should also check out the Franklin rafting notes on the PWS website at www.parks.tas.gov.au. All expeditions should register at the booth at the point where the Lyell Hwy crosses the Collingwood River, 49km west of Derwent Bridge.

The trip down the Franklin, starting at Collingwood River and ending at Sir John Falls, takes between eight and 14 days, depending on river conditions. Shorter trips on certain sections of the river are also possible. From the exit point at Sir John Falls, you can be picked up by a Strahan Seaplanes & Helicopters (p241) seaplane, or by West Coast Yacht Charters' yacht *Stormbreaker* (p241) for the trip back to Strahan.

The upper Franklin, from Collingwood River to the Fincham Track, passes through the bewitchingly beautiful Irenabyss Gorge and you can scale Frenchmans Cap as a side trip. The lower Franklin, from the Fincham Track to Sir John Falls, passes through the wild Great Ravine.

Franklin River Rafting   RAFTING
(☑0422 642 190; www.franklinriverrafting.com; 70 Dillons Hill Rd, Glaziers Bay; 8/10-day trip $2695/2995) Excellent eight- and 10-day trips from Collingwood Bridge, with trips on the *Stormbreaker* back to Strahan. The longer trip includes the chance to climb Frenchmans Cap.

Tasmanian Expeditions   RAFTING
(☑1300 666 856; www.tasmanianexpeditions.com.au; ☻9-day trip $2695) Classic Franklin River trip, with a boat back to Strahan.

Water By Nature   RAFTING
(☑0408 242 941, 1800 111 142; www.franklinrivertasmania.com; 5/7/10-day trips $1980/2440/2980) This outfit provides five, seven and 10-day trips and you get to fly out of the Gordon River in a seaplane. Also offers climbs of Frenchmans Cap.

Cradle Mountain–Lake St Clair National Park

Cradle Mountain – that perfect new-moon curve of rock that photographers love to capture reflected in mirror-still waters – has become something of a symbol of Tasmania. It's perhaps the best-known feature of the island and is regarded as the crowning glory of the 1262-sq-km Cradle Mountain–Lake St Clair National Park. The park's glacier-sculpted mountain peaks, profound river gorges, lakes, tarns and wild alpine moorlands extend from the Great Western Tiers in the north to Derwent Bridge in the south. The park encompasses Mt Ossa (1617m), Tasmania's highest peak, and Lake St Clair, the deepest lake (200m) in Australia, brimming with the clear, fresh waters of this pristine environment.

The legendary adventure within the park is the celebrated Overland Track, a week-long hike that's become something of a holy grail for bushwalkers. The 65km track, stretching from Cradle Mountain to Lake St Clair (Leeawuleena or 'sleeping water' to Tasmania's Indigenous people), is an unforgettable journey through Tasmania's alpine heart.

Less well known is that Cradle Mountain is a fabulous wildlife-watching destination as well – sightings of wombats, Bennett's wallabies and pademelons are almost guaranteed, with Tassie devils and platypuses also possible.

Cradle Mountain–Lake St Clair National Park

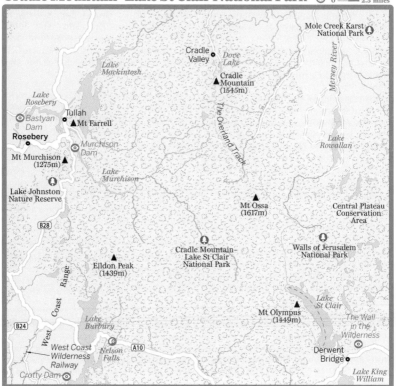

👁 Sights

Devils@Cradle
WILDLIFE RESERVE

(☑03-6492 1491; www.devilsatcradle.com; 3950 Cradle Mountain Rd; adult/child $18/10, family $45-60, night feeding tours adult/child $27.50/15, family $70-90; ⊙10am-4pm, tours 10.30am, 1pm & 3pm, night tours 5.30pm) This excellent wildlife park is filled with Tasmanian devils, a wombat or two, and elusive eastern and spotted-tail quolls. Here you can learn about the facial tumour disease that's threatening the devils' survival. You can visit on your own at any time, but try getting here at tour times to really get the most from your visit. The mainly nocturnal animals are observed most spectacularly at feeding time (5.30pm); there's an additional night feeding time at 8.30pm during daylight saving.

In addition to the tours, which take 45 minutes, there's a DVD presentation in a room with detailed information panels.

Wilderness Gallery
GALLERY

(☑03-6492 1404; www.wildernessgallery.com. au; Cradle Mountain Rd; admission $7, free for Cradle Mountain Hotel guests; ⊙10am-5pm) At the Cradle Mountain Hotel complex, on the road into Cradle Mountain, this impressive gallery showcases incredible environmental photography. It also has a fascinating **Tasmanian Tiger Exhibition**, complete with the only thylacine-skin rug in existence.

🏃 Activities

Walking the Overland Track
This is Tasmania's iconic alpine journey: a 65km, six- to eight-day odyssey with backpack through incredible World Heritage–listed mountainscapes from Ronny Creek, near Cradle Mountain, to Lake St Clair. The track ends on the northern shore of Lake St Clair – from here you can catch the ferry (p256), or walk the 15km Lakeside Track

back to civilisation. If you have experience of camping and multi-day hikes, good fitness and are well prepared for Tasmania's erratic weather, it's a very achievable independent adventure. Inexperienced walkers should consider going with a guided group.

Most hikers walk the Overland Track during summer when alpine plants are fragrantly in flower, daylight hours are long and you can work up enough heat to swim in one of the frigid alpine tarns. The track is very busy at this time and is subject to a crowd-limiting permit system. The track is quiet and icily beautiful for experienced walkers in winter. Spring and autumn have their own charms, and fewer walkers than in summer (though the permit system still applies).

Apart from the permit season, when a north–south walking regulation is enforced, the track can be walked in either direction. The trail is well marked for its entire length. Side trips lead to features such as **Mt Ossa**, and some fantastic **waterfalls** – so it's worth budgeting time for some of these. Apart from in the dead of winter, you can expect to meet many walkers each day.

There are unattended huts with bare wooden bunks and coal or gas heaters spaced a day's walking distance apart along the track, but don't count on any room inside in summer – carry a tent. Campfires are banned and you must carry a fuel stove for cooking.

The walk itself is extremely varied, negotiating high alpine moors, rocky scree, gorges and tall forest. A detailed description of the walk and major side trips is given in Lonely Planet's *Walking in Australia*. For further notes on the tracks in the park, read *Cradle Mountain–Lake St Clair and*

Walls of Jerusalem National Parks by John Chapman and John Siseman. A handy pocket-sized reference for the walk is the PWS's *The Overland Track: One Walk, Many Journeys*, which has notes on ecology and history plus illustrations of flora and fauna you may see along the way. You can get all the latest on the track and walk planning at www.parks.tas.gov.au. The reference map for the track and surrounds is the 1:100,000 *Cradle Mountain–Lake St Clair* map published by Tasmap.

Walking Cradle Valley

Cradle Valley has some of the most accessible trailheads in the park. The following is by no means an exhaustive list:

Knyvet Falls (25 minutes return) Begins opposite Cradle Mountain Lodge.

Crater Lake (two hours return) Climb up to this lake-filled crater from the Ronny Creek car park.

Cradle Valley Walk (two hours one-way) An easy 8.5km walk from the interpretation centre to Dove Lake. It's boardwalked as far as Ronny Creek (5.5km); the rest of the track to Dove Lake can get quite muddy and is sometimes closed after heavy rain.

Dove Lake Circuit (two- to three-hour loop) Go all the way around the lake from Dove Lake car park, with near-constant Cradle Mountain views.

Cradle Mountain Summit (six to eight hours return) A tough but spectacular climb with incredible views in fine weather; not recommended in bad visibility or when it's snowy and icy in winter. Can begin at either Dove Lake car park or Ronny Creek.

ℹ LICENCE TO WALK

The Overland Track is struggling under the weight of its own popularity. Recent years have seen 9000 walkers tread its paths annually and only careful management will prevent this route from being loved to death. To help keep walker numbers manageable and the walking experience one of wilderness, not crowd dodging, the following rules apply.

➡ There's a booking system in place from 1 October to 31 May, when a maximum of 34 independent walkers can depart each day.

➡ There are fees of $200/160 per adult/child aged five to 17 and concession, to cover the costs of sustainable track management (these apply from October to May only).

➡ The compulsory walking direction from October to May is north to south.

There's a booking system for walking permits on the Overland Track website at www.parks.tas.gov.au, or call ☎03-6165 4254 for more information. Bookings open on 1 July.

Walking Cynthia Bay

If you're at the southern, Lake St Clair end of the national park, these are our pick of the day-hikes on offer:

Larmairremener tabelti (one hour return) Aboriginal cultural-interpretative walk that winds through the traditional lands of the Larmairremener, the Indigenous people of the region. It starts at the visitor centre and loops through the lakeside forest before heading along the shoreline back to the centre.

Platypus Bay Circuit (30 minutes return) From Watersmeet, near the visitor centre.

Shadow Lake Circuit (four to five hours return) Mixture of bush tracks and boardwalks through rainforest, stringybark trees and sub-alpine forests.

Mt Rufus Circuit (seven to eight hours return) Climbs Mt Rufus through alpine meadows and past lakes and sandstone outcrops with fine views over the Franklin River.

Lake St Clair Lakeside Walk Catch the ferry to Echo Point (three to four hours back to Cynthia Bay) or Narcissus Hut (five to seven hours back to Cynthia Bay) and walk back along the lakeshore.

FAMILY WALKS

Although it depends on the age of your kids, many of the walks in Cradle Valley are suitable for children of reasonable fitness. If your kids are *really* young, the following might appeal.

Rainforest Walk & Pencil Pine Falls (10 minutes return) Begins at the interpretation centre. It's boardwalked and easy, but quite spectacular.

Enchanted Nature Walk (25 minutes return) Begins near Cradle Mountain Lodge and runs alongside Pencil Pine Creek; accessible for prams and wheelchairs for most of the way.

Weindorfers Forest Walk (20 minutes return) Begins next to Waldheim Cabins and climbs up through the forest; not pram or wheelchair accessible.

Ronny Creek (20 to 25 minutes return) The boardwalks that mark the start of the Overland Track are ideal for families, with wombats in abundance.

Other Activities

Cradle Country Adventures   HORSE RIDING
(📞1300 656 069; www.cradleadventures.com.au) Horseback is a great way to get around the Cradle Mountain area, with eight half- or full-day rides to choose from, as well as longer trails (two to four days). It also organises quad-bike tours just outside World Heritage areas.

Cradle Mountain Canyons   CANYONING
(📞1300 032 384; www.cradlemountaincanyons.com.au; adult $105-210, child or concession $85-190; ⊙departures 8.30am, 9.30am & 1.30pm Nov-Apr) Scramble, abseil and climb down a procession of pools and waterfalls while wearing a snug-fitting wetsuit. Choose between the Lost World Canyon (for beginners) or Dove Canyon or Machinery Creek (both for more advanced canyoning) and see the region's extreme beauty up close and personal. Cradle Mountain Canyons' office is located adjacent to the Cradle Mountain Visitor Information Centre.

🖙 Tours

Tasmanian Expeditions   WALKING
(📞1300 666 856; www.tasmanianexpeditions.com.au; ⊙Oct-early May) Tasmanian Expeditions does a six-day Overland Track trek (from $1995), plus a range of other hikes through the national park and beyond.

Cradle Mountain Huts   WALKING
(📞03-6391 9339; www.cradlehuts.com.au; Oct-late Dec, Apr & May $3050, late Dec-Mar $3300; ⊙tours Oct-Apr) If camping isn't for you, then you can take a six-day guided walk in a small group (four to 10 people) along the Overland Track, which includes accommodation in private huts.

Tour fee includes meals, national park entry fee and transfer to/from Launceston. Gear hire is also available.

McDermott's Coaches   BUS TOUR
(📞03-6394 3535; www.mcdermotts.com.au) A Park Explorer Tour (adult/child $35/20) will get you conveniently to the park's bus-accessible highlights for a spot of walking. McDermott's also does an evening wildlife-spotting tour ($55/40) that combines seeing the devil feeding at Devils@Cradle and night-time wildlife spotting in a 4WD. Trips leave from the Cradle Mountain Transit Centre. National park entry is additional.

A day tour from Launceston is also available; see the website.

WATCHING WILDLIFE AT CRADLE MOUNTAIN

Cradle Mountain is one of the easiest places in Australia to see wildlife in abundance. In addition to the following, it's possible to see Tasmanian devils, echidnas, spotted-tailed quolls and eastern quolls.

Common wombat Seen regularly throughout the park, but best found along the Ronny Creek valley before dusk.

Tasmanian pademelon This small, plump, wallaby-like creature is commonly seen throughout the park, especially around accommodation such as Cradle Mountain Hotel.

Bennett's wallaby Not as common as the pademelon, but still seen regularly, including around Ronny Creek.

Platypus Present in most of the park's rivers, but try Ronny Creek close to dawn or dusk.

Grayline　　　　　　　　　　BUS TOUR
(☑03-6234 3336, 1300 858 687; www.grayline. com) Offers a day coach tour from Launceston to Cradle Mountain (adult/child from $148/74), including a hike around Dove Lake, on Monday, Wednesday, Friday and Sunday, leaving at 8.30am and returning at 5pm.

Cradle Mountain Helicopters　SCENIC FLIGHTS
(☑03-6492 1132; www.cradlemountainhelicopters. com.au; Cradle Mountain Rd; 20-minute flights adult/child from $245/150; ⊙late Sep-Jun) You can get a spectacular bird's-eye view over Tasmania's alpine heart by taking a helicopter joy ride. The choppers leave from the airstrip next to the visitor centre, and you can get all your postcard-perfect shots of sights such as Cradle Mountain, Dove Lake and little-seen Fury Gorge.

☆✿ Festivals & Events

Tastings at the Top　　　　　　FOOD
Cradle Mountain Lodge is the venue for this renowned winter foodie event, a three-day festival of gastronomic delights held in May or June.

⨇ Sleeping & Eating

⨇ Cradle Valley

Some of the accommodation here is self-catering, but there's no supermarket, so bring your own supplies.

Discovery Holiday Parks Cradle Mountain　　　　　CARAVAN PARK $
(☑03-6492 1395; www.discoveryholidayparks.com. au; Cradle Mountain Rd; unpowered/powered sites per 2 people $36/46, dm $32, cabins from $144, cottages from $159; P@🛜) This bushland complex is 2.5km from the national park.

It has well-separated sites, a YHA-affiliated hostel, a camp kitchen and a laundry, and self-contained cabins.

Waldheim Chalet & Cabins　　　CABIN $
(☑03-6491 2271; d $70, extra adult/child $25/10) Set in forest near the original Weindorfers' chalet are some rustic wood-lined cabins with bunks sleeping eight, six and four. Each has kitchen facilities and there's a shared shower and toilet block. Despite its simplicity, this is a lovely place to stay in a gorgeous setting.

★Cradle Mountain Highlanders Cottages　　　COTTAGE $$
(☑03-6492 1116; www.cradlehighlander.com. au; Cradle Mountain Rd; d $125-285; P) This is the best-kept secret at Cradle Mountain! The genuinely hospitable hosts have a charming collection of immaculately kept self-contained timber cottages. All have wood or gas fires, queen-sized beds, electric blankets and continental-breakfast provisions. Three cabins include a spa, and all are serviced daily.

The surrounding bush is peaceful and filled with wildlife that will most likely pay you a visit.

Cradle Mountain Hotel　　　　HOTEL $$
(☑03-6492 1404, 1800 420 155; www.cradlemountainhotel.com.au; Cradle Mountain Rd; d from $169; P@🛜) This large complex is the first you come to on the way into Cradle Valley, and heralds its presence with a grand porticoed gate. Though the public areas are pleasantly timbered and log-fire-warmed, the rooms are, frankly, rather motel-ish. Get one on the front side to ensure a rainforest view.

There's a decent buffet restaurant (adult/child $38/19), or the more refined Grey Gum à la carte restaurant (mains from $28).

THE WEINDORFERS' LEGACY

If not for the forward-looking vision of one Gustav Weindorfer, Cradle Mountain might never have been incorporated into a national park. Weindorfer, an Austrian immigrant, first came to Cradle in 1910 and built a wooden cabin, Waldheim (German for 'Forest Home'), in 1912. Weindorfer and his Australian wife, Kate, took their honeymoon at Waldheim and fell in love with the area. Recognising its uniqueness, they lobbied successive governments for its preservation.

Kate Weindorfer had a passion for botany and became an expert in the area's bushland and flora, encouraging Gustav's appreciation of the landscape. Their spirit was tenacious – in those days a horse and cart could only get within 15km of Cradle Mountain, and from there they walked to Waldheim while packhorses carried supplies. The Weindorfers encouraged visitors to come to this remote place and share in its marvels.

Kate died in 1916 from a long illness, and Gustav moved to Waldheim permanently, devoting his life to preserving the mountain area he loved. He died in 1932, and almost 40 years later Cradle Mountain was finally declared a national park.

The original chalet burnt down in a bushfire in 1974, but was rebuilt using traditional carpentry techniques and stands as a monument to the Weindorfers. Just inside the doorway is Gustav's original inscription: 'This is Waldheim/Where there is no time/And nothing matters'.

★ **Cradle Mountain Lodge** LODGE $$$
(☑ 1300 806 192, 03-6492 2103; www.cradlemountainlodge.com.au; Cradle Mountain Rd; d $189-870; P ✷ @ ☎) When this mountain resort of wooden cabins emerges from the swirling mist on a winter's day, you can't help but be charmed by its ambience. Most rooms wear a contemporary feel and some have open fires, the lodge puts on dozens of activities and guided walks, and the Waldheim Alpine Spa offers relaxing massages and beauty treatments.

**Cradle Mountain
Wilderness Village** CHALET, CABIN $$$
(☑ 03-6492 1500; www.cradlevillage.com.au; Cradle Mountain Rd; d $169-299; P @ ☎) When you walk into the reception here on a clear day, you'll be treated to some exceptional views of Cradle Mountain. There are some quite luxurious chalets and cabins set peacefully in the trees, and they're painted in perfect eucalypt greys and greens.

Cradle Wilderness Cafe CAFE $
(☑ 03-6492 1024; Cradle Mountain Rd; mains $8-11; ☺ 8am-9pm Dec-Mar, 9am-5pm Apr-Nov) This cafe, next to the visitor centre, does coffee, light meals and snacks. Drop by to pick up last-minute sandwiches for your walk. There's pasta and pizza in the evening in summer.

Tavern Bar & Bistro BISTRO $$
(☑ 03-6492 2100; www.cradlemountainlodge.com.au; mains $16-29; ☺ noon-8.30pm) Hearty mountain fare and a roaring open fire give this unpretentious place at Cradle Mountain Lodge its charm. It's all about pasta, burgers, steaks and salmon, and it has a good kids menu. There's also live music some Wednesdays at 8.30pm.

★ **Highland
Restaurant** MODERN AUSTRALIAN $$$
(☑ 03-6492 2100; 2/3/5-course meal $62/72/95; ☺ 6-9pm) Arguably Cradle Mountain's premier eating experience, this fine-dining restaurant at Cradle Mountain Lodge does dishes such as Tasmanian rack of lamb or quail roulade in a refined setting.

Road to Cradle Mountain

Lemonthyme Lodge HOTEL $$
(☑ 03-6492 1112; www.lemonthyme.com.au; Dolcoath Rd, Moina; lodge d from $135, cabins $295-395; @) Off Cradle Mountain Rd at Moina is this secluded mountain retreat offering cabins, some with spa, and rooms in the main lodge with shared facilities – though the word is that these rooms can be noisy. Hang out by the roaring fire before dinner in the restaurant. There's animal feeding nightly at 8.30pm and good walks on the property.

Driving to Cradle Mountain from Devonport, turn onto the gravel Dolcoath Rd, 3km south of Moina, and follow it for a scenic 8km to get here.

Cradle Chalet
BOUTIQUE HOTEL **$$**

(☑03-6492 1401; www.cradlechalet.net.au; 1422 Cradle Mountain Rd, Moina; d $175-240) Attractive timber chalets in a bushland setting. You can soak up the peace from your own private deck, or chat with the friendly hosts, who are a mine of regional advice. The rooms include continental breakfast, and evening meals are by arrangement. No kids under 15.

🛏 Cynthia Bay

Lake St Clair Lodge
LODGE **$$**

(☑03-6289 1137; www.lakestclairlodge.com.au; unpowered/powered sites per 2 people $25/30, dm/d $40/110, cottages $185-550; P @) Unpowered bush-camping sites on the lakeshore, and powered caravan spots. The backpackers lodge has two- to four-bunk rooms and kitchen facilities. There are also upmarket self-contained cottages. In the main building opposite the Lake St Clair visitor centre there's a cafe, serving a hearty menu to fill you up before or after a bushwalk. Last orders at 6.30pm.

You can camp for free at Fergy's Paddock, 10 minutes' walk back along the Overland Track. You'll need your parks pass. There are pit toilets, and fires aren't allowed, so take a fuel stove for cooking.

🛏 Derwent Bridge & Bronte Park

Derwent Bridge is 5km from Lake St Clair and has a few good accommodation options.

Bronte Park Holiday Village
HOTEL **$$**

(☑03-6289 1126; www.bronteparkvillage.com.au; 378 Marlborough Hwy, Bronte Park; unpowered/powered sites $15/25, d $120-130, cottage d $140) Just off the Lyell Hwy, 30km east of Derwent Bridge, this place has a variety of accommodation, plus a bar and restaurant. The hotel can also arrange a spot of fishing with local guides, or evening wildlife-spotting tours.

Derwent Bridge Wilderness Hotel
HOTEL, PUB **$$**

(☑03-6289 1144; www.derwentbridgewildernesshotel.com.au; Lyell Hwy; dm $35, d with/without bathroom from $145/125; P ❄ @) This chalet-style pub has a high-beamed roof and a pleasingly country feel: enjoy a beer or a hot drink in front of the massive log fire. The hostel and hotel accommodation is plain but comfortable, and the restaurant serves commendable pub fare, including excellent roasts, pastas, steaks and soups with hot crusty bread.

Derwent Bridge Chalets & Studios
COTTAGE **$$**

(☑03-6289 1000; www.derwent-bridge.com; Lyell Hwy; d $145-245; P @) Just 5km from Lake St Clair (500m east of the turn-off), this place has one-, two- and three-bedroom self-contained cabins and studios, some with spa, but all with full kitchen and laundry facilities, and bush at the back porch. They're unremarkable, but clean and comfy.

Hungry Wombat Café
CAFE **$**

(Lyell Hwy; mains $6-16; ⊘8am-6pm summer, 9am-5pm winter) Part of the service station, this friendly cafe serves breakfasts that'll keep you going all day. For lunch there are soups, sandwiches, fish and chips, pies, wraps and burgers, and there's a range of all-day snacks, coffees and cakes. Everything's homemade and jolly good. There's a small grocery section, too, and it gives tourist info.

❶ Information

Cradle Mountain Visitor Information Centre (☑03-6492 1110; www.parks.tas.gov.au; 4057 Cradle Mountain Rd; ⊘8am-5pm, reduced winter hours) The Cradle Mountain visitor centre is just outside the park boundary. Here you can buy your park passes, get detailed bushwalking information and maps, weather condition

---

DON'T MISS

WALL IN THE WILDERNESS

On your journey between Derwent Bridge and Bronte Park, don't miss the **Wall in the Wilderness** (☑03-6289 1134; www.thewalltasmania.com; adult/child $10/6; ⊘9am-5pm Sep-Apr, to 4pm May-Aug). This amazing creation is a work of art in progress. Wood sculptor Greg Duncan is carving a panorama in wood panels depicting the history of the Tasmanian highlands. The scale is incredible – when it's finished, which will take an estimated 10 years, the scene will be 100m long.

Though the tableau is large-scale, it's carved with breathtaking skill and detail – from the veins in the workers' hands, to the creases in their shirts, to the hair of their beards. The Wall is 2km east of Derwent Bridge, and is definitely worth making time to check out.

ℹ PARK ACCESS & WEATHER CONDITIONS

Traffic at the Cradle Valley entrance to the park is strictly controlled and once the vehicle quota (or parking capacity) is reached, the boom gates won't open to let vehicles in until enough vehicles have left; this can be a particular problem in the morning.

To keep traffic out of the park itself, most access is now by shuttle bus. Buses run every 10 to 20 minutes between about 8am and 8pm in summer (reduced hours in winter) from the Cradle Mountain Transit Centre (by the visitor centre) where you park your car. The fare is included in a valid parks pass. Buses stop at the ranger station interpretation centre, Snake Hill, Ronny Creek and Dove Lake. Because of the way the shuttle bus operates, we recommend that you visit the interpretation centre on your way out of the park, rather than on the way in. There is limited parking for cars (no campervans) at Dove Lake on a first-come, first-served basis. You'll need a valid parks pass.

Whatever time of the year you visit, be prepared for cold, wet weather in Cradle Valley and on the Overland Track; it rains on seven out of 10 days, is cloudy on eight out of 10 days, the sun shines all day only one day in 10, and it snows in Cradle Valley on average 54 days each year. You could find yourself camping in the snow at any time of year, but you also need to be aware of sunburn, not just in summer. Winds can be extreme.

updates and advice on bushwalking gear, bush safety and bush etiquette. The centre has toilets, a small shop-cafe and Eftpos (cash out may be available). It also accepts credit-card payment. There are no ATMs.

There's no drinking water to fill up with here, only bottled water to buy in the shop.

Lake St Clair Visitor Information Centre
(☑ 03-6289 1172; www.parks.tas.gov.au; Cynthia Bay; ⊘ 8am-5pm) Cynthia Bay, on the southern boundary of the park, has the Lake St Clair visitor centre. It provides park and walking information and has displays on the area's geology, flora, fauna and Aboriginal heritage. If you've forgotten your rain gear you can pick up some waterproof attire in the shop here.

Ranger Station Interpretation Centre
(⊘ 8.30am-5pm during daylight saving, to 4pm in winter) Just inside the park boundary at Cradle Valley is the ranger station interpretation centre. At the time of writing, it was building an auditorium for video presentations on the natural history of Cradle Mountain and the tracks in the area. There are also Aboriginal cultural displays.

ℹ Getting There & Away

BUS

Tassielink (☑ 1300 300 520; www.tassielink. com.au) Services to Cradle Mountain Transit Centre from Launceston via Devonport – pick-up at the ferry terminal can be arranged. Destinations from Cradle include Launceston ($61.50, 3¼ hours), Devonport ($42.40, two hours) and Strahan ($42.40, three to four hours). It also has a Hobart–Lake St Clair service ($53.60, 2½ hours).

To get from Launceston to Lake St Clair ($106.50), take the Tassielink service to Queens-town, overnight there, then take the Strahan–Hobart bus to Lake St Clair the following day.

For Overland Track walkers, there's a Launceston–Cradle Mountain and Lake St Clair–Hobart package costing $102. Tassielink also does baggage storage and transfers while you're on the track ($10 per bag). A bushwalkers' package from Launceston to Cradle Mountain and Lake St Clair to Launceston costs $135.

CAR & MOTORCYCLE

If driving, fill up with petrol before heading out to Cradle Mountain – prices are higher there than in the towns. The road north from Bronte Park to Great Lake (35km) is mostly gravel. Though it's usually in a good condition, it's worth checking with a local before you depart.

ℹ Getting Around

Unless you absolutely need your car, avoid overcrowding on the narrow road to Dove Lake and take the shuttle bus from next to the visitor centre.

Lake St Clair Ferry (☑ 03-6289 1137; www. lakestclairlodge.com.au; one-way adult/child $40/20) Lake St Clair Lodge operates bushwalkers' ferry trips to and from Narcissus Hut at Lake St Clair's northern end. The boat departs Cynthia Bay three times daily (9am, noon and 3pm) year-round (or on demand, minimum six people), reaching Narcissus Hut about 30 minutes later. Winter departures may be reduced, so always ring ahead.

If you're using the ferry service at the end of your Overland Track hike, for which bookings are essential, you must radio the ferry operator when you arrive at Narcissus to reconfirm your booking. You can also ride the ferry from Cynthia Bay to Echo Point (adult/child $35/17), and then walk back to Cynthia Bay (two to three hours).

THE SOUTHWEST

Tasmania's southwest corner is about as wild as it's possible to get in this plenty-wild state. It's an edge-of-the-world domain made up of primordial forests, rugged mountains and endless heathland, all fringed by untamed beaches and turbulent seas. This is among the last great wildernesses on Earth: a place for absorption in nature, adventure and isolation.

Much of the southwest is incorporated into the Southwest National Park, some 6000 sq km of largely untouched country. Just one road enters the southwest, and this only goes as far as the hydroelectric station on the Gordon Dam. Otherwise, all access is by light plane to the gravel airstrip at Melaleuca, by sailing boat around the tempestuous coastline, or on foot.

This remote country was home to Tasmanian Aboriginals for about 35,000 years, and apart from periodic burning here by the first inhabitants, which helped form the buttongrass plains, the southwest bore little human imprint before hydroelectric dams drowned a great swathe of it in 1972.

For the well-prepared visitor, this part of Tasmania is an enticing adventure playground. There are challenging, multi-day walks (as well as shorter wanders), remote sea kayaking on the waterways of Bathurst Harbour and Port Davey, and ancient forests to explore. Those who prefer aerial pleasures can take a mind-blowing abseil down the curvaceous wall of the Gordon Dam, or swoop over the valleys and mountains on a scenic southwest joy flight.

Maydena

POP 224

Maydena is a quiet little town in the Tyenna Valley, surrounded by hills and eucalypt forests, just 12km west of Southwest National Park on the way to Strathgordon.

⊙ Sights & Activities

Take Junee Rd north out of town for about 10 minutes and you'll come to the start of the 10-minute walk to the mouth of Junee Cave. Here, a waterfall cascades out of the cave mouth that is part of a 30km-long series of caverns known as the Junee River karst system. The system includes Niggly Cave, reputedly the deepest cave in Australia, at 375m. Cave divers make hair-raising journeys through the flooded underground passageways, but other visitors can't enter.

Maydena Adventure Hub   ADVENTURE SPORTS
(☑1300 720 507; www.adventureforests.com.au; ⊙9am-5pm Oct-Mar, pre-booked tours only Apr-Sep) Maydena Adventure Hub can take you on a top-of-the-world adventure (adult/child $62/50) to the amazing Eagle's Eyrie, set in alpine vegetation at 1100m with fantastic 360-degree panoramas over the southwest mountain ranges. Travel is in a 4WD bus and advance booking is essential. The Adventure Hub also rents out mountain bikes and rail-track riders – pedal-powered rail carts.

There's also a cafe serving lunches and snacks (mains $8 to $20).

CRADLE COUNTRY & THE WEST MAYDENA

TOURS IN THE SOUTHWEST

There are a few tours available for those who'd like to tackle the southwest in a small group, with an experienced guide organising much of the gear and the logistics.

Tasmanian Expeditions (☑1300 666 856, 03-6331 9000; www.tasmanianexpeditions.com.au) Tasmanian Expeditions offers numerous walking-tour options in the southwest, including the five-day Mt Anne Circuit (per person $1595), the seven-day Port Davey Track ($2495) and the 16-day Port Davey and South Coast Track ($4495).

Roaring 40s Kayaking (☑0455 949 777; www.roaring40skayaking.com.au; 3/7-day trip $2150/2990) To experience this wilderness from the water, consider a sea-kayaking adventure. From November to April, Roaring 40s Kayaking offers camp-based kayaking trips exploring Port Davey and Bathurst Harbour with access by light plane to and from Hobart.

Par Avion (☑03-6248 5390; www.paravion.com.au; adult/child half-day $320/240, full day $420/360, 2-night trip per person $1950) You can swoop over the southwest from the air on a scenic small-plane flight with this Hobart-based operator. On a clear day you can see the whole of this corner of Tasmania as you buzz over wild beaches and jagged peaks before landing at Melaleuca. Half-, full- and three-day/two-night expeditions are possible.

🛏️ Sleeping & Eating

⭐ **Giants' Table & Cottages**   COTTAGE $$
(☑️ 03-6288 2293; www.giantstable.com.au; Junee Rd; cottage $125-180) Named for the giant trees in the Styx, these were once simple workers' cottages. Now done up, they're spacious, wood-heated and come in various configurations: one sleeps up to 10. There's also a **restaurant** (bookings essential) serving hearty fare to fill you after a day's adventuring. Platypuses are a frequent sight in the property's ponds, and echidnas sometimes wander through.

Maydena Country Cabins   CABIN $$
(☑️ 03-6288 2212; www.maydenacabins.com.au; 46 Junee Rd; d $165) There are cosy timber-lined one- and two-bedroom cabins here with glorious mountain views and – something you don't expect in Tasmania – a small herd of friendly alpacas just dying to pose for a photo with you. There's also an in-house B&B option, and the friendly owners are a mine of information on the area.

Lake Pedder Impoundment

At the northern edge of the southwest wilderness lies the Lake Pedder Impoundment, a vast flooded valley system covering the area that once cradled the original Lake Pedder, a spectacularly beautiful natural lake that was the region's ecological jewel. The largest glacial outwash lake in the world, its shallow, whisky-coloured waters covered 3 sq km and its wide, sandy beach made an ideal light-plane airstrip. The lake was home to several endangered species and considered so important that it was the first part of the southwest to be protected within its own national park. But even this status ultimately failed to preserve it and Lake Pedder disappeared beneath the waters in 1972.

These days, trout fishing is popular here. The lake is stocked, and fish caught range from 1kg to the occasional 20kg monster. Small boats or dinghies are discouraged because the lake is 55km long and prone to dangerously large waves. Boat ramps exist at Scotts Peak Dam in the south and near Strathgordon in the north.

There are two campgrounds near the lake's southern end. The **Edgar Camping**

Ground FREE has pit toilets, water, fine views of the area and usually a fisher or two – in wet weather it's less attractive as it's exposed to cold winds. There's also **Huon Campground** (campsite d $10, extra adult/child $5/2.50), hidden in tall forest near Scotts Peak Dam.

Strathgordon

Built to house Hydro Electric Commission (HEC) employees during the construction of the Gordon Dam, Strathgordon is still the base for those who operate the power station today. About 2km past the ex-Hydro settlement is **Lake Pedder Lookout**, with good views over the lake. A further 10km west is the **Gordon Dam** itself. From the car park, walk down a flight of steps that takes you along the perfect curve of the dam wall.

🏃 Activities

Aardvark Adventures   ADVENTURE SPORTS
(☑️ 0458 127 711, 03-6273 7722; www.aardvarkadventures.com.au; per person $215) At Gordon Dam you can abseil over the edge of the dam wall with Hobart-based Aardvark Adventures, which organises abseiling trips here (suitable for beginners, minimum two people). You can do two different abseils, and then the big one: 140m right down the wall. It's claimed to be the highest commercial abseil in the world.

🛏️ Sleeping

Accommodation and meals may be available at the Lake Pedder Chalet, although access is often restricted to those working at the power station.

Teds Beach   CAMPGROUND $
(campsite per 2 people $13, extra adult/child $5/2.50) There's a campground at Teds Beach, beside the Lake Pedder Impoundment, with toilets and electric barbecues. No fires permitted.

ℹ️ Information

Hydro Tasmania Visitor Centre (⊙ 9am-6.30pm) The Hydro Tasmania visitor centre at Strathgordon has interpretation on the dams, including two huge mock-up models of the power station, and maps of the mountains and the lakes in 3D.

THE GIANTS OF THE STYX & UPPER FLORENTINE

The Styx: even the name is evocative, speaking of the ancients and underworlds. If you come to the Tasmanian Styx, you'll be absorbed in a domain of ancient tall trees and forests so mysteriously beautiful you'd be forgiven for thinking you have indeed crossed to another world. Tasmania's Styx Valley and the nearby Upper Florentine Valley have also become known for something far more of this world: the logging of old-growth forests, and the fight to save them. Despite a landmark agreement between conservationists and the timber industry in 2010, the future of logging in the area remains uncertain and conservationists continue their campaign to fully protect both areas in a national park, which would be added to the Tasmanian Wilderness World Heritage Area.

In the rich and heavily watered soils of the Styx Valley, trees grow exceptionally tall. The *Eucalyptus regnans* (swamp gums) here are the loftiest trees in the southern hemisphere, and the highest hardwood trees on Earth. Trees of up to 95m in height have been recorded in the valley, and many of the trees in what's known as the Styx Valley of the Giants reach more than 80m above the ground.

Southern visitor centres stock Forestry Tasmania's *Styx* brochure and the Wilderness Society's *Styx Valley of the Giants* brochure. The latter has detailed driving directions, a walking map and interpretation. It can also be downloaded from www.wilderness.org.au/campaigns/forests/styx_walking_guide.

In the Upper Florentine, there are several walks varying from 15 minutes to two hours. The Tiger Valley Lookout is one hour from the car park and has awe-inspiring views over the peaks and forests of the southwest.

Note: the roads here are unsealed and, though manageable by 2WD vehicles, are slippery after rain. Watch out for log trucks. Boom gates may restrict access to some of the features described in the self-drive tours.

Southwest National Park

The state's largest national park is made up of remote, wild country – forest, mountain, grassy plains and seascapes. Here grows the Huon pine, which lives for 3000 years, and the swamp gum, the world's tallest flowering plant. About 300 species of lichen, moss and fern – some very rare – festoon the rainforests, and the alpine meadows are picture-perfect with wildflowers and flowering shrubs. Through it all run wild rivers, their rapids tearing through deep gorges and waterfalls plunging over cliffs.

Fit, experienced bushwalkers can explore the area on tough multi-day walks. One short walk is the Creepy Crawly Nature Trail, an easy 20-minute stroll through rainforest with child-friendly interpretative signage. Its start is about 2km after the Scotts Peak turn-off from the Strathgordon Rd.

Further south, the road leaves the forest near Mt Anne, revealing wonderful views of the surrounding mountains in fine weather. To the west lies the Frankland Range, while to the south is the jagged crest of the Western Arthur Range.

Get your national parks pass and information about the southwest at the Mt Field National Park visitor centre (p90).

Activities

Day Walks

From Scotts Peak Rd you can climb to Mt Eliza, a steep, five-hour return walk, giving panoramic views over the Lake Pedder Impoundment and Mt Solitary. Another challenging eight-hour walk for experienced hikers is from Red Tape Creek (29km south of the main road, along Scotts Peak Rd) to Lake Judd.

From the Huon Campground at the Lake Pedder Impoundment, the best short walk follows the start of the Port Davey Track through forest and buttongrass plain. Mt Wedge is a popular five-hour return walk (signposted off the main road) and has great views of the Lake Pedder Impoundment and Lake Gordon. There's also the 15-minute Wedge Nature Trail from the car park.

Multi-Day Walks

The best-known walks in the southwest are the 70km Port Davey Track between Scotts Peak Rd and Melaleuca (four or five days), and the considerably more popular, 85km South Coast Track between Cockle Creek and Melaleuca.

The South Coast Track takes six to eight days to complete, and hikers should be prepared for weather that could bring anything from sunburn to snow flurries. Par Avion (☑03-6248 5390; www.paravion.com.au) flies bushwalkers into or out of the southwest, landing at Melaleuca, and there's vehicle access to Cockle Creek on the park's southeastern edge. Detailed notes to the South Coast Track are available in Lonely Planet's *Walking in Australia,* and there's comprehensive track information at www.parks.tas.gov.au.

Of the more difficult walks that require a high degree of bushwalking skill, the shortest is the three-day circuit of the Mt Anne Range, a challenging walk with some difficult scrambling. The walk to Federation Peak, which has earned a reputation as the most difficult bushwalking peak in Australia, will take a highly experienced walker seven to eight days. The spectacular Western Arthur Range is an extremely difficult traverse, for which seven to 11 days are recommended.

❶ Getting There & Away

From November through March, **Evans Coaches** (☑03-6297 1335; www.evanscoaches.com. au) operates an early morning bus from Hobart to the start (and finish) of the Mt Anne Circuit, and to Scotts Peak Dam. Evans also runs a bushwalker pick-up/drop-off service at Cockle Creek, at the end of the South Coast Track.

Melaleuca

Melaleuca is little more than a couple of buildings hidden in the bush and a white quartzite gravel airstrip with a wooden shed for an airport. As you fly in, you'll see the workings of the earth from the tin mining carried out by hardy bushmen over the years. In the trees by Moth Creek is the house lived in for over 40 years by the southwest's most legendary resident, Deny King. All around are buttongrass plains, mountains, water and wilderness. Walkers can overnight in a basic hut, and there's camping nearby. You can also visit the excellent bird hide, where you might see the extremely rare orange-bellied parrot.

Bushwalkers' flights by Par Avion (www. paravion.com.au; one-way/return $200/390) deposit walkers at the Melaleuca airstrip. They also pick up here by arrangement, and can leave food drops for hikers coming in to Melaleuca on the Port Davey Track. Flights run on demand, so book well ahead, especially in the summer season. Note: gas canisters and fuels such as Shellite and methylated spirits cannot be carried on the planes. You must purchase them at the airline office and pick up at your destination.

Understand
Tasmania

Tasmania Today

There's an expression from the 1980s: 'Wake up Australia, Tasmania is floating away!' Mainlanders mightn't have been too interested in Tasmania back then, but these days Australia is awake to the Apple Isle's loveliness. Sea- and tree-change migrants are escaping to the island, reversing the historical drift of young Tasmanians heading north for careers or study. Tasmania's astounding natural beauty, fab food and compact cities have become essential antidotes to the more pressured urban lifestyles to the north.

Best on Film

The Hunter (2011) Willem Dafoe goes hunting for the last Tasmanian tiger.

Van Diemen's Land (2009) Cannibal convict Alexander Pearce escapes from Macquarie Harbour.

The Sound of One Hand Clapping (1998) A father and daughter at odds in Tasmania's Central Highlands.

The Tale of Ruby Rose (1988) Ruby gets spooked in the wilds after dark.

Captain Blood (1935) Legendary Tasmanian Errol Flynn swashbuckles his way towards Olivia de Havilland.

Best in Print

The Narrow Road to the Deep North (Richard Flanagan; 2014) From Hobart to the Thai–Burma Death Railway. The 2014 Man Booker Prize winner.

In Tasmania (Nicholas Shakespeare; 2004) A British spin on the island's history, heritage and culture.

Thylacine (David Owen; 2003) Poignant recounting of the tragic demise of the Tasmanian tiger.

Into the Woods: the Battle for Tasmania's Forests (Anna Krien; 2012) Pro- and anti-logging conflict in Tasmania's forests, courtrooms and media.

For the Term of His Natural Life (Marcus Clarke; 1874) Classic account of convict life at Port Arthur.

An Outdoor State of Mind

The modern Tasmanian identity is mirrored in the island's ancient and remarkable landscape. Dark foliage and craggy peaks are whipped by notorious winds, and stunted winter days are infused with the stark clarity of southern light. This Gothic environment fosters a keen sense of adventure and an understated resilience. Rather than hiding indoors behind sandstone walls, Tasmanians embrace their wilderness: getting into it, over it, or on top of it is something the Tasmanian work-life balance absolutely mandates. Beneath woollen beanies and layers of thermals and Gore-Tex, locals are ready to launch into the bush given the slightest excuse.

Tasting Tasmania

A highlight of any Tasmanian trip is getting stuck into the island's food and drink, especially fresh seafood, luscious fruits, craft beer and stellar wines. This cool-climate combo is a hit with both Australian and international chefs: local salmon is served in the restaurants of Tokyo, while whiffy Tassie cheeses provide the perfect finish to meals in Melbourne and Sydney bistros. And how about the whisky! Hobart's Sullivans Cove whisky won the gold medal at the 2014 World Whisky Masters in London – a coveted prize rarely won by anyone other than traditional Scottish producers. There are now over a dozen whisky distillers across the state producing superb single malts. And, of course, the classic Tasmanian snack on-the-run remains the curried scallop pie – a peppery, lurid-yellow concoction sheathed in pie pastry that will fuel your wilderness adventure, solve your morning hangover or prepare you for tomorrow's.

The Urban Vibe

Hobart and Launceston's growing urban fizz is proving irresistible to ex-Tasmanians, who are heading back home, confident they're not missing out on anything that Melbourne, Sydney or London can offer. Well, maybe not London...but Hobart does have water views to rival Sydney's, and continues to evolve into a cosmopolitan hub with craft-beer bars, hipster coffee hang-outs, an awesome art-house cinema, gourmet providores and farmers markets. Meanwhile, Launceston has been busily transforming itself from 'bogan' backwater into a boutique river city full of students on the run from the books. If you're after a live band or a beer, you're in the right town.

Small Island, Big Issues

The passionate environmental debates that regularly erupt in Tasmania often overflow to become federal issues. More than ever, there's conflict over what the big island thinks the little island should be protecting. Should it fight for a close-knit community, jobs for locals and a sequestered way of life? Or should it be for the wilderness, justly famous beyond these island shores? Either way, Tasmanian issues continue to inform the broader Australian political debate, reflecting an increased global focus on the melding of commercial and environmental imperatives.

Tourism Tasmania

The marketing of Tasmania as a tourist destination remains (arguably) the most distinctive, well-informed and savvy campaign in Australia. Affordable airfares from Melbourne, Sydney and Brisbane, plus increased global internet exposure, have also bolstered the island's tourism sector. Well-run local businesses are reaping the benefits, with wilderness tours, outdoor activities and tailored foodie experiences leading the charge. And it's not just air traffic: dozens of cruise ships pull into the Hobart and Burnie waterfronts every summer, depositing thousands of curious travellers with cash to splash in local shops, bars and eateries. Tasmania's accommodation operators have lifted their collective game, banishing (mostly) the kitsch, faux-colonial trimmings of the past in favour of classy contemporary interiors and attentive service. For a day or for a month, Tasmania is now both a good-looking and reliable place to visit.

POPULATION: **514,700**

AREA: **68,401 SQ KM**

GDP: **$24,905 MILLION**

GDP GROWTH: **1.2%**

INFLATION: **2.5%**

UNEMPLOYMENT: **6.8%**

if Tasmania were 100 people

34 would have Australian ancestry
34 would have English ancestry
8 would have Irish ancestry
7 would have Scottish ancestry
17 would have other ancestry

national parks & reserves
(% of land use)

national parks & reserves — 41
other — 59

population per sq km

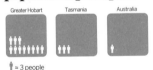

Greater Hobart · Tasmania · Australia

≈ 3 people

History

Tasmania's short written history is bleak and powerful. But like the rest of Australia, it has a much longer story, that of its *palawa*, or 'first man', the term some Tasmanian Aboriginals use to describe themselves. Depicted as a people all but wiped out in an attempted genocide, their culture survives today, despite the fact that their home became Britain's prison island in the first half of the 19th century.

Along Tasmania's west coast, stone engravings have been found, thought to be important symbols of Tasmanian Aboriginal beliefs. The island's Indigenous population also had a knowledge of astronomy.

Tasmanian Aboriginal Peoples

The Land Bridge & the Ice Age

Tasmania was part of the super-continent Gondwana until it broke away and drifted south some 160 million years ago. Aboriginal people probably migrated across a land bridge that joined Tasmania to the rest of Australia at least 35,000 years ago. Sea levels were much lower then and the Tasmanian climate much drier and colder. Aboriginal peoples settled the extensive grasslands on the western side of Tasmania, where they hunted wallabies. When the last ice age ended between 18,000 and 12,000 years ago, glaciers retreated, sea levels rose and tall forests became established on Tasmania's western half. In the east, rainfall increased and new grasslands developed. Cut off by the rising sea, Tasmania 'floated away' from mainland Australia, and a distinctive existence began for the people, animals and plants of the island.

Living on the Island

The culture of the Tasmanian Aboriginals diverged from the way people were living on the mainland, as they developed a sustainable, seasonal culture of hunting, fishing and gathering. The islanders produced sophisticated boats and used them to hunt seals and mutton birds on and around the offshore islands.

Those who remained in the west lived mainly on the coast. Aboriginal women collected shellfish (mussels, abalone and oysters), the remains of which comprise the enormous middens still found around Tasmania's coastline. Both men and women wore necklaces of shell.

TIMELINE	12,000–8000 BC	1642	1700s
	Tasmania's Aboriginal peoples – part of Australia's original Indigenous population who arrived on the continent 60,000–35,000 BC – are separated from the mainland when sea levels rise following the last ice age.	Dutch explorer Abel Tasman eyeballs Tasmania and lands at Blackmans Bay south of Hobart. He names the island Van Diemen's Land after a Dutch governor.	Visiting Captain Bligh plants the isle's first apple tree. Three centuries later the growers of the Huon Valley still toast their good fortune with zingy cider.

They sheltered in bark lean-tos and protected themselves from the island's cold weather with furs and by applying a thick mix of ochre, charcoal and fat to their skin.

Sails, Guns & Fences

European Discovery

The first European to spy Tasmania was Dutch navigator Abel Tasman, who bumped into it in 1642. He named this new place Van Diemen's Land after the Dutch East Indies' governor. It's estimated there were between 5000 and 10,000 Aboriginals in Tasmania when Europeans arrived, living in 'bands' of around 50 people, each claiming rights over a specific area of land and being part of one of nine main language groups.

European sealers began to work Bass Strait in 1798, raiding tribal communities along the coast and kidnapping Aboriginal women to act as forced labour and sex slaves. The sealers were uninterested in Aboriginal land and eventually formed commercial relationships with the Aboriginals, trading dogs and other items so they could take Aboriginal women back to their islands.

The Black Wars

In 1803 Risdon Cove on the Derwent River just north of Hobart became the site of Australia's second British colony (after Sydney). One year later the settlement relocated to Sullivans Cove, the site of present-day Hobart, where the Hobart Rivulet offered a reliable water supply.

Despite initial friendly exchanges and trade, an unknown number of peaceable Aboriginal people were killed during this early period, as European fences and farming encroached on their hunting grounds and significant places. In return Aboriginal people began to carry out their own raids. In 1816 Governor Thomas Davey produced his 'Proclamation to the Aborigines', which represented settlers and Indigenous Tasmanians living together amicably – in direct contrast to the realities of a brutal conflict.

By the 1820s these territorial disputes had developed into the so-called Black Wars, as Aboriginal people increasingly refused to surrender their lands, women and children without a fight. In 1828 martial law was declared by Lieutenant-Governor Arthur. Aboriginal groups were systematically murdered, arrested or forced at gunpoint from districts settled by whites – arsenic on bread and steel traps designed to catch humans were used. Many more succumbed to European diseases against which they had no immunity.

Meanwhile around Bass Strait, a disapproving Van Diemen's Land establishment contemptuously termed the descendants of sealers and

Looking for a convict in your family tree? To help with genealogy searches, check the website of the Tasmanian Family History Society (www.tasfhs.org).

1788	1798	1803	1804
The First Fleet arrives at Sydney with its cargo of convicts. More than 200 years later, family connections to these colonists are still a badge of honour for contemporary Australians.	'Straitsmen', a rough bunch of sealers, make their home and their living in Bass Strait. It's a tough life, characterised by long periods working this unforgiving stretch of water.	The Lady Nelson arrives in Risdon Cove north of Hobart, and Australia's second British penal settlement is established. The site is returned to the Tasmanian Aboriginal community in 1995.	The Risdon Cove settlement relocates to Sullivans Cove (the present-day Hobart waterfront). Another settlement at George Town on the island's north coast is also established.

Aboriginal women 'half-castes', applying continual pressure on Bass Strait islanders to adopt European farming ways and assimilate with mainlanders.

Historic Bridges

Richmond Bridge (p83)

Ross Bridge (p130)

Campbell Town's Red Bridge (p132)

The Black Line

As the Black Wars continued the British were growing concerned about how it might look to the world if their actions led to the extinction of an entire race of people. In 1830, in an attempt to contain all Aboriginals on the Tasman Peninsula for their security and to preserve their culture, a human chain of 2200 men known as the Black Line was formed by settlers and soldiers, moving through the settled areas of the state from Moulting Lagoon, through Campbell Town to Quamby Bluff. Three weeks later this farcical manoeuvre had succeeded in capturing only an old man and a boy, and confirmed settlers' fears that they couldn't defeat the Aboriginals by force of arms. The *Hobart Courier* mocked the exercise: it had cost half the colony's annual budget. In turn it must have given the Aboriginal people an awful sense that their time was running out.

A Parallel Prison

Following the failure of the Black Line, Lieutenant-Governor Arthur consented to George Augustus Robinson's plan to 'conciliate' the Aboriginal people. In effect Robinson enticed and cajoled virtually all of the Aboriginals in mainland Tasmania to lay down their arms, leave their traditional lands and accompany him to new settlements. In doing so he became the first European to walk across much of the state, adding the title of explorer to that of missionary. There is strong historical evidence that the people of Oyster Bay, including their prominent chief Tongerlongetter, whom Robinson regarded as 'a man of great tact and judgement', followed him to a succession of settlements in the Furneaux Islands based on the promise of sanctuary and land. Instead, they were subjected to attempts to 'civilise' and Christianise them, and made to work for the government.

After enduring a number of moves, including to Sarah Island on the west coast, Tasmania's Indigenous inhabitants were finally settled at Wybalenna (Black Man's Houses) on Flinders Island. One by one the people began to die from a potent mixture of despair, homesickness, poor food and respiratory disease. In 1847 those who had managed to survive petitioned Queen Victoria, complaining of their treatment and referring to the 'agreement' they thought Robinson had made with Lieutenant-Governor Arthur on their behalf. Wybalenna was eventually abandoned and the survivors transferred to mainland Tasmania. Of the 135 who had been sent to Flinders Island, only 47 lived to make the journey to Oyster Cove, south of Hobart. The new accommodation here

1807	1811	1822–53	1824
First settlers arrive from Norfolk Island on the Lady Nelson and found New Norfolk. A replica of the Lady Nelson today offers tall-ship sailings on the Derwent River.	Governor Lachlan Macquarie arrives from Sydney and draws up initial plans for Hobart's streets. Public buildings erected at this time include the Mt Nelson Signal Station.	Convicts are imprisoned at various penal settlements around the state, including Sarah Island and Port Arthur. For some it (eventually) presents the opportunity of a new start.	The Cascade Brewery opens in Hobart under the shadow of Mt Wellington, making it Australia's oldest continuously operating brewery.

proved to be substandard and the Aboriginals once again experienced the criminal neglect of the authorities, and growing demoralisation. Within a decade, half of the 47 were dead.

Mapping Van Diemen's Land

Nearly 130 years after Abel Tasman's able efforts, Tasmania was visited by a series of other European sailors, including captains Tobias Furneaux, James Cook and William Bligh. Between 1770 and 1790 they all visited Adventure Bay on Bruny Island and believed it to be part of the Australian mainland, rather than an island off an island (off an island).

In 1792 Admiral Bruni D'Entrecasteaux explored the southeastern coastline more thoroughly, mapping and naming many of its features. Many major landmarks in this area still bear the French names he gave them.

In 1798 Lieutenant Matthew Flinders circumnavigated Van Diemen's Land and proved that it was indeed an island.

Australia's Second Settlement

In the late 1790s Governor King of NSW decided to establish a second settlement in Australia, south of Sydney Cove. Port Phillip Bay in Victoria was initially considered, but the site was rejected due to a lack of water on the Mornington Peninsula and, in 1803, Tasmania's Risdon Cove was chosen. A year later, the settlement was moved 10km south to the present site of Hobart on the other side of the Derwent River. The threat of French interest in the island suggested the need for a settlement up north; a site called George Town was proclaimed on the Tamar River in 1804.

That same year 74 convicts were shipped out to Van Diemen's Land, with 71 soldiers, plus their 21 wives and 14 children. Penal settlements were built in the island's most inhospitable places. Macquarie Harbour, on the harsh west coast, became Tasmania's first penal site in 1822, and by 1833 roughly 2000 convicts a year were sent to this end-of-the-earth colony as punishment for often-trivial crimes.

The community quickly developed a very particular character: lawlessness and debauchery were rife. Nascent Van Diemen's Land was dominated by a mentality of 'If it grows, chop it down; if it runs, shoot it'. Yet it was also defined by great pioneering innovation and courage.

Exploring Coast to Coast

The establishment of George Town in 1804 attracted new settlers, resulting in a demand for more land. Settlers initially spread along the island's southeast coast towards Port Arthur, along the east coast and around the Launceston area. By 1807 an overland route from Hobart to Launceston

Historic Pubs

Knopwood's Retreat (p76), Hobart

Man O'Ross (p132), Ross

Stanley Hotel (p224)

Deloraine Hotel (p208)

Royal Oak (p184), Launceston

HISTORY MAPPING VAN DIEMEN'S LAND

The reference to 'Truganini in chains' in the Midnight Oil song *Truganini* is not factually correct. It's more likely to be a metaphor for the appalling treatment of Tasmania's Aboriginal people.

1830	1853	1856	1870s
The Black Line, a slow-moving human chain of 2200 men, fails to flush out Tasmania's Aboriginal inhabitants. The intention was to corral all Aboriginals on the Tasman Peninsula south of Eaglehawk Neck.	The Anti-Transportation League lobbyists succeed in ending convict transportation. In the 50 years from 1803, an estimated 75,000 convicts made the forced journey to Van Diemen's Land.	The state changes its name from Van Diemen's Land to Tasmania in an attempt to distance itself from the taint of the convict era.	Gold and tin are discovered in the state's north, signalling the beginning of mining activity in Tasmania. Organised opposition to the industry only begins to take hold a century later.

had been forged. Stone was readily available for construction work and many early stone buildings still survive. Some of the best examples of these buildings can be found in Richmond and in Ross and Oatlands along the Midland Hwy.

To the settlers, Tasmania's big unknowns were its rugged western and central hinterlands, where difficult, mountainous country barred the way. The first Europeans to cross the island were escapees from Macquarie Harbour – many escaped, but only a few survived the journey to Hobart Town.

In 1828 George Frankland was appointed Tasmania's surveyor-general. Determined to map the entire state, he sent many surveyors on long, arduous journeys during the 1830s, often accompanying them. By 1845, when Frankland died, most of the state was roughly mapped and catalogued.

TRUGANINI'S LEGACY

One of the last surviving full-blooded Tasmanian Aboriginals, Truganini lived through the white invasion of her land, and her death has become a symbol of the attempted genocide of her people.

Truganini was born on Bruny Island in 1812, the daughter of Mangana, the chief of the Nuenonne people. Along with her husband, Woureddy, she left her island home to travel with George Robinson – accounts also suggest she lived with sealers as a young woman, an experience that left her unable to bear children. When she was older, Truganini lived with fellow Tasmanian Aboriginals in the derelict environment of Wybalenna on Flinders Island and afterwards at the disastrous Oyster Cove settlement.

It is remarkable, given the times, that Truganini lived into her 60s. When she died in Hobart in 1876, the Tasmanian government declared that she was the last of the island's Indigenous peoples and that her race was extinct (in fact, she was outlived by Suke and Fanny Cochrane, two women of tribal parentage). The announcement of her death, and the resulting funeral procession through Hobart, aimed to 'end the native problem'. The demise of the Tasmanian Aboriginal race was taken as fact – and still endures in some encyclopedias and school history lessons.

Against her wishes to be buried in the mountains behind Oyster Cove, or dropped deep into the D'Entrecasteaux Channel, Truganini's 4ft-tall skeleton was instead displayed for many years as a public curio in the Tasmanian Museum. Much to the chagrin of the Royal Society in Tasmania, other parts of her contested remains were shipped to Britain by the Royal College of Surgeons in London and were only repatriated in 2002. It took more than a lifetime for Truganini's wishes to be granted and her ashes finally scattered in the channel beside her beloved Bruny Island. You can visit a memorial to Truganini at the Neck on Bruny Island, and there's a memorial on Mt Nelson behind Hobart, at the top of the Truganini Track.

1916	1932	1934	1935
Tasmania's first national parks are established at Freycinet and Mt Field – a strong foundation for the state's future reputation for pristine wilderness areas.	Born in Stanley in 1879, Joseph Lyons becomes Australia's first (and only) Tasmanian prime minister. The suburb of Lyons in Canberra is named after him in 1965.	Construction of the 7km Pinnacle Rd up Mt Wellington begins, creating employment for thousands of men during the Depression.	Debonair Tasmanian Errol Flynn stars in Captain Blood, a rollicking tale in which his character is sold as a slave to Olivia de Havilland, escapes and becomes a pirate.

Building roads across the mountainous west was difficult and many were surveyed across all sorts of landscapes before being abandoned. But in 1932 the Lyell Hwy from Hobart to Queenstown was finally opened for business, linking the west coast and Hobart.

Convict Life

Sarah, Maria & Arthur: the Worst of the Worst

The actual site of the first penal settlement in Tasmania was on small Sarah Island, in Macquarie Harbour on the west coast. The prisoners sent there were those who had committed further crimes after arriving in Australia. Their severe punishment was hard manual labour, cutting down Huon pine in the rainforest. It's believed conditions were so dreadful that some prisoners committed murder in order to be sent for trial and execution in Hobart.

The number of prisoners sent to Van Diemen's Land increased in 1825. In the same year the island was recognised as a colony independent of NSW, and another penal settlement was established, this one off the east coast on Maria Island, where prisoners were treated more humanely.

In 1830 a third penal settlement was established at Port Arthur on the Tasman Peninsula. Shortly after its construction, the other two penal settlements closed – Maria Island in 1832 and Sarah Island in 1833.

Punishments meted out to convicts at Port Arthur included weeks of solitary confinement. The worst prisoners were sent to work in the coal mines of the nearby Saltwater River, where they were housed in miserably damp underground cells. A visit to Port Arthur evokes the terrible conditions suffered by prisoners during this era.

A Name Change & a New Image

In 1840 convict transportation to NSW ceased, resulting in an increase in the number of convicts being sent to Van Diemen's Land; there was a peak of 5329 new arrivals in 1842. In 1844 control of the Norfolk Island penal settlement (in the Pacific Ocean, 1610km northeast of Sydney) was transferred from NSW to Van Diemen's Land and by 1848 'VDL' was the only place in the British Empire to which convicts were still being transported.

Vociferous opposition to the continued transportation of convicts came from free settlers, who in 1850 formed the Anti-Transportation League to successfully lobby for change. The last convicts transported to the colony arrived in 1853.

Van Diemen's Land had been the most feared destination for British prisoners for more than three decades. During those years a total of 74,000 convicts had been transported to the island. The majority of these people had served out their sentences and settled in the colony, yet so

---

Experience Convict Life

Port Arthur Historic Site (p105)

Coal Mines Historic Site (p104)

The Female Factory sites in Hobart (p57) and Ross (p130)

Darlington (p142) on Maria Island

HISTORY CONVICT LIFE

1936	1945	1967	1972
The last known thylacine (aka Tasmanian Tiger) dies in Hobart's Beaumaris Zoo. Wild sightings continue into the 21st century, but no evidence of the species' continued survival is ever produced.	The epic 1170km Sydney to Hobart Yacht Race is run for the first time. The winning time of 43 hours, 23 minutes and 12 seconds, set by Wild Oats IV in 2012, is the current race record.	Tasmania's deadliest bushfires kill 62 people, injure over 900 and leave more than 7000 homeless. The 'Black Tuesday' fires impacted on 2640 sq km, from the Midlands to the D'Entrecasteaux Channel.	Lake Pedder is flooded as part of a hydroelectric scheme. The Lake Pedder Restoration Committee (www.lakepedder.org) is now committed to restoring the lake to a natural wilderness state.

terrible was its reputation that in 1856 – the year it achieved responsible self-government – it changed its name to Tasmania in an attempt to free its image once and for all from the shackles of its past.

Tasmanian culture has since undergone a transition from shame, and an increasing number of Tasmanians of European descent now identify with their convict past. There has also been an increase in pride in being Tasmanian and, driven by compelling tourism marketing and a burgeoning food-and-wine scene, the state's positive and cosmopolitan profile is far removed from the negative preconceptions of just a few decades ago.

Gold, but no Great Rush

Historic Walking Tours

Hobart Historic Tours (p61)

Louisa's Walk (p61), Hobart

Launceston Historic Walks (p177)

In the 1870s gold was discovered near the Tamar River, as was tin in the northeast. These discoveries prompted a deluge of international prospectors. In the northeast hundreds of Chinese miners arrived, bringing their culture with them. The themed Trail of the Tin Dragon (p165) tourist path through the northeast highlights this aspect of the state's history.

Mining was a tough way of life and most people didn't make their fortunes. Individual prospectors grabbed the rich, easily found surface deposits, but once these were gone the miners had to form larger groups and companies to reach deeper deposits, until eventually these either ran out or became unprofitable to work. The Beaconsfield Mine & Heritage Centre (p189) north of Launceston is still operational and can be visited today.

Once it was realised there was mineral wealth to be found, prospectors randomly explored most of the state. On the west coast, discoveries of large deposits of silver and lead resulted in a boom in the 1880s and an associated rush at Zeehan. In fact, so rich in minerals was the area that it ultimately supported mines significant enough to create the towns of Rosebery, Tullah and Queenstown. Geological exploitation went unchecked, however, and by the 1920s copper mining at Queenstown had

---

IN THE NATIONAL TRUST WE TRUST

As you explore Tasmania you'll often come across gracious old heritage estates and properties managed by the **National Trust** (☎03-6344 6233; www.nationaltrust.org.au/tas). Many are staffed by volunteers and have rather specific opening hours, but if you do fancy a spot of time travel, be sure to talk with the attendants: they are often passionately knowledgeable about local stories and heritage. Step onto the well-worn flagstones of the Georgian Regency mansion **Clarendon** (p197) near Evandale, the convict-built **Franklin House** (p175) in Launceston and the colony's first lawyer's digs, **Runnymede** (p58) in Hobart. All are well worth a visit.

1975	1982	1982–3	1996
Hobart's Tasman Bridge collapses, killing 12, when the ore carrier Lake Illawarra crashes into it. Seven of the dead were crew members.	Taking in the Southwest, Franklin–Gordon Wild Rivers and Cradle Mountain–Lake St Clair National Parks, the expansive Tasman Wilderness World Heritage Area is established.	The Franklin River Blockade is staged to oppose construction of a dam in the area, and is ultimately successful. The action is a substantial boost to Tasmania's conservation lobby.	The massacre of 35 people at the Port Arthur Historic Site stuns the world and eventually results in stricter gun-control laws in Australia.

gashed holes in the surrounding hills, while logging, pollution, fires and heavy rain stripped the terrain of its vegetation and topsoil. The environment has only begun repairing itself over the past few decades.

The rich belt of land from Queenstown to the north coast is still being mined in several places, but this is now being done with a little more environmental consideration and fewer visible effects than in the past.

Tasmania in the 20th Century

Although it was ignored in the initial federal ministry, Tasmania officially became a state when Australia's Federation took place in 1901. For Tasmanians, as for mainlanders in the new Commonwealth of Australia, the first half of the 20th century was dominated by war, beginning with the dispatch of a contingent of 80 Tasmanian soldiers to South Africa and the Boer War, through the Great War and WWII, with the Depression of the 1930s thrown in for bad measure.

The state's post-WWII economy was reassuringly buoyant, with industrial success embodied by Bell Bay's aluminium refinery and the ongoing developments of the powerful Hydro-Electric Commission. However, by the 1980s it had suffered a worrisome decline. Subsequent years saw economic unease reflected in climbing 'brain drain' levels to the mainland (especially among the under-30s) and falling birth rates.

Saving the Wilderness

Since the early 1970s, the key influence on Tasmanian history has been the ongoing battle between pro-logging companies and environmental groups. Tasmania is a state that's poorer and has less employment opportunities than mainland states, but it's also an island with world-beating wilderness and scenic beauty. With these two contemporary markers of Tasmanian society, the ideological fault lines often evident in Tasmanian history are not difficult to trace back and understand.

In 1910 Austrian Gustav Weindorfer reached the summit of Cradle Mountain. Throwing his arms out, he declared that the magnificence of the place, 'where there is no time and nothing matters', was something the people of the world should share. It later became a national park. In the 20th century the extinction of the thylacine and the flooding of Lake Pedder led to the birth of the green movement in 1972, when concerned groups got together to form the United Tasmania Group. Ten years later, thousands of people acted to stop the damming of the Franklin River. Leaders in these movements became a force in Australian federal politics – the Greens Party, under the leadership of Tasmanian Bob Brown, who was a senator from 1996 until 2012.

History Museums

Queen Victoria Museum & Art Gallery (p173), Launceston

Tasmanian Museum & Art Gallery (p53), Hobart

Narryna Heritage Museum (p57), Hobart

Anglesea Barracks (Map p50), Hobart

Low Head Pilot Station Museum (p191)

1997	1998	2008	2010
Homosexuality is finally decriminalised in Tasmania. In 2010 Tasmania becomes the first state to recognise same-sex marriages performed in other jurisdictions as registered partnerships.	The Sydney to Hobart Yacht Race is marred by tragedy when hurricane-force conditions cause five boats to sink with the loss of six lives.	Prime Minister Kevin Rudd apologises to Australia's Aboriginal stolen generations. Tasmanian Aboriginal activist Michael Mansell questions whether financial compensation will follow.	Signed in December 2010, the 'Statement of Principles' agreement is promoted as a peace deal between the pro-forestry and pro-environmental groups in Tasmania.

Tasmania in the 21st Century

Backed by strong tourism campaigns, vocal supporters in mainstream media, a respected arts scene and the emergence of several excellent local brands that wind up in shopping trolleys across the country, Tasmania's image change is crystallising as it fosters its reputation as a 'pure' holiday isle and lifestyle haven.

The long-running debate between pro-logging groups, pro-pulp-mill corporations and conservationists keen to protect Tasmania's old-growth forests and wild heritage continues. In 2010 a breakthrough was achieved with the signing of the 'Statement of Principles' agreement – a 'peace deal' between pro-forestry and pro-environmental groups. Following this, in 2011 the 'Tasmanian Forests Intergovernmental Agreement' was signed by Australian prime minister Julia Gillard, Tasmanian premier Lara Giddings and conservation and forestry groups, creating new areas of forest reserves while guaranteeing ongoing native and plantation timber access for the forestry industry. In 2012 the key protagonist on the pro-logging side of the debate – forestry company Gunns Ltd – was placed in voluntary administration.

The Tasmanian Forests Intergovernmental Agreement was passed into law by the Tasmanian parliament in 2013, but was subsequently repealed by a new conservative state government in 2014. A six-year moratorium period came into effect, after which the impact of resuming logging in Tasmania's old-growth forests is to be re-examined.

Indigenous Rights

Of course, Truganini and Suke and Fanny Cochrane were not the last Tasmanian Aboriginals. They may have been the last 'full-blooded' representatives of their race, but countless Tasmanians of mixed heritage survived.

Over recent decades the state's Indigenous population has found a new voice, sense of community and identity. Tasmanian Aboriginals continue to claim rights to land and compensation for past injustices. Acknowledgement of the treatment meted out to Indigenous peoples by Europeans has resulted in the recognition of native titles to land. In 1995 the state government returned 12 sites to the Tasmanian Aboriginal community, including Oyster Cove, Risdon Cove, Kutikina Cave and Steep Island. Wybalenna was added to this list in 1999, and areas of Cape Barren and Clarke Islands in 2005.

APOLOGY

In 1997 the Tasmanian parliament became the first in Australia to formally apologise to the Aboriginal community for past actions connected with the stolen generations.

2011	2011	2014	2014
Tasmania's first female premier – Lara Giddings, from the left-wing Labor Party – is elected, keeping the top job until 2014.	Controversial Tasmanian timber company Gunns Ltd sells the Triabunna woodchip mill to cashed-up environmentalists Graeme Wood and Jan Cameron, before going into receivership in 2012.	Tasmania author Richard Flanagan reaches the pinnacle of global literary success, winning the Man Booker Prize for his novel The Narrow Road to the Deep North.	Hobart 16-year-old Jack Hale wins the Australian 100m sprint title in 10.13 seconds (with a bit of a tailwind) – the world's fastest teenager in 2014.

Gourmet Tasmania

Tasmania has been dubbed the 'providore island' – an astute moniker given the state's booming food and wine scenes. Super seafood, juicy berries and stone fruits, splendidly calorific dairy products, craft beers, excellent cool-climate wines and winning whisky compete for your attentions on the Tasmanian menu.

Around the state, organic farms, orchards, vineyards and small enterprises are busy supplying fresh local produce, and buyers (restaurants, markets, providores and individuals) are snapping it up. Dishes on menus throughout Australia feature Tasmanian oysters, scallops and salmon, and King Island cream appears on dessert menus from Sydney to Perth. Hobart and Launceston eateries offer even more in the way of locally sourced and seasonal goodies.

Visitors may find themselves sometimes underwhelmed by menus in some country towns, especially if the local pub is the only eatery. However, excellent providores are popping up around the island, so a DIY Tasmanian picnic is usually an option.

Travellers who want to eat their way around the Apple Isle should go to www.discovertasmania.com.au – click on 'What to Do' then 'Food and Drink' and start planning your next meal.

Local Produce

Seafood

Like the rest of Australia, Tasmania is 'girt by sea' (...referencing the national anthem, and the inevitable Australian schoolkid's question: 'Dad, what does 'girt' mean?'). It's a no-brainer that the seafood here is magnificent, harvested from some of the cleanest ocean water on the planet.

Essential specialities include oysters on Bruny Island, at Coles Bay and at Barilla Bay near Hobart; and ocean trout from the waters of Macquarie Harbour. Deep-sea fish such as trevalla (blue eye) and striped trumpeter are delicious, as is the local Atlantic salmon, extensively farmed in the Huon estuary and D'Entrecasteaux Channel south of Hobart. Squid (calamari), rock lobster (known as crayfish in these latitudes), abalone, scallops and mussels are also menu regulars.

From a humble curried scallop pie or fish and chips at Hobart's Constitution Dock, to an innovative meal at one of Hobart's gourmet restaurants, Tasmania is a spectacular seafood destination.

Download the *Tasmanian Fruits Farm Gate Guide* from the Fruit Growers of Tasmania website (www.fruitgrowerstas.com.au). This annual publication lists the best places to secure a drive-in, pick-your-own summertime vitamin hit of stone fruit, cherries and berries.

Meat

Tasmania is known for its high-quality beef, based on a natural, grass-fed (as opposed to grain-fed) production system and free from growth hormones, antibiotics and chemical contaminants. Beef from King Island and Flinders Island is sublime, and if you see it on a menu and the wallet allows, tuck into premium Wagyu beef from Robbins Island, also in Bass Strait. Flinders Island also farms prime lamb. Cape Grim, on the north-western tip of mainland Tasmania, has also gained market traction for its beef, especially in Launceston's better restaurants. These meats have also made the grade in upmarket restaurants throughout Australia, and command a ransom in overseas markets such as Tokyo.

Game meats also feature on menus, with quail, wallaby, kangaroo and farmed venison often available. Wallaby and kangaroo meat is tender, lean, flavoursome and packed with protein – if you can banish the imagery of these doe-eyed animals cavorting in the wild from your mind, you're in for a treat.

Fruit

Tasmania's cool climate equates to fabulous berries and stone fruit; picking your own (in season) is a great way to enjoy them. Sorell Fruit Farm (p99) near Hobart is a favourite – it gives visitors the opportunity to pick all sorts, including raspberries, cherries, apples and pears. Impromptu stops at roadside stalls in the Huon and Tamar Valleys offer the chance to buy freshly picked fruits. Other places worth a visit include Christmas Hills Raspberry Farm Cafe (p209) near Deloraine, Kate's Berry Farm (p146) outside Swansea, Eureka Farm (p159) in Scamander and Hillwood Berry Farm (p190) near George Town.

Jams, sauces, fruit wines, ciders and juices made from Tasmanian fruits are also excellent. Many varieties are available at gourmet food stores and providores and from stalls at Hobart's Salamanca Market. Tasmanian cider, in particular, has had a real resurgence of late, filling the bar taps in pubs around the state and across Australia. Don't miss the Apple Shed (p119) in Huonville for a jug or a tasting paddle of Willie Smith's best brew, and Spreyton Cider Co (p206) near Latrobe in the northwest.

Cheese

Tasmania has an impressive cheese industry, somewhat hampered by the fact that all milk here must be pasteurised, unlike in Italy and France. Despite this legal inconvenience, the results are fabulous – just slap some local leatherwood honey over a slice of blue cheese for tasty confirmation.

Visit the Pyengana Dairy Company (p162), not far from St Helens, for sensational cheddar. Grandvewe Cheeses (p116), just south of Woodbridge, produces organic cheese from sheep and cow's milk. Ashgrove Farm Cheese (p209) near Deloraine conjures up traditional cheeses such as Rubicon red, smoked cheddar and creamy Lancashire, while the Bruny Island Cheese Co (p115) produces Italian and French styles.

Food Festivals

Taste of Tasmania (p63), Hobart around New Year's Eve.

Taste of the Huon (p122), Huonville in March.

Festivale (p177), Launceston in February.

Savour Tasmania Food Festival (p63), statewide in May.

TOP 10 FARM GATES & ARTISAN PRODUCERS

Chat with the farmer, fruiterer or orchard owner at these top spots to pick up the freshest of local Tasmanian produce.

Get Shucked Oyster Farm (p115), Bruny Island

King Island Dairy (p231), King Island

Sorell Fruit Farm (p99), Sorell

Freycinet Marine Farm (p152), Coles Bay

Cherry Shed (p206), Latrobe

House of Anvers (p206), Latrobe

Honey Farm (p211), Chudleigh

Grandvewe Cheeses (p116), Woodbridge

Cradle Coast Olives (p217), Ulverstone

Pyengana Dairy Company (p162), Pyengana

In providores and restaurants, keep an eye out for the superb brie from King Island Dairy (p231). If you do find yourself on King Island, a visit to the walk-in refrigerated tasting room here is one of the more generous foodie experiences you'll ever have (don't eat beforehand).

Other Items

Not content with seafood successes and champion cheese, Tasmanian producers are getting creative and showing off their agricultural skill, growing or harvesting some wonderfully diverse products, including buckwheat, walnuts, wasabi, wakame (a type of seaweed) and saffron. Black truffles are being harvested in the north of Tasmania, with an idea to capture the European market during the French off season.

Tasmania also produces fantastic honey, chocolate and fudge, mushrooms, asparagus, olive oil, mustards and relishes. To stock up, check out Hobart's Farm Gate Market (p48) and Salamanca Market (p53), Launceston's Harvest (p185) market, or hit providores statewide.

Where to Eat

Fine Dining

Tasmania's best fine-dining restaurants rival anything on the Australian mainland, and local chefs are renowned for making the most of the excellent local produce. Menu items can be expensive (mains sometimes exceeding $35), but diners are guaranteed innovative and thoughtful interpretations of local seafood, beef and lamb, partnered with the best Tasmanian wines.

In Hobart, Blue Eye (p72) and Ethos (p70) are outstanding. Meanwhile, Stillwater (p182) still delivers Launceston's most interesting high-end tastes. Elsewhere on the island, Edge (p153) at Coles Bay, Xanders (p225) in Stanley, Piermont (p146) in Swansea and the Home Hill Wines (p121) restaurant in Huonville are all excellent.

Cafes

Like the rest of Australia, Tasmania has fallen hard for coffee, and the humble bean is taken super seriously at cafes such as Pilgrim Coffee (p69), Retro Café (p71) and Pigeon Hole (p74) in Hobart, and at Sweetbrew (p181) and the Blue Café Bar (p182) in Launceston.

Cafes are travellers' best options for breakfast and brunch; expect to pay around $12 to $18 for main-course menu items. You will find good cafes outside of Hobart and Launceston, but they are less prevalent. As an alternative, B&B accommodation generally provides a calorific start to the day.

Pubs

The quality of Tasmanian pub food swings between gourmet and grossly outmoded. Upmarket city pubs brim with ethnic flavours and innovation, while utilitarian country pubs proffer a more predictable slew of schnitzels, roasts and deep-fried seafood. Pub bistro meals (main courses generally $18 to $30) come with the added ambience of a rear dining room; while counter meals in the front bar (mains usually $12 to $20) are quick-fire, no-frills affairs, accompanied by blokey airs.

In Hobart, the Shipwright's Arms Hotel (p68), the New Sydney Hotel (p77) and the Republic Bar & Café (p77) plate up the city's best pub grub, while Launceston's finest meal with a cold beer can be found at the Sportsmans Hall Hotel (p182). The Man O'Ross Hotel (p132) in Ross is also a solid option.

Listing foodie haunts, wineries, breweries, distilleries and other purveyors of gastronomic bounty, the *Tasmania Wine & Gastronomy Map with Breweries and Distilleries* is an essential for galloping gourmets. Pick one up online at www.vwmaps. com/australi-an-wine-maps/ tasmania or in Hobart's main bookshops.

For some pre-trip inspiration, check out the SBS Television series Gourmet Farmer (www.sbs. com.au/shows/ gourmetfarmer), in which Sydney food critic Matthew Evans moves to Cygnet in southeast Tasmania to try his hand at organic farming. It's a highlights reel of gorgeous scenery and fab Tassie produce.

Vegetarian Options

Vegetarian eateries and menu selections are becoming more common in large towns and tourist areas. Tasmanian cafes usually have a few vegetarian options, but vegans will find the going much tougher. Indian and Asian eateries are the best bet for vegetarians in Hobart, or swing by Fresh on Charles (p182) or Garden of Vegan (p183) in Launceston.

Tasmanian Wine

Since the mid-1950s, Tasmania has been building a rep for quality cool-climate wines, characterised by full, fruity flavours and high acidity. Today vineyards across the state are producing sublime pinot noir, riesling and chardonnay, with many producers focusing on sparkling wine as their future.

Tasmania can be split into three key wine regions: the north around Launceston; the east around Swansea; and the south around Hobart. There are plenty of large, professional outfits with sophisticated cellar doors, but you'll also find smaller, family-owned vineyards with buckets of charm.

Some wineries' tastings are free, while most charge a small fee refundable if you buy a bottle.

The North & East

The Tamar Valley and Pipers River areas north of Launceston are Tasmania's best-known wine regions, and are home to a number of big-name wineries, including Ninth Island Vineyard (p186), Pipers Brook (p192) and Jansz Wine Room (p192). Velo Wines (p186), just out of Launceston, and Delamere Vineyards (p192) in Pipers River are two of our small-scale faves.

Wineries are also dotted down the east coast from Bicheno to Dunalley, including the well-respected Freycinet Vineyard (p143) and Devil's Corner (p143) near Swansea.

The South

A major producer in Hobart's northern suburbs (next to MONA!) is Moorilla (p58). Established in 1958, it's the oldest vineyard in southern Tasmania. Just east of Hobart, the Coal River Valley is home to an increasing number of wineries, most notably Frogmore Creek (p83) and Puddleduck Vineyard (p83).

Foodie Tours & Cooking Courses

Herbaceous Tours (p62), tours ex-Hobart.

....

Long Lunch Wine Tour Co (p62), tours ex-Hobart.

....

Gourmania (p61), tours ex-Hobart.

....

Agrarian Kitchen (p88), cooking courses near New Norfolk.

....

Red Feather Inn (p194), cooking courses in Hadspen.

TOP FIVE TASMANIAN CRAFT BEERS

Craft-beer boffins may want to time their Tasmanian sojourn around November's **Tasmanian Beerfest** (p63). Otherwise look for the following microbrews in Tasmania's pubs and bars:

Moo Brew (www.moobrew.com.au) Standout beers include a zingy *hefeweizen* and a hoppy pilsner. An offshoot of the impressive Moorilla winery operation at MONA north of Hobart.

Seven Sheds (p214) Specialises in a malty Kentish ale, plus seasonal brews and honey-infused mead. In Railton.

Iron House Brewery (p158) On the east coast near Scamander. Makes a crisp lager, hoppy pale ale and a Czech-style pilsner.

Two Metre Tall (p86) Real ale and ciders, with ingredients sourced from its farm in the Derwent Valley. Friday night and Sunday afternoon 'Farm Bar' sessions are a hoot.

Van Dieman Brewing (www.vandiemanbrewing.com.au) Based near Evandale. Produces six beers, including the English-style Jacob's Ladder amber ale.

Further south, in the Huon Valley area, you'll find Hartzview Vineyard (p116), Panorama Vineyard (p119) and Home Hill Wines (p120). Cross over the ferry to Bruny Island Premium Wines (p115) – Australia's southern-most vineyard – or continue south to Dover and St Imre Vineyard (p124) for Hungarian-style wines.

Tasmanian Beer

The definitive example of Tasmanian parochialism is the traditional local loyalty to regionally brewed beer. In the south it's Cascade, brewed in South Hobart; in the north Launceston's James Boag's flies the flag. Until quite recently you could draw an invisible line from Strahan through Ross to Bicheno, north of which no sane publican would serve Cascade. South of this hoppy division, any mention of Boag's would provoke confusion and ridicule. These days things are much less definitive and you'll find Cascade and Boag's both freely available in 'enemy territory'.

Cascade highlights include the very drinkable premium lager, a pale ale, the ever-present draught and saucy winter stouts. Boag's produces similar beers to the Cascade brews, such as its premium lager and draught.

Tasmanian Whisky

In recent years Tasmania, with it's chilly Scotland-like highlands and clean water, has become a whisky-producing hot spot. There are about a dozen distillers around the state now, bottling superb single malts for a growing international market. Sullivans Cove Whisky, based at Cambridge near Hobart, has been racking up world whisky awards but doesn't as yet have a cellar door you can visit. If you're keen for a wee dram, stop by Lark Distillery (p53) in Hobart, Redlands Estate Distillery (p88) in the Derwent Valley, Nant Distillery (p133) in Bothwell or Hellyers Road Distillery (p217) in Burnie.

When We Eat: A Seasonal Celebration of Fine Tasmanian Food and Drink by Liz McLeod, Bernard Lloyd and Paul County is the companion guide to *Before We Eat*. It covers the availability of seasonal foods in the state, accompanied by great recipes and photographs.

GOURMET TASMANIA TASMANIAN BEER

Wilderness & Wildlife

Tasmania is the size of a small European country – plenty of room for the island's unique flora and fauna to live, thrive and survive. A roll call of quirky species reinforces Tasmania's unique appeal, and travellers have plenty of opportunities – both structured and spontaneous – to see a Tasmanian devil, a platypus, a Cape Barren goose... The backdrop to this animal hubbub is the state's amazing wilderness, comprising some of the planet's most important natural heritage areas.

The website of the Parks & Wildlife Service (www.parks.tas. gov.au) is an absolute gold mine of information on the Tasmanian wilderness and how best to access it. Download fact sheets on national parks, bushwalks, plants and wildlife, camping grounds within parks and loads more.

Tasmanian Wilderness

Adrift some 240km south of Victoria, across tumultuous Bass Strait, Tasmania is Australia's only island state and also its smallest. Including its offshore islands, Tasmania's surface area is 68,401 sq km – slightly smaller than Ireland and slightly larger than Sri Lanka. To the east is the Tasman Sea, separating Australia and New Zealand; to the south and west the Southern Ocean rolls nonstop to Antarctica. Most folks fly into Tasmania from mainland Australia in an hour or two at the most. It seems so accessible, but really, this island is a long way from anywhere. Walking through the Tasmanian wilderness, the sense of remoteness is palpable and utterly delicious.

Rugged but Beautiful

Welcome to Australia's most compact, yet diverse, state. Unlike much of mainland Australia, flat land is a rarity here. Tasmania's highest mountain, Mt Ossa, peaks out at just 1617m, but much of the island's interior is extremely vertiginous. One indication of the lack of level ground is the proximity of central Hobart and Launceston to some rather impressive hills – life in the suburbs here often involves having steep driveways and strong leg muscles!

Tasmania's intricate coastline is laced with coves and beaches, shallow bays and broad estuaries – the result of river valleys flooding as sea levels rose after the last ice age. By contrast, the island's Central Highlands were covered by a single ice sheet during that ice age. This bleak (but amazingly beautiful) landscape remains a harsh environment, dotted with lakes, dappled with winter snow and completely unsuitable for farming.

Showing the scars of recent glaciation, most of Tasmania's west coast is a twisted nest of mountain ranges, ridges and formidable ocean beaches. The climate here is inhospitable: the coastline is pummelled by uncompromising seas and annual rainfall clocks in somewhere upwards of 3m. But on an overpopulated planet, this kind of wilderness is increasingly rare; the west's cliffs, lakes, rainforests and wild rivers are among Tasmania's greatest attractions and irresistible temptations for walkers, adventurers and photographers.

By the time the rain clouds make it over to the east coast, they've usually dumped their contents out west, and have become fluffy and benign rather than grey and menacing. The east coast is sunny and beachy, with a sequence of laid-back holiday towns and photogenic white-sand beaches.

The fertile plains of the Midlands area is Tasmania's agricultural heartland – east of the harsh Central Highlands, but not so far east that rainfall becomes an anomaly.

National Parks & Reserves

A greater percentage of land – around 40% – is allocated to national parks and reserves in Tasmania than in any other Australian state. The Tasmania Parks & Wildlife Service (PWS) manages around 800 reserves, including 19 national parks, covering over 27,000 sq km. More than 2000km of superb walking tracks, unique flora and abundant fauna combine to create a mecca for naturalists, bushwalkers, wildlife watchers, campers and photographers. Roughing it in the wild is always an option – trek through the inspiring natural beauty of the southwest, or escape civilisation on a raft down the free-flowing Franklin River – but guided walks, scenic flights and river cruises also open this world up to travellers seeking a gentler Tasmanian experience.

National Parks

Tasmania's 19 national parks are awesome, in the truest sense of the word. Walk along a trail and scale a peak, or visit a few parks and come to grips with the island's environmental diversity, which includes highland lakes, surging rivers, ocean-swept beaches, craggy coves, wildlife-rich islands, jagged ranges and lush temperate rainforest.

Public access to the national parks is encouraged as long as safety and conservation regulations are observed. The golden rules: don't damage or alter the natural environment, and don't feed wild animals. Most of the parks are easily accessed by vehicle, but two – Savage River in the heart of the Tarkine wilderness, and the Kent Group of islets in Bass Strait – are virtually inaccessible. Walls of Jerusalem National Park has no road access directly into the park itself, but there is a car park a steep 30-minute walk down from the park boundary.

When to Visit

Most people visit Tasmania's national parks during summer (December to February) to enjoy long days and warm weather (although Tasmania can receive snow in December!). Visiting outside these months sees smaller crowds and seasonal diversity: autumn features mild weather and the changing colours of deciduous beech forests; winter sees snow on the peaks; spring brings on a surge of wild flowers.

Park Fees

Visitor fees apply to all national parks, even when there's no rangers' office or roaming ranger on duty. Funds from entry fees remain with the Parks & Wildlife Service and go towards constructing and improving walking tracks, camping grounds, toilets, lookouts and picnic facilities, as well as funding a program to train new rangers and the popular summer 'Discovery Ranger' activities for younger visitors.

There are two main types of passes available for short-term visitors: 24-hour and holiday passes. A 24-hour pass costs $12/24 per person/vehicle; a holiday pass lasts for eight weeks and costs $30/60 per person/vehicle. Vehicle passes cover up to eight people. Annual passes ($96 per vehicle) and two-year passes ($123 per vehicle) are also available if you're a frequent visitor.

For most travellers the eight-week holiday pass is the best bet. Passes are available at most park entrances, at many visitor centres, aboard the *Spirit of Tasmania* ferries, from Service Tasmania (p36) and online at www.parks.tas.gov.au.

There are myriad camping options within Tasmania's national parks – see www.parks.tas.gov.au for info. If you plan on camping in super-popular Freycinet National Park from 18 December to 10 February or over Easter, you'll need to fill out a ballot entry online.

Access & Facilities

Information centres with walking information and history and ecology displays are at both ends of Cradle Mountain–Lake St Clair National Park, as well as at Freycinet, Mt Field and Narawntapu National Parks.

The 16 most accessible parks (ie not the Savage River, Kent Group and Walls of Jerusalem National Parks) all have short walking tracks, toilets, shelters and picnic areas for day visitors to use; many also have barbecues. The entire Tasmanian Wilderness World Heritage Area and most national park areas have been declared 'fuel-stove only' to protect the natural environment – this means no campfires. Dogs are definitely not allowed in any of the national parks.

Established camp sites are available in all accessible parks, except for the Hartz Mountains, Mole Creek Karst and Rocky Cape National Parks. Some sites are free, while others have a small charge per person (generally $6 to $13 for an unpowered site) in addition to park entry fees. Ben Lomond, Cradle Mountain–Lake St Clair, Freycinet, Maria Island and Mt Field National Parks also have accommodation options inside their boundaries, ranging from rustic huts to five-star resorts. Click on 'Recreation' then 'Camping' on www.parks.tas.gov.au for detailed information for each park.

There are short walks suitable for wheelchair users and some prams at the Cradle Mountain–Lake St Clair, Freycinet, Mt Field, Tasman and Franklin–Gordon Wild Rivers National Parks (though wheelchair users may require assistance on these walks).

World Heritage Areas

The internationally significant **Tasmanian Wilderness World Heritage Area** (www.parks.tas.gov.au/wha) contains the state's four largest national parks – Southwest, Franklin–Gordon Wild Rivers, Cradle Mountain–Lake St Clair and Walls of Jerusalem – plus the Hartz Mountains National Park, the Central Plateau Conservation Area, the Adamsfield Conservation Area, a section of Mole Creek Karst National Park, the Devils Gullet State Reserve and part of the Liffey Falls State Reserve.

The region achieved World Heritage status in 1982, acknowledging that these parks make up one of the planet's last great, temperate wilderness areas. An area nominated for World Heritage status must satisfy at least one of 10 criteria – the Tasmanian Wilderness World Heritage Area fulfilled a record seven categories! The area comprises a grand 15,840 sq km – around 20% of Tasmania.

In 1997 the Macquarie Island World Heritage Area was proclaimed for its outstanding geological and faunal significance. Cruises (p305) are possible to this remote sub-Antarctic island 1500km southeast of mainland Tasmania.

The Tasmanian Wilderness World Heritage Area is one of only 197 natural World Heritage areas in the world. To find out what gives these places 'outstanding universal value', check out http://whc.unesco.org/en/list.

Access & Tours

Most of the World Heritage area is managed by the Parks & Wildlife Service as a publicly accessible wilderness. To get into the true heart of the area usually means trudging off on a long-range bushwalk with a tent and a week's supply of food – either independently or on a guided hike. For a considerably less demanding experience, there are also scenic flights available departing Hobart, Strahan and Cradle Valley near Cradle Mountain.

Other Protected Areas

In addition to the national parks, the Parks & Wildlife Service manages nearly 800 other terrestrial reserves. This brings the sum total land in Tasmania protected as one kind of reserve or another up to 50.1%. Most reserves are established around a significant, protected feature – often wildlife – but have fewer regulations than national parks, often allowing mining, farming, forestry or tourism development to occur. Many are small sites and include caves, waterfalls, historic sites and some coastal regions. Usually there are no entry fees to these areas, except where the government has actively restored or developed the area.

TASMANIA'S NATIONAL PARKS

PARK	FEATURES	ACTIVITIES	BEST TIME TO VISIT
Ben Lomond National Park	alpine flora, the state's main ski field	walking, skiing, rock climbing	year-round
Cradle Mountain–Lake St Clair National Park	moorlands, mountain peaks, the famed Overland Track, Australia's deepest fresh-water lake	walking, scenic flights, wildlife spotting	year-round
Douglas-Apsley National Park	dry eucalypt forest, river gorges, water-falls, wildlife, waterhole swimming	walking, swimming	summer
Franklin–Gordon Wild Rivers National Park	two grand wilderness watercourses, deep river gorges, rainforest, Frenchmans Cap, Aboriginal sites	rafting, river cruises (from Strahan)	summer
Freycinet National Park	picturesque coastal scenery, Wineglass Bay, granite peaks, great beaches, walks	walking, abseiling, sea kayaking, scenic flights, fishing	year-round
Hartz Mountains National Park	alpine heath, rainforest, glacial lakes, views of the southwest wilderness	walking, wild flowers	spring, summer
Kent Group National Park	Bass Strait islets (mostly inaccessible), fur seals, seabirds, historical significance	wildlife watching	year-round
Maria Island National Park	traffic-free island with convict history, peaceful bays, fossil-filled cliffs	walking, mountain biking, swimming	spring, summer
Mole Creek Karst National Park	more than 200 limestone caves and sinkholes, some open to the public	caving, walking	year-round
Mt Field National Park	abundant flora and fauna, alpine scenery, high-country walks, Russell Falls, Mt Mawson ski field	walking, skiing, wildlife watching	year-round
Mt William National Park	long sandy beaches, protected Forester kangaroos	walking, fishing, swimming	spring, summer
Narawntapu National Park	north-coast lagoons, wetlands, tea-tree mazes, native wildlife	swimming, walking, wildlife watching	summer, autumn
Rocky Cape National Park	bushland, rocky headlands, Aboriginal caves, exceptional marine environment	swimming, fishing, walking	summer, autumn
Savage River National Park	cool temperate rainforest inside the Tarkine wilderness; utterly secluded, no road access	walking	summer
South Bruny National Park	wild cliffs, surf and swimming beaches, heathlands, wildlife	walking, swimming, surfing, wildlife spotting, eco-cruises	spring, summer
Southwest National Park	vast multi-peaked wilderness; one of the world's most pristine natural wonders	walking, swimming, scenic flights, mountaineering, sea kayaking	summer
Strzelecki National Park	mountainous slice of Flinders island, rare flora and fauna	walking, rock climbing, wild-life watching, swimming	summer
Tasman National Park	spectacular sea cliffs and rock forma-tions, offshore islands, forests, bays and beaches, the new Three Capes Track	walking, diving, surfing, eco-cruises, fishing, sea kayaking	year-round
Walls of Jerusa-lem National Park	spectacular, remote alpine and mountain wilderness, no road access	walking	summer

Categories of Reserves

Categories of reserves managed by the PWS include state reserves such as the Hastings Caves State Reserve in the southeast and the Liffey Falls State Reserve southwest of Launceston; conservation areas such as the Arthur Pieman Conservation Area in the state's northwest and the Bay of Fires in the northeast; nature reserves; game reserves; regional reserves; historic sites such as the Richmond Gaol; and nature recreation areas such as Humbug Point Nature Recreation Area near St Helens in the northeast.

Marine Reserves

The PWS also manages seven offshore marine reserves and 14 marine conservation areas, together covering 1351 sq km, or around 7.9% of Tasmania's state coastal waters. Fishing or collecting living or dead material within Tasmanian marine reserves is illegal. Reserves include Tinderbox near Hobart, around the northern part of Maria Island, around Governor Island off the coast at Bicheno, at Port Davey and Bathurst Harbour in the southwest and Macquarie Island. See www.parks.gov.tas.au for detailed information.

Tasmanian Wildlife

Many of the distinctive mammals of mainland Australia – the marsupials and monotremes isolated here for at least 45 million years – are also found in Tasmania. But the island's fauna is not as varied as that of the rest of Australia, and there are relatively few large mammals here – no koalas and few big kangaroos, for example. Smaller mammals proliferate, but can be difficult to spot in the bush. Fortunately there are plenty of wildlife parks around the state where you can get a good look at them.

Also on view here are a dozen endemic bird species, some impressive snakes and creepy-crawlies and whales cruising the coastline.

Marsupials

Marsupial mammals give birth to partially developed young that they then protect and suckle in a pouch. The island's best-known marsupials are of course the Tasmanian tiger and Tasmanian devil. Resembling a large dog or wolf with dark stripes and a stiff tail, the Tasmanian tiger (aka thylacine) was officially declared extinct in 1986. Tasmanian devils look nothing like the Warner Bros cartoon character – they're small, nuggety, black-and-white beasts...but they do have voracious appetites and combative dispositions.

Kangaroos & Wallabies

Both the kangaroo and wallaby species found in Tasmania are related to those found on the mainland, but they're generally smaller than their northern kin. Tasmania's largest marsupial is the Forester kangaroo *(Macropus giganteus)*. Following increasing pressure from the growth of farming, Narawntapu National Park in the state's north and Mt William National Park in the northeast have been set aside to preserve these impressive animals.

The Bennett's wallaby *(Macropus rufogriseus)* thrives in colder climates (Tasmania certainly fits the bill) and is often seen angling for food at Cradle Mountain–Lake St Clair and Freycinet National Parks. They may seem cute, but please don't feed them. Animals in the wild should be feeding themselves: giving them processed foods such as bread crusts or biscuits not only teaches them to rely on visitors as their main food source, it can cause a fatal disease called 'lumpy jaw'. Bennett's wallabies are smaller than Forester kangaroos – just over 1m tall at the most – but like all native animals they can sometimes be aggressive. It is best to approach with caution.

In 1964 the original cartoon series featuring 'Taz', the Warner Bros Tasmanian devil character, lasted just five short episodes. Such was the cult status Taz achieved, however, that he was resurrected for three seasons of his own show in 1991.

TAZ

Tasmanian Devils

Assuming the thylacine is no more, the Tasmanian devil *(Sarcophilus harrisii)* is the largest carnivorous marsupial in the world. Devils mostly eat insects, small birds, rodents and carrion and can often be seen at night feasting on roadkill – a habit that unfortunately often leads to them becoming roadkill themselves. Mature devils are about 75cm long, with short, stocky bodies covered in black fur with a white blaze across their chests.

Sadly, Devil Facial Tumour Disease (DFTD; a fatal, communicable cancer) infects up to 75% of the wild population. Quarantined populations have been established in places such as Maria Island, but efforts to find a cure have thus far proved fruitless. Check out www.tassiedevil.com.au for more on DFTD and the efforts underway to eradicate it.

Possums

There are several varieties of possum in Tasmania. The sugar glider *(Petaurus breviceps)* has developed impressive webs between its legs, enabling it to glide effortlessly from tree to tree. The most common and boldest of the species is the brushtail possum *(Trichosurus vulpecula)*, which lives and sleeps in trees, but descends to the ground in search of food. Brushtails show little fear of humans and regularly conduct late-night food heists at camping grounds (you've been warned!). Don't forget to zip up your tent and carefully store leftover food, and don't panic if you hear something akin to an asthmatic Darth Vader roaming around outside your hut: possums hiss and growl at each another, particularly during mating season. A shyer (and much quieter) relation is the smaller ringtail possum *(Pseudocheirus peregrinus)*.

See black-and-white footage of a Tasmanian tiger at the Tasmanian Museum & Art Gallery in Hobart, or on YouTube. For an insightful read, pick up David Owen's *Thylacine* (2011) or Col Bailey's *Shadow of the Thylacine* (2013). For a Hollywood spin, check out surly Willem Dafoe in *The Hunter* (2011).

WILDERNESS & WILDLIFE TASMANIAN WILDLIFE

TIGER, TIGER, BURNING BRIGHT

The story of the Tasmanian tiger (thylacine), a striped, nocturnal, dog-like predator once widespread in Tasmania and in parts of mainland Australia, has two different endings.

Version one says thylacines were hunted to extinction in the 19th and early 20th centuries, with the last captive tiger dying in Hobart Zoo in 1936. Harangued, diseased and deeply misunderstood, the thylacine didn't stand much of a chance once European interests started to encroach on its terrain. It was officially declared extinct in 1986, the requisite 50 years after that last, lonely thylacine died. No specimen, living or dead, has been conclusively discovered since then, despite hundreds of alleged sightings.

Version two maintains that thylacines continue a furtive existence deep in the Tasmanian wilderness. Scientists dismiss such ideas, suggesting that inbreeding among limited numbers of survivors would have put an end to the species just as readily as the hunters' rifles.

But such is the ongoing fascination with the thylacine that sightings still occasionally make the nightly news, however frustratingly unconfirmed they may be (no-one ever seems to have a camera handy...and if they do, digital images these days are all too easily doctored and debunked). The tantalising possibility of surviving tigers also makes them prime corporate fodder: Tasmanian companies plaster tiger imagery on everything from beer bottles to licence plates and record labels.

In recent years scientists at Sydney's Australia Museum began scripting another possible ending to the tiger saga. Kicking off version three of the story, biologists managed to extract DNA from a thylacine pup preserved in alcohol since 1866. Their aim was to successfully replicate the DNA, with the long-term goal of cloning the species. Needless to say, there were many obstacles and the project drew criticism from those who would rather have seen the money spent on helping current endangered species. In 2005 the project was shelved due to the poor quality of the extracted DNA, but work done since by the University of Melbourne has raised the possibility of future success.

WILDLIFE UNDER THREAT

Since Europeans arrived, Tasmania has lost more than 30 species of plants and animals – most famously, the thylacine, or Tasmanian tiger. Currently over 600 types of flora and fauna are listed under the state's Threatened Species Protection Act.

Among Tasmania's threatened birds are the forty-spotted pardalote, orange-bellied parrot (which breeds in Tasmania then wings it back to mainland Australia) and wedge-tailed eagle. Tasmania is also home to the largest invertebrate in the world, the giant freshwater crayfish, whose numbers have been so depleted by recreational fishing and habitat destruction that it's now illegal to take any specimens from their natural habitat.

Introduced species are also having an impact. In 2001 it was reported a fox had been spotted near Longford in the state's north. Fox predation puts nearly 80 of the island's indigenous land species at enormous risk because of their vulnerability to attack from an animal against which they have no defence. Subsequent reports of the European red fox in other parts of the state confirmed the animal had been deliberately introduced to Tasmania, probably for the purposes of hunting. A full-time fox taskforce has been set up by the state government. If you see a fox, phone the **Fox Hotline** (☏1300 369 688).

Wombats

Weighing up to 35kg, Tasmania's subspecies of the common wombat *(Vombatus ursinus tasmaniensis)* is a very solid, powerfully built marsupial with a broad head and short, stumpy legs. Wombats live in underground burrows that they excavate, and are usually very casual, slow-moving characters, partly because they don't have any natural predators to worry about. Maria Island and Cradle Mountain are good places to see them. Another subspecies, *Vombatus ursinus ursinus,* once lived on all the Bass Strait islands, but is now only found on Flinders Island.

Other Endemic Marsupials

Like the Tasmanian devil, the Tasmanian pademelon *(Thylogale billardierii,* aka the rufous wallaby) is unique to the island – a small, rounded species sometimes seen hiding in forests. It's a notoriously shy creature, which you'll be lucky to see in the wild – tread quietly if you do spot one.

Other endemic marsupials include the Tasmanian bettong *(Bettongia gaimardi),* found exclusively in the east of the state and growing only to a compact 2kg; and the carnivorous eastern quoll *(Dasyurus viverrinus),* approximately the size of a domestic cat. The eastern quoll was declared extinct on the Australian mainland in 1964 (the last known sighting was believed to be in Sydney's exclusive eastern suburb of Vaucluse!), but it's common and fully protected in Tasmania.

In 2010 the Tasmanian state government developed a plan for 100,000 brushtail possums to be killed and processed for overseas sale each year. The *Wildlife Trade Management Plan for the Commercial Harvest and Export of Brushtail Possums in Tasmania* is now in place, carefully managing quotas and wild numbers.

Monotremes

The platypus and echidna are the world's only two living monotremes – mammals that lay eggs.

Monotremes are often regarded as living fossils, and although they display some of the intriguing features of their reptile ancestors (egg-laying, and that their reproductive, defecatory and urinary systems utilise a single outlet), they suckle their young on milk secreted from mammary glands.

Platypuses

Up to 50cm long, the platypus *(Ornithorhynchus anatinus)* lives in fresh water and burrows into riverbanks. It has a leathery, duck-like bill, webbed feet and a beaverish body. You're most likely to see one in a stream or lake, searching out food in the form of crustaceans, worms and tadpoles with its electro-sensitive bill. They're notoriously shy: if you want to spot one in the wild, look for telltale lines of small bubbles tracking across the surface of a waterway and sit very still! Latrobe in the northwest bills itself as the 'Platypus Capital of the World'.

Echidnas

The land-based echidna *(Tachyglossus aculeatus)* is totally different to the platypus. It looks similar to a porcupine, and is covered in impressively sharp spikes. Echidnas primarily eat ants and have powerful claws for unearthing their food and digging into the dirt to protect themselves when threatened. They're common in Tasmania, but if you approach one all you're likely to see up close is a brown, spiky ball. However, if you keep quiet and don't move, you might be lucky – they have poor eyesight and will sometimes walk right past your feet.

Birds

Tasmania has a wide variety of seabirds, parrots, cockatoos, honeyeaters, hawks, owls, falcons, eagles and wrens, flitting through the undergrowth, on the prowl at night and soaring around sea cliffs. There are 12 species endemic to Tasmania, including the forty-spotted pardalote, black currawong, Tasmanian thornbill, green rosella and Tasmanian native hen. If you're a mad-keen twitcher, sign up for a comprehensive tour with Bruny Island's Inala Nature Tours (p113). Inala is also a driving force behind October's annual Bruny Island Bird Festival (p113).

Black Currawongs

The black currawong *(Stepera fuliginosa),* found only in Tasmania, lives primarily on plant matter and insects, but will sometimes kill small mammals or infant birds. You'll often see this large, black, fearless bird goose-stepping around picnic areas.

Mutton Birds

The mutton bird is more correctly called the short-tailed shearwater *(Puffinus tenuirostris).* It lives in burrows in sand dunes and migrates annually to the northern hemisphere. These small birds fly in spectacular flocks on their way back to their burrows (the same ones every year) at dusk. They are still hunted by some Tasmanians, notably around Flinders Island, and there are certain places where you will occasionally see cooked mutton bird advertised for sale.

Penguins

The little penguin *(Eudyptula minor)* is the smallest penguin in the world, and lives in burrows in Tasmania's sand dunes. Penguin spotting is a drawcard activity for tourists and is particularly fun for kids. Visitors can see Tassie's penguins waddle from the ocean to their nests just after sunset at Bruny Island, Burnie, Bicheno, Low Head and Penguin (naturally). Bring a picnic, settle in to watch the sun go down and enjoy the show.

Snakes & Spiders

Like the rest of Australia, there are plenty of creatures in Tasmania that can do you a disservice.

There are three types of snake here, and they're all poisonous. The largest and most venomous is the tiger snake *(Notechis scutatus).* There's also the copperhead *(Austrelaps superbus)* and the smaller white-lipped whip snake *(Drysdalia coronoides).* Bites are rare, as most snakes are generally shy and try to avoid humans. Tiger snakes can sometimes get a bit feisty, particularly in the late summer and especially if you tread on one (watch your step when stepping over logs into sunny patches where they may be basking). If you are bitten, don't try to catch the snake

WILDERNESS & WILDLIFE TASMANIAN WILDLIFE

WOMBAT DEFENCES

If threatened, a wombat will often dive head first into one of its tunnels, blocking the entrance with its extremely tough rear end, which is clad in extra-thick skin.

for identification, as there's a common antivenin for all three species. Instead remain as still as possible, bandage the bite site firmly and get someone else to ship you to hospital for treatment.

An eight-legged local with a long reach (up to 18cm) is the Tasmanian cave spider *(Hickmania troglodytes),* which spins horizontal mesh-webs on the ceiling of a cave to catch insects such as cave crickets (it's harmless to humans). On the toxic side of the fence are the Tasmanian funnel-web, redback and white-tailed spiders. If you're bitten by a funnel-web or redback, seek immediate medical attention. White-tailed spider bites aren't life-threatening, but can be painful and sometimes cause ulceration.

Whales

The Mammals of Australia, edited by Ron Strahan, is a complete survey of Australia's somewhat offbeat mammal species. Every species is illustrated and much of what's known about them is covered in individual species accounts, written by the nation's experts.

Southern right whales *(Eubalaena australis)* migrate annually from Antarctica to southern Australia to give birth to their calves in shallow waters. So named because they were the 'right' whales to kill, they were hunted to the point of extinction around Tasmania while sustaining a lucrative industry. Numbers have recovered: they're now regularly seen migrating along the east coast (in November and December especially). Whales have also made a return to Hobart's Derwent River estuary, where they were once so plentiful that locals joked they could walk across the river on their backs.

Long-finned pilot whales *(Globicephala melas)* are also common, and sadly are often involved in beach strandings around the Tasmanian coast.

Tasmanian Flora

Tasmania's myriad flora ranges from the dry forests of the east, through the alpine moorlands and buttongrass plains of the centre, to the temperate rainforests of the west. Many of the state's plants are unlike those found in the rest of Australia, with ties to species that grew millions of years ago when the southern continents were joined at the hip as Gondwana. Similar plants are found in South America and fossilised in Antarctica.

The Parks & Wildlife Service website (www.parks.tas.gov.au) has comprehensive information on Tasmanian flora: click on 'Nature & Conservation' then 'Plants'.

Pines

Many of Tasmania's trees are unique to the state – the island's native pines are particularly distinctive. The best known is the Huon pine which can live for thousands of years. Other slow-growing island pines include the King Billy pine, celery-top pine and pencil pine, all of which exist commonly at higher altitudes and live for around 500 years. Some pencil pines on the Central Plateau have managed to hang in there for 1000 years, but they're especially vulnerable to fire.

Huon Pine

Prized by shipwrights and furniture makers for its rich, golden hue, rot-resistant oils, fine grain and fragrance, Tasmania's Huon pine *(Lagarostrobos franklinii)* is one of the slowest-growing and longest-living trees on the planet. Individual trees can take 2000 years to reach 30m in height and live to 3000 years, a situation overlooked by 19th-century loggers and shipbuilders, who plundered the southwest forests in search of this 'yellow gold'. Fortunately it's now a protected species. Most of the Huon pine furniture and timber work you'll see around the state is recycled, or comes from dead trees salvaged from riverbeds and hydroelectric dams. Some older trees remain: one 2500-year-old beauty can be viewed during cruises on the Gordon River.

CHALLENGES FOR BUSHWALKERS

A notable component of the understorey in Tasmanian forests is the infamous horizontal scrub, a plant that can make life hell for bushwalkers if they veer off established tracks. More familiar (and considerably more benign) is buttongrass (*Gymnoschoenus sphaerocephalus*). Growing in thick clumps up to 1m high, this uniquely Tasmanian grass prefers broad, swampy areas like the many flat-bottomed valleys in the Central Highlands, pressed out by glacial action during ice ages. Buttongrass plains are usually muddy and unpleasant to walk through – in many places the Parks & Wildlife Service has incorporated sections of elevated boardwalk enabling hikers to steer clear of the mud.

Another interesting specimen is the cushion plant, which is found in alpine areas and at first sight resembles a green rock. In fact, it's an extremely tough, short plant that grows into thick mats ideally suited to helping it cope with its severe living conditions. It's not so tough, however, that it can tolerate footprints – stepping on one can destroy thousands of tiny leaves, which take decades to regenerate.

Beech & Eucalyptus

The dominant tree of the wetter forests is myrtle beech, similar to European beeches. Tasmania's many flowering trees include the leatherwood, which is nondescript most of the year but erupts into bright flowers during summer. Its white and pale-pink flowers yield a uniquely fragrant honey.

Many of Tasmania's eucalyptus trees also grow on the mainland, but down on the island they often grow ludicrously tall. The swamp gum (*Eucalyptus regnans;* known as mountain ash on the mainland) can grow to 100m in height and is the tallest flowering plant in the world. Look for it in the forests of the southwest, where you'll also find the state's floral emblem, the Tasmanian blue gum (*Eucalyptus globulus*).

In autumn you might catch an eyeful of the deciduous beech, the only truly deciduous native plant in Australia. It usually grows as a fairly straggly bush with bright green leaves. In autumn, however, the leaves become golden and sometimes red, adding a splash of colour to the forests. The easiest places to see this lovely autumnal display are the Cradle Mountain–Lake St Clair and Mt Field National Parks.

Horizontal Scrub

The skinny horizontal scrub (*Anodopetalum biglandulosum*) is a feature of the undergrowth in many parts of Tasmania's southwest. It grows by sending up thin, vigorous stems whenever an opening appears in the forest canopy. The old branches soon become heavy and fall over, then put up shoots of their own. This continuous process of growth and collapse creates dense, tangled thickets – bushwalkers have been rumoured to completely disappear into it when venturing off the beaten track. You can see twisted examples of horizontal scrub in the southwest's forests and in the Hartz Mountains.

King's Lomatia

This member of the *Proteaceae* family has flowers similar to those of the grevillea, and grows in the wild in only one small part of the Tasmanian Wilderness World Heritage Area. Studies of the plant's chromosomes have revealed that it's incapable of reproducing sexually, which is why it must rely on sending up shoots to create new plants. Further research has shown that there's absolutely no genetic diversity within the population, which means that every king's lomatia in existence is a clone. It's the oldest known clone in the world, thought to have been around for at least 43,600 years.

Environmental Politics in Tasmania *Anna Krien*

It was the loss of Lake Pedder that first divided Tasmanians. In spite of its national park status, the glacial lake with a pink quartz beach was flooded in 1972 to create the Gordon Dam. Tasmania was, and still is, consistently passed over for manufacturing investments, and the state government was intent on luring industry to the island with the offer of cheap electricity.

Anna Krien's debut book, *Into the Woods: The Battle for Tasmania's Forests* (2010), won both the Queensland and Victorian Premier's Literary Awards in 2011.

The 1960s was also a heady time of naturalist and hiking groups, as a newfound appreciation of the Australian landscape was emerging and protesters seemed to converge at the lake. Ignoring a nationwide petition to save Lake Pedder (with over 250,000 signatures, it was the largest conservation petition at the time in Australia's history), both state political parties declared the lake a 'non issue'. This led to the formation of the United Tasmania Group (later to become the Greens), which became the first political Green party in the world, and has haunted the island's entrenched two-party political system ever since.

Saving the Franklin River

In 1976 when the Franklin River fell in the sights of the Hydro-Electric Commission (HEC) the activists were ready. Lessons learned from the failure of saving Lake Pedder came to the fore as they ignited a nationwide campaign that would become the most famous environmental fight in Australia's history. At its peak, hundreds of people swarmed to the wild river's edge to protest, as workers and bulldozers cut a path to the banks. A core political team, led by Greens leader Bob Brown, pushed for a national referendum on the river's fate.

In 1981 the pressured federal Liberal party offered a compromise – voters could choose between a 'big' dam and a 'little' dam. Almost half of Australian voters scrawled 'NO DAM' across the scrap of paper and dropped them into the ballot boxes with disdain. A third of Tasmania's voters did the same. Sniffing the wind, leader of the federal Labor opposition, Bob Hawke, told a crowd gathered at a 'Save the Franklin' rally, that he would protect the Franklin if he were elected. His wife Hazel, standing beside him, wore yellow dangly earrings with 'No Dam' placarded on them.

Finally, in 1983, after 1272 protesters had been arrested, 1324 charges laid and 447 people jailed in the island's maximum-security prison including Bob Brown, who went from prison to taking a seat in state parliament in a four-week turnaround, the federal election swung to the Labor party. Tasmania's state government tried to repeal federal orders to reverse construction on the river in the High Court, but lost by one vote. It was the local conservation movement's first victory, and the Wilderness Society was formed – now a nationwide advocacy group and major player in the island's conservation. But the victory was not without a large degree of trauma and bitter division. Hours after the river's safety was ensured and hundreds of jobs therefore dismissed, a 2000-year-old protected tree was axed, drilled and filled with diesel and set alight.

Logging & Woodchipping Industries

To this day, the division continues. But the conservation movement's enemy is no longer hydro-electricity. It is the logging industry, in particular – woodchipping. According to the *Wood Resource Quarterly,* in 2013 Australian woodchip exports rose to 3.3 million tonnes. Plantation timbers account for much of the export market, but native forests are still being logged for woodchips.

In 1972 four companies had locked-in contracts for Tasmanian native forest woodchips to the value of $460 million. Initially promoting their work as an act of frugality, woodchip companies claimed they were simply using the 'waste on the forest floor' left behind by loggers. Loggers who had been selectively felling mature trees for sawlogs for generations, however, accused the newcomers of taking away their future yield. Woodchippers had introduced 'clearfelling' – wherein they literally mowed a logging coupe flat by carting away useful trees and burning the rest. It became clear that the 'waste' the loggers left behind, was the actual forest. Fights broke out between the two crews, but the chippers took priority. Woodchips were an accountant's dream – cheap public forest, a resource extraction method that requires little delicacy or skill, quick turnaround, and a seemingly insatiable market in Japan and China, who turned the high volume, low-value product into pulp and paper. Soon loggers were instructed to cut all sawlog trees in one swoop, whether the resource was mature or not, and let the chippers take the rest.

Excepting a few mills on the mainland licensed to chip the butts and heads of trees felled for sawlog purposes (as well as use of the residue from sawmills) this ideology of waste efficiency is mostly spin.

Semantics & Stickers

Many Australians refer to Tasmania's forests conflict as the 'forest wars' and in this vein, like all wars, visitors to the island will need to wade through a significant amount of propaganda and spin.

It can be a semantic nightmare. Conservation groups produce aerial shots of scarred charcoal swathes of land, using words such as 'Hiroshima' and 'rape', while pro-timber organisations respond with photographs revealing a 'tapestry' of new growth. Even more confusing are the statistics. From state forestry and the timber industry, you'll hear that 45% of the island's forests are protected, 95% of 'high quality' wilderness is in reserves and 79% of all old growth forest is safe from logging. From green groups however, 30% of Tasmania's original forest is protected from logging and 70% has either been destroyed or is still available for logging.

It's often said that each glut of car stickers in Tasmania signals a new chapter in the feud. Visitors to the island may want to keep an eye out for these as well as for the wildlife. The Franklin River campaign produced pro-dam stickers that read 'Save a job, shoot a Green', 'Fertilise the Forest: Doze in a Greenie' and 'Keep Warm This Winter: Burn a Greenie'.

See the website of Forestry Tasmania (www.forestrytas.com.au) for its views on how both sides of the Tasmanian logging debate – economic and environmental – can be managed sustainably.

ENVIRONMENTAL POLITICS IN TASMANIA ANNA KRIEN LOGGING & WOODCHIPPING INDUSTRIES

In response, 'No Dam' was plastered defiantly across the country. More recent stickers include 'Save the Styx', 'Tasmania: The Corrupt State' and 'I love Tassie's forests, so SUE me', alluding to the Gunns 20 case in 2004, which saw local woodchipping company Gunns Limited bring a $6.3 million lawsuit against 20 protesters.

Gunns & the Pulp Mill

A 21st-century addition to bumpers and rear windscreens was a 'No Pulp Mill' sticker, in regards to a $2.3 billion pulp mill proposed by Gunns Limited in the Tamar Valley. And while the prospect of the pulp mill didn't have quite the same romantic appeal as the Franklin River or Lake Pedder, it did, however, broaden the depth of the island's green movement into a coalition of convenience. In particular, residents of the Tamar Valley proved more difficult to deal with than Gunns expected; many disbelieved the company's claims that their health, their economies and the environment would be taken into consideration and would be unaffected by the mill.

Gunns' monopoly compromised local timber workers' bargaining power when it came to their rights, wages and compensation. The com-

SIMPLE STEPS FOR SAVING THE FORESTS

Tasmania's wild and scenic beauty, along with a human history dating back 30,000 years, is a priceless heritage available to all of us. The waterfalls, wildlife, wild rivers, lovely beaches, snowcapped mountains and turquoise seas are abundant and accessible for locals and visitors alike.

Because we are all creations of nature – the curl of our ears is fashioned to pick up the faintest sounds of the forest floor – we are all bonded to the wilds. Yet around the world, wilderness is a fast-disappearing resource and Tasmania is no exception.

Truckloads of the island's native forests, including giant eucalypt species producing the tallest flowering plants on earth, arrive at the woodchip mills, en route to Japan and China. After logging, the forests are firebombed and every wisp of fur, feather and flower is destroyed. These great forests, built of carbon, are one of the world's best hedges against global warming. They are carbon banks. Yet they are being looted, taken from our fellow creatures and all who come after us. The log trucks on Tasmania's highways are enriching banks of a different kind.

Over two decades ago, people-power saved Tasmania's wild Franklin and Lower Gordon Rivers, which nowadays attract hundreds of thousands of visitors to the west coast. Those visitors, in turn, bring jobs, investment and local prosperity. Saving the environment has been a boon for the economy and employment.

The rescue of Tasmania's forests relies on each of us, and there are plenty of ways we can help. We can help with letters or phone calls to newspapers, radio stations or politicians; with every cent donated to the forest campaigners; and in every well-directed vote. The tourist dollar speaks loudly in Tasmania, so even overseas travellers, who cannot vote, should take the opportunity to write letters to our newspapers and politicians. With each step we take, we move toward ending this destruction of Tasmania's wild and scenic heritage.

Dr Bob Brown
Former senator and leader of the Australian Greens, Bob Brown was elected to the Tasmanian parliament in 1983 and first elected to the Senate in 1996. His books include The Valley of the Giants (The Wilderness Society, with Vica Bayley, 2005), and Optimism – Reflections on a Life of Action (Hardie Grant Books, 2014). Read more about Bob Brown at www.bobbrown.org.au.

pany also leased vast swathes of state land, enjoyed first buyer's rights over much of the state's unprotected native forest and was the biggest private landowner on the island. Its directors also appeared to have a direct line to the state's political powerbrokers.

Prior to Gunns' announcing its pulp mill proposal in 2005, the state government rolled out a 'Pulp Mill Taskforce'. The $1.4 million tax-paid initiative, which included a touring promotional minibus, sought to convince locals that the island needed a pulp mill. Controversially, Labor premier Paul Lennon appeared on pro-pulp-mill TV advertisements and it was reported in the *Tasmanian Times* that he also had a Gunns' building subsidiary do his home renovations during an independent assessment of the company's mill proposal. During this time, the independent panel was blighted with numerous resignations, as three key members – Christopher Wright, a retired Supreme Court judge; Dr Warwick Raverty, known as the country's 'go to' pulp mill expert; and Julian Green, a senior bureaucrat – accused the state government and Gunns of intimidation and bullying. Adding to this quagmire of controversy, two board members – former premier Robin Gray and director John Gay – were forced to resign by the company's own investors, who demanded that Gunns receive globally recognised ethical certification before any progress on the pulp mill could be made.

Gunns' finances subsequently went into a tailspin from which it has not recovered. In 2011 the company sold its Triabunna woodchip mill to millionaire Tasmanian conservationists Jan Cameron (co-founder of Kathmandu) and Graeme Wood (founder of Wotif.com). Following this, in 2012 Gunns went into voluntary administration. At the time of writing, the site of the proposed pulp mill remains empty.

The Wilderness Society (www.wilderness.org.au) is a national not-for-profit environmental organisation that got its start in Tasmania in the 1970s, protesting against the construction of the Hydro-Electric Commission dam that flooded Lake Pedder. Check the website for issues currently on their agenda.

The Statement of Principles

In 2010 the *Statement of Principles* agreement regarding the state's forest wars was negotiated. This pact – largely driven by broad opposition to the pulp mill – is widely believed to be different to the past 30 years of forestry inquiries, impact statements, court cases, legislation and subsequent amendments and agreements, all of which also claimed to be the last of their kind but seemed only to further entrench the conflict. This recent roundtable discussion between the forest industry, timber workers *and* conservation groups, has produced a carefully worded statement proposing to phase out logging the island's native forests for commodities such as woodchips, and has called for a moratorium on the logging of high-conservation-value forests.

The *Statement of Principles* didn't congeal into something more concrete until 2011, with the signing of the *Tasmanian Forests Intergovernmental Agreement* (TFIA). The delay was mainly due to the federal government not being willing to hand over funding without careful thought – and with good cause. In 2005, in a deal struck between then-prime minister, John Howard, and premier Paul Lennon, $250 million was given to the island's timber industry to restructure and shift into a sustainable future. A subsequent investigation by the Australian National Audit Office suggested that the distribution of these funds was rushed, not transparent and failed commonly accepted standards for grants.

The Tasmanian Forests Intergovernmental Agreement & Beyond

Following on from the establishment of the *Statement of Principles*, in 2011 left-wing Labor Australian prime minister Julia Gillard and Tasmanian premier Lara Giddings signed the *Tasmanian Forests Intergovernmental Agreement,* along with environmental groups, union bodies and forestry associations. The TFIA struck an accord between Tasmania and the Australian Commonwealth, guaranteeing a sustainable supply of plantation and native timber for the forestry industry while establishing new old-growth forest reserves within the state. The $277 million agreement allocated funds towards regional development projects, protection and management of old-growth forests, and community and mental-health support.

The TFIA was finally passed into legislation by state parliament in 2013. Then in 2014 a new conservative Liberal Tasmanian state government was elected on a platform of reducing unemployment, ousting Labor who had held power for 16 years. The Tasmanian parliament promptly voted to abandon the TFIA. This turn of events enshrined a six-year moratorium period, after which the logistics and impact of resuming logging in old-growth areas will be reassessed. It seems the momentary truce between Tasmania's pro- and anti-logging factions has ended. Perhaps these divisions are too deeply embedded in economy, politics, community and morality to ever be resolved.

A change of attitude on the island is required. Tasmania is a beautiful, but poor state. Many of those that want to protect the wilderness say the island can survive on tourism, while those who are 'pro-development at all cost' rely on short-term job creation via government capitalisation projects and natural resource extraction. In truth, neither of these economies can keep the island afloat alone, and nor are they the only options. As many locals will tell you, there is a lot more to Tasmania than trees.

The **Tasmanian Conservation Trust** (www.tct.org.au) is the state's primary nongovernmental conservation organisation. In addition to managing its own campaigns, the TCT has been active in its support of other community based environmental organisations including the National Threatened Species Network and the Marine and Coastal Community Network.

ENVIRONMENTAL POLITICS IN TASMANIA ANNA KRIEN

Survival Guide

Directory A–Z

Accommodation

Accommodation in Tasmania includes camping grounds, hostels, B&Bs, guesthouses, eco-resorts, heritage and boutique hotels and motels. Main tourist centres are often fully booked in summer, over Easter and on public holidays – book ahead. Weekend visits are popular with mainland Australians – look for cheaper midweek and off-peak packages for good discounts.

In most areas you'll find seasonal price variations. Over summer (December to February) and in school and public holidays, prices are highest. The cooler winter off-peak season (June to August) offers lower rates.

Ask about car parking when booking accommodation for central Hobart and Launceston.

Discover Tasmania (www. discovertasmania.com) Tasmania's official tourism website offers online accommodation booking.

Green Getaways Australia (www.greengetawaysaustralia. com.au) Concise listings of environmentally aware accommodation.

Tasmanian Accommodation (www.tasmanianaccommodation.com) Comprehensive listings of all kinds of island accommodation.

Tasmania Luxury Accommodation (www.tasmaniluxuryaccommodation.com. au) Resorts, boutique hotels and luxury B&B accommodation: high-end stuff.

Camping

Camping in most national parks requires you to purchase a parks pass and then pay a small (unpowered) site fee (usually couple/child/family $13/2.50/16, additional adult $5). Facilities are generally pretty basic, but often include toilets, picnic benches and fireplaces (BYO wood). There are also plenty of free camp sites in national parks, with minimal facilities. Forestry Tasmania also offers a few simple camp sites.

Other than at a few particularly popular places (eg Freycinet National Park on the east coast) it's not possible to book national park camp sites...so arrive early! Organise national parks passes in advance (unless there's a park visitor information centre where you can purchase one on-site). Camping fees are payable either on-site in deposit boxes, or at visitor centres.

Parks & Wildlife Service (www.parks.tas.gov.au) Click on 'Recreation', then 'Camping'. Also the hub for info on national parks passes.

Camping Tasmania (www. campingtasmania.com) A deep reservoir of Tasmanian camping info.

Caravan Parks

Tasmania also has plenty of commercial caravan parks, with hot showers, kitchens and laundry facilities. Unpowered sites for two people generally fall into the $20 to $30 price bracket; powered sites usually range from $30 to $37. Some parks offer cheap dorm-style accommodation and on-site cabins. Cabin configurations vary, but expect to pay $90 to $150 for two people in a cabin with a small bathroom and kitchenette.

Caravan Parks Tasmania (www.caravanparkstasmania. com) Comprehensive website, detailing all of Tasmania's caravan parks.

Guesthouses & B&Bs

Tasmania's B&Bs occupy everything from restored convict-built cottages to upmarket country manors and

---

BOOK YOUR STAY ONLINE

For more accommodation reviews by Lonely Planet authors, check out http://lonelyplanet.com/hotels/. You'll find independent reviews, as well as recommendations on the best places to stay. Best of all, you can book online.

beachside bungalows. Some places advertised as B&Bs are actually self-contained cottages with breakfast provisions supplied. Only in the cheaper B&Bs will bathroom facilities be shared. Some B&B hosts may cook dinner for guests (usually 24 hours' notice is required). Rates usually range from $140 to $300 per double.

Beautiful Accommodation (www.beautifulaccommodation. com) A select crop of luxury B&Bs and self-contained houses.

Hosted Accommodation Tasmania (www.tasmanianbedandbreakfast.com) B&Bs, homestays and farmstays.

Oz Bed & Breakfast (www.ozbedandbreakfast.com) Nationwide website with good Tasmanian listings.

Hostels

The established YHA network in Tasmania comprises just four hostels, but backpacker accommodation can be found in most major towns. Often you'll need to supply your own bed linen, or sheets can be rented for around $5. Sleeping bags are usually a no-no.

INDEPENDENT HOSTELS

Tasmania has plenty of independent hostels, but standards vary enormously. Many are old rabbit-warren pubs that have been transformed into backpackers, with rowdy bar areas and makeshift bathroom facilities, while others are converted motels where all rooms have private bathrooms. Newer purpose-built hostels generally have tidier facilities, with good communal areas and plenty of bathroom space. Other good places are small, intimate hostels where the owner is also the manager.

Independent backpacker establishments typically charge $25 to $30 for a dorm bed and $70 to $80 for a twin or double room with shared bathroom (upwards of $100 if there's a private bathroom).

Backpacker Tasmania (www.backpackertasmania. com) Backpacker listings around the state.

YHA HOSTELS

Tasmania has four hostels as part of the **Youth Hostels Association** (YHA; Map p54; ☑03-6234 9617; www.yha.com. au). They are in Hobart, Bridport, Strahan and Coles Bay. YHA hostels offer dorms, twin and double rooms, and cooking and laundry facilities. The vibe is generally less 'party' than in independent hostels. Most have noticeboards offering shared rides and advertising seasonal and part-time work.

Nightly charges start at $25 for members; hostels also take non-YHA members for an extra $3. Australian residents can become YHA members for $42 for one year ($32 if you're aged between 18 and 25). Join online or at any YHA hostel. Families can also join: just pay the adult price, then kids under 18 can join for free.

The YHA is part of Hostelling International (www. hihostels.com). If you already have HI membership in your own country, you're entitled to YHA rates in Tasmanian hostels.

Hotels & Motels

In Tasmania's cities, hotel accommodation is typically comfortable and anonymous, often with a heritage bent (though some newer contemporary options are appearing). Aimed at business travellers and midrange tourists (doubles generally upwards of $160), they tend to have a restaurant/cafe, room service, gym and various other facilities.

Midrange drive-up motels have similar facilities to hotels (tea- and coffee-making, fridge, TV, bathroom). There's rarely a cheaper rate for singles, so they're a better option if you're travelling as a couple or a group of three. Prices reflect standards, but you'll generally pay

between $120 and $160 for a room.

Innkeepers Collection (☑1300 130 269; www.innkeeper.com.au) Hotels, motels, lodges and apartments.

Pure Tasmania (☑1800 420 155; www.puretasmania.com. au) Upmarket hotels and resorts in Hobart, Launceston, Strahan, Cradle Mountain and Freycinet National Park.

Pubs

Some Tasmanian pubs have been restored – the new Alabama Hotel in Hobart is a prime specimen – but generally, pub rooms remain small and weathered, with a long amble down the hall to the bathroom. They're usually central and cheap – singles/doubles with shared facilities from $60/90; more if you want a private bathroom – but if you're a light sleeper, avoid booking a room above the bar and check whether a band is playing downstairs that night.

Self-Contained Apartments & Cottages

Holiday units in Tasmania are largely self-contained midrange affairs, rented on either a nightly or weekly basis. They often have two or more bedrooms – cost-effective for families and groups. Self-contained historic cottages are pricier, starting at around $200 per night, but often include breakfast provisions.

Cottages of the Colony (www.cottagesofthecolony. com.au) Self-contained historic cottages around the state.

Home Away (www.homeaway. com.au) Self-contained historic cottages and rental properties.

Tas Villas (www.tasvillas. com) Self-catering accommodation.

Other Accommodation

Long-term Accommodation
If you want to stay longer in Tasmania, noticeboards in universities, hostels, bookshops and cafes are good places to start. Shared-flat vacancies are also listed in the classified sections of the daily newspapers: Wednesday and Saturday are the best days to look. Online, check out Gumtree (www.gumtree. com.au).

WWOOFing See Willing Workers on Organic Farms (www.wwoof. com.au) for info on working on farms in return for bed and board.

Activities

Are you the outdoors type? If you're looking to do some bushwalking, fishing, rafting, sea kayaking, sailing, scuba diving or surfing, Tasmania could be your personal promised land!

Bureau of Meteorology (www.bom.gov.au/tas) Tasmanian weather can be fickle: check the forecast before you head into the wilds.

Canoe Tasmania (www.tas. canoe.org.au) Canoe and kayak club info around the state.

Inland Fisheries Service (www.ifs.tas.gov.au) Info on fishing regulations around the state.

Parks & Wildlife Service (www.parks.tas.gov.au) Click on 'Recreation' for oodles of bushwalking and camping info.

Royal Yacht Club of Tasmania (www.ryct.org. au) Swing the boom and hoist the spinnaker – sailing advice around the island.

Service Tasmania (www. service.tas.gov.au) For detailed bushwalking maps; outlets around the state.

Tasmanian Scuba Diving Club (www.tsdc.org.au) Get your goggles on and get underwater; scuba advice and events.

Tassie Surf (www.tassiesurf. com) Daily surf photos and weather updates.

Tourism Tasmania (www. discovertasmania.com) Extensive outdoor-activity info; click on 'What to Do' then 'Outdoors & Adventure'.

Trout Guides & Lodges Tasmania (www.troutguidestasmania.com.au) Trout-fishing guides and Central Highlands accommodation options.

Discount Cards

See Tasmania Attractions Pass (☑1300 366 476; www. seetasmaniapass.iventurecard.com; adult/child 3 days $199/112, 7 days $255/146, 10 days $365/155) Allows free entry to over 35 attractions and activities around Tasmania, including national parks, National Trust properties and big-ticket drawcards such as Port Arthur Historic Site and Tahune AirWalk. Children's rates apply up to age 15. Passes can be purchased online. The passes aren't cheap, however, and can only be used on consecutive days, so do some research to determine if it's a worthwhile investment. Alternatively, 'flexi' pass options allow you to visit five or seven sights

Climate

Strahan

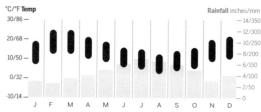

HOBART

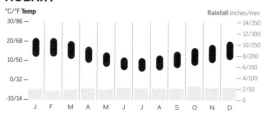

LAUNCESTON

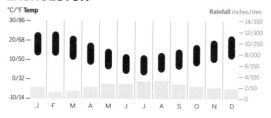

over a three-month period. Five-ticket flexi passes cost adult/child $169/99; seven-ticket passes are $219/125.

Senior Cards Travellers over 60 with some form of identification (eg a Seniors Card – www.seniorscard.com.au) are often eligible for concession prices. Most Australian states and territories issue their own versions of these, which can be used Australia-wide.

Student & Youth Cards The internationally recognised International Student Identity Card (www.isic.org) is available to full-time students aged 12 and over. The card gives the bearer discounts on accommodation, transport and admission to various attractions. The same organisation also produces the International Youth Travel Card (IYTC), issued to people under 26 years of age and not full-time students, and has benefits equivalent to the ISIC. Also similar is the International Teacher Identity Card (ITIC), available to teaching professionals. All three cards are available online or from student travel companies ($30).

Electricity

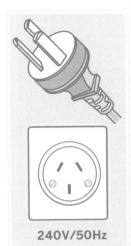

240V/50Hz

Food

For the low-down on what to expect when you sit down to eat in Tasmania, have a read of the Gourmet Tasmania chapter (p273).

Gay & Lesbian Travellers

It wasn't always the case, but Tasmania is now considered by G&L rights groups to have greater equality in criminal law for homosexual and heterosexual people than most other Australian states. But beyond the law, a lack of discrimination outside of urban centres should never be assumed.

Gay Tasmania (www.gaytasmania.com.au) Accommodation and travel info.

Q Switchboard (☎1800 184 527; www.switchboard.org.au) Telephone counselling, information and referrals.

TasPride (www.taspride.com) Based in Hobart, but a Tasmania-wide support group. A good source of info on upcoming events, including November's annual TasPride Festival.

Health

Availability & Cost of Health Care

Facilities As per the rest of Australia, Tasmania has an excellent health-care system: a mixture of privately run medical clinics and hospitals alongside public hospitals funded by the Australian government. There are also excellent specialised public-health facilities for women and children in major centres.

Medicare The Medicare system covers Australian residents for some health-care costs. Visitors from countries with which Australia has a reciprocal health-care agreement – New Zealand, the Republic of Ireland, Sweden, the Netherlands, Finland, Italy, Belgium, Malta, Slovenia, Norway

and the UK – are eligible for benefits specified under the Medicare program. Online see www.humanservices.gov.au/customer/dhs/medicare.

Medications Painkillers, antihistamines for allergies and skincare products are widely available at chemists throughout Tasmania. You may find that medications available over the counter in some countries are only available in Australia by prescription. These include the oral contraceptive pill, some medications for asthma and all antibiotics.

Health Care in Remote Areas

In Tasmania's remote locations, there could be a significant delay in emergency services reaching you in the event of serious accident or illness. An increased level of self-reliance and preparation is essential.

Consider taking a wilderness first-aid course, such as those offered at the **Wilderness Medicine Institute** (www.wmi.net.au). Take a comprehensive first-aid kit that is appropriate for the activities planned, and ensure that you have adequate means of communication. Tasmania's sometimes limited mobile-phone coverage can mean that additional radio communication is important for remote areas.

Insurance

Worldwide travel insurance is available at www.lonelyplanet.com/travel_services.

You can buy, extend and claim online anytime – even if you're already on the road. For information on car insurance, see p000.

A good travel insurance policy covering theft, loss and medical problems is essential. Some policies specifically exclude designated 'dangerous activities' such as scuba diving, skiing and even bushwalking. Make sure the policy you choose fully covers you for your activity of choice.

You may prefer a policy that pays doctors or hospitals directly rather than requiring you to pay on the spot and claim later. If you have to claim later, make sure you keep all documentation. Check that the policy covers ambulances and emergency medical evacuations by air.

Internet Access

Access You'll find internet access in libraries, cafes, hotels and hostels, plus government-funded Online Access Centres, which operate in 69 Tasmanian towns. For a complete listing of these centres, see www.linc.tas.gov.au/findus.

Wi-fi Wireless access is fast becoming a given in most Tasmanian accommodation (even across some entire town centres), but access is still limited in more isolated areas such as Bruny Island and the southeast. If you're a Telstra customer, you should be able to access the internet via your smartphone in most parts of the island.

Legal Matters

Most travellers will have no contact with Tasmania's police or legal system. If you do, it's most likely to be while driving.

Driving There's a significant police presence on Tasmanian roads – police have the power to stop your car, see your licence

(you're required to carry it), check your vehicle for roadworthiness and insist that you take a breath test for alcohol (and sometimes illicit drugs).

Drugs First-time offenders caught with small amounts of illegal drugs are likely to receive a fine rather than go to jail, but the recording of a conviction against you may affect your visa status.

Visas If you remain in Australia beyond the life of your visa, you'll officially be an 'overstayer' and could face detention and then be prevented from returning to Australia for up to three years.

Arrested? It's your right to telephone a friend, lawyer or relative before questioning begins. Legal aid is available only in serious cases; for Legal Aid office info see www.legalaid.tas.gov.au. However, many solicitors do not charge for an initial consultation.

Money

In this book, prices refer to the Australian dollar.

ATMs & Debit Cards

Tasmanian cities are flush with ATMs, but they're often absent in smaller towns. If there is a bank in a small town, it will often only be open two or three days a week. Local post offices sometimes act as agents for the Commonwealth Bank, although they are open only restricted weekday hours. In towns where there are no banks, you'll sometimes find a multi-card ATM in the local grocery store or petrol station.

Debit Cards For international travellers, debit cards connected to the international banking networks – Cirrus, Maestro, Plus and Eurocard – will work fine in Tasmanian ATMs. Expect substantial fees. A better option may be prepaid debit cards (such as MasterCard's 'Cash Passport' cards) with set withdrawal fees and a balance you can top up

from your bank account while on the road.

Credit Cards

Credit cards such as MasterCard and Visa are widely accepted for most accommodation and services, and a credit card is essential (in lieu of a large deposit) to hire a car. They can also be used to get cash advances over the counter at banks and from many ATMs, depending on the card – but be aware that these withdrawals incur immediate interest. Diners Club and American Express cards are not as widely accepted.

For lost credit cards contact the following.

American Express (1300 132 639; www.americanexpress.com.au)

Diners Club (1300 360 060)

MasterCard (1800 120 113; www.mastercard.com.au)

Visa (1800 450 346; www.visa.com.au)

Taxes & Refunds

Goods & Services Tax The GST is a flat 10% tax on all goods and services – accommodation, eating out, transport, electrical and other goods, books, furniture, clothing etc. There are exceptions, however, such as basic food items (milk, bread, fruit and vegetables etc). By law the tax is included in the quoted or shelf price, so all prices are GST-inclusive.

Refund of GST If you purchase goods with a total minimum value of $300 from any one supplier no more than 30 days before you leave Australia, you are entitled under the Tourist Refund Scheme (TRS) to a refund of any GST paid. The scheme only applies to goods you take with you as hand luggage or wear onto the plane or ship. For details, see the website of the **Australian Customs & Border Protection Service** (1300 363 263, 02-6275 6666; www.customs.gov.au).

Opening Hours

Banks	9.30am-4pm Mon-Thu, to 5pm Fri
Post offices	9am-5pm Mon-Fri, some Sat morning in cities
Pubs & bars	11am-midnight daily
Restaurants	breakfast 8-10.30am, lunch noon-3pm, dinner 6-9pm
Shops	9am-5pm Mon-Fri, 9am-noon or 5pm Sat, late-night shopping to 9pm Thu or Fri

Sunday trading for retailers is becoming more common in Tasmania, but is limited mainly to Hobart and Launceston.

Restaurants in the main eating strips of Hobart and Launceston keep longer hours than usual, but in regional Tasmania most eateries adhere to limited hours. Outside of the peak tourist season, it's sometimes necessary to book for dinner to make sure a particular establishment opens.

Photography

If you're not happily snapping away with your smartphone, digital cameras, memory sticks and batteries are sold prolifically in cities and town centres. Try electronics stores (Dick Smith, Tandy) or the larger department stores. Many internet cafes, camera stores and large stationers (Officeworks, Harvey Norman) have printing facilities.

Check out Lonely Planet's *Travel Photography* guide.

Public Holidays

The holidays listed are statewide unless otherwise indicated.

New Year's Day 1 January

Australia Day 26 January

Hobart Regatta Day 2nd Monday in February (southern Tasmania)

Launceston Cup Last Wednesday in February (Launceston only)

King Island Show 1st Tuesday in March (King Island only)

Eight Hour Day 2nd Monday in March

Easter March/April (Good Friday to Easter Tuesday inclusive)

Anzac Day 25 April

Queen's Birthday 2nd Monday in June

Burnie Show 1st Friday in October (Burnie only)

Launceston Show 2nd Thursday in October (Launceston only)

Hobart Show 3rd Thursday in October (southern Tasmania)

Flinders Island Show 3rd Friday in October (Flinders Island only)

Recreation Day 1st Monday in November (northern Tasmania)

Devonport Show Last Friday in November (Devonport only)

Christmas Day 25 December

Boxing Day 26 December

School Holidays

The Christmas/summer school-holiday season runs from mid-December to late January. Accommodation often books out. Book early for *Spirit of Tasmania* ferry services. Three shorter school holiday periods occur during the year. They fall roughly from early to mid-April, late June to mid-July, and late September to early October.

Safe Travel

Tasmania is a relatively safe place to visit, but you should still take reasonable precautions. Don't leave hotel rooms or cars unlocked and don't leave your valuables unattended or visible through a car window. Avoid walking around in cities by yourself after dark.

PRACTICALITIES

➧ **Currency** The Australian dollar comprises 100 cents. There are 5c, 10c, 20c, 50c, $1 and $2 coins, and $5, $10, $20, $50 and $100 notes.

➧ **Magazines** *Tasmania 40° South* (www.fortysouth. com.au) is a glossy quarterly magazine with food, travel and wildlife stories.

➧ **Newspapers** *The Mercury* (www.themercury.com. au) covers Hobart and the south; *The Examiner* (www. examiner.com.au) covers Launceston and the north.

➧ **Radio** Tune in to ABC radio; check out www.abc.net. au/radio.

➧ **TV** Watch the ad-free ABC, the multicultural SBS, or one of two commercial stations, WIN (the equivalent of Channel Nine) and Southern Cross (a mash-up of Channels Seven and Ten), plus additional digital channels.

➧ **Weights & Measures** The metric system is used throughout Australia.

GOVERNMENT TRAVEL ADVICE

Tasmania can seem a long way from global strife, but if you're heading beyond these island shores, the following government websites offer travel advisories and information on current hotspots.

Australian Department of Foreign Affairs & Trade (www.smarttraveller.gov.au)

British Foreign & Commonwealth Office (www.gov. uk/fco)

Government of Canada (www.travel.gc.ca)

US State Department (www.travel.state.gov)

At the Beach

Surf beaches can be dangerous places if you aren't used to the conditions. Undertows (or 'rips') are the main problem. If you find yourself being carried out by a rip, the important thing to do is just keep afloat – don't panic or try to swim against the current, which will exhaust you. In most cases the current stops within a couple of hundred metres of the shore: you can then swim parallel to the shore for a short way to get out of the rip and make your way back to land.

Insects

In the warmer months of the year, expect mosquitoes, especially around sunset. Insect repellents will deter them, but it's best to cover up. Ticks are found in moist bushy areas and can be avoided by covering up in light clothing. Most people experience little or no symptoms of bites, but occasionally paralysis or allergic reaction to their toxins can occur. If you find a tick lodged somewhere on your body, gently remove it with a pair of fine-pointed tweezers by grasping as close to the skin as possible.

Jack jumper ants have a black body and orange pincers. They are aggressive and can sometimes 'jump' from the vegetation. Bull ants (aka inchmen) are larger, with dark browny-red bodies.

Bites from both cause an allergic reaction, followed by devilish itching. Signs of an ant nest can include small pebbles at the entrance to the hole.

Leeches

Leeches may be present in damp rainforest conditions: bushwalkers often find them on their legs or in their boots. Salt or a lighted cigarette end will make them fall off. Do not pull them off, as the bite is then more likely to become infected. Clean and apply pressure if the point of attachment is bleeding. An insect repellent may keep them away and gaiters are a good idea when you're walking.

Sharks

Despite the bad rep, shark attacks are rare in Tasmania, with only four deaths in the last 50 years in state waters.

Snakes

Tasmania is home to three snake species: tiger, white-lipped and lowland copperhead snakes– see www. parks.tas.gov.au/wildlife/reptile/snakes.html. All three are venomous, but they are not aggressive and, unless you have the ill fortune to stand on one, it's unlikely you'll be bitten. Snakes are most active in summer and are often spotted on bushwalking trails around the state.

To minimise your chances of being bitten, always wear boots, socks and long trousers (ideally gaiters) when walking through undergrowth. Don't put your hands into holes and crevices and be careful if collecting firewood.

Spiders

There are only a couple of spiders to watch out for in Tasmania. The white-tailed spider is a long, thin, black spider with a white tip on its tail. It has a fierce bite that can lead to local inflammation. It is a ground scavenger and can sometimes crawl into piles of stuff left on the floor. The disturbingly large huntsman spider has a non-venomous bite. Seeing one will more likely impact on your blood pressure and/or underpants.

Telephone

Australia's main telecommunication companies all operate in Tasmania.

Telstra (☏13 22 00; www. telstra.com.au) The main player, with the best mobile coverage. Offers landline and mobile-phone services.

Optus (www.optus.com.au) Telstra's main rival. Landline and mobile-phone services.

Vodafone (☏1300 650 410; www.vodafone.com.au) Mobile-phone services.

Virgin (☏1300 555 100; www. virginmobile.com.au) Mobile-phone services.

Information & Toll-Free Calls

➡ Numbers starting with 190 are usually recorded information services, charged anything from 35c to $5 or more per minute (more from mobiles).

➡ Toll-free numbers beginning with ☏1800 can be called free of charge from anywhere in Australia, though they may not be accessible from certain areas or from mobile phones.

➡ Calls to numbers beginning with ☏13 or ☏1300 are

charged at the rate of a local call – the numbers can usually be dialled Australia-wide, but may be applicable only to a specific state or STD (Subscriber Trunk Dialling) district.

➡ Telephone numbers beginning with either ☑1800, ☑13 or ☑1300 cannot be dialled from outside Australia.

International Calls

➡ When calling overseas you need to dial the international access code from Australia (☑0011 or ☑0018), the country code and the area code (without the initial ☑0).

➡ If calling Australia from overseas the country code is ☑61 and you need to drop the ☑0 in the state/territory area codes.

➡ The **Country Direct Service** (☑1800 801 800) connects callers in Australia with operators in nearly 60 countries to make reverse-charge (collect) or credit-card calls.

Local Calls

➡ Local calls from private phones cost 30c and are untimed.

➡ Local calls from public phones cost 50c and are untimed.

➡ Calls to mobile phones attract higher rates and are timed.

Long-Distance Calls & Area Codes

➡ Australia uses four long-distance STD area codes:

STATE/ TERRITORY	AREA CODE
ACT	☑02
NSW	☑02
NT	☑08
QLD	☑07
SA	☑08
TAS	☑03
VIC	☑03
WA	☑08

➡ STD calls can be made from virtually any public phone and are cheaper during off-peak hours (7pm to 7am).

➡ Long-distance calls (more than 50km away) within these areas are charged at long-distance rates, even though they have the same area code.

➡ When calling from one area of Tasmania to another, there's no need to dial ☑03 before the local number.

➡ Local numbers start with ☑62 in Hobart and southern Tasmania, ☑63 in Launceston and the northeast, and ☑64 in the west and northwest.

Mobile (Cell) Phones

Numbers Local numbers with the prefix ☑04 belong to mobile phones.

Reception If you're not on the Telstra network, coverage can be patchy outside of Hobart, Launceston, Burnie, Devonport and the Midland Hwy. It may be worth purchasing a Telstra prepaid SIM card, though you'll still struggle in remote parts of the state.

Networks Australia's digital network is compatible with GSM 900 and 1800 (used in Europe), but generally not with the systems used in the USA or Japan. For overseas visitors GSM 900 and 1800 mobiles can be used in Australia if set up at home first – contact your service provider before you travel.

Providers It's easy enough to get connected short-term: the main service providers (Telstra, Optus, Virgin and Vodafone) all have prepaid mobile systems. Buy a starter kit, which may include a phone or, if you have your own phone, a SIM card and a prepaid charge card. Shop around between the carriers for the best offer.

Phonecards & Public Phones

A variety of phonecards can be bought at newsagents, hostels and post offices for a fixed dollar value (usually $10, $20 etc) and can be used with any public or private phone by dialling a toll-free access number and then the PIN number on the card. Shop around.

Most public phones use phonecards; some also accept credit cards. Old-fashioned coin-operated public phones are becoming increasingly rare (and if you do find one, chances are the coin slot will be gummed up or vandalised beyond function).

Time

Australia is divided into three time zones:

➡ Western Standard Time (GMT/UTC plus eight hours) applies in Western Australia

➡ Central Standard Time (GMT/UTC plus 9½ hours) covers the Northern Territory and South Australia

➡ Eastern Standard Time (GMT/UTC plus 10 hours) covers Tasmania, Victoria, New South Wales and Queensland

Daylight Saving

Daylight saving in Tasmania begins on the first Sunday in October and ends on the first Sunday in April. These arrangements are in line with Victoria, New South Wales, South Australia and the ACT. Daylight Saving does not operate in Queensland, Western Australia or the Northern Territory.

Toilets

Toilets in Tasmania are sit-down Western style (though you mightn't find this prospect too appealing in some remote spots).

See www.toiletmap.gov.au to search for public-toilet locations.

Tourist Information

Tasmanian Travelways

(www.travelways.com.au) The online version of the *Tasmanian Travelways* tourist newspaper.

Tourism Tasmania (☎03-6238 4222; www.discovertasmania.com) Tasmania's official tourism promoters. The main Tasmanian Travel & Information Centre in Hobart is a helpful spot for planning statewide travel and can handle bookings of all sorts.

Local Tourist Offices

Tasmania's main visitor information centres supply brochures, maps and local info and can often book transport, tours and accommodation. They generally open from around 8.30am or 9am to 5pm or 5.30pm weekdays, with slightly shorter hours on weekends. Info centres in smaller towns are usually staffed by volunteers (chatty retirees), resulting in less-regular opening hours.

Travellers with Disabilities

An increasing number of accommodation providers and key attractions have access for those with limited mobility, and tour operators often have the appropriate facilities: call ahead to confirm. Also check out the *Hobart CBD Mobility Map* from Hobart's visitor information centre.

Several agencies also provide information:

National Information Communication & Awareness Network (Nican; ☎02-6241 1220, TTY 1800 806 769; www.nican.com.au) Australia-wide directory providing information on access, accommodation, sports and recreational activities, transport and specialist tour operators.

ParaQuad Association of Tasmania (☎03-6228 9500; www.paraquadtas.org.au) Information for disabled travellers. Download *The Wheelie Good Guide*.

Parks & Wildlife Service (☎1300 827 727; www.parks.tas.gov.au) *Parks for all People* (PDF download) outlines access for mobility-impaired visitors to Tasmania's national parks and reserves. Click on 'Recreation' then 'Disabled Access'.

Visas

All visitors to Australia need a visa – only New Zealand nationals are exempt, and even they sheepishly receive a 'special category' visa on arrival. Application forms for the several types of visa are available from Australian diplomatic missions overseas, travel agents or the website of the **Department of Immigration & Citizenship** (DIAC; ☎13 18 81; www.immi.gov.au). Visa types:

eVisitor (651)

➡ Many European passport holders are eligible for a free eVisitor visa, allowing stays in Australia for up to three months within a 12-month period.

➡ eVisitor visas must be applied for online (www.immi.gov.au/e_visa/evisitor.htm). They are electronically stored and linked to individual passport numbers, so no stamp in your passport is required.

➡ It's advisable to apply at least 14 days prior to the proposed date of travel to Australia.

Electronic Travel Authority (ETA; 601)

➡ Passport holders from eight countries that aren't part of the eVisitor scheme – Brunei, Canada, Hong Kong, Japan, Malaysia, Singapore, South Korea and the USA – can apply for either a visitor ETA or business ETA.

➡ ETAs are valid for 12 months, with stays of up to three months on each visit.

➡ You can apply for an ETA online (www.eta.immi.gov.au), which attracts a nonrefundable service charge of $20.

Visitor (600)

➡ Short-term Visitor visas have largely been replaced by the eVisitor and ETA. However, if you're from a country not covered by either, or you want to stay longer than three months, you'll need to apply for a Visitor visa.

➡ Standard Visitor visas allow one entry for a stay of up to three, six or 12 months, and are valid for use within 12 months of issue.

➡ Apply online at www.immi.gov.au; costs range from $130 to $335.

Work & Holiday (462)

➡ Nationals from Argentina, Bangladesh, Chile, Indonesia, Malaysia, Poland, Portugal, Spain, Thailand, Turkey, the USA and Uruguay aged between the ages of 18 and 30 can apply for a Work and Holiday visa prior to entry to Australia.

➡ Once granted, this visa allows the holder to enter Australia within three months of issue, stay for up to 12 months, leave and re-enter Australia any number of times within those 12 months, undertake temporary employment to supplement a trip, and study for up to four months.

➡ For details see www.immi.gov.au/visas/pages/462.aspx. Application fee $420.

Working Holiday (417)

➡ Young (aged 18 to 30) visitors from Belgium, Canada, Cyprus, Denmark, Estonia, Finland, France, Germany, Hong Kong, Ireland, Italy, Japan, South Korea, Malta, Netherlands, Norway, Sweden, Taiwan and the UK are eligible for a Working Holiday visa, which allows you to visit for up to 12 months and gain casual employment.

➡ Holders can leave and re-enter Australia any number of times within those 12 months.

➡ Holders can only work for any one employer for a maximum of six months.

➡ Apply prior to entry to Australia (up to a year in advance) – you can't change from another tourist visa to a Working Holiday visa once you're in Australia.

➡ Conditions include having a return air ticket or sufficient funds ($5000) for a return or onward fare. Application fee $420.

➡ Second Working Holiday visas can be applied for once you're in Australia, subject to certain conditions; see www.immi.gov.au/visas/pages/417.aspx.

Visa Extensions

If you want to stay in Australia for longer than your visa allows, you'll need to apply for a new visa (usually a $335 Visitor visa 600) via www.immi.gov.au. Apply at least two or three weeks before your visa expires.

Volunteering

Volunteering is an excellent way to meet people and visit some interesting places, with a number of worthy projects active in Tasmania.

Conservation Volunteers Australia (☑1800 032 501; www.conservationvolunteers.com.au) Helps volunteers get their hands dirty with tree planting, walking-track construction and flora and fauna surveys.

Greening Australia (☑1300 886 589; www.greeningaustralia.org.au) Helps volunteers get involved with environmental projects in the bush or in plant nurseries.

Volunteering Tasmania (☑1800 677 895; www.volunteeringtas.org.au) Useful resource bringing volunteers and volunteer projects together.

Willing Workers on Organic Farms (WWOOF; ☑03-5155 0218; www.wwoof.com.au) WWOOFing is where you do a few hours work each day on a farm in return for bed and board. Most hosts are concerned to some extent with alternative lifestyles, and have a minimum stay of two nights. Join online for $70. You'll get a membership number and a booklet listing participating enterprises ($5 overseas postage).

Women Travellers

Tasmania is generally a safe place for women travellers, although the usual sensible precautions apply. It's best to avoid walking alone late at night in major towns. When the pubs close and there are drunks roaming around, it's probably not a great time to be out on your own.

Work

Casual work can usually be found during summer in the major tourist centres, mainly working in tourism, hospitality, labouring, gardening or farming.

Seasonal fruit picking is hard work and pay is proportional to the quantity and quality of fruits picked. Harvest is from December to April in the Huon and Tamar Valleys.

Grape-picking jobs are sometimes available in late autumn and early winter, as some wineries still hand-pick their crops.

Australian JobSearch (www.jobsearch.gov.au) Myriad jobs across the country.

Harvest Trail (www.jobsearch.gov.au/harvesttrail) Harvest job specialists.

National Harvest Telephone Information Service (1800 062 332) Advice on when and where you're likely to pick up harvest work.

Seek (www.seek.com.au) General employment site; good for metropolitan areas.

Travellers at Work (www.taw.com.au) Excellent site for working travellers in Australia.

Transport

GETTING THERE & AWAY

Tasmania is the land under 'the land down under'. It's a long way from just about everywhere and getting here usually means hopping on a flight.

There are no direct international flights to Tasmania. Visitors to the island state will need to get to one of Australia's mainland cities and connect to a Tasmania-bound domestic flight to Hobart, Launceston or Devonport. Melbourne and Sydney (and, to a lesser extent, Brisbane) airports have the most frequent direct air links to the island. Also popular is the *Spirit of Tasmania* passenger and car ferry, sailing between Melbourne and Devonport in Tasmania's north.

Flights, cars and tours can be booked online at lonelyplanet.com/bookings.

Entering Tasmania

Security at mainland Australian airports has increased in recent years, both in domestic and international terminals, but Tasmania's arrivals procedures are generally less time-consuming. You may, however, encounter quarantine-control 'sniffer' dogs in baggage claim areas, nosing their way through the luggage in search of illegal fruit, vegetables and whatever else they're trained to detect.

Air

There are major airports in Hobart and Launceston, as well as smaller operations at Burnie/Wynyard and Devonport. (Burnie/Wynyard airport is officially known as Burnie Airport, but is actually 19km west of Burnie, in the town of Wynyard. Some Tasmanians call the airport 'Burnie', others call it 'Wynyard'...so we refer to it as 'Burnie/Wynyard').

Flights are getting ever cheaper: it's straightforward to find a one-way flight to Hobart or Launceston for $100 to $150 from Sydney or Melbourne.

Airports
Burnie/Wynyard Airport (☑03-6442 1133; www. burnieairport.com.au; 3 Airport St, Wynyard) On the southern edge of Wynyard, 19km west of Burnie.

Devonport Airport (☑13 13 13; www.devonportairport. com.au; Airport Rd, Devonport) About 10km east of central Devonport.

Hobart Airport (☑03-6216 1600; www.hobartairport.com. au; Strachan St, Cambridge) At Cambridge, 19km east of Hobart.

Launceston Airport (☑03-6391 6222; www.launcestonairport.com.au; 201 Evandale Rd, Western Junction) About 15km south of Launceston, on the road to Evandale.

CLIMATE CHANGE & TRAVEL

Every form of transport that relies on carbon-based fuel generates CO_2, the main cause of human-induced climate change. Modern travel is dependent on aeroplanes, which might use less fuel per kilometre per person than most cars but travel much greater distances. The altitude at which aircraft emit gases (including CO_2) and particles also contributes to their climate change impact. Many websites offer 'carbon calculators' that allow people to estimate the carbon emissions generated by their journey and, for those who wish to do so, to offset the impact of the greenhouse gases emitted with contributions to portfolios of climate-friendly initiatives throughout the world. Lonely Planet offsets the carbon footprint of all staff and author travel.

Airlines

Jetstar (☎13 15 38; www.jetstar.com.au) Qantas' low-cost airline. Direct flights from Melbourne and Sydney to Hobart and Launceston.

Qantas (☎13 13 13; www.qantas.com.au) Direct flights from Sydney, Brisbane and Melbourne to Hobart and Launceston. QantasLink (the regional subsidiary) offers flights between Melbourne and Devonport.

Regional Express (Rex; ☎13 17 13; www.regionalexpress.com.au) Melbourne to Burnie/Wynyard and to King Island.

Tiger Airways (☎03-9999 2888; www.tigerairways.com.au) Melbourne to Hobart.

Virgin Australia (☎13 67 89; www.virginaustralia.com.au) Direct flights from Melbourne, Sydney, Brisbane and Canberra to Hobart, and from Melbourne, Brisbane and Sydney to Launceston.

Sea

Cruise Ship

During summer passengers from hefty international cruise ships regularly disembark onto the Hobart and Burnie waterfronts. Contact **P&O Cruises** (☎1300 159 454; www.pocruises.com.au) to see what's sailing. The **TasPorts** (www.tasports.com.au) website lists all the expected cruise-ship arrivals.

Just about the only way to see the remote Macquarie Island, proclaimed Tasmania's second World Heritage area in 1997, is to take one of the sub-Antarctic islands cruises scheduled by New Zealand-based **Heritage Expeditions** (☎1800 143 585; www.heritage-expeditions.com).

Ferry

Two **Spirit of Tasmania** (☎03-6421 7209, 1800 634 906; www.spiritoftasmania.com.au) ferries ply Bass Strait nightly in each direction between Melbourne and Devonport on northern Tasmania's coast. The regular crossing takes around 11 hours, departing

INTERSTATE QUARANTINE

There are stringent rules in place to protect the 'disease-free' agricultural status of this island state: fresh fruit, vegetables and plants cannot be brought into Tasmania. Tourists must discard all such items prior to their arrival (even if they're only travelling from mainland Australia). There are sniffer dogs at Tasmanian airports, and quarantine inspection posts at the Devonport ferry terminal. Quarantine officers are entitled to search your car and luggage for undeclared items. See http://dpipwe.tas.gov.au/biosecurity/quarantine-tasmania for detailed info.

either mainland Australia or Tasmania at 7.30pm and arriving at 6.30am. During peak periods, including Christmas, Easter and key holiday weekends, the schedule is amended to two sailings per day, departing at 9am and 9pm. Check the website for details.

Each ferry can accommodate 1400 passengers and around 650 vehicles and has restaurants, bars and games facilities. The ships' public areas have been designed to cater for wheelchair access, as have a handful of cabins.

DEPARTURE POINTS

The Devonport terminal is on the Esplanade in East Devonport; the Melbourne terminal is at Station Pier in Port Melbourne.

CABIN & SEATING OPTIONS

There is a range of seating and cabin options. 'Ocean Recliner' seats are the cheapest – a bit like airline seats (BYO earplugs and eye mask if you actually want to get some sleep). Cabins are available in twin or three- or four-berth configurations, with or without porthole windows. Or you can up the ante to a 'deluxe' cabin with a queen-size bed, TV and two windows. All cabins have a private bathroom. Child, student and pensioner discounts apply to all accommodation, except for deluxe cabins. Prices do not include meals, which can be purchased on board from the restaurant or cafeteria.

FARES

Fares depend on whether you're travelling in the peak period (mid-December to late January and Easter), or in the off-peak period (all other times). For the peak season and holiday weekends, booking ahead as early as possible is recommended.

One-way online prices (per adult) are as follows. Fares per person come down if there's more than one person per cabin. It's cheaper again if you're prepared to share a cabin with same-gender passengers who aren't travelling with you (mini dormitories!). Fares listed here are the less-flexible, non-refundable 'Spirit Fare' prices (conditions are similar to discount airlines). Check online for specials.

FARE	PEAK	OFF-PEAK
Ocean Recliner seat	$187	$96
Inside three- or four-berth cabin	$203	$129
Inside twin cabin	$248	$162
Deluxe cabin	$417	$326
Daytime sailings (seats only)	$161	n/a
Standard vehicles	$83	$83
Campervans up to 7m in length	$145	$102
Motorcycles	$58	$58
Bicycles	$5	$5

GETTING AROUND

The easiest, most flexible way to see Tasmania is to drive. But don't make the mistake of drawing up exhaustive itineraries with carefully calculated driving times between each destination. Though this is sometimes necessary to catch a particular tour, or to check in at a pre-booked B&B, you'll find many roads here to be wiggly two-lane affairs: getting from A to B usually takes longer than you think.

Many people also make the mistake of thinking they can see all of Tasmania's top attractions (Cradle Mountain, Freycinet National Park, Hobart, Port Arthur) in one week, madly dashing west, east, north and south. Slow down, or you may need a holiday when you get home!

Public transport is adequate between larger towns and popular tourist destinations (buses only – no trains!), but visiting remote sights can be frustrating due to irregular or nonexistent services. Rent a car to make the most of your time; competition keeps rental prices reasonable.

Air

Distances within Tasmania are far from huge, so air travel within the state is not very common. Of more use to travellers are the air services for bushwalkers in the southwest, and flights to King and Flinders Islands.

Par Avion (☏1800 017 557; www.paravion.com.au) Flies regularly from Launceston to Cape Barren Island (one-way from $124) just south of Flinders Island. Also runs scenic flights over the east coast and southwest, plus bushwalker transport between Hobart and Melaleuca (one-way from $230) for the South Coast Track or Port Davey Track.

Sharp Airlines (☏1300 556 694; www.sharpairlines.com) Flies between Melbourne (Essendon Airport) and Flinders Island (one-way $245), and Launceston and Flinders Island ($181). Also services King Island from Launceston ($282) and Burnie/Wynyard ($214).

Bicycle

Cycling Tasmania is one of the best ways to get close to nature (and, it has to be said, to log trucks, rain, roadkill...). Roads are generally in good shape, and traffic outside the cities is light. If you're prepared for occasional steep climbs and strong headwinds, you should enjoy the experience immensely.

Transport It's worth bringing your own bike, especially if you're coming via ferry: bike transport on the *Spirit of Tasmania* costs just $5 each way year-round. Another option is buying a bike in Hobart or Launceston and reselling it at the end of your trip – hit the noticeboards in backpackers, or bike shops in the major centres.

Rental Bike rental is available in the larger towns, or there are a number of operators offering multi-day cycling tours or experiences such as mountain biking down Mt Wellington in Hobart.

Road Rules Note that bicycle helmets are compulsory in Tasmania, as are white front lights and red rear lights if you're riding in the dark. See www.biketas.org.au for more information.

Boat

There are a few handy regional ferries around Tasmania, accessing the islands off the island.

Bruny Island Ferry (☏03-6273 6725; www.brunyislandferry.com.au; Ferry Rd, Kettering; car return $30-35, motorcycle/bike/foot passenger $5/5/free) Runs at least eight times a day from Kettering

to Bruny Island in Tasmania's southeast. To effectively explore Bruny, you'll need your own car or bicycle.

Furneaux Freight (☏03-6356 1753; www.furneauxfreight.com.au; Main St, Bridport; adult/child/car return $140/90/550) Small weekly passenger and car ferry from Bridport in Tasmania's northeast to Lady Barron on Flinders Island.

Maria Island Ferry (Map p141; ☏0419 746 668; www.mariaislandferry.com.au; adult/child return $35/25, bike/kayak $10/20) Runs a twice-daily service from Triabunna on the east coast to Maria Island National Park, carrying passengers and bicycles. Reduced services during winter.

Bus

Tasmania has a reasonable bus network connecting the major towns and centres, but weekend services can be infrequent. There are more buses in summer than in winter, but smaller towns are still not serviced terribly frequently. Small operators run useful services along key tourist routes and to smaller regional towns. The two main players – Tassielink and Redline – don't currently offer multi-trip bus passes.

Popular routes and fares include the following.

Bicheno Coach Service (☏03-6257 0293, 0419 570 293; www.freycinetconnections.com.au) From Bicheno to Coles Bay on the east coast, continuing to the start of the walking tracks in Freycinet National Park. Also connects with Tassielink buses to/from Hobart at the Coles Bay turn-off.

Calow's Coaches (Map p178; ☏03-6376 2161, 0400 570 036; www.calowscoaches.com) Services the east coast (St Marys, St Helens, Bicheno) from Launceston.

Evans Coaches (☏03-6297 1335; www.evanscoaches.com.au) Bushwalker services between Geeveston and Cockle Creek in the southeast (for the South Coast Track).

Lee's Coaches (Map p178; ☎03-6334 7979; www.lee-scoaches.com) Services the East Tamar Valley region from Launceston. Buses stop on Brisbane St.

Manions' Coaches (Map p178; ☎03-6383 1221; www.manionscoaches.com.au; 168 Brisbane St) Services the West Tamar Valley region from Launceston. Buses stop on Brisbane St.

Redline Coaches (☎1300 360 000; www.tasredline.com.au) The state's second-biggest operator. Services the Midland Hwy between Hobart and Launceston, and the north-coast towns between Launceston and Smithton.

Sainty's North East Bus Service (Map p178; ☎0400 791 076, 0437 469 186; www.saintysnortheastbusservice.com.au) Buses between Launceston and Lilydale, Scottsdale, Derby and Bridport.

Tassielink (☎03-6235 7300, 1300 300 520; www.tassielink.com.au) The main player, with extensive statewide services. From Hobart buses run south to Dover via the Huon Valley, southeast to Port Arthur, north to Launceston via the Midlands Hwy, to the east coast as far as Bicheno, and to Queenstown on the west coast via Lake St Clair.

From Launceston buses run south to Cressy, to Hobart via the Midlands Hwy, and west to Devonport, continuing to Strahan on the west coast via Cradle Mountain and Queenstown. Express services from the *Spirit of Tasmania* ferry terminal in Devonport to Launceston and Hobart also available.

Car & Motorcycle

Travelling with your own wheels gives you the freedom to explore to your own timetable, and you can crank up the AC/DC as loud as hell!

You can bring vehicles from the mainland to Tasmania on the *Spirit of Tasmania* ferries, so renting may only be cheaper for shorter trips. Tasmania has the usual slew of international and local car-rental agencies.

Motorcycles are a cool way to get around the island: the climate is OK for bikes most of the year.

Automobile Associations

Under the auspices of the **Australian Automobile Association** (AAA; ☎02-6247 7311; www.aaa.asn.au), the **Royal Automobile Club of Tasmania** (RACT; Map p50; ☎03-6232 6300, roadside assistance 13 11 11; www.ract.com.au; cnr Murray & Patrick Sts, Hobart; ⊙8.45am-5pm Mon-Fri) provides an emergency breakdown service to members, with reciprocal arrangements with services in other Australian states and some overseas organisations. Also good for tourist literature, maps and accommodation and camping guides.

Driving Licence

To drive in Australia you'll need to hold a current driving licence issued in English from your home country. If the licence isn't in English, you'll also need to carry an International Driving Permit (IDP), issued in your home country. Your home country's automobile association can usually issue one on the spot (bring a passport photo). These permits are valid for 12 months.

Fuel

In small towns there's often just a pump outside the general store, but all the larger towns and cities have conventional service stations. Most are open from 7am to around 10pm daily, plus you'll find a few 24-hour openers in Hobart and Launceston.

Unleaded petrol, diesel and gas are all widely available. In small rural towns,

prices often jump about 10c per litre from urban rates, so fill up before leaving a bigger centre.

Insurance
THIRD-PARTY INSURANCE
Third-party personal-injury insurance is included in vehicle registration costs, ensuring that every registered vehicle carries at least minimum insurance. We recommend extending that minimum to at least third-party property insurance – minor collisions can be amazingly expensive.

RENTAL VEHICLES
When it comes to hire cars, understand your liability in the event of an accident. Rather than risk paying out thousands of dollars, consider taking out comprehensive car insurance or paying an additional daily amount to the rental company for excess reduction – this reduces the excess payable in the event of an accident from between $2000 and $5000 to a few hundred dollars.

EXCLUSIONS
Be aware that if travelling on dirt roads you usually won't be covered by insurance unless you have a 4WD (read the fine print). Also, many insurance companies won't cover the cost of damage to glass (including the windscreen) or tyres.

Purchase
If you're touring Tassie for several months, buying a secondhand car may be cheaper than renting. You'll probably pick up a car more cheaply by buying privately online rather than through a car dealer, but buying through a dealer does have the advantage of some sort of guarantee.

Online, check out Car Sales (www.carsales.com.au) or Gumtree (www.gumtree.com.au).

LEGALITIES

When you buy a car in Tasmania, you and the seller need to complete and sign a Transfer of Registration form. Inspections or warrants of fitness aren't required, but ensuring the vehicle registration is paid becomes your responsibility. See www.transport.tas. gov.au/online/vehicles for details.

It's also your responsibility to ensure the car isn't stolen and that there's no money owing on it: check the car's details with the **Personal Property Securities Register** (☑1300 007 777; www. ppsr.gov.au).

Rental

Practicalities Before hiring a car, ask about any kilometre limitations and find out exactly what the insurance covers. Note that some companies don't cover accidents on unsealed roads, and hike up the excess in the case of any damage on the dirt – a considerable disadvantage as many of the top Tasmanian destinations are definitely off-piste! Some companies also don't allow their vehicles to be taken across to Bruny Island.

Costs International company rates start at about $55 for a high-season, multi-day hire of a small car. Book in advance for the best prices. Small local firms rent cars for as little as $30 a day, depending on the season and the duration of the hire. The smaller companies don't normally have desks at arrival points, but can usually arrange for your car to be picked up at airports and the ferry terminal in Devonport.

Autorent-Hertz (☑1800 030 222; www.autorent.com. au) Also has campervans for hire and sale.

Avis (☑13 63 33; www.avis. com.au) Also has 4WDs.

Budget (☑1300 362 848; www.budget.com.au) Car rental.

Europcar (☑1300 131 390; www.europcar.com.au) Car rental.

Lo-Cost Auto Rent (☑03-6231 0550; www.locostautorent.com) Branches in Hobart and Launceston.

Rent For Less (☑1300 883 728; www.rentforless.com. au) Branches in Hobart and Launceston.

Selective Car Rentals (☑1800 300 102; www. selectivecarrentals.com.au) Branches in Hobart, Launceston and Devonport.

Thrifty (☑1800 030 730; www.thrifty.com.au) Car rental.

CAMPERVANS

Companies for campervan hire – with rates from around $90 (two-berth) or $150 (four-berth) per day, usually with minimum five-day hire and unlimited kilometres – include the following.

Apollo (☑1800 777 779; www. apollocamper.com) Also has a backpacker-focussed brand called Hippie Camper.

Britz (☑1300 738 087; www. britz.com.au)

Cruisin' Tasmania (☑1300 664 485; www.cruisintasmania. com.au) Campervan rental.

Maui (☑1300 363 800; www. maui.com.au) Campervan rental.

Tasmanian Campervan Hire (☑1800 807 119; www. tascamper.com) Specialises in two-berth vans.

MOTORCYCLES

Tasmanian Motorcycle Hire (☑0418 365 210; www. tasmotorcyclehire.com.au) has a range of touring motorbikes for rent from around $120 per day (cheaper rates for longer rentals); see the website for full pricing details. Based in Launceston.

Road Conditions & Hazards

Road conditions in Tasmania are generally pretty good, but there are a few hazards to watch out for en route.

4WD TRACKS

Anyone considering travelling on 4WD tracks should read the free publication *Cruisin' Without Bruisin'*, available online from the Parks & Wildlife Service (www.parks.tas.gov.au): click on 'Recreation' then 'Other Activities'. It sets out a code of practice to minimise your impact on the regions you drive through.

BLACK ICE

In cold weather be wary of 'black ice', an invisible layer of ice over the tarmac, especially on the shady side of mountain passes. Slippery stuff.

CYCLISTS & LOG TRUCKS

Cycle touring is popular on some roads, particularly on the east coast in summer. When encountering bicycles, wait until you can pass safely to avoid clipping, scaring or generally freaking out cyclists. Log trucks piled high and coming around sharp corners also demand caution.

DISTANCES

Distances may appear short when you peruse a map of Tasmania, especially compared with the vast distances on mainland Australia. But many roads here are narrow and winding, with sharp bends and occasional one-lane bridges. Getting from A to B usually takes longer than expected.

UNSEALED ROADS

Most of the main roads around Tasmania are sealed and in good nick, but there are also many unsealed roads leading to off-the-beaten-track spots. Ask your car-rental company if they're cool with you going off-tarmac.

WILDLIFE

Watch out for wildlife while you're driving around the island, especially at night – the huge number of carcasses lining highways tells a sorry tale. Many local animals are nocturnal – try to avoid driving in rural areas at dusk and after dark. If it's unavoidable, slow down. If you do hit and injure an animal, contact the **Parks & Wildlife Service** (☑03-6165 4305; www.parks.tas.gov.au) for advice.

Road Rules

Cars are driven on the left-hand side of the road in Tasmania (as they are in the rest of Australia). An important road rule is to 'give way to the right' – if an intersection is unmarked (unusual), you must give way to vehicles entering the intersection from your right.

The speed limit in built-up areas is 50km/h. Near schools, the limit is 40km/h in the morning and afternoon. On the highway it's 100km/h or 110km/h.

Random breath tests are common. If you're caught with a blood alcohol level of more than 0.05% expect a fine and the loss of your licence. Talking on a mobile phone while driving is also illegal (excluding hands-free technology).

Hitching

Hitching is never entirely safe in any country in the world, and we don't recommend it. Travellers who decide to hitch should understand that they are taking a small but potentially serious risk. People who do choose to hitch will be safer if they travel in pairs and let someone know where they are planning to go.

People looking for travelling companions for car journeys around the state often leave notices on boards in hostels and backpacker accommodation. Online, www.needaride.com.au is a good resource.

Local Transport

Metro Tasmania (☑13 22 01; www.metrotas.com.au) operates local bus networks in Hobart, Launceston and Burnie, offering visitors inexpensive services around the city suburbs and a few out-of-the-way areas, including the Channel Hwy towns south of Hobart, and Hadspen south of Launceston. Check online for schedules and fares.

Tours

Backpacker-style, outdoorsy and more formal bus tours offer a convenient way to get from A to B and check out the sights on the way. Operators include the following.

Adventure Tours (☑1800 068 886; www.adventuretours.com.au) An Australia-wide company offering one- to seven-day

ROAD DISTANCES (KM)

	Burnie	Deloraine	Devonport	Geeveston	Hobart	Launceston	New Norfolk	Oatlands	Port Arthur	Queenstown	St Helens	Scottsdale	Smithton	Sorell	Strahan	Swansea
Deloraine	100															
Devonport	50	50														
Geeveston	381	281	331													
Hobart	328	228	278	53												
Launceston	137	51	87	254	201											
New Norfolk	290	190	240	91	38	197										
Oatlands	246	146	196	136	83	118	79									
Port Arthur	386	286	336	148	95	258	133	140								
Queenstown	148	204	198	312	259	251	221	261	354							
St Helens	293	207	243	304	251	156	247	168	299	407						
Scottsdale	197	111	147	314	261	60	257	178	318	311	96					
Smithton	88	188	138	469	416	225	378	334	474	236	381	285				
Sorell	316	216	266	78	25	188	63	70	70	284	229	248	404			
Strahan	183	222	209	353	289	271	253	370	388	41	405	330	224	325		
Swansea	264	164	214	189	136	136	174	114	181	395	118	214	352	111	352	
Triabunna	314	214	264	139	86	186	124	131	131	345	168	264	402	61	249	50

These are the shortest distances by road; other routes may be considerably longer.
For distances by coach, check the companies' leaflets.

tours around Tasmania, including hostel accommodation.

Jump Tours (☎0422 130 630; www.jumptours.com) Youth- and backpacker-oriented three- and five-day Tassie tours.

Tarkine Trails (☎0405 255 537; www.tarkinetrails.com.au) Green-focused group offering guided walks in the Tarkine wilderness, the Walls of Jerusalem and the Overland Track.

Tasmania Tours (☎1800 994 620; www.tasmaniatours. com.au) Multi-day coach tours around the island, from four to 13 days. Prices include accommodation.

Tasmanian Expeditions (☎1300 666 856; www. tasmanianexpeditions.com.

au) Offers an excellent range of activity-based tours: bushwalking, cabin-based walks, rafting, rock climbing, cycling and sea kayaking.

Tasmanian Safaris (☎1300 882 415; www.tasmaniansafaris.com) Multi-day, all-inclusive, eco-certified 4WD tours ex-Launceston, heading to Hobart via the east coast. There's bushwalking, bush camping and lots of wilderness. Canoe trips also available.

Under Down Under (☎1800 064 726; www. underdownunder.com.au) Offers pro-green, nature-based, backpacker-friendly trips. There are tours from three to nine days.

Train

For economic reasons, passenger rail services in Tasmania sadly ceased in the late 1970s. There are a couple of small, scenic tourist routes still running, however, including the **West Coast Wilderness Railway** (☎03-6471 0100; www.wcwr.com. au) between Queenstown and Strahan (34km) and the **Ida Bay Railway** (☎0428 383 262, 03-6298 3110; www. idabayrailway.com.au; 328 Lune River Rd; adult/child/family $30/15/75; ⊙9am-5pm) in the southeast.

Behind the Scenes

SEND US YOUR FEEDBACK

We love to hear from travellers – your comments keep us on our toes and help make our books better. Our well-travelled team reads every word on what you loved or loathed about this book. Although we cannot reply individually to your submissions, we always guarantee that your feedback goes straight to the appropriate authors, in time for the next edition. Each person who sends us information is thanked in the next edition – the most useful submissions are rewarded with a selection of digital PDF chapters.

Visit **lonelyplanet.com/contact** to submit your updates and suggestions or to ask for help. Our award-winning website also features inspirational travel stories, news and discussions.

Note: We may edit, reproduce and incorporate your comments in Lonely Planet products such as guidebooks, websites and digital products, so let us know if you don't want your comments reproduced or your name acknowledged. For a copy of our privacy policy visit lonelyplanet.com/privacy.

OUR READERS

Many thanks to the travellers who used the last edition and wrote to us with helpful hints, useful advice and interesting anecdotes:

Brian Rieusset, David Thames, Garry Greenwood, Jan Lehmann, Janice Blakebrough, Jon & Linley Dodd, Kevin Callaghan, Lisa Walker, Megan McKay, Melanie Tait, Owen Boscheinen, Peter Mill, Richard Scott, Sally McDonald, Trevor Mazzucchelli and Urs Grueter.

AUTHOR THANKS

Anthony Ham

Heartfelt thanks to Tasmin Waby; to Ben Cade, Yolanda Paredes, Liam and Naia for being such fine companions of the road; and to countless Tasmanians who shared their passion and expertise for this wonderful corner of the earth. To Marina, Carlota and Valentina – os quiero.

Charles Rawlings-Way

Huge thanks to Tasmin for the gig, and to our highway-addled co-author Anthony. Thanks also to the all-star in-house Lonely Planet production staff, and the friends who helped us out on the road and dished the local low-down, particularly Mark, Cath, Fred, Lucy and the kids in Hobart, and Helen in Launceston. Special thanks as always to Meg, my road-trippin' sweetheart, and our daughters Ione and Remy who provided countless laughs, unscheduled pit-stops and ground-level perspectives along the way.

Meg Worby

A big thank you to Tasmin, once again. Kudos to the in-house team at Lonely Planet for turning our many weeks of exploration into this most reliable of handheld devices. Cheers to all our Tasmanian friends for great company and insider tips. Love to the small and unflappable travellers, Ione and Remy, who saw snow for the first time on this trip. Thank you, as ever, to Charles: a pro.

ACKNOWLEDGMENTS

Climate map data adapted from Peel MC, Finlayson BL & McMahon TA (2007) 'Updated World Map of the Köppen-Geiger Climate Classification', Hydrology and Earth System Sciences, 11, 1633–44.

Cover photograph: Dove Lake, Cradle Mountain, Ian Woolcock/Shutterstock ©

THIS BOOK

This 7th edition of Lonely Planet's *Tasmania* was researched and written by Anthony Ham, Charles Rawlings-Way and Meg Worby. The previous edition was written by Brett Atkinson and Gabi Mocatta. Anna Krien wrote the Environmental Politics in Tasmania chapter. The guidebook was produced by the following team:

Destination Editor Tasmin Waby

Product Editors Kate Mathews, Katie O'Connell

Senior Cartographer Julie Sheridan

Book Designer Cam Ashley

Assisting Editors Andrew Bain, Susan Paterson, Gabrielle Stefanos, Ross Taylor, Saralinda Turner

Cartographers James Leversha, Alison Lyall

Cover Researcher Naomi Parker

Thanks to Daniel Corbett, Anna Harris, Karyn Noble, Lauren O'Connell, Martine Power, Dianne Schallmeiner, Ellie Simpson, Samantha Tyson, Lauren Wellicome

Index

Bonorong 83

Map Legend

Sights
- Beach
- Bird Sanctuary
- Buddhist
- Castle/Palace
- Christian
- Confucian
- Hindu
- Islamic
- Jain
- Jewish
- Monument
- Museum/Gallery/Historic Building
- Ruin
- Shinto
- Sikh
- Taoist
- Winery/Vineyard
- Zoo/Wildlife Sanctuary
- Other Sight

Activities, Courses & Tours
- Bodysurfing
- Diving
- Canoeing/Kayaking
- Course/Tour
- Sento Hot Baths/Onsen
- Skiing
- Snorkelling
- Surfing
- Swimming/Pool
- Walking
- Windsurfing
- Other Activity

Sleeping
- Sleeping
- Camping

Eating
- Eating

Drinking & Nightlife
- Drinking & Nightlife
- Cafe

Entertainment
- Entertainment

Shopping
- Shopping

Information
- Bank
- Embassy/Consulate
- Hospital/Medical
- Internet
- Police
- Post Office
- Telephone
- Toilet
- Tourist Information
- Other Information

Geographic
- Beach
- Gate
- Hut/Shelter
- Lighthouse
- Lookout
- Mountain/Volcano
- Oasis
- Park
- Pass
- Picnic Area
- Waterfall

Population
- Capital (National)
- Capital (State/Province)
- City/Large Town
- Town/Village

Transport
- Airport
- Border crossing
- Bus
- Cable car/Funicular
- Cycling
- Ferry
- Metro station
- Monorail
- Parking
- Petrol station
- Subway station
- Taxi
- Train station/Railway
- Tram
- Underground station
- Other Transport

Note: Not all symbols displayed above appear on the maps in this book

Routes
- Tollway
- Freeway
- Primary
- Secondary
- Tertiary
- Lane
- Unsealed road
- Road under construction
- Plaza/Mall
- Steps
- Tunnel
- Pedestrian overpass
- Walking Tour
- Walking Tour detour
- Path/Walking Trail

Boundaries
- International
- State/Province
- Disputed
- Regional/Suburb
- Marine Park
- Cliff
- Wall

Hydrography
- River, Creek
- Intermittent River
- Canal
- Water
- Dry/Salt/Intermittent Lake
- Reef

Areas
- Airport/Runway
- Beach/Desert
- Cemetery (Christian)
- Cemetery (Other)
- Glacier
- Mudflat
- Park/Forest
- Sight (Building)
- Sportsground
- Swamp/Mangrove

OUR STORY

A beat-up old car, a few dollars in the pocket and a sense of adventure. In 1972 that's all Tony and Maureen Wheeler needed for the trip of a lifetime – across Europe and Asia overland to Australia. It took several months, and at the end – broke but inspired – they sat at their kitchen table writing and stapling together their first travel guide, *Across Asia on the Cheap*. Within a week they'd sold 1500 copies. Lonely Planet was born. Today, Lonely Planet has offices in Franklin, London, Melbourne, Oakland, Beijing and Delhi, with more than 600 staff and writers. We share Tony's belief that 'a great guidebook should do three things: inform, educate and amuse'.

OUR WRITERS

Anthony Ham

Devonport & the Northwest, Cradle Country & the West Anthony was born in Melbourne, grew up in Sydney and has spent much of his adult life travelling the world. He recently returned to Australia after ten years living in Madrid and brings to this guide more than fifteen years' experience as a travel writer. As a recently returned expat, Anthony is loving the opportunity to rediscover his country and indulge his passion for wilderness. He brings to the book the unique perspective of knowing the land intimately and yet seeing it anew as if through the eyes of an outsider. Check out his website, anthonyham.com.

Charles Rawlings-Way

Co-author: Hobart & Around, Tasman Peninsula & Port Arthur, the Southeast, Midlands & Central Highlands, the East Coast, Launceston & Around As a likely lad, Charles suffered in school shorts through Hobart winters. Ice on the puddles, snow on Mt Wellington...he dreamed of one day living somewhere warmer. Now that he does (Adelaide) and the world is hotting up, Hobart is looking good again! Returning to Tasmania on reconnaissance, he was thrilled to discover that his old home town has good coffee now, Launceston has a craft beer hipster bar and there's still snow on Mt Wellington. Charles has penned 20-something Lonely Planet guidebooks. Charles also co-authored the Plan Your Trip, Understand and Survival Guide sections of this book.

Meg Worby

Co-author: Hobart & Around, Tasman Peninsula & Port Arthur, the Southeast, Midlands & Central Highlands, the East Coast, Launceston & Around Tucking in to a creamed scallop pie in Hobart and pondering erstwhile Tasmanian Errol Flynn, Meg realised that a love of beauty, a lust for adventure and a yearning for tights must naturally have begun here. She is a former member of Lonely Planet's languages, editorial, web and publishing teams in Melbourne and London. This is her ninth Lonely Planet guidebook as co-author, with another dashing Tasmanian. Meg also co-authored the Plan Your Trip, Understand and Survival Guide sections of this book.

Contributing Authors

Anna Krien wrote the Environmental Politics in Tasmania chapter. Her debut book, *Into the Woods: The Battle for Tasmania's Forests* (Black Inc, 2010), won both the Queensland and Victorian Premier's Literary Awards in 2011. Her writing has appeared in the *Big Issue*, *Frankie*, the *Age*, the *Monthly* and the *Griffith Review*, and has been selected for *Best Australian Essays* and *Best Australian Stories*.

Published by Lonely Planet Publications Pty Ltd
ABN 36 005 607 983
7th edition – November 2015
ISBN 978 1 74220 579 3
© Lonely Planet 2015   Photographs © as indicated 2015
10 9 8 7 6 5 4 3 2 1
Printed in China